SCIENCE ANNUAL

A Modern Science Anthology for the Family

1990

ACKNOWLEDGMENTS

Sources of articles appear below, including those reprinted with the kind permission of publications and organizations.

ON THE ROAD TO IO, Page 8: Reprinted with permission of the author; article first appeared in AIR & SPACE/SMITHSONIAN, December 1988/January 1989.

WOMEN IN SPACE, Page 22: Reprinted with permission of the author; article first appeared in *Space World,* November 1988.

IN SEARCH OF PLANET X, Page 29: Reprinted from the July/August 1988 issue of *The Planetary Report,* the bimonthly magazine of The Planetary Society, 65 N. Catalina Avenue, Pasadena, CA 91106.

EXPLORING THE FORCES OF SLEEP, Page 38: Copyright © 1988 by The New York Times Company. Reprinted by permission.

BRUSHES WITH DEATH, Page 44: Reprinted with permission from *Psychology Today* magazine. Copyright © 1988 (PT Partners, L.P.).

THE PERILS OF POT, Page 47: *American Health Magazine* © 1988.

DISASTER DYNAMICS, Page 53: Reprinted with permission from *Psychology Today* magazine. Copyright © 1988 (PT Partners, L.P.).

WHAT'S BEHIND BLINKING?, Page 59: Reprinted by permission from the December 1988 issue of *The Sciences,* published by the New York Academy of Sciences, 2 East 63rd Street, New York, NY 10021.

THE EXERCISE FIX, Page 63: Reprinted with permission from *Psychology Today* magazine. Copyright © 1988 (PT Partners, L.P.).

DESIGNER PROTEINS, Page 70: Shawna Vogel/ © 1988 Discover Publications.

BANKING ON SEEDS, Page 76: Reprinted with permission of the author; article first appeared in *Audubon,* the magazine of the National Audubon Society.

IMAGES OF IMMUNITY, Page 82: Reprinted from *FDA Consumer,* March 1988, U.S. Food and Drug Administration.

SERENDIPITOUS SHIPWRECK, Page 87: Reprinted by permission from *Sea Frontiers,* © 1988 by the International Oceanographic Foundation, 3979 Rickenbacker Causeway, Virginia Key, Miami, FL 33149.

IS YOUR COMPUTER SECURE?, Page 98: Reprinted from the August 1, 1988, issue of *Business Week* by special permission, copyright © 1988 by McGraw-Hill, Inc.

ERASABLE OPTICAL DISKS, Page 106: Reprinted with permission, FORTUNE, © 1989 The Time Inc. Magazine Company. All rights reserved.

ELECTRONIC BULLETIN BOARDS, Page 110: Reprinted with permission of the author; article first appeared in SMITHSONIAN, September 1988.

TOKENS OF PLENTY, Page 119: Reprinted with permission from SCIENCE NEWS, the weekly newsmagazine of science, © 1988 by Science Service, Inc.

ANATOMY OF A HURRICANE, Page 128: Prepared expressly by Dr. Robert C. Sheets, Director, National Hurricane Center, Coral Gables, FL.

SEASONS, SEAS, AND SATELLITES, Page 136: Reprinted with permission of the author; article first appeared in AIR & SPACE/SMITHSONIAN, February/March 1988.

RHYTHM AND CLUES, Page 142: Reprinted with permission from *Insight;* © 1988 Insight. All rights reserved.

TAKING FEAR OUT OF NUCLEAR POWER, Page 158: Reprinted with permission, FORTUNE, © 1988 The Time Inc. Magazine Company. All rights reserved.

HYDROGEN: FUEL OF THE FUTURE?, Page 166: Reprinted from the November 28, 1988, issue of *Business Week* by special permission, copyright © 1988 by McGraw-Hill, Inc.

CONSERVATION COMES OF AGE, Page 170: Adapted from the book *State of the World 1988,* published by the Worldwatch Institute, 1775 Massachusetts Avenue, Washington, DC 20036.

WINGING INTO HISTORY, Page 178: By Joan Ackermann-Blount and William Oscar Johnson, reprinted courtesy of *Sports Illustrated* from the May 2, 1988, issue. Copyright © 1988, Time Inc. ALL RIGHTS RESERVED.

HANDLING HOSPITAL WASTE, Page 195: Copyright 1988 by Ellen Kunes and reprinted with the permission of Omni Publications International, Ltd.

POLLUTION'S ASSAULT ON ANTIQUITY, Page 210: Reprinted with the permission of *Archaeology Magazine,* Vol. 41, No. 4. (Copyright the Archaeological Institute of America, 1988.)

THE REVOLUTION IN HEART TREATMENT, Page 222: Copyright © 1988 by The New York Times Company. Reprinted by permission.

HEALING WITH LASERS, Page 229: Reprinted by permission of *Prevention.* Copyright 1988, Rodale Press, Inc. All rights reserved.

BODIES TO ORDER, Page 242: Reprinted from *Stanford Medicine.* Copyright 1988, The Board of Trustees of the Leland Stanford Junior University.

STAFF

EDITORIAL

Editorial Director
Bernard S. Cayne

Executive Editor
Joseph M. Castagno

Managing Editor
Doris E. Lechner

Copy Editors
David M. Buskus
Meghan O'Reilly

Proofreader
Stephan Romanoff

Indexer
Pauline M. Sholtys

Manuscript Typist
Susan A. Mohn

Art Assistant
Elizabeth Farrington

Contributing Editors
Elaine Pascoe
Philip A. Storey

Editorial Librarian
Charles Chang

Art Director
Eric E. Akerman

Production Editor
Diane L. George

Production Assistant
Sheila Rourk

Manager, Picture Library
Jane H. Carruth

Chief, Photo Research
Ann Eriksen

Photo Researcher
Paula J. Kobylarz

Photo Assistant
Jeanne A. Schipper

Financial Manager
Jean Gianazza

Staff Assistant
Freida K. Jones

MANUFACTURING

Director of Manufacturing
Joseph J. Corlett

Senior Production Manager
Christine L. Matta

Assistant Production Manager
Barbara L. Persan

CONTRIBUTORS

JOAN ACKERMANN-BLOUNT, Contributor, *Sports Illustrated*
Coauthor, WINGING INTO HISTORY

H. ALDERSEY-WILLIAMS, Contributor, *Popular Science*
SAVING VENICE

THOMAS B. ALLEN, Free-lance writer; former editor, *National Geographic*; author, *War Games*
ELECTRONIC BULLETIN BOARDS

MARK ALPERT, Reporter, *Fortune*
ERASABLE OPTICAL DISKS

JOHN ANDERSON, Senior research scientist, Jet Propulsion Laboratory, Pasadena, CA
IN SEARCH OF PLANET X

J.S. BAINBRIDGE, JR., Contributor, *Smithsonian*
FROGS THAT SWEAT POISON

ANDREW BAUM, Professor of medical psychology, Uniformed Services University of the Health Sciences, Bethesda, MD
DISASTER DYNAMICS

BERYL LIEFF BENDERLY, Free-lance writer
IMAGES OF IMMUNITY

BRUCE BOWER, Staff writer, *Science News*
REVIEW OF THE YEAR: BEHAVIORAL SCIENCES

WILLIAM J. BROAD, News science reporter, *The New York Times*
THE PHYSICS OF THRILLS

ANTHONY J. CASTAGNO, Energy consultant; manager, nuclear information, Northeast Utilities, Hartford, CT
REVIEW OF THE YEAR: ENERGY

THELMA CHANG, Free-lance writer
ON THE ROAD TO IO

MILES CUNNINGHAM, Writer, *Insight* magazine
A CRYONIC FUTURE

RIC DOLPHIN, Senior writer, *Maclean's*
GLIMPSES OF CREATION

ALAN DURNING, Researcher, Worldwatch Institute, Washington, DC
Coauthor, CONSERVATION COMES OF AGE

ERIK ECKHOLM, Deputy science and health editor, *The New York Times*
EXPLORING THE FORCES OF SLEEP

GLENN EMERY, Senior editor, *Insight* magazine
UNTANGLING TRAFFIC'S TROUBLED FUTURE

EDMUND FALTERMAYER, Board of editors, *Fortune*
TAKING FEAR OUT OF NUCLEAR POWER

CHRISTOPHER FLAVIN, Researcher, Worldwatch Institute, Washington, DC
Coauthor, CONSERVATION COMES OF AGE

WINIFRED GALLAGHER, Senior editor, *American Health*
THE PERILS OF POT

DANIEL GOLEMAN, News science reporter, *The New York Times*
THE PSYCHOLOGY OF THRILLS

ELEANOR GRANT, Science writer
THE EXERCISE FIX

DAN GUTMAN, Contributor, *Discover*
THE SCIENCE OF FOUL PLAY

JEFFREY H. HACKER, Free-lance writer
THE CHANGING WORLD OF MAPS
THE MYSTERY OF EASTER ISLAND
REVIEW OF THE YEAR: TECHNOLOGY
IN MEMORIAM

KATHERINE M. HAFNER, Staff editor, *Business Week*
IS YOUR COMPUTER SECURE?

KATHERINE HARAMUNDANIS, Free-lance writer; formerly research associate, Smithsonian Astrophysical Laboratory, Cambridge, MA; coauthor, *An Introduction to Astronomy*
REVIEW OF THE YEAR: ASTRONOMY

JOHN A. HART, Contributor, *Animal Kingdom*
Coauthor, TRACKING THE RAIN FOREST GIRAFFE

TERESE B. HART, Contributor, *Animal Kingdom*
Coauthor, TRACKING THE RAIN FOREST GIRAFFE

BRUCE HATHAWAY, Assistant editor, *Smithsonian*
GOOD VIBES FROM QUARTZ

TOM HEPPENHEIMER, Contributor, *Science Impact Letter*
STEALTH TECHNOLOGY

GLADWIN HILL, National environmental correspondent—retired, *The New York Times*
REVIEW OF THE YEAR: THE ENVIRONMENT

ELLEN HOFFMAN, Free-lance writer
HAVE OFFICE, WILL TRAVEL

ERIC HOFFMAN, Free-lance writer; author, *Adventuring in Australia*
THE PECULIAR PLATYPUS

PETER HOFFMAN, Contributor, *Business Week*
HYDROGEN: FUEL OF THE FUTURE?

JACK C. HORN, Senior editor, *Psychology Today*
REACTIONS TO RADON

JAMIE JAMES, Contributor, *Discover* magazine; coauthor, *Kourion*
BIGFOOT OR BUST

WILLIAM OSCAR JOHNSON, Senior editor, *Sports Illustrated*
WINGING INTO HISTORY

SHIRLEY KRAUS, Managing editor, *Stanford Medicine*
BODIES TO ORDER

ELLEN KUNES, Contributor, *Omni*
HANDLING HOSPITAL WASTE

MARC KUSINITZ, Free-lance science/medical writer; author, *Drugs and the Arts, Celebrity Drug Use, Drug Use Around the World*
REVIEW OF THE YEAR: PHYSICAL SCIENCES

STEVEN LALLY, Associate editor, *Prevention*
HEALING WITH LASERS

RICHARD LIPKIN, Writer, *Insight* magazine
RHYTHM AND CLUES

FRANK LOWENSTEIN, Free-lance writer; formerly assistant editor, *Oceanus* magazine
SEASONS, SEAS, AND SATELLITES

DENNIS L. MAMMANA, Resident astronomer, Reuben H. Fleet Space Theater and Science Center, San Diego, CA
REVIEW OF THE YEAR: SPACE SCIENCE
AMERICA RETURNS TO SPACE

WILLIAM H. MATTHEWS III, Regents' professor of geology emeritus, Lamar University, Beaumont, TX
REVIEW OF THE YEAR: EARTH SCIENCES

MARTIN M. McLAUGHLIN, Free-lance consultant; former vice-president for education, Overseas Development Council, Washington, DC
Coauthor, REVIEW OF THE YEAR: PAST, PRESENT, AND FUTURE

CARL NYLANDER, Director, Swedish Institute of Classical Studies, Rome
POLLUTION'S ASSAULT ON ANTIQUITY

ELAINE PASCOE, Free-lance writer
THE 1988 NOBEL PRIZE FOR PHYSIOLOGY OR MEDICINE
FORESTS AFIRE
THE 1988 NOBEL PRIZES FOR PHYSICS AND CHEMISTRY

BRUCE PATERSON, Contributor, *Consumers' Research* magazine
CAFFEINE: VICTIM OR VILLAIN?

DOUG PERRINE, Outdoor educator and free-lance photo-journalist
Coauthor, SERENDIPITOUS SHIPWRECK

PAUL PERRY, Founding editor, *Second Wind*
BRUSHES WITH DEATH

IVARS PETERSON, Mathematics/physics editor, *Science News*
TOKENS OF PLENTY

DEBRA PLYMATE, Air-traffic controller; member, Professional Women Controllers and The Ninety Nines
WOMEN IN SPACE

HOWARD M. SCHMECK, JR., Science correspondent, *The New York Times*
THE REVOLUTION IN HEART TREATMENT

ANNE M. SCHWARTZ, Editor, *Audubon Activist,* published by the National Audubon Society
BANKING ON SEEDS

ROBERT C. SHEETS, Director, National Hurricane Center, Coral Gables, FL
ANATOMY OF A HURRICANE

JOANNE SILBERNER, Associate editor, *U.S. News & World Report*
REVIEW OF THE YEAR: BIOLOGY

FRANK SLIFKA, Marine naturalist and free-lance photographer
Coauthor, SERENDIPITOUS SHIPWRECK

JOHN A. STERN, Chairman, psychology department, Washington University, St. Louis, MO
WHAT'S BEHIND BLINKING?

DOUG STEWART, Contributor, *Discover* magazine
SKY SCRAPING

PHILIP A. STOREY, Staff editor, *Academic American Encyclopedia*
REVIEW OF THE YEAR: COMPUTERS AND MATHEMATICS

BOB STROHM, Editor-in-chief, *National Wildlife* magazine
REVIEW OF THE YEAR: WILDLIFE

ROBERT SULLIVAN, Staff writer, *Sports Illustrated*
A WHALE OF A TALE

JENNY TESAR, Free-lance science and medical writer; author, *Parents as Teachers, Introduction to Animals, Preparing for the SAT and Other Aptitude Tests*
THE ALASKA OIL SPILL
REVIEW OF THE YEAR: HEALTH AND DISEASE
NURSING: A CHANGING PROFESSION

SHAWNA VOGEL, Associate editor, *Discover* magazine
DESIGNER PROTEINS

PETER S. WELLS, Professor of anthropology and director, Center for Ancient Studies, University of Minnesota
Coauthor, REVIEW OF THE YEAR: PAST, PRESENT, AND FUTURE

WENDY WILLIAMS, Contributor, *National Wildlife*
AN ABUNDANCE OF SWANS

CONTENTS

ASTRONOMY AND SPACE SCIENCE

ASTRONOMY AND SPACE SCIENCE

The space shuttle topped the astronomy/space science news in 1988. But not overshadowed were advances in infrared astronomy, the still-unfolding drama of SN 1987A, and the spirit of international cooperation in space research.

ASTRONOMY

by Katherine Haramundanis

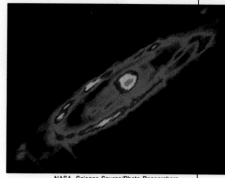

NASA–Science Source/Photo Researchers

Scientists use infrared images to study the structure of distant galaxies.

The Solar System

The sunspot cycle, on the rise since 1986, reaches its maximum from 1988 to 1992. During this period, frequent solar flares will disrupt radio and telephone communications, damage electronic systems in satellites, create radiation hazards to astronauts and aircraft passengers at high altitudes, and can even alter the orbits of artificial satellites. Correlations of the sunspot cycle with weather, although possible, have not yet been clearly proven. ■ New observations of the Sun suggest that there may be important differences between the composition of the Earth and the Sun. If so, the models we currently use for the origin and evolution of the solar system would change. ■ Detailed observations gathered new information on the planets: tectonic activity has been detected on Venus; Nereid, a moon of Neptune, has a diameter of about 410 miles (660 kilometers) and a highly irregular shape; Ariel and Miranda, satellites of Uranus, show evidence of "solid ice volcanism"; the rings of Uranus may be continuously generated by a "grinding" process of unseen moonlets. ■ Sodium and potassium vapor have been found in the atmosphere of the Moon. ■ A refined theory of solar system formation indicates that the terrestrial planets (Mercury, Venus, Earth, Mars) were formed by fundamentally different mechanisms than the giant planets (Jupiter, Saturn, Uranus, Neptune). ■ Halley's comet has two "heartbeats": one from its cloud of dust and gas, the other from its jets of dust; both arise from pressure from the solar wind. ■ Chiron, an asteroid, has brightened as it approaches the Sun, acting more like a comet than an asteroid. Owing to its unstable orbit, Chiron may in time become more obviously a comet. ■ Meteoroid streams have also been associated with a number of asteroids. ■ The Martian atmosphere continues to be debated. The detection of deuterium on Mars suggests the planet once had a dense, warm atmosphere. "Fluvial" features on Mars may have been caused by water released during volcanos or heated underground, which then emerged to flow across the surface.

Photos: National Radio Astronomy Observatory, Green Bank

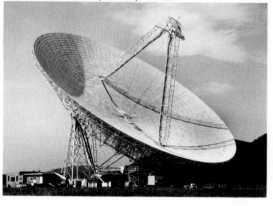

The fracture of a stressed steel plate caused the radio telescope at the National Radio Observatory in Green Bank, West Virginia, to suddenly collapse last November. No definite plans have been made to replace the instrument.

The Milky Way

A nova, an AM Herculis system, may have been a binary with a cool normal star and a highly magnetized white dwarf held together by gravity. The strong gravitational field of the white dwarf pulled matter from its companion, eventually causing the nova explosion. Without the magnetic field, the matter falling into the white dwarf would simply form an accretion disk. With the magnetic field, the matter is drawn to the magnetic poles, causing the nova to brighten. ■ A planetary nebula may be created by the interactions within a binary system—for example, between a large, bluish cool star and a small, hot, reddish companion. The two stars coalesce and form a nova explosion, throwing off the shell, which then becomes a planetary nebula. ■ Wolf-Rayet stars, 20 to 100 times more massive than the Sun, may be remnants of old supernovas, or possibly old binary systems. ■ An unusual white dwarf, 0950+139, has been discovered in Nebula EGB 6 about 1,500 light-years away. The white dwarf seems to have recently ejected a glowing cloud of gas. Current theory holds that white dwarfs are dying stars on a one-way trip to stellar death; the new observations indicate that at least this white dwarf is doing just the opposite, becoming more active. ■ Pulsar PSR 1957+20, a member of a binary system with an eclipsing companion about 20 times the mass of Jupiter and larger than the Sun in diameter, has been shown to be in an act of "stellar cannibalism." The pulsar is consuming its companion in a feast that will last another 100 million years. ■ Spectral observations (not yet confirmed) of the yellowish star HD114762 indicate that it may have a dim companion with a mass between that of Jupiter and a small star. ■ Globular clusters, ancient members of our galaxy that occur as clumps of some 1 million stars, cruise in very eccentric, sometimes retrograde orbits throughout our galaxy. Some contain pulsars. Such orbits point to violent and early beginnings; their form and trajectories are as yet unexplained. The more metal-rich clusters are younger. ■ The Puppis A supernova may be the site of an explosion in the expanding gas shell from a previous supernova that occurred 3,000 years earlier.

The Universe

Observations continue to extend our view into the mysteries of the universe. The phenomena of infrared imaging techniques have helped us find primitive galaxies just forming, at distances of perhaps 15 billion to 17 billion light-years. ■ New observations of elliptical galaxies indicate that, contrary to previous theory, they contain gas and stars of all ages. This finding eliminates them as a standard with which to map the expansion of the universe. ■ Astronomers have found the farthest known galaxy: called 4C41.17, it has a redshift of 3.8 and may be 15 billion light-years away. ■ Supernova 1987A has been tracked for more than 700 days, far longer and in much greater detail than any other supernova in history. Astronomers believe the supernova derives its energy from the decay of the radioactive elements cobalt 56 and cobalt 57. But the cause of the explosion of the compact blue supergiant progenitor Sk 202-69 remains unexplained. ■ Remarkable observations of M31, the Great Andromeda Spiral, provide the most detailed view to date of the gas in the center of the huge galaxy. Unexplained features include a small spiral deep inside M31's spheroidal bulge, and threadlike structures plunging into the center from every angle. Some astronomers suggest that the Great Spiral may have a black hole with the equivalent of perhaps 50 solar masses at its center. ■ IRAS 14348-1447, an infrared object, is an extremely bright colliding galaxy system, possibly a dust-shrouded quasar.

Scientists need to discover the rate of expansion and the average density of the universe to verify any of the proposed models of the future of the universe. In the "closed" model (left), the great density of matter creates gravity strong enough to stop the universe from expanding and start it contracting. In the "saddle" model (center), the matter only slows the rate of expansion. In the "open" model (right), the universe expands fast enough to avoid any contraction.

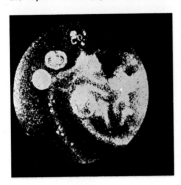

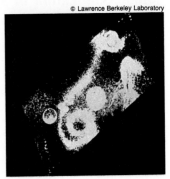

SPACE SCIENCE
by Dennis L. Mammana

The Space Shuttle

On September 29, 1988, the space shuttle *Discovery* rode into space after nearly two years of modifications and tests. During their successful mission, *Discovery* astronauts deployed a communications satellite, performed dozens of scientific experiments, and returned to America the dream of space exploration. (See also the article beginning on p. 14.)

Two months later the space shuttle *Atlantis* carried five astronauts, all military officers, into orbit on a top-secret military mission. They launched a powerful new $500 million spy satellite to peer with radar eyes through clouds and darkness at military operations in Eastern Europe and the Soviet Union.

But this was not the only progress made by the U.S. military. On January 8, an unmanned Delta rocket launched a 3-ton (2.7-metric ton), $250 million military satellite into space as part of the most complex and costly experiment yet in the Strategic Defense Initiative ("Star Wars") antimissile program.

In preparation for the future, the National Aeronautics and Space Administration (NASA) unveiled on December 19 an ambitious space blueprint that would establish a manned lunar observatory and put astronauts on Mars or its tiny moon Phobos by early in the next century.

International cooperation in space research gained momentum as well. At

AP/Wide World

Americans rejoiced when the U.S. space-shuttle program finally started up again.

the Moscow summit in May, the USSR offered to carry American scientific instruments on its future flights to Mars, while the U.S. agreed to help select a landing site for an unmanned Soviet Mars craft to be launched in 1994.

On the day *Discovery* returned to space, the U.S. signed an agreement with 11 other nations to cooperate on the detailed design, development, operation, and utilization of a permanently manned space station. Participating countries are the U.S., Canada, Japan, and the nine member nations of the

European Space Agency (ESA): Belgium, Denmark, France, the Federal Republic of Germany, Italy, the Netherlands, Norway, Spain, and the United Kingdom.

The $23 billion facility, known as Space Station Freedom, will serve as a stepping-stone for human exploration of our solar system. The 440-foot (135-meter)-long station will weigh about 175 tons (160 metric tons), and will orbit 220 miles (350 kilometers) above Earth. Nineteen shuttle flights will be needed to ferry materials and personnel back and forth beginning in 1994.

Commercialization of Space

In early 1988 President Ronald Reagan signed a new National Space Policy that strongly supports U.S. commercial space ventures, and issued a 15-point Commercial Space Initiative that encourages the government to buy commercial space goods and services.

Payload Systems, Inc., became the first American firm to contract with the Soviet Union to carry commercial payloads into orbit. The agreement calls for flights of scientific experiments that

could help benefit the American pharmaceutical, biotechnology, and chemical industries.

In an attempt to become the first privately owned company in the rocket-launching business, the American Rocket Company (AMROC) successfully completed a test firing of its 70,000-pound-thrust hybrid rocket motor on September 2. With this test, AMROC passed the last milestone before it tests a single booster on a suborbital flight.

Arianespace, the private company that markets and directs launch operations of Ariane boosters, successfully launched three satellites on board its new Ariane 4 rocket on June 15, 1988, from the European Space Agency's launching pad in French Guiana. One, the Pan American Satellite, is billed as the "world's first private international satellite." As of June 16, 1988, Arianespace had booked 67 launch-service contracts, nearly half of them European.

Foreign Space Programs

The Soviet Mir space station remained active during the year, and cosmonauts continued to be ferried to and from the station aboard Soyuz craft.

On December 21, Mir cosmonauts Vladimir Titov and Musa Manarov returned to Earth after spending 366 days on Mir. They broke the previous record for long-duration spaceflight by passing Yuri Romanenko's record of 326 days.

The first Soviet space shuttle rose from its pad at the Baikonur Cosmodrome in Soviet Central Asia on November 15. Named Buran (Russian for "snowstorm"), the 100-ton (90-metric-ton) craft is virtually identical in size and shape to the American shuttle. But unlike its American counterpart, the Soviet shuttle is completely liquid-fueled, and its Energia booster can lift nearly four times more weight.

While the Soviets hailed the success of the unmanned Buran's two-orbit maiden voyage, they will not schedule a manned shuttle mission until every one of the craft's systems has been tested.

Soviet planetary research continued onward as well. On July 7 and 12, the U.S.S.R. successfully launched two spacecraft—Phobos I and II—on a 400-million-mile (640-million-kilometer) journey to Mars.

Once at Mars, their goal was to conduct a series of chemical, magnetic, and gravity experiments on the Martian moon Phobos. A spiderlike landing craft would descend to the moon's surface and hop about to get a good look at the terrain. But on the night of August 29, an incorrect radio signal sent one of the robot craft wobbling out of control.

Just one week later, the Soviets suffered another problem. A Soviet cosmonaut and an Afghan astronaut spent 25 harrowing hours stranded in Earth orbit, when maneuvers for landing their craft failed. Aboard the craft were Commander Colonel Vladimir Lyakhov and copilot Captain Abdul Ahad Mohmand of the Afghanistan Air Force.

The intense space drama began on the morning of September 6, when an infrared sensor incorrectly told onboard computers that the craft was improperly oriented for landing. They tried to land again, but failed when the capsule's deceleration motor burned for six seconds instead of the required 230 seconds.

Tensions ran high. Although the men had enough oxygen, food, and water for two days, carbon dioxide was rapidly building up inside the cabin. The U.S. considered launching the space shuttle *Discovery* on a rescue mission,

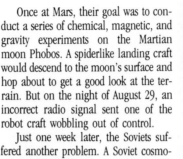

© Tass from Sovfoto

In 1988, the Soviets launched Buran ("snowstorm"), their first space shuttle. The 100-ton craft, virtually identical in size and shape to the American shuttle, can lift nearly four times more weight.

but rejected the idea because several days would be required to reach the stranded space travelers.

Fortunately, their third attempt at landing worked perfectly, and their Soyuz TM-5 craft landed safely on the following day.

In other space programs, the Japanese announced their development of a single-stage-to-orbit spaceplane for early next century. All early designs use air-breathing engines for atmospheric flight, and liquid hydrogen/liquid oxygen rockets for space propulsion. One could make its way into orbit by 1996.

In July, India suffered its second setback in 15 months as its powerful five-stage rocket plunged only minutes after lift-off into the Bay of Bengal. It carried on board a satellite to survey forest deterioration, mineral deposits, and water reserves.

Israel sent an experimental satellite into orbit in September—the first step toward developing a reconnaissance satellite that would make Israel less dependent on the U.S. Code-named Ofek (Horizon), the craft remained in space for about a month, collecting data on solar energy and the Earth's magnetic field.

A computer malfunction stranded the crew of Soyuz TM-5 in space for 25 hours.

© Tass from Sovfoto

On The Road To IO

by Thelma Chang

The images were startling. During rapid hit-and-run flybys of Jupiter in 1979, cameras aboard the two Voyager spacecraft witnessed at least eight volcanic eruptions on the surface of Io, one of the giant planet's moons. The volcanoes spewed forth huge umbrella-shaped plumes, one at least 180 miles (290 kilometers) high and 720 miles (1,160 kilometers) wide. Boiling sulfur pits dotted Io's surface, colorful lava flows poured from volcanic craters, and gaseous sulfur dioxide appeared over one volcanic area. Io, the most geologically active body in the solar system, was soon being compared to Dante's Inferno.

Galilean Discoveries

Although some observations of Jupiter's moons had been made from Earth and the Pioneer spacecraft, little was known about them until the Voyager missions. The four largest, discovered by Galileo in 1610 and known as the Galilean moons ever since, revealed their individual characters in 1979. Europa is covered with a crust of ice resembling a cracked eggshell, which suggests the presence of liquid water beneath. Ganymede has mountains and valleys and exhibits evidence of plate tectonics similar to Earth's continental drift. Callisto, the farthest of the four from Jupiter, is apparently a cold and barren world. Io, the closest to Jupiter, is mottled red and brown and about the size of our Moon. It is the only body in the solar system besides Earth known to exhibit volcanism. (However, there is evidence of volcanic activity on Venus.)

Scientists hope that investigations of Io's volcanic activity may shed light on Earth's own volcanism. They look to another Galileo—this one a spacecraft—to fill in some blanks. Scheduled for launch from a space shuttle in October 1989, Galileo will operate within the Jovian system for nearly two years, skimming 20 to 100 times closer to the moons than the Voyagers and scrutinizing the giant planet and its "miniature solar system" as never before. Technologically superior to the Voyagers, Galileo carries 11 scientific instruments on its orbiter portion, and six others on a probe that will provide the first direct sampling of Jupiter's atmosphere.

While the Voyager observations functioned as quick snapshots, the Galileo observations will provide long-term views of Io's volcanoes. "You want to know how this all fits into a longer history," says Jay Goguen, resident research associate at the Jet Propulsion Laboratory (JPL) in Pasadena, California. "For example, Voyager I and II took pictures of the volcanoes just four months apart, but even within that short time, Pele, one of the largest ones, had shut down and stopped. . . . And also there was evidence observed by William Sinton [of the University of Hawaii] that in the period between the two Voyagers, there was an eruption that turned on, did its thing, then turned off. When Voyager II got there, you could see a dark spot and a big, bright halo, which looked much like other volcanoes."

Celestial Pinball

Galileo's first task is to leave Earth, something that has proved frustratingly difficult. Originally it was to have been launched by shuttle in 1982, boosted out of orbit by an Inertial Upper Stage, then slung to Jupiter by a gravity assist from Mars. When that schedule slipped, Galileo's new launch window required a more powerful upper stage, the Centaur.

When *Challenger* exploded, not only was Galileo stranded, but rethinking led to the abandonment of the liquid-fuel Centaur. Reteamed with the Inertial Upper Stage and unable to use Mars for a helping hand, Galileo needed to find a new route to Jupiter. The result will be an elaborately meandering journey called VEEGA (Venus-Earth-Earth-Gravity Assist), a form of celestial pinball among the planets.

VEEGA makes for an ingeniously plotted itinerary. Once in Earth orbit, Galileo will be boosted not to Jupiter but to Venus. There the planet's gravity will slingshot the spacecraft back to Earth for another boost out to the asteroids. Two years later the spacecraft will intercept Earth's orbit again for a final assist to Jupi-

The Galileo space probe will soon shed new light on Io, a moon of Jupiter. Viewed from the surface of the moon Europa, Io appears dwarfed by the giant planet.

ter. The journey will last six long years, but its benefits include opportunities to scrutinize asteroids and the far side of the Moon.

No Loitering

As the orbiter reaches the Jovian system, it will fly within 600 miles (965 kilometers) of Io, a maneuver intended to brake the spacecraft for insertion into orbit around Jupiter and allow it to listen as its probe enters the Jovian atmosphere. Galileo will make its most intensive studies of Io at this point, says Fraser Fanale, the spacecraft's satellite working group chairman.

Galileo can't loiter in Io's neighborhood, however: at that distance, Jupiter's intense radiation would soon prove deadly. ''We'll get most of the intensive Io data within hours of the [one] encounter,'' Fanale says. ''But even when we're not dealing with Io—say we're at Europa's orbit doing something else—we can make observations of Io as well as Voyager

The Galileo probe (left) will fly within 600 miles of Io before going into orbit around Jupiter. During its brief swing around the planet, Galileo will drop an instrument package to sample the gases of Jupiter's atmosphere and transmit the data back to Earth.

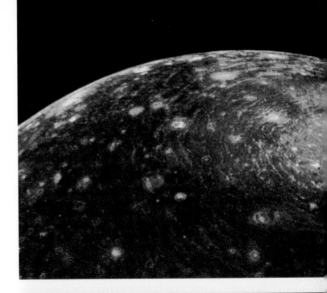

The earlier Voyager probes have provided glimpses of the other Galilean moons of Jupiter. Callisto (top) is cold and barren. Europa (middle) has an icy crust resembling a cracked eggshell. The mountains and valleys of Ganymede (bottom) show evidence of continental drift.

did.'' Once inside the Jovian system, Galileo will sweep past the outer moons on a route that takes in 12 looping encounters with Europa, Ganymede, and Callisto. ''My job is to make sure the project does all these encounters with the best coverage and resolution,'' says Fanale. ''Different distances are sometimes better for different things. . . . For [wide-area] coverage you want to be far away. For high resolution you want to be close. For an occultation [eclipse] you have to be behind the planet. For morphology you want shadows. But the guy who wants a compositional angle, the last thing he wants is shadows. He wants flat lighting.''

Fanale has high hopes for Galileo's high-resolution camera, the near-infrared mapping spectrometer (NIMS), which he describes as ''a marriage of a spectrometer and an image system.'' Each pixel—one of the many elements that make up a NIMS image—includes both visual and spectrographic information. ''You can either slice it one way or slice it another,'' says Fanale. For example, a scientist can take a NIMS image and have a computer color-code the pixels that have recorded, say, sulfur or basalt. He could even create a false-color image that color-codes every substance pictured. ''With NIMS we can actually see a compositional image,'' Fanale says. ''That's a very powerful technique that can do, in about half an hour, the work of 100 geologists working 100 years in the Andes. We're looking at Io with something that can measure while it's imaging.''

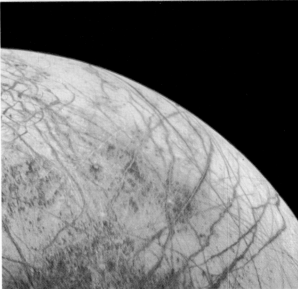

Understanding Volcanoes

Galileo's observations could lead to a better understanding of volcanism on Earth. In our few thousand years of recorded history, Earth has never experienced Io's level of volcano activity. Enormous eruptions may have occurred earlier, however. For example, the Kimberly diamonds, from a volcanic vent in South Africa, must have been formed under great pressure deep inside the ground, then forced to the surface by a tremendous eruption.

''There are periods on Earth when volcanism is active and not so active for reasons we don't fully understand, so it's important to see if those irregularities in activity level also exist on

Illustrations: JPL

Io," says Thomas McCord, Galileo scientist and chairman of the geosciences division of the Hawaii Institute for Geophysics. "Then, if we find another planet with this characteristic, we can compare it to Earth to better understand the volcanism process."

We do know that Earth's volcanism results from interior heat created by the radioactive decay of such elements as uranium, potassium, and thorium. The heat generated through such processes should be proportional to the planet's volume—yet Io, though much smaller than Earth, has more intense interior heating; its proximity to Jupiter may partly account for this.

Tidal Flexing

Scientists agree that Jupiter exerts tidal forces on its satellites and that friction caused by the tides creates heat. Io, the Galilean moon closest to the planet, is not only susceptible to the gravitational effects of Jupiter, it also feels the tug from the outer moons. Io is continually squeezed by a process called tidal flexing, much like being held in a fist that keeps tightening and relaxing.

"That's what provides the heat on Io," says the University of Hawaii's Sinton. "Io is just about the distance from Jupiter as our Moon from Earth. But Jupiter's mass is 318 times greater than Earth's, and on Io the tides are that much stronger. More than that, Jupiter's gravity causes Io to move around it in 1.7 days, much faster than the 28 days it takes our Moon to move around the Earth. So not only is Io getting squeezed, it's getting squeezed faster, and that heats it up even more."

The huge plumes spewed from Io's volcanoes, especially the spectacular 180-mile (290-kilometer)-high plume above Pele, indicate the extremes of Io's volcanism. Sinton, who has studied Io for eight years to gather data on a massive lava lake named Loki, points to a picture of Mount St. Helens smothered by a cloud of cinder and ash. "If we imagine that we took away the Earth's atmosphere and a lot of its gravity," he says, "that cloud would rise substantially higher," though not nearly to the height of Io's plumes. The scientists studying Io hope that once they have identified the eruptions' composition, they can begin to understand the mechanism that hurls them so high.

Sulfur and Silicates

There are two candidates for the materials involved in the volcanism: silicate—molten rock like Earth lava—and liquid sulfur, which is not as common on Earth. Sulfur has been detected on Io, but some believe that it may not be as common as silicate, existing mainly like "paint on the surface," according to Robert Howell of the astronomy and physics department at the University of Wyoming. Favoring the silicate argument are recent observations by a JPL group, which detected a volcanic explosion that was too hot to be liquid sulfur. Furthermore, fluid sulfur would be unable to support the mountain ranges seen on the satellite. A point in favor of the sulfur, however, is the fact that Io is so dry. "Once you get rid of water," Howell says, "sulfur is one of the things left that is volatile." Most likely, both types of eruptions are present on Io.

Another puzzle is Io's torus, a doughnut of glowing ions—charged particles—that accompanies Io in its orbit around Jupiter. "It may be that the volcanoes provide the atoms to the torus," says JPL's Jay Goguen. "The material comes off Io's surface by impacts of energetic particles. . . . It's hoped that by watching the volcanoes and the changes in the torus, you can demonstrate a link between volcanic activity and the source of materials in the torus."

Earthbound Observations

Periodically, project scientists have observed Io from facilities located, suitably enough, atop another volcano—Mauna Kea, on the island of Hawaii. (At 13,796 feet [4,200 meters], Mauna Kea's summit is above 40 percent of Earth's atmosphere, so its telescopes are especially sensitive.) Even from the most powerful telescope, Io appears as a mere pinpoint of light, but with the help of computers and special filters, scientists have been able to make some observations. "One of the most important factors about this research is to find out where the erupting volcanoes are so that Galileo will know where to point the cameras," says Goguen. "It's also important to look at Io [from Earth] at the same time Galileo is looking at it, because you want to know how ground-based measurements relate to what the spacecraft is seeing."

Other Earth observations will help. Scientists worldwide are in the process of organizing an International Jupiter Watch to coordinate Earth-based observations with Galileo's. "We want to have coverage of Io, Jupiter, and the whole system—not just from one location on Earth, but from such places as Australia, Chile, the Canary Islands, Japan, the U.S. mainland observatories," says Sinton.

© Ron Miller

Aside from the Earth, Io is the only body in the solar system known to exhibit volcanic activity.

In 1991 scientists can also take advantage of an occultation, a relatively rare occurrence in which the Earth is in a position to observe one satellite cover up another, and the moons' paths appear "edge on." When one satellite's edge crosses a volcano, there's a sudden drop in reflected light, allowing astronomers to measure the volcano's size. Meanwhile, in Hawaii, Mauna Kea's 33-foot (10-meter) Keck Telescope, the largest of its kind, is scheduled for completion in 1991.

Io's volcanism is, of course, only one facet of the Galileo project, which employs an estimated 700 people, including engineers, managers, technicians, and 115 renowned national and international scientists who make up 17 different investigation teams. Despite delays, they've weathered the disappointments and continue to pull it together. JPL's Torrence Johnson, chairman of the Galileo Project Science Group, is responsible for coordinating the craft's 17 onboard investigations involving six nations, a job not unlike that of an activities director on an ocean cruise. "It's interesting in that you have to be worried about looking at all aspects of the Jovian system at once," says Johnson, whose youthful appearance belies the fact that his experience extends back to Voyager. "While we're dealing with people from all over, it's without conflict because the culture is one of scientific experiments, so we share the same wavelength in that respect. We worry about the right measurements, the right everything."

"I, as an investigator, probably spend about three solid months each year simply planning the mission," says Galileo scientist Thomas McCord. "There are dozens of investigators who spend various amounts of time. It comes out to hundreds of years of effort, and that's just the science."

Galileo's delays have been frustrating for its investigative team: by the time Galileo returns its data in 1995, about 20 years will have gone into the project. William Sinton will have retired from the university system by then, and others may not be around for the payoff. "One investigator from California has already died," notes Fanale. "[But] even if we're not here, it's critical that we do a full-up beautiful mission because Galileo has an impact for all of us."

America Returns to Space

by Dennis L. Mammana

Its name was *Discovery,* and it rose atop a majestic fountain of fire into the clear blue Florida sky. Below, hundreds of thousands of spectators crowded the roadsides and beaches for a glimpse of history, and millions more watched on television. The date of the historic launching: September 29, 1988.

Thirty-two months had passed since the last shuttle cleared that same tower. It was only a minute later that we heard those bone-chilling words: "Go at throttle up." But a response never came. Instead, *Challenger* burst into a blinding fireball, its smoldering remains plunging into the cold Atlantic miles below.

© Roger Ressmeyer/Starlight

America roared back to space with the successful launching of the shuttle Discovery in September 1988. The liftoff ended a 32-month interruption in shuttle launches during which a reorganized NASA examined and improved nearly every aspect of the space program.

"Back to the Future!" "The Dream Is Alive: Go Discovery!" And the message lights in New York City's Times Square proudly said it all: "America Returns to Space!"

Challenger Disaster

It was on a cold January morning in 1986 that the nation's great dream of space exploration turned into its worst nightmare.

On that day an "O-ring" on a solid-fuel rocket booster didn't seal. Hot gases escaped and turned the shuttle *Challenger* into a burning fireball. Seven astronauts died that morning— among them a New Hampshire schoolteacher who had captured the imaginations of children with her dream of reaching for the stars.

To assure that such a disaster would never occur again, President Ronald Reagan appointed a 13-member commission, headed by former Secretary of State William P. Rogers. Its job was to investigate the possible causes of the *Challenger* explosion, and to recommend ways of preventing similar accidents in the future.

In their painstaking four-month probe, the panel reassembled the chain of events that led to the explosion, and discovered a complex series of mistakes, oversights, and misjudgments that contributed to it.

The commission found that the National Aeronautics and Space Administration (NASA) had become too intent on achieving its launch schedule, perhaps at the expense of safety. They further discovered that the shuttle's solid-fuel rocket boosters were fitted with incorrectly designed O-rings that lost their sealing ability in cold weather. On the frigid morning of the tragedy, the O-rings leaked hot gases that burned their way through the thin skin of the giant external tank, causing the fuel to ignite.

The Rogers Commission then outlined ways in which the shuttle booster's joint and seal might be redesigned, and how astronauts themselves might be involved in making decisions about shuttle design and launch.

Changes at NASA

To clean up its problem-riddled administration and improve worker morale, NASA underwent a major change itself. In May 1987, the popular

Everyone watching *Discovery* on this day remembered. As the gleaming white craft rolled gracefully onto its back and soared out over the Atlantic, the eyes of the world became riveted. Then, as that fateful 73-second mark neared, hearts pounded faster and faster. Those words were heard again: "Go at throttle up" . . . and were followed by a cheery, "Roger, go."

And *Discovery*—America's 26th shuttle mission—roared its way back into space.

Some cheered; some wept. Some merely gazed in silent awe. The pride of the nation was proclaimed on T-shirts, coffee mugs, hotel signs, and newspapers: "Return to Flight!"

The newly designed astronaut suits contain a parachute, an oxygen supply, and a life raft for ocean returns.

James C. Fletcher returned as the agency's chief administrator, a job he had held for eight years during the 1970s. (Fletcher resigned the position in April 1989.) NASA also established a new office of safety where employees can report safety problems in strict confidence.

Astronauts were given a major role in flight operations, and several moved into top management positions. Rear Admiral Richard Truly, who piloted the second test flight of the *Enterprise* in 1981, took over the agency's office of space flight. Captain Robert Crippen, a veteran of four shuttle missions and the pilot of the first shuttle flight in 1981, was appointed deputy director of shuttle operations.

A New *Discovery*

To those who watched the lift-off, the shuttle looked much the same as *Challenger*. But beneath its surface lay a totally changed craft.

Hundreds of changes had been made. Some were relatively minor, such as repositioning thermostats to keep cabin temperatures more comfortable, and changing fasteners on panels to permit easier access by the crew. But others were more critical.

On the orbiter alone, 210 modifications were made, including rewiring; improvements to brake, steering, and landing systems; stronger wings; and better heat-absorbing tiles. One hundred improvements were made to vehicle software, 145 to the solid-fuel rocket boosters, and 35 to the orbiter's main engines. And high on NASA's list was fixing the flawed joints between the stacked cylinders that make up the solid-fuel rocket boosters (SRBs).

NASA and Morton Thiokol, Inc., the SRB manufacturers, designed new, tighter joints between booster segments, added a third rubberized O-ring, and improved insulation to prevent burning gases from reaching the O-ring seals. As an extra safety measure, tiny heaters were added to the joints to protect them from cold.

Escape Systems

NASA also incorporated several systems to help astronauts escape in emergency situations. On the launch pad, the astronaut walkway atop the 34-story gantry was outfitted with heat sensors and water sprinklers. Two additional escape baskets were installed to enable astronauts and workers to slide down 1,200-foot (366-meter) cables to safety anytime before the final 30 seconds of countdown.

Two new landing sites in Africa were added to provide astronauts more flexibility in emergency situations—one at an abandoned Strategic Air Command (SAC) base near Ben Guerir, Morocco, 40 miles (64 kilometers) north of Marrakech, and the other at an airport in Banjul, Gambia, in northwestern Africa.

If, however, the shuttle must make an unscheduled return and no adequate runway can be reached, the orbiter could be set on a controlled glide at 25,000 feet (7,600 meters), and the hatch blown open with explosive bolts. The astronauts can then slide down an aluminum-and-steel escape pole and parachute into the ocean.

Such an escape is possible only because each astronaut's newly designed space suit is now equipped with a parachute, an oxygen supply, and a life raft for ocean returns. Once safely in the water, the astronauts can signal their location with a tiny radio.

If a crippled shuttle does reach a runway during an emergency, the astronauts can blow open the side hatch and pop open an inflatable slide similar to those used in commercial aircraft, and slide to safety on the ground.

Let's Do Launch

In addition to hardware changes, NASA's preflight inspections and launch rules have become more rigorous as well. Under the new policies, fuel cannot be loaded into the shuttle's huge external tank if the temperature has averaged less than 41° F (5° C) during the previous 24 hours. Further, the craft may not be launched if the temperature is below 37° F (2.7° C) with a light wind, or below 47° F (8.3° C) with no wind.

In addition, no craft can be launched if the wind blows at more than 27 miles (43 kilometers) per hour, if it is raining at the launching pad or within the flight path, if there is lightning within 11.5 miles (18.5 kilometers) of the pad, or even if the shuttle might fly through any of certain types of clouds.

Passing the Tests

To make sure that all systems were operating properly, engineers tested the shuttle parts under the most extreme conditions imaginable.

On August 30, 1987, scientists and engineers gathered at the Morton Thiokol test range

Left: NASA; above: © Keith Meyers/NYT Pictures

In an emergency, astronauts can set the shuttle on a controlled glide at 25,000 feet and escape by sliding down a pole (left) and parachuting safely into the sea. Astronauts can evacuate a shuttle on the runway using an aircraft-style inflatable slide (above).

some 25 miles (40 kilometers) west of Brigham City, Utah, to watch the first full-scale test of the newly designed booster rocket.

The signal was given, and the rocket was ignited. A 500-foot (150-meter)-long plume of fire shot from the booster's end, and the rocket burned more than a million pounds of fuel during its two-minute test.

During the test, some 520 instruments recorded the rocket's vital signs, enabling scientists to proclaim it an overwhelming success. This marked the first bright sign in the shuttle program in many months.

Engineers still weren't satisfied. Over the next 12 months, four more tests followed, each more ruthless. The rocket was intentionally assembled with holes, gaps, depressions, and sep-

Before resuming regular flights, NASA conducted five test-firings of the shuttle's redesigned solid rocket motor.

arations in the insulation and seals of the five major joints to see if hot gases would penetrate and scorch backup seals.

By August 18, 1988, the final test was completed. The redesigned joints and other components appeared to have withstood heat and stresses more extreme than they would ever encounter in a real launch.

Just one week before this final booster test, engineers ignited *Discovery*'s three main engines for their final—and flawless—22-second "flight readiness" test.

These successes did not come easy, however. Throughout the summer a nagging series of problems surfaced and forced five announced launch dates to be abandoned.

A leak in a 0.5-inch (1.25-centimeter) metal line leading to a small fuel tank took technicians on a two-day, round-the-clock search in July. Late that same month, a mysterious hydrogen leak sprung up on the launch pad, and a few days later a sluggish fuel valve postponed the main-engine firing test.

But finally the craft was ready, proclaimed by some to be the safest space vehicle in existence. Preparations for launch began.

Nearly two years had passed since an American shuttle left pad 39B, and the U.S. had fallen far behind in basic space research. During this time, unemployment in the Cape Canaveral area rose to 6.5 percent. The Soviets launched dozens of satellites, sent two scientific probes to Mars, and ferried cosmonauts between Earth and its Mir space station. The U.S. also lost countless commercial clients who chose to have their satellites launched by the European Space Agency or by China rather than wait for the U.S. space program to return to form.

If the U.S. was to make its space comeback, this was the time. And NASA wasn't taking any chances. They planned this mission as a "test flight" to make sure everything worked as planned—both in space and on the ground.

On Board *Discovery*

When *Discovery* left its launch pad on September 29, 1988, five veterans of space flight were aboard—the first time since the *Apollo 11* flight to the Moon in 1969 that such importance was given to a mission.

Navy Captain Frederick H. (Rick) Hauck, a physicist and test pilot, was commander. Piloting the craft was Air Force Colonel Richard O. Covey. Riding along as mission specialists were Marine Lieutenant Colonel David C. Hilmers; George (Pinky) Nelson, a former astronomer; and John M. Lounge, an astrophysicist and former Navy pilot.

Once *Discovery* eased safely into orbit 180 miles (290 kilometers) above the Earth, the astronauts were anxious to begin work. "We're looking forward to the next four days," said Hauck. "We have a lot to do, and we're going to have a lot of fun doing it."

They began immediately with the successful deployment of the Tracking and Data Relay Satellite, or TDRS, to increase NASA's communications with other satellites and shuttles.

Once it was sent on its way into a geosynchronous orbit some 22,000 miles (35,400 kilometers) overhead, the astronauts settled back to conduct dozens of scientific experiments. These ranged from studying the effects of microgravity on blood viscosity, to photographing lightning bolts in the atmosphere below, to testing a new method of communications using infrared light. The experiments also included two student investigations of zero-gravity crystal growth that had been lost in the *Challenger* explosion.

There were some glitches, however. On the second day of the flight, a special 3-foot (1-meter) communications antenna in the cargo bay wouldn't rotate properly, and had to be retracted and stowed unused for the duration of flight. Temperatures inside the cabin rose to around 80° F (27° C) because water inside one of the air-conditioning systems froze after launch.

Few shuttle missions are all work and no play, and this one was certainly no exception. For their first wake-up call on Friday morning, the crew received a surprise. From a sound sleep, they were awakened by: "Gooooood morning, *Discovery*! Rise and shine. Time to start doing that shuttle shuffle. Hey, here's a little song coming from the billions of us to the five of you." It was comedian Robin Williams,

Five veterans of space flight manned the historic flight of the shuttle Discovery: *(clockwise from left front) Richard Covey, pilot; David Hilmers, George "Pinky" Nelson, and John Lounge, mission specialists; and the mission commander, Frederick Hauck.*

greeting the astronauts with a line from his movie *Good Morning, Vietnam.*

On Sunday, as the crew prepared to return from the first shuttle mission in nearly two years, they paid tribute to their *Challenger* comrades who died blazing a trail into space for future generations.

In a moving memorial service, Commander Hauck said: "Today, up here where the blue sky turns to black, we can say at long last: 'Dear friends, we have resumed the journey that we promised to continue for you.' "

Return to Earth

On Monday, October 3, after 64 orbits and 1.7 million miles (2.7 million kilometers), the crew of *Discovery* began their long descent to Earth. Nearly half a million people gathered in the southern California desert to greet *Discovery*'s historic return.

After two spectacular sonic booms at 50,000 feet (15,250 meters), the shuttle appeared in the sky, banked sharply to the left, and made its final approach.

At 9:37 A.M. Pacific time, *Discovery*'s wheels touched down on the dry lake bed at Edwards Air Force Base, greeted by the cheers and tears of a nation. Within minutes the 26th U.S. shuttle mission rolled to a stop. Over their radio the astronauts heard the proud voice of Capcom: "Welcome back, *Discovery*—a great ending to a new beginning!"

During the flight, only 10 problems were documented, and those were relatively minor. Initial inspections of the 97-ton (88-metric-ton) craft revealed that no major repairs were needed before its next flight, and only six of the 30,000 tiles in the heat shield will need to be replaced. "The vehicle looks beautiful," said John J. Talone, Jr., ground processing manager at Kennedy Space Center. "It looks as good or better than any vehicle we've brought back."

Said Admiral Truly: "We're going to have to make sure we do the same on the second flight, the third flight, and all flights in the future. I'm convinced we can continue to do that."

Future Directions

Not clear, however, is the direction of NASA's "new beginning." Many questions remain. What purpose will the shuttle serve? What role will it play in the launching of commercial and military satellites? For the construction of a U.S. space station? For the launching of manned and unmanned scientific missions throughout the solar system? At present, no one knows for sure.

Nevertheless, construction began in August 1987 on a new $2 billion orbiter to replace *Challenger*. Scheduled for its maiden voyage in February 1992, the orbiter will be named in a contest among the nation's schoolchildren.

The new shuttle will include a parachute system in its tail section to help slow down the vehicle as it rolls down the runway. Such an innovation will extend the lifetime of the orbiter's brakes and enable the use of shorter runways at the various emergency sites around the world and at Cape Canaveral.

On the day of *Discovery*'s launch, the U.S. and 11 other countries signed an agreement to cooperate on the design, development, and operation of a permanently manned space station to serve as an international research laboratory and in the development of new space transportation technologies.

The astronauts conducted dozens of experiments in orbit. As part of an investigation submitted by students, Pinky Nelson photographed zero-gravity crystal growth.

NASA

From liftoff to landing, flight controllers at the Johnson Space Center monitored every step of the Discovery *mission.*

By recent estimates, at least 20 shuttle flights will be required to erect the $19 billion station, with additional flights each year to ferry people, supplies, and equipment back and forth—beginning in 1994. No long-term plans will be put into place until the shuttle is flying regularly again. The present schedule calls for five missions to fly the first year after *Discovery,* and nine the following year, with as many as a dozen a year by the mid-1990s.

Most will be in service to ferry a two-year backlog of scientific missions into space. These include the Magellan radar mapper to Venus; the Hubble Space Telescope, which has been called "potentially the most significant tool for scientific discovery in our lifetime"; a Spacelab mission called Astro-1; the Galileo mission to Jupiter; the Mars Observer; and the Ulysses probe over the Sun poles.

For the distant future, the Marshall Space Flight Center is funding a modest study of a heavy-lift vehicle called "Shuttle C" (for "cargo"), and exploring ways to extend the current shuttle's time in orbit.

NASA is also developing an advanced booster system that will enable the shuttle to carry an extra 12,000 pounds (5,400 kilograms) of cargo into orbit—an increase equivalent to 2.4 additional shuttle missions a year on a 14-flight schedule.

The Dream Is Alive

With the successful launch of *Discovery,* the nation's eyes are again aimed toward space.

Two thousand Kennedy Space Center workers laid off after the *Challenger* accident have been rehired or replaced. And unemployment in the Cape area has returned to its pre-accident level of only 4.7 percent.

A telephone survey of more than 1,500 adults while *Discovery* was in orbit revealed that an astonishing 73 percent believe that the shuttle program was "worth continuing" despite risks and costs—an increase of 7 percent in just two years.

And the nation's shuttle program—not so long ago felled by an unimaginable tragedy—seems bound for greatness once again.

NASA

Women in Space

by Debra Plymate

T he sky's the limit'' has been uttered for decades, but how many women take the saying literally? Traditionally, woman's role has been attached to domestic responsibilities that bind her to the Earth. Even today, with women moving into the competitive world of corporate management, many continue to assume primary responsibility for the management of home and children, and most women do not grow up with the notion that flying is a practical pursuit.

Adventurous Aviatrixes

For women the long road to space began in the early days of aviation. While the Wright brothers were experimenting with flying machines, their sister Katherine was home tending to domestic chores. One wonders, then, what they thought when Blanche Scott soloed a Curtiss pusher biplane in 1910, not even seven years after they had achieved the first powered flight by man in the history of the world. Amelia Earhart was a baby in Atchison, Kansas, when the Wright brothers invented the airplane. A few years later, she saw her first airplane at the Iowa State Fair. By the 1920s she had dared to fly. After becoming the first woman to cross the Atlantic by air, Earhart also became, in 1932, the first woman to fly solo across the Atlantic,

In 1983, astronaut Sally Ride became the first American woman to fly in space when she served as a mission specialist aboard the space shuttle Challenger.

and, in 1935, made the first solo flight by man or woman from Honolulu, Hawaii, eastward across the Pacific to Oakland, California.

In 1937 Earhart took off in her twin-engine Lockheed Electra on a world equatorial flight that ended somewhere in the Pacific, where she tragically disappeared after covering more than 22,000 miles (34,500 kilometers). To this day, she is remembered not only as a preeminent aviatrix, but as a heroine to all American women.

While Earhart was striving for distance records, Jacqueline Cochran was filling the record books with speed records. Cochran set more records than any other pilot—male or female—in aviation history. She became interested in aviation in the early 1930s, and by 1932 was a licensed pilot. An ambitious businesswoman and entrepreneur, Cochran acquired a cosmetic-manufacturing company and flew herself around the country on business-related trips.

During World War II, Cochran founded the Women Air Force Service Pilots (WASPs) and was the only woman to fly a bomber in England. In May 1953, in the shadow of Chuck Yeager, she became the first woman to fly faster than the speed of sound.

While Cochran was in Europe in the 1940s, a 12-year-old named Jerrie Cobb began flying with her Air Force father. She became a ferry pilot, delivering airplanes around the world, won numerous flying awards, and became an executive with Rockwell's Aero Commander Division. By 1960 Cobb had logged more than 10,000 hours in all types of aircraft. And more than 20 years before the first American woman would fly in space, Cobb was selected as the first woman in the Mercury astronaut candidate testing program.

Early Astronaut Criteria
During the late 1950s, the National Aeronautics and Space Administration (NASA) was assigned the responsibility for developing and carrying out the mission of manned spaceflight. Aeromedical consultants established a plan for astronaut selection calling for males aged 25–40, less than 5 feet, 11 inches (180 centimeters) tall, with at least a bachelor's degree. Candidates had to have qualifications in physical, mathematical, biological, or psychological sciences; technical or engineering work experience in research and development; or operation of aircraft, balloons, or submarines. Because of

classified aspects, however, this plan was not approved.

In 1958 President Eisenhower stipulated that volunteers for the space program be drawn from the ranks of military test pilots. The Pentagon provided a list of more than 100 pilots on active duty. From interviews, medical and written tests, and rigorous laboratory examinations at Lovelace Clinic in Albuquerque, New Mexico, and Wright Air Development Center in Dayton, Ohio, the first seven American astronauts were selected and announced to the public in May 1959.

Randolph Lovelace, who was responsible for screening candidates for the Mercury program, decided to see if women might also be suitable for spaceflight. Twenty outstanding women pilots were recruited and sworn to secrecy. By February 1960, the first, Jerrie Cobb, had passed the grueling physical tests and moved on to the next phases of testing. The other women were tested two at a time at the Lovelace Clinic. Twelve passed the first phase and were eager to follow Cobb, who by that time had completed subsequent training, including in the Multiple Axis Space Test Inertia Facility (MASTIF) at Lewis Research Center.

Woman Eschewed
To say these women were eager to go into orbit would be an understatement. Not only did they endure extreme physical demands and discomforts—ice-water injections in their ears or swallowing 3 feet (1 meter) of rubber tubing—all made sacrifices in their personal and professional lives. It came as a severe blow when NASA Administrator James Webb, in July 1961, ordered discontinuance of the program.

When NASA revealed the participation of women in the Mercury program, the media responded with chauvinistic quips like "Astrodolls," "Spacegals," "Astrotrix," and "Astronettes." As a result of public pressure to announce the role of women in the space program, Jerrie Cobb was appointed as a consultant to NASA Administrator James Webb; she was never consulted.

NASA continued to remain indifferent to a woman-in-space concept in spite of a visit to the United States by Russian space scientists in 1961, when they announced a female cosmonaut training program. NASA effectively barred women from becoming astronaut candidates by upholding the qualification requirement of military test pilot experience. Jackie Cochran, the only woman in the country who could meet this qualification, was beyond the age limit.

In 1962 Jerrie Cobb and Jane Hart went to Washington to plead with Vice President Johnson to sponsor a woman-in-space program. Instead of the assistance they had hoped for, he responded by arranging congressional hearings. Cobb and Hart, testifying before the House Space Subcommittee in July 1962, claimed discrimination by NASA, and argued that education requirements had been waived for John Glenn, who lacked a degree in a physical or biological science or in engineering. Glenn testified that "if we can find women that demonstrate that they have better qualifications than the men around them . . . we would welcome them with open arms." Cobb, in fact, had over 10,000 hours as a pilot—in contrast to Glenn's 5,000 hours and Scott Carpenter's 2,900 hours. Ultimately, however, Congress refused to authorize a coed program for astronauts.

In 1963 the Soviet Union achieved the world's first spaceflight by a woman when they sent Valentina Tereshkova into orbit. Tereshkova, a textile factory worker with no technical background, went on a world tour extolling the virtues of the Soviet system. "As you can see," she proclaimed, "on Earth, at sea, and in the sky, Soviet women are the equal of men." But it would be almost 20 years before another Soviet woman would go into space.

Soviet cosmonaut Valentina Tereshkova pioneered female space travel in 1963 as the pilot of Vostok 6.

Intensive Testing

During those 20 years, NASA employed increasing numbers of women in professional roles, such as mathematicians and engineers. Women also participated in experiments to determine the effects of weightlessness in the environment of outer space.

The first major biomedical research project to obtain physiological data on the reaction of women to conditions that would be experienced on the shuttle took place at NASA's Ames Research Center. In September 1973, 12 Air Force nurses volunteered for five weeks of tests to observe the reaction of women to increased gravity. The volunteers were spun in a centrifuge to simulate G-loads. When centrifugal forces were great enough to cause blackout from diminished blood flow to a subject's brain, the centrifuge was stopped.

In 1977 a San Francisco newspaper advertisement solicited volunteers for a study to determine whether women could withstand the stresses of spaceflight. Of 70 responses, 10 women were chosen to spend three and a half weeks in a windowless, soundproof enclosure at Ames in simulated orbital flight. These tests alternated between periods of strenuous activity and bed rest while doctors measured the results of changing atmospheric pressure and the effects it had on circulation. Endurance exercises on treadmills and bicycles were also conducted. The daily cycle of flight in space was simulated with a total of 16 hours of daylight and eight hours of darkness in 16 increments of 90 minutes every 24 hours. This simulated an orbit of the Earth every hour and a half. The bed-rest portion of the experiment covered nine days, the length of a typical shuttle mission, during which time the subjects were not allowed to get up, sit, or raise their knees. Because they were not allowed to raise their heads, they wore prismatic glasses for reading and bathed in a horizontal shower they jokingly nicknamed the "cookie oven."

After the rest period, the women were spun in a centrifuge to produce the same high G-forces that would be experienced during reentry. Other than incidents of boredom and short temper during the tests (and, for a few days, weakness, wooziness, light-headedness, and medically unexplained tingling in the feet— all of which are common to astronauts), the conclusion was that spaceflight would have no adverse effect on women, and that their reactions appeared no different from those of men.

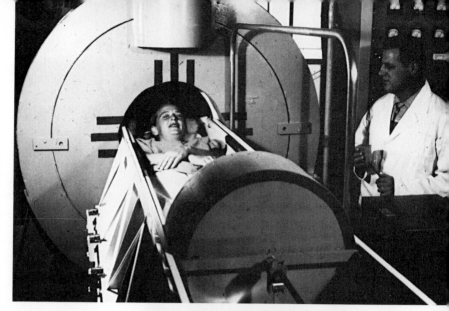

Jerrie Cobb (right), Myrtle Cogle (below), and ten other women pilots passed the grueling physical and psychological tests required for astronaut selection. In July 1961, soon after they had entered a second phase of testing, NASA abruptly discontinued the female astronaut program. Fifteen years would pass before NASA would again allow women to apply for astronaut openings.

Scientists, however, continued to question the effects of space on the female physiology. In November 1978, the Human Research Center at Ames conducted a similar study on older women. Eight women between the ages of 45 and 55 completed nearly a month of tests encompassing simulated orbit. Again scientists concluded that women could withstand the stresses of spaceflight, regardless of age.

As recently as 1984, subjects at Johns Hopkins Medical Center were tested in horizontal bed rest to simulate weightlessness to ascertain whether conception is possible in space. Changes in body-fluid composition and volume before and after exercise were examined to reveal how female hormones and reproductive ability might be affected by spaceflight. Results showed that menstrual cycles were lengthened by low gravity, but that it was unknown how the reproductive organs would function in complete weightlessness. The study also concluded that space should not affect a fetus, since the womb also simulates a low-gravity environment.

Concurrently, research into the effects of weightlessness on bone loss was under way at Washington University in St. Louis, Missouri. Significant bone loss from calcium depletion had been noted in astronauts in the Skylab program. Women astronauts are more at risk than men, since they have smaller frames, lose more bone mass due to hormone decline with age, and ingest fewer calories, and thus, less calcium.

Women Finally Welcomed

On July 8, 1976, NASA announced openings for astronauts to fly on the new space shuttle, and, for the first time, women were encouraged

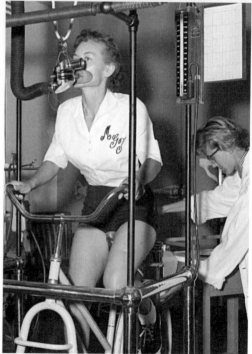

Both photos: Lovelace Medical Center

to apply. It had been 10 years since NASA had selected new astronauts. The new spacecraft would be spacious enough to have, among other features and amenities, toilet facilities for women. In the sex-discrimination-awareness era of the 1970s, NASA was finally ready for equality. Of 5,680 new mission-specialist applicants, 1,251 were women. Of the 35 astronauts accepted, six were women.

In early 1977 Sally Ride, a graduate student at Stanford University in Palo Alto, Cali-

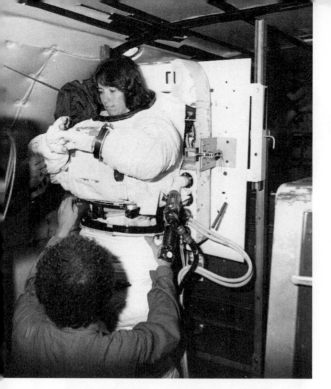

By the late 1970s, astronaut candidate Anna Fisher and a handful of other women were serious contenders for crew openings on upcoming space shuttle flights.

fornia, saw NASA's "call for astronauts" announcement in the university's newspaper. A physics student nearing completion of her doctoral thesis, Ride expected her future to be in research and teaching. The timing of NASA's decision to include women as candidates for shuttle flights was serendipitous. Little did Ride know, when she decided to apply, that she was to become the most revered woman aviator since Amelia Earhart.

The new selection committee used realistic physical requirements, such as vision correctable to 20/20 and height from 60 to 76 inches (152 to 193 centimeters), along with a psychiatric examination and interview. At the insistence of Carolyn L. Huntoon, Johnson Space Center's deputy chief for personnel development, the women were not questioned about aspects that were not considered in selecting men, i.e., plans to have children or spousal career considerations. On January 16, 1978, Ride was notified of her selection for the job of mission specialist on a space shuttle flight.

American Women in Space

On July 18, 1983, aboard *Challenger,* Ride became the first American woman to enter a world once dominated by male test pilots. Dur-

ing the seven-day flight, Ride and fellow astronaut John Fabian were responsible for the operation of a 50-foot (15-meter) mechanical arm that deployed a $40 million communications satellite.

A year later, on August 30, 1984, Judith Resnik became the second American woman to orbit Earth, aboard *Discovery.* Among her many assigned duties on the seven-day flight, Resnik was responsible for extension and retraction of a 102-foot (31-meter) experimental solar panel from *Discovery*'s cargo bay. The panel, a prototype auxiliary power source to extend future missions, was the tallest structure ever deployed in space.

Also aboard *Discovery* with Resnik was Steven Hawley, Ride's then-husband. When asked at the time what he thought of his wife being selected for flight before him, he said, "If they hadn't picked her, I'd be mad."

Interestingly, while many early female aviation pioneers appeared independent to the point of being unmarried or, at best, aloof mates, half of the first six women astronauts were married to fellow astronauts. The first astronaut couple was Rhea Seddon and Robert Gibson, and Seddon holds the distinction of being the first astronaut to have a baby.

The flight of *Challenger* in October 1984 was the first American space mission to have two women on the same flight. Along with Sally Ride, the first woman to fly in space twice, was Kathryn Sullivan, who became the first American woman to walk in space. She and astronaut David Leestma spent three and a half hours outside the shuttle. As a team, they connected a fuel line between a tank containing toxic hydrazine fuel and an empty tank as a rehearsal for the refueling of a Landsat satellite that had exhausted its fuel. After finishing, Leestma said, "You want to stay out here an extra minute?" Reluctant to end the space walk, Sullivan replied, "Twist my arm."

Optimizing Selection Possibilities

In the decade since the first group of women was inducted, four subsequent selections of shuttle astronaut candidates—in 1980, 1984, 1985, and 1987—included nine additional women. Of the 45 applicants selected since 1984, 43 were either military personnel or employees of NASA, even though civilians make up the vast majority of applicants. Of the two nonmilitary or non-NASA personnel selected, one was G. David Low, son of a former deputy

At NASA's weightless environment facility (right) and in all other phases of training, women undergo the same rigorous preparation for space travel required of men. Once in space, duties both inside and outside (below) the spacecraft are assigned without regard to sex.

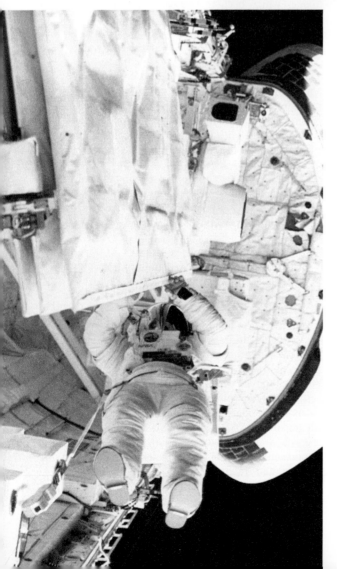

administrator of NASA, who was working at the Jet Propulsion Laboratory (JPL) under contract to NASA. The other was Mae Jemison, a physician and the first minority woman to be selected.

For aspiring astronauts with scientific qualifications, employment with NASA as an engineer or scientist would improve their likelihood of becoming astronauts. In 1974 women represented 10.8 percent, a fourfold increase. During fiscal year 1987, 20.2 percent of the agency's total hires in the scientific and engineering occupations were women.

Carolyn Spencer, before applying for the astronaut candidate program, worked as a materials engineer at Marshall Space Flight Center, preparing experimental equipment for Space Processing Applications Rocket (SPAR) flights. She had dreamed of space ever since watching, from her high school near Cape Canaveral, the launch of a Redstone rocket carrying Alan Shepard in May 1961.

Spencer went on to earn a degree in astronautical engineering, spending part of each college year at a NASA field center as a cooperative student. There she met Mary Helen Johnston, who had viewed the same Redstone rocket from another high school in the area. Johnston had earned a doctorate in metallurgical engineering, specializing in solidification of materials, crystal growth, and X-ray diffraction. Johnston and Spencer collaborated on materials-

Women have shared in the tragedies as well as the triumphs of the space program. Judith Resnik (front), Christa McAuliffe (fourth in line), and five other astronauts perished in the 1986 Challenger *explosion. Sally Ride served on the commission that investigated the accident.*

processing experiments flown on SPAR missions, experiments that have shown that absence of gravity (as in Earth orbit) contributes to the uniformity of structure in casting. Their research will lead to development of a methodology for preselection of structures for specific uses and manufacturing.

Already a Legacy

The 1986 *Challenger* accident took the lives of seven crew members, including Judith Resnik and teacher Christa McAuliffe. Following the disaster, President Reagan appointed Sally Ride to the Rogers Commission, which was responsible for investigating the accident. Upon completion of the investigation, she was assigned to NASA headquarters as a special assistant to the administrator for long-range and strategic planning, managing studies that will help the nation choose its next major goal in space. These studies culminated in the August 1987 release of *NASA Leadership and America's Future in Space*, which became known simply as "The Ride Report." Ride left NASA in the fall of 1987, accepting a fellowship at the Stanford University Center for International Security and Arms Control.

Sally Ride's flight firmly established an equal role for women in the space exploration program. She will be remembered for her professional accomplishments in the space program, as will Judith Resnik and Christa McAuliffe, who gave their lives in exploration of the newest frontier—space.

The future is bright for women in aeronautical research and space exploration. Role models in a variety of interesting space-related jobs can be found at every organizational level. In just over 50 years, the ranks of American women pilots have swelled to 42,000, a 326 percent increase. The military services have been training women pilots at an ever-increasing rate since 1970; because of this, it is likely that women will be qualified to be flight commanders on the *Freedom* Space Station.

Judging from the past achievements of women, future decades hold an incalculable panorama of new opportunities for women. As America moves ahead to explore, develop, and settle the inner solar system, there will be less focus on the contributions of women because of the peculiarity of their sex—but more based on merit and skill as women avail themselves of opportunities without the obstacles of prejudice, custom, and tradition.

in search of
PLANET X

by John Anderson

F or those interested in planetary exploration, there could hardly be a more fundamental question than whether or not there are undiscovered planets in our solar system. Only 58 years ago, in 1930, Clyde Tombaugh, working at Lowell Observatory, discovered the planet Pluto. In 1977 a search of the sky by Charles T. Kowal of the California Institute of Technology (Caltech) revealed the giant asteroid Chiron, initially hailed by the press as a tenth planet. In 1978 James L. Christy and Robert Harrington of the U.S. Naval Observatory discovered Pluto's satellite, Charon.

Yet Chiron is much too small to qualify as a planet, and even Pluto and Charon, with diameters of 1,425 miles (2,300 kilometers) and 800 miles (1,280 kilometers), respectively, are more like satellites than planets, at least from the standpoint of size. Even the mean density of the

Planet X, theorized to lie somewhere beyond the orbit of Pluto, would benefit little from the Sun's energy.

Pluto-Charon system, only about two times as dense as water, is more typical of large satellites—such as Ganymede, Callisto, and Titan—that are combinations of rock and ice.

Although the Pluto-Charon system and Chiron would be fascinating to study and explore, the possibility of a tenth planet offers us something far different, a planet on the scale of the Earth or perhaps larger. The term "Planet X," coined by American astronomer Percival Lowell before the discovery of Pluto, is used for any undiscovered planet outside Neptune's orbit. Some believe that such a planet exists, but there is not a single shred of hard evidence for any planets outside of the nine known ones.

What appears to some as compelling indirect evidence that a Planet X may exist may in fact be pointing to something quite different, perhaps something even more tantalizing. In fairness, it should be pointed out that some in the scientific community do not consider the indirect evidence at all compelling, and instead look to faulty data for explanations.

In this article, evidence, taken seriously by some, that borders on mysticism—such as ancient Babylonian texts, numerology, and mythology—has been ignored. Although possibly valuable for other scholarship or for inspiration, such material is inappropriate within the context of the scientific method. So what evidence do we have?

First of all, there is no convincing theoretical argument that the planetary system ends at Neptune. Before William Herschel's discovery of Uranus in 1781, the outermost known planet was Saturn. In 1846 Urbain Jean Joseph Leverrier realized that perturbations in Uranus' orbit could be explained if another massive planet orbited the Sun outside of Uranus. He sent his calculations to Johann Gottfried Galle, who discovered Neptune the same night he received Leverrier's prediction. With Galle's discovery, the radius of the known solar system increased to 30 times the average distance between Earth and the Sun (30 astronomical units). One astronomical unit (abbreviated AU) is equal to approximately 93 million miles (150 million kilometers).

Yet the distance of the hypothetical Oort Cloud of comets is more than 1,000 times farther from the Sun than Neptune, while the nearest star, Alpha Centauri, is over 9,000 times farther than Neptune. To get an idea of the scale of that distance, let a U.S. dime represent the solar system within Neptune's orbit. Then the distance to Alpha Centauri is about 89 yards (82 meters). There is still plenty of room for more planetary orbits about the Sun.

Searching with Telescopes

Since Herschel and Galle's searches of the sky with telescopes resulted in the discovery of two planets about 15 to 17 times more massive than Earth, it is hardly surprising that at least a few people were eager to carry on the search with the improved instruments of the 20th century. The most extensive search, spanning the years 1929 to 1943, was conducted by Clyde Tombaugh at the Lowell Observatory near Flagstaff, Arizona. After 14 years of persistent work and the discovery of Pluto, he was convinced that no other planet visible with his 13-inch (33-centimeter) telescope existed within a large portion of the sky north and south of the ecliptic, the plane cut by Earth's orbit about the Sun. (All the known planets except Pluto orbit in about the same plane.) In a wider region, no brighter planets existed.

Yet Tombaugh left one-third of the sky out of his survey. Some of the neglected region was near the celestial South Pole and hence inaccessible from Flagstaff. Other neglected regions, though in the Northern Hemisphere, were far from the ecliptic, where planets are less likely. Later, between 1977 and 1984, Charles T. Ko-

American astronomer Clyde Tombaugh discovered Pluto during a 14-year search of the heavens, but found no evidence of Planet X.

JPL researchers are studying discrepancies in the orbits of the nine known planets for indications of a tenth planet.

© Roger Ressmeyer

wal used the 48-inch (122-centimeter) Schmidt Telescope at Palomar Observatory to survey a region 15 degrees north and south of the ecliptic. Because of the Schmidt Telescope's larger aperture, Kowal was able to include dimmer stars not available to Tombaugh. He found no planets.

It is unlikely that anyone in the future will repeat these efforts of Tombaugh and Kowal, who examined literally tens of millions of stars. The next extensive search for planets will probably be done with automated instruments, freeing the observer from the thousands of hours required to compare hundreds of photographic plates taken at the telescope.

It is sometimes difficult to understand why no one has seen a planet larger than Earth. But considering the number of candidate objects in the sky, practically all of them invisible to the naked eye, one can get an idea of the difficulty of selecting one out of about 100 million possibilities.

Influencing Orbits

For that reason, scientists have shifted their emphasis from surveying a large region of the sky toward identifying likely regions for Planet X and then concentrating the search there. With this new approach, some of us have been trying to cast the search for Planet X in terms of grav-

itational influences on the orbits of known objects in the solar system.

Actually, attempts to locate Planet X through its effects on other bodies have a long ancestry. The discoveries of both Neptune and Pluto were preceded by mathematical calculations showing systematic errors in the orbit of Uranus. Pluto was, in fact, found near the location predicted by Percival Lowell from his calculations.

However, in light of Pluto's small mass, it is clear that the ninth planet could not have caused the disturbances in the orbits of Uranus and Neptune that Lowell noted. Nevertheless, after its discovery and well into the 1950s, some astronomers were convinced that unless Pluto had a mass at least as big as Earth's, the observed orbital disturbances of Uranus and Neptune could not be explained.

By the 1960s it was becoming clear that Pluto's influence was insufficient to explain the irregular orbits of Uranus and Neptune; at the same time the data that were so important to Lowell began arousing suspicion. At the U.S. Naval Observatory and at the Jet Propulsion Laboratory (JPL), researchers decided to disregard the older data and to concentrate solely on information obtained with instruments whose hardware and data-reduction procedures were well understood.

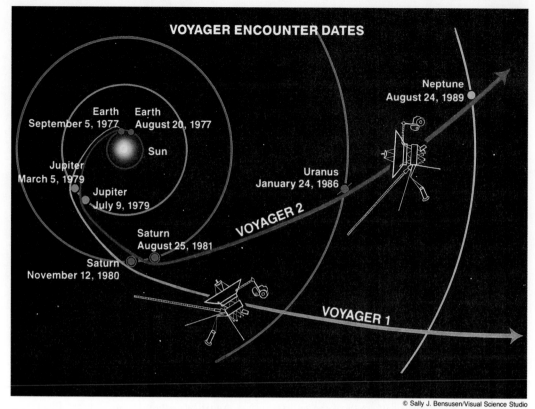

VOYAGER ENCOUNTER DATES

Earth
September 5, 1977

Earth
August 20, 1977

Sun

Jupiter
March 5, 1979

Jupiter
July 9, 1979

Uranus
January 24, 1986

Neptune
August 24, 1989

Saturn
August 25, 1981

Saturn
November 12, 1980

VOYAGER 2

VOYAGER 1

© Sally J. Bensusen/Visual Science Studio

Data gathered during Voyager 2's Neptune flyby and subsequent journey may help solve the Planet X question.

Particularly at JPL, where the emphasis is on computing planetary orbits for the space program, the data on Uranus and Neptune were severely limited to first include only observations made at the U.S. Naval Observatory with either the 6- or 9-inch (15.25- or 22.8-centimeter) transit-circle instruments (telescopes that can measure planetary positions very precisely), and then to include only data taken after 1911, when a further improvement in instruments, the impersonal micrometer, was introduced. Using those data, as well as data extending all the way back to 1846, astronomers at the U.S. Naval Observatory concluded in 1971 that the current model of the outer solar system is incomplete. This finding could imply undiscovered planets. (It should be recalled that when unexplained motions were detected in Mercury's orbit about 100 years ago, it took Albert Einstein's 1916 theory of general relativity to reconcile the discrepancies.)

More recently, R. S. Gomes and S. Ferraz-Mello in Brazil have analyzed essentially the same data, but extending to 1982. They determined, with a reliability of greater than 99 percent, that there is an unaccounted influence on the motion of the orbit of Neptune. They also concluded that we cannot rule out a source of gravitational attraction, including the possibility of a tenth planet with a mass about that of Earth.

The discrepancies in the orbits of Uranus and Neptune are most noticeable over the years since 1846. The unexplained motions account for at least 2,700 miles (4,400 kilometers) in the location of Neptune and at least 1,700 miles (2,800 kilometers) in the location of Uranus.

New Insights from Pioneer

Puzzled by these discrepancies, a program was undertaken a few years ago to examine the orbits of Pioneer 10 and 11 for unexplained motions. Pioneer 10 had an encounter with Jupiter in December 1973. Pioneer 11 visited Jupiter in December 1974 and then proceeded to Saturn. Both spacecraft are leaving the solar system on orbits that take them far beyond Uranus and Neptune. Pioneer 10 is now 43.5 AU out, almost one and a half times farther from the Sun than Neptune, and Pioneer 11 is at a distance of 25.6 AU, well beyond the orbit of Uranus.

The two spacecraft are being tracked by the NASA/JPL Deep Space Network (DSN) with radio equipment that allows the spacecraft's motions to be determined accurately at interplanetary distances. No unexplained motions were found that could be attributed to Planet X; such information nevertheless tells something about the characteristics of the hypothetical tenth planet's orbit. We know, for example, that there can be no planets of Earth size within 40 AU or so of either Pioneer spacecraft.

We will continue to monitor the motions of the two Pioneer spacecraft for perhaps another five years, after which their power sources will become too feeble for radio tracking. For now the search for Planet X must be guided by the unexplained motions of Uranus and Neptune and by the negative results from the DSN data. But at least one other piece of indirect evidence is significant.

Simulating Orbits

Thomas C. Van Flandern and Robert Harrington of the U.S. Naval Observatory have shown with computer simulations that a planet with peculiar orbital characteristics and a few times bigger than Earth could explain both peculiarities of Pluto's orbit and the fact that Triton, Neptune's large satellite, revolves in a clockwise direction while other major satellites and planets in the solar system move counterclockwise. In the scenario analyzed by Van Flandern and Harrington, Planet X passed sufficiently close to Neptune in the distant past that it expelled one of its satellites (Pluto) and reversed the motion of Triton.

If this happened, Planet X is now in a peculiar orbit of its own with a period of about 800 years and a present distance about three times the distance of Neptune from the Sun. Robert Harrington has been searching the sky for this planet, but has found nothing yet. It is interesting that the planet he seeks is consistent with the Uranus and Neptune data as well as the negative results from the two Pioneer spacecraft.

So does Planet X exist? Nobody knows. It is an interesting possibility, and certainly well worth the search, but admittedly not all share this view. Nonetheless, whatever the form of the direct or indirect evidence, there will always be a few people sufficiently motivated by the possibility of success to carry on the tradition of planet-hunting.

The Deep Space Radar Detector can track space probes for five years after they leave the known solar system.

JPL

BEHAVIORAL SCIENCES

BEHAVIORAL SCIENCES

In 1988 researchers discovered that schizophrenia may have some genetic origins. Studies were carried out on memory, hyperactive children, and AIDS patients. A sound method of increasing children's language skills was tested.

by Bruce Bower

© Erika Stone/Photo Researchers

Children may express depression or anxiety through hyperactive behavior.

Hyperactive Children

Psychiatrists are taking a close look at the families of hyperactive children in an effort to improve treatments for the controversial disorder. Researchers at the Eisenhower Army Medical Center in Fort Gordon, Georgia, found hyperactivity often reflects a youngster's depression or anxiety. The parents of hyperactive children also reported elevated levels of depression and anxiety in themselves. Many had experienced a number of stressful events, such as divorce or hospitalization, in the previous year.

It is difficult to prove a link between parents' problems and a child's hyperactivity, say the scientists. But effective treatment often must go beyond giving a child the stimulant drug Ritalin, they contend. Ritalin can calm hyperactive behavior in some cases, but there are recurring concerns that the drug is prescribed too freely for all sorts of behavior problems.

The Georgia psychiatrists run support groups for parents of hyperactive children, where parents begin to unravel the ways in which family members habitually interact and reinforce one another's behavior. Hyperactive youngsters also learn to regulate their heartbeat through biofeedback training, a process that helps improve their concentration and self-control.

Emotion and AIDS

Preliminary work at the University of Miami School of Medicine found that anger and a sense of vigor are linked to stronger immune responses among homosexual men in the early stages of infection with the AIDS (acquired immune deficiency syndrome)-causing virus. The virus is referred to as HIV.

Immunity was also stronger among HIV-infected men who openly vent their emotions and say they want to get on with life despite having severe problems. In other studies, this type of "fighting spirit" predicts longer survival among cancer patients.

The Miami scientists studied 49 homosexual men whose HIV infection was newly diagnosed. Those reporting more vigor, anger, venting of emotions, and determination to get on with life possessed more active natural killer cells, one type of infection-fighting cell in the immune system. Lymphocytes, another type of immune cell, responded more vigorously to chemical stimulation.

Investigators at the University of California at San Francisco reported, however, that immune function did not increase among HIV-infected men given stress-management training and group support. The men attended eight two-hour weekly sessions and an all-day retreat where training was provided in relaxation techniques (such as yoga and meditation), good health habits (such as exercise and nutrition), and stress management.

Men who attended the program did, however, decrease their average number of sexual partners. A comparison group of HIV-infected men who did not receive training increased their average number of sexual partners in the same period.

Regular exercise seems to help newly diagnosed AIDS victims manage stress.

© Co Rentmeester/The Image Bank

Flashbulb Memories

Remember what you were doing when you learned the space shuttle *Challenger* had exploded? You probably do, and a recent psychological theory suggests such a major event activates a special type of memory that creates a permanent "flashbulb memory" of your experiences just before, during, and after learning of the startling event.

But flashbulb memories tend to fade and are not always accurate, reported psychologists at Johns Hopkins University in Baltimore, Maryland. These recollections may be vivid, but they have much in common with normal memory.

The researchers administered questionnaires to 45 people within a week of the January 28, 1986, space shuttle explosion, and 27 of the subjects completed another questionnaire nine months later. Subjects reported where they were and what they were doing at the time,

© AP/Wide World

People can often recall the exact circumstances under which they learned of such startling events as the assassination attempt on President Reagan in 1981.

how they heard about it, and how they reacted upon learning of the explosion. There was much consistency in responses at one week and nine months, but there was also a substantial increase in "don't remember" responses, and a shift from specific to general answers.

Another researcher, who questioned people one month and seven months after the 1981 assassination attempt on President Reagan, found more specific and consistent memories among those who reported the most surprise upon learning of the event.

Genetics of Schizophrenia

Scientists located genetic markers for schizophrenia in seven Icelandic and English families. The markers apparently lie near a gene that predisposes its bearers to schizophrenia.

Schizophrenia refers to a group of severe mental disorders with symptoms such as delusions, hallucinations, apathy, and an inability to take care of one's basic needs. A schizophrenic does not have a split personality, as many people

commonly believe. About one person in 100 has some form of schizophrenia.

The families in the new study have many schizophrenic members. Markers were located with chemical substances that slice samples of genetic material at precise locations. The markers turned up predominantly in family members with schizophrenia or related disorders.

Researchers are still a long way from identifying the gene they think lies near

the markers. But once they do, genetic counseling, at least for people with a large number of schizophrenics in their families, may be possible. Analysis of the gene may also lead to better drug treatments for schizophrenia.

In another study, investigators found the same genetic markers did not turn up in schizophrenic members of a large Swedish family. This suggests that a number of genes may be involved.

Reading and Language

Parents who changed the way they read picture books to their children, by adopting a few simple techniques to increase a child's active participation, substantially boosted the youngster's language development. Psychologists at the State University of New York at Stony Brook trained parents of 2- to 3-year-old children to ask open-ended questions while reading stories, rather than reading the stories straight through or posing "yes/no" questions. One example is asking

"What is Eeyore doing?" instead of "Is Eeyore lying down?"

Children whose parents read to them in this way for one month did far better on tests of vocabulary and verbal expression than children whose parents did not undergo the one-hour training.

How parents talk to their children makes a big difference in language development. A child who actively responds to what a parent reads readily acquires reading and speaking skills.

Open-ended questions during storytime enhance a child's verbal skills.

© Erika Stone/Photo Researchers

Exploring The Forces of Sleep

by Erik Eckholm

I t's 2:30 in the morning, you've got a crucial interview during the day, and you find yourself desperately thrashing in bed. Worry over what you're going to say has given way to panic over whether, given how sleepy you'll surely be, you will be able to speak coherently at all. If this sounds familiar, relax, because the news from the world of science is good. If you care enough about tomorrow's challenge for it to keep you awake, a growing body of research shows, you'll probably rise to the occasion and do just fine.

Photos: © Lou Manna

A volunteer sleeps while electrodes transmit readouts of her vital signs to a specialist, who monitors the data for signs of a sleep disorder. Such data has revealed that sleep patterns change as a person ages.

After a bad night's sleep, you might not be able to stay alert throughout a long, monotonous meeting, and it wouldn't be safe to make a long drive. But studies indicate that even if you have hardly slept for days, when faced with an important task, you can perform as well as ever. Personal resilience and drive, it seems, can temporarily overcome drowsiness. In addition, biological rhythms play a crucial role in determining how awake or sleepy one feels. These daily rhythms, physiological changes that ordinarily make one feel alert during the day and sluggish at night, are so powerful that they affect performance even more than the sheer amount of sleep does.

Inborn Sleep Requirements

Everywhere, the majority of adults sleep from seven to eight hours a day, according to Dr. Wilse B. Webb, professor emeritus of psychology at the University of Florida. He says that one in 100 needs only 4½ hours, and another one in 100 sleeps 10½ hours. Individual requirements are inborn; people who fight their natural sleep needs are in for a constant battle that is bound to test their willpower. When the will to stay awake flags—during boring, routine activities, for example—sleepiness inevitably triumphs, producing the urge to nod off during the day.

But in years of studies, Dr. Webb has tested the abilities of the sleep-deprived and found that even after three or four days without sleep, people can perform tasks requiring intense concentration without impairment. What they lose is persistence and, especially as time passes, alertness. "You don't become less smart," Dr. Webb says. "You just can't keep on producing."

After inadequate sleep, it's the little things that suffer—with possibly dangerous consequences. In desert war games, Dr. Webb notes, Israeli soldiers defend themselves in battle just fine, even when they get almost no sleep for several days. What they forget to do is to follow a prime rule of desert warfare: to fill their canteens at every opportunity. "If something is important enough, if you're motivated or excited by it, you can overcome the effects of sleepiness," adds Dr. Mary A. Carskadon, an associate professor of psychiatry and human behavior at Brown University Medical School. But if you push things too far, especially if you continue in an activity that is monotonous but requires constant vigilance, such as driving, "you may be courting catastrophe."

Circadian Rhythms

In recent years, researchers seeking to understand the function of sleep and its effects on performance have turned more and more to the study of daily, or circadian, biological rhythms. While these rhythms—cyclical changes in hormone levels and body temperature—vary somewhat among individuals, most people fall into the same pattern. For example, body temperature usually rises during the day, correlating with alertness, and falls at night, when people start to feel drowsy. Circadian rhythms are influenced by such environmental cues as daylight, but also operate independently of them. When a person's internal clock is not synchronized with the time of day, problems occur, among them jet lag and, bedraggled workers may be pleased to know, the Monday-morning blues.

People on the East Coast who enjoy carousing late at night and sleeping until noon on weekends are, in terms of their biological clocks, shifting themselves to Denver or Los Angeles, observes Dr. Daniel Wagner, a neurologist at the Sleep-Wake Disorders Center at the New York Hospital–Cornell Medical Center in White Plains. When these people rise early and go to work on Monday, they suffer the malaise that results from their body rhythms being out of sync with their schedules. Experiments in which people have lived temporarily in caves or in windowless rooms, without cues about the time, show that the natural daily sleep-wake cycle is about 25 hours. The reason for this inherent tendency to lengthen the day is unknown, but it explains why most people find it easier to stay up late than to get up early, and suffer less severe jet lag when they fly west than east.

Biological Trough

Research has also found a definite biological "trough" in midafternoon, a dip in alertness that happens in spite of how much you slept the night before, how big your lunch was, or how boring a meeting is. Interestingly, the tendency to feel drowsy in the afternoon seems to develop naturally at puberty; 10-year-olds remain brightly alert all day. The findings, says Dr. Carskadon, suggest that the urge to rest after lunch is, like the more powerful one at night, biologically based. The "siesta" cultures may have the right idea.

Circadian rhythms appear to affect alertness even more than sleep deprivation does, at least in the short run, says Dr. Richard M. Coleman, an instructor in psychiatry and behavioral sciences at Stanford University Medical School and author of *Wide Awake at 3:00 A.M.* People asked to complete a routine task on a computer terminal every hour for 24 hours generally do well during the day and poorly after midnight, hitting the nadir at three or four in the morning. But their performance picks up again at 7:00 or 8:00 A.M., indicating that the inner clock partially overcomes the effects of sleep loss. Even after a poor night's sleep—four or five hours for people used to eight—subjects perform better during the day than they do at night. After several successive nights of inadequate sleep, however, Dr. Coleman says that circadian rhythms might not compensate for sheer exhaustion.

But some people perform best early in the morning or late at night. In part this seems to reflect differences in their biological clocks. Such variations are usually of little consequence, unless a "morning" or a "day" person must work at night.

Employees on the graveyard shift can seldom keep their work schedules and their inner clocks aligned, and this has alarming implications for the workers as well as for society. It is no coincidence, sleep researchers assert, that the major accidents at Three Mile Island in Pennsylvania, Bhopal in India, and the nuclear power plant at Chernobyl in the Soviet Union all happened deep in the night, when most operators are least alert. Even the small biological trough in the afternoon seems to undermine the performance of some kinds of tasks. Statistics show a rise in the frequency of car accidents attributable to sleepiness in the middle of the afternoon.

Clockwise Rotation

The biological clock is flexible enough to adjust to slight changes in a person's work schedule; but in many industries, rotations in shift work are so drastic that they play havoc with body rhythms, leaving employees unable to sleep at home and impairing their productivity at work. Scientists are now applying their knowledge of circadian rhythms to industrial management to help make shift work more bearable for employees.

A recent experiment with officers in the Philadelphia Police Department provided tangible evidence that some methods of rotating shift work are indeed better than others. The experiment was conducted by the Center for Design of Industrial Schedules, a nonprofit organization directed by Dr. Charles A. Czeisler, an associate professor of medicine at the Harvard Medical School who is associated with Brigham and Women's Hospital. Philadelphia, Pennsylvania, police officers normally work on one shift for six straight days, followed by two days off, and then change shifts. This schedule requires the policemen to adjust their sleep habits every eight days, which is nearly impossible. The strain takes a toll: officers feel tired on the job and are involved in a lot of automobile accidents while on patrol.

For 11 months last year, 220 officers worked on a new schedule intended to minimize the disruption of their internal rhythms. The policemen stayed on the same shift for three weeks at a time instead of one. Then their shifts moved forward—from day to evening, and evening to overnight, for example—instead of the reverse, which had been customary. This "clockwise" rotation reduced the burden of

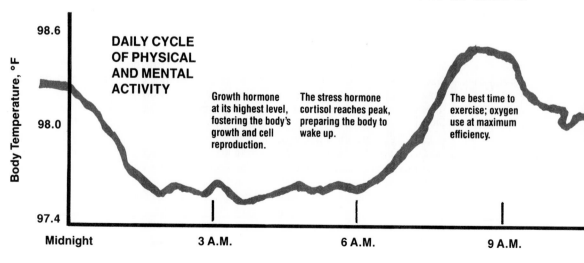

DAILY CYCLE OF PHYSICAL AND MENTAL ACTIVITY

Body Temperature, °F

98.6 — 98.0 — 97.4

Growth hormone at its highest level, fostering the body's growth and cell reproduction.

The stress hormone cortisol reaches peak, preparing the body to wake up.

The best time to exercise; oxygen use at maximum efficiency.

Midnight   3 A.M.   6 A.M.   9 A.M.

change on circadian rhythms by taking advantage of their 25-hour cycle and the resulting inclination for most people to stay up late. In addition, fewer officers were required to work the early-morning shift, statistically a low-crime period. The number of consecutive workdays was also cut from six to four, which gave the officers a chance to catch up on their sleep.

In a survey at the end of the experiment, most officers said they slept better at home and suffered less fatigue on their job. Policemen and their families said they were happier with the new schedule. The use of alcohol and tranquilizers to induce sleep was cut in half, the incidence of policemen falling asleep while at work declined by 29 percent, and the incidence of on-the-job automobile accidents was 40 percent lower than in previous years.

Micro-arousals

Circadian rhythms are not the only factors that influence whether you get a good night's sleep. Many experts believe that the deepest stages of sleep, known as "slow-wave" sleep, the times when you are hardest to wake, are important for producing a well-rested feeling. Whether or not

A drowsy person may succumb when lack of sleep and tedious circumstances reinforce the body's natural instinct to rest after lunch. Measurements of body temperature versus time of day further suggest that alertness hits a temporary trough around three o'clock in the afternoon.

Productivity peaks; brain most active.

Alertness hits temporary trough, but most people say they feel happier than at any other time of day.

Alertness improves; heart rate peaks. The speed with which a person can add and multiply numbers — or run the 50-yard dash — picks up.

Body temperature drops, alertness flags; stress hormone falls to lowest level; people get sleepy.

| 12 Noon | 3 P.M. | 6 P.M. | 9 P.M. | Midnight |

this is true, research suggests that the degree to which people feel rested depends more than anything else on the number of times they awaken during the night. For a variety of reasons, ranging through the tossing of a restless bedmate, anxiety, and serious medical problems, you may awaken repeatedly. Although these arousals may last only seconds and be forgotten by morning, they leave you feeling that you didn't sleep well, without knowing why.

"Micro-arousals" of less than 10 seconds are frequent among people over 50, who may have hundreds a night. Older people also wake up outright more often and take longer to fall asleep, which explains why half of all men and women over 50 complain of insomnia, more than twice the proportion of younger age groups. Changes in sleeping patterns are a frequent accompaniment of aging, observes Dr. Charles Herrera, the director of the Sleep Disorders Program for the Middle-Aged and Older Adult at the Mount Sinai Medical Center in New York City. The total time in the deep stages of sleep diminishes, and, Dr. Herrera has found, elderly people lose "plasticity," becoming less able to cope with jet lag and shift work.

Sleep Disorders

Although these changes are normal, certain other sleep problems, which can afflict people of all ages, are potentially dangerous and deserve medical attention. These include insomnia that is specifically linked to depression, medicines, or illness; narcolepsy, a neurological disorder that causes a frequent and uncontrollable urge to sleep; and, above all, the disturbance known as sleep apnea, from the Greek for "want of breath." People with sleep apnea stop breathing as many as several hundred times during the night for anywhere from about 30 seconds to one minute at a time. The spells may trigger heart attacks or strokes, but the more common dangers arise from the insidious daytime effect of sleep apnea: attacks of extreme drowsiness, which undoubtedly account for many car accidents and some stalled careers as well. The syndrome generally doesn't strike until middle age, when it is most common in obese men; in the later years, it afflicts many women, too.

Just about everyone has at one time or another suffered from insomnia, ranging from occasional trouble falling asleep to chronically fitful nights. One way to help prevent it, says Dr. Wagner of New York Hospital–Cornell Medical Center, is to wake up at the same time each day regardless of when you fall asleep, to synchronize your sleep-wake cycles with your daily schedule. Some people virtually condition themselves to staying awake in bed by reading books, doing crossword puzzles, and analyzing reports from the office. Dr. Wagner and other

Passengers flying east suffer the most from jet lag because their bodies must adjust to an earlier wake-up time.

© Yvonne Hemsey/Gamma-Liaison

Late-night revelers who sleep until noon on weekends find their biological clocks disrupted on Monday morning.

sleep specialists advise such people to leave these materials out of their bedrooms and to avoid certain other activities—such as exercising, eating large meals, and drinking caffeinated beverages—late in the evening.

Most doctors who treat sleep disorders discourage their patients from using sleeping pills. While they usually countenance pills for coping with insomnia caused by temporary stresses, such as the loss of a job, they caution that all available medications lose their effectiveness after a few weeks, even as they create physical and psychological dependence. Sleeping pills also produce abnormal sleep patterns and reduce alertness the next day.

Not to Worry

Doctors used to recommend a snort of liquor as a soporific, but no longer do. "Most people will probably have a better day after a bad sleep than if they drank themselves to sleep or took sleeping pills," says Dr. Ernest Hartmann, the director of sleep centers at Newton-Wellesley Hospital and West-Ros-Park Mental Health Center near Boston, Massachusetts. While a few drinks can indeed knock a person out, research has shown that alcohol suppresses the initial cycles of REM (rapid eye movement) sleep, when active dreaming occurs. The REM phase then rebounds with a vengeance, resulting in nightmares and frequent awakenings in the middle of the night. In fact, many experts describe the delirium tremens suffered by alcoholics as a waking REM state. Even a single nightcap can aggravate sleep apnea.

If insomnia is persistent and severe, medical or psychological help may be necessary. Regularly awakening in the middle of the night, for example, may be a sign of depression or alcoholism. For the occasional insomniac, though, the message the experts convey is not to worry. "If you're lying in bed trying to sleep, and for some reason you're getting more wide awake instead, that's the time to get up and do something else," recommends Dr. Hartmann. "Read a book or watch TV; lying there for two hours worrying just makes it worse."

And, in any case, Dr. Hartmann observes, "After a bad night, you can do better than you think you can."

© Liz Pyle/New Scientist

Brushes With DEATH

by Paul Perry

Raymond Moody chose to study psychiatry, he explains, "because it's the study of human peculiarity." And his own area of special interest, many would say, is indeed peculiar. In 1975 he published a book called *Life After Life,* in which he described the remarkable mental journeys of people who had come close to death but had not died.

People's near-death experiences (NDEs), as Moody called them, involved "out-of-body" experiences and other common characteristics, such as being sucked through a tunnel and greeted by happy people, some of them long-dead relatives.

A poll conducted by the Gallup Organization in 1981 revealed 15 percent of the American adults polled report a near-death experience. There are more than 100 support groups that exist in order to help people to better understand these events, as well as a professional journal and a quarterly newsletter.

Former Skeptics

Following the publication of *Life After Life,* Moody was subjected to attacks by medical colleagues who doubted his reports. Looking back, however, he says that it was good to have skeptics around: "Many of them tried hard to prove me wrong and ended up becoming believers themselves." Moody presents the evidence for NDE in his recent book, *The Light Beyond.*

One former skeptic is Michael Sabom, an Atlanta, Georgia, cardiologist who first heard about Moody's work in 1977 and doubted it all. But when he started casually surveying his patients, he was amazed at the number who did report NDEs. Sabom conducted a study of his own that has become a benchmark in NDE research. He examined the NDEs of 116 people, dividing their experiences into three types: autoscopic (an out-of-body experience), transcendental (entry into a "spiritual realm"), and experiences that mix the two. He talked to 32 people who claimed to have observed their own resuscitation by emergency-room doctors, and he compared their descriptions with the "educated guesses" of patients who had undergone resuscitation but had not had out-of-body experiences. He found that 23 of 25 patients in the comparison group made major mistakes in describing the resuscitation procedure, while none of the patients claiming out-of-body experiences made a mistake.

These results, Sabom says, are compelling evidence that the people who were out-of-body had a unique visual perspective on the hectic emergency-room activity. And coupled with the mental transformations seen in people following an NDE, they have convinced Sabom that something is happening as these people are snatched from death. "I don't think this stuff should be sensationalized as it has been in some instances," Sabom says. "It should be looked at as part of the normal living and dying process. If people would look at NDEs in that light, they might not seem so weird."

Many people who have come close to death report having had a near-death experience, a set of events that often includes moving along a tunnel toward a bright light.

The researcher Moody credits most with legitimizing his work is Kenneth Ring, a University of Connecticut psychologist. Where Moody's evidence is largely anecdotal, Ring has been conducting empirical work on NDE. Through considerable pleading and explaining at several Connecticut hospitals, Ring was able to find and interview 102 people about their NDEs. He was able to show that religion, race, and age are unrelated to whether a person has an NDE, and he was also able to confirm Moody's finding that the NDE is a positive experience that transforms personality.

Perhaps the most interesting current research is that of Melvin Morse, a Seattle,

Washington, pediatrician. In one study he has attempted to answer the most basic of all questions related to NDE: Does a person really have to be "near death" to have one of these experiences? To answer the question, he culled 202 medical records to find 11 young patients who had survived "critical illness"—a condition he defines as one with a mortality rate greater than 10 percent. He compared them with 40 patients of the same age who had survived serious illnesses having low mortality rates.

Although none of the seriously ill had had NDEs, 7 of the 11 critically ill had memories that included at least one of the following: being out-of-body (six patients), entering darkness

Knowing Near Death

There are nine traits that define the near-death experience, though it is rare for anyone to experience all nine. The presence of at least one of these symptoms is enough to constitute a near-death experience, according to psychiatrist Raymond Moody.
• *A sense of being dead.* At first, many people don't realize that the experience they are having has anything to do with being near death. They find themselves floating above their body and feeling confused. They wonder, "How can I be up here, looking at myself down there?"
• *Peace and painlessness.* An illness or accident is frequently accompanied by intense pain, but suddenly during a near-death experience, the pain vanishes. According to research by psychologist Kenneth Ring, 60 percent of people who have had a near-death experience report peace and painlessness.
• *Out-of-body experience.* Frequently people feel themselves rising up and viewing their own bodies below. Most say they are not simply a point of consciousness, but seem to be in some kind of body. Ring says 37 percent have out-of-body experiences.
• *The tunnel experience.* This generally occurs after an out-of-body experience. For many, a portal or tunnel opens, and they are propelled into darkness. Some hear a "whoosh" as they go into the tunnel, or they hear an electric vibration or humming sound. The descriptions are many, but the sense of heading toward an intense light is common to almost all tunnel experiences. Twenty-three

percent of Ring's subjects reported entering darkness, which some describe as entering a tunnel.
• *People of light.* Once people pass through the tunnel, they usually meet beings of intense light; this light permeates everything as it fills them with feelings of love. As one person said, "I could describe this as 'light' or 'love,' and it would mean the same thing." They frequently meet up with friends and relatives who have died, though the glowing beings can't always be identified. In Ring's research, 16 percent saw the light.
• *The Being of Light.* After meeting several beings of light, there is usually a meeting with a Supreme Being of Light. To some, this is God or Allah; to others, simply a holy presence. Most want to stay with the Being of Light forever.
• *The life review.* The Being of Light frequently takes the person on a life review, during which life is viewed from a third-person perspective, almost as though watching a movie. An important difference from cinema, however, is that the person not only sees every action, but also its effect on people in his or her life. The Being of Light helps put the events of life in perspective.
• *Rising rapidly into the heavens.* Some people report a "floating experience," in which they rise rapidly into the heavens.
• *Reluctance to return.* Many find their unearthly surroundings so pleasant they don't want to return. Some even express anger at their doctors for bringing them back.

(five), being in a tunnel (four), deciding to return to their bodies (three), peaceful or positive emotions (three), visions of dead relatives (one), or reaching a heavenly border (one). Morse concluded that to have a near-death experience, one must actually be near death.

Spiritual Survival?

Moody is intrigued by the scientific research his work has initiated. But he is even more intrigued by the most fundamental question underlying the whole enterprise: Does something in each of us survive death? "After years of listening to these things, I believe that something does," Moody says.

The aspect of the NDE that convinces Moody of spiritual survival is the out-of-body experience, which he considers proof that *something* leaves the body as the end draws near. He describes baffling cases to bolster his argument. One example: a woman who had been blind for 50 years was able to describe the instruments that were used in her resuscitation following a heart attack—right down to their colors.

Moody hears hundreds of these stories each year. He is constantly intrigued by them, yet even more convinced that science won't answer the final question: Do we survive death? "The answer to that question," he concludes, "isn't one for science. It is what faith is all about."

Near Death or Altered State?

Paul Kurtz, chairman of the Committee for the Scientific Investigation of Claims of the Paranormal, takes issue with some of the conclusions drawn by Raymond Moody. He notes that there are any number of explanations for the variety of encounters that make up NDEs. NDEs are not unlike other out-of-body experiences (OBEs) that are commonly encountered and do not occur in near-death situations. People who have had an OBE report a similar sense of separation from the body, even a hovering sensation and a "bird's-eye view." It is not necessary to explain this phenomenon as "astral projection"—that is, an actual departure from the body. It is much like the so-called "hypnagogic" and "hypnopompic" states, the twilight states we pass through between waking and sleeping. We know that patients who are unconscious or semiconscious may still hear what is going on around them.

There are reasonable physiological explanations for NDEs. We know that when the body is badly injured, the heart stops, the brain is deprived of oxygen, and cerebral anoxia occurs. Its effects are well documented. At first there may be a sense of well-being, probably the result of the brain's endorphin response to extreme trauma. As more neurons are damaged by lack of oxygen, the brain's ability to make critical judgments becomes impaired, reality becomes vague or illogical, and hallucinations occur. Psychopharmacologist Ronald Siegel has suggested that NDEs are similar to the

hallucinatory experiences induced by drugs, which are directly related to states of excitement and arousal in the central nervous system, and are accompanied by disorganization in the brain's regulation of incoming stimuli. Just as psychedelic drugs can trigger such neuronal frenzy, so, too, can anesthetics, fever, exhaustion, injuries—and probably the emotional and physiological processes involved in dying. The bright light often associated with NDE is a common hallucination and may be the result of some optical peculiarity, such as phosphenes, that arises during an altered state of consciousness. The light experience may also result if the central nervous system mimics the effect of light on the retina. Siegel notes that he is able to create the tunnel experience in volunteers under laboratory conditions.

Others have suggested that a kind of "depersonalization" process may be at work during an NDE. What this means is that the NDE is actually a psychological reaction to the prospect of facing imminent death, a coping mechanism used to struggle with a distressing, traumatic situation. There is no question that people can be profoundly moved by an existential brush with mortality, an experience that can dramatically alter one's values and outlook on life. That Moody's subjects have experienced profound personality change is not surprising—but it is hardly evidence for an afterlife. Belief in such a realm requires a leap of faith beyond the available scientific evidence.

the PERILS of POT

by Winifred Gallagher

America just can't decide what to do about marijuana. Some people equate smoking pot with sipping wine, others with abusing hard drugs. Most rank it somewhere in between. The confusion is awkward but understandable: marijuana is the nation's most popular but perhaps least understood illegal psychoactive substance.

So far, studies of pot's health effects suggest what many who've smoked it would predict: for most people, occasional use probably isn't particularly harmful. Heavy use over long periods is likelier to be dangerous, although the kind of expensive, long-term studies that proved the destructive effects of tobacco and alcohol remain to be done. At present, those who seem most at risk include young people, pregnant and nursing women, heart patients, and the emotionally unstable. Harvard psychiatrist and drug researcher Norman Zinberg summarizes the inadequate and conflicting data this way: "Nothing's been proved, but there's reason to worry."

There's a pressing reason to learn more about marijuana's effects: the pot on the street has increased in strength and potential harmfulness. Thousands of professional growers, many of them in northern California, have transformed American homegrown from a cottage industry into a multibillion-dollar-a-year agribusiness. These knowledgeable farmers use sophisticated technologies like hydroponics to cultivate pot powerful enough to command astronomical prices—more than $100 an ounce in big cities.

Recent studies show there are plenty of customers, though not quite as many as there used to be. Pot smoking peaked in 1978, and has declined since, especially among teenagers. The number of high school seniors who smoke it daily fell by over half from 1978 to 1986. However, the drug remains enormously popular:

Marijuana smoked today may have a THC level 10 times higher than the level typical of pot in the 1960s.

Professional growers use selective breeding, hydroponics, and other sophisticated agricultural techniques to produce the high-potency strains of "homegrown" marijuana (left) that have captured the American market. Not to be outdone, government agents now use a variety of advanced imaging and detection techniques that have greatly increased the number of "busts" (below) for pot cultivation.

some 62 million Americans have tried it, and 18 million smoke it regularly. Many of today's smokers are the baby boomers who first lit up in the 1960s and 1970s. But some have found that the drug that mellowed them as hippies can make them uptight as yuppies.

One reason that pot smoking makes many graying members of the Woodstock generation anxious these days is that even occasional use can jeopardize their livelihoods: many face tests to detect traces of the drug in their urine as a condition of employment. Even long-ago indulgence can damage reputations, as Judge Douglas Ginsburg learned when he was forced to withdraw himself from consideration for the U.S. Supreme Court.

The uncertainty over almost every aspect of marijuana has created confusing, contradictory policies. At the same time that the practice of urine testing spreads, laws in many states increasingly treat users with leniency. Although smokers can still be jailed in some states, they are now merely fined in others where the drug has been "decriminalized." In Alaska they can even legally grow their own. Smoking marijuana continues to become more socially acceptable, but the question still remains: Is it safe?

What Pot Is, How It Works

Marijuana is not a simple—or even a single— drug. Its wide range of effects on body and mind are caused by the more than 400 chemicals of the *Cannabis sativa* plant, especially the 60 or so that are unique to it—the cannabinoids. Some of these may contribute only minimally to the "high," but THC (delta-9-tetrahydrocannabinol) produces most of the psychoactive effects. While the potency of street drugs varies greatly, the average concentration of THC by weight has increased from 1 percent or less in the 1960s and 1970s to anywhere from 4 to 10 percent in the 1980s.

When marijuana is smoked, THC enters the lungs, passes into the bloodstream, and is carried to the brain in minutes. Both THC and its chemical by-products dissolve in fatty tissue—such as the brain, the adrenals, the gonads, and the placenta—and remain there for three or more days. (These chemicals can be detected in the urine of frequent smokers for four weeks or more.) It's worrisome that these compounds linger in the body and accumulate with repeated smoking, but there's no evidence yet that they cause harm.

In the brain itself, according to Dr. B. Martin, a professor of pharmacology at the Medical College of Virginia in Richmond, THC seems to turn on a number of biochemical systems. In low concentrations, it may cause two or three changes; in stronger doses, 10 or 12. Says Martin: "The high is probably a combination of effects—sedation, euphoria, and perceptual alterations—each caused by a separate mechanism." He thinks that molecules of THC produce their effects by fitting into special receptor cells in the brain, like keys in locks. If Martin and his colleagues could prove the existence of the receptors, their discovery would suggest that a THC-like biochemical occurs naturally—the body's own version of marijuana. "Such a substance could serve in the maintenance of mental health," Martin says, "perhaps by helping the individual to calm down or protect himself against stress."

High Anxiety

During the marijuana high, which lasts for two to four hours after smoking, users often experience relaxation and altered perception of sights, sounds, and tastes. One of pot's most common side effects is the "munchies"—a craving for snacks, especially sugary ones. Participants in a study at Johns Hopkins ate more snacks—and consumed more calories per day—while they had access to marijuana in a social situation.

The high can be subtle and somewhat controllable, and intoxicated users can seem sober to themselves and others. But this *feeling* of sobriety is one of pot's greatest risks to well-being. Hours after the sensation of being stoned is over, the drug can still impair psychomotor performance.

The user's coordination, visual perceptions, reaction time, and vigilance are reduced, which can make it dangerous to drive, fly, or operate machinery. In a study done at Stanford University, simulated tests of pilots' skills showed that the pilots were affected for up to 24 hours after smoking, although they felt sober and competent. Another California study showed that a third of the drivers in fatal car crashes had been smoking marijuana. Driving under the influence of pot may be especially

dangerous, because the driver may not know when his abilities are also curtailed for hours after smoking. This delayed effect could be a serious problem for students, especially frequent smokers. Because the duration and extent of marijuana's psychomotor effects are not known for sure, the practice of testing urine to determine workers' competence is very controversial. "For the first two to four hours, say, on a Saturday night, the drug decreases one's ability to think, drive, and work," says Dr. Reese Jones, a drug researcher and professor of psychiatry at the University of California, San Francisco. "But it's yet to be determined if those effects are still present on Monday morning."

Dr. Robert Millman, director of the alcohol and drug abuse service of the New York Hospital–Payne Whitney Clinic, agrees. "Most of the urine screenings that test positive for drugs pick up signs of pot—a very widely used drug," he says. "Companies are confused about what to do—should they fire everybody?"

Evaluating marijuana's impact on mental ability is difficult, but gauging its effects on emotional health is even more so. Responses are subjective and unpredictable. Marijuana is often associated with a feeling of mellowness, but it causes anxiety as well. It might make one user drowsy, and another—or the same user on a different occasion—hyperactive. One smoker becomes chatty, another withdrawn.

The strength of the drug, frequency of use, and physiological differences among users—for example, in body size and neural sensitivity to the drug—help account for the wide range of reactions. "About a third of people who smoke it feel no effects, a third feel ill, and a third feel high," says Dr. Renaud Trouvé, a drug researcher and assistant professor of anesthesiology at Columbia-Presbyterian Medical School in New York City.

What Timothy Leary and others called "set and setting"—the mental state of the user and the environment in which the drug is taken—also plays a part in emotional reactions to marijuana. According to Millman, many people now in middle age found smoking pot relaxing as youths within the laid-back 1960s counterculture. As they've increased in age, power, and responsibility, they've tuned out, turned off, and dropped in.

"There's a natural history to marijuana use," he says. "The baby boomers have acquired a sense of their vulnerability and of the finiteness of time—'This is my life we're talking about!'" he says. "Feeling lethargic and giving up control make them anxious now."

That fear of losing control, or even one's mind, can induce paranoia and anxiety—pot's most common unpleasant side effects—in people who would not have had these problems if they hadn't taken the drug, according to Millman. Moreover, he says, "marijuana can open a door to psychosis in predisposed persons similar to the action of many hallucinogens like LSD." Many doctors suspect that in these rare instances of users losing touch with reality, the drug has simply activated a latent psychiatric problem. Because of marijuana's potential for stirring up the psyche, psychiatrists say those with preexisting disorders should stay away from it.

However, after Harvard's Dr. Norman Zinberg, author of *Drug, Set, and Setting,* studied a group of marijuana smokers, he concluded that "essentially, marijuana doesn't cause psychological problems for the occasional user." Many of his colleagues agree. Most of Zin-

Marijuana, now California's leading cash crop, brings in billions of dollars a year to the state's illegal growers.

© Tina M. Mori

berg's subjects described the drug as not particularly deleterious to normal functioning, and difficult (though not impossible) to abuse; they tended to restrict smoking to leisure time and special occasions, often planned around food.

Deadheads and Other Potheads

The researchers' consensus on long-term heavy marijuana smokers is bleaker, although hard data are more elusive than those on the drug's acute effects. For the vast majority of users, pot isn't physically addictive. It ranks far below drugs such as cocaine and heroin—or alcohol and tobacco—in inviting compulsive use. Nonetheless, a significant number of smokers use the drug frequently, often daily. Such regular use is one of the most obvious signs of a serious marijuana problem; heavy daily smokers are usually at least a bit out of it.

Being out of it is less noticeable in the countries where the three large field studies of chronic users were conducted than in the fast-paced United States. Marijuana is widely accepted in Jamaica and Costa Rica, and within certain subcultures in Greece. These studies found that pot smokers were by and large as healthy—and functioned as well—as nonsmokers. However, although these surveys didn't prove any major, permanent health consequences of long-term pot use, that doesn't mean there aren't any. Researchers caution that the subjects of these studies were mostly poorly educated, working-class adults who have lower standards for productivity and health than middle-class Americans. And it took decades, not years, to determine the serious risk now known to be associated with alcohol and tobacco.

For those who look on pot as a buffer against stress, so-called "self-medication" can be dangerous: the person who smokes in an effort to "treat" his depression, anxiety, or personality quirks may only add to his trouble. The psychological problem most often associated with chronic marijuana smoking is the "amotivational syndrome." Those thought to have it—many of them teens and young adults—show diminished goal orientation, passivity, and an inability to master new problems. However, the syndrome poses a chicken-or-egg question: Does heavy pot use cause poor motivation, or vice versa?

New York Hospital's Millman prefers the term "aberrant motivation" to describe the inert attitude of some heavy smokers. "When parents

© J. L. Atlan/SYGMA

Nancy Reagan and other celebrities have made "just say no" a rallying cry for antidrug efforts across the country.

arrive at my office with a son in a ponytail and a tie-dyed shirt, they don't have to say a word. The kid is abusing drugs and doing badly in school and at home—but somehow he can get himself to a Grateful Dead concert in Ohio with seven dollars in his pocket. He doesn't lack motivation; he's just focusing it in the wrong direction."

Millman, who thinks such flawed motivation is caused by the combination of pot and preexisting psychological problems, has found that some adolescents smoke grass not only to escape from their troubles, but to explain them. Such self-handicapping protects their egos against feelings of failure. "Many of the kids I see have made pot smoking the rationalization for psychopathology—they and their peers can say they act weird because of dope, rather than because they have an untreated learning disability or an emotional disorder," he says.

Children and teenagers are endangered by any drug, because their bodies and minds—especially their judgment—are immature. A study of middle-class adolescents dependent on marijuana, reported in the May 1987 issue of the journal *Clinical Pediatrics,* helped identify those who may be at highest risk from the drug. Many were learning-disabled, had family histories of alcoholism, and personal and academic problems. Their parents—and, in some cases, therapists—hadn't suspected their pot smoking for a year after they started, perhaps because other problems may have disguised the drug use.

The connection between pot and poor motivation and learning disabilities is particularly troubling in an era when 28 percent of students drop out of high school. The sedation, skewed psychomotor functioning, and involvement with other drugs and drug-abusing peers associated with marijuana make any use by teens unwise. A kid who tries pot also has an estimated 10 percent risk of becoming a daily smoker—and frequent use, at this age, can become truly disastrous.

Revving Up the Heart

Proof of the physical risks of marijuana is as elusive as proof of its dangers to the mind. The lack of comprehensive long-term human studies and the limits of animal research frustrate scientists like Renaud Trouvé. He's convinced that marijuana stresses the heart, lungs, and immune and endocrine systems, particularly when it's used frequently. "As for the short-term physiological effects of marijuana, one can believe what is written," he says. "As for the long-term effects, we just don't know."

For example, it seems reasonable that pot smoking would be bad for the lungs. Marijuana contains more tar and carcinogens than tobacco and is inhaled longer and harder. But while heavy users do show a measurable airway obstruction and seem more prone to bronchitis and sinusitis, no links to serious lung diseases like cancer or emphysema have been established. In fact, perhaps the worst threat to the lungs of pot smokers is the herbicide paraquat, which was sprayed widely on marijuana fields, especially in Mexico. The use of the chemical, which can cause severe lung damage, has been discontinued, although it's being considered as a way to deter growers in California and Hawaii.

The effects of marijuana on the reproductive system also seem ominous, but remain unproved. The drug temporarily lowers the level of the sex hormone testosterone in men, and decreases the number, quality, and motility of sperm, but the impact on fertility is unknown. However, testosterone also helps govern puberty's changes in boys. Some researchers think that low levels of the hormone could impair adolescent development.

Women who smoke heavily may have menstrual irregularities, and may even fail to ovulate. When pregnant monkeys, rats, or mice are exposed to heavy doses of pot, their offspring are more likely to have a low birth weight or to be stillborn. There's no clear proof that marijuana causes birth defects, but pregnant and nursing women are urged to treat pot with the same caution they give to alcohol and tobacco.

Similarly grim but inconclusive observations suggest that marijuana use can adversely affect other organs and systems in the body. Some researchers have found that marijuana can cause microscopic brain-cell damage in monkeys—but human brain damage hasn't been shown. Some studies suggest that marijuana can suppress immune function to some extent, but scientists don't yet know whether that degree of dysfunction affects health. What's more, marijuana increases the heart rate by as much as 90 beats per minute. This added workload could be very dangerous for those with cardiovascular disorders such as angina, but there's no evidence that it causes any permanent harm to healthy hearts.

Toward a Sound Pot Policy

What state-of-the-art marijuana researchers tell experts is that we need to know more. In 1982 the Institute of Medicine published ''Marijuana

and Health,'' a 188-page report based on solid research and compiled by a committee of 21 scientists. Its conclusion, echoed by many marijuana researchers today: ''Marijuana has a broad range of psychological and biological effects, some of which, at least under certain conditions, are harmful to human health. Unfortunately, the available information does not tell us how serious this risk may be.''

The uncertainty that surrounds marijuana use is compounded when it's compared to the nation's other drugs—both legal and illegal. Despite increasing decriminalization and public tolerance of pot, half of all drug arrests made by local police in 1985—almost 500,000— involved marijuana, according to *The New York Times*. Many citizens consider this police enforcement an inappropriate use of resources that could be used to fight the greater menace of deadly drugs like heroin and cocaine—or, for that matter, tobacco and alcohol, which cause hundreds of thousands of deaths each year.

It's unlikely that either of these two legal, lethal drugs would be lawful if they were discovered today. ''The light use of marijuana is certainly not as bad for you physically as alcohol or tobacco,'' says Harvard's Zinberg. ''Our drug policy is based on morals, not on health considerations. The person with a drink in his hand says to himself, 'I'm bad enough, but that guy smoking pot over there is worse.' ''

Zinberg says the best approach toward a sound policy on marijuana would be continued decriminalization accompanied by 15 years of serious long-term research. By then the public would have enough information to make personal choices and public policy decisions. Reese Jones believes that, regardless of policy changes, marijuana's popularity may gradually die out as the group of heavy users ages.

The one point on which all those concerned with marijuana agree is that having so little knowledge of the drug is dangerous. Despite its prevalence and the unanswered questions about its use, federal support for pot research, still in its infancy, has decreased—diverted to less-used but ''hotter'' drugs like cocaine. ''I'm a researcher with conservative views on drug use who hasn't found the hard data on the health effects of marijuana,'' says Jones. ''There's a lot of uncertainty about it—you can't say it's unsafe, but there's no proof it's benign, either. We should be studying it to find out, but all the research money is going to help figure out how to detect it in people's urine instead.''

Calamities of human origin tend to have a much greater impact on their victims than do natural disasters. People directly affected by the December 1988 plane crash in Lockerbie, Scotland (above) will likely suffer psychological repercussions far longer than will evacuees from a flooded neighborhood (left).

Disaster Dynamics

by Andrew Baum

Natural disasters fascinate people. The raw power of nature smashing into the concrete and brick of human settlements, the violent winds, the raging waters—all symbolize the eternal battle between us and the elements. In many cases, we win. By building dams to reduce flooding, by predicting and preparing for storms and earthquakes, we can often minimize serious damage and loss of life. But our control is limited. All too often, natural forces wreak havoc—physically, socially, and psychologically—when we can't restrain them.

Whom Do You Blame?

In recent years we have been hearing more about different kinds of disasters: leaking toxic-waste dumps that contaminate our homes and drinking water; nuclear power plants that release radiation into the air; asbestos insulation that threatens the health of workers, homeowners, and schoolchildren. These calamities, often undramatic and undetected for years, may cause individual distress and social disruption greater than disasters brought on by natural forces.

The fact that these are caused by people rather than by nature seems to affect the way we react to them. Although there are exceptions, technological calamities, especially when they involve toxic substances, can cause more severe or longer-lasting mental and emotional problems than do natural disasters.

There seem to be several reasons for this. One is that the former give us someone to blame. Following the accident at the Three Mile Island nuclear power plant, for example, lawsuits were filed and protests organized to stop reopening of the plant. Similar actions have taken place at Love Canal and in other communities affected by leaking toxic chemicals. As the lawsuits and recriminations drag on for months and years, people constantly relive the horror and stress of the event.

Natural disasters don't normally produce these continuing reminders of calamity. Whom do you blame for an earthquake? While we may criticize public officials for not coping properly with the damage or for not giving enough warning, we can't blame them for the event itself. It was, we say, an act of God, and we move on to do what we can to diminish its effects.

Blaming others also affects our sense of control over the world. Research has suggested that losing this feeling of control lessens our ability to cope with stress of all kinds. We never thought human beings had much power over natural disasters, so we don't feel that we have lost control and allowed a blizzard or tornado to hit. A leaking toxic-waste dump or a major plane crash is another matter. Since we like to believe that our technology is under control, such disasters may shake our feeling of power over our creations. Suddenly the beast of technology is prowling free.

The years of protests following the accident at Three Mile Island kept the stress of the incident fresh in people's minds.

© Brad Bower/Picture Group

The gradual onset of drought and the prospect of eventual relief help farmers cope psychologically with exceptionally dry weather (above). By contrast, the removal of asbestos from schools and other buildings (left) does little to reassure those whose future health remains in jeopardy from years of inhaling asbestos fibers.

No End in Sight

The seemingly endless nature of technological calamities is another factor that can make them more stressful. Natural disasters are usually swift, powerful events that sweep across an area suddenly and are gone. There are exceptions to this—droughts and some floods are slow in building, and provide some warning as they intensify and persist for days, weeks, or longer. But the most common natural disasters, such as tornadoes and hurricanes, strike fiercely with little warning, cause visible destruction, and disappear as suddenly as they arrive.

Natural catastrophes usually reach their low point quickly. When a storm strikes, it does its worst and moves on. The danger is over, and recovery can begin. Much the same is true of an earthquake; although there may be tremors and aftershocks, there is a point at which danger has been replaced by the need to rebuild.

Many technological threats, in contrast, lack a clear beginning or end. At Three Mile Island, for example, the emergency unfolded

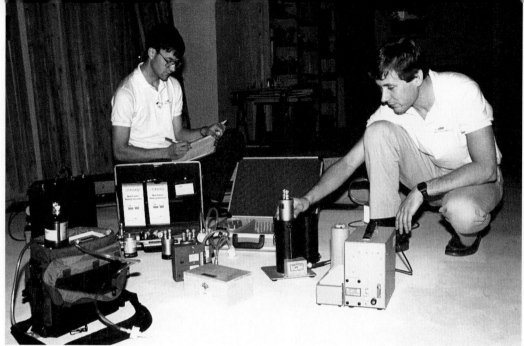

Many people whose homes test positive for radon still doubt that a naturally occurring gas could pose a hazard.

REACTIONS TO RADON

Just as people feel less stressed by natural disasters than by technological ones, they seem to take natural hazards less seriously than those caused by human beings. Public officials in New Jersey have learned this the hard way over the past few years in cases involving radon, an invisible, odorless, and tasteless gas produced by the natural decay of uranium and radium. When it enters and remains in homes or other poorly ventilated buildings, the highly concentrated gas can become dangerous. The Centers for Disease Control (CDC) in Atlanta, Georgia, estimate that radon causes somewhere between 5,000 and 30,000 lung cancer deaths in the United States each year.

When tests showed radon at potentially dangerous levels in homes in northern New Jersey, the state's Department of Environmental Protection (NJDEP) released information about the threat through newspapers, radio, and TV. Homeowners were advised to have radon levels monitored, and to take remedial action if the levels exceeded the Environmental Protection Agency (EPA) recommendation of 4.2 picocuries of radiation per quart (4 picocuries per liter) of air.

To see how well the message was get-ting through, the NJDEP commissioned several surveys beginning in April 1986 to measure public awareness of the danger and see what people were doing about it. Neil D. Weinstein of Rutgers University and colleagues Peter M. Sandman and Mary Lou Klotz found that the chief response had been apathy. Only half of the homeowners had even thought about having their homes tested, and very few had actually done so.

At the American Psychological Association meeting in 1987, Weinstein reported that even the few people who had had their homes tested underestimated the threat. "When people who know that radon can cause lung cancer are asked how serious it would be if they became ill from radon, only half say it would be serious or very serious. . . . Very few are taking prudent protective measures."

While "apathy" seems an accurate description of this reaction to naturally occurring radon, it doesn't fit the storm created in Vernon, New Jersey, when the radon threat had a human cause. Thousands of drums of contaminated dirt from the site of an abandoned factory that had used radium to make luminous watch dials were stored near homes

slowly. It was more than a week before most people could believe that the danger of radiation was past, and many living in the area are still worried.

The unusual reaction to the 1972 Buffalo Creek flood in West Virginia illustrates how human causation seems to affect our reactions to disaster. Most studies of flood victims show that their feelings of distress—anxiety, depression, and other symptoms—increase rapidly immediately after the disaster and then die away fairly quickly. Within a year, most victims have recovered, although some of the symptoms may return if people are reminded of the event. The Buffalo Creek flood, however, created long-lasting emotional upheaval, evident among many victims two years after the flood, and in some cases up to 14 years later. What made Buffalo Creek different?

Following several days of rain, a coal-slag dam at the head of the middle fork of Buffalo Creek collapsed suddenly, unleashing millions of gallons of water in an enormous wave. The muddy water roared through the valley, crashing off the walls of the hollow and washing away almost everything in its path. Many people were asleep in their homes as the wave hit. If they awoke, they found that their valley had been changed forever. The land itself had been disfigured; homes, automobiles, and trailers had washed away; and many of their neighbors were dead. The community, which had been very cohesive before the flood, was uprooted and smashed beyond recognition.

This tremendous death, destruction, and lost sense of community certainly contributed to the unusually severe, long-lasting emotional stress in the Buffalo Creek area. But another difference between this and most other floods was the issue of human responsibility. The rain itself was not sufficient to create the flood. It was brought on by the collapse of a coal-slag dam built by the mining company. People built the dam, and it failed.

in the towns of Montclair and Glen Ridge. To end the problem, state officials decided to mix clean dirt with the contaminated dirt (which was fairly low in radioactivity to begin with) to reduce the radiation to below the EPA danger level. They then planned to move the mixture to an abandoned quarry in a rural area and convert the quarry into parkland.

Weinstein described what happened next: "When Vernon, the town picked out to be the recipient of this good fortune, heard about the plan . . . the reaction was incredible. In this sleepy rural area of 20,000 people, rallies attracting 3,000 and 10,000 people were held. A 3-mile (4.8-kilometer) caravan drove across the state and surrounded the governor's mansion.

"Civil-disobedience training sessions were held in anticipation of a need to block the entrance to the quarries, and more extreme groups, the Radical Underground and the Raiders, were apparently ready to shoot out the tires of arriving trucks or blow up bridges if the feared radon came by train. In the face of this vehement opposition, and the state's total inability to convince anyone in Vernon that the risk was really negligible, the government backed down and started looking for other disposal mechanisms."

Weinstein believes that several related factors—having someone to blame, the resulting anger, and the question of who was responsible for taking action—help explain these sharply different reactions to radon. When there is someone or something people can blame for a risk, they act. In Vernon the enemy was the government, which said that carting in radon didn't pose any risk, an idea that the people of Vernon found "presumptuous and outrageous. . . . Anger at the state and alarm at radon are deeply intertwined. In fact, anger seems to be far more powerful a mobilizer than fear."

These two examples reconfirm a general psychological truth: people are normally more willing to blame someone else for a problem than to deal with one personally by taking individual action. Getting them to act is particularly hard when people can't see the problem directly and it supposedly exists in their own homes, where they normally feel safe and comfortable. Under these circumstances, the researchers point out, "It is extremely difficult to get people to take any precautions more burdensome than switching from aspirin to Tylenol."

JACK C. HORN

Toxic Substances

The issue of when the worst is over is particularly stressful when toxic substances are involved. The potential for contamination from human-caused accidents or neglect is seemingly endless: illegal dumping, inadequate safeguards, and accidental releases of toxins have created standing hazards throughout the U.S.

In addition to the physical harm toxins can do, their presence (past or current) can make people uneasy about the possible results of exposure. Many of the health consequences of toxin exposure, such as cancer or genetic abnormalities, take years to develop or become evident. As a result, people who fear or know that they were exposed may worry for years about what will happen to them.

Research my colleagues and I have done at Three Mile Island and at toxic-waste sites suggests that such worry and uncertainty are associated with stress that persists for years. Chronic stress and the emotional, hormonal, and immunological changes associated with it may cause or exacerbate many illnesses. And since public officials often lose credibility following a disaster, the information they release to reduce fears—such as data on the low rate of actual exposure to radiation or other toxins—may actually serve to increase these fears.

When we compared a group of people living near Three Mile Island with a similar group elsewhere, we found that the Three Mile Island group reported more physical complaints, such as headaches and back pain, as well as more anxiety and depression. We also uncovered long-term changes in levels of hormones—such as epinephrine, norepinephrine, and cortisol—that the body secretes during stress. These hormones affect bodily functions, including muscle tension, cardiovascular activity, overall metabolic rate, and the immune system.

Not everyone we studied in the Three Mile Island area showed these symptoms. In general, three main factors, individually or in combination, distinguished the people who were less affected by stress from those who showed more symptoms: their coping style, social support, and assumption of responsibility. First, the people who concentrated on controlling their emotions showed fewer symptoms of stress than those who tried to change the situation itself in various ways, such as by campaigning against the reopening of the plant. Second, those who had more friends and family to depend on generally reported fewer emotional problems. And third, people who accepted more responsibility for what had happened to them after the accident, rather than blaming others for all their troubles, seemed to do better.

Our observations at Three Mile Island support the idea that long-term psychological problems are more likely after technological disasters than after natural ones. But this belief is based largely on studies that are different in a number of ways, such as their measures of mental health, their methods of selecting victims and control subjects to study, and the time lag between the disaster and the study. These differences make precise comparisons difficult.

Natural versus Manmade Disasters

We have begun comparative studies of natural and technological disasters that avoid these problems. One preliminary study compared the effects of technological failure that exposed some people to hazardous chemicals leaking from a waste dump with those of a flood that caused widespread community disruption and property damage. We compared people living near the dump with those in the flood area, and also with a control group, similar in age, background, and other demographic characteristics, whose neighborhood had not been flooded and was not near any hazardous-waste site.

We collected the same physiological and psychological data from the three groups nine months after the announcement of the toxic hazard and ten months after the flood. People who had lived near the toxic-waste site reported greater distress and exhibited the same kinds of stress-related physiological changes we observed in people living near Three Mile Island. The flood victims, on the other hand, expressed little continuing distress and showed few stress-related physiological changes; their responses were similar to those of our control subjects.

Factors other than different causes could have produced the different long-term effects in these cases. It seems that most of us are better able to adjust to and recover from problems created by natural catastrophes than those posed by technological accidents and oversights. With fast-growing populations and the rapid spread of technological change, the possibility of technological disasters or toxic accidents is widespread. As we work toward minimizing their occurrence, we must also learn more about the psychological and biological changes they induce, and how their detrimental effects on mental and physical health can be alleviated.

What's Behind BLINKING?

by John A. Stern

Quesada/Burke/© 1989 DISCOVER PUBLICATIONS

O ur most delicate sensory equipment is surprisingly vulnerable to attack. The eyes, when open, are exposed to everything from dust and smoke to sharp objects and blows to the face. To be sure, much of the eye is protected by the skull: each socket, composed of seven fused bones and padded with fat, absorbs all but the most severe affronts. But roughly one-tenth of the eye's total surface— the almond-shaped portion that peers out into the world and gathers light—has nothing between it and the atmosphere. The body protects this vital asset by blinking.

Fifteen thousand times a day, on average, we blink, partly to rinse our eyes of debris, partly to cleanse and polish their outer surfaces. During the blink itself, which may last no longer than a tenth of a second, a flap of the thinnest skin in the human body, reinforced with tough

cartilagelike fibers, snaps shut. Then the lids retract, coating the eyes in a film of tears. This rinsing, while important, requires a blink only once or twice a minute, when the tears dissolve. Yet most people blink far more often than that: on average, 15 times a minute—much more often than seems necessary.

Crucial Instants

Why human beings blink so frequently has never been a pressing question. Most 18th- and 19th-century scientists merely observed blinking as naturalists might, offering no theory for its purpose or its timing. The first important insights came in 1895, when it was suggested that blinking is related to fatigue caused by reading. By 1927 Eric Ponder and W. P. Kennedy, who monitored the blinking of subjects in hothouses at the University of Edinburgh, had de-

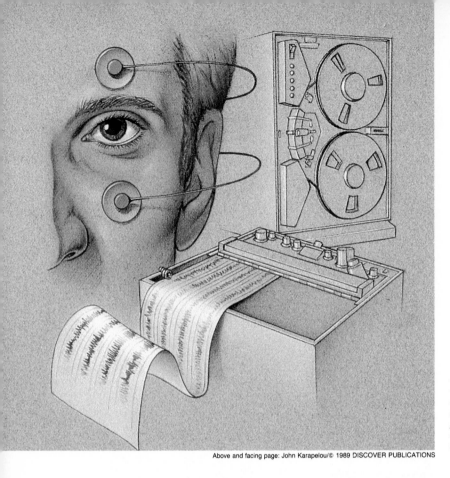

Electrodes measure the frequency and duration of blinks by sensing the change in voltage that the blinks produce. A polygraph machine or tape recorder stores the information.

Above and facing page: John Karapelou/© 1989 DISCOVER PUBLICATIONS

termined that a person will blink at the same rate whether trekking across the Gobi Desert, where the eye's coating of tears presumably would evaporate more quickly than elsewhere, or strolling through the rain forests of Brazil.

Ponder and Kennedy also learned that rates of blinking vary according to the tasks a person performs. People engaged in wholly visual activities—finding a path through a maze or drawing a line between two parallel lines—blink less frequently. They also found that fatigued individuals blink more often than rested ones. Other scientists determined that subjects blink frequently if angered or excited, or when speaking, hinting at some unexplained relationship between blinking and the mind.

Only recently, though, has there been considerable evidence that blinking may be psychologically—as well as physiologically—significant. Measurements of the rate of blinking, as well as the timing and duration of blinks, have shown that the movement may provide clues to the state of the brain. Just as cardiologists glean information about the heart from electrocardiograms, psychologists and neurologists can discern—from electrical measurements of the eyes

and the brain—how blinking varies according to whether a person is alert, bored, anxious, or concentrating. These measurements suggest that each blink may occur at the crucial instant in which we stop seeing and start thinking.

Endogenous Blinks

Like heartbeats, blinks can take several forms. Besides the blinks that cleanse the eye, there are those associated with unexpected circumstances (such as loud noises), as well as the voluntary flaps of the eyelids that may express anger or incredulity. Another type, the so-called endogenous blink, is neither voluntary nor elicited by any external threat.

In the decades following Ponder and Kennedy's experiments, researchers observed the rate of endogenous blinks under a variety of circumstances. Studies by the British psychologist G. C. Drew in 1951, for example, demonstrated that people blink with decreasing frequency as a visual task becomes more difficult. But it was not until the 1970s, when psychologists began to consider the exact timing and duration of blinks in relation to different tasks, that a clearer picture of the phenomenon began to take shape.

By then scientists had developed the expertise to examine blinking more closely, using cameras and infrared lights, and electrodes to gauge the electrical bursts from nerves and muscles around the eyes. Such techniques made it possible to study how eyelid movements coincide with mental processes.

The first and most obvious lesson was that an increase in alertness reduces both the rate and the duration of blinks. A person reading a novel blinks about six times a minute; someone engaged in conversation blinks more than twice as often. Likewise, in flight simulators, aviators blink half as often when manning the pilot's position as when sitting in the copilot's seat. Pilots also tend to blink for shorter intervals than copilots. What's more, if the simulated mission is especially difficult (if the objective is to track an enemy jet or fly close to the ground), both pilot and copilot blink less than they normally would. Drivers blink less often on city streets (where there are traffic lights, pedestrians, and other distractions) than when speeding down rural interstate highways, again indicating that the need to remain alert affects the pattern of blinking. Even more intriguing is the finding that, in a potentially dangerous situation—when one is passing another vehicle—blinks are nearly always inhibited as the eyes pass from the road to a peripheral area (such as the speedometer or a rearview mirror) and back to the visual field of most importance.

A more subtle effect on blinking seems to occur when a person is bored. One experiment required people to determine whether a 40-minute series of tones or lights was long or short. Since the stimuli were brief, and regularly spaced, they eventually bored the subjects. Over the course of the experiment, the fraction of a second that the subjects' eyes were shut during blinks grew by more than 30 percent. Apparently, when the brain judges incoming information to be less than compelling, it allows itself to rest, and blinks last longer.

Anxiety also is reflected in blinking. Novice helicopter pilots blink more often than instructors, and women with anxiety disorders blink more often than calmer women do. Witnesses under cross-examination by antagonistic attorneys blink more frequently than those facing friendly lawyers. When a person answering a question has to face another person—rather than an inanimate object—during his response, blinking increases. And when such a subject faces someone who asks questions requiring di-

A device using infrared light could monitor the alertness of pilots by tracking the frequency of their blinks. Each blink would block the reflection of the invisible infrared beam off their eyes. The same device could rouse tired drivers and warn others to steer clear.

rect yes-or-no answers, blinking rates rise still higher. This connection between blinking and apprehension explains why television newscasters are instructed not to blink, in order to appear calmer and more controlled—and, thus, unflappable before the cameras. It may even account for why presidents and other public officials seem to blink far more frequently when facing hostile questions than when responding to queries for which they have prepared. So far, though, psychologists have no explanation of why anxiety elicits blinking.

Sensory Episodes

The relationship between memorizing and blinking seems clearer. Subjects asked to commit a series of letters or numbers to memory are most likely to blink shortly after the appearance of the information to be stored. The more letters the subjects are asked to memorize, the more time elapses between the presentation and the blink; the brain needs twice as long to store six characters as it does two. The same holds for unfamiliar foreign-language characters: the blink after two characters comes after a longer interval than the blink after just one. It seems likely, then, that a blink indicates the moment at which the memory forms, and that this occurs only when the brain anticipates no additional material.

This conclusion is bolstered by additional research into the relationship between blinking and decision making. When subjects are asked to distinguish between a short tone and a long one, the blink typically begins close to the end of the long stimuli but well after the end of the short one. The decision that a tone is long can be made before the stimulus is finished: as soon as the mind realizes the tone is not short, it is possible to deduce it must be long. (With a short tone, the brain waits another instant to be sure it is not long.) The number of correct decisions a subject makes is related to when the blink begins and to how long it lasts: when subjects blink during a tone, they tend to make many more errors. When blinking occurs before or after a tone, however, the number of correct decisions rises, suggesting that at its most efficient, the brain orders a blink when it has enough information to make a good decision. A similar pattern occurs during reading. People are most likely to blink as their eyes reach the end of a line, or when they fail to understand it and reread the three or four previous words for additional information. The brain seems to need to pause between significant sensory episodes; the blink marks the pause.

Mental Punctuation

These experiments indicate that blinking serves as a kind of mental punctuation. The brief, infrequent blinks of low-flying pilots and city drivers are like commas, dividing the images speeding before their eyes into manageable units. When blinks last longer and arrive more frequently, during the formation of memories or the making of decisions, they are more like periods, providing a fuller, more complete interruption of the influx of visual information that allows the brain briefly to think—to store or mull over information, in addition to merely taking it in. Measurements of brain-wave activity seem to corroborate this notion. During blinking there is an increase in alpha waves, which are characteristics of the brain in its most relaxed, restful moments.

If blinking is a form of punctuation, it may explain the curious fact, reported by a number of early researchers, that the same task triggers different rates of blinking in different individuals. Arithmetic puzzles, for example, cause some people to blink more, others less. A person whose blinking rate declines as she figures out the solution to, say, the problem of adding 4 to the product of 18 and 14, may be formulating the answer visually, imagining the numbers in her mind's eye just as they might appear on a piece of paper. Because the image of the numbers is important—just as the image of the terrain below a jet is crucial to a pilot—the individual will seldom blink, in an attempt to freeze the picture. Another person's blinking rate may rise during the exercise, because his brain is ordering a blink at the end of every stage of problem solving. The differences in how individuals think, in other words, may be reflected in how they blink.

President Bush and just about anybody else will tend to blink more often during an impromptu press conference.

© Cynthia Johnson/Gamma-Liaison

The
EXERCISE
FIX
by Eleanor Grant

© Rick Smolan/Woodfin Camp & Assoc.

Healthy or not, running addicts would rather pursue their activity than suffer from exercise withdrawal.

The long winter months take a heavy toll on the recreational athlete. Many let their running shoes gather dust in closets or allow their bicycles to lean dejectedly against cellar walls. They resign themselves to watching their sleek lines grow softer, and some may even be grateful for the rest.

There are others, however, who brave the slush-locked streets or the grinding tedium of laps on an indoor track rather than miss their daily dose of exercise. For them a day off is an irritant, a missed week is a severe trial, and a month off is a life crisis of catastrophic proportions. They are people such as Richard, an executive in his early 30s who found himself unable to give up his daily 7- to 8-mile (11- to 13-kilometer) run, even though it interfered with his job and made strangers of his children. "When I run, I feel very energized, proud of myself, and have more confidence," Richard says. "If I don't run, I feel like a slob: lazy, heavy, and tired. I won't last long at my job if I don't spend the necessary hours there; but if I don't run, I won't be very good at it, either. . . . Running is my life. It makes me feel like a complete person, and I need to do it every day." Richard is addicted to exercise.

Positive Addiction?

Researchers have known of the addictive qualities of running and other aerobic sports for some time. At first, exercise addiction seemed harmless, and many believed it was beneficial. Psychiatrist William Glasser, who popularized the concept in his 1976 book *Positive Addiction,* contrasted compulsive running with the use of alcohol or drugs to cope with life's problems; running neither destroyed the mind nor pickled the liver, he argued, but instead strengthened both body and soul.

Soon, however, the focus shifted to the darker side of exercise addiction. In 1979 psychologist William Morgan found that addicted runners continued to run even when it put their jobs, their family relationships, and their health in jeopardy. This reinforced an observation made by many physicians and sports-medicine specialists: some "recreational" athletes push themselves to the point of injuries such as shin-splints or stress fractures, then refuse to rest and recuperate, causing greater and perhaps permanent damage.

Exercise Withdrawal

The reason exercise addicts keep punishing themselves probably lies in what happens when they don't run, swim, bicycle, or work out. Connie Chan, a psychologist at the University of Massachusetts at Boston, has studied the psychological consequences of being unable to exercise. Chan and psychologist Hildy Y. Grossman compared 30 male and female runners who had been laid low by minor injuries for at least two weeks with a similar group who continued to run. Those who could not run displayed more

Most exercise addicts have taken up aerobic sports as adults to get in shape or lose weight.

signs of depression, anxiety, and confusion than did those who could, and they were far less happy with themselves and their bodies. Like other addictions, exercise appears to have withdrawal symptoms.

Chan has treated dozens of running addicts and has learned that they have some common characteristics. Addicts must run daily to function normally, and they become irritable, tense, and anxious if unable to exercise for a few days. These are the short-term symptoms of exercise withdrawal. When unable to run for longer periods of time, addicts can experience more drastic symptoms—including depression; lack of energy; loss of interest in eating, sex, and other activities; decreased self-confidence and self-esteem; insomnia; and weight loss or gain. They continue to run while injured, and organize their lives around exercise and related activities, ignoring their families and careers.

Edward Colt, an endocrinologist and former medical director of the New York City marathon, believes that exercise addiction is very widespread: "I think that all—100 percent—of the people who exercise regularly are addicted to some extent." But not everyone agrees that the problem is so extensive; some, including Morgan, now question its very existence. Morgan no longer studies the issue; he

feels that the concept of exercise addiction is extremely murky, and no one has ever confirmed that exercise is addictive in the same way that drugs and alcohol are.

Endorphin Junkies

One popular—but unproved—theory is that athletes become hooked on endorphins, the body's natural painkillers, which surge into the brain and bloodstream during strenuous exercise. Colt and his colleagues have done studies that show runners do have elevated endorphin levels after exercise, but no one has demonstrated that these substances actually have physiologically addictive effects. It's more likely that the "runner's high" is a feeling of well-being that comes with release of stress.

Endorphins might contribute to exercise addiction, perhaps by dulling the pain of aching muscles or battered bones that would otherwise tell people that they are overdoing it, but Chan thinks that the roots of the problem run much deeper: for the addict, exercise fulfills profound psychological needs.

The typical addict is usually not a world-class athlete; more likely, he or she is one of millions who have taken up aerobic sports in adulthood as a way of getting in shape or losing weight. People who stick to an aerobic-exercise regimen usually find themselves not only slimming down and firming up, but also feeling more relaxed and better able to cope with stress.

Potential addicts develop a heady sense of control over their bodies and feel invincible when running. They are intense individuals whose jobs often do not produce quantifiable results, and in their increasing mileage and other "personal bests," they discover a source of measurable achievement. For many, these results are a revelation, a self-affirmation that helps to overcome deeply buried fears of powerlessness and personal inadequacy. Eventually, exercise becomes much more than a form of recreation or a path to physical fitness. It is the root of their psychological well-being, the touchstone of their identities.

Escape or Compulsion?

Some exercise fanatics are single professionals who would rather hit the streets or the gym after work than confront an empty house. For some, workouts meet their needs for social contact; for others, exercising is a way to avoid thinking about an empty social calendar. For all such fanatics, this heightens their sense of dependence on exercise.

Chan and Colt have found that many exercise addicts show a history of compulsive behavior. "In my experience, many [running addicts] are replacing one addiction with another," Colt says. "I've seen many former workaholics, alcoholics, gamblers, and smokers."

True to form, these addicts do not seek help willingly. "There's only one thing they want," says Colt, "and that is to find a doctor who will provide the magic cure that will allow them to keep running." Chan agrees, saying, "As long as they're able to run, [addicts] don't see a problem." Many of the exercise addicts whom Chan treats are referred to her by physicians, frustrated when their patients will not stop running long enough to let overtraining injuries heal. By the time disabled runners reach her door, most are already deep in the throes of withdrawal and are more than a little bewildered by their symptoms.

"It's one thing to expect physical changes when you're not allowed to run, but exercise addicts are not prepared for the psychological repercussions," Chan says. "One of the things I offer them is reassurance that withdrawal is common and that they can get through it and get back in shape."

Diversify Activity

Chan helps patients identify how they benefit from running psychologically, in terms of self-esteem and stress control, and explores with them other activities that might offer similar rewards. She often suggests joining a hiking club or pursuing educational interests. If an injury does not preclude all exercise, she encourages patients to walk, swim, or participate in whatever physical activity possible to minimize withdrawal and maintain conditioning. To help patients cope with stress, Chan often tells them to relive a favorite run in their minds.

Once addicted athletes are physically well enough to start exercising again, Chan advises them to take it slow at first and diversify their physical activities, perhaps by taking up a sport that stresses a different set of muscles, tendons, and ligaments. They also need to become more involved with activities and people who are not connected to the exercise ritual.

Chan does not try to get people to give up exercise altogether: "I love to run. I would never tell anyone not to run." But with any exercise program, she says, moderation is the key to gaining the greatest benefits, both physical and psychological. Those who depend exclusively on one activity for a sense of well-being are flirting with addiction. In the long run, it doesn't work.

To some running addicts, participating in a marathon represents an affirmation of their own self-worth.

© Peter Sibbald/Picture Group

BIOLOGY

BIOLOGY

Through innovations and policy decisions, the products of biotechnology moved closer to widespread use in 1988. Discoveries in genetics challenged current dogma. New species and new habits for old species were discovered.

by Joanne Silberner

A bioengineered mouse (above) became the first animal to be patented. Researchers fused genes from a sheep and a goat to form a "geep" (below right) with traits of both species.

Biotechnology and Agriculture

The U.S. Patent and Trademark Office, making good on a promise to allow the patenting of genetically engineered animals, granted the world's first animal patent to Harvard University in April. The patent, granted for mice implanted with a gene that predisposes them to breast cancer, extends to "transgenic nonhuman mammals," any mammal implanted with genes from another animal. The process was developed at Harvard. In November the Du Pont Company announced plans to sell the mice. Researchers can use the transgenic mice to study how cancer-related genes cause cancer, and determine whether drugs can be used to halt the process.

Policymakers continued to debate the fate of new agricultural breeds. The Patent Office might require farmers to pay royalties for subsequent generations of genetically engineered livestock. One of the first examples of new livestock is a geep, a cross between a sheep and a goat. More-conventional breeds loaded with foreign genes that make them grow bigger or faster are more likely to put the policy to a practical test.

While policymakers continued to argue about the safety of altering the genes of animals and plants, scientists continued to devise and test new products. Crop Genetics International of Maryland conducted the first outdoor test of an engineered pesticide—a corn bacterium loaded with a gene from another bacterium that produces an insect-killing enzyme. The hope is that the hybrid bacteria, when injected into corn plants, will protect the corn from insect pests.

The U.S. Office of Technology Assessment (OTA) issued a report saying that

Top: AP/Wide World; above: UC Davis

the several dozen open-air tests of genetically altered organisms show that with precautions, field testing of genetically altered organisms appears to be safe.

Ancient Life

A fossil find pushed the age of insects back 15 million years. Conrad C. Labandeira of the University of Chicago identified a well-preserved insect fossil as being 390 million years old, suggesting that the creature's own ancestors made landfall 421 million to 408 million years ago—much earlier than previously thought.

Researchers at the University of California at Los Angeles (UCLA) ran a computer comparison of the organizations of genes in several species suggesting that all life could have evolved from single-cell organisms that lived in near-boiling water. Hailed as landmark research by some scientists, the findings are disclaimed by others. Researchers at the University of California at San Diego sought to test the hypothesis by duplicating, in the laboratory, the conditions that exist at hot-water vents on the ocean floor. Chemical studies they carried out indicated that the temperature and pressure found at the vent sites are too great to allow the complex chemical organization necessary for the beginning of life to occur.

Scientists found the fossil of an insect that lived 390 million years ago.

AP/Wide World

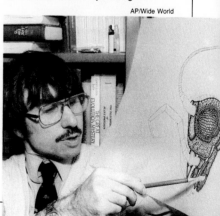

Insects and Plants

Researchers from the Massachusetts Institute of Technology (MIT) and several other institutions announced the discovery of one of the two most numerous types of plankton in the ocean. Although such species might seem hard to miss, the other common species was just discovered 10 years ago. The newly noticed plankton escaped detection for so long because they are small—one-fiftieth the diameter of a human hair—and almost invisible in the light sources used in conventional microscopes. The researchers found the plankton with the help of a laser. The plankton live in low-light conditions 330 feet (100 meters) beneath the ocean's surface at concentrations of up to 100,000 cells per milliliter. At this concentration, 10 gallons (37 liters) would contain as many of the plankton as there are people on earth.

More-dangerous organisms continued to threaten the health and welfare of people. Locusts, swarming in clouds of 150 square miles (389 square kilometers), caused serious devastation across Africa. And bee specialists predicted that so-called killer bees, a cross between a docile species and an aggressive African bee accidentally released in Brazil, will continue their migration from South America, reaching Texas by 1990 if control efforts fail. When angered or threatened, the bees attack en masse, and have killed at least 350 people in Central and South America.

According to the Boston-based Center for Plant Conservation, over 10 percent of the 25,000 plant types native to the U.S. could disappear from the wild. They identified a total of 680 plants that could be extinct by the year 2000.

© Darrell Lister

Hive busting: nothing seems to slow the killer bees on their northbound trek from Latin America.

Animal Behavior

© Charles Palek/Animals Animals

Cliff swallows are the only birds known to transfer partially incubated eggs among each others' nests.

One way to produce many offspring is to get someone else to bring up the children, giving the parents the time and energy to have more offspring of their own. Some species of birds lay eggs in the nests of other birds, even in the nests of other species. One theory held that such parasitism might be due to the birds mistaking someone else's nest for their own. Two Yale ornithologists observed colonial cliff swallows in Nebraska, and found that some of the birds laid eggs in their own nest and then carried them in their beaks to someone else's nest. The observation proved that,

at least for cliff swallows, parasitism was not simply a mistake in identification.

Honeybee queens now have one less secret from bee researchers. Simon Fraser University bee specialists have identified five chemicals used by the queens to control their broods. A queen exudes this chemical mix, and the worker bees lick it off and spread it throughout the colony. A man-made version of the chemicals fooled bees into thinking their queen was present after she had been removed, so that they didn't select a new queen or build a new home for the queen. It also attracted honeybee swarms.

Genetics

A long-held theory in biology claims that continuous mutations allow a species to survive environmental changes. If a change in temperature occurs, for example, those individuals in a species whose randomly mutated genes aid in cold-weather living will survive and reproduce, and eventually most of the colony will be the high-temperature type. Two researchers from Harvard University now

suggest that bacteria can deliberately mutate in order to survive a change in environment.

The researchers grew a line of bacteria that can't use the milk sugar lactose for food in an environment where lactose was the only food. The pattern of growth indicated that there were more mutations after the cells were placed in the new environment, and mutations of other

genes did not occur more often. The finding, the researchers assert, reopens the question of how and why mutations actually occur.

In a new method of gene transplantation, a team of Italian scientists discovered that sperm cells in solution with segments of foreign DNA captured and tightly incorporated large amounts of the foreign genetic material.

DESIGNER PROTEINS

by Shawna Vogel

Your body contains millions of different proteins, but the absence of just one can seriously disrupt life. Take the enzyme triosephosphate isomerase, or TIM, which enables your body to nearly double the energy it makes from one molecule of the sugar glucose. "If you have none of it," says Harvard biochemist Jeremy Knowles, "you can just about live. But you're not very healthy, because you're making only half the energy that you could. If you were to see a lion, for instance, you couldn't run. You'd just stand there and look at it. This little protein gives you the extra energy you'd need to charge off."

Other proteins may not save us from a predator, but they are just as crucial. Some are structural: collagen provides the scaffolding for connective tissue, keratin for hair and nails, myosin and actin for muscle fibers. Still others—such as enzymes, hormones, and antibodies—orchestrate essential bodily functions.

For decades, biochemists have dreamed of wresting control over the enormous power wielded by these biological workhorses. But only recently have the new techniques of molecular biology enabled researchers to determine the structural code of some proteins, splice the genes that dictate their shape into bacteria, and mass-produce them. The first fruits of this biotech revolution—human insulin, human growth hormone (HGH), and tissue plasminogen activator, which dissolves blood clots during a heart attack—are already on the market. In the pipeline are relaxin, a hormone used to relax the birth canal during labor; erythropoietin, which stimulates the growth of red blood cells; and a protein called CD4, a receptor that the AIDS virus binds to—it could act as a decoy to the virus in patients stricken with the disease.

Outdoing Nature

But a second phase of the revolution is already in the making. Not content with copying existing proteins, biochemists are hoping to improve on them and even invent some proteins of their own to outdo those designed by nature.

The pace of their research has picked up significantly with the availability of a technique, introduced in the early 1980s, called site-directed mutagenesis, which lets biochemists replace one or more links in the snarled amino acid chains that make up proteins. By substituting some amino acids for others, they can make delicate changes in a protein's structure and, since structure determines function, change the way it behaves.

This tool allows biochemists to envision exciting new protein products—from drugs custom-tailored for fewer side effects, to industrial catalysts that will work in extremes of heat or pH or when strong chemicals are present. But researchers worldwide are still thwarted by enormous ignorance. The proteins that occur in nature have had some 4 billion years of evolution to perfect their individual structures. Each is a specific combination of amino acids, arranged in different sequences to form chains that can be anywhere from 50 to more than 1,000 amino acids long. Moreover, each chain folds itself into a unique three-dimensional shape that is critical to the protein's function.

Speeding Up Reaction

The function that most interests protein engineers is the ability of enzymes to catalyze—promote and speed up—a wide variety of chemical reactions. A typical enzyme can be imagined as an expediter; it holds together molecules by binding to them, and keeps them stabilized so that a reaction can occur between them. When the reaction is finished, the enzyme is freed (unchanged by the experience) to begin its job again. If it weren't for the enzyme, the molecules might take millions of years to undergo a change that can take less than a second.

The region of the enzyme that stabilizes the reacting molecules is called its active site. Like a lock and key, the shape of this site meshes perfectly with the shape of the molecules. In some enzymes the active site promotes the linking of two molecules; in others it hastens the

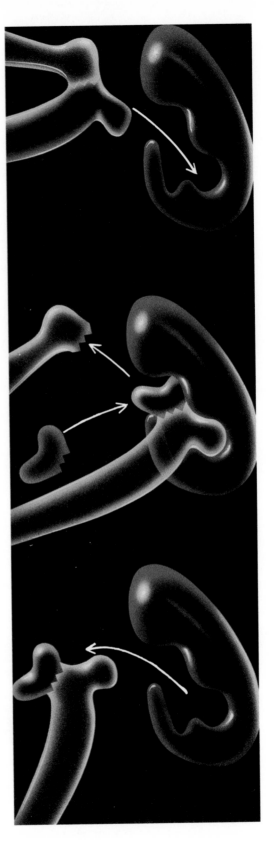

Much research has concentrated on modifying the action of enzymes, a type of protein that promotes and speeds up chemical reactions in the body without undergoing any chemical changes itself. Biochemists already know much about the action of trypsin, a digestive enzyme that breaks down food protein chains. Like two pieces in a jigsaw puzzle (top), trypsin (in red) and the protein chain (yellow) mesh together perfectly. The trypsin binds to the chain and breaks off a piece of it (center). A water molecule (blue) replaces the broken-off piece, and the enzyme moves away (bottom), chemically unaltered. Any change in trypsin's structure would alter its action entirely.

Above: George Kelvin/© 1988 DISCOVER PUBLICATIONS; facing page: Andrew Christie/© 1988 DISCOVER PUBLICATIONS

splitting of one molecule into two, or changes the molecule in some other way. The active site in the digestive enzyme trypsin, for example, is a specifically shaped pocket that cradles two adjacent amino acids in the protein chains in food and expedites their separation.

Change an amino acid in this pocket and you change its shape, thus altering trypsin's ability to work. Even replacing an amino acid that is just part of the enzyme's infrastructure may deprive the enzyme of some activity. Inevitably the replacement will differ from the original in some characteristic—size, chemical reactivity, electric charge—and cause a slight shift in the position of the rest of the amino acids that could disturb the active site. Very subtle shifts can have drastic effects, as researchers have discovered in their tinkering. Indeed, protein engineers often lament that what these past few years have shown is that they really don't know that much about how proteins work.

Bleach and Mussel Glue

Some biochemists, nevertheless, have already made proteins with modified functions that could prove to be useful products in the not-too-distant future. BioPolymers in Farmington, Connecticut, for example, has been experimenting with a glue that mussels use to attach themselves to wet surfaces. The adhesive is apparently ideal for watery bonding tasks like repairing teeth, setting fractured bones, or mending displaced corneas. Modifications to the glue's amino acid sequence have produced versions that set faster, bond more strongly, or degrade more quickly to suit specific uses. At

the Massachusetts Institute of Technology (MIT), Gregory Petsko is substituting amino acids in glucose isomerase, an enzyme used to make high-fructose corn syrup, for those that tend to degrade when the enzyme is exposed to the high temperatures used in manufacturing. Similarly, researchers at Genencor in San Francisco have substituted one amino acid for another in subtilisin, an enzyme used in detergents. The amino acid they replaced is altered by bleach, a change that renders the enzyme useless. Their modified version should remain active longer when bleach is used in laundry.

In these cases, researchers are using what might be called the top-down approach—that is, substituting amino acids in proteins whose three-dimensional shapes are already known. This critical information enables them to make sense of what would otherwise be an inscrutable string of amino acids, and to alter, for example, only the amino acids in the protein's functional site. Without knowing how the protein chain folds, there's really no way to tell which amino acids are just scaffolding and which are important to function.

Resolving Structure

Resolving a protein's three-dimensional structure, however, is enormously time-consuming. It involves aiming X rays at the crystallized form of the protein and then analyzing the patterns of the diffracted rays—a process that can take months, or even years. Right now, out of millions of proteins, the structures of roughly 300 are known; only 10 or 20 new structures are added to the list each year.

The glue that mussels secrete to adhere to wet surfaces may have human uses if scientists can modify its structure.

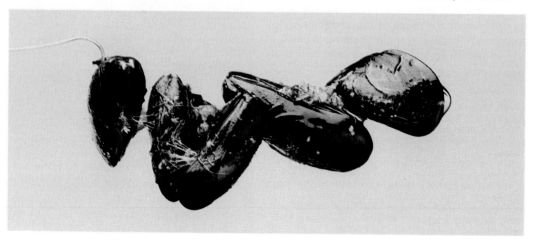

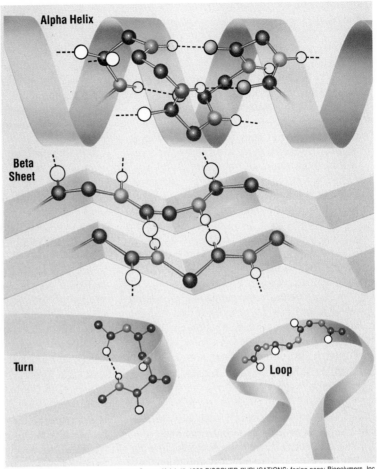

Alpha Helix

Beta Sheet

Turn

Loop

The amino acid sequences that make up protein chains repeatedly fold into one of four basic shapes: alpha helices (top), beta sheets (center), turns (bottom left), or loops (bottom right).

Above: George Kelvin/© 1988 DISCOVER PUBLICATIONS; facing page: Biopolymers, Inc.

Although computers may eventually speed up this laborious process, no computer can yet bypass X-ray crystallography and predict, simply on the basis of the amino acid sequence, how a protein will look when it's folded up. Once the overall structure is known, computers can help researchers model the effects of specific amino acid substitutions. But even then numerous approximations must be made.

Therein is a bottleneck. The number of known amino acid chains for proteins is growing all the time, and the numbers are likely to swell now that work has begun on sequencing the human genome. (Once the DNA sequence of a gene is known, biologists can usually determine the amino acid sequence of the protein it codes for.) But without the ability to predict what these protein chains will look like when they're folded up, a huge pool of proteins with potential medical and industrial benefits will lie untapped. "It used to be that protein folding was considered a dark, arcane subject studied by musty and dusty physical biochemists in small meetings in unheard-of places," says MIT biologist Jonathan King. "But now an enormous number of applications are out there, just waiting for the solution to this problem."

Indeed, the ultimate goal of protein engineering—building functional proteins from scratch, instead of relying on nature's designs or co-opting her to do the building—is contingent upon finding the solution. Protein engineers long to build proteins shaped specifically to bind to target molecules. A protein, for example, that selectively attaches itself to the enzyme reverse transcriptase could block the AIDS virus from replicating and spreading. Proteins that bind to pollutants could clean contaminated water or soil. And ones that simply cut polymers into lengths at specific sites could be enormously useful chemical scissors in the plastics industry. Without understanding how protein

Any foreign substance that gets into the bloodstream—from bacteria and viruses to toxins—has the potential to muck up our health. To protect us, the immune system rapidly makes proteins called antibodies, which recognize the undesirable substances, bind to them, and mark them for destruction. Antibodies can be made to an almost unimaginably large range of substances, and each homes in on its target with great precision. It's this combination of diversity and specificity that has long interested researchers.

Enzymes also are proteins that act by binding to specific substances, but, unlike antibodies, they don't merely hang on to their targets, but transform them by catalyzing a chemical reaction.

For years, biochemists wondered whether they could combine the best features of both kinds of protein. Finally, in December 1986, two groups in California, one at the Research Institute of Scripps Clinic and the other at the University of California at Berkeley, announced that they had managed to do just that. They had made a catalytic antibody, or "abzyme," pointing the way to a whole new class of substances that have the versatility of antibodies plus the chemical properties of enzymes.

Abzymes could act as drugs to break up proteins in, say, cancer cells. Or they could be used to cut proteins at specific sites, a long-sought tool that would let biologists snip proteins into pieces the way they snip DNA with restriction enzymes.

To make antibodies to almost any substance, biologists inject a small sample of the target molecule into a mouse to coax its immune system into producing antibodies shaped to fit that specific molecule. The immune-system cells that make the antibodies are then fused with other cells in the lab. Researchers can then select and clone the ones that spew out copies of the antibody.

chains take on their shapes, such possibilities live mainly in biochemists' imaginations.

Researchers believe the rules of folding are somehow written in a protein's amino acid sequence. "It's a lot like origami [the art of Jap-

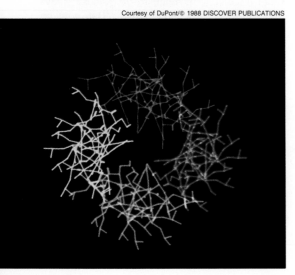

DuPont chemists have already built simple versions of proteins called ion channels from scratch.

Courtesy of DuPont/© 1988 DISCOVER PUBLICATIONS

anese paper folding]," says Jane Richardson, a biochemist at Duke University Medical Center. "Like a folded piece of paper, a protein contains traces of how it was made, but it's extremely difficult to decipher the clues by unfolding it." Biochemists tinkering with existing proteins are gradually gathering information about how each amino acid contributes to the overall structure. But this top-down approach is too selective for a few researchers. "Modifying naturally occurring sequences," says Richardson, "is a great way of asking subtle questions, but it's not a good way of asking dumb questions. And we're really still at that stage."

Building from Scratch

Richardson and a handful of others prefer to tackle the problem a different way: from the bottom up. They're not fiddling around with existing proteins, but building their own from scratch. These would-be protein architects are building on unknown territory.

Their attempts have been aided by recent studies that have uncovered nature's fondness for repeatedly using and reusing certain structures. There is some method, after all, to the apparent madness of a folded protein. Portions

The challenge facing the researchers was to induce the mouse to create an antibody that not only binds to the molecule but hastens the desired reaction. The trick, they reasoned, was to make an antibody that fits the shape of the molecule as it's actually undergoing the reaction—when the molecule is in its so-called transition state. Since this state is highly unstable and fleeting, they had to fake it: they constructed a stable analogue of the unstable transitional molecule. Injected into a mouse, it made antibodies tailored to that shape.

The ruse worked. In experiments the antibody to the counterfeit molecule bound tightly to the real molecule and catalyzed the desired reaction.

Compared with natural enzymes, which speed up the pace of reactions about 1 billionfold, the first abzymes weren't too swift. The very simple kinds of reactions they promoted (involving, for example, one substance reacting with water) were only about 1,000 times faster than they would have been

without a catalyst. Nevertheless, they showed that the approach was viable.

The Scripps group has since upped the rate of its abzyme reaction to 7 million times that of the uncatalyzed reaction, much closer to the speed of enzymes. Several groups have recently succeeded in making abzymes for more complex and useful reactions, and now work on abzymes that will split the bonds linking amino acids in proteins. Abzyme engineers have basically had to rely on letting the mouse do its thing—and then picking the best of the antibodies it produced. But soon they'll be able to take these mouse-made abzymes and tinker with their amino acid sequences by using the protein engineer's technique of site-directed mutagenesis.

"Now that is lovely," says Harvard biochemist Jeremy Knowles, "because it allows these abzyme characters to refine the catalytic antibody." Of course, it also puts them in the same boat as protein engineers—painfully aware of how much they still have to learn about nature's craft.

of the amino acid chain commonly assume one of four basic configurations: alpha helices, which look like corkscrews; tightly wound loops; sharp turns or kinks in the chain; and beta sheets, strands that weave back and forth to form twisted ribbons. "The view that is beginning to emerge," says Penn State biochemist George Rose, "is that a protein may be a sort of mix-and-match ensemble of modular units."

By designing a circle of alpha helices, chemist William DeGrado and his colleagues at Du Pont have built simple versions of proteins called ion channels, which control the traffic of certain substances in and out of cells. Ion channels act like pores through the cell membranes; when open, they allow electrically charged ions—like sodium, potassium, or calcium—to pass through. DeGrado's primitive channels can even be somewhat selective, permitting passage, say, only to positively charged ions that are less than a certain size. DeGrado has also built other proteins with simple, easily made cylindrical shapes called 4-helix bundles. He hopes to attach functional sites to these prefab proteins, including a site that will bind to metals. Such proteins could be useful for cleaning up toxic waste.

Nature herself has apparently adopted this kind of piecewise construction in many enzymes. The large barrel shape of TIM, the protein that keeps us from being food for lions, is duplicated in about a dozen other enzymes. "Interestingly," says Harvard's Knowles, "the active sites of those twelve enzymes are all at one end, at the same end, of this barrel. So one begins to wonder whether in primordial time there was this stable, folded scaffolding, and nature made catalysts by changing individual amino acids, just like we are doing now."

Most likely, the various efforts of protein engineers will end up working to their advantage. By testing out small changes in a protein's chain, biochemists will gradually learn how each amino acid contributes to the protein's overall form. As each piece falls into place, they'll be that much closer to the day when they can predict a protein's shape from its amino acid sequence. Others will tackle the problem a different way, first dreaming up simple structures they want to build, and then trying to invent the sequences that fold into them. Somewhere along the road, the two approaches—top-down and bottom-up—may give biochemists the insight they need to gain mastery over proteins.

Banking on Seeds by Anne Schwartz

On Sutton Mountain in the dry canyon-lands of eastern Oregon, above a water-fall that flows only in spring, grows one of a handful of known stands of the arrowleaf thelypody, *Thelypodium eucosmum*. It is in the mustard family, a tall, showy, purple-flowered perennial. Endemic to a region that has been grazed for most of this century, the plant has the misfortune of being delectable to cows. It once flourished in riparian areas in three or four coun-ties, but has retreated to the few moist places that cows just can't reach.

It's not easy for people to reach, either. Three of us have hiked several miles and scram-bled over crumbled columns of basalt timrock to collect the plant's seed. I am with botanist Julie Kierstead, curator of the Berry Botanic Garden rare-plant seed bank in Portland, Oregon, and Nature Conservancy ecologist Jimmy Kagan. Kagan coordinates the Oregon Natural Heritage Program, which keeps track of the state's rare flora and fauna. He rediscovered this population of arrowleaf thelypody in 1982.

It is July, the waterfall is bone-dry, and the plant's seeds should be ripe. Kierstead instructs us to collect from at least 50 plants—if we can find that many—so that our sample is geneti-cally diverse, but to take only one or two seed-pods from each, so as not to impair the plants' reproductive ability. "If a lot of seeds have already fallen out," she warns, "we'll just have to take what we can get." Kierstead searches along one draw leading down into the waterfall, and back up another. Kagan scouts the main draw. I head down another, nervously. We're out of shouting range. I'm told there are rattle-snakes around.

When we finally regroup, Kagan's wax-paper collecting bags are stuffed with the plant's siliques—long, skinny, twin-chambered seed pods peculiar to mustards. Kierstead has a smaller take. I've come up empty-handed after crisscrossing the streambed and looking under every juniper, where the plants are supposed to grow. "When they're blooming, they just jump out at you," Kagan reports. But at this stage, the seed stalks are brown, and the plants are hard to see. "They hide in plain sight," Kier-stead says, offering me some small comfort.

That evening we meet up with Cheryl McCaffrey, a U.S. Bureau of Land Manage-ment (BLM) botanist new to the district. Many of Oregon's threatened plants grow on land managed by the BLM, and she wants to get a feel for the plants—and the people with whom she'll be dealing. The next day the four of us set out to find several more rare plants, including Howell's thelypody (*Thelypodium howellii* ssp. *spectabilis*), another pretty, purple-flowered mustard. It has just three remaining toeholds, all in the Powder River Valley in northeast Oregon. Like its relative on Sutton Mountain, it is what Kagan calls an "ice-cream plant" to cows. Both thelypodiums are high-priority species—plants for which convincing evidence exists for listing under the Endangered Species Act.

Edging toward Extinction

The seeds we gather on this trip hold much of what remains of the genetic variability of the two species—a constellation of plant traits that can never be recaptured once lost. Kierstead will store them in the Berry Botanic Garden's seed bank, where they should remain viable for at least 50 years. Berry will also grow out some plants on its grounds. If either thelypodium dis-appears from the wild, the garden will have its germ plasm, or hereditary material, and the hor-ticultural knowledge needed to restore it.

Of the approximately 25,000 to 30,000 species, subspecies, and varieties of vascular plants native to the United States, about 3,000—more than a tenth of the total—are thought to be edging toward extinction. Berry's work with the rare thelypodiums—involving *ex-situ*, or off-site, conservation—is part of a new response by botanical gardens to the urgency of this situation. Joining in a network called the Center for Plant Conservation, 19 gardens from Hawaii to Massachusetts have made an unprec-edented commitment to creating reserves, on their grounds, of the endangered plants in their biogeographic regions.

Off-site conservation might not seem like news to those who have followed the efforts to save peregrines or condors by breeding them in captivity and reintroducing them into the wild. Like zoos, botanical gardens represent a tre-mendous resource for conserving endangered species in a protected environment, and for con-ducting biological research needed to protect species in the wild. Yet, surprisingly, they are a resource largely untapped. Botanists who seek out rare plants and horticulturists who tend the plant collections back at the botanical gardens seem to exist in two different worlds. "Bota-

Botanical gardens have developed banks to preserve the seeds of some 3,000 varieties of endangered plants native to the U.S., thereby preventing their extinction.

nists often don't have the faintest idea of how to grow things," says Julie Kierstead. "And horticulturists may not have the faintest idea of where they grow in the wild."

To date, the preservation of beleaguered plants has been accomplished largely by protecting their habitats. To save the arrowleaf thelypody, for example, the Nature Conservancy is trying to arrange a land swap between the owners of the plant site and the BLM; if it goes through, the conservancy will work to assure that the BLM manages the site properly as a research natural area, a spot designated by the federal government as ecologically significant.

Off-site Preservation

Conservationists dedicated to habitat preservation are understandably worried that growing plants off-site might be perceived as an acceptable alternative to saving rare-plant habitat in the wild—especially in difficult situations, such as when an endangered plant gets in the way of powerful development interests. "It's a touchy situation to come in with an *ex-situ* plan and deal with people who are used to working with *in-situ* conservation," Kierstead says. "They're fairly skittery—afraid it may undo years and years of work."

But preservationists can't always act quickly enough or save every population of a rare plant. Everyone has stories about stands destroyed by dam construction or roving cows or bulldozers before anyone could prevent it.

To provide some insurance against situations like these—a second line of defense—two young Boston botanists, Donald Falk and Frank Thibodeau, came up with the idea for a botanical garden–based, off-site program. The final design for their Center for Plant Conservation took shape in discussions with Peter Ashton, director of Harvard University's Arnold Arboretum in Jamaica Plain, Massachusetts, and Jonathan Shaw, then director of the New England Wild Flower Society's Garden in the Woods, a native-plant garden in nearby Framingham. Their goal was nothing less than to create a national collection of endangered plants—a sort of Library of Congress of rare-plant genes.

Several botanical gardens, such as the North Carolina Botanical Garden and the Waimea Arboretum and Botanical Garden in Hawaii, were already working to protect endangered species; and during the previous decade, the botanical community had done some soul-searching along these lines. "I think it was the

right time for the idea," says Falk. Conservation groups were also receptive. The Nature Conservancy lent its computer files on endangered plants, as did the Office of Endangered Species at the U.S. Fish and Wildlife Service.

In April 1984, the center opened shop, with Falk and Thibodeau as codirectors. It operates out of a renovated attic in the administration building at the Arnold Arboretum and has a staff of seven, including four botanists.

The Berry Botanic Garden

As part of the Center for Plant Conservation, the Berry Botanic Garden is responsible for plants native to the West Coast, from Washington to northern California and as far east as the Cascade Mountains. Just a decade ago, Berry's six, mostly wooded acres belonged to Rae Selling Berry, an extraordinary plantswoman. She created there a very unusual species garden for plants she collected from all over the world, especially primroses, rhododendrons, and alpines. She also grew a great many native northwestern wildflowers. When she died in 1976, having left no provision for continuing the garden (her children, in fact, had planned to sell it for a housing subdivision), her gardening friends in Portland and around the world raised money to buy the land. In 1979, when it became a botanical garden, it already had a good collection of natives, including many rare species.

Its offices are in Mrs. Berry's large white frame house. As we sit in the comfortable kitchen, Julie Kierstead tells me about Berry's endangered-plant program. The garden really has two overlapping programs—the Center for Plant Conservation and the Seed Bank for Rare and Endangered Plants of the Pacific Northwest, which also includes plants from the dry eastern part of Oregon. The two thelypodiums we collected, while not technically in Berry's territory under the center, will be grown out and maintained as part of the center's collection.

Saving the Seeds

We set off on a tour of the garden. The first stop is the mudroom, where the seed bank, an old Amana freezer, is lodged unceremoniously. Looking inside, I see four trays of vials. Kierstead explains that each vial represents about 40 hours of work. Most of the seeds are gathered for her by volunteers, amateur and professional botanists who get out in the field to look for rare plants. Kierstead herself cleans the seeds, counts or weighs them, and bottles them. Care-

A vial of seeds for preservation represents many hours of lab work. Botanists must count, clean, desiccate, and freeze the contents of each vial of seeds collected. Endangered plants include Nelson's checkermallow (above left), and a type of evening primrose (left).

ful records of each collection are entered into the computer files.

Before the seeds go into the freezer, they must spend several weeks in a desiccator; otherwise, the water they contain would freeze and puncture the cell membranes. Every five years or so, following accepted seed-banking procedures, Berry will thaw out the seeds and test their germination rates.

Seed banking is the easiest, cheapest, and most compact way of saving the genetic diversity of a species. But some seeds don't take to freezing or drying, and for these a "full," self-perpetuating collection of 50 plants must be maintained under the center's guidelines. (The current scientific thinking is that a population of this size holds about 95 percent of a species' possible genetic permutations.) It's not easy to keep a large troop of rare plants alive and reproducing. As Kierstead notes, "In a garden setting, you more or less expect to lose a certain number of things every year. And when you have to manage something knowing that you can't replace it, it becomes a lot more critical.

When botanists find an endangered plant at a threatened site, they gather its seeds and store or plant them elsewhere.

When something dies, you can't just say, 'Oh well . . . darn!' ''

Fortunately, the seeds of most of the plants with which Berry is working can be stored. But Berry's gardeners will grow at least a few plants of each species so they can figure out how to propagate it and keep it alive. Kierstead also believes it important for a garden to display rare plants: ''People don't get excited about conservation unless there's something real. The average person—even the gardener who's really interested in plants—will likely never see an endangered species in the wild.''

Of the dozen or so endangered species Berry is now working with, perhaps two-thirds have not yet grown large enough to be planted out in the garden. A small greenhouse shelters plants that are being started from cuttings; just outside are rows of plastic cups sprouting seedlings. Cold frames house young plants that need extra protection. Eventually, Berry hopes to be able to cultivate all of the 60 or so endangered species in its territory.

The garden's director, David Palmer, a lean, red-haired Englishman, is working near the greenhouse. Palmer supervises the three paid gardeners as well as a number of volunteers. Few of the plants have ever been grown before, and next to nothing is known about their germination and growing requirements. The gardeners try to match a plant's habitat, he says, although sometimes a plant behaves very differently in a garden.

Endangered Plant Menagerie

Kierstead takes me through the rock garden, which slants up a gentle incline behind the house. Here rare and endangered species grow among the garden alpines. She quickly reels off Latin names: *Penstemon peckii*, endemic to the eastern slope of the Cascades; *Luina serpentina*, known from only one place in central Oregon, where it grows in sparsely vegetated soils; *Arabis koehleri* var. *koehleri*, whose seed came from plants that survived blasting during the retrofitting of a dam.

Other threatened natives grow in the perennial beds of the Lily Garden, which was recently redesigned to be more of a meadow garden, better suited to natives. This is where the two thelypodiums will go. She shows me a few specimens of the silvery phacelia *(Phacelia argentea),* a dune plant of the southern Oregon coast, where it is being crowded out by a European beach grass, trampled by cattle, and overrun by dune buggies.

My tour concludes with a walk through the woodland area and the primrose collection begun by Mrs. Berry. We head back to the kitchen for lunch. Tomorrow we'll be collecting seed from a recently discovered stand of Barrett's penstemon *(Penstemon barrettiae),* a rare Columbia River Gorge endemic. It grows on a cliff near the Bonneville Dam that is about to be blasted to make way for a new navigation lock, and the garden is helping to reestablish it elsewhere on the dam's grounds.

The blasting took place this summer; the seed collected at the time of my visit has been stored; the cuttings taken have all done well. But not every plant can be preserved through seed collecting and cultivation. Terrestrial orchids,

for example, have so far resisted all attempts to grow them. No one has been able to unravel the details of their symbiosis with soil fungi. Indeed, little beyond taxonomy is known about most of our rarest species: their survival and reproductive strategies, ecology, genetics, and biochemistry remain a virtual mystery. By gathering information on how to grow endangered species and by making them more accessible for research, the Center for Plant Conservation has the potential to advance our understanding greatly. What biologists learn about a species should contribute much to its long-term preservation in the wild.

Don Falk cautions, "I think everyone still views this as a grand experiment. The whole idea will take a few years to prove itself." Although 200 of the most endangered species in the United States have been brought into cultivation by the gardens in the center's network, the sheer number of plants that await preservation is a daunting challenge. Says Frank Thibodeau: "One of the things that pushes us onward is the notion that there needs to be at least an attempt to work with any plant that is really at the edge of extinction."

Plant preservation in action: volunteers transplant rare Barrett's penstemons in a safe place after finding a stand of the endangered flowers growing on a cliff scheduled for blasting.

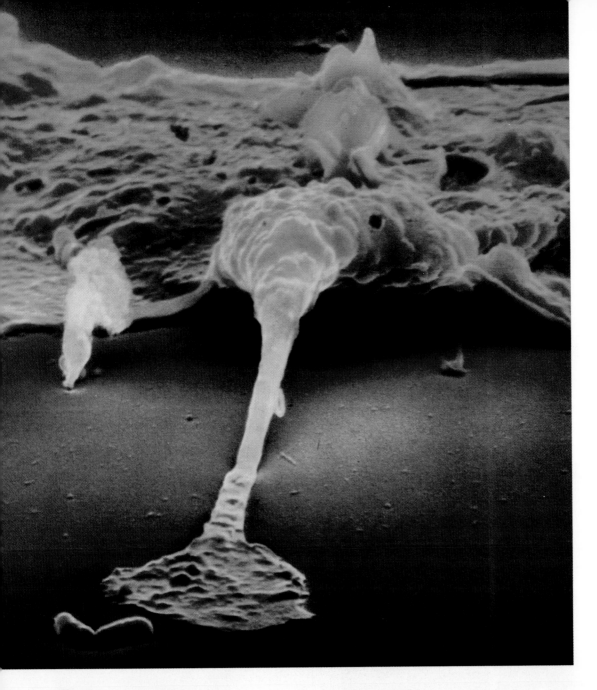

IMAGES of IMMUNITY

by Beryl Lieff Benderly

O pen any newspaper these days, or turn on any newscast, and a mysterious new vocabulary leaps out at you: "T cells," "receptors," "immunosuppression"—terms rarely heard outside the research laboratory even five years ago. But that was before AIDS, organ transplants, and other newsmaking developments in immunology transformed the jargon of this once esoteric medical specialty into the subject of daily headlines and the language of major public policy debates.

It's a language in which people—even those fresh from high school or college biology courses—still are not very fluent. Scientific understanding of the immune system has exploded since AIDS (acquired immune deficiency syndrome) burst onto the public health scene in 1981. Cancer research and organ transplants have added their own impetus to the worldwide effort to understand our bodies' defenses. Nearly every week now brings new findings on what has become medical science's fastest-moving frontier.

Frontiers are what the immune system is all about—the frontier between the human body and its invaders, the boundary between "self" and "foreign" matter. A subtle and complicated task faces the specialized organs and cells that make up the immune system: to recognize and destroy dangerous intruders without doing undue damage to the body's own tissues. And so a subtle, complicated, and superbly economical system has evolved to meet this basic survival need—so great are the subtlety and complexity, in fact, that some basic procedures still puzzle researchers.

Immunity's Military-like Organization

The immune system is unlike any of the body's other major mechanisms. It's not a plumbing setup like circulation, or an electronic switching network like the nervous system, or a freight-handling mechanism, like digestion. Indeed, many of its vital components don't even stay put, but instead move freely through the body, pervading both fluids and tissues. It works in the blood, in the lymph, and even inside the organs of other systems. One way to understand immunity is not to think of a mechanical device, but to imagine instead a highly mobile, thoroughly disciplined military organization. Like a well-run army, it includes training and support bases, crack units of specialized troops, a sophisticated communications network, and an extremely effective intelligence service.

Indeed, surveillance units on constant alert compose the body's first line of defense. Like vigilant border guards or rooftop plane spotters, specialized cells constantly search for and identify unwelcome aliens. Using highly specific signals, they then summon fighters expert in

just the type of combat required to overcome the particular foe. Meanwhile, other troops join in the fray or supply needed equipment. Finally, effective disposal units move in to mop up.

A modern defense establishment includes frogmen, paratroops, commandos, ski troops, artillery, infantry, tank battalions, antiaircraft batteries, and other specialists in searching out and destroying many kinds of enemies. Similarly, the immune system has components equipped to find and kill such varied attackers as bacteria, viruses, foreign chemicals, and even the body's own cells undergoing threatening changes.

Lymphocyte "Boot Camp"

The foot soldiers of the immune system are white blood cells, or lymphocytes; large numbers of them man bases in the lymph nodes and spleen and also circulate throughout the body. They arise as immature, undifferentiated stem cells in the bone marrow, but later grow into specialized cells with particular functions. Like raw army recruits, new lymphocytes report to "training bases" where they mature and acquire their special features. Those that attend boot camp in the thymus gland are called T (or thymus-medicated) cells. T cells, or T lymphocytes, include killers, which fight the enemy directly; helpers, which aid in the recognition and attack; and suppressors, which turn off the immune response when the battle is won. T cells serve a variety of regulating, communicating, and combat functions.

The training ground for B cells, or B lymphocytes, has not yet been definitely located, but researchers suspect that they mature in the tonsils, the lymph nodes, and lymph tissue in the gut. The main function of B cells is to produce antibodies that attack specific antigens (a general term for anything that triggers an immune response).

Although the two main classes of lymphocytes differ in many respects, they share two features that make the immune response possible. They can recognize and become activated by specific molecules, and in their active mode they can rapidly reproduce copies of themselves. Thus, unlike a volunteer army, which must entice recruits into joining up, embattled lymphocytes can simply clone battalions of reinforcements, as needed, on the spot.

The crucial ability of lymphocytes to identify other entities arises from receptors that dot their outer surfaces. Each receptor is, in effect,

Immunity in action: a patrolling macrophage sends out a cellular extension called a pseudopod ("false foot") to engulf and destroy an invading bacterial cell.

Photo, facing page: Courtesy of Lennart Nilsson © Boehringer Ingelheim International GMBH

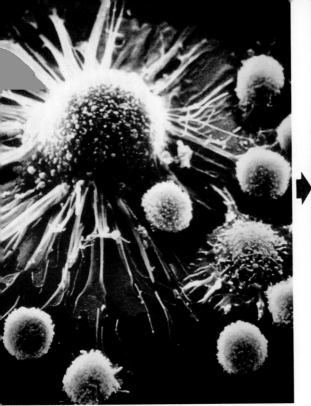

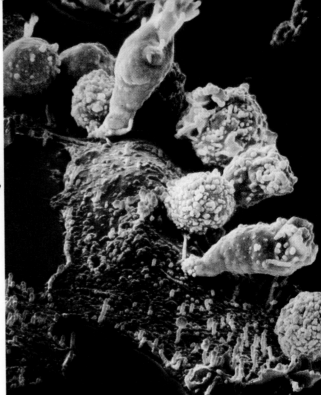

Killing a cancer cell. A squadron of killer T cells, drawn to the telltale antigens of a cancer cell, prepares to take lethal action against the abnormal structure.

Next, the normally round killer cells set upon the cancer cells, transforming their shape as they wage chemical warfare to penetrate the cell membrane of their prey.

a molecular lock capable of accepting only a single key. When a lymphocyte encounters its target molecule—which may be a part of an invading organism, or on the surface of another cell, or moving freely through the body fluids—a receptor locks onto it, and the lymphocytes become "activated." The activated cell is then ready to carry out its designated function in the cause of immunity, whether it be fighting, signaling, coordinating, or helping. Receptors also play an important part in the immune system's internal communications. Cells signal one another by emitting appropriate molecules that are then recognized by other, receptive cells. T cells, in particular, produce a number of different signaling and control chemicals known as lymphokines.

Enemy Recognition

Given the immense number of invaders, attackers, and signaling chemicals potentially present in human blood and tissue, one of the immune system's most remarkable features is that its members, as a group, can precisely recognize and react to so many different ones. They accomplish this through a judicious combina-

tion of extreme specialization and great variation. Each individual B and T cell, for example, has one—and only one—kind of antigen receptor; it is permanently committed to recognizing only that intruder and no other. By random mutation, though, the body produces vast numbers of lymphocytes with slightly different receptors; the variations may number in the millions. Since each lymphocyte can make many identical copies of itself, any given lymphocyte can vastly increase the body's sensitivity to a particular antigen. This ability to replicate also creates a "memory" of the invaders so that, upon a second encounter with an antigen, the body has the ability to more quickly deploy its defenses. This is also the principle of vaccination—to confer protection against an antigen by exposing a person to it through a harmless inoculation.

The immune army includes numerous other components. Natural killer cells, for example, are lymphocytes specially designed to eliminate tumor cells. Macrophages—lymphocytes whose Greek name "big eaters" indicates both their size and one of their main functions—can digest unwanted organisms and materials.

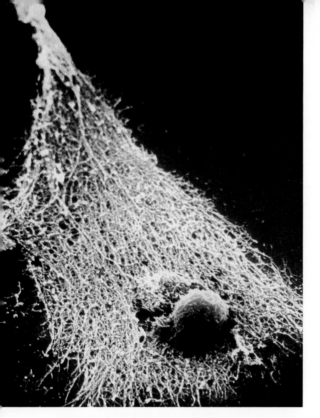

Mission accomplished, the ruptured cancer cell has spilled out its contents and died. All that remains of the cancer cell is a collapsed network of fibers.

They also help coordinate other immune system functions. Antibodies—large, complex protein molecules produced by B cells—bind to particular antigens, puncture their membranes, and kill them by allowing their contents to drain out. Still other proteins, called the complement, enhance the antibodies' ability to destroy cells.

Strategy against Bacteria

Bringing all these forces to bear against an enemy requires both a grand strategy and ingenious tactics. Suppose, for example, that *Salmonella* bacteria have hitched a ride on your dinner. As the invaders make their way into the body, they scatter bits of themselves—antigens that can be recognized as foreign invaders by the right lymphocyte. On their scavenging rounds, macrophages pick up these pieces of molecular debris and carry them about, rather like banners.

If you are resistant to this infection, the macrophage will soon, literally, bump into a T cell that recognizes this antigen. The T cell raises the alarm, emitting a shower of signaling chemicals, and the antibody response swings into action. The appropriate B cells, alerted by

the signal, start churning out antibody, which makes its way through the bloodstream to the enemy. Appropriate T cells gather to coordinate operations and help the B cells. Complement molecules also converge and, in doing so, call in the macrophage cleanup squad. The antibody tackles the invaders, trying to pierce their outer membranes and disperse their fluids. The macrophages, spurred on by the complement, attempt to gobble the enemies up. Once the combined defensive forces have the intruders on the run, suppressor T cells give the all clear, the immune response slows, and the system returns to its usual state of watchful readiness.

Strategy against Viruses

If the invader is a virus, however, a different strategy comes into play. These wily enemies work under cover and from within; they infiltrate the body's cells and commandeer them into producing more viruses. When a cold virus enters your body, for example, the immune system's task is to find and destroy "self" cells gone haywire. The same holds for the cells that have become cancerous—that have become a subversive force bent on overrunning the body's normal cells. The defending immune system must recognize both these types of turncoat cells by antibodies carried on their outer surfaces. Two classes of troops undertake the attack: natural killer cells, lone hunters that roam the body on search-and-destroy missions; and killer cells, T cells turned into killers under orders of a lymphokine, interleukin.

Given the crucial position of the T cells in both sounding the alarm and organizing the battle, a person without a proper T-cell defense is clearly open to all kinds of dangerous diseases. And that is precisely what happens in AIDS. The AIDS virus kills T4 lymphocytes, which play a central role in initiating and coordinating the immune response. In ways not yet fully understood, the virus apparently also disables macrophages, leaving the body defenseless against the cancers and infectious diseases that eventually prove fatal to those afflicted with the disease.

Mistaken Identification

Not all malfunctions of the immune system involve infectious agents, though. Sometimes the cells overdo their vigilance and mount an attack against substances that are harmless, or even beneficial. An allergy, for example, is a case of mistaken identity—the body mistakes

Photos, above and facing page: Courtesy of Lennart Nilsson © Boehringer Ingelheim International GMBH

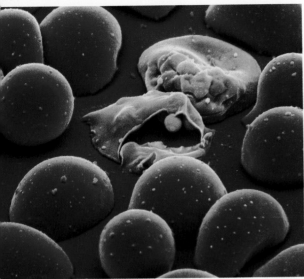

© Lennart Nilsson

When a red blood cell infected by malaria parasites bursts, it releases hoards of protozoa ready to attack healthy cells. The presence of the protozoa in the bloodstream provokes a counterattack by the immune system.

major challenge to physicians is keeping the body from attacking a transplanted liver, kidney, or heart. The drug cyclosporine has been useful in preventing organ rejection. Cyclosporine apparently blocks production of interleukin, a signaling chemical needed to turn T cells into killers and launch the immune attack. Using this drug, therefore, doctors can deliberately suppress the immune response that would ordinarily protect the transplant recipient against foreign tissues. Although this keeps the patient from rejecting the new organ, it also reduces protection against ordinary invaders. (The same principle applies for many types of chemotherapy used against cancer, which temporarily suppress the marrow's ability to produce lymphocytes.)

When bone marrow itself is transplanted, a reverse rejection can occur. In graft-versus-host disease, the lymphocytes from the transplanted marrow identify the recipient's tissue as foreign. Immunosuppressive drugs, given for the first six months, can help control this response during the lifetime of the existing mature lymphocytes. New lymphocytes appear not to reject the host.

Harnessing the Power of Immunity

The immune system's immense power to combat disease holds great promise for better health as medical science learns to harness the body's own defenses for the war against major killers. Already doctors have developed methods of producing immune substances outside the body, and then using them to step up the natural attack against diseases. Interferon, which blocks the reproduction of viruses, has been used in experimental cancer therapies. Last year it was approved by the U.S. Food and Drug Administration (FDA) to treat patients with hairy cell leukemia, a rare and usually fatal cancer. Experiments have shown success in using interleukin to increase the number of killer T cells deployed against cancer tumors. Of even broader potential usefulness, a group of hormones called hematologic growth factors has recently been used to encourage growth of certain blood cells, including disease-fighting lymphocytes.

As researchers understand more about the immune system, hope grows that some of humankind's deadliest enemies may come under medical control. And so does the certainty that more and more Americans will soon be learning the strange new language of immunology.

such innocuous items as eggs or ragweed pollen for harmful invaders and calls out powerful chemical defenses, including histamine and leukotrienes. These substances help in the fight against real enemies by making the blood vessels more permeable—easier for the relatively large white cells to pass through on the way to battle. But, in this case, they are simply annoying nuisances that bring on the rashes, sneezing, wheezing, and other afflictions so familiar to allergy sufferers.

The immune mechanism can even turn dangerous. In autoimmune diseases—arthritis, lupus, rheumatic fever—the immune system falsely identifies certain of the body's own tissues as foreign, and moves in for the kill. Antibodies against the *Streptococcus* bacterium— the microbe that causes the common "strep throat," for example—are known to be involved in rheumatic heart disease, which can follow some cases of strep throat. Thus, although strep throat in itself is not a particularly dangerous infection, prompt treatment is critical to prevent the more serious consequences of rheumatic heart disease.

Organ Rejection

Sometimes the foreign matter the immune system attacks is not threatening but beneficial, as in the case of lifesaving organ transplants. A

Serendipitous Shipwreck

by Frank Slifka and Doug Perrine

Triumph may sometimes spring from disaster, but the mechanisms by which this occurs are often so unpredictable that even the most astute minds are unable to forecast the turn of events. Yet the history of science is replete with examples of great advances resulting from unfortunate mishaps—the discovery of penicillin from the accidental contamina-

Two highly territorial species of angelfish (right), rarely seen in close proximity, flourish side by side in the underwater oasis created by the Arimora (top) near Egg Island in the Bahamas. Nutrients leaking from the shipwreck support an unusual variety of sealife.

The Arimora *offers more than abundant food. The golden coney, Spanish hagfish (above), and other colorful fish can seek shelter in the wreckage. Other creatures, such as a giant hermit crab (above, bottom) and a southern stingray (right), blend into the background.*

tion of a bacterial culture, for example. Such lucky chance occurrences are called *serendipity*, and often come cloaked in the guise of misfortune. Certainly the crew of the 260-foot (79-meter) steel freighter *Arimora* must have had no inkling of the potential contribution their ship was to make to marine science as it made its way through the Northeast Providence Channel one dark night in May 1970.

The voyage from South America carrying a load of guano-based fertilizer bound for the farmlands of Europe had been completely routine until the ship neared the northern tip of Eleuthera Island in the Bahamas. The fire erupted in the galley so suddenly and spread with such devastating speed that the crew soon ceased all efforts to control it and began to think of saving themselves. The possibility of an explosion was a real danger. The captain swung the ship around and headed at full speed toward the nearest land: a tiny speck of rock named Egg Island, after the seabird eggs that the early explorers found there. Where the sea bottom sloped up from 25 to 15 feet (7.6 to 4.6 meters),

the ship ran hard aground, striking the limestone bottom with such force that the keel cracked. All of the crew were able to escape ashore and were rescued by fishermen from the community of Spanish Wells, on St. George's Cay, 7.5 miles (12 kilometers) to the east.

Underwater Fire

The fire continued to smolder for three months, leaving the *Arimora* a total ruin. Underwater, a different sort of "fire" burned away all life in the area. As the waves washed out the high-

The wreckage of the Arimora creates numerous surfaces upon which primitive sealife can attach and reproduce. Delicate feather duster worms (above) spend much of their lives clinging to the side of the ship. Tubelike formations of nudibranch eggs (right) spread out like tentacles from the Arimora's hull.

Both photos: © Frank Slifka

phosphate fertilizer, the concentration in the water surrounding the wreck rose to levels too high for living things to survive. For several years afterward, fishermen reported that the area was barren, much like a lawn that has been burned by an overapplication of fertilizer. Gradually, however, the leaching of fertilizer slowed, and life began to return to the area. As various life-forms began to reestablish themselves, a miraculous thing happened. The area surrounding the wreck began to "bloom" like a garden. Luxuriant fields of algae grew up around the wreck, attracting small invertebrates and hordes of herbivorous fish. Predators followed—snappers, groupers, and rays.

Today the *Arimora* is like an oasis in the middle of a relatively barren hard-bottom plain. Yellow stingrays by the dozens cover the bottom surrounding the ship, and schools of giant parrot fish pick at algae growing on the ship's sides. A giant oval of lush green, brown, and red algae covers the bottom for about 55 yards (50 meters) in any direction from the ship.

Nutrients—essential chemicals for the growth of living things—are of great interest to both biologists and farmers because they control the amount and type of organisms that can be found in any ecosystem. In most aquatic systems, nitrogen and phosphorus seem to be the limiting nutrients—the ones that are in short supply. A number of experiments have been conducted in freshwater lakes to artificially enrich the systems, but environmental regulations have made such experimentation in the ocean almost impossible. If the captain of the *Arimora* had applied for a permit to conduct phosphate-enrichment studies of the Eleuthera flats, he would certainly have been denied.

Opportunity for Study

The accidental stranding of the ship, however, serendipitously created an unusual research opportunity that marine scientists, through the efforts of the authors, have only recently been made aware of. In 1987 scientists from the University of Miami Rosenstiel School of Marine and Atmospheric Science (RSMAS) and Florida Institute of Technology (FIT) descended upon the "accidental enrichment experiment" site.

Dr. Kerry Clark and graduate student Duane DeFreese of FIT collected specimens of opisthobranch sea slugs. Clark, an authority on Atlantic opisthobranchs, recently published a paper that predicted a correlation between nutrient levels and diversity of sea slugs. Interestingly, the authors have found over a dozen species of slugs on the wreck and the bottom surrounding it, including one that appears to be unknown to science. Clark and DeFreese, however, were impressed not so much with the diversity of slugs as with the density. One species, *Elysia ornata,* is so common that as many as 300 have been found in an area approximately 13 by 20 feet (4 by 6 meters). This slug, which the authors call the salt-and-pepper sea slug for the white and black dots on its back, has been observed feeding primarily on the algae *Bryopsis*. This and two other types of algae present, species *Cladophora* and *Polysiphona,* are usually reliable indicators of a high-nutrient environment.

Large numbers of opisthobranch egg cases were also found, indicating that the wreck is an active breeding site for these mollusks. Underwater photographer Jeff Hamann, who publishes a "nudi calendar" of color photographs of nudibranchs, visited Spanish Wells and found 11 species of sea slugs in a single weekend! Hamann collected a specimen of *Chromodoris nyala* at the wreck site, a species that has not been recorded since the original description 20 years ago.

RSMAS biology professor Alina M. Szmant, who is a specialist in nutrient cycling and coral growth, made a preliminary visit to the wreck of the *Arimora* and found it to be a "very unusual site." She found colonies of coral, especially the finger coral *Porites* species and brain coral *Diploria* species, growing both on the hull of the ship and on the bottom around it, sticking up through the algal mat. She hopes to conduct experiments to determine if the growth rate of the coral is being affected by the high-nutrient load. She was particularly intrigued by the fact that the corals were surrounded by algae, but were not being smothered by them. She is hoping to discover if the corals have some defensive mechanism to prevent being overgrown by the algae.

School of Angels

RSMAS ichthyologist Arthur A. Myrberg, who is an authority on fish ecology and behavior, did a preliminary census of fish at the wreck. He recorded 66 species of fish from 26 families, and believes that more are present. As with the sea slugs, though, he found that the numbers of species present were not as impressive as the numbers of individuals within certain of the species. He observed large shoals of gray angelfish *(Pomacanthus arcuatus),* counting 53 individuals within an area of approximately 480 square yards (400 square meters). The authors have observed even more on some occasions, counting up to 75 before losing track. Such large aggregations of this species are highly unusual because, as Myrberg points out, "One rarely, if ever, sees more than a pair within a large foraging area." He adds, "Clearly something is happening here that does not happen on a usual coral reef."

The gray angelfish were observed feeding on the green fingerlike algae *Codium* species and on beds of mixed red, green, and brown algae, which contained large numbers of macro-invertebrates. It may be that the unusual gregarious behavior of the angelfish here is related to the elevated food supply. The fish's behavior may also be affected by the lack of shelter such as that provided by a coral reef.

Future studies at the site of this serendipitous accident may shed more light on the role of nutrients in the marine environment and factors affecting the behavior and distribution of marine organisms, as well as providing some insights into the wise use of artificial reefs. The wreck is under consideration by the Bahamas National Trust for preservation as a marine sanctuary, which would benefit this rare and unusual underwater oasis.

PHYSIOLOGY OR MEDICINE

by Elaine Pascoe

For the first time since 1957, the Nobel Prize in Physiology or Medicine was awarded to researchers who developed important drug treatments while working for drug companies. The 1988 prize was shared by two Americans, Gertrude B. Elion and George H. Hitchings, and a Briton, Sir James Black.

Elion and Hitchings, working for the Burroughs Wellcome Company, collaborated in the development of a series of drugs that became standard in the treatment of leukemia, gout, malaria, and other ailments. Research conducted by Black, who was associated with Smith-Kline Beckman Corporation and Imperial Chemical Industries, led to revolutionary drug treatments for heart disease and ulcers. In both cases, much of the research had been done in the 1950s and 1960s; the years since then have proved the value of the treatments.

The principles established by these researchers, meanwhile, have been used to develop a number of other essential drugs for treatment of a variety of disorders. "While drug development had earlier mainly been built on chemical modification of natural products, they introduced a more rational approach based on the understanding of basic biochemical and physiological processes," the Nobel citation said.

Nuclear Metabolism

In the mid-1940s, Hitchings and Elion began to explore the differences in the nuclear metabolism of human cells, cancer cells, parasites, bacteria, and viruses. At the time, research into nucleic acids, which control heredity and cell function, was in its infancy; little was known about the ways that the enzymes that make up nucleic acids are formed and put together. But the two researchers quickly realized that if they could detect variations in the way different kinds of cells handle these enzymes, or nucleotides, they would find points of attack against disease.

Focusing on two enzymes, purine and pyrimidine, Elion and Hitchings first studied the formation of nucleic acids in harmless bacteria. They found that certain conditions, including the presence of folic acid or a combination of purines, were essential if the bacteria were to reproduce their nucleic material and multiply. The next step was to find substances that would block the formation of the acids—thus preventing cell division and multiplication—without damaging human cells.

The work had an obvious application in cancer treatment, specifically in blocking the rapid white-cell multiplication characteristic of leukemia. The first drug that the researchers developed was abandoned when it proved to be too toxic for human use. But in the 1950s, at the Sloan-Kettering Institute, Hitchings and Elion developed two drugs that were effective against leukemia: 6-mercaptopurine and thioguanine. Both are still used to treat the disease.

Searching for other anti-cancer drugs, the researchers altered 6-mercaptopurine to form azathioprine (Imuran) in 1957. It was not effective against cancer, but it had another action: it was able to suppress the body's immune response. That made the drug useful in treating autoimmune conditions, including se-

George Hitchings and Gertrude Elion (below), and Sir James Black shared the 1988 Nobel Prize in Physiology or Medicine. Drs. Hitchings and Elion were honored for developing drugs to treat leukemia, gout, malaria, and other diseases.

© Tannenbaum/SYGMA

vere rheumatoid arthritis, and in organ transplants, where it prevented the body from rejecting donated organs. Other immunosuppressants have been developed since, but azathioprine is still in use. Allopurinol (Zyloprim and Lopurin) likewise began with an attempt to create an anticancer drug; after it was found to block an enzyme that facilitated uric acid buildup, it was used to treat gout.

The two researchers applied the same principles to develop drugs for the treatment of infectious diseases: pyramethamine (Daraprim and Fansidar), which is effective against the parasite that causes malaria; and trimethoprim (Bactrim and Septra), which fights fungal and bacterial infections, including the *Pneumocystis carinii* pneumonia

that is a leading cause of death among AIDS patients. In 1977 they developed acyclovir, effective in treating herpes virus infections. Following the principles established by Elion and Hitchings, other researchers synthesized AZT (azidothymidine), the only drug approved for the treatment of AIDS in the United States.

George Herbert Hitchings was born in Hoquiam, Washington, on April 18, 1905. He earned bachelor's and master's degrees at the University of Washington in Seattle and a doctorate in biochemistry at Harvard. After teaching for nine years, he joined Burroughs Wellcome in 1942. He remained with the company until his retirement in 1984, rising to become vice president for research and a company director. After retirement he

continued his association as a consultant at the Wellcome Research Laboratories in Research Triangle, North Carolina.

Gertrude Belle Elion was born on January 23, 1918, in New York City and graduated from Hunter College with a degree in biochemistry in 1937. Unable to find a laboratory that would hire a woman chemist, she taught high school while working toward a master's at New York University. World War II opened up more opportunities for women, however, and in 1944 she was hired as Hitchings' laboratory assistant. She soon became a colleague, collaborating fully in the drug research. At her retirement from Burroughs Wellcome in 1983, she was head of experimental therapeutics; like Hitchings, she continued as a consultant.

Blocking Cell Receptors

Black's research, like that of the U.S. researchers, focused on the specific biochemical operations of cells; but it took a very different approach. The seed came from a paper by Raymond P. Ahlquist of the Medical College of Georgia, in Augusta, who suggested in the 1940s that the neurotransmitters epinephrine and norepinephrine stimulate cells through two types of receptors, alpha and beta, on the cell surfaces. The two-receptor theory helped explain the dual action of these body chemicals, which cause both contraction and relaxation of smooth tissues

such as the heart and blood vessels. In some conditions the action is harmful—by prompting an increase in heart rate and contraction of blood vessels, for example, the chemicals are a factor in high blood pressure and heart disease.

Black reasoned that if a chemical compound could be found that would lock into the receptor sites, the effects of epinephrine and norepinephrine would be blocked. In 1960 he succeeded in developing propranolol (Inderal), the first clinically useful member of a group of drugs called beta-blockers that did just

that. Propranolol, which contained a chemical side chain that mimicked the neurotransmitters, fit into the beta-receptors and prevented the neurotransmitters from exciting heart tissues.

Beta-blockers were first used to treat high blood pressure and the pain of angina pectoris. Later, after studies showed that propranolol decreases the death rate among heart-attack survivors by as much as 25 percent, it became part of standard therapy in heart disease. Further work led to the development of similar beta-blockers, which are useful in treating migraine headaches as well as various heart problems.

Meanwhile, Black's work with beta-blockers led him to research in the action of histamine, a body chemical involved in inflammation. Histamine's effects range from the bronchial constriction of allergic reactions to the production of stomach acids associated with ulcers. Antihistamines, which were developed in the 1950s, were only partly effective and did nothing for ulcers.

Black theorized that, again, two types of receptors must be involved—and that antihistamines blocked only one. The research spanned 14 years, but his theory proved correct: in 1972, he developed cimetidine (Tagamet), which prevents histamine from acting on cells by block-

Sir James Black was honored for developing beta blockers and ulcer drugs.

BETA BLOCKERS: A WEAPON AGAINST HEART DISEASE

Unmedicated Heart

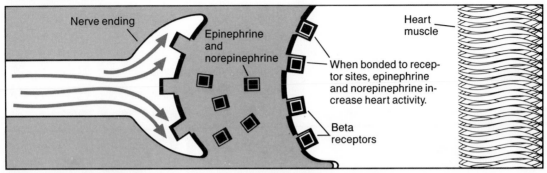

Heart Treated with Beta Blockers

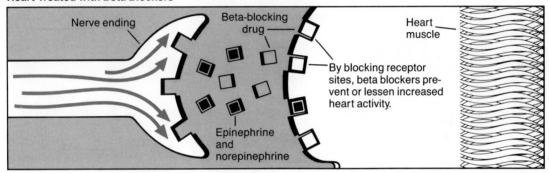

ing H-2 receptors on the cell surfaces. Because it halts the production of stomach acid associated with histamine, it became a standard treatment for ulcers.

James Whyte Black was born on June 14, 1924, in Uddington, Scotland. He earned degrees in medicine and surgery at the University of St. Andrews in 1946 and, for the next 12 years, taught physiology. In 1958 he joined Imperial Chemical Industries and began his work on beta-blockers.

Following his success with propranolol, Black became head of SmithKline & French Laboratories in England and, later, director of the Therapeutic Research Division of Wellcome Research Laboratories there. In 1973 he joined the staff of King's College Hospital Medical School at the University of London. He was knighted in 1981 and heads the James Black Foundation, a private research foundation supported by Johnson & Johnson.

Immunosuppressants, drugs that suppress the immune system, help prevent the body from rejecting a transplanted organ.

© Levon Parian/SYGMA

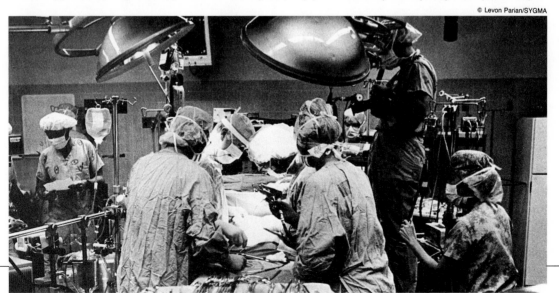

COMPUTERS
AND
MATHEMATICS

COMPUTERS AND MATHEMATICS

Computer criminals made headlines by spreading "viruses" through several networks. In mathematics, at least one old problem resisted new solutions. Meanwhile, educators struggled to improve the quality of math teaching.

by Philip A. Storey

Wall Street uses electronic "display books" to match buy and sell orders.

Computer Trading

The stock market continued to recover from the October 19, 1987, crash caused, in part, by computerized trading that accelerated a dive of record proportions—508 points in just a single trading day.

Wall Street was taking a multi-pronged approach to the problems created by computer trading. First, controls called circuit breakers were instituted: all computer trading halts when the Dow Jones Industrial Average falls 250 points in a single day. Second, massive new computing power was being unleashed in the stock exchanges to keep closer track of trades.

Many insiders voiced concerns that the new solutions will not work: computer technology may allow traders to sell more frantically than ever just before the Dow reaches that magic 250-point dip. One expert told *The Wall Street Journal:* "Wall Street's use of computers has moved through three stages. It went from being an operational tool to being a competitive edge, until today it is survival gear."

Hackers and Viruses

Hackers and viruses drove computer news from the business section to the front page several times in 1988. (*Hackers* are computer hobbyists who electronically break into others' computer systems. *Viruses* are computer programs designed to "self-replicate" much like their biological counterparts.)

Hackers have managed to penetrate some of the country's most sensitive computer networks.

Hackers managed to penetrate several sophisticated computer systems in the United States—even networks used by major universities and the U.S. Defense Department. Most disturbing was the disclosure that, over the course of several years, a West German computer-hacker group had broken through the security of at least 30 military and research computers. Several members of the group were arrested in March 1989 in connection with the security breaches.

On November 2, 1988, Robert Morris, Jr., a 23-year-old graduate student at Cornell University, injected a computer virus—as a prank—into a nationwide computer network. The virus slowed—or "crashed"—more than 6,000 computers. Although no data were reported lost, researchers spent hours—or, in some cases, days—expunging the virus from their computers. Morris intended his virus program to leave just one copy of itself in each computer to which it was transmitted in the Arpanet computer network jointly shared by the scientific research community and the military. Due to a fault in the program, the virus replicated itself repeatedly inside each computer, rapidly filling up the available computer memory and rendering the machine inoperable.

Incidents of contamination by computer viruses are causing concern among military security experts, business people, and bankers. How easily can a high-tech terrorist do damage? Some viruses, unlike the one Morris created, are intended to destroy data. Many software firms have marketed programs that safeguard against viruses, but computer-security experts warn that hackers may just discover new ways to circumvent the antiviral programs.

A New Personal Computer

Steve Jobs has introduced an innovative new personal computer produced by his fledgling company, NeXT Inc. Jobs, who cofounded the successful Apple Computer company (which he left in 1985), has introduced a number of innovative machines before, including the enormously popular Apple II and Macintosh personal computers.

According to Jobs, the NeXT computer will cause a revolution in higher education. Its sales will, in fact, be initially limited to teachers and students.

NeXT has dazzling features, including a magneto-optical disk drive that can access disks that hold 300 times more data than conventional magnetic disks. Its powerful signal processor can act as a modem, play music, and synthesize the human voice. Sleek design features complete the package. Industry insiders nonetheless predict the NeXT computer will run into tough competition in a marketplace already rife with personal computers. The NeXT computer should sell for about $6,500.

© Doug Menuez/Picture Group

Steve Jobs claims that his latest introduction, the NeXT computer, has the power of a mainframe.

An Assault on Fermat's Last Theorem

The mathematics community was abuzz with excitement over news that Fermat's Last Theorem may have finally been solved by a Japanese mathematician. The theorem concerns a simple equation: $x^n + y^n = z^n$ (x, y, z, and n must be positive integers). When $n = 2$, the equation has an infinite number of solutions, such as $3^2 + 4^2 = 5^2$, or $5^2 + 12^2 = 13^2$. But when n equals any number higher than 2, the equation apparently has no solutions. Proving this theorem, short of

multiplying an infinite series of numbers, has thus far proven to be an impossible endeavor.

The problem became one of the most notorious in all of mathematics because of a note that Pierre de Fermat, a distinguished French mathematician, wrote about it in his notebook more than 350 years ago: "I have discovered a truly remarkable proof of this theorem which this margin is too small to contain." Fermat, however, never recorded the

proof, and the problem has intrigued and confounded generations of mathematicians ever since.

Utilizing new methods from the field of differential geometry, Yoichi Miyaoka of Tokyo Metropolitan University claimed to have discovered a proof of Fermat's Last Theorem. But his proof did not hold up under the intense scrutiny of his fellow mathematicians. Fermat's Last Theorem still remains the Holy Grail of mathematics.

Mixed Results from Math Study

Almost every high school graduate in the United States can handle simple arithmetic, according to a 1988 report by the Educational Testing Service. But the data showed that no progress had been made in the teaching of the more complex

mental tasks that employers require of their employees.

Only half of the 17-year-olds could solve math problems at the junior high school level. Fewer than one in 15 could cope with high school problems requir-

ing several steps or involving algebra or geometry. And only 7 percent of the 17-year-olds were deemed prepared for college-level science education.

The report noted that most of the gains seen in basic skills were the result of improvements among students living in the Southeast and among black and Hispanic students. A "back to the basics" teaching approach, which has become widespread since the early 1970s, has proven its success, the report said.

On the down side, the report said that most mathematics teaching was dull, and chided teachers for not making more use of calculators, computers, and other new technological devices. The report found that most high school students perceive mathematics to have limited application in their future.

A "back-to-basics" approach to teaching math has improved fundamental skills.

© Paul Conklin/Uniphoto Picture Agency

© Don B. Stevenson

Is Your Computer SECURE?

by Katherine M. Hafner

D onald Gene Burleson resented authority. He denounced federal income taxes
as unconstitutional and boasted that he
hadn't paid any since 1970. The pudgy, 40-
year-old programmer also complained that his
salary at USPA & IRA Co., a Fort Worth,
Texas, securities trading firm, was too low. He
often had heated arguments with his superiors.

"He was so fanatical about everything," says former coworker Patricia Hayden. But she adds:
"He could do anything with a computer."

Evidently he could. Two days after USPA
fired him in 1985, the company alleges, Burleson entered its headquarters and planted a program that once each month would wipe out all
records of sales commissions. USPA discovered
the break-in two days later. But it lost 168,000
records before disabling the program. Burleson
is now awaiting trial on charges of "harmful
access to a computer," a felony in Texas. If
convicted, he faces up to 10 years in jail.

Violent Shutdown

The Burleson caper is just one in a string of
recent events that point to the alarming vulnerability of computer systems—and the businesses
and government agencies that rely on them.
Hackers have invaded sophisticated data networks—even those at the Pentagon. Accidents,
such as the May 1988 fire at an Illinois Bell
switching station outside Chicago, have dis-

America's computer systems stand threatened by everything from hackers and viruses to high-tech thieves, disgruntled workers, and even natural disasters. Some companies go so far as to store their highly sensitive computer tapes and disks in a mountainside vault in Phoenix.

rupted communications in entire towns for weeks at a time. But nearly all experts agree that the foremost threat, which accounts for at least 80 percent of security breaches, is of internal origin: "The real problem is errors, omissions, or well-thought-out acts by individuals who have authorized access to data," says Lawrence L. Wills, in charge of selling data-security software for IBM.

Whether the fault lies with a disgruntled employee, a hacker, simple human ineptitude, or a natural disaster, disabling a vital computer and communications system can be as easy as cutting a critical power line or typing a few commands on a keyboard. The threat is eloquently simple: computer networks and the information they handle are assets a company can't do without. But often they aren't adequately protected, and the consequences of that exposure can be disastrous. Without computers, "we cannot run our plants; we cannot schedule; we cannot bill or collect money for our product; we can't design our product," says G. N. Simonds, executive director of management information systems at Chrysler Corporation. "In essence, we very quickly shut the company down."

The potential for trouble is even greater in the service industries that now dominate the economy. Every workday, U.S. computer networks transmit close to $1 trillion among financial institutions, an amount equal to 25 percent of the gross national product. When a software problem fouled up record keeping in the Bank of New York's government securities trading operations in 1985, other banks temporarily stopped trading with it. The Fed had to lend the bank $24 billion to keep it operating until the problem was fixed. An airline the size of American Airlines could lose up to $34,000 in booking fees each hour its reservations system is down.

Little wonder that businesses are worried—and reacting. To protect its vast reservations system in Tulsa, Oklahoma, American Airlines built a $34 million underground facility with 1-foot (30.5 centimeter)-thick concrete walls and a 42-inch (107-centimeter)-thick ceiling. Anyone who scales the barbed wire faces a security system that includes a retina scanner, a James Bondian device that detects unauthorized

personnel by the unfamiliar pattern of blood vessels in their eyeballs. Indeed, a booming industry has developed to help protect computers, ranging from scores of consultants to sellers of hardware and software impediments to intruders.

High-tech Thievery

Despite such defenses, however, systems remain vulnerable. High-tech thieves steal $3 billion to $5 billion annually in the U.S. alone, according to consultants at accounting firm Ernst & Whinney in Cleveland, Ohio. And computer crime pays well: in an average stickup, security experts say, a bank robber grabs $5,000. By contrast, the average electronic heist nets $500,000. In electronic funds networks, "you have $15,000-a-year clerks transferring $25 million a day," says Ronald Hale, research manager at the Bank Administration Institute in Chicago. For some the temptation is too great.

In early July 1988, a group of insiders wired $54 million from the London office of Union Bank of Switzerland to another Swiss bank, complete with the correct authorization codes. A malfunction in the second bank's computer delayed the transaction, and auditors discovered it and froze the funds before they could be collected. First National Bank of Chicago foiled a $70 million embezzlement scheme only because the two employees who masterminded it made a dumb mistake: they tried to overdraw on the accounts they were stealing from.

Often even hackers depend on inside help. A band of teenage programmers, calling themselves "phrackers," has been giving fits to Pacific Bell and other phone companies with a simple con game. Posing as fellow employees, they call phone company representatives and cajole them into releasing computer passwords. Says one 17-year-old phracker: "It works surprisingly well." Inside the company computer, phrackers cause mayhem by disconnecting service to customers or changing work orders.

Now changes in computer technology are making mischief easier. Increasingly, minicomputers and personal computers are being spread through offices and networked together. Such "distributed processing" multiplies the potential points of access. "When computerization was centralized, the computers were in one room behind locked doors," says Edwin B. Heinlein, a computer security consultant in San Rafael, California. "Now it's a hell of a mess."

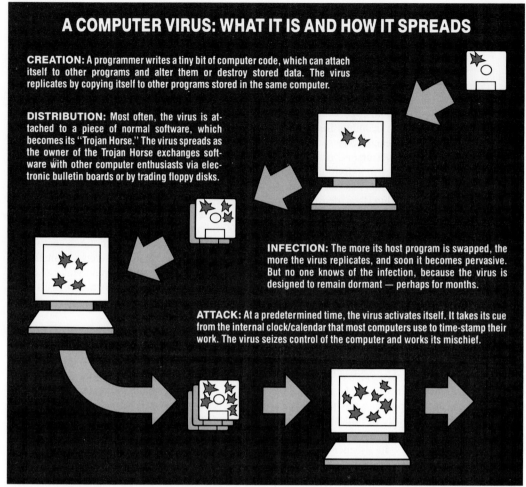

A COMPUTER VIRUS: WHAT IT IS AND HOW IT SPREADS

CREATION: A programmer writes a tiny bit of computer code, which can attach itself to other programs and alter them or destroy stored data. The virus replicates by copying itself to other programs stored in the same computer.

DISTRIBUTION: Most often, the virus is attached to a piece of normal software, which becomes its "Trojan Horse." The virus spreads as the owner of the Trojan Horse exchanges software with other computer enthusiasts via electronic bulletin boards or by trading floppy disks.

INFECTION: The more its host program is swapped, the more the virus replicates, and soon it becomes pervasive. But no one knows of the infection, because the virus is designed to remain dormant — perhaps for months.

ATTACK: At a predetermined time, the virus activates itself. It takes its cue from the internal clock/calendar that most computers use to time-stamp their work. The virus seizes control of the computer and works its mischief.

© Rob Doyle/*Business Week*

With 33 million desktop machines in use, hundreds of thousands of individuals have acquired the technical skill to "penetrate most systems," says Gerald E. Mitchell, director of data security at IDS Financial Services in Minneapolis.

Using international phone links, a group of West German hackers took repeated strolls through the computers of the National Aeronautics and Space Administration (NASA) in 1988, as well as through several U.S. military networks. NASA spent three months changing passwords and clearing out "trapdoor" programs that the intruders had planted to give them access. Another German hacker spent nearly two years cruising through unclassified data in U.S. Defense Department and other research computers around the world until he was stopped in 1988. And NASA's Jet Propulsion Laboratory (JPL) in Pasadena, California, was invaded by hackers yet to be identified.

The Insidious Virus

Even companies with good security have run into a new and insidious problem: the computer virus. Like microorganisms, these replicate and spread. They're tiny bits of software, often quickly written, that hide in larger programs and then pounce unpredictably. Some simply deliver a surprise message on the screen. Others can wipe out every shred of information in a computer.

What especially worries corporate computer managers is that somehow these destructive programs could migrate to mainframe computers and do serious damage to the most sensitive corporate data. Says Jeffrey M. Hoffman, a computer specialist at Atlantic Richfield Company (Arco): "The PC world is the lightly protected gateway to the host computer world." Although most large computer systems employ mechanisms that isolate computer code, reducing the opportunity for a virus to spread, the threat exists—even for Big Blue. Although the company plays down the incident, in December 1987, a viruslike program infiltrated IBM's 145-country electronic mail network, forcing the entire system to be shut down.

When such incidents occur, the victim company often has failed to employ some surprisingly simple measures. Experts say, for instance, that companies should outlaw such mundane passwords as a birthday or a spouse's name. NASA concedes that it was using ''inappropriate'' passwords that were easy to guess. IBM's Wills urges companies to remind workers not to log on to a computer and then leave it unattended, nor share passwords with co-workers. He is also a proponent of written computer security policies, complete with security clearances.

Need to Know

IBM has five classes of data, from unclassified, with no restrictions, to ''registered IBM confidential,'' available only to employees with a predetermined need to know. After the December 1987 incident, which began when a West German law student sent a self-replicating Christmas greeting into a European academic research network, IBM tightened controls over its electronic networks.

It's crucial, say experts, to treat computer security as a management, not a technology, problem. For example, programs running on Marine Midland Bank's central computer are ''encapsulated'' so that employees can use only what's needed to perform their jobs—and can't browse through the system.

Physical barriers are important, too, and there are lots of new ones. Electronic card keys, or ''smart cards,'' with embedded microchip memories and processors, are starting to be used as ID cards for workers. They can be programmed with volumes of personal data and authorization codes that are hard to fake. Some smart cards change passwords every 60 seconds. But even such cards have a flaw: they can be stolen. More secure, some experts think, are biometric devices, which identify people according to physical quirks. Machines can now scan voice inflections, handprints, and even typing habits.

Still, common sense may be the best protection—and less intrusive. For example, USPA could have thwarted Donald Gene Burleson by thinking faster. The company procras-

tinated before changing its computer passwords, a crucial mistake: as a computer security officer, Burleson was one of three people at the company who knew everyone's password.

Cover-up

A similar mistake caught up with Wollongong Group, a software company in Palo Alto, California. Ming Jyh Hsieh, a 38-year-old Taiwanese émigré who worked as a customer support representative, was fired in late 1987. Two months later Wollongong noticed that someone was logging on to its computers at night via modem. Some files had been copied or damaged. After tracing the calls to Hsieh's nearby home, police seized her personal computer, along with disks containing Wollongong's proprietary software, estimated to be worth millions of dollars. She was arrested, charged with illegal access to computers, and, if convicted, faces up to five years in prison.

Wollongong had crippled Hsieh's access code, but the company suspects that she somehow obtained another worker's. Since the incident, Wollongong periodically changes passwords and account numbers. ''Any company that doesn't is asking to be kicked,'' says Norman Lombino, Wollongong's marketing communications manager.

One advantage for computer crooks is that their victims often keep quiet, notes consultant Robert H. Courtney, Jr. Statistics are hard to come by. But experts estimate that only 20 to 50 percent of computer crimes are ever reported. Particularly for banks, a successful fraud is a public relations disaster. Burleson's break-in at USPA might never have come to light had he not sued for back pay—thus encouraging a countersuit. ''No one wants to display their managerial shortcomings,'' says Courtney. In one extreme case, Courtney says, an insurance company executive used his personal computer to scan claim records needed to commit a $13 million fraud. The company found out and fired him. But to avoid a scandal, it gave him a lavish going-away party.

Bringing the problem into the open may be the only way to improve security, however. Take viruses. These wily programs most often find their way into corporate computer systems when an employee inadvertently introduces them. Computer enthusiasts from New York to New Delhi use electronic bulletin boards on communications networks such as The Source to ''chat'' by computer. One of their favorite pastimes is swapping programs—any one of which can include a virus that attaches itself to other programs in a computer.

No one knows how many viruses have been planted. But John D. McAfee, a virus expert at InterPath Corporation, a security consulting firm in Santa Clara, California, says there have already been 250,000 outbreaks. He estimates that 40 of the nation's largest industrial companies have been infected.

Pakistani Flu

Worldwide computer networks take viruses on some remarkable journeys. Recently the *Providence Journal-Bulletin* was infected by the Pa-

kistani Brain—two years after that program began circulating. Nobody knows how it got to Rhode Island. But before it was through, it had infected 100 of the paper's personal computer hard disks. Basit Farooq Alvi, a 19-year-old programmer from Punjab province, says he wrote the virus not to destroy data, but as a warning to would-be software pirates. The virus would interfere only with bootlegged copies of his package, a program for physicians. Other programmers, however, have given it a pernicious twist: now versions of the brain often carry instructions to wipe out data files. And some of these versions have spread to Israel, Europe, and the U.S.

Below: © Biophoto Associates/Photo Researchers; bottom: © Alexander Tsiaras/Photo Researchers

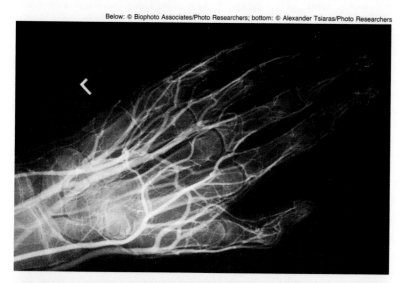

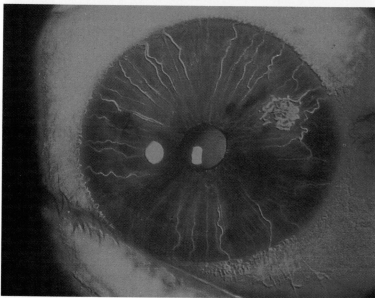

Computer security starts with denying unauthorized personnel access to sensitive data banks. Already, some companies require an employee to pass one hand beneath an electronic camera before entering a sensitive area. The camera identifies the employee by means of his or her subcutaneous vein patterns (above). Other companies grant clearance only after a retina scanner has verified the unique pattern of blood vessels in the employee's eye (left).

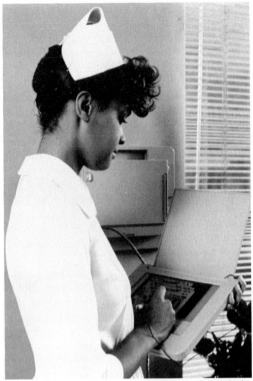

Courtesy of Linus Technologies, Inc.

Some hospital computers now rely on handwriting-recognition systems to limit the personnel who have access to the medical records of patients.

Even a well-meant virus can have unfortunate side effects. Richard R. Brandow, the 24-year-old publisher of a Montreal computer magazine, and coworker Pierre M. Zovile created a benign virus to dramatize the pervasiveness of software piracy. Point proved: in two months, Brandow says, illegal copying had transferred the virus to 350,000 Macintoshes around the world. When the internal clocks on these machines hit March 2, 1988, the first birthday of the Mac II computer, each machine displayed Brandow's "universal message of peace to all Macintosh users."

Vaccine Programs

It was a nice thought. But Marc Canter, president of a small Chicago software publisher, says that Zovile's virus wasn't innocuous. It caused Canter's computer to crash and infected disks that he supplied to software producer Aldus Corporation in Seattle, Washington. For three days, Aldus unwittingly transferred the virus onto copies of its Freehand illustration program on its assembly lines. Aldus pulled back the tainted

disks, but not before some of them were received by customers.

As with many computer security problems, the chief weapon against viruses is employee awareness, says Arco's Hoffman. After a virus invaded Macs at Arco's Dallas office, then spread to another Arco office in Anchorage, Alaska, the company told employees not to use software of questionable origin.

There also are more than a dozen "vaccine" programs, including Interferon, a package that Robert J. Woodhead, an Ithaca, New York, author of computer games, offers free. Woodhead says each virus has a unique pattern, which his software can identify. It then erases the virus. Another method, in use at Lehigh University's computer labs since a virus struck there a few years ago, is to test suspicious software by setting the computer clock to Christmas, New Year's, or April Fools' Day—dates on which many viruses are set to detonate.

Viruses have caused such consternation that Congress is mulling tougher federal laws. A House bill introduced in July 1988 would make it a federal crime to insert a malicious virus into a computer. Basic computer-crime laws are already on the books in 48 states, and business and industry leaders are looking for government agencies to set guidelines for security standards. Under the Computer Security Act of 1987, the National Bureau of Standards (NBS) is charged with doing that. But agency budget cuts are expected to slow the process, industry officials say. In Japan, meantime, the government gives a tax break to companies purchasing facilities and hardware to guard their systems.

Even without such incentives, U.S. companies are spending huge sums on computer security. They can be anything from software to control access to the mainframe, costing $35,000 a copy, to hardware that scrambles data so it can't be understood if a phone line is tapped. In 1982 only 10 percent of IBM mainframes had data security software, according to a survey by market researcher Computer Intelligence. Now the figure is 35 percent.

To foil hackers, many companies are installing dial-back systems on computers. These ensure that an incoming call is from an authorized number. A large mainframe may have hundreds of "ports" for remote computers—with callback units costing $600 to $700 per port. Additional encryption hardware for encoding data can cost $1,200 per communications line. With the most to lose, banks are a big market for such equipment. They disguise data by encrypting it, and many use message-authentication techniques to ensure that what is received over phone lines matches what was sent.

Modem Meltdown

In the wake of the Chicago fire, there's also new interest in "disaster recovery"—restoring operations after fires, floods, earthquakes, or sabotage. For years, companies have shipped computer tapes with sensitive records to vaults such as that run by Data Mountain Inc. in Phoenix, Arizona, where gun-toting guards watch over a 2,000-square-foot (186-square-meter) room chiseled out of rock.

But the phone company blaze in the Chicago suburb of Hinsdale lent a new urgency to such planning. "The story has gotten out to Europe, Asia, and Australia," says Dave Haeckel, a principal with Arthur Andersen & Co., a Big Eight accounting firm that does computer consulting. That's been a boon for disaster-recovery specialists such as Comdisco Inc. "I've never seen anything like this," says Raymond Hipp, president of Comdisco Disaster, which collects fees of $100 million annually from 1,000 customers to maintain backup systems. Comdisco says it can restore computer service in 24 hours.

Such a promise may be worthless if phone lines have melted, as they did in Hinsdale. "Nobody had really focused on the lack of redundancy in the Bell operating companies' networks," notes Hipp. Local phone companies relay computer signals to a long-distance carrier such as American Telephone & Telegraph Company (AT&T) or a data network such as Tymnet, which relays the signal to a local phone company that picks it up for the customer. Without that last link, the most sophisticated computer network may be useless.

Most of the time, phone company backup systems route calls around trouble spots. But in Hinsdale, a worst-case scenario occurred. The automated phone-switching facility was unstaffed and lacked the kind of fire-suppression system used in computer centers. There was no

Fingerprint matching has found increasing use as a means of preventing unauthorized access to computer data bases.

London Picture Service from British Trade Office

Computer Calamities

• **Viruses and Other Malicious Software.** These potentially devastating programs are usually planted by means of a "Trojan Horse"—a seemingly normal package hiding a destructive program that can wipe out a computer's data files. Antiviral programs can be used to detect viruses. Employees should be prohibited from loading untested software into the system.

• **Fires, Floods, Power Failures, Earthquakes.** A few precautions can prevent acts of God from becoming data disasters. Copies of data should be stored at another site. Backup computers should be set up. Disaster-recovery services guarantee restoration of normal data processing within hours of a crisis.

• **Sneak Attacks by Outside Hackers.** Simple passwords won't stop these technoterrorists from breaking in by telephone. Data should be encrypted and the computer programmed to accept calls only from authorized telephones. At night, disk drives containing sensitive data should be shut down.

• **Wiretaps and Electronic Eavesdropping.** It's easier than most companies think for outsiders to tap the telecommunications lines that connect their computers. Advanced cryptographic techniques can scramble messages, and special enclosures can contain the emissions that electronic eavesdroppers are able to intercept and decode.

• **The Enemy Within: Employee Tampering.** The number one security threat is employees, whose theft, sabotage, or ineptitude can cause havoc. Employees should have access only to the systems and data needed to do their jobs. Lock up machines that do critical tasks. Change passwords frequently.

alarm at the local fire station, because Illinois Bell feared that the fire department couldn't put out a computer fire without causing excessive damage.

The result: thousands of homes and businesses, including headquarters offices of McDonald's Corporation and Motorola Corporation, were cut off. Large businesses restored communications with emergency microwave radio systems. But seven local businesses have filed lawsuits to recover losses caused by the outage.

Computer customers, as well, want better security features from hardware and software suppliers. Many companies are considering making AT&T's Unix software—or its derivatives—a standard to smooth the connections between different brands of machines. But since Unix was designed to make it easy for computers to share files and programs, it's also susceptible to break-ins, says Judith S. Hurwitz, editor of *Unix in the Office,* a newsletter.

For instance, phrackers in California, after cracking the password system on one Unix computer last year, used the same approach to unlock Unix-based systems at phone companies all over the country. Now AT&T is making Unix more secure. Similarly, Digital Equipment Corporation (DEC) says it has patched software holes that let West German Chaos Club members break into its VAX computers.

Hi-tech Hijacking

Concern over computer security will mount as companies do more electronic transactions. In the $55 billion textile business, for instance, sales data, new orders, shipment information, inventory receipts, and invoices are beginning to flow directly from one company's computer to another's via a pipeline called Electronic Data Interchange (EDI). Other companies, such as makers of automobile parts, are using EDI to send items directly to customers, and therefore bypassing warehouses. The potential for fraud and theft is enormous. "There have always been attempts to divert products," says Peter Browne, president of Profile Analysis, a Ridgefield, Connecticut, consulting firm. "Now it can be done electronically."

Corporations are left in a bind: they need to expand computerized information and transaction-processing systems to compete. But the more they do, the greater their risk. "Our society must do something to control the problem," says Ernest A. Conrads, director of corporate security at Westinghouse Electric Corp. "If not, our information system can't grow the way technology will allow us to." In the long run, that could have more profound economic consequences than all the hackers, viruses, and disaster-induced computer failures combined.

ERASABLE OPTICAL DISKS

by Mark Alpert

I magine a new form of information storage that would hold encyclopedic amounts of data but could slip into a personal computer or workstation as easily as a floppy disk does— and could be erased and written on again several million times without the least sign of wear. Well, it's finally here. Over the past year, Japanese electronics giants and American high-tech firms have introduced the first erasable optical disks, along with the disk drives that put information on them and get it off again.

Reading by Laser

Unlike the magnetic floppy disks, hard disks, and tape cartridges that store data in most of today's computers, optical disks use laser light to record and read information, just as do the compact-disk recordings that are supplanting LPs. The new technology promises to give computer users what they have been clamoring for: lots of reusable memory in a form that can be removed from the machine at the end of the workday for use at home or while traveling. Many computer users, especially those in security-conscious government agencies, don't like leaving their data unprotected when they go home. Because they cannot remove high-capacity hard disks, the most popular storage devices for personal computers (PCs), some users go so far as to put their computers under lock and key overnight.

One famous trendsetter, Steve Jobs, the cofounder of Apple Computer, has included a Canon optical disk drive as the primary storage device for the workstation from his new company, NeXT. IBM, Hewlett-Packard, and other computer makers are carefully eyeing the market but have yet to plunge in, partly because the optical-disk drives available thus far are slower and more expensive than the best magnetic-storage devices. Lingering differences over compatibility could also hold back the young technology. So, while optical drives were the

High-capacity erasable optical disks can be written on and erased millions of times without deteriorating.

hottest new products at the industry's fall trade shows, it's not yet clear how much of a dent they will make in the $23-billion-a-year worldwide disk-drive market.

The full name for the new technology is magneto-optical storage: the disk drive combines a laser and a magnetic coil, which work in tandem. Because the laser can read a bit of data only 40-millionths of an inch across, an optical disk the size of a CD can hold vast quantities of information—the entire text of the *Encyclopedia Americana,* for example, or every telephone listing in New York and New England. But until recently the optical disks suffered from a serious drawback: you could record information on them, but you couldn't erase it.

The breakthrough came in 1987, when teams of engineers at 3M and other disk makers discovered almost simultaneously how to make an ultrathin magnetic layer that could be written on and erased millions of times without deteriorating. The introduction of erasable optical-disk products followed like a tidal wave, much of it originating in the Orient. Many of Japan's largest electronics companies have come forward with optical disks or optical-disk drives or both.

Timed for Optical

The principal U.S. entrant so far is Maxtor Corp. of San Jose, California, which sold $300 million worth of conventional hard-disk drives last year. Maxtor has chosen to take on the foreign Goliaths with an optical drive that can put a full gigabyte of data—1 billion bytes, the equivalent of 500,000 typewritten pages or 2,800 floppy disks—on a single optical disk only 5¼ inches (13⅓ centimeters) in diameter, the same size as most floppies. That's more than half again as much as the capacity of the Japanese drives. Maxtor engineers named their product the Tahiti, figuring they could probably afford to vacation there if the disk drive succeeds. Maxtor and Verbatim, an Eastman Kodak subsidiary headquartered in Charlotte, North Carolina, have also introduced systems that record data on an even smaller 3½-inch (8.9-centimeter) optical disk.

Most of the players in this game, including Jobs, are betting that erasable optical disks will eventually become the storage medium of choice for everything from desktop workstations

HOW AN ERASABLE DISK WORKS

BLANK DISK

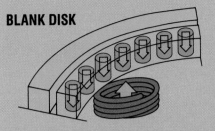

Each data-storage spot on a blank disk is magnetized in the same direction; here its north pole points downward. The magnetic orientation cannot be changed unless the disk is heated.

WRITING

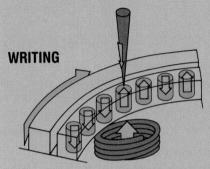

To inscribe digitized data, an infrared laser heats selected data-storage spots on the disk. A magnetic coil flips the north pole up to signify a binary 1 or leaves it down for a binary 0.

READING

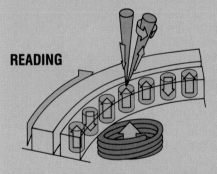

On a weaker setting, the laser bounces off the disk. The light is polarized clockwise or counterclockwise, depending on which way the data spot is magnetized. The disk drive reads the signals.

ERASING

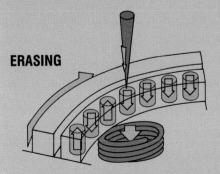

The magnetic coil reverses field. The laser heats all data spots, causing them to orient downward again.

to data libraries that networks of users have access to. "Once every 20 years we see a transition to a new storage technology," says W. Michael Deese, vice president for optical systems at the U.S. subsidiary of Sony; the parent company developed the audio CD jointly with Philips NV of the Netherlands. "The market is now timed exactly right for optical."

The earliest computers stored their data on bulky reels of magnetic tape. Later machines used magnetic disks that provided much faster access to information. IBM passed a milestone in 1973 when it developed a system that could store at least 30 million bytes of information on a single magnetic disk. Because of its capacity, the system was called the Winchester hard-disk drive, supposedly after the .30-caliber hunting rifle. The hard disks in most Winchester drives are erasable but not removable. The beauty of the erasable optical disk is that it combines the high storage capacity of a Winchester disk with the ease of removal of a floppy.

Removable and Reliable

"Removability will be the most important tool for the sale of the optical product in its early stages," predicts George Scalise, CEO of Maxtor. "The typical executive has up to 60 megabytes—about 165 floppy disks' worth—of financial data or sales plans or other information in his or her computer files," says Donald Strickland, vice president of Verbatim. "If you can carry that information with you when you travel, then you can transfer your computerized office to anywhere in the world."

The other great advantage of optical disks is reliability. Perhaps the most dreaded experience in using a PC is a "head crash." That's what happens when the magnetic reading device, or head, of a disk drive collides with the spinning disk and sends invaluable data into oblivion. Head crashes are not uncommon with Winchester drives because the magnetic head is just 15-millionths of an inch above the disk. "With a high-capacity drive, if you lose 50 megabytes of information, that's 25,000 pages down the drain," says computer analyst Aharon Orlansky. There's no chance of a head crash in an optical-disk system. The laser is a full one-sixteenth inch (1.5 millimeters) above the disk, which is coated with a protective layer of plastic or chemically strengthened glass.

The first generation of optical-disk drives does have limitations, though. The most advanced Winchester hard-disk-drive systems can

© Jim Richardson

Erasable optical disks will not find widespread use until manufacturers agree on standards that make the disks compatible with each other's systems.

hold almost as much data as optical drives and can store and retrieve those data three to 10 times faster. Also, the great majority of Winchester drives cost less than $1,000, while the erasable optical drives range from $1,000 to $6,000. Makers of the optical drives are confident that performance will improve and prices will fall with each new generation of products. But Winchester disk drives continue to become faster and cheaper, usually doubling their performance every two to three years.

Potential Applications

Many analysts see the market splitting right down the middle, with optical systems becoming the predominant device for long-term document storage, and magnetic systems retaining control over the fast "scratch pad" uses in workstations and PCs. "It's a horse race, and I don't think the optical horse will catch up to the magnetic horse until the middle or late 1990s," says Bob Katzive, vice president of Disk/Trend, a market-research firm in California.

For this reason, most forecasts for the growth of the optical-storage market are on the conservative side. Katzive estimates that sales of erasable optical-disk drives will increase from virtually nothing today to $900 million by 1991, with most of the drives going into document-storage systems rather than workstations or PCs. Users who need to update their data constantly—airlines, banks, and insurance companies, for example—will probably want to stick with the faster magnetic systems for now.

The first widespread applications of the erasable optical disk are likely to be in market niches where maximum speed is not critical but high storage capacity and removability are. For example, Autometric, an engineering-services company in Alexandria, Virginia, has started using an erasable optical-disk system to store highly complex Landsat satellite photographs of the earth's surface. Each requires 280 megabytes to cover 13,225 square miles (34,253 square kilometers). Says senior scientist William J. Cox: "We've never been able to put the whole picture in one place before."

Currently, optical-disk drives are being sold by companies such as Advanced Graphic Applications of New York City, which mix and match disk drives and disks from various manufacturers and provide the software to make them all work together. For optical-disk systems to become the truly dominant storage technology, however, they will have to be incorporated into the workstations and PCs offered by major computer makers. Says Deese: "I wouldn't be surprised to see IBM enter the market. It has made its interest known."

Fans of the erasable optical disk point out, too, that even if the disks don't replace magnetic-storage systems on most computers, there's lots of room for the new technology to thrive anyway. Edward Rothchild, head of a San Francisco consulting firm for optical-disk companies, estimates that only 2 percent of all information is stored on magnetic media, while 3 percent is stored on microfilm and 95 percent on paper. "The dominant form of information storage today is file cabinets," Rothchild says. "Paper is the real target for replacement by optical storage." Optical disks last longer than magnetic tapes, which must be rerecorded every two or three years to preserve their data. And retrieval of information is considerably faster than is possible with microfilm or microfiche.

3M, a major supplier of recording media, was quick to recognize the opportunity and became an early leader in the race to manufacture low-cost erasable optical disks, which currently sell for $150 to $250 apiece. (A floppy disk costs about $1.50.) The Minnesota-based giant faces tough competition from Sony, the Maxell

subsidiary of Hitachi, and a joint venture between Philips and Du Pont that is manufacturing disks for the Maxtor drive. "They will become a commodity product eventually," says Roger Hilde, manager for erasable media at 3M.

Near-term Outlook

Before that happens, however, the competitors must agree on standards, so that a user can slip any maker's disk into any other maker's drive. In the rush to bring optical products to market, several companies developed systems before standards had been set for the technology. The Canon optical-disk system used by NeXT, for example, is not compatible with the others.

It's barely possible that all these companies have missed the boat. Engineers at IBM, Tandy, and Matsushita are now studying other optical-recording technologies—phase change and dye polymer—that could eventually make the magneto-optical systems obsolete. But there wouldn't be so many companies introducing erasable optical products right now if they didn't sniff the sweet scent of impending profits. "It will be a gradual growth, but by the year 2000, optical systems will take over," declares John Kondo, technical and marketing director for Olympus. "The market is wide open."

An erasable optical disk (lower left) holds 30 percent more data than the bulkier hard disk (top) and 1,400 to 2,800 times as much as the floppy disk (right).

Electronic Bulletin Boards

by Thomas B. Allen

I am making a telephone call by tapping the number keys—2775990—on my computer's keyboard. Somewhere, in another computer, a telephone rings. I hear a dial tone, then a high-pitched whine. On the screen of my computer monitor, the word "CONNECTED" appears. And then: "Welcome to the EAST COAST PUB NET! A Free Information Exchange for Writers, Graphic Artists, Photographers, Editors, and Publishers. Enjoy." I log on to the computer in a simple ritual: in response to questions, I type my name, city, and state, and a password that will enable me to call the board again and prove I am not an imposter. A computer-style menu pops up, and from Pub Net's offerings I select "conferences," which includes one called Writers, Editors, and Other Word Mongers.

Pub Net, I am informed, allows conference members to contribute poems or (very) short stories—no longer than 99 lines. Keystroke by keystroke, I follow instructions to open the Pub Net anthology. In a few seconds I see this relaxed message: "O.K. folks here is using the conference for what it is intended."

By pushing the down-arrow key, I scroll through the torrent of words pouring onto the screen: a poem based on Greek myth, a surge of sonnets, a delicate strand of haiku (an unrhymed form of Japanese verse), a kindly comment about the haiku from a conferee who identifies himself as Yukio Iura. He has a message for "ALL": we should know about Machi Tawara, a Japanese language teacher whose poetry booklet sells in the millions in Japan. He types: "Is it alright for you to say 'Marry me'/After drinking couple cans of beer . . . ?"

Reach Out and Touch

Yukio Iura is there and not there. His words, typed weeks before, linger in this nowhere place called an electronic bulletin board. He is reaching out to touch people by posting a modern version of the weather-beaten notices that fluttered on the wall of the old town hall.

The boards present messages and conferences on subjects as diverse as the whims of the human heart and mind. A sampler, from several hours of browsing: astronomy, comic books, motorcycles, skydiving, artificial intelligence, music, investments, medicine, mathematics, and "harmless jokes." A New York City bulletin board offers conferences on such topics as aging, alcoholism, death, eating disorders, and psychopathology.

I logged on to a discussion about transactional analysis: "Once this process begins [the rewriting of the life script], self-acceptance is soon to follow." The writer then veered off to say, "Whenever you discuss abstract ideas, they seem to float away into the clouds."

Abstract or not, the ideas kept bounding onto the board, and the phrases had the air of an academic discussion: "I'm not sure I understand your point fully," or "As you must realize," or "I *DO* think the topic is one that should be researched."

The analysts, like the Pub Net group, use the boards to exchange information through a medium that combines the convenience of the telephone with the massive memory of the personal computer. Many who use the bulletin board system—BBS to enthusiasts—believe that they have discovered a form of communication that can revolutionize the way we exchange information.

Yukio Iura puts his messages on boards like Pub Net. He also has his own board, which he runs with the zeal of a true believer. A Japanese banker who works for the Institute of International Finance in Washington, D.C., he says, "I see what I do as personal liaison between the United States and Japan."

On his board, Yukio discusses such subjects as Japanese culture and international economics. He runs as many as 21 conferences, exchanging messages and ideas with about 500 callers. I met him first on the boards—he fre-

Computer enthusiasts contribute and exchange information using electronic bulletin boards.

From the sublime to the ridiculous: topics running the gamut from classical music to cartoon characters (above) can find their way onto an electronic bulletin board. A system operator, or "sysop" (below), sets the rules, regulating who logs on, how long the caller stays on, and the type and quantity of information uploaded or downloaded.

quents several in the Washington area—and then dialed his board and asked if we could meet in person, a rare event in the BBS world. In this world, people argue, chat, and exchange information without hearing each other's voices, without ever seeing each other. They spend hours, usually at night, reading words, writing words, seeing ideas and thoughts scroll by, staring at their monitors, never at a human face.

The Sysop

As the custodian of a board, Yukio is a "sysop"—a system operator. A sysop sets the rules, deciding what a caller must do to log on, how long the caller can stay on, and what the caller can take (or "download") from the board. "Some boards are very strict. Some even want a donation," he says. "My board is generous. I let a caller on for 60 minutes at a time, and I let him download to almost the sky's the limit."

Callers can upload information from their computers to a board or download offerings from a board to the caller's computer. Many of the programs are the proud creations of highly talented hackers who want to show off their handiwork to appreciative peers. (A clock program I downloaded from Pub Net, for instance, replaces my computer's coldly precise digital time with a more human-sounding phrase. So instead of flashing, say, ''12:08'' on the screen, the computer gives the time as ''A few minutes past twelve.'')

''I do not have many techies on my board,'' Yukio says. (Techies are, as you might guess, technical whizzes who love to write and tinker with computer programs.) ''My callers download documents much more than they do programs.'' Typical documents are bibliographies of Japanese writers available in English, a short biography of the poet Machi Tawara, and an essay by Yukio about consumerism in Japan.

''My board,'' Yukio says, ''is a way of saying thanks to Americans who taught me how to use computer technology. I feel that operation of a board is one of the best ways to show my appreciation.'' When he returns to Japan, he will leave the board to his successor.

A sysop, like someone behind a one-way mirror, is invisible but able to observe. Callers have no way of knowing whether the sysop is watching them or has gone off and left the board on automatic. A young Washington woman tells of having trouble downloading a program from a BBS. ''All of a sudden,'' she recalls, ''a message flashed on the screen. It addressed me by name and politely asked me if I could use some help. I felt like God was talking to me.''

The message came from Kurt Riegel, director of national astronomy centers for the National Science Foundation, and sysop of Astro, a board that informs callers about such celestial matters as the coming of comets and the cataloging of stars. Astro attracts callers from throughout the United States and Europe. ''And the other day,'' Kurt told me, ''someone logged on from Brazil.''

Kurt let me watch him in his sysop role one night at Astro headquarters—a room in his home on a quiet street in Arlington, Virginia. On the table before him were a computer, its monitor, a keyboard, and a telephone, to which a device called a modem was connected. The rest of the table was cluttered with stacks of floppy disks and computer manuals.

User Aliases

A caller's modem (*mo* for modulation, *dem* for demodulation) changes, or modulates, the computer's letters and numbers into audible tones. The high-pitched whistling tones are transmitted over telephone lines to Kurt's modem, which demodulates the signals. His computer then restores the signals to the original letters and numbers, which then appear on his monitor.

''I don't pay much attention to security,'' Kurt said. ''And of course there is no way to

A file called Trashcan enables a bulletin board sysop to recognize problem users and promptly dump them.

Many electronic bulletin boards have restrictions that protect the personal privacy of the callers.

check on whether someone is using his or her real name. But I do have this.'' As he spoke, he brought up on the screen a file called Trashcan, which contained a list of words that he, as sysop, had seen being used as caller aliases. There were the usual four-letter words, along with many others, including Alien, Darth, Oz, Starfleet, and Psycho. ''When the bulletin board sees anyone trying to register by using any of Trashcan's words,'' Kurt said, ''the user is dumped and disconnected.''

Kurt's fingers poked about the keyboard. ''My job is primarily throwing away stuff. There's an unbelievable amount of junk.'' He scanned messages, deleting old ones and rearranging the rest of them.

Most Astro callers want to discuss serious topics. One, for example, asked a technical question about the way the Doppler shift could affect communication with extraterrestrials. Kurt responded with an equally technical answer. Incoming messages may be addressed to ALL, to the sysop, or privately to another registered caller. (One message looked at first like a report of a new supernova. A new star, ''primarily pink in color,'' had been born to an astronomer and his wife.) The sysop sees all messages, including the private ones. About 20 percent of Astro's messages are private.

Callers to some boards can get privacy through aliases. A few boards, particularly those that encourage freewheeling conferences, urge participants to cloak their identities. ''Women use aliases quite often, for protection, I guess,'' says Mike Cuthbert, who runs a popular radio talk show in Washington, D.C. '' 'Mr. Spock' is a doctor, an obstetrician. I know of at least one other doctor who doesn't use his real name.

''I'm in a lot of boards—with my real name—and I get ideas for my shows. I like the boards. They give people a chance to talk without the usual hang-ups. There's usually no mention of body shape or questions about looks, and no 'Are you sexy?' We have fine conversations, especially on the more intellectual boards, where they chase away the techies.''

Most forms of communication provide clues about the communicators. On radio, Mike Cuthbert's resonant voice is readily recognized. Pen pals can get clues from each other's handwriting. Strangers on a telephone can make geographical assumptions from drawl or psychological assumptions from intonations and pauses. Even Morse code senders have a recognizable touch. But board users get no reliable cues about each other's appearance, age, sex, or background.

An Invisible World

Because the on-line world is rarely organized and always invisible, information about it is hard to come by. But its growth is known to be phenomenal. One of the most extensive systems of bulletin boards is called FidoNet. In 1984 it consisted of 300 boards; by 1987 there were 2,000 in a network encompassing Europe, Asia, Africa, South America, and Australia.

I asked D. Thomas Mack, the man most responsible for founding the bulletin board world, how many boards are on-line at any given hour. ''Probably in the five years that electronic bulletin boards have been out there, I'd say there have been anywhere from 50,000 to 100,000 boards,'' he told me. ''But if you ask me how many are currently operating, I would say anywhere from 1,000 to 5,000.

''Boards are like wives, dogs, and swimming pools,'' he continued. ''Everyone has one once. And so people put up a bulletin board to see what will happen. They fail to see that it will take a lot of time. The maintenance of a board, like that of a pool or a dog or a marriage, gets too much for them and they quit.''

Mack created RBBS-PC (Remote Bulletin Board System–Personal Computer), a popular software program for connecting computers through telephones and modems. Without RBBS-PC or a program like it, bulletin board communication is not possible. Mack distributes RBBS without charge because he believes that a bulletin board is ''a contribution to a community, just like a barn raising was. It's a 21st-century technology that's grounded in the concept of user helping user.''

''Unlike radio, newspapers, and television, RBBS-PC provides a vehicle within which information can be exchanged! That is what makes RBBS-PC so unique,'' Mack wrote in a commentary accompanying downloaded versions of the program. ''Because the exchange is written, it is structured. Because it is structured, it can be thoughtful. . . . RBBS-PC provides every personal computer owner with his own 'soap-box' in a national Hyde Park.''

But BBS users tend to cluster around local phone numbers, as in a neighborhood park, rather than spending money to dial distant boards. So local sysops usually compile long lists of area BBS phone numbers and offer them for downloading. Often, though, the numbers produce not a modem's whine but a human one—an irate voice saying the household no longer includes a BBS. Or the number may be answered by a cheery phone-company recording that says the phone has been disconnected.

"Flaming" Language

On these short-lived chatter boards, as serious computer communicators call them, the screen pulsates with short messages, sometimes in lowercase, sometimes in PASSIONATE CAPITAL LETTERS. The sentences slam into each other as each person types a comment and the squabbling scrolls down the screen. When an antifeminist broke into a conference on women's rights, a woman typed her response, then sputtered: ''My computer is smoking.''

Extremely violent language is called ''flaming.'' One board has a regular conference called Flamers/Get Rid of Your Anger. Because of the lack of visual or audible cues, emotional BBSers must resort to symbols. In a good mood, they will add a signal for a smile—or type ''tee-hee'' or ''grin'' or ''hug.'' When flaming flares, however, they will INSULT EACH OTHER IN CAPITALS.

Most inhabitants of the BBS world want to exchange information, not insults. Typical callers roam the boards—BBSing, they call it—not to lurk but to upload and download. There is an understanding among the program swappers that those who take must also give.

Many sysops keep track of ''download/upload ratios'' and chide program hogs for monopolizing on-line time; it may take half an hour or more to download a long program. Harassed sysops, who combine the virtues of a drill sergeant and a favorite auntie, must ration users. Complex rules govern access to the most popular, program-laden boards.

Some BBSers are strictly private; only registered callers, using passwords, can log on.

Callers vent their frustrations on electronic bulletin boards using violent language called ''flaming.''

Commercial information-service boards, which are not considered part of the BBS network, charge subscribers for the downloading of information, such as stock market prices.

Uncle Sam is the sysop of a surprising number of boards. I lurked on BBSers at the Department of Commerce, the Census Bureau, the Department of Education, and many other agencies on U.S. Government lists. Imagine my surprise when I dialed the U.S. Bureau of Prisons and was told: ''If you have accidentally found this board and are not a government employee or other authorized visitor, you are NOT welcome here! REPEATED LOG-ON TRIES WILL BE REPORTED TO LAW ENFORCEMENT AUTHORITIES!!!''

A caller who logs onto a bulletin board but does not contribute information is said to be "lurking."

containers, and stole some goods. The captain of the *Urundi . . .* took the attackers by surprise and they fled.''

Community Computing

This electronic advice to mariners is an example of how BBSers are rapidly spreading from the PC world of hackers and other hobbyists to the world at large, where the PC-phone-modem hookup is gaining new respect. Just as the U.S. Government is reaching out with this latest form of communication, so are states and cities.

In Cleveland the Society for Public Access Computing was formed in 1987 to help found ''Electronic Cities,'' a community computing system. The system was founded in Cleveland by Dr. Thomas Grundner, who is a faculty member at Case Western Reserve University.

Responding to simple computer commands, the visitor to ''Electronic Cleveland'' signs a guest book and wanders through the city, choosing such stops as Government House, University Circle, the Post Office, the Hospital, the Schoolhouse, the Arts Center, and the Courthouse. Each stop offers interactive communication and information about what is going on at the real-world version of the electronic way station. Government House was still being built when I entered. The blueprint calls for a system that will let the on-line citizen log on to ''electronic offices'' of local, state, and federal

I did receive permission (and a short-term password) from the Defense Mapping Agency to dial the somewhat restricted board operated by the DMA's Navigation Information Network. After a few keystrokes, ''PIRATES''— yes, in capitals—appeared.

The warning involved the West German ship *Urundi*, which ''was attacked by pirates while dropping anchor in Freetown harbor, Sierra Leone. The pirates, who were armed with knives and axes, climbed on board the ship after approaching it on a motorboat, smashed in 6

On a special electronic bulletin board for schoolchildren, kids discuss everything from acid rain to culinary likes and dislikes.

Scientists in the U.S. and the Soviet Union have set up a bulletin board to compare notes on global warming trends.

elected representatives. In each office the visitor will be able to download a newsletter and leave messages in a mailbox.

On an international level, scientists in the United States and the Soviet Union have set up a bulletin board network to compare notes on global warming trends. This streamlined technology makes it possible for American scientists to communicate with their Soviet colleagues without the expense or protocol problems of face-to-face meetings in either country.

Classrooms are also going on-line. A growing number of schools—plans are for as many as 10,000—are linked through the National Geographic Kids Network, a collaboration of the National Geographic Society, the National Science Foundation, and Technical Education Research Centers of Cambridge, Massachusetts. Late last year a field test of the network dispatched pupils of 31 schools to

ponds and creeks from Massachusetts to California. The kids, from fourth through sixth grade, then tested the water for acidity and typed their findings into the network to compare results. A scientist at a central computer analyzed the data, put the information into map and chart form, and then uploaded the results back into the network.

Megan Andrew, of the North Dickinson Elementary School in Carlisle, Pennsylvania, was shocked at what appeared on her classroom monitor. "The worst," she said, "was finding out that we had the most acid in our rain and it is going to kill the fish."

Sometimes the youngsters on the network just talk to each other about everyday things. "I'm the only kid in my class that lives on a farm," a fourth grader typed. ". . . I've been living on the farm all my life. My favorite food is sweet corn. I hate peas."

From a fifth grader in Virginia: "We live in a small town about two hours away from Richmond, our capital. There are about 400 kids in our school. The food in our cafeteria is terrible."

Networked Kids Discuss Classroom Pets

And at an on-line school in Massachusetts: "We had a discussion on whether or not to include Kirsten's antfarm as a pet. Shauna said it wasn't, because the ants do not share our environment. Then, we wondered if we should include the fish. We took a vote of the whole class before we decided that the antfarm was not a pet."

Farther up the electronic street is the New School for Social Research's Connected Education Program. Students do not go to the New

Late into the night, some serious users are absorbed in a world of display screens and digital readouts.

School's New York City campus. They stay home and dial up a bulletin board that presents lectures and assignments. They can log on to lectures such as "Artificial Intelligence and Real Life," type questions, and get responses from other students and lecturers.

On-line computer classmates can drop in at the Connect Ed Cafe, where they electronically socialize with other students and faculty members. They can also go to a computer library to read or print out computer-stored documents written by Connect Ed faculty members and visiting lecturers.

For the foreign students—they dial in from Europe, Japan, and Singapore—there is Connect Ed's on-line tutoring in written English as a second language. And for prospective graduates there are conferences on jobs, including ones involving computer networks.

Seminar members—there may be as many as 25—read the faculty member's launching comments, write comments of their own, and then discuss the topic with one another. Unlike off-line students, who file into a lecture hall and listen, on-line students can absorb their professor's words at any time they want and from anywhere they happen to be.

Paul Levinson, the founder of Connected Education, is a member of the New School's faculty and an associate professor of communications at Fairleigh Dickinson University. A major advantage of what he calls "Electures," Levinson says, is the students' ability to participate "when they are at their best" and without "the anxieties that occur in face-to-face groups." He believes that computer conferences may greatly help the shy ones who do not perform well in the classroom.

"Fingers fluttering lightly on keyboards in the privacy and convenience of homes," Levinson writes in his book *Mind at Large,* "may be more faithful servants of the intellect than tongues wagging in smoke-filled restaurants and crowded halls."

I lurked at the Connect Ed Cafe a couple of times and listened in on conversations. People did not RAISE THEIR VOICES. The talk was civilized and reminiscent of countless conversations in countless colleges over countless years. There were solemn discussions about the state of the universe, the meaning of reality, and the search for absolute truth. Wistfully, I wished I were there. And then I suddenly realized that, electronically, I *was* there. This was a nowhere place, and, as part of it, I could be anywhere.

Tokens of Plenty

by Ivars Peterson

One, two, three, four. . . . We learn to count at such an early age that we tend to take the notion of abstract numbers for granted. We know the word "two" and the symbol "2" express a quantity that can be attached to apples, oranges, or any other object. We readily forget the mental leap required to go from counting specific things such as apples to the abstract concept of number as an expression of quantity.

Just such a leap may have occurred roughly 5,000 years ago among people living in ancient Mesopotamia, a fertile region watered by the Tigris and Euphrates rivers in the Middle East. Ten thousand years ago, counting was a concrete affair. Residents of small agricultural settlements kept track of their goods by maintaining stores of baked clay tokens—one token for each item, different shapes for different types of items. A marble-sized clay sphere would stand for a bushel of grain, a cylinder for an animal, an egg-shaped token for a jar of oil.

Thousands of years later, the growth of villages into cities and the increasing complexity of human activities forced a shift to more efficient means of data storage. The token system evolved into a kind of shorthand in which signs indicating standard measures of grain, impressed on a clay tablet, came to represent not grain or any other specific commodity, but the concept of pure quantity. The coupling of signs for numbers with pictorial symbols for specific goods—the beginning of writing—provided ancient accountants with the tool they needed to record the varied activities of a city's citizens.

It was a revolution in both accounting and human communication, says archaeologist Denise Schmandt-Besserat of the University of Texas at Austin. For the first time, it provided a reckoning system applicable to any and every item under the sun. It put an end to a cumbersome scheme in which particular tokens were used for counting different goods. It also made taxation on a broad scale feasible.

Precursors of Writing

For Schmandt-Besserat, this new picture of the origin of abstract numbers and the beginning of writing is the culmination of nearly two decades of study that began with a search for the earliest examples of the human use of clay. "I wanted to find out how clay was discovered, for what and when, so I went from museum to museum to review clay collections from the times between 10,000 and 6000 B.C.," says Schmandt-Besserat. "I was looking for things like bricks and pots. Instead, I was surprised to find all these little clay objects. Nobody really knew what they were."

Archaeologist Denise Schmandt-Besserat has proposed that ancient accounting systems based on clay tokens evolved into the modern concept of abstract numbers.

Courtesy Schmandt-Besserat

Ancient Mesopotamians used plain clay tokens in assorted shapes to represent quantities of various farm products.

The objects, recovered from archaeological sites ranging from Turkey and Palestine to Syria and Iran, came in a variety of geometric shapes, including cones, spheres, disks, cylinders, and pyramidlike tetrahedrons. Some appeared to be miniature models, an inch (2.5 centimeters) or less in size, of animals, tools, and other natural or human-made items. Others bore markings such as incised lines. Sometimes excavators found only a few specimens; occasionally they encountered large collections of these mysterious objects.

Traditionally, archaeologists separated these objects into different categories according to shape, and tried to guess the use of each particular class of objects. For instance, the disks, they thought, may have been lids for small jars, and the spheres could have been marbles.

In contrast, Schmandt-Besserat tackled the problem from the point of view of what these objects had in common: they were all made of clay. They were similar in size and manufactured in roughly the same way.

"It was obvious to me they belonged together," Schmandt-Besserat says. Once these objects, or tokens, came to be considered as a group, their role in counting and record-keeping gradually became clearer.

"Within a year I realized that I was dealing with the precursors of writing," Schmandt-Besserat says. "But it took me a long time to see their connection with counting and numbers."

It was like working on a puzzle, she says. It meant tracking the development of writing on clay tablets backward in time, from what are known as cuneiform symbols back to pictographs, and then to token shapes.

"Unfortunately, very few pictographic signs can be traced back and identified with tokens," says Schmandt-Besserat. "There are many tokens with no known translation."

Visual Patterns

The first appearance of clay tokens in the archaeological record coincides with the development of agriculture, especially grain cultivation, in the period from 8000 to 7500 B.C. People in Mesopotamia, once mainly hunters and gatherers, began settling in villages and relying on a farm economy based on grain.

Archaeological studies of the period show evidence of grain cultivation in fields surrounding villages, the construction of communal silos for storing grain, and a rapid increase in population. In such a setting, individual farmers needed a reliable way to keep track of their goods—especially the amount of grain stored in shared facilities. The answer they found was to fashion clay tokens, or counters, in the form of simple geometric shapes with plain, unmarked surfaces.

The Sumerians, as the people living in this region were called, used different token shapes for different types of goods. Cones and spheres referred to the two most common Sumerian measures of grain: a small unit roughly equivalent to a liter, and a larger one approximately equal to a bushel. Larger cones and spheres and flat disks probably signified even larger measures of capacity. Cylinders and lens-shaped tokens represented animals.

In such a system, two clay spheres represented two bushels of grain, and two egg-shaped tokens represented two jars of sesame oil. There were as many tokens of a certain shape as there were of that item in the farmer's store. The concept of "two," or any other number, as a quantity didn't exist.

"Representing units of real goods in a one-to-one correspondence, these counters were doubtless lined up in front of accountants, who organized them according to types of goods, producers or recipients, entries or expenditures,'' Schmandt-Besserat says. They could even be arranged in visual patterns to facilitate estimation and counting of items at a glance.

Growing Complexity

This token system persisted practically unchanged for almost 4,000 years, spreading over a large geographic area. The next major change was the appearance of more elaborate tokens, especially in early cities in southern Mesopotamia, alongside the well-established system of simple counters. Though similar in size, material, and color, and fabricated in much the same way as their plainer cousins, the new tokens bore various surface markings and showed a greater variety of shapes, including twin cones, bent coils, and miniature models of tools, utensils, containers, and various animals.

These elaborate tokens, one of the first signs of increasing urbanization and the growing complexity of Sumerian society, were probably used for items such as manufactured products—the output of Sumerian workshops. For instance, incised cones, egg shapes, and diamondlike rhomboids represented quantities of processed foods such as loaves of bread, jars of refined oil, and vessels of beer. In the textile industry, disks and parabolic tokens with linear markings signified different types of fibers, cloths, and finished garments, whereas incised cylinders and rectangles stood for strings and mats. Other tokens represented luxury goods such as perfumes and various kinds of metalwork.

The advent of complex tokens coincided with the rise of powerful central governments and the construction of monuments and great temples, beginning around 3350 B.C. Art from that period shows the pooling of community resources and the management and redistribution of goods to support an elite, and for celebrating large community festivals that required considerable planning and the bringing together of vast quantities of goods.

Tokens were used to manage these massive tasks. ''They provided, for the first time, a precise system for keeping records, and thus were a means of control and power in the hands of the leadership,'' Schmandt-Besserat says. ''Indeed, complex tokens clearly seem to be associated with the world's first system of coercive taxation and redistribution of goods.'' Scenes from Sumerian art show punishments such as beatings, hinting that even then citizens did not always pay their taxes willingly.

Complex tokens, excavated from an ancient Sumerian city, come in a variety of shapes and often bear markings or perforations (top). Each shape represents a particular item, such as a trussed duck (center), a jar of oil, a sheep, a garment, or units of land, string, or metal (bottom). The more elaborate tokens also reflect the growing urbanization of ancient Sumeria, the increased output of manufactured goods from its workshops, and the development of trade networks among early Mesopotamian cities.

Sumerian clerks stored plain tokens in clay globes, or envelopes (left). To indicate what each envelope contained, they pressed the token into the soft clay surface before sealing and baking the envelope, leaving a distinctive set of imprints. A pictographic clay tablet from an Iranian excavation (below) carries the symbols for the numeral 33 (three wedges and three circles) and the sign for a jar of oil. The inscription thus reads "33 jars of oil."

Numerals and Writing

Throughout this later period, both simple and complex tokens coexisted, one associated with products of the granary and farm, the other with products of the urban workshop. In fact, temple excavations reveal the Sumerians handled the two kinds of tokens separately and stored them differently.

Sets of simple tokens were stored in clay globes, or "envelopes," that often bore markings indicating what was enclosed, and seals that may have recorded transactions (perhaps contracts, receipts, or even IOUs). The envelope markings were important because the enclosed tokens, once sealed in their clay cocoon, were hidden from view. Initially, temple clerks probably marked the envelopes simply by pressing tokens into the soft clay surface before sealing and baking it—making visible the number and shape of tokens enclosed. Excavated specimens show circular markings of various diameters and depths, and wedges of different lengths and widths.

Complex tokens couldn't be stored in clay envelopes because they left indecipherable impressions. Instead, they were often perforated and could be strung together and attached to a clay tag, which apparently served to identify the account.

In Schmandt-Besserat's view, these two categories of tokens and their different means of storage evolved into Sumerian script. The plain tokens gave rise to numerals, while the complex

tokens, with their patterns of inscribed lines, gave rise to writing.

One key step was realizing that once the envelopes were marked, it was no longer necessary to keep the tokens themselves. It would do just as well to mark the appropriate shapes on a clay tablet and to forget about the rest.

At the same time, the markings on complex tokens also could be inscribed, using a stylus, directly onto a clay tablet instead of on the token itself. For example, an incised ovoid token would be replaced by a neatly drawn oval with a slash across it. Such pictographic signs would indicate the nature of the items being recorded.

The result was a new, more practical, less cumbersome data-storage system. It was easier to handle a few clay tablets with neatly aligned signs than a large collection of loose tokens. It also became clear that using a stylus was

The precise record-keeping that evolved from clay tokens quickly gave rise to systems of coercive taxation and redistribution of goods. Ancient art suggests that even back then, citizens did not always pay their taxes willingly.

quicker than making an impression of every individual token.

Then came the great leap, perhaps the deed of an accountant who arguably could be given the title *Homo mathematicus*. Around 3000 B.C., someone had the bright idea that, instead of representing, say, 33 jars of oil by the symbol for a jar of oil repeated 33 times, it would be simpler to precede the symbol for a jar of oil by numerals—special signs expressing numbers. Moreover, the same signs could be used to represent the same quantity of any item.

The new signs were symbols for the two basic measures of grain—used in a novel fashion. The wedge (impressed cone) came to stand for 1, and the circle (sphere) for 10. There were no special symbols for other numbers.

This economical notation spread rapidly. It was no longer necessary to have differently shaped counters for different items. Anything of importance could be expressed compactly and flexibly on clay tablets. This accounting system fulfilled the needs of an emerging state bureaucracy, increasing the amount of information recorded and making possible a comprehensive system of taxation.

Clay tokens themselves became obsolete by 3000 B.C., replaced by pictographic tablets that could express not only "how many" but also "where, when, and how." With the introduction of a new type of stylus, pictographic writing developed into cuneiform notation. The resulting record-keeping system was so efficient and convenient that it was used in the Middle East for the next 3,000 years. Eventually, it was displaced by Aramaic script written with a flowing hand on papyrus, which proved to be even more efficient.

Meanwhile, the ancient Babylonians adopted and modified the Sumerian system for dealing with abstract numbers. From there the system traveled to Greece, at length becoming part of the great flowering of mathematics in the ideas of Pythagoras, Euclid, and Archimedes.

Mastering Abstraction

"This story is, in essence, a study in the stages whereby human culture slowly, and then even more quickly, mastered the art of abstraction," Schmandt-Besserat says. Whether a similar process leading to the concept of abstract numbers occurred in other civilizations, such as the Chinese or Maya, isn't known. "Nobody has looked into the development of counting there," she says. "Everybody always assumes abstract counting is a given."

The invention of abstract numbers must be accorded a prominent place among the greatest of human contrivances, Schmandt-Besserat says. Too frequently, in studies of the development of mathematics, the invention of zero and the advent of place notation are heralded as major accomplishments of the civilized world, while abstract numbers are mistakenly regarded as intuitive.

"This is simply not the case," Schmandt-Besserat asserts. The token system is just one piece of evidence proving that counting was not spontaneous, but rather the product of a long, slow cultural evolution.

EARTH SCIENCES

EARTH SCIENCES

The year 1988 was marked by major earthquakes around the world. Earth scientists made significant fossil discoveries, probed the inner earth, and learned more about the earth's crustal plates.

by William H. Matthews III

Earthquakes and Seismology

A severe earthquake—measuring 6.9 on the Richter scale, with aftershocks of up to 5.8—struck Armenia on December 7. The cities of Leninakan, Spitak, and Kirovakan were devastated; 25,000 people were killed; thousands were injured; and more than 500,000 were left homeless. The catastrophic quake occurred in a zone of seismic activity where moving crustal plates converge.

On August 20 a temblor of 6.5 magnitude rocked parts of Nepal and India, killing more than 980 people. The strongest quake to hit the Himalayas in 500 years, the tremors were apparently caused by movements generated in the Indian plate (which comprises the Indian subcontinent) as it presses against the Asian plate. A destructive earthquake hit southwestern China on November 6. This magnitude-7.6 quake caused about 1,000 deaths and left some 100,000 people homeless.

A wide area of southern California was rattled by a 4.5 quake on June 26. Felt 50 miles (80 kilometers) away, the quake was centered near Upland, California. And a magnitude-6.0 earthquake struck northeastern Canada on November 25. The temblor generated seismic waves that were felt from the Great Lakes to the Atlantic Coast.

© Tass from Sovfoto

The powerful earthquake that struck Armenia last December killed thousands and left thousands more homeless. Aftershocks complicated relief efforts.

Meteorology and Climatology

Kevin E. Trenbeth and his colleagues at the National Center for Atmospheric Research (NCAR) in Boulder, Colorado, attributed the summer's severe Midwestern drought to unusual cooling of El Niño (a large ocean current in the equatorial Pacific). This, combined with other events, displaced the rain-laden jet stream enough so that it passed over North America farther north than it usually does, according to Trenbeth's theory. The same weather anomaly apparently caused the heavy monsoons and flooding that Bangladesh experienced in 1988.

In another NCAR project, Denver's Stapleton International Airport has been testing a Doppler radar and monitoring equipment that can spot microbursts—deadly downdrafts that can appear without warning. Microbursts, or wind shears, have been responsible for many airplane crashes. In the test of the prototype equipment, pilots were successfully warned away from the microbursts.

The drought and heat wave of 1988 provided a surge of business to private companies that prepare weather forecasts and other weather information tailored to the specific needs of clients.

Courtesy of Accu-Weather

Paleontology and Fossils

The use of new exploration techniques led to more information about the dinosaurs. "Sonic geophysical imaging" has made it possible to differentiate dinosaur bones from the surrounding rock by the length of time it takes sound waves to pass through each material. This tool is being used to unearth the remains of "Seismosaurus," a plant eater that was at least 110 feet (33.5 meters) long and weighed 40 tons (36 metric tons) or more. Computerized axial tomography, or CAT, scanning has been used to produce images of an embryo in a dinosaur egg found in Utah. This 150-million-year-old egg contains what is probably the oldest known dinosaur embryo. In Colorado, paleontologists discovered 6-foot (about 2-meter) dinosaur pelvic bones. They represent what may turn out to be the largest known dinosaur.

A peculiar dinosaur skull, previously incorrectly classified, was identified as a pygmy tyrannosaur possibly related to modern birds. Found in Montana in 1942, the skull's braincase is riddled with air canals used to cool the brain. And two exceptionally huge dinosaurs—"Supersaurus" and "Ultrasaurus"—have now been shown to be unusually large specimens of *Brachiosaurus*, rather than distinct species of supergiants.

In Charleston, South Carolina, geologists discovered fossils of the largest known flying seabird. It appears to be a relative of the cormorants and pelicans and lived about 30 million years ago. The bird had a wingspread of 18 feet (5.5 meters) and may have weighed as much as 90 pounds (41 kilograms). Meanwhile, a new fossil bird found in Spain is believed to be the oldest known flier. It appears to be intermediate between *Archaeopteryx*, the oldest known bird, and modern birds.

Debate continued over the causes of the mass extinctions at the Cretaceous-Tertiary (K-T) boundary. A new theory proposes that the widespread death of ocean plankton after an impact could have caused a worldwide heat wave that triggered the extinction of other animals. Geologists working in Texas found evidence suggesting that a huge tsunami hit the Gulf Coast. Other scientists suggested that at least two extraterrestrial bodies crashed into the earth.

Below: © AP/Wide World; right: © NYT Pictures

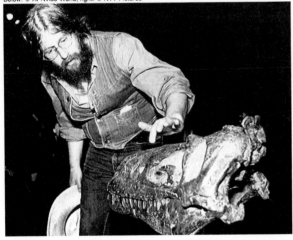

Scientists identified a dinosaur skull (left) as belonging to a small cousin of the tyrannosaurs (below). Its formal name Nanotyrannus lancensis means "pygmy tyrant."

Earth Structure and Plate Tectonics

New ideas were proposed about the condition of the earth at the time of its formation 4.6 billion years ago. The new theory suggests that the center of the earth was originally hot, instead of cold, as once thought. (The traditional view holds that our planet condensed into a solid as it densified out of a vast rotating cloud of gas, dust, and rock.) The new conclusion was reached by geologists working at the Rennselaer Polytechnic Institute (RPI) through the spectral analysis of reflected light from distant asteroids. Their research shows that certain asteroids have been subjected to powerful blasts of intense light early in their history. The origin of these fiery blasts is not definitely known, but there is a possibility it could have been an explosive outburst from the young sun.

The discovery of massive rocks buried deeply beneath the flat plains of the Midwest suggests a mountain range the size of the Himalayas may have cut across eastern Ohio more than 1 billion years ago. Results of geophysical surveys have revealed very thick layered rock formations some 2 miles (3.2 kilometers) beneath the earth's surface. These structures, 4 to 6.5 miles (6.5 to 10.5 kilometers) thick and about 100 miles (161 kilometers) wide, were on the surface during Precambrian time about 1.3 billion years ago. Some of the formations in eastern Ohio plunge as much as 24 miles (39 kilometers) underground.

© N. Reynard-Figaro/Gamma-Liaison

ANATOMY of a HURRICANE

by Dr. Robert C. Sheets

Shortly after noon on September 12, 1988, Kingston, Jamaica, lay under the eye of Hurricane Gilbert. The city had already endured the leading edge of the storm; but, sheltered by mountains to the north, it had not felt its full fury. Now, as the relatively calm storm center moved off to the west and the wind direction shifted from the north to the south, Gilbert unleashed its full power.

Within minutes, violent winds were ripping the roofs off buildings, felling trees, and downing power and telephone lines. With communications knocked out, ham radio operators reported sustained wind speeds of 121 miles (195 kilometers) per hour and gusts to 147 miles (235 kilometers) per hour. At Manley International Airport, the wind tossed airplanes about like so many plastic models. Debris flew everywhere. Surging tides flooded low-lying areas. Blowing spray and rain were so heavy that observers could not see more than a few feet beyond their windows.

As Gilbert pounded Jamaica, officials at the National Hurricane Center (NHC) in Coral Gables, Florida, pored over computer models and electronic displays to update their forecast of the storm's strength and direction. Calls went out to the areas directly in its path—the Cayman Islands, Cuba, Mexico. The center's director and hurricane specialists briefed the press on the storm's progress, fielding thousands of phone and direct television interviews.

After battering Jamaica for six hours, the storm center moved off to the west. The toll: 45 dead, some 500,000 homeless, four-fifths of the island's houses damaged or destroyed, and roughly $2 billion in damage. But Gilbert had only begun to flex its muscles. Before it was over, the hurricane would become the storm of the century, with sustained winds of 185 miles (300 kilometers) per hour and gusts of over 200 miles (320 kilometers) per hour.

Birth of a Storm

As is the case with the majority (60 to 70 percent) of the hurricanes that form in the North Atlantic from June to November each year (the official hurricane season), Gilbert began as a cluster of clouds moving off the northwest coast of Africa. The embryo of the storm—first observed by satellite on September 3—was associated with a tropical wave: a wrinkle in the uniformly eastern flow of the trade winds. Over the next several days, the system moved westward across the Atlantic in the trade wind belt. Then,

on September 8, as it approached the Lesser Antilles, its showers and thunderstorms began to coalesce. Satellite pictures showed that the system had developed the counterclockwise, cyclonic circulation typical of North Atlantic tropical storms. With wind speeds still under 39 miles (63 kilometers) per hour, it was classified as a tropical depression.

The process by which the system formed and subsequently strengthened depended on at least three conditions: warm surface waters, high humidity, and the ability to concentrate heat in the vertical. The latter factor depends on winds at all levels of the developing system to be essentially from the same direction at the same speed. A storm like Gilbert begins to form when air is warmed by contact with the water (gaining sensible, or measurable, heat) and is moistened by evaporation from it (gaining latent heat that will later be released through condensation). The need for these conditions explains why hurricanes form only in warm months over warm waters.

As the air warms, it rises, spiraling inward toward the center of the system. And the closer

A hurricane rotates around an eye (facing page), its region of lowest pressure. To fill the low-pressure void, moist air rushes toward the eye, spiraling upward to create an eye wall (below). Once atop the eye, the air cools and descends back into the storm. Outside the eye, towers of warm moist air form updrafts that produce rain bands.

Insight Magazine/Melody Warford

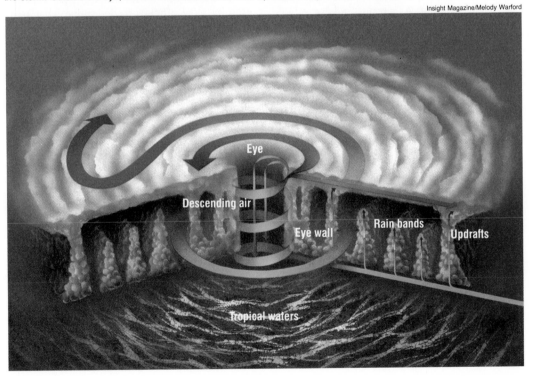

it gets to the center, the faster it moves. The reason is partial conservation of angular momentum—the same principle that causes a figure skater to spin slowly with arms extended and to spin faster with arms tucked in. The strong winds created by the moving air produce turbulent seas, and huge amounts of spray become suspended in the air. The suspended spray in turn increases the rate of evaporation, so that the storm begins to feed on itself.

In a hurricane the center is a relatively calm area, the eye. The most violent activity takes place in the area immediately around the eye, called the eyewall. There, as the spiraling air rises and cools, moisture condenses into tiny droplets, forming clouds and rainbands. The condensation releases latent heat, which causes the air to rise still farther; and that in turn results in more condensation. The result is a column of rapidly rising air that produces an intense low-pressure area near the storm center.

At the top of the eyewall (about 50,000 feet, or 15,250 meters), most of the air is propelled outward in an anticyclonic flow. (Without this flow, the air's upward motion would be stifled, and pressure at the center of the storm would begin to rise.) However, some of the air moves inward and sinks into the eye. This air is warmed rapidly by compression; and as it warms, its moisture-holding capacity increases and the air dries out. As a result, in intense hurricanes, the eye becomes nearly cloud-free.

At the middle to upper levels of the storm, the temperature is much warmer in the eye than outside it. This temperature difference creates a large pressure differential across the eyewall, contributing to the violence of the storm. Hurricane-force winds can produce waves 50 to 60 feet (15 to 18 meters) high in the open ocean. When the storm meets land, the combination of low pressure and high winds produces a dome of high water—the storm surge—that is pushed ashore and floods low-lying areas.

Tracking Gilbert

By September 9, when the system that would become Gilbert came within range of reconnaissance aircraft, satellite pictures indicated that the clouds were rapidly becoming better organized. The aircraft (which are operated by the Air Force and the National Oceanic and Atmospheric Administration [NOAA] and fly directly into a storm's eye) soon found that wind speeds were over 39 miles (63 kilometers) per hour. The system therefore was designated tropical storm Gilbert. (Each year, hurricanes and tropical storms are named in alphabetical order from a list approved by the U.N. World Meteorological Organization [WMO].) It moved through the Lesser Antilles late that day.

Gilbert then strengthened rapidly. Late on September 10, with winds blowing at 74 to 95 miles (120 to 153 kilometers) per hour, it reached category 1 status on the Saffir/Simpson scale used to measure hurricane strength. About twelve hours later, it attained category 2 status—with winds of 96 to 110 miles (154 to 177 kilometers) an hour—and took direct aim at the island of Jamaica.

At the NHC in Coral Gables, several types of satellite images flowed into computers and electronic display systems and were filtered, enhanced, colorized, animated, and analyzed by the satellite meteorology staff. Cloud motions were used to estimate currents at various levels in the atmosphere around the hurricane, while data from aircraft pinpointed the exact motion of the storm and its strength and wind field distributions. Along with surface observations from land stations, ships and buoys, and weather balloons throughout the region, this information was fed into computer models to determine the extent of the hurricane, its changes with time, and expected storm surge heights and areas of inundation—information that would be used by local officials to determine what areas needed to be evacuated.

As the storm center passed south of the Dominican Republic, an electronic display of satellite pictures showed a massive, rotating cloud system that covered most of the eastern half of the Caribbean, with the hurricane's eye clearly visible. Based on the computer models, the NHC forecast that the center of Gilbert would pass directly over Jamaica shortly after noon on September 12. John Blake, director of the Jamaican Meteorological Services, discussed the situation over a restricted telephone line with the director of the NHC. By the early afternoon of September 11, the "hurricane watch" issued early in the day for Jamaica (warning of the possibility of a hurricane) was upgraded to a "hurricane warning" (indicating the probability of a hurricane within the next 12 to 24 hours).

With reports indicating that Gilbert was rapidly gaining strength, Jamaica prepared for the onslaught of a major hurricane with winds in excess of 100 miles (160 kilometers) an hour. Residents in low-lying areas that might be cov-

© Richards/Gamma-Liaison

Director Robert C. Sheets (standing) and his associates at the National Hurricane Center review satellite images, computer models, and aircraft-reconnaissance data to predict most accurately the future course of a hurricane.

ered by the storm surge, those in potential flash-flood areas, and those in substandard housing were moved to places of refuge as fast as resources permitted.

The NHC, meanwhile, in its capacity as the Regional Tropical Meteorological Center of the WMO, provided guidance and advice for countries throughout the region. Several phone calls were made to the meteorological services of Cuba and Mexico and to government officials in the Cayman Islands to discuss the storm's probable impact and the wording for warnings. Similar discussions were held with officials in south Florida and with other branches of the National Weather Service. Complete forecast and warning packages were produced every six hours, with intermediate advisories at three-hour intervals.

A Record Storm

Gilbert struck Jamaica as a category 3 hurricane—a storm with winds of 111 to 130 miles (178 to 209 kilometers) per hour—and continued to strengthen. It reached category 4 status—winds of 131 to 155 miles (210 to 249 kilome-

ters) per hour—before its center passed about 20 miles (32 kilometers) south of Grand Cayman Island at 9:00 A.M. on September 13. The maximum sustained surface winds near the storm center approached 140 miles (225 kilometers) per hour at this time.

Then, less than two hours after passing Grand Cayman, Gilbert became a rare category 5 hurricane, with winds in excess of 155 miles (250 kilometers) per hour. And by 6:00 P.M. on September 13, the storm attained the lowest sea-level pressure ever measured in the Western Hemisphere: 26.22 inches (888 millibars) of mercury. (Pressure is considered the most accurate measure of storm strength, with lower pressure indicating a stronger storm.) It is likely that the hurricane reached a minimum pressure as low as 26.15 inches (885 to 886 millibars) of mercury between measurements taken by reconnaissance aircraft.

By comparison, the lowest pressure measured in deadly Hurricane Camille of 1969 was 26.73 inches (905 millibars). The previous record was 26.34 inches (892 millibars), recorded in the violent but small 1935 Florida

As it swept across the Yucatán Peninsula, Hurricane Gilbert packed enough punch to drive heavy cargo ships ashore.

Keys hurricane. Among factors cited as contributing to Gilbert's strength were the fact that the storm strengthened over very warm waters and that its eye was much smaller than average, which had the effect of concentrating the hurricane's energy.

Hurricane strength in general is unrelated to overall size. However, very strong hurricanes usually have relatively small eyes—less than 10 miles (16 kilometers) in diameter. But, in addition to its strength, Gilbert was huge. As the storm approached Mexico, satellite pictures showed that its circulation covered the entire western half of the Caribbean, Central America, and the southeastern Gulf of Mexico.

The center of Hurricane Gilbert moved across the east coast of the Yucatán Peninsula near Cozumel on the morning of September 14. It was the first landfall of a category 5 hurricane in the Western Hemisphere in nearly 20 years. (The last occurrence was in 1969, with Hurricane Camille.) Cancún and other resort areas were hit hard. At Cancún Beach, the 20-foot (6-meter) storm surge picked up a Cuban freighter several miles offshore and tossed it ashore like a toy boat.

As the center moved inland over the large landmass of the peninsula, the source of energy for the core—warm water—was cut off. The inner eyewall then weakened, nearly dissipating by the time the center had crossed the Yucatán. However, the tentacles of Gilbert reached well out over the Gulf of Mexico and the Caribbean, maintaining the hurricane's outer strength.

In fact, the stronger winds began spreading out over an even larger area than before, until they covered large portions of the Gulf ahead of the center. These strong winds stirred up the waters, bringing cool water from below to the surface. The effect of these cooler waters was to additionally reduce the energy that the storm would normally absorb. This helped limit the strength of the showers and thunderstorms at the storm's core.

In the nearly two days it took for the storm to move from Yucatán across the southwestern Gulf to northern Mexico, the central pressure remained nearly constant. The inner eyewall never reformed, and started to reappear only near landfall on the Mexican coast. However, with the storm's strength spreading farther from the center, hurricane-force winds and high tides were felt along the lower Texas coast, well away from the core.

Hurricane Gilbert finally met its demise as it moved inland over northern Mexico. While moving over land or cold water cuts off the source of energy for hurricanes, the spin-down rate is somewhat slower over water than over land, where surface friction contributes to the process.

As hurricanes move inland and spin down, they generally carry with them large amounts of moisture-laden air. In Gilbert, this moisture produced heavy rains and flash floods over northern Mexico. More than 200 people lost their lives in Mexico because of the storm, as a result of flash floods in the Monterrey area. Gilbert also produced tornadoes in Texas (a common occurrence when hurricanes move inland).

It Could Have Been Worse

Gilbert left widespread destruction in its wake, but the damage could have been worse. Luck played a role in limiting it. Over Jamaica the hurricane moved westward at a steady 14 miles (22 kilometers) per hour, thus limiting the period of heavy rain and high winds. Had the hurricane's forward speed slowed or stalled, the height of the storm surge could have doubled, resulting in much more extensive coastal flooding. The extended periods of heavy rains and high winds could have produced massive flash flooding (the greatest threat to life posed by hurricanes in much of the Caribbean and Central America) and destroyed many more buildings.

Similarly, there was considerable destruction on Grand Cayman, but a combination of factors reduced the potential for damage. If the center had passed 8 to 10 miles (13 to 16 kilometers) closer to the island, the destruction would probably have increased by more than a factor of two because the island would have been hit with much stronger winds. (Insurance statistics indicate that damage may be proportional to as much as the fourth power of the wind speed as building design thresholds are exceeded.) Data from reconnaissance aircraft showed that the flight-level wind in the north eyewall was well over 150 miles (240 kilometers) per hour; but just 10 miles (16 kilometers) farther north, the winds at that level were about 110 miles (177 kilometers) per hour. The data also showed that the eyewall was surrounded by an area relatively free of showers and thunderstorms. It was apparently this area that passed over Grand Cayman.

Below: © Richards/Gamma-Liaison; facing page: © S. Dorantes/SYGMA

Hurricane Gilbert unleashed its full fury on Jamaica, leaving 45 dead, 500,000 homeless, and thousands of houses destroyed. The island may take years to recover fully.

Gilbert's high winds blew aircraft around like toys at the Kingston, Jamaica, airport (right). By the time the storm reached the Texas coast (above), its strength had largely dissipated, although it provided much-needed rain.

Grand Cayman did record a maximum sustained wind of 137 miles (220 kilometers) an hour, with a gust of 155 miles (250 kilometers) an hour, but these extreme conditions were not experienced for a prolonged time. The final factors that prevented more damage were that buildings were generally well constructed and that most structures were on the west end of the island. The cyclonic circulation primarily produced onshore winds on the north and east coasts, with much shorter periods of onshore wind on the west and south coasts.

Timely and accurate warnings were also credited with keeping loss of life to a minimum. Frequent updates on the storm's progress were provided by the NHC for the broadcast networks, local television and radio stations, and print media throughout the region. A Spanish-speaking meteorologist provided briefings for Hispanic stations. Several broadcasters produced extended public service programs and documentaries. And more than 100,000 callers dialed the Hurricane Hotline number (900-410-NOAA)—sponsored as a public service by NBC News, *USA Today*, and AT&T in cooper-

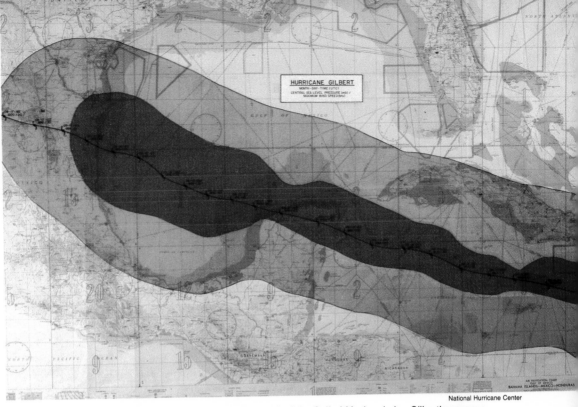

Winds of hurricane (red) and tropical-storm (orange) force lashed the Gulf of Mexico during Gilbert's passage.

ation with the NHC—to hear a recorded announcement of the latest advisory.

Finally, in spite of the damage Gilbert generated, the storm had a beneficial aspect: as its remnants moved toward the Northeast across the United States, it brought some much-needed rain to the drought-stricken Midwest.

A Record Year

The 1988 Atlantic hurricane season produced 11 named storms, five of which reached hurricane strength. The number of named storms was slightly above the long-term average of nine to 10, and the number of hurricanes was slightly below the average of six. However, 1988 will be remembered as a season of record-breaking hurricanes.

In addition to Gilbert, Hurricane Joan broke intensity records. Joan was a category 4 hurricane on the Saffir/Simpson scale when it struck Nicaragua on October 22. There had never been a record of a hurricane of this intensity at so low a latitude in the western Caribbean. Joan's minimum pressure at landfall near Bluefields, Nicaragua, was 27.46 inches (930 millibars), and the storm had sustained winds of nearly 135 miles (217 kilometers) per hour.

Joan earned another distinction when it crossed Central America from Atlantic to Pacific and was renamed tropical storm Miriam—a rare, though not unprecedented, event.

Joan and Gilbert combined to produce more than $5 billion in damage and more than 500 deaths throughout the Caribbean, Central America, and Mexico. When a later hurricane, Helene, reached full strength, 1988 became the first year since 1961 to experience three hurricanes with strengths of category 4 or more.

While Texas felt the fringe of giant Hurricane Gilbert, the United States on the whole was not severely affected by the 1988 hurricanes. Tropical storms Beryl, Chris, and Keith and Hurricane Florence made landfall on the continental United States. Beryl and Florence struck in eastern Louisiana and Mississippi, while Chris moved inland near the Georgia–South Carolina border. Keith, a large late-season storm just below hurricane strength, affected most of the west coast of Florida and, later, central Florida and the east coast north of Palm Beach. Total direct damage from these storms was estimated to be near $60 million—an amount well below the annual average of more than $1 billion over the past decade.

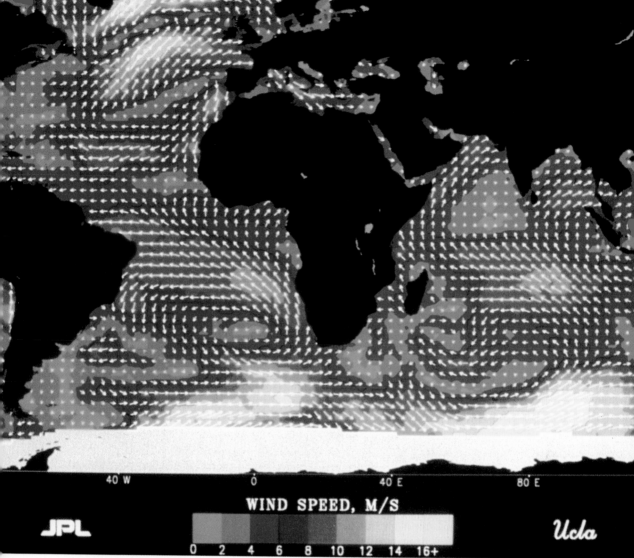

WIND SPEED, M/S

40 W   0   40 E   80 E

JPL

0 2 4 6 8 10 12 14 16+

Ucla

JPL/NASA & University of California, Los Angeles

Seasons, Seas, and Satellites

by Frank Lowenstein

NASA's Seasat satellite used radar to take 350,000 wind measurements over the world's oceans. In the resulting map (above), arrows indicate wind direction; arrow length and color contouring signify speed.

W hen Kathryn Kelly began studying the Pacific Ocean's California Current in 1979, oceanographers pictured it as an aquatic interstate off North America's West Coast—wide and smooth, with only gradual changes in speed and few branch currents. But when Kelly looked at the satellite images on which she was to base her doctoral dissertation, she saw the equivalent of a mountain road—narrow and rough, intersected by jets of water curling out from the coast. Most of the oceanographers with whom she worked, she recalls, thought such a picture of the current "couldn't possibly be real."

Kelly herself had doubts. As she stared at the twisting, mysterious lines on the satellite images, she says, "I kept thinking, *Where's the California Current?*" She even drew arrows on her photographs where she expected the current to be. But as she compared the satellite images to theoretical models and some puzzling data collected by ships at sea, Kelly became convinced that the satellite photos were showing something that oceanographers didn't even know existed.

Two years later scientists using traditional oceanographic methods verified the existence of the small California coastal eddies that are now known as "squirts." The work of Kathryn Kelly—now an assistant scientist at Woods Hole Oceanographic Institute in Massachusetts—was no longer on the fringes of oceanographic science.

New Discoveries

Satellite imagery has revealed new features in the ocean, features that are too large and change too quickly to be detected easily from ships. Moreover, by providing vast amounts of data collected at regular, frequent intervals, satellites have allowed oceanographers to study already-known features in greater detail than was previously possible. Today, says Robert Chase, formerly with Woods Hole and presently a professor of aerospace engineering sciences at the University of Colorado at Boulder, "we're finding out every day that the ocean is not what we thought it was."

Oceanography isn't what it once was, either. Even as satellites began playing a significant role, a trend developed within the discipline itself. While some oceanographers used satellites to further traditional studies of oceanic currents and the composition of the seas, others began a multidisciplinary examination of the roles oceans play in the ecology and climate of the entire earth.

For example, satellites are especially effective at discovering eddies. Vortices thrown off by currents large and small, eddies can be up to 200 miles (320 kilometers) in diameter and travel hundreds of miles over several years. From satellite studies, oceanographers now know that eddies help distribute nutrients throughout the ocean. The nutrients influence plant growth, which in turn affects the atmosphere's carbon dioxide balance. And by stirring up the seas, eddies speed up the dispersal of equatorial heat around the globe and thus affect winds and weather worldwide.

The techniques and equipment necessary to understand the global impact of the oceans are relatively new. When the institution at Woods Hole, the foremost research organization in its field, was founded in 1930, it had two major assets: its location at the end of a narrow peninsula on Cape Cod, Massachusetts, and its sail-powered research vessel, the *Atlantis* (for which

Researchers retrieve an instrument package used to collect data underwater. Although satellites provide the big picture, oceanographers still depend on research vessels to get on-site measurements to compare with data from space.

the fourth space shuttle was named). These lean times gave rise to the stereotype of the "hairy-chested oceanographer out in heavy weather taking samples with a bucket," according to John Steele, Woods Hole's director. The science has since become more complex, but until recently oceanographers were still limited by the speed—rarely more than 12 knots—at which their research vessels traveled. Furthermore, regions such as the Antarctic were almost totally inaccessible. Ships were simply unable to collect enough data to allow scientists to understand the oceans that cover 71 percent of our planet's surface.

30,000 to 50,000 grid points scattered around the world, Wolff says. A clear understanding of long-term climatic trends requires a more thorough knowledge of the circulation of the oceans, the cycling of nutrients within the oceans, and the rate of growth of oceanic plants. Only satellites can gather much of the information necessary to understand these basic processes.

Meteorologists and astronomers caught on to the potential of satellites about a decade before the oceanographers. With oceanographic studies, going into space takes you further from the action. "Once you get up high, you have to

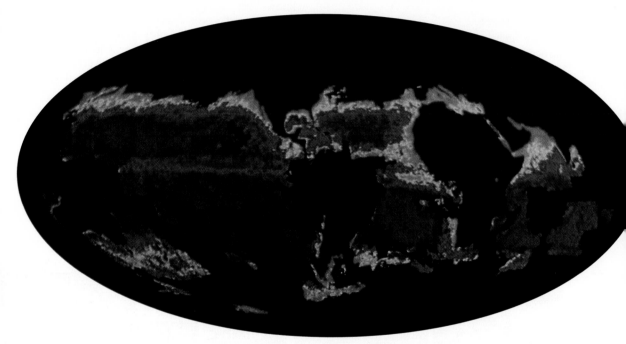

© Eugene Feldman/NASA

A composite of images from the Coastal Zone Color Scanner satellite reveals that the highest concentrations of chlorophyll (red and yellow) generally hug the continental coasts, while the lowest levels (blue) occur in midocean.

Grid Points

Oceanographers base their research on the conditions at the "grid points," places where key parameters such as temperature and wind speed are regularly measured. "In models we're using now, we have a few thousand grid points surrounding the globe," says Paul Wolff, assistant administrator for Ocean Services and Coastal Zone Management at the National Oceanic and Atmospheric Administration (NOAA). But to understand the oceans well enough to determine their effect on climate, for example, will require

learn to look through the atmosphere," says Stan Wilson, chief of the National Aeronautics and Space Administration's (NASA's) Oceanic Processes Branch. "Once you do see through the atmosphere, you're essentially only looking at the surface" of the oceans. That can be misleading. For example, satellites can measure sea-surface temperatures over large areas. But while temperature patterns observed at the surface generally extend several hundred feet below, sometimes they vary significantly from those just below the surface.

Polar Polynyas

Despite their drawbacks and relatively recent acceptance, satellites have already contributed significantly to oceanographic knowledge. They have discovered uncharted polynyas—ice-free areas in the Arctic and Antarctic that scientists believe are important for the biological productivity of polar waters. No one knew of the existence of Antarctica's Weddell Sea polynya, which can be up to 100 miles (160 kilometers) long, until satellites spotted it in 1974.

Off the coast of South Africa, satellites have been used to study the course of the Agulhas Current, which is so complex that over the course of about 150 miles (240 kilometers), its flow often includes a nearly complete loop. Without satellites, notes Chase, tracing the movements of the Agulhas would require so many ships that it "would cost you the better part of the GNP."

Satellites have also given oceanographers insights into how their science interacts with climatology, biology, geography, and even political science, among other fields. Today, notes John Steele, "If you're an oceanographer, you're interested in desertification in Africa, mud slides in California, the wheat crop in the Midwest."

Monitoring the Greenhouse Effect

"Man is altering the planet," says James J. McCarthy, professor of biological oceanography at Harvard University. "We have altered the atmosphere. The greenhouse effect is real. The planet is warming. We don't know the consequences of these actions for what NASA has called 'the habitability of the planet.'"

The greenhouse effect, a global warming caused by increased levels of carbon dioxide and other gases in the atmosphere, could trigger climatic changes—a rise in sea level due to the melting of polar ice, greater rainfall in East Africa and the Sahara, and milder conditions in the Arctic and the wheat-growing regions of the Soviet Union. But few scientists are willing to speculate on how dramatic these changes will be. "When climate starts to change, all bets are off," notes Richard Houghton, associate scientist at the Woods Hole Research Center.

One reason for the uncertainty is a fundamental lack of understanding of how carbon (including carbon dioxide), nitrogen, sulfur, phosphorus, and other elements are cycled through the environment. According to Houghton, to-

day's best models cannot account for the movements of about 2.2 billion tons (1.9 billion metric tons) of carbon each year—more than is released by all the cars, power plants, and factories in the United States. Current estimates of how much carbon dioxide is removed from the atmosphere by oceanic processes may not apply once large-scale climatic changes begin.

Oceanic plants, like those everywhere, store carbon dioxide, but the seas can hoard it in other ways as well: gases continuously diffuse back and forth between the ocean and the atmosphere. When the ocean's surface waters cool and descend into the depths, they carry some gases into long-term storage with them. As a result, the deep oceans store about 60 times as much carbon as the atmosphere holds.

The oceans also directly affect the distribution of heat and moisture around the world. Winds drive ocean currents, which in turn warm or cool the air above them, generating new winds. The heat moved about by ocean currents moderates world climate, keeping equatorial regions habitable and preventing the poles from entering perpetual deep freeze. But "we lack real measures of the amount of heat carried poleward by the oceans," wrote Chase in an article he recently coauthored.

Many oceanographers spend much more time in front of a computer terminal than they do at sea.

© Caroline Sheen

Vintage tools of oceanography include a Nansen bottle for seawater samples (on windowsill) and a current meter.

EYES ON THE OCEAN

To implement global programs, oceanographers look to a series of satellites scheduled for launch in the early 1990s. A few replace older, less sophisticated satellites, but most will provide oceanographers with entirely new capabilities.

If the Pentagon approves its funding, the Navy Remote Ocean Sensing System could be the first of the new breed of oceanographic satellites to arrive in orbit. Its instruments will measure wind speed and direction at the ocean surface, wave height, the ocean surface's shape and temperature, the location of sea ice, and precipitation over the seas. Much of this data is intended primarily for military use.

Oceanographers are particularly interested in measurements from a NASA "scatterometer" scheduled to fly aboard the Navy satellite. The scatterometer uses radar to measure very small waves, known as capillary waves, on the surface of the oceans. The waves, which are driven by local winds and vanish as soon as the winds die, are reliable indicators of wind speed and direction—key parameters in any model of ocean currents. At present, ocean surface wind speeds are known only at locations where ships or coastal buoys can take measurements. By using present satellites to track cloud movements, oceanographers can determine atmospheric wind speeds. They can then extrapolate wind speeds at the ocean surface; such measurements, however, are notoriously imprecise.

Topex/Poseidon is a joint U.S.-French satellite scheduled for launch in December 1991 aboard an Ariane 4 rocket. Its satellite altimeter will be able to measure the shape of the ocean surface with radar. Knowing the ocean's shape helps oceanographers trace surface currents, which create differences of a few feet in surface height. Because variations in earth's gravitational field create bumps and dips of up to several hundred feet in the ocean's surface height, oceanographers must first subtract the much larger gravity-induced variations. The Geopotential Research Mission, a pair of satellites that together would precisely measure the gravitational variations, is still in the conceptual stage at NASA.

In 1978 the Coastal Zone Color Scanner (CZCS) was launched on NASA's Nimbus-7. It was expected to operate for one year, but continued to function until June 1986. In the

Big Payoffs

Satellites will provide useful new perspectives on oceanic plants, winds, and currents, but they can't do everything. Oceanographers maintain that ships will always be needed to confirm satellite data and look at processes that occur too deep in the ocean for satellites to see.

Even if the ships endure, Steele's hairy-chested oceanographer may become an anachronism. "The days when an oceanographer could do meaningful research by himself—that's sort of passé," Wolff says. "I see oceanography as a big science with big computer models." Big computer models require big computers and large groups of scientists working together, so Wolff expects the science to become concentrated at two or three institutions that can afford such large-scale projects. Ships will become accessories to satellites, like puppets dangling at the end of heavenly strings.

Not all scientists are sure this view of oceanography is for the best. "There's still a hell of a lot we need to understand about the ocean itself," Steele says, though he admits that "to do both [large-scale satellite programs and extensive ship-based research] would require a doubling in the funding of ocean science."

Wolff notes that a lack of accurate models of the interaction between the ocean and the atmosphere "will soon become the biggest source of error in the two- or three-day weather predictions." Increasing the accuracy of those forecasts by even 15 percent would save several billion dollars annually in the United States.

But Chase is looking for even bigger payoffs from accurate long-term climate predictions. "If I can sit down and tell a farmer in Iowa that he's making a mistake planting winter wheat this year," he says, "the economic impact would be phenomenal. If you could tell people in the Sahel, 'You should not stay here because the Sahara Desert is going to take over. . . .' " For many oceanographers, this is the real promise of satellites.

1960s oceanographers on ships and airplanes had proven that the wavelengths of light reflected from the ocean surface are directly related to the local concentration of chlorophyll (which makes water greener), and that chlorophyll concentration is an accurate index of aquatic biological activity. Marine phytoplankton account for at least 30 percent of the earth's photosynthesis activity, so tracking and understanding small sea plants is crucial to the development of a theory of the global carbon dioxide cycle. Experiments with the CZCS have demonstrated the feasibility of studying phytoplankton using satellite observations.

Now, scientists are eager to continue this research with a new color scanner. "The only way you can get [information on chlorophyll concentration] globally is from a satellite with an ocean color instrument," notes D. James Baker, president of Joint Oceanographic Institutions, Inc., a project-planning and -coordinating body directed by representatives of 10 U.S. oceanographic institutions. The most likely home for such an instrument is the Landsat 6 satellite, scheduled for launch in 1991. According to a spokesman for EOSAT, the satellite's operators, Landsat 6's color sensor has capabilities even more advanced than the CZCS's.

In early 1990 the European Space Agency (ESA) plans to launch ERS-1 (for Earth Resources Satellite). It will carry both an altimeter and a synthetic aperture radar, which is especially useful for looking at sea ice. Two other satellites with synthetic aperture radars have been proposed: the Canadian Radarsat, which is still in the planning stages, and a Japanese earth-monitoring satellite that may be launched by 1992.

By the turn of the century, these satellites, too, will need replacement, and already scientists are planning for the next generation of instruments and space platforms. Meanwhile, oceanographers' appreciation of the long-term measurements ocean satellites can provide is growing. University of Colorado professor Robert Chase is looking forward to the day when all the satellites now on the drawing boards are in orbit. If our understanding of the oceans and their role in global climate is ever to improve, says Chase, "the only way it's going to happen is by increasing the frequency and length of observations." And the only way that's going to happen is with satellites.

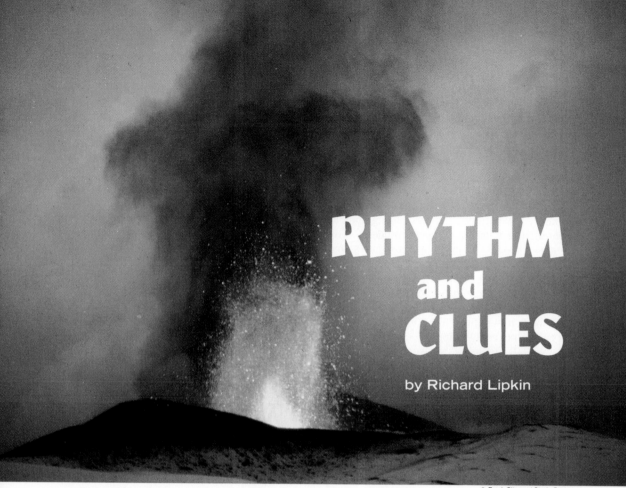

RHYTHM
and
CLUES

by Richard Lipkin

© Frank Siteman/ Stock, Boston

The heavenly motions are nothing but a continuous song for several voices, to be perceived by the intellect, not by the ear." When Johannes Kepler, the great astronomer, wrote that in 1619, he was thinking about cycles in the universe. He saw the universe as a harmony of spheres, with the planets as big, lumpy balls wobbling around a great sun, and the solar system as a cyclic machine.

It is now known that every 93,408 years the solar system completes one full cycle around the center of the galaxy, with the assembly of planets assuming the same configuration. Rhodes W. Fairbridge, professor emeritus of geology at Columbia University, has nicknamed it the APR cycle—All Planets Restart.

Are Cycles Related?

That cycles exist in nature is common knowledge today: roughly every 24 hours, the Sun ascends on Earth's eastern horizon; the Moon appears in its sky about every 25 hours; ocean tides rise and fall nearly every 12.5 hours.

Linked to longer-term solar and lunar cycles are weather cycles. As the Sun's temperature rises and then falls every 11 years, and as the Moon's gravity alters its tug on Earth's atmosphere each 18.6 years, so, too, does Earth's atmosphere get warmer and cooler and more and less pressurized every two decades, resulting in a 20-year cycle of floods and droughts. In the animal kingdom, one finds all sorts of odd cycles. Every 3.86 years, Norwegian lemmings leap from cliffs to the sea in droves. Each 9.7 months, on Ascension Island, a British territory in the South Atlantic near Africa, terns swarm in to hatch their eggs. In the woods of Canada, the population of lynx has risen and fallen regularly every 9.6 years since at least 1735, records reveal.

The big question puzzling researchers is whether any of these and the thousands of other known cycles in nature are related—whether, as early scientists had pondered, deeply embedded in the universe there might be a pulse to which all smaller cycles somehow are attuned.

In the case of long geologic cycles, the evidence is persuasive. According to Michael R. Rampino, a geologist at New York University and the National Aeronautics and Space Administration (NASA), and editor of "Climate: History, Periodicity, and Predictability," Earth undergoes geologic cycles that, in some cases, take millions of years to complete, correlating with other, larger cycles in the solar system.

The largest known cycle occurs in the Milky Way galaxy, which vaguely resembles a pinwheel-shaped disk that rotates once every 250 million years. Embedded in one of its pinwheel spokes is Earth's own solar system, which bobs up and down in the Milky Way "like a horse on a carousel," writes Rampino. Doing so, the Sun and Earth pass through the galaxy's midline about every 30 million years. As the solar system plunges through dense clouds of gas, dust, and comets, it is bombarded by comets, some similar in size and shape to Halley's. They pelt Earth and its neighboring planets and tumble toward the Sun.

Naturally occurring events seem to follow distinct rhythmic patterns. Scientists believe a relationship may exist between such apparently dissimilar patterns as the 30-million-year cycle of volcanic activity (facing page) and the 76-year orbit of Halley's Comet (below) around the Sun.

Back on Earth, scientists see some interesting parallels. It just so happens that roughly every 30 million years, comets rain down on Earth. The planet itself has always gone through cyclic geologic upheavals. In one case, more than 60 million years ago, lava deep within Earth surged and fractured its crust. Volcanoes boomed. On a plain now part of western India, volcanic flooding filled the land. A continental plate split, while volcanic ash darkened the sky and cooled the atmosphere.

"All in all," writes Rampino, "it was a time of extraordinary activity, more intense than the Earth had experienced for some 30 million years."

Inexplicable Synchrony

Rampino believes the upheavals on land and in space were not coincidences. Drastic changes in sea level, comet showers, large shifts in Earth's molten core and crust all occur in roughly 30-million year cycles. Much of the planet's physical history, in his opinion, is likely linked to bigger cycles in the galaxy, which in turn affect smaller-scale cycles in the solar system and on Earth.

The notion of some larger timekeeping mechanism for Earth's cycles, an ancient idea that resurfaced during the late 17th century, is looking more and more plausible these days. The difficulty, in the deepest scientific sense, is discerning the correct causal relationship, if there is any, among the many obvious cycles.

The first good evidence that Earth's processes have rhythms came from investigations of extinctions of marine life. During the early 1980s, David M. Raup and J. John Sepkoski, Jr., two paleontologists at the University of Chicago, showed that nearly every 26 million years, many species of sea life simultaneously went belly-up. Rampino and colleagues, in larger studies of sea life, reptiles, and mammal fossils, found a larger extinction cycle, at 30 million years. Such long-term Earth processes as seafloor spreading, volcanic activity, mountain building, and changes in the oceans themselves all occurred in roughly 30-million–year synchrony.

These are very long-term cycles. In the atmosphere, in the animal kingdom, and in human society, there are thousands of other short-term cycles that sometimes inexplicably fall into synchrony.

Every eight years, for example, the average levels of barometric pressure, of precipita-

The rise and fall of the tides provide one of the most familiar examples of natural cycles. The range in height between high and low water can be quite dramatic.

tion, and of the growth rates of pine trees and sweet potatoes hit their highs and lows at the same time. So do the prices of sugar, butter, pig iron, and stocks; the production levels of cotton, coal, crude petroleum, cigarettes, and lead; even the abundance of red squirrels.

That such statistical data exists is due to the efforts of Edward R. Dewey. An economist at the Department of Commerce during the 1920s and 1930s, he became obsessed with cycles and started to assemble an enormous collection of cycle data. Intrigued by cycles in business, banking, labor, and the production of goods, Dewey in 1941 chartered a Foundation for the Study of Cycles, now affiliated with the University of California at Irvine. During his 37 years

as president of the foundation, Dewey amassed an extraordinary amount of data on cyclic phenomena, more than 3,000 documented cycles.

Making It Official

When scientists at the foundation notice a steady pattern among reams of data, they subject the pattern to analyses before they deem it an official cycle. Much of the information has been culled from historical, business, geologic, and other scientific records.

There are, for example, hundreds of well-known eight-year, 9.2-year, 9.6-year, and 18.2-year cycles, each unique, but all pulsing in synchrony. Every 9.2 years the abundance of grasshoppers and partridge, the number of patents issued in the United States, and the water levels in U.S. lakes follow the same statistical pattern. On the 18.2-year circuit are the numbers of U.S. marriages, flood levels of the Nile, the rate of residential building construction, and levels of U.S. immigration, each rising and falling along the same lines.

Even today, no one, including Jeffrey H. Horovitz, executive director of the cycle foundation, can say with certainty why, how, or even if these cycles are related; the suggestion that they are sounds implausible. But equally implausible from a statistical point of view is that randomness alone could explain hundreds of coincidences.

Rather, Horovitz contends that although the exact mechanisms relating sunspots and meteorologic cycles, lunar and geologic cycles, climate and crop, flora and fauna cycles are not fully understood, the coincidences of similar cycles are too pervasive to be explained by mere chance.

Horovitz suggests the following line of potential causality among some natural cycles: cycles of the Sun affect Earth's magnetosphere in a regular and recognizable way. When "rung like a bell by a solar storm," he says, Earth's outer atmosphere gets stirred up. The barometric pressure rises and falls. There are storms. The weather synchronizes with the Sun's activities. Temperatures rise and fall, as do levels of rainfall.

These weather cycles in turn affect plant life, which withers and flourishes in demonstrable cycles. Those organisms that eat the plants are affected as well. Their populations rise and fall in relation to what they eat. Affected, too, by weather and atmospheric changes are people, whose moods and business activities are well known to be influenced by everything from blizzards and monsoons to subtler atmospheric changes like humidity or a stretch of gray days.

Cycles Beget Cycles

Consequently, if the logic holds, cycles affect cycles affect cycles. They do not merely oscillate independently in a vacuum, but affect each other—and eventually human beings. Many cycles are probably related through long causal chains that are too complex to spot easily. Thus, these disparate cycles, examined en masse, should serve as indicators, Horovitz says, offering suggestions as to how various elements of the solar system, ecosystem, and biosphere might affect each other.

Cycles of nonliving systems such as earthquakes are more easily identified and documented than cycles involving biological or social phenomena. Yet the latter exist, too. There are well-established cycles in economics and business—such as in the rate of small-business failures, industrial bond yields, auto sales, or cheese consumption. Industrial production cycles are known by most businessmen—a six-year cycle in aluminum or steel. Airplane traffic surges every 5.5 years. There are microeconomic cycles, too, such as the number of sales orders for particular items received by General Electric Company or Goodyear Tire & Rubber Company.

Dewey found evidence of cycles in the incidence of disease, mob behavior, and crime. Membership in religious organizations rises and falls steadily every nine years. Murder, rape, and aggravated assault all have monthly and seasonal patterns. Even wars: between the years 1050 and 1915, for instance, he discerned a 142-year war cycle from data on international battles.

At the cutting edge of cycles research, says Horovitz, are large-scale cycles in mental health. Psychiatrists report regular patterns in the number of "crisis visits" and "stress days," when everyone seems to clamor for help. Scheduled to begin soon is a 12-year global study of mental health cycles, based on the successful outcome of a recently completed two-year pilot study.

Even old ideas, such as that of life's cyclic nature, regularly rise and fall in popularity. "The same Nature which delights in periodical repetition in the skies is the Nature which orders the affairs of earth," Mark Twain wrote. "Let us not underrate the value of that hint."

© B. Daemmrich/Stock, Boston

Scientists have determined that even human behavior seems to follow regular patterns. Church attendance (above) and cheese consumption (below) rise and fall in periodic cycles. Economic activity such as steel production and tire sales also conforms to cycles.

© Jon A. Rembold/*Insight* Magazine

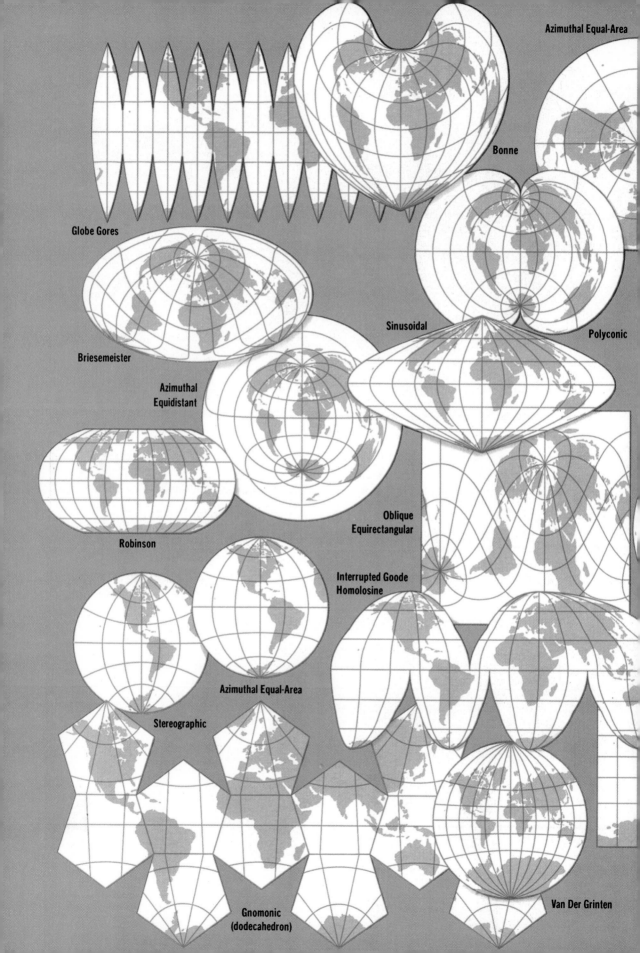

Azimuthal Equal-Area

Globe Gores

Bonne

Briesemeister

Sinusoidal

Polyconic

Azimuthal
Equidistant

Robinson

Oblique
Equirectangular

Interrupted Goode
Homolosine

Stereographic

Azimuthal Equal-Area

Van Der Grinten

Gnomonic
(dodecahedron)

Orthographic

Globe Rosette

Perspective

Miller Cylindrical

The Changing
WORLD
of MAPS

by Jeffrey H. Hacker

In a recent test of basic geography, a group of U.S. college students was asked to locate some well-known places on a map of the world. According to their answers, Africa is located in North America, the Soviet Union can be found in Central America, and the "state" of Atlanta borders North Carolina.

That kind of response, given time and again by U.S. students at every level, underscores a growing national embarrassment: "geographic illiteracy." Nor is the problem confined to young people. In a 1988 study commissioned by the National Geographic Society, some 75 percent of American adults could not locate Vietnam on a world map. Fewer than half could find Great Britain, France, or Japan. And, most amazingly of all, one in seven Americans could not even locate the United States.

The problem of geographic illiteracy has generated increasing concern in the U.S. educational community. More and more schools are making geography a required course. Teaching methods and curricula are being reformulated. New textbooks and other learning materials—for students and adults alike—are being created.

Not coincidentally, the campaign for map literacy comes precisely at a time when maps themselves are being reassessed, redrawn, and in some cases hotly debated. New designs have been introduced. New technologies, from satellite images to digital plotting, have created a host of highly specialized maps with important new applications. Politics have come to bear as never before. Even psychologists are taking interest, plumbing the depths of what they call "cognitive mapmaking."

Often regarded as staid, static, and noncontroversial, the art and science of cartography continues to change and chart new realms. The more it becomes science, the more it becomes art—and vice-versa.

Global Projections—Mercator to Robinson

Users of the common world map might be surprised to learn that Greenland is only about the size of Mexico. Since Ptolemy in the second century, cartographers have wrestled with the problem of drawing the round earth on a flat sheet of paper. They have long known that images on world maps necessarily distort the shapes of landmasses and oceans. In the widely used projection drawn by the Flemish mapmaker Gerhardus Mercator in 1569, Greenland appears larger than all of South America.

For centuries, cartographers have struggled to create flat maps that render the earth's round surface without distortion. The Robinson projection (far left, center), recently adopted by the National Geographic Society, comes relatively close.

Over the centuries, hundreds of variations have been tried—from circles, ellipses, and ovals, to hearts, stars, and butterflies. Because no single world map is perfect, choosing one depends on the purpose of the user. When Mercator devised his projection in the 16th century, it was for the specific purpose of aiding navigators on the high seas; the constant lines of bearing enabled seamen to chart a straight course between two points. The Mercator projection became so well known, however, that people began to misuse it for geographical reference.

Although the Mercator projection remains the most widely used map of the world, its distortions of size and shape have led to the adoption of others. In 1922, for example, the National Geographic Society selected the Van Der Grinten projection as its standard world map. The Van Der Grinten projection, patented in 1904 by Alphons Van Der Grinten, was seen as a useful compromise between distortions of spatial relations and those of size and shape.

A number of alternatives have been developed since Van Der Grinten's, and in 1988—its centennial year—the National Geographic Society announced another new standard. It replaced the Van Der Grinten projection with the Robinson projection, created in 1963 by the recognized dean of U.S. cartographers, Arthur H.

American college students consistently misidentify the locations of foreign countries, states, and even the United States itself. Such widespread geographic and map illiteracy has alarmed educators throughout the country.

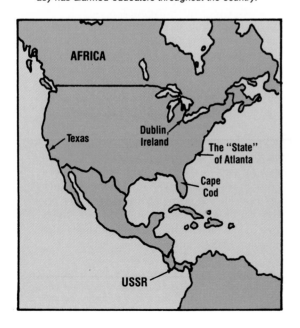

Robinson of the University of Wisconsin at Madison. The Robinson projection represents a further step toward accuracy of landmass size and shape. Greenland, for example, appears only 60 percent larger than reality, compared to 400 percent larger on Van Der Grinten and 1,500 percent larger on Mercator. Greenland, of course, is the biggest problem; landmasses closer to the equator are much more accurately drawn.

In designing his projection, Robinson took a somewhat unusual approach for a modern cartographer. Instead of relying entirely on mathematics and computers, he began by visualizing how each country *ought* to look on a map. Only then did he turn to math and computers to delineate their shapes. "Mapmaking is as much an art form as a science," he says. "What I really did was create a portrait of the earth."

Robinson's "portrait" is widely expected to become the norm for cartography in the U.S. In distributing the maps through its magazine, the National Geographic Society will cause a fundamental change in the way millions of people view the world. For whatever the degree and type of distortion, the representation becomes the reality in the mind of the map user.

Ethnocentrism and the Peters Projection

In addition to such technical matters as distortion of distance, size, and shape, ethnic and cultural issues have risen to the forefront of modern cartography. Some mapmakers have argued that common world projections—the Mercator in particular—are "Eurocentrically biased"; that is, that Europe and the entire Northern Hemisphere are shown larger relative to South America and Africa than they really are.

The pervasiveness of a Eurocentric bias, as well as the power of maps in dictating world views, was evidenced in a 1987 study sponsored by the International Geographic Union. More than 4,000 first-year college students from 54 countries were asked to draw a map of the world in 30 minutes, showing as many nations as time and memory allowed. According to geographer Thomas F. Saarinen, who conducted the study, most of the students depicted the world as centered in Europe. Even in such countries as Singapore, Thailand, and Hong Kong, most students visualized Europe in the middle. Saarinen believes that the bias occurs because the Mercator projection has been used for so long.

The most outspoken critic of Eurocentric mapping has been the German historian and car-

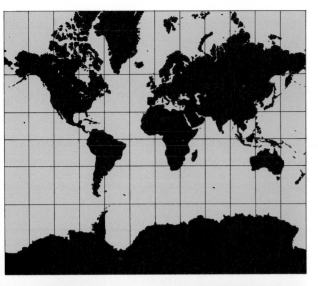

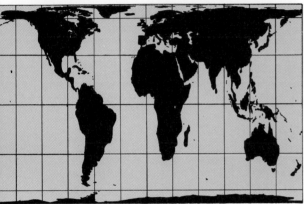

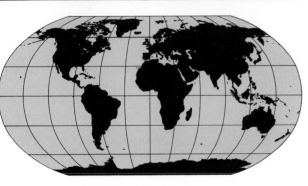

The Mercator projection (top), the most familiar and widely used map today, originated in the 1500s as an aid for navigation. Its distortion in favor of northern landmasses gave rise to charges of a "Eurocentric" bias. The controversial Peters projection (center) went to the opposite extreme, elongating equatorial countries to twice their actual length. The Robinson projection (bottom) comes closer to geographic reality than do any of its predecessors. Its high degree of accuracy was achieved by first visualizing what each country should look like on a map; then their shapes were delineated using computers and mathematics.

tographer Arno Peters. Peters notes that the less prominent regions on the Mercator map include important parts of the Third World that are populated by dark-skinned peoples. He concludes that the Mercator projection reflects a racist attitude, drawing its popularity from an exaggeration of white-dominated areas.

To correct the bias, Peters announced in 1973 that he had developed a new projection that represents all peoples of the world on an equal basis—especially the three-quarters of humankind living in the Third World. Promoting his map as the only one that meets global social concerns, Peters has achieved a worldwide distribution estimated at more than 16 million copies in six languages. The Peters projection has been adopted by several agencies of the United Nations, the World Council of Churches, and a number of other organizations.

Rarely in the field of cartography has any development sparked such controversy as the Peters projection. Several objections have been raised. First, scholars have pointed out that Peters' "new" projection is actually the same as one rendered in 1855 by James Gall of Scotland. Second, Peters' claims that his map meets every cartographic need and should be used to the exclusion of all others are said to be misleading. No projection is perfect, Peters' included. In addition to abandoning such qualities as linear scale and proportional distance, the Peters projection fails to meet his claim of proper area representation. Although industrialized nations are shown halfway between the equator and North Pole with very little distortion of shape, Third World countries near the equator are vertically elongated by a ratio of two to one. This has led Arthur Robinson to object on aesthetic grounds as well. "The landmasses," he says, "look like wet, ragged, long winter underwear hung out to dry on the Arctic Circle."

Political and Other Distortions

The world of mapmaking received another jolt in September 1988, when the chief cartographer of the Soviet Union acknowledged that for 50 years, government authorities had deliberately falsified virtually every public map of the country. According to an interview in the official press by Viktor R. Yashchenko, head of the Geodesy and Cartography Administration of the Council of Ministers, a number of rivers, mountains, peninsulas, and other features were misplaced; roads, towns, and other landmarks were either moved or omitted entirely; boundaries

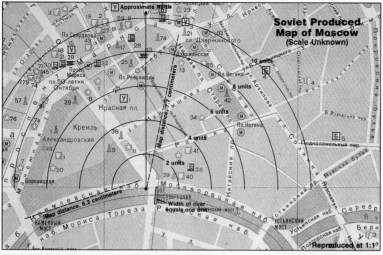

Soviet Produced Map of Moscow
(Scale Unknown)

Map distance 13.3 centimeters

8 units
6 units
4 units
2 units

Width of river equals one unit

Map distance, 6.2 centimeters

Reproduced at 1:1?

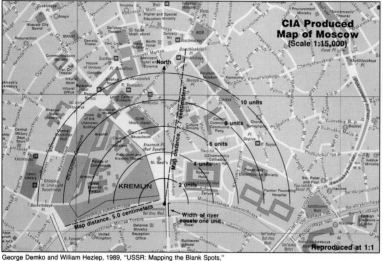

CIA Produced Map of Moscow
(Scale 1:15,000)

North

10 units
8 units
6 units
4 units
2 units

KREMLIN

Map distance, 5.0 centimeters

Width of river equals one unit

Reproduced at 1:1

George Demko and William Hezlep, 1989, "USSR: Mapping the Blank Spots,"
FOCUS 39(1). The American Geographical Society, New York, N.Y.

In 1988, the chief Soviet cartographer admitted that government authorities had deliberately falsified virtually every public map published in the country for 50 years. A Soviet-produced map of downtown Moscow (top) has no known scale. In order to compare the Soviet map with a CIA-produced map of the same area (bottom), the width of the river on each of the maps has been arbitrarily designated as a "unit of distance." The street plan 10 units out from the river differs significantly between the maps. Owing to its greater detail and high accuracy, the CIA map is in considerable demand on the Moscow black market.

were shifted; and scales were altered. The campaign of distortion was begun under Stalin in the 1930s and directed by the secret police. The purpose was to frustrate foreign intelligence operations and aerial bombings.

In his interview Yashchenko also announced that Moscow had agreed to release accurate maps, which have existed for decades but have been classified as state secrets. The willingness to make them public, he said, reflected President Mikhail Gorbachev's policy of *glasnost* (openness) and a relaxation of "mistrust and spy mania." Moscow also was embarrassed by protests from its own citizens. "We received numerous complaints," said Yashchenko. "People did not recognize their motherland on maps."

The intentional distortion of maps for political, economic, and other reasons is nothing new, of course. In Roman times, cartographers abandoned the scientific techniques developed by their Greek predecessors, designing maps specifically for administrative and military purposes. For centuries the standard map of the world featured a grossly exaggerated representation of the Roman Empire. Later, during the 16th and 17th centuries, New World explorers often wrote their reports and drew their maps to elicit monetary support from patrons, to promote the new lands with prospective colonists, or simply to enhance their own reputations. Says map historian Anne W. Tennant of the Denver Art Museum: "Their reports and charts— flawed, exaggerated, and downright erroneous as they frequently were—supplied the raw material upon which the early atlases were based."

The long history of distortion and falsification underscores the need for continuing vigilance against the intrusion of political and other interests in the science of cartography. Yet the announcement in the Soviet press also suggested that the emergence of new technologies has made misrepresentation on maps an almost lost cause. As Yashchenko said in his interview, "This work [of map distortion] became senseless with the appearance of space photography," which enabled other countries to make extremely accurate maps from satellite data.

The View From Space

The technological advances of recent decades have opened up vast new realms for the ancient art and science of mapmaking. Remote sensing from space and electronic data processing have provided powerful new means of gathering information, transforming it into maps of fantastic detail, revising and altering the images at the press of a button, and in many cases replacing conventional printed maps with maps displayed on a screen and stored on a computer chip.

Remote sensing, by airborne or satellite radar and by instruments known as "multispectral scanners," complements and frequently replaces conventional aerial photography and land surveys in providing comprehensive views of geographic features. They have made it possible, for the first time, to map the entire world in detail. Every unexplored region on the globe is exposed to close, continuous scrutiny.

The new radar technology provides a precise picture of earth topography. Known as side-looking or synthetic-aperture radar, the system sends pulses of ultra-high-frequency radio signals toward the target and detects the faint echo that bounces back. The relative time it takes for the signal to return provides a precise measure of relative elevation. The echoes are recorded on film and transformed by laser into a holograph-like three-dimensional image.

The multispectral scanner, carried on Landsat satellites, captures visible light just as a conventional camera does, but it also detects electromagnetic (near-infrared) radiation that is imperceptible to the human eye. The scanner has myriad valuable applications. Since different objects on earth—whether animal, vegetable, or mineral—all reflect sunlight in a different way, each one has its own "spectral signature." Thus, remote-sensing multispectral scanners can distinguish areas of dense vegetation, barren land, water, urban sprawl, and a host of other features. On the maps they generate, the various features are represented in different colors. From their perch in space, multispectral scanners can even distinguish such characteristics as clear or polluted water, healthy or diseased crops, deciduous or coniferous trees, and the mineral content of soil.

Digital Mapping

The transformation of satellite data into a map involves a complex intermediate step. Data from remote-sensing devices are encoded in a staggering number of digital impulses; a single "picture" taken by a civilian Landsat satellite contains some 250 million bits of information. These impulses are turned into map images by powerful computers and graphics systems. In a multiyear, multimillion-dollar project, the U.S. Government is developing a digitized mapping

"Geosystems" combine digital maps and computer databases to generate highly detailed maps of everything from geological indications for oil exploration (below) to the market-penetration potential of a fast-food franchise.

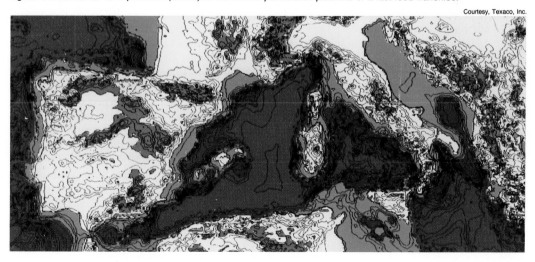

A few taps on a keyboard can produce an amazing array of demographic and geographic data (left). A few more taps combine the data into a highly specialized digitized map (above).

system in which users will be able to illustrate such features as population density, land use, the presence of minerals, traffic patterns, and utility lines almost instantaneously.

The marriage of such detailed digital maps with computer databases has created a versatile new tool called a "geosystem." A geosystem actually consists of two databases: one containing the maps, and the other containing more specific information needed by the user. Examples of the latter might include demographic breakdowns, sales figures, or market potential. Today geosystems are helping U.S. companies make key planning decisions in an increasing number of areas. Oil companies are using them to create maps that show rock formations, previous oil strikes, land-leasing terms, and other essential information. Fast-food chains are using them to measure the performance of existing franchises and to select the best sites for new ones. Even overnight delivery services use them to dispatch trucks and planes.

Cognitive Mapping

At the same time that modern technologies are generating more accurate and comprehensive maps of everything, a new branch of psychology is focusing on the subjective differences in the way people see the world and map it in their minds. Researchers in this fledgling field of "cognitive psychology" resist the kind of absolute, rigid schematics based on mathematical formulations and high-tech imagery. Instead, they seek to describe the curious distortions we all apply to our surroundings. According to Reginald Golledge of the University of California at Santa Barbara, a pioneer of cognitive psy-

chology, "People don't think in Euclidean geometry. They still put monsters in their maps."

The study of cognitive mapping goes beyond mere recognition that people view their surroundings in subjective, nongeometric ways. Researchers attempt to record the *ways* people orient themselves, and to interpret those viewpoints in a useful way. In the latter endeavor, the disciplines of math, statistics, and the scientific method come very much into play.

In a rigorous study of geographic orientation to new surroundings, Golledge and his colleagues were able to identify some distinct patterns. Newcomers to an area initially orient themselves by setting up a series of landmarks—or "anchor points"—and recognizing the routes that connect them; no overall picture is yet established. The accumulation of such knowledge tends to continue for about six months, at which time the person begins to discard unimportant landmarks. After this sorting out and consolidation process is completed, the person begins setting up second- and third-level anchor points. Only then does a broad picture finally begin to emerge.

Golledge's allusion to modern map "monsters" reflects another key aspect of the relationship between people and their surroundings. In the mental "maps" we all carry, there are always places we instinctively fear and avoid. These may be decaying inner cities for some, wealthy suburbs for others, heavy traffic areas, high-crime areas, or the neighborhood in which one's mother-in-law lives. As in the case of anchor points, map monsters vary among people of different ages, sexes, ethnic backgrounds, economic levels, and the like.

The processes of mental mapmaking, especially as they can be distinguished in groups, suggest an alternative to the cluttered street maps that are themselves so monstrous to many people. New maps would be designed for specific user groups, identifying the most logical landmarks and omitting unnecessary details. For example, maps for children might show traffic lights and mailboxes instead of street names. Maps for tourists might show only the most popular attractions and most direct routes. Maps for newcomers might even be computer-customized to show the home, workplace, and nearest shopping center.

"It's amazing the number of people who say to me, 'I just can't read maps,' " says Golledge. "There's got to be some way to take all this mystery away from cartography. . . ."

Toward Map Literacy

In his novel *Tom Sawyer Abroad*, Mark Twain has Tom and Huckleberry Finn carried off from Missouri in a balloon. Floating eastward, they wonder if they have crossed Illinois. Huck is sure they haven't; Tom asks how he can tell.

"I know by the color. We're right over Illinois yet," says Huck. "And you can see for yourself that Indiana ain't in sight."

"What's color got to do with it?" asks Tom.

"It's got everything to do with it. Illinois is green, Indiana is pink. You show me pink down there, if you can. No sir; it's green."

"Indiana *pink*? Why, what a lie!"

"It ain't no lie; I've seen it on a map, and it's pink."

"Seen it on the map! Huck Finn, do you reckon the States was the same color out-of-doors as they are on the map?"

"Tom Sawyer, what's a map for? Ain't it to learn you facts?"

While Huck's literal-minded view exaggerates what we have come to know as "map illiteracy," his logic reflects precisely the point many modern educators have made about the teaching of geography today. The emphasis on facts, they say, has made geography the subject kids love to hate—the tedious memorization of capital cities, mountain ranges, and principal crops. Central to the revival of geographic education, say the experts, is the use of more innovative teaching methods that add a broader dimension to the litany of place names. In studying the geography of Switzerland, for example, students would not only learn about its Alpine terrain, 26 cantons, and dairy production, but they would also learn about its history of isolation, its languages, and its bucolic way of life.

Just as critical to geographic literacy are some basic understandings about maps—how they are made, how they are used, and how they vary. With all the innovations and technological improvements of recent decades, the perfect map remains as elusive as facts themselves. Differences in perspective, variations in purpose, and even deliberate distortions have made the art and science of cartography no more certain and no less static than the world as people see it.

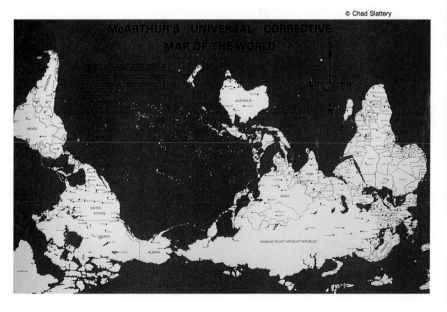

© Chad Slattery

Cognitive mapping studies the subjective way in which people see the world and map it in their minds. An Australian, for instance, might visualize his homeland as top and center on a world map.

ENERGY

ENERGY

As economists and environmentalists worried about future energy demands, the U.S. used record amounts of energy in 1988. The nuclear power industry remained troubled, but exciting advances were made in solar power.

by Anthony J. Castagno

© Michael Sargent/The White House

James Watkins (far left) will serve as President Bush's Secretary of Energy.

The U.S. Energy Picture

The United States used more energy in 1988 than ever before—more than 80 quadrillion Btu's (British thermal units, a measure of energy expenditure)—and imported more oil than in any other year since 1979. Meanwhile, headlines told of the global warming trend known as the "greenhouse effect," which was caused, at least in part, by burning fossil fuel. Yet oil consumption in the United States continued rising, and nonfossil energy sources such as nuclear power provoked increasing controversy.

President George Bush named retired Admiral James Watkins as his energy secretary. Watkins, a veteran of the Navy's nuclear submarine program and formerly chief of naval operations (CNO), was charged with resolving problems at the nation's nuclear weapons production facilities, all of which are managed by the Department of Energy (DOE). These facilities, plagued by troubles that came to light in 1988, may cost more than $150 billion over the next two decades for cleanup and upgrades, according to a report prepared for the government.

Nuclear

Nuclear power continued producing an increasing share of the country's electricity requirements, growing from 17.7 percent in 1987 to approximately 20 percent in 1988. By year's end there were 109 plants licensed in the United States and more than 410 worldwide.

While nuclear power supplied approximately 16 percent of the world's

Despite opposition, the Seabrook nuclear plant may soon begin operating.

© Seth Resnick/Picture Group

electricity, it supplied about a third of that used in Western countries. In some countries, such as France and Belgium, nuclear power supplied more than two-thirds of the total electricity demand.

Controversy continued to surround the U.S. nuclear power industry in 1988, and the future of several plants was uncertain. Voters in California, Nebraska, and Massachusetts faced ballot questions to close down nuclear plants, but each measure was defeated. Emergency planning issues continued to keep the stalled Seabrook (New Hampshire) and Shoreham (New York) nuclear power plants on the sidelines and in the headlines even after President Reagan signed an executive order giving the federal government clear jurisdiction.

In January, Seabrook's main owner, Public Service Company of New Hampshire (PSNH), filed for bankruptcy, becoming the first utility in modern times to take that step. By year's end a bankruptcy court was considering several options—including a proposal by PSNH to restructure under federal control, a proposal from the state to establish a public power authority, proposals from neighboring Vermont and Maine utilities to merge with PSNH, and proposals from at least two other New England utilities to buy the service territory and non-Seabrook assets of PSNH.

In 1987, for the first time in history, a kilowatt-hour of nuclear electricity became more expensive than coal electricity. Although nuclear fuel held a substantial cost advantage over coal fuel, operating and maintenance expenses pushed total costs about a tenth of a cent higher than coal, 2.18 cents versus 2.07 cents per kilowatt-hour. Both remained significantly lower than other sources, as natural gas cost 2.89 cents and oil cost 3.74 cents per kilowatt-hour.

Research into new, safer reactor designs was stepped up in 1988, some involving passive safety systems in the traditional water-cooled design, others relying on gas or liquid sodium as their primary coolant (see also page 158).

Oil

Throughout the year the Organization of Petroleum Exporting Countries (OPEC) tried repeatedly to reach accord on production quotas and price-fixing. Prices tumbled to just over $10 a barrel before an agreement reached at the November OPEC meeting brought prices back into the mid-teens.

OPEC production throughout 1988 was well over the "ceiling" quota of 17.4 million barrels per day, frequently hitting peak levels of 21.5 million barrels. With demand for OPEC oil averaging around 19 million barrels a day, the overflow has created an enormous glut.

Worldwide, production of oil averaged 60 million barrels a day, nearly 10 million barrels over demand. OPEC, which once supplied more than 60 percent of all the oil in the world, now supplies about 30 percent, substantially reducing its influence in controlling this valuable commodity.

In the United States, according to the American Petroleum Institute, demand for oil continued growing, increasing about 3.2 percent to 17.2 million barrels per day. This was the highest level since 1979, but still was less than 1978's record demand of 18.8 million barrels per day.

At 7.2 million barrels a day, oil imports have increased 45 percent in the past three years. With domestic production at its lowest point in twelve years—and continuing to decrease (a 2.9 percent decrease in 1988 alone)—the trend of the past few years is expected to continue, a trend that the Government Accounting Office (GAO) warns could result in another oil crisis in the 1990s. In the United States, imports now supply 41.4 percent of demand, up from 31.5 percent in 1985, and approaching the record 48 percent of 1977.

Gasoline, which accounts for 43 percent of the oil used in the U.S., was plentiful and priced at levels close to those of 1987, averaging approximately $1 per gallon. But gasoline prices rose dramatically in the first half of 1989.

© Terrence McCarthy/NYT Pictures

The price of oil rose sharply in early 1989, despite plentiful supplies.

Solar Technology

In early 1988 one of DOE's solar research projects, conducted at Sandia National Laboratories in New Mexico, scored a breakthrough with the development of a photovoltaic solar cell that is 31 percent efficient. This is more than twice as high

Special lenses can focus the equivalent of 1,000 suns onto one solar cell.

Sandia National Laboratories

as the 15-percent efficiency of solar cells now used in calculators, and even exceeds the 30 percent barrier once considered the maximum, leading to speculation of efficiencies of 35 to 38 percent. This compares to 34 percent efficiency for fossil fuel–burning plants, and opens the door to future widespread use of the sun for generating electricity.

Costs for existing—and improving—photovoltaic solar technology have been dropping dramatically for more than a decade, but solar-produced electricity still costs about four times as much as that produced through conventional means. As this cost differential decreases and as efficiencies increase, there is a very real potential that by the year 2000, solar could be supplying 1 percent—6 billion watts—of the country's electricity supply, or enough to meet the overall energy needs of some 3 million people.

Electricity

Demand for electricity grew by nearly 5 percent in 1988 over 1987, with demand during peak levels exceeding that expected for the early 1990s.

Strong industrial growth, coupled with a record cold winter and a record hot summer, led to an unprecedented demand for electricity—and a record number of appeals to consumers to curb usage—as utilities in many parts of the country scrambled to stretch available supplies of electricity by imposing voltage reductions, or "brownouts."

In addition to voltage reductions, these utilities sought to increase their supplies by "wheeling" (shipping large amounts of electricity from one part of the country to another), and by buying huge amounts of electricity from Canada. There also was increased use of cogeneration and electricity produced by small private companies, and renewed calls for additional conservation.

Hochtemperatur-Reaktorbau GmbH

Taking Fear Out of
NUCLEAR POWER

by Edmund Faltermayer

Jinxed by runaway construction costs and reviled for putting humanity at needless risk, nuclear power seemed destined for gradual abandonment. That was last year. Amid mounting evidence that the earth is warming because of the greenhouse effect, splitting atoms to generate electricity is getting new respect. Unlike coal or oil, nuclear power creates neither acid rain nor carbon dioxide, which is believed to be mainly responsible for the planet's rising temperature.

Protecting the Public

By happy coincidence, companies that build reactors are working on a medley of new models, some of which have begun to allay concerns about safety. With new humility following the accidents at Three Mile Island and Chernobyl, the nuke makers are relying heavily on ''passive'' design features to protect the public. In future versions of the water-cooled reactor, which dominates the industry, simple gravity flow from emergency tanks would protect the

Innovative reactor designs and stringent employee procedures may help reduce anxiety over nuclear safety. In a helium-cooled reactor (facing page), fuel pellets have ceramic coatings that seal in radioactivity. At plants in the U.S. and abroad, workers pass through detectors (right) to measure any exposure to radioactivity.

nuclear core for several days or longer even if all else failed. One proposed version of a gas-cooled reactor would offer still greater peace of mind. In the worst imaginable situation, with the control-room crew inattentive and the core entirely deprived of coolant, no significant radioactivity would be released—ever.

The new models are badly needed, if only for political and psychological reasons. Only giant strides in safety will overcome antinuclear passions and permit streamlining of the elaborate regulatory and judicial processes that have stopped atomic expansion in its tracks. No U.S. utility has ordered a reactor since 1978. Why fight a battle in which any self-professed environmental group—or just a few people scared of nukes in their community—can tie up a project indefinitely merely by hiring a lawyer? Why risk the kind of strong political opposition, reaching up to Governor Mario Cuomo, that forced New York's Lilco to abandon the $5.3 billion Shoreham reactor in June 1988 before it could light a single lamp?

The political climate might change, and the country might get the power it is going to need, if the industry's critics are moved by design improvements to alter their stance. The most respected watchdog group is the Union of Concerned Scientists, which has called for the phasing out of existing reactors. Robert Pollard, the group's senior nuclear safety engineer, is wary of all the newfangled nukes and wants to be shown that they will live up to the claims made for them. But he allows that at least one new model—a gas-cooled reactor—"sounds eminently workable."

Ah, but wouldn't the cost of added nuclear safety make the kilowatts prohibitively expensive? Not at all, insist the reactor builders. Safer reactors, they say, are also simpler and cheaper to build. Standardization would save money, too. A major curse of U.S. nuclear power has been a plethora of custom-built plants, nearly all different. The Nuclear Regulatory Commission (NRC), which oversees reactor safety, hopes to O.K. a master design for each improved reactor in advance, thus speeding regulatory approvals for each project.

Since most of the U.S. is awash in generating capacity these days, utilities can wait a few years before they place orders. Some buyers may not be utilities at all, but the emerging species of independent generating companies. It would take until the middle or late 1990s—about the time electricity demand is expected to catch up with supply—before detailed design work, regulatory approvals, and construction could be completed on the advanced nukes.

Defense in Depth

The fact that safer reactors can be built does not mean that existing ones are unacceptably hazardous. The U.S. now gets 20 percent of its electric power from 108 reactors; 14 more are under construction and in no apparent danger of being idled like Shoreham and New Hampshire's Seabrook facility. Some other industrial countries rely more heavily on the atom—

among them France (70 percent), Belgium (66 percent), and South Korea (53 percent). None of the non-Communist world's power reactors are built like the tricky Chernobyl unit that blew its concrete roof in 1986, causing 32 deaths in the worst civilian nuclear disaster ever. Nevertheless, people near the plants live with potential danger in somewhat the same way that the Dutch who live below sea level face the possibility of flooding if a dike gives way.

The U.S. nuclear industry's answer has long been what it calls "defense in depth." In the case of water-cooled reactors, four barriers plus automatically controlled standby pumps are supposed to keep the radioactivity of a crippled reactor from reaching the world outside. Three such "dikes" were breached or circumvented in history's second most serious power-reactor accident, at Pennsylvania's Three Mile Island (TMI) in March 1979. But the last and most formidable barrier, the thick, steel-reinforced containment building, kept in nearly all the lethal stuff. No one was injured.

For 40 minutes the uranium core was partly or almost entirely uncovered by coolant. More than half the fuel elements melted into a blob at the bottom of the reactor vessel—a billion-dollar blob for General Public Utilities (GPU), which is spending that amount just to clean up. Yet while core damage was greater than anyone suspected at the time, the release of radioactive elements constituting a serious health hazard was negligible—in the case of radioactive iodine, one-millionth or less of Chernobyl's release. Milk from nearby goat herds picked up

two to three times as much radioactive iodine from the Russian disaster thousands of miles away as it did from the TMI mishap next door.

Norman Rasmussen, a Massachusetts Institute of Technology (MIT) nuclear engineer, ran a landmark study before the TMI accident calculating the mathematical probability of releases from U.S.-type nuclear plants serious enough to cause 10 or more premature cancer deaths. The reassuring odds: about once in 3 million reactor-years of operation. The TMI accident and more recent studies, Rasmussen says, suggest that nukes are "substantially safer" than previously thought. Certainly the operators are more on their toes than a decade ago. TMI-1, the surviving sister reactor of the ruined TMI-2, has a revamped control room. The Institute of Nuclear Power Operations in Atlanta, Georgia, set up after TMI by utilities as a clearinghouse for safety information, reports a decline in safety-related incidents. Slack discipline gets harsh punishment. At Philadelphia Electric Company's Peach Bottom plant last year, some members of a night crew were found asleep or playing video games. They were suspended, reassigned, or demoted; the company's chairman took early retirement.

Water-cooled Reactors

Water-cooled reactors, alas, function in such a way that no one can rule out a far more dangerous accident than TMI—one with even worse consequences than Chernobyl. The odds are ludicrously small, but that no longer assuages the

In the worst-case scenario of equipment failure and control room errors, the fuel cores of water-cooled reactors—the dominant type in the U.S.—could overheat and leak radioactivity in as little as 20 minutes if no one took corrective action. Advanced versions of this reactor would stretch the grace period to three days. PIUS reactors have a backup pool of borated water that would keep the core cool for a week. Gas-cooled reactors offer an 8-hour response time, but even then, only minute amounts of radioactivity would leak. The other two designs offer unlimited response times if safety devices fail.

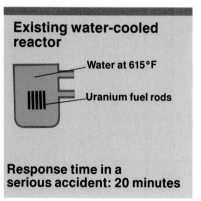

Existing water-cooled reactor

Water at 615°F
Uranium fuel rods

Response time in a serious accident: 20 minutes

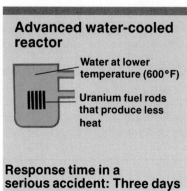

Advanced water-cooled reactor

Water at lower temperature (600°F)
Uranium fuel rods that produce less heat

Response time in a serious accident: Three days

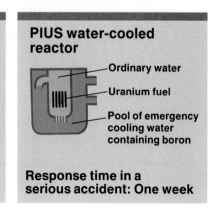

PIUS water-cooled reactor

Ordinary water
Uranium fuel
Pool of emergency cooling water containing boron

Response time in a serious accident: One week

public. Vice president James Moore of Westinghouse, the biggest U.S. reactor builder, sounds almost like a nuke-basher when he declares: "We gain very little when we explain that the potential for a radiation release is one in 10 million, if we have to acknowledge that it could theoretically happen tomorrow. We are selling our wares to nervous human beings, not to statisticians."

Critics of water-cooled reactors point out that at full power the temperature inside their uranium-oxide fuel pellets reaches 3,300° F (1,815° C), high enough to melt the zirconium alloy cladding that surrounds the fuel rods. Only the water holds it below melting temperature. In the course of keeping the reactor cool, the water picks up enough heat to produce the steam that drives generators. But if all the water suddenly vanished because of a pipe break, the cladding—one of the barriers against radioactive releases—could begin melting in seconds.

That possibility, defenders say, is based on a wildly farfetched combination of things gone wrong. Robert Long, a vice president at GPU's nuclear subsidiary, says that in the worst believable sequence of events, a reactor's operators have at least 20 minutes before they must begin worrying about damage to the fuel core. At TMI, where the operators for a time did the opposite of what was necessary, it was more than an hour before core damage began.

Sodium and Boron

Instead of emphasizing multiple barriers and "engineered systems"—an array of emergency pumps and automatic controls—the new designs look to nature for a helping hand. One approach, used in rival proposals by General Electric (GE) and Rockwell International, is to abandon water as a coolant in favor of liquid sodium, which has a far higher boiling point and superior ability to absorb unexpected heat surges.

A water reactor's coolant must be kept at high pressure—up to 150 times atmospheric pressure—lest it turn to steam. Liquid sodium needs no pressurization. If pumps circulating the coolant broke down, the liquid sodium itself, along with the natural circulation of air around the outside of the reactor, would prevent fuel damage indefinitely. One worry, however, is that liquid sodium reacts violently when exposed to air or water. The reactor vessel would have to be double walled, with the space between filled with nitrogen as an added precaution.

PIUS is not a pope, but another intriguing reactor design, developed at Asea Brown Boveri, a big Swedish electrical equipment maker. The letters stand for "process inherent, ultimate safety." Based on the natural tendency of liquids of different densities to separate, PIUS is a water-cooled reactor surrounded by a large pool of cold, heavier water containing boron. Under normal operation the borated water, which halts nuclear reactions by absorbing neutrons, would be kept at bay not by a valve but by the sheer pressure of the regular coolant. If the regular coolant were suddenly lost, the heavier fluid would rush in without human intervention, keeping the core safely cooled for a week while the operators deliberated their next move.

The main drawback of both PIUS and sodium-cooled reactors is that prototypes have never been built. Says Chairman James J. O'Connor of Commonwealth Edison in Chicago, Illinois, a major operator of nuclear plants: "It would be unrealistic for a utility to order, in the near future, a reactor based on a technology that has yet to be proven commer-

Illustrations: © John Pirman

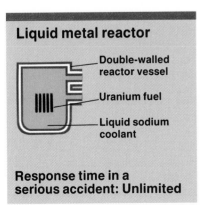

Liquid metal reactor

Double-walled reactor vessel

Uranium fuel

Liquid sodium coolant

Response time in a serious accident: Unlimited

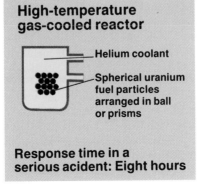

High-temperature gas-cooled reactor

Helium coolant

Spherical uranium fuel particles arranged in ball or prisms

Response time in a serious acident: Eight hours

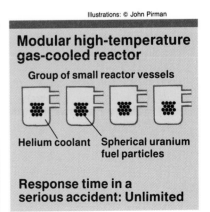

Modular high-temperature gas-cooled reactor

Group of small reactor vessels

Helium coolant   Spherical uranium fuel particles

Response time in a serious acident: Unlimited

cially viable.'' The Electric Power Research Institute (EPRI) in Palo Alto, California, a utility-supported group, is putting most of its money for advanced reactor research into the familiar water-cooled workhorse. The reason, says Karl Stahlkopf, who runs the effort, is that ''we know where the devils are.''

Prolonged Breathing Spells

Devils aplenty have been cast out of an improved water-cooled reactor design jointly developed by GE, Hitachi, and Toshiba. Tokyo Electric Power Company has signed up for two units, and construction will begin in the early 1990s. Westinghouse, which is also working on an advanced model with Japanese partners, hopes to announce an order before long. Nothing radical is planned in either case—only a host of evolutionary refinements in controls, pumps, and other equipment that cut the chances for trouble.

The big leap in safety would come with compact new versions on the drawing boards at Westinghouse, GE, Combustion Engineering, and Babcock & Wilcox, a subsidiary of McDermott Inc. During the 1960s and 1970s, reactors kept getting bigger, reaching a maximum capacity of 1,400 megawatts, enough to power a city of 700,000. The Westinghouse model AP600—the letters stand for ''advanced, passive,'' and the capacity is 600 megawatts—is a more appropriate size for an era when utilities expect to grow in smaller increments.

The AP600 is a far more easygoing design than today's reactors. Fuel and water temperatures would both be lowered, reducing the concentration of heat that must be removed if there is an accident. When present reactors lose their coolant, pumps powered by emergency diesel generators are supposed to keep the core covered with water from an external tank. The AP600 would be safe even if the diesels failed to kick on. The reactor would sit directly beneath tanks containing a total of 400,000 gallons (1.5 million liters) of water. In a severe accident, valves would open automatically from the change in pressure alone, and gravity would deliver a Niagara of emergency coolant.

The AP600 would offer a prolonged breathing spell. Even if everyone in the control room died and all power were cut off, the core would remain undamaged for 72 hours. Richard Slember, general manager of Westinghouse's energy systems unit, says that three days is only the minimum expectation: ''Some of our engineers think we could go forever.'' The containment building, in fact, would be designed so that natural air circulation around the walls would prevent later overheating. After several weeks the temperature of a crippled reactor tapers off to a less worrisome level.

Gas-cooled Reactors

Every design mentioned so far has one limitation. The fuel core, whether cooled by liquid sodium or water, must be kept covered to prevent damage. Something could go awry: those passive valves just might not open as they should. In the end the builders must fall back on probability calculations showing that the passive safeguards are virtually certain to work—a proposition that may not impress critics.

Enter the gas-cooled reactor. Depending on the type, its core can survive without coolant for periods ranging from hours to eternity. That is a mighty arresting fact. But like Shi'ite and Sunni Muslims, executives in the nuclear industry and the utilities are sharply divided over whether gas-cooled reactors are ready to play a big role in cranking out kilowatts. To nuclear engineer Lawrence Lidsky, who runs gas-cooled reactor research at MIT, the issue is already settled. ''The water-cooled reactor in any incarnation,'' Lidsky says, ''is inherently an exceedingly complex, unforgiving device.'' The U.S. embraced it prematurely and sidetracked other reactor concepts, says Lidsky and others in the gas-cooled gang, because it was a spin-off from the nuclear Navy.

Such talk infuriates the water-cooled crowd, which worries that enthusiasm for the gas-cooled reactor could divert energies from improving their baby. Gas-cooled reactors will have their place early in the next century, says EPRI's Stahlkopf. But only advanced water reactors will be ready within 10 years, when the country will need more kilowatts.

Nonsense, counter companies working on the gas-cooled concept. Among them is General Atomics of San Diego, California, once controlled by Chevron but in private hands since 1986. General Atomics has more than two decades' experience with gas reactors. Other players include West Germany's Siemens, which also builds water-cooled reactors, and HRB, a German company that designs the gas-cooled type. The Soviet Union is getting interested in gas-cooled technology, and the Japanese Government is weighing a proposal to build a $690 million research reactor.

Water treated with neutron-absorbing boric acid cools spent fuel rods and contains their radioactivity (above). The rods sometimes remain in the pools for years. To meet stringent safety codes, nuclear power plants undergo almost continuous maintenance (below).

Gas-cooled reactors use radically different fuel elements, which hold in enormous amounts of radioactivity at the source. By an automated process, General Atomics and HRB coat spheres of uranium fuel, no larger than grains of sand, with multiple layers of ceramic materials to a diameter of 0.04 inch (1 millimeter). The most heat-resistant and radiation-proof material is silicon carbide. The coatings perform the same containment role as that giant concrete structure at TMI.

The ceramic layers cannot melt, although ultimately they vaporize. Not until the particles reach a temperature of 3,300° F (1,815° C)—well above the level encountered when a reactor suddenly loses all coolant—does some radioactivity begin to leak out. The particles are clustered by tens of thousands in graphite fuel elements. General Atomics packs them into hexagonal prisms 4 feet (1.2 meters) high; the Germans embed them in ''pebbles'' the size of billiard balls.

Hardly anyone disputes the inherent safety of gas-cooled reactors. The big issues are their reliability and competitiveness. Britain and France together built dozens of them in the 1950s and 1960s, and they ran fine. But because they were cooled with carbon dioxide, effi-

© Bob Mahoney/Picture Group

Nuclear power plants use specially designed, remote-control robots to survey radiation-contaminated areas.

ciency was low; the plants converted only 28 percent of the heat from the chain reaction to electricity. France long ago switched to water-cooled reactors, which achieve efficiencies of around 34 percent, and Britain later followed.

Cooling with Helium

Helium-cooled gas reactors do even better. The U.S., West Germany, and Britain built experimental helium reactors in the 1960s. At the time the attraction was not safety but the high temperatures that are achieved, useful both in power generation and in such industrial processes as chemical manufacturing and coal gasification. All three reactors performed well; the West German one is still chugging away. By the mid-1970s, General Atomics had orders from utilities for 10 commercial-size plants.

Then a series of setbacks nearly killed off the helium reactor. When energy conservation hit, utilities canceled nine of the orders. The only commercial helium reactor in the U.S.— Public Service Co. of Colorado's 330-megawatt plant at Fort St. Vrain, within view of the Rocky Mountains near Denver—flopped economically. The fuel has performed splendidly as a containment device since the plant went into service in 1974. Because radiation within the plant is extremely low, a recent visitor was allowed to walk on top of the concrete-shelled reactor when it was at 80 percent power without the usual safety suit or dosimeter (a device used to measure radioactivity).

A design flaw unrelated to safety has played hob with operations. In other gas-cooled units, the circulators that keep helium moving in and out of the reactor are lubricated with oil. The Colorado circulators use water. From time to time, water leaks into the reactor, and the plant must be shut down to remove it. Though the reactor is up and running much of the time, the utility took a $101 million after-tax hit in 1986 and wrote off most of its investment.

If the tale stopped there, gas-cooled reactors might rate a place among technology's also-rans. But in the past year, the outlook has brightened.

A motorist speeding down the Autobahn near Hamm, northeast of West Germany's Ruhr region, cannot miss the high cooling tower of the world's only other big helium reactor. The 300-megawatt facility, unromantically known as the THTR—an abbreviation for thorium high-temperature reactor—is on-line and performing satisfactorily.

No water woes here. The reactor, using traditional oil-lubricated circulators, first generated current at 100 percent of capacity in September 1986. In the past 19 months, it has run at full power roughly two-thirds of the time, converting heat to electricity at an impressive 41 percent efficiency. Klaus Knizia, who heads one of the utilities that owns it, told a recent nuclear conference: "As a prototype, the reactor has lived up to expectations. We are confident that it will prove to be reliable." HRB says it is ready to build a 550-megawatt model that would have generating costs comparable to those of large water-cooled reactors.

The Hamm reactor's neighbors can sleep soundly. Martin Heske, a nuclear engineer who works at the plant, says that in the worst conceivable accident, all devices for removing heat from the core would conk out. In that event, it would take eight hours before the fuel heated up to 3,600° F (1,980° C). The resulting radioactivity would be so small that the authorities would not require the local population to evacuate, Heske says, but locally grown lettuce and other vegetables might become unsafe to eat.

By shrinking a gas-cooled reactor, designers can offer a grace period without limit. Both General Atomics and its West German collaborators are pitching modular reactors as the ultimate in atomic safety. In the American design,

The disposal of hazardous wastes remains one of the most controversial aspects of the nuclear power industry.

four 135-megawatt modules, each in an individual below-ground concrete silo, would make up a unit with a total capacity of 540 megawatts. The reactor vessels would be 22 feet (6.7 meters) in diameter—just small enough so the ground can absorb sufficient heat to prevent fuel damage in a serious mishap.

"We get our safety from abject simplicity," says Linden Blue, one of two brothers who own General Atomics. "The fuel temperature in the core can never exceed 2,900° F (1,600° C)." In the worst accident, studies by General Atomics conclude, people living right at the plant fence would pick up a trivial dose of radioactivity—less than air passengers, for example, get from natural sources on a round trip from coast to coast.

Economic Competitiveness

Pretty heady stuff, all right, concedes the water-cooled faction. But what are the economics? Why rush to the modular reactor when no successful prototype exists? Gas Cooled Reactor Associates, an organization supported by utilities with about a third of U.S. generating capacity, has looked into the competitiveness question. Big sections of the modules, it says, could

be built efficiently in factories and shipped to the silos. The organization's study claims a four-module nuke could produce power 10 percent cheaper than a coal-fired plant.

A four-module prototype could cost $1.5 billion to $1.7 billion to build. Utilities that would sell the power could raise about two-thirds of the amount, General Atomics says. But they probably could not come up with the rest—the heavy additional costs in a first-of-a-kind undertaking. To make up most of the gap, lobbyists for the gas-cooled reactor cause are looking to the Department of Energy (DOE), which until now has been less enthusiastic about the idea than some congressmen.

In the hot new design race, both gas-cooled and water-cooled models may survive and coexist. For buyers, the choice will come down to a trade-off between radiation risk and business risk—between a proven performer with a smidgen of worry and an even safer design still in its youth. The power may be no bonanza in either case. But kilowatts from coal and oil will probably be just as costly. And new worries about the greenhouse effect are turning fossil-fuel plants into bad guys just when nuclear power is poking its nose out of the doghouse.

HYDROGEN: *Fuel of the Future?*

by Peter Hoffmann

To a small band of determined advocates, the idea of a "hydrogen economy" has been a dream. After all, hydrogen is one of the most abundant chemical elements in the world. And as a fuel, it is completely nonpolluting: burn it, and all you get is lots of energy and a little bit of steam. There's one big problem, though. Most of the world's hydrogen is tied up with oxygen in the form of water. Splitting those molecules to obtain hydrogen takes as much energy as it releases as fuel.

So only a handful of researchers have led the search for economical ways to produce hydrogen. But that was before warnings that carbon dioxide produced from burning fossil fuels was probably responsible for the greenhouse effect, a devastating global warming. The hydrogen economy could beat that problem by using nonfossil energy, such as solar, to extract a pollution-free, transportable fuel from water. Suddenly, eager scientists are betting on hydrogen. "Sometime in the 21st century, hydrogen will be a major part of our energy infrastructure," predicts James R. Birk, a research director at Electric Power Research Institute (EPRI) in Palo Alto, California.

Power Surge

The utilities haven't made statements like that since the energy crisis of the 1970s, when almost any alternative fuel was in vogue. But

Hydrogen may be tomorrow's source of abundant, nonpolluting energy. Already, the space shuttle uses energy from fuel cells that produce electricity from hydrogen.

now EPRI, the research arm of the industry, has even hosted a conference on hydrogen. A number of projects to demonstrate hydrogen's potential are under way—from using solar energy to produce hydrogen in Saudi Arabia to powering airplanes in the Soviet Union and electrifying homes in the United States.

That new interest doesn't mean hydrogen will fuel the family car—or the local utility—anytime soon. It still faces the technological stumbling blocks that have dogged it all along—how to make it cheaply and store it efficiently. But if the researchers tackling those problems succeed, hydrogen could help reduce the amount of fossil fuels the world burns.

Indeed, there aren't many places where hydrogen couldn't be used. In its liquid form, highly flammable hydrogen is already a staple fuel for rockets, and, handled carefully, can be burned just as easily in land-based vehicles and aircraft. During the energy crisis, utilities experimented with fuel cells, which produce electricity directly from a chemical reaction—no heat—for backup power. Smaller versions can generate power for factories, homes, or even electric vehicles.

Fueling the researchers' faith in converting water to an economical source of energy is the steady climb of solar-cell efficiencies. Just four years ago, commercial cells based on amorphous silicon could convert less than 5 percent of the sunlight that struck them to electricity. Now cells with efficiencies of 7 percent are on the market, and laboratory versions are approaching 15 percent. Such cells, if located in the Southwest, could split water into hydrogen that could be delivered to fuel pumps for the equivalent cost of $1.55 to $2.00 per gallon of gasoline, predict Joan M. Ogden and Robert H. Williams of Princeton University's Center for Energy and Environmental Studies.

Unfortunately, it would take a lot of solar power to make a dent in the amount of fuel required by U.S. vehicles. EPRI's Birk figures that would require 400,000 megawatts of electricity—two-thirds of the nation's present capacity. The Princeton scientists estimate that the job would entail covering a 24,000-square-mile (62,000-square-kilometer) area in solar cells.

Solar cells are not the only way to generate electricity without pollution, however. Canada's Hydro Quebec, with its enormous hydroelectric facility on James Bay, for years has recognized the potential for using its off-peak power to make transportable hydrogen. Now it may have a customer. The utility and the European Community (EC) may spend $3.4 million to study making hydrogen in Canada for export to Europe.

Algae and Bugs

Some organisms, too, can extract hydrogen from the water. At Oak Ridge National Laboratory (ORNL), a group led by Elias Greenbaum is harnessing the photosynthetic talents of green algae. Greenbaum has reported light-to-hydrogen conversion efficiencies of up to 10 percent—as good as many solar cells. Greenbaum thinks he can hike efficiency levels enough to make large-scale hydrogen-producing ponds economical.

At Texas A&M University, researcher Nigel Packham is setting loose carefully chosen bacteria in fermentation tanks to munch on waste vegetable matter. Packham thinks that within a decade he will be able to make hydrogen even more cheaply than with solar cells.

Still, making hydrogen is just part of the problem. To compete with other fuels, storage must become more efficient, too. A light gas in its natural state, hydrogen is costly to compress and liquefy. So most researchers are experi-

Most of the world's hydrogen is tied up with oxygen in the form of water. Scientists at the Oak Ridge National Laboratory have found that green algae placed in an atmosphere of pure helium will use the energy of sunlight to separate hydrogen from water molecules.

© Kelly Scott Walli/The Oak Ridger

A LIFT FOR HYDROGEN

In his gray suit and overcoat, Aleksei A. Tupolev looks like the model of a courtly Old World banker. But to his audience at the recent 7th World Hydrogen Energy Conference in Moscow, Tupolev seemed more like the Christopher Columbus of the coming alternative energy age.

At Moscow's flashy new Center for International Trade, aviator-designer Tupolev described the history-making flight in April 1988 of a triple-engine commercial jet airliner that was partially powered by liquid hydrogen. For the first time since sketchy Soviet press reports of the flight, Tupolev confirmed that the right-side engine of his modified TU-155 commercial jet ran on hydrogen during its entire 21-minute flight.

That fact is important to hydrogen and aviation specialists in the West, who recall that a twin-engine American B-57 Air Force bomber also flew partially on liquid hydrogen some 30 years ago. The engine, however, used hydrogen for periods of only 20 minutes or so during the flight.

The West is still interested in hydrogen-powered aircraft. In the early 1980s, Lockheed Corporation tried to interest some Western governments in building a hydrogen-fueled commercial aircraft. That failed, but now the U.S. Defense Department's National Aerospace plane project, which would fly from a runway into space, is being designed to run on hydrogen. The Air Force will soon decide whether to go ahead with the $3.5 billion project.

Any plane powered by hydrogen will require special safety features. In Tupolev's plane the liquid hydrogen is carried in a stainless-steel tank, which takes up most of the rear passenger compartment. To cut the risk of explosions, electrical wires were spark-proofed, and hydraulic and conventional fuel lines were relocated.

Safety concerns make it unlikely that passenger aircraft will be fueled by hydrogen. But the rockets that launch both the U.S. and Soviet space shuttle use hydrogen. And, with Tupolev's experiment, the Soviets may have gained the high ground in the race to build a self-propelled spaceplane.

menting with metallic alloys that sop up hydrogen and release it when warmed. But these so-called hydrides can hold only 1 percent of their weight in hydrogen.

While that's all right for running utility fuel cells, it's not so hot for vehicles. Daimler-Benz, which is testing hydrogen-powered cars, says the performance of its retrofitted vehicles has suffered 20 to 25 percent. That's because the container needed to give the vehicles a range of 100 miles (160 kilometers) on a tankful of hydrogen adds 615 pounds (280 kilograms)—and lots of wear and tear—to each vehicle.

Help could come from Japan. Seijirau Suda, a professor at Tokyo's Kokugakuin University and one of the world's leading hydride researchers, thinks an international research group he formed last fall can triple storage efficiency to 3 percent by weight within three years.

And he is trying a type of hydride based on magnesium that has up to six times the storage capacity of other materials.

Despite the hurdles, some big hydrogen projects are on the drawing boards. Interest is especially high in West Germany. There industry and government spend an estimated $200 million per year on hydrogen research, and this spring a Research and Technology Ministry commission recommended spending an additional $555 million by 1992.

The Vapor Belt

Clearly, one reason for West Germany's enthusiasm is concern for its environment. German forests have been ravaged by acid rain, yet the country's alternatives to fossil energy are limited. The 1986 accident at the Soviet Union's Chernobyl nuclear plant hardened public oppo-

HYDROGEN AT WORK

• Daimler-Benz and BMW have tested cars fueled by hydrogen; Daimler is now considering buses. The Soviets have been testing vans, automobiles, and a forklift truck.

• The Soviet Union has flown a jet fueled partly by hydrogen. In the United States, the Defense Advanced Research Projects Agency (DARPA), the National Aeronautics and Space Administration (NASA), and the Air Force are developing a single-stage, earth-to-orbit plane that would use hydrogen.

• Large fuel cells, in which a chemical reaction produces electricity as hydrogen and oxygen recombine, have been tested as backup power for utilities in New York City and Tokyo.

• Dow Chemical and Canada's Ballard Technologies will test a fuel cell to power electric cars. Elenco, a joint venture of the Belgian Nuclear Assn. and Dutch State Mines, is developing an electrical bus.

• Three German companies—Ingenieur Kontor Luebeck, Howaldtswerke Deutsche Werft, and Ferrostaal—are conducting sea trials of a superquiet submarine that is powered by a fuel-cell system built by Siemens.

• Germany's Frauenhofer Institute for Solar Energy Systems and Chronar Corporation in the United States are developing self-contained hydrogen systems for homes and buildings. They consist of solar panels to produce the hydrogen and storage systems to hold it. The fuel can then be used directly for heat or cooking and in fuel cells to produce electricity.

such a scheme, the German and Saudi Arabian governments plan to build a 350-kilowatt solar plant that would make hydrogen near Riyadh. In Bavaria a government-backed consortium that includes BMW, Messerschmitt-Bolkow-Blohm, and Siemens plans a $27 million, 500-kilowatt solar hydrogen plant.

The U.S., however, is not so gung ho. The Department of Energy (DOE) spent a mere $3 million last year on hydrogen research, and even that is a decline from $3.8 million in 1984. "There is a terrible tendency in the U.S. to take the short-term view," says John Appleby, director of the Center for Electrochemical Systems and Hydrogen Research at Texas A&M. But if the greenhouse effect keeps the heat on, even the U.S. Government may find itself agreeing with a growing number of hydrogen optimists.

Photos below: © Mercedes-Benz; facing page: © Tass from Sovfoto

At Daimler-Benz, hydrogen-fueled cars need a 615-pound tank to hold enough fuel for a 100-mile trip. The added weight greatly reduces performance. As a vehicular fuel, hydrogen will more likely find use in buses and trucks.

sition to nuclear power, and Germany's northern climate doesn't lend itself to large-scale solar-energy development. "If you want solar energy, you have to import it," says Carl-Jochen Winter, an official at Germany's aerospace agency. "You need an energy carrier—and that's hydrogen."

Already Germany is testing that idea. German researchers envision solar plants in sun-rich countries in the Middle East or North Africa producing hydrogen that can be moved north by pipeline, truck, or ship. To test the viability of

© David Walberg/*Time* Magazine

CONSERVATION COMES OF AGE

by Christopher Flavin and Alan Durning

When the Ford Foundation completed a landmark study in 1974 of energy needs in the United States, it presented a sobering vision of the future. Even in the most optimistic scenario, the nation's energy use was predicted to rise by almost 20 percent by 1987.

Since that report was published, however, U.S. energy use has actually fallen, even though the economy has expanded by more than 35 percent. Most of the other market-oriented industrial economies of North America, Western Europe, and the Far East have also become more efficient. Australia and Canada improved by 6 percent since 1974, for example, while Japan improved by 31 percent, a remarkable gain since it already had one of the world's most efficient economies in 1974.

The savings from energy conservation around the globe now total $250 billion annually—the cost of the oil, gas, coal, and nuclear energy that is no longer needed each year. Clearly, consumers, companies, and nations have realized that energy efficiency is one of the best buys in town.

Besides saving money, energy efficiency can lessen the world's dependence on Middle East oil and ease tension in the Persian Gulf. It can lessen acid rain, which is wreaking destruction on the forests of central Europe. It can reduce rising carbon dioxide levels that may be the harbingers of catastrophic climate change.

But not all countries have been successful in using energy more efficiently. While data for centrally planned countries are difficult to obtain, available evidence indicates that these nations are lagging behind. The Soviet Union has not bettered its record since the early 1970s, and remains the world's least energy-efficient industrial economy.

The rising cost and dwindling supply of energy have spurred development of energy-efficient technologies. In the steel industry, oxygen-fired furnaces can change molten iron into steel in 45 minutes, a job that takes traditional open-hearth furnaces 8 hours and twice the energy.

An energy-efficiency gap has also opened among developing nations. Newly industrializing economies—such as Taiwan, South Korea, and Brazil—have begun to incorporate state-of-the-art industrial machines and processes. But most of the Third World is lagging farther and farther behind. Many nations are still going through the early, energy-intensive phases of industrialization and are subsidizing energy prices. As a result, imported oil continues to place a heavy burden on foreign exchange, and the lack of progress in improving efficiency will make it increasingly difficult for these countries to compete in international markets.

International economic competitiveness is not just an issue for the Third World. In 1986 the United States used 10 percent of its gross national product to pay the national fuel bill, compared to only 4 percent for Japan. Relative to Japan, the United States is effectively paying a $200 billion energy-inefficiency tax each year, making its economy less competitive. Some experts worry that the current pace of conservation is too slow to prevent potentially disastrous climate change.

Still, the United States has made a tremendous improvement in the past 15 years. In addition, the changes have been remarkably unobtrusive, caused by subtle shifts in the economy and by technological improvements, rather than by dramatic life-style changes such as buying tiny cars. A new American office building, for example, has about the same lighting levels and temperatures as older ones, but uses less than half as much electricity. Even large luxury cars now get 20 to 25 miles per gallon.

The main reason that efficiency has come so easily is that higher energy prices have spurred engineers, managers, and consumers to use better technologies. Some governments have helped speed the process. The United States has enacted efficiency standards for buildings, appliances, and automobiles. In addition, tax credits and subsidies are available, and new institutions have been created to open new avenues of investment. Some utilities, for example, are now being rewarded by regulators for putting money into the efficiency of their customers' buildings.

No country, however, has even begun to tap the full potential for further improvements. Because of technologies now coming on the market, efficiency gains of at least 50 percent compared to current levels are available in every sector of the economy.

Home and Office

One example is buildings. Winston Churchill once said, "We shape our buildings and afterwards our buildings shape us." Churchill understood that we have become an indoor breed, spending most of our lives inside walls we have built. We now also spend a substantial share of our resources to heat, cool, and light buildings. In 1985 buildings in the combined industrial-market economies used the equivalent of 16.7 million barrels of oil per day—almost as much as the entire production of the Organization of Petroleum Exporting Countries (OPEC).

The typical building in these countries uses 25 percent less energy than it did in 1973, saving the equivalent of 3.8 million barrels of oil every day—more than the output of the North Sea. But these gains pale beside what is possible. The technology now exists to construct buildings that use one-third to one-tenth as much energy as today's structures.

While retrofitting existing buildings with insulation and other conservation measures typically cuts energy consumption by one-quarter, the biggest potential for gains comes from new structures. The average U.S. home now consumes 160 kilojoules of heating energy per square meter of floor space per degree-day. By contrast, new Swedish houses use just 65. Recently built superefficient homes in Minnesota use an average of 51 kilojoules, and some individual units in Sweden go as low as 18.

These savings result from superinsulation—doubling the normal insulation and building an airtight liner into the walls. Superinsulated houses are so airtight that they require mechanical ventilation to remove indoor air pollutants. Heat radiating from people, stoves, and appliances warms the houses, requiring little auxiliary heating. Superinsulation adds about 5 percent to building costs, but the energy savings usually pay for the extra expense in about five years.

There are now more than 20,000 superinsulated homes in North America, with perhaps 5,000 more built every year. But they represent less than 1 percent of new-housing construction. Home buyers tend to discount long-term costs like energy, so builders put their efforts into cosmetic selling points, rather than efficiency. As one housing expert explains, when American home buyers must choose between better insulation and luxuries like a Jacuzzi whirlpool bath, "the Jacuzzi wins out most of the time."

Offices, hospitals, and other commercial buildings also offer considerable room for improvement. Sweden now requires that all new structures use less than 1.0 kilojoule per square meter of floor space per year. If all U.S. commercial buildings were that efficient, our energy consumption would be 9 percent lower.

The most important feature of efficient new commercial buildings is "intelligence." These "smart" buildings monitor outdoor and indoor temperatures, sunlight, and the location of people—sending heat, cooled air, and light only where they are needed. Analysts calculate that air-conditioning bills could be cut in half just by using air conditioners that measure temperatures outside and then ventilate rather than cool whenever possible.

Other efficiency gains, for both commercial and residential buildings, come from improved windows. As much energy now leaks

A well-insulated building requires much less energy to heat during the winter and cool during the summer.

© Billy E. Barnes/Stock, Boston

through American windows every year as flows through the Alaskan pipeline. By adding a special "heat mirror" film that lets in light without letting out heat, for example, a window's insulation value can be doubled. Advanced technologies that may be economical in the 1990s could give windows the same insulation value as ordinary walls.

Appliances are a potential source of savings. The average refrigerator in American homes now consumes 1,500 kilowatt-hours of electricity every year. But a model currently on the market, a Whirlpool, uses only 750. And yet this is only the beginning. A Danish prototype consumes 530, and one study suggests that the number could cost-effectively drop to as low as 200 kilowatt-hours per year.

Heating and cooling technologies can also be made far more efficient. Conventional gas furnaces, for instance, send a quarter of their heat up the chimney. But new condensing furnaces reabsorb much of that heat by cooling and condensing exhaust gases. They cut fuel use by 28 percent, reduce air pollution, and make chimneys obsolete, requiring only small exhaust vents.

Lighting, which consumes about 20 percent of U.S. electricity, offers some of the largest and most economical savings now available. Perhaps 40 large U.S. power plants could be given early retirement simply by switching to currently available—and cost-effective—lighting technology. Compact, screw-in fluorescent bulbs, for example, are more than four times as efficient as traditional incandescent ones—and last ten times as long. Furthermore, every improvement in lighting efficiency reduces heat production and therefore saves on air-conditioning. The California Energy Commission calculates that in Fresno, every 100-watt savings on lighting means an additional 38-watt savings on air-conditioning.

If the industrial-market economies have yet to tap all of the potential of energy conservation, the rest of the world lags even further behind. In Eastern Europe and the Soviet Union, buildings tend to be leaky and poorly insulated. In developing countries, structures present starkly different images. In the countryside, buildings are spartan, and fuelwood is the dominant energy source. Because fuelwood use is so inefficient, total energy consumption measured in units of heat is high.

Cities across the Third World house the swelling urban underclass, which inefficiently

Today's office buildings maintain the lighting levels of 15 years ago while using only half as much electricity.

uses fuelwood, charcoal, or more expensive fuels. Meanwhile, members of a relatively wealthy elite consume energy with the same—or more—profligacy as their industrial-country counterparts. For this modern sector, which takes the bulk of national commercial energy, high-efficiency technologies are crucial. Indeed, better air conditioners make even more sense in Manila than in Manhattan.

Miserly Automobiles

Although buildings consume large amounts of energy, transportation ranks as the largest and most rapidly growing drain on the world's oil reserves. Transportation burns fully 63 percent of the oil consumed in the United States, more than the country itself produces. Worse, much of the world appears set on replicating this unhealthy condition. Already passenger cars around the world consume one of every six barrels of oil produced. Meanwhile, the burning of fossil fuels to move people and cargo releases more than 700 million tons (635 million metric tons) of carbon into the atmosphere annually,

contributing to a possible greenhouse effect. In fact, the average American car pumps its own weight in carbon into the atmosphere each year.

The major problem is overreliance on the automobile. Young, rapidly growing cities, especially those in developing countries, have the opportunity to plan for enormous energy savings early on by designing residential and work areas that do not require people to travel long distances by car. But even mature cities can save energy by reducing dependence on the automobile. Van pools, buses, and railroads, for example, require a quarter as much fuel to move each passenger as private cars or airplanes do. Railways and ships, meanwhile, use less than a third as much fuel as trucks to move freight. Only when walking, bicycling, and using public transit become the norm in the world's major urban centers can oil dependence be cut substantially.

Some gains, however, can be made by improving the average fuel efficiency of cars. New American automobiles have nearly dou-

The plastic body panels, aluminum parts, aerodynamic design, and lean-burning engine of the Honda CRX HF (above) deliver a gas mileage of over 50 miles per gallon. A Whirlpool refrigerator now on the market (left) consumes only half as much electricity as the average refrigerator.

bled their fuel economy since 1973, but still have not closed the efficiency gap with Europe and Japan.

These countries have produced several innovative, fuel-efficient models that are already on the road. The sporty two-seat Honda CRX HF, for example, uses plastic body panels and aluminum parts to save weight, good aerodynamics to cut wind drag, and a special lean-burning engine. It gets over 50 miles per gallon (mpg). Subaru has replaced the standard gearbox entirely on one of its models, opting instead for a continuously variable transmission (CVT). In CVTs a belt transfers engine power to the drive shaft as it runs around two adjustable pulleys, giving the car an unlimited number of gears and allowing the engine to run at a rela-

tively constant, more efficient speed. Subaru found that this technology improved fuel efficiency by at least 20 percent over a three-speed automatic transmission.

Even more exciting innovations are under development. Toyota's prototype AXV is one standout, combining an advanced diesel engine with a continuously variable transmission. The car is spacious enough to accommodate an entire family—a remarkable achievement considering that its estimated fuel economy is an astounding 98 mpg.

Although some efficiency technologies appear expensive, the resulting vehicles may cost little more than today's models. If fuel-economy innovations were fully integrated into the normal cycle of turnover in plant and equipment, it would cost an additional $59 to $90 to bring most U.S. cars into the 38- to 53-mpg range by 1990. By the year 2000, cars could average 51 to 78 mpg for an additional $120 to $330 apiece (in 1980 dollars)—less than the price of a good car stereo.

Despite this modest cost, however, market forces alone are unlikely to boost efficiency enough to head off growing oil dependence and greenhouse warming. Although the cost of saving gasoline is far below the cost of buying it, car buyers seem not to care about fuel economy once it is above a certain threshold. As a result, society's interests require policies such as standards and consumer incentives to continue to push fuel economy up.

Industry's Gains

While government involvement may be needed to reduce fuel use in transportation, it is less crucial for industry, where increased efficiency often means higher profits. In fact, industry has led the way in improving energy efficiency during the past 15 years. Overall, the energy intensity of the industrial sector in countries belonging to the Organization for Economic Cooperation and Development (OECD) has fallen a remarkable 30 percent since 1973. In particular, Denmark and Japan made unprecedented gains, with 7 percent annual savings between 1979 and 1984. In the United States, industrial energy use in 1986 was actually 17 percent lower than in 1973, despite a 17 percent increase in production.

Physicist Marc Ross of the University of Michigan believes that the gains in the United States have two causes. About 45 percent is attributable to a shift towards less energy-intensive materials and goods. For example, production of steel and cement has fallen, while electronic gadgets proliferate. In addition, many energy-intensive raw materials are now imported from other countries. The other 55 percent can be traced to more-efficient equipment and processes.

Industry's use of oil has fallen particularly rapidly; almost half the oil consumed now serves as raw material for products rather than as fuel.

But even after these advances, industry still uses 37 percent of the total energy supply of the industrial-market economies, and as much as 60 to 70 percent in many developing nations. In addition, North American industry is still much more energy-intensive than the industries of Europe and Japan, and recent declines in oil prices may lull some industries into complacency, delaying additional improvements.

A few widely used technologies hold immense potential for savings. In the United States, 95 percent of industrial electricity goes for electromechanical drives, electrolysis, and heating—all of which can be made more efficient. The Electric Power Research Institute estimates that simply adding variable-speed controls to many electric devices is enough to offset the added energy that will be used by all the new electricity-using industrial technologies projected to be introduced by the year 2000.

Major energy savings are also being made in the production of chemicals, the cement industry, and the steel industry. In industrial countries, for example, traditional open-hearth steel furnaces have largely been replaced by more-efficient basic-oxygen furnaces and electric-arc furnaces that recycle scrap steel and cut energy needs by half.

In 1988, the United States imported more than 3 million barrels of oil per day, a 45 percent increase in just three years. Many of the new "efficiency technologies" aim at reducing our dependence on foreign energy sources.

© Martin Rogers/Stock, Boston

Cogeneration

One of the greatest opportunities to improve industrial energy efficiency lies in cogeneration. By installing a small boiler and electric generator within a plant, a company can produce electricity by using heat that would normally be wasted.

Such systems are hardly a new idea; they were widely used early in the century, but most of them were abandoned in the rush to build central electricity-generating plants. In the United States, cogeneration reached a low of 10,475 megawatts in 1979; in Europe, it is still widely used in urban-district heating systems. Denmark has required since 1972 that all new power facilities include cogeneration.

In the past decade, however, industrial cogeneration has grown explosively in the United States. The reason is the Public Utility Regulatory Policies Act of 1978, which allows industry to sell power to utilities at a fair market price. More than 47,000 megawatts of cogeneration—with as much generating capacity as 47 large nuclear plants—were registered with the Federal Energy Regulatory Commission as of October 1, 1987. Some of the largest users include the oil industry, which taps such systems to produce steam for enhanced oil recovery; the chemical industry, which can use petroleum by-products as fuel; the food-processing industry, which has large heat requirements; and the pulp and paper industry, which burns wood wastes.

In addition, the world's biggest industrial countries appear to be in the midst of a structural shift away from the processing of basic materials. Growing affluence, saturation of the market for energy-intensive materials, and the emergence of new high-technology products are helping to usher in this new era. And as a result, most industrial-market countries are unlikely to use as much energy for industry in the year 2000 as they did a quarter-century earlier.

What Lies Ahead?

The Club of Rome's 1972 warning that the world would run out of fuels and raw materials appears contradicted by the fact that the world today faces a glut rather than a shortage of fossil fuels. But that glut is itself a product of temporary shortages and soaring prices, which stimulated production and helped boost conservation. And the effects of energy use on the global environment may force us to set stringent limits on the burning of fossil fuels.

Investment in energy efficiency is the most effective response to a number of problems, for it simultaneously invests in lowered oil dependence, reduced air pollution, and climate protection. Doubling the fuel efficiency of a typical European car, to 50 mpg, lowers its annual fuel bill by almost $400; cuts emissions of nitrogen oxides, hydrocarbons, and carbon monoxide; and reduces carbon emissions by half, or 450 kilograms annually. A similar improvement for

Cogeneration plants recycle "waste" heat to generate energy. At Chevron Corporation's refinery in El Segundo, California, exhaust gas from huge electricity-producing turbines goes to a boiler where it heats water to produce steam. The steam provides the heat needed in many steps of the oil-refining process. Technicians monitor the entire process electronically.

Greater reliance on mass transportation could significantly reduce the vast amount of fuel used for automobiles.

the world as a whole would make a substantial contribution to climate protection.

Energy efficiency is also the best way for industrial countries to reduce their dependence on imported oil. In the United States, for example, the increase in the average fuel efficiency of automobiles—from 13.1 mpg in 1973 to 17.9 mpg in 1985—cut U.S. gasoline consumption by 20 billion gallons per year, lowering oil imports by 1.3 million barrels per day, two-thirds of the peak production from the rich oil fields of Alaska. The country could save another 1.9 million barrels per day by the year 2000 by raising new-automobile fuel efficiency to 45 mpg in 1995, according to a recent study by Deborah Bleviss of the International Institute for Energy Conservation.

Conserving energy will also reduce air pollution, and it is the most effective weapon against the ultimate environmental threat—climate change. Improving worldwide energy efficiency by 2 percent annually would keep the world's temperature within 2° F of current levels, avoiding such catastrophic effects as rising sea levels and dramatic shifts in the positions of the world's deserts and agricultural zones.

The investments needed to sustain a 2 percent rate of improvement in energy efficiency during the next decade or two can be justified on purely economic grounds. The world has al-

ready achieved an annual energy savings of more than $250 billion compared to 1973, mostly as a result of private investment decisions rather than government policies. Each additional 2 percent of savings would reduce bills by about $20 billion annually, but would cost only $5 billion to $10 billion to achieve.

The pace of energy conservation could be vastly increased if governments were to create more incentives to invest in efficiency. A joint commitment of the United States and the Soviet Union could help protect the climate from the greenhouse effect, for example, since together the two countries account for 42 percent of the carbon now entering the atmosphere.

The Third World is also critical to any long-term energy scenario. In these countries the challenge will be meeting the energy needs of the poor without repeating the mistakes of the rich. Only rapid advances in energy efficiency and a decentralized, agriculturally based development path can allow developing nations to combine improved living standards with limited energy supplies.

Achieving the full potential of energy efficiency will require a fundamental change in governments around the world. Energy policy must emerge from the obscure corners of energy ministries to become the centerpiece of national —and international—economic philosophy.

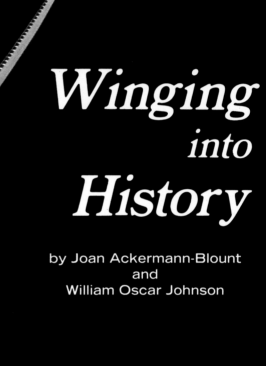

Winging *into* *History*

by Joan Ackermann-Blount
and
William Oscar Johnson

Three thousand, five hundred years ago, when the legendary inventor Daedalus took flight from imprisonment on the island of Crete, he flew on wings he had painstakingly made of low-grade wax and feathers scrounged from molting seabirds. It was all very low tech, very Greek, for he had only the old wax-and-feather technique to work with and knew nothing of high-modulus Thornel carbon fiber, polystyrene foam, Kevlar, and Mylar. He did not have information about a glycogen-replacing fluid that might sustain him during the exhausting wing-flapping exertions of flight. Nor did he have access to a flight simulator for preflight practice or any inkling of what his maximum aerobic capacity (VO2 max, for short) might be. Nor did Daedalus have assistance from physiologists, meteorologists, directors of flight operations, corporate sponsors, a Norwegian weather station, a dozen Massachusetts Institute of Technology (MIT) undergraduates, an MIT professor of aerodynamics, and a Yale professor of classics, to name a few. Operating nicely without all of this support, the mythological Daedalus flew over the Aegean Sea, although no one is sure how far he got from Crete or where he went or whether he landed safely.

Last year quite another kind of Daedalus—a frail, 70-pound (32-kilogram), man-powered aircraft, half-dragonfly and half-bicycle, that had taken 15,000 hours and $1 million to build and had benefited enormously from all of the techniques, technology, and technicians just listed—performed a historic flight, a magic merger of high tech and classic Greek heroism that thrilled the world.

At 7:06 A.M. on Saturday, April 23, 1988, the pink-and-silver pedal-driven ultralight craft called Daedalus 88 was propelled down the runway of a military airfield in Iráklion, Crete's largest city, assistants running alongside to support the wings until the plane was airborne. It was bound for the volcanic island of Santorin 74 miles (120 kilometers) away. The pilot and the power of the plane was a suitably godlike Greek athlete, Kanellos Kanellopoulos, 31, an iron-muscled local hero who has won 14 Greek national cycling championships. His job was to keep Daedalus 88 aloft by endlessly pumping pedals that powered a drivetrain through two

gearboxes, which, in turn, kept an 11-foot (3.3-meter) polystyrene foam propeller whirling.

Kanellopoulos and the 35-member support operation, which included four other pilots and two extra planes, had been hung up on Crete for three weeks waiting for optimum—and very rare—weather conditions: calm seas, southerly winds of three knots or less, temperatures under 70° F (21° C), and visibility to the horizon. As it turned out, the weather came up beyond anyone's wildest dreams. Moving steadily, and at times almost swiftly, on energy produced by Kanellopoulos' churning legs—as well as by a lovely, blessed tail wind that got up to 10 knots—Daedalus 88 floated gallantly along 30 to 50 feet (9 to 15 meters) above the surface of Homer's wine-dark sea. A flotilla of Greek Navy and Coast Guard vessels, spectator boats, and motorized rubber rafts ready to pick up the pilot should the fragile craft suddenly plunge into the water cruised below the silent plane. At one point the project's command boat asked the ever-pumping, ever-perspiring cyclist how he felt, and Kanellopoulos replied, "I feel well, cold and cool." Every 15 minutes he radioed reports on how much he was sweating and how much fluid he was drinking.

Triple-Record Setter

Daedalus 88 was designed to maintain an average speed of 15 miles (24 kilometers) per hour, but on this day the wind and Kanellopoulos combined to produce an average of 18.9 miles (30.4 kilometers) per hour. Thus, as the plane advanced closer and closer to the black sand of Santorin's Perissa Beach, it was clear that the trip was going to take far less time than anyone had anticipated. Technical experts on the project had estimated that the journey might take as long as six hours, but as Kanellopoulos got to within 33 feet (10 meters) of the beach, it was just 11:00 A.M.—a mere three hours and 54 minutes after takeoff. A crowd of 500 shouted and waved from the sand as the giant, insectlike aircraft—its wingspan is 112 feet (34 meters), which is 4 feet (1.2 meters) longer than that of a 727 jet—floated toward land. Then the cheers abruptly turned to cries of alarm.

A sudden head wind had come up, bringing the frail plane almost to a stall for a moment. Kanellopoulos banked until Daedalus 88 was parallel to the beach, but another gust battered the craft. To everyone's horror, the tail snapped off. Then both wings tilted upward, and the plane dropped into the sea.

Greek mythology came to life when the pedal-powered Daedalus flew from Crete to the island of Santorin.

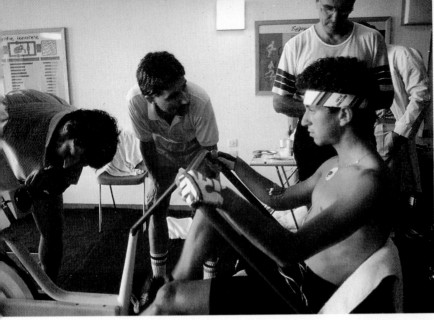

There was only an instant of anxiety for the fallen pilot. Kanellopoulos' sandy head bobbed up in the waves, and he swam almost casually to shore. He emerged streaming water and grinning brightly. When everything was added up, *Daedalus 88* and its Greek hero-pilot had set three records: (1) the 74-mile (120-kilometer) journey was the longest straight-line human-powered flight ever, beating the 22.3-mile (36-kilometer) crossing of the English Channel in 1979 by Bryan Allen in the *Gossamer Albatross;* (2) the trip broke the absolute distance record for human-powered flight set by fellow Daedalus Project member Glenn Tremml, 28, who used a *Daedalus 88* prototype called *Light Eagle* to fly 36.4 miles (58.5 kilometers) at Edwards Air Force Base in California in January 1987; (3) the trip broke the duration record for a human-powered flight. The old mark of two hours and 49 minutes had been set by Allen during his 1979 Channel crossing.

Triumphant Feat

The joyous, dripping Kanellopoulos told reporters and merrymakers at the beach, "This is a triumph for science, for man, and for history." Indeed, it was a triumph of organization and innovation that was worthy of a space shot, altogether a remarkable achievement. As Steve Bossolari, the MIT professor of aeronautics who was in charge of flight operations on Crete, put it, "The flight was an unparalleled combination of theoretical, computational, and experimental research in aerodynamic capabilities."

Suffice it to say that it was never simple. "We all used to build model airplanes and rock-

ets," says John Langford, program manager for Daedalus, one day in March 1988 as he is supervising some of the last testing stages of the venture. "The models just got bigger and bigger." Langford is sitting in his office at MIT's Lincoln Laboratory Flight Facility in Concord, Massa-

Kanellos Kanellopoulos, the winner of 14 Greek national cycling championships, pedaled the Daedalus for four grueling hours across the Aegean. Flying the Daedalus differed greatly from bicycle riding, however. The Daedalus pilot sat in a recumbent position that prevented the full leg extension typical of bike riding.

© Lane Stewart/Sports Illustrated

chusetts; the three clocks over his head are set for local time, California time, and Athens time. Downstairs in a hangar, a dozen engineers and helpers, who have been working night and day for months, are painstakingly piecing together *Daedalus 88.* Its twin craft, *Daedalus 87,* had recently been "tweaked" (that's MIT-speak for bent out of shape) in a crash on Rogers Dry Lake at Edwards Air Force Base in California, and would need more than a few "kluges" (MIT for repairs) before being transported along with two other ultralights to Crete late in March of 1988.

Langford, 30, who is on leave from the Institute for Defense Analysis in Alexandria, Virginia, led the construction of two human-powered planes when he was an undergraduate student at MIT. The first was called *Chrysalis.* The second, named *Monarch,* won first prize in the Royal Aeronautical Society's Kremer World Speed Competition in 1984. "I gave talks about the *Monarch,*" says Langford, "and people kept asking me what we were going to do next. I said that I thought we now had the technology to duplicate Daedalus' flight, and if anyone was interested in financing the project, he could sign up in the back of the room. It was kind of a joke, really."

The punch line turned out to be a three-year project with about $1 million worth of corporate funding, as well as moral and practical support from MIT, the Smithsonian, Yale, the National Aeronautics and Space Administration (NASA), and the government of Greece. The project was organized into a three-phased plan. Phase 1 was a feasibility study of the flight with research into aerodynamics, structures, meteorology, and physiology. Phase 2 was the building of a prototype, the *Light Eagle.* Phase 3 was the flight of *Daedalus 88* over the Aegean.

Technological Advances

What began as a whimsical flight of fancy afforded significant breakthroughs both in aeronautical technology and human physiology. To design and build the bike that flies, Langford called on some buddies from his undergraduate days: Mark Drela, an assistant professor of aeronautics at MIT who had a reputation for being able to test theoretical airfoils in the simulated wind tunnel of his mind; Harold (Guppie) Youngren, a senior aerodynamics engineer for Lockheed-California Company who had won a prestigious model-rocket competition in Bulgaria; Robert Parks, a senior research engineer at Lockheed Missiles & Space Company who built the gearboxes for the aircraft; and Juan Cruz, who quit his job at Beech Aircraft Corporation in Wichita, Kansas, and moved to Boston, bringing with him an invaluable knowledge of high-modulus graphite materials. "If you think of the structure as a bird," says Cruz, "my assignment was to design the bones. The pilot is the muscle. Mark's job was to design the feathers, the aerodynamics, and Guppie's was to make sure the bones fit inside the feathers."

However the plane was structured, the flight would demand an enormous effort from the pedaler-pilot—an effort that one of the project members predicted would be comparable to running two marathons back-to-back. "This is very different from anything," says Tremml, one of the pilots on the project. "You have to put out a constant amount of power. The power you're putting out the first minute is the same as the middle minute and the last minute."

"I think they're pushing the physical limits," says Greg Zack, another pilot, "but I wouldn't be here if I didn't think it could be done."

New structures formulated for the flight (in particular an airfoil with 30 percent less drag than those used on previous human-powered aircraft) and new materials (especially the new types of graphite-epoxy used in the plane's fuselage) were essential elements in the construction of a pedal-driven aircraft capable of flying record-breaking distances. The design of the craft was dictated by the amount of power its engine—the pilot, that is—could supply. His ability to provide the necessary power (3.1 watts per kilogram of pilot weight) for such a long period of time was made possible largely by a new glycogen-replacing beverage developed by Ethan Nadel, a physiologist at Yale. Nadel spent hours and hours testing and selecting the "engines" for the project. In essence, he was their mechanic.

Pilot Training

Each of the 200 or so men and women who applied for spots as pilots—most of whom responded to ads placed in cycling magazines—was given a VO2 max test to measure aerobic capacity and mechanical power production. If the candidate scored a high VO2 max, he or she underwent a second test on an ergometer, a stationary bike. The athlete was required to perform at 70 percent of aerobic capacity and power production for four grueling hours. This placed them at the outer limits of endurance performance research.

"Several physiologists were skeptical," says Nadel, who adds that elite athletes now routinely perform at levels beyond those conceivable only a few years ago. Ultimately five endurance athletes, including, of course, Kanellopoulos, went into final training for the flight. "We didn't know who would get to fly when conditions were right," says Tremml. "It was up to fate." Fate, a native of Greece, was kind to its nearest of kin: each of the pilots was con-

stantly in training, and each would be ready to fly when his turn came. Kanellopoulos was simply scheduled to fly on Saturday. He made the most of his opportunity.

Had Kanellopoulos not made it to Santorin, another plane and another pilot could have been called on. After all, the pilots had spent months in intensive training the likes of which no one had ever experienced. Zack, who had been racing bicycles in top-class national events for two years, had said, "The flight of the *Daedalus* will be like an intense 100-mile [160-kilometer] pro race. But flying it is totally different from riding a bike. In a recumbent seat, you can't duplicate the leg extension you use on a road bike. On a bike you use different muscles, a different percentage of the power stroke. Your seat position isn't the same. Your butt doesn't get so sore in an upright position. And 15 miles [24 kilometers] an hour in the *Daedalus* is *screaming*."

If it's not quite like riding a bike, it's not really like flying, either. "The airplane is so light and so large and so slow," says Tremml, "it doesn't feel like flying. It feels like you're floating. Very slowly. Very gently. I just use one finger to steer the *Light Eagle*."

But nothing was gentle about the tests and training the latter-day Daedaluses underwent. One day in a hospital room at Edwards, for example, Zack was pedaling hard for six hours in a semirecumbent position on an ergometer and staring at a video flight simulator that was hooked up to the bike. "I'm going to avoid the mountains; there's turbulence up there," he said, manipulating the rudder-elevator stick gently with his right hand to avoid the approaching bright green mountains on the screen. Zack was sweating hard. He was wearing only running shorts, a heart-rate monitor on his chest, and a catheter plugged into his arm to allow blood samples to be drawn. "Everyone needs to be reassured that the engine isn't gonna putz out," said Zack. "If the flight was gonna be a cakewalk, they wouldn't put us through this misery."

The purpose of this awful six-hour ride, which each pilot suffered that week, was twofold: to test the athletes' endurance one month before the first possible flight from Crete, and to test the special fluid-replacement drink that Nadel had developed along with Dr. James Whittam of the Shaklee Corporation, which hopes to market it. The drink would be essential, serving both as fuel with a high carbohy-

Just yards short of shore, a sudden wind gust battered the Daedalus, *causing its tail to snap off. Although the craft dropped into the sea, the pilot emerged unharmed and exuberant (below). The* Daedalus *flight set new records for longest straight-line and absolute-distance human-powered flight, and for longest duration of a human-powered flight.*

Both photos: © Charles O'Rear/West Light

drate content to supply energy, and as a coolant to keep the pilot from dehydrating.

"An athlete might sweat up to 30 grams a minute to dissipate heat," says Ethan Nadel, whose beverage has been dubbed Ethan-all by his cohorts. "That equals 3 pounds [1.4 kilograms] of water per hour, or 18 pounds [8 kilograms] after six hours. You lose sodium when you sweat. That's why we have to keep supplying sodium."

"This stuff blows away other drinks," says Frank Scioscia, another pilot, referring to the high-energy concoction. "I've lost 8 pounds [3.6 kilograms] in cycling competitions. After the six-hour test, I didn't lose anything. I weighed exactly the same."

Myth Becomes Reality

But beyond the commitment to high-tech tools, always looming behind the project was the ancient legend of the man who flew himself out of prison. To keep that in sharp and inspiring focus, Daedalus hired its own classicist. Sarah Morris, a professor at Yale, was the resident expert on Greek myths. According to Morris, who is writing a book about the mythological Daedalus, he was known in classical Greece as a sculptor, architect, and metal craftsman. Among many other impressive projects, Daedalus built the labyrinth in which he and his son, Icarus, were imprisoned on Crete. Icarus tried to escape on wax-and-feather wings with Daedalus, but he ignored his father's warning not to fly too close to the sun. Alas, his wax melted, and Icarus fell to the sea amid a blizzard of feathers, supplying moral grist for Christians ever since.

In one sense, *Daedalus 88* was reminiscent of Icarus' flight, for it, too, ended up as wreckage in the Aegean Sea. Except that *Daedalus 88* had carried a man aloft for 74 miles (120 kilometers) before it went down. Miraculous? Mythical? No, it was just a terrific, even inspiring, example of man working at his best. As Langford says, "There is no practical application or financial interest in this flight. We did it purely for the symbolism of doing it."

THE ENVIRONMENT

THE ENVIRONMENT

The events of 1988 etched ever more starkly the growing confrontation between mankind's activities and the environment. The world's inhabitants must balance their living patterns with the preservation of their planet.

by Gladwin Hill

© Shepard Sherbell/Picture Group

Swedish scientists track balloons that monitor the depletion of the ozone layer now occurring in Arctic regions.

Saving the Skies

International concern mounted in 1988 about drastic global climatic changes possibly under way as a result of the world's industrial activities. One such process is the apparent depletion of the stratospheric layer of ozone (a concentrated form of oxygen) that shields the earth from potentially lethal ultraviolet radiation from the sun. Another process is the "greenhouse effect"—a buildup of atmospheric carbon dioxide from combustion activities—which tends to trap excessive heat close to the earth.

In 1987, 46 nations endorsed a treaty to halve production of two major industrial chemical groups, chlorofluorocarbons and halons, that are believed to cause ozone depletion through chemical reactions. The compounds are widely used in plastic foam, cleaning agents, refrigerants, and other products. In mid-1988 new studies of the problem moved the head of the Environmental Protection Agency (EPA), Lee M. Thomas, to urge that the international pact be reinforced to provide for total elimination of the two chemicals. Du Pont, the biggest maker of these chemicals, announced it would end production of the troublesome substances by the year 2000, and meanwhile ready substitutes for the market by 1990.

Ozone depletion, originally observed over the South Pole, may be occurring in more-populated Arctic regions of Canada, Scandinavia, and the Soviet Union. American scientists organized a major six-week expedition for 1989 to gather data on the Arctic situation.

Data on the "global warming" threat are rather indefinite as well. Still, representatives of 35 nations conferred at Geneva, Switzerland, on steps to collect information and "formulate responses." The most probable strategies likely will entail the curbing of fossil fuel burning and improving the efficiency of combustion to produce less gaseous residues. Without constraints, some scientists believe that trapped heat could radically alter weather patterns and melt global ice caps, causing catastrophic rises in ocean levels.

Some speculate that the "greenhouse effect" already has manifested itself in the severe drought that hit the U.S. Midwest farm belt and contributed to the 1988 fires at Yellowstone National Park. But there was no immediate scientific confirmation of such a link.

Oil spills in Pittsburgh, in Alaska, and elsewhere hampered clean water efforts.

© AP/Wide World

Cleaner Water

Abatement of water pollution progressed. The EPA reported that 87 percent of the nation's public sewer systems met a July 1988 deadline for installing two-stage sewage treatment; 423 large plants were still not in compliance. The agency said that, since the 1972 Clean Water Act, the government had spent $45 billion on sewerage improvements, and the states some $15 billion. Outlays will have to reach $140 billion by early in the next century to achieve the law's goals.

Whither Waste?

Garbage precipitated an ongoing series of small crises in 1988 on both the domestic and international fronts.

Along the mid-Atlantic coast of the U.S., beaches in several states had to be closed temporarily due to noxious medical refuse. Overseas, grubby ships laden with wastes from numerous nations plied between Europe and Africa seeking dumping grounds. Most often they were turned away; the few recorded acceptances created internal political furor. There even were tentative negotiations to ship wastes from the United States to Great Britain.

The turmoil resulted from a collision between economics and growing worldwide environmental sensitivity. In the bygone era of nearby community dumps, waste disposal in the United States cost only a few dollars per truckload. But today, with viable dumping grounds ever more distant, and the waste flow ever bigger and with more toxic substances, disposal may cost as much as $2,500 per ton for transport or processing. Some areas in Africa had been accepting foreign wastes for fees as low as $3 per ton. But 1988 brought a Third World repudiation of any perceived role as a dumping ground for Western garbage. In Africa, national waste-acceptance contracts were voided, officials imprisoned, and penal-

© Bart Bartholomew/NYT Pictures

Consumers who separate returns by material help lower the cost of recycling.

ties as severe as death enacted for trafficking in foreign wastes.

With ocean dumping under everwidening international sanctions, wastes can only be buried, burned, or recycled. In the United States, waste volume has nearly doubled since 1960; meanwhile, disposal landfills have dwindled from 18,000 to 6,000 in the past decade. Calling the waste problem ''staggering,'' the EPA drafted minimum standards for municipal dumps, and a program of federal assistance to communities that establish recycling. Congress also enacted a law to monitor dangerous refuse from medical facilities. (See also p. 209.)

In a related development, inquiries disclosed hazardous concentrations of radioactive wastes dumped indiscriminately at a dozen federal plants making nuclear weapons constituents. Cleanup costs were projected to run into billions of dollars.

The scheduled opening of the nation's first nuclear-waste repository, a half mile (0.8 kilometer) underground near Carlsbad, New Mexico, was postponed indefinitely. Doubts arose in many circles about how effectively it might contain contaminants such as plutonium. Plutonium remains radioactive for 280,000 years.

Love Resurgent

A decade ago, disclosure of alarming accumulations of chemical wastes at Love Canal, near Niagara Falls, New York, required the evacuation of nearly 1,000 families and touched off a nationwide discovery of similar dumps. Last year, however, authorities in New York declared the community partly safe for reoccupancy.

In the $250 million cleanup, hundreds of homes were razed and thousands of tons of contaminated soil and debris removed. Some 1,300 former residents had shared a $20 million settlement of a lawsuit against the dumpers of the waste and local officials.

Soil tests confirmed that half of the Love Canal area could be resettled.

© Phil Matt/NYT Pictures

The Alaska
Oil Spill

by Jenny Tesar

Top: © Al Grillo/Picture Group; above: © B. Nation/SYGMA

In March 1989, a damaged tanker spilled more than 11 million gallons of oil into Alaska's Prince William Sound. The oil sullied beaches, injured wildlife, and threatened the delicate ecological balance of the region.

O il: they call it black gold. But in Alaska, it became a black plague, despoiling the land, killing countless animals, and leaving a legacy that already has had economic, political, and environmental repercussions.

On the evening of March 23, 1989, the oil tanker *Exxon Valdez* left Valdez, Alaska, carrying 1.26 million barrels of crude oil. The ship was bound for southern California, where its black gold would be refined, producing gasoline for the nation's voracious consumers. But the tanker never arrived. Less than three hours later, at 12:04 A.M. on March 24, it struck Bligh Reef at the northern end of Prince William Sound.

Underwater rocks tore open eight of the tanker's fifteen giant cargo holds, emptying about 265,000 barrels of oil—more than 11 million gallons—into the icy waters. It was the largest oil spill in North American history.

Had cleanup crews and equipment been deployed promptly, much of the ensuing damage caused by the oil spill could have been avoided. Instead, precious cleanup time was wasted. Wrote *Time* magazine writer George J. Church: "The story . . . resembled a Greek tragedy updated by Murphy's Law."

From the Bay to the Sound

What happened in Prince William Sound had its beginnings in 1968, when vast petroleum and natural-gas deposits were discovered in the Arctic coastal plain, or North Slope, around Prudhoe Bay. Following years of debate over environmental concerns and how to move the oil to American markets, the oil companies and the federal government settled on an 800-mile (1,300-kilometer)-long trans-Alaska pipeline, which would run from Prudhoe Bay south to the ice-free port of Valdez.

Work began on the pipeline in 1975, and was completed in 1977, at a cost estimated at more than $10 billion. In addition to the pipeline, the system includes a 14-tanker terminal at Valdez and 12 pumping stations. The system was designed and built by the Alyeska Pipeline Service Company, a consortium formed by eight oil companies (including Exxon). Alyeska also operates the system, which can carry more than 2 million barrels of oil a day. And the consortium assumes responsibility for cleaning up oil spills.

In January 1987, following pressure by environmentalists, Alyeska filed a contingency plan with the U.S. Government that detailed how it would handle a 200,000-barrel spill in Prince William Sound. It boasted that it would have cleanup equipment at the scene within five hours. It also said: "It is highly unlikely that a spill of this magnitude would occur. Catastrophic events of this nature are further reduced because the majority of tankers calling on Port Valdez are of American registry and all of these are piloted by licensed masters or pilots."

A Different Reality

The *Exxon Valdez* left port at 9:10 P.M. on March 23 under the command of a harbor pilot. Soon after the harbor pilot left the tanker, Captain Joseph J. Hazelwood radioed Coast Guard traffic control and asked for permission to change sea-lanes to avoid floating chunks of ice—a common hazard at that time of the year. Hazelwood received permission to move eastward into the empty northbound (incoming) lane, and then return to a southwesterly course. Shortly thereafter, Hazelwood went to his cabin, handing over the ship to the third mate, Gregory Cousins, who was not certified by the Coast Guard to pilot a vessel through island-dotted Prince William Sound. This violated Exxon policy, which calls for the captain to remain in command until the ship has reached the open ocean.

The Exxon Valdez *spilled its cargo when an underwater reef tore open eight of the tanker's fifteen giant holds.*

Exactly what happened next remained unclear for weeks after the accident. It was alleged that Hazelwood had put the ship on autopilot after changing to the eastward direction, without informing either Cousins or Robert Kagan, the new helmsman. The ship continued to travel east, moving beyond the sea-lanes into an area of rocky reefs. When Cousins, realizing that the ship was headed toward Bligh Reef, commanded Kagan to correct the course, precious moments were lost before they noticed that the ship was not responding to manual steering. By then it was too late. The first of two collisions occurred, and oil began leaking from the ship.

Nine hours after the accident, Hazelwood's blood-alcohol level was tested and found to be 0.06 percent, greater than the 0.04 percent the Coast Guard considers acceptable for ship captains. (Alcohol begins to impair the brain's ability to function when the blood-alcohol level reaches 0.05 percent—a level obtained by drinking 2 to 3 ounces of whiskey.)

It is not known why the blood tests were administered so late; certainly the delay meant that Hazelwood's condition at the time of the accident may never be known. His blood-alcohol level may have been significantly higher than 0.06 percent, however. Assuming that Hazelwood had had no alcohol after the accident, and that his body metabolized at the normal rate, then his blood-alcohol level at the time of the accident was about 0.19 percent. This is almost double the 0.10 percent level at which most states consider automobile drivers to be legally intoxicated.

Hazelwood had a history of alcohol problems. He was twice convicted of drunken driving, and in 1985 underwent treatment for alcohol abuse. Though his automobile driver's license was revoked and he was not permitted to drive a car, he retained his ship license, and Exxon allowed him to keep piloting.

Following the accident and the blood-alcohol-level test, Exxon fired Hazelwood, and the state filed criminal charges against him, including piloting a ship while under the influence of alcohol. These were the first criminal charges ever filed against an oil tanker captain in Alaska.

According to Coast Guard officials, the tanker moved beyond the range of their radar well before the accident. Budget cuts had reduced the Coast Guard traffic-control staff in Valdez, and the radar used to monitor the ship was not as powerful as one that had been used in the past. Had they used a more powerful radar and maintained contact with the *Valdez*, they could have warned Cousins of the impending danger. The accident also might have been avoided had the Coast Guard's radar been electronically linked to the harbor's vessel-traffic system so that an alarm would sound automatically if a tanker wandered out of its correct path.

Botched Cleanup Efforts

"We are out here working our hearts out without accomplishing anything because there's no one in charge, and that's the real problem," said Jim Aguiar, a fishing boat captain, to Roberto Suro, a reporter for *The New York Times*. The date: three weeks after the accident—weeks marked by delay, confusion, and bungled efforts to contain and clean up the spilled oil.

When oil is released into water, it naturally disperses in four ways: (1) a large percentage gradually evaporates; (2) some mixes with water to form an emulsified mixture that scientists call *mousse*; (3) some is broken up by waves and turbulence into tiny droplets, which remain in suspension; (4) a small percentage dissolves, including the most poisonous and carcinogenic compounds.

For cleaning oil spills, three methods are available:

Containment and Collection. Boats are used to place floating booms in a ring around the oil, containing the oil so it can be collected. Either pumps or skimmers are used to remove the oil from the water's surface. The oil is then stored for later disposal. This method works well only in calm water, and it is expensive and time-consuming. It has to be done quickly, before the oil spreads over too large an area. Also, its potential value in a large spill such as that in Prince William Sound has been questioned, simply because it is difficult, if not impossible, to gather enough equipment quickly enough.

Dispersants. These detergentlike chemicals, which generally are sprayed on oil spills from low-flying helicopters and planes, break up the oil into tiny drops, making it easier for natural chemical and biological processes to break down the oil. Wave action is usually needed to mix the chemicals with the oil, although Exxon spokesman Les Rogers says that the dispersant used by his firm, Corexit, works even in calm seas. Dispersants are inexpensive and can be used on large spills. According to Alyeska's contingency plan, dispersants

Boats placed floating booms (above) around the spill to prevent the oil from spreading. The oil contained by the booms was then pumped or skimmed from the water's surface. By the time the booms were in place, however, thousands of gallons of oil had already washed up on nearby beaches (left).

Top: © B. Nation/SYGMA; above: © Karen Jettmar/AllStock

should be the chief method of breaking up the oil in a large spill. However, they must be applied quickly, before the oil spreads and is converted to mousse.

Burning. Surface oil can be burned if the oil slick is continuous and thick. The process is inexpensive, feasible for large spills, and probably the fastest way to remove oil from water. Like the other methods, it is effective only in the earliest stages of a spill. Another drawback is that burning pollutes the air with thick clouds of acrid black smoke. And it is difficult to heat the

oil to a high enough temperature to ignite, especially in cold Arctic waters—Exxon used lasers to keep some patches of the slick burning.

None of these methods was deployed quickly enough or extensively enough to have much effect on the spill in Prince William Sound. The oil converted to mousse, and by March 28, Dennis Kelso, Alaska's commissioner of environmental conservation, said, "We are past the opportunity to recover much oil. . . . We have a spill that's on the move, and we're looking at defensive measures to save

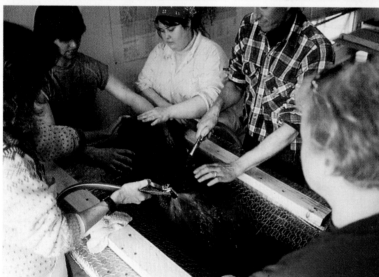

The spreading oil saturated the fur of thousands of sea otters that live in Prince William Sound. If not quickly removed, the oil ruins the insulating properties of the otter's fur. Volunteers worked around the clock to rescue and clean the creatures before they froze to death.

what we can.'' For example, by early April the state and local fishermen had placed plastic booms across the entrances to four bays that are prime salmon hatcheries, hoping to keep the spilled oil away from the hundreds of millions of salmon fry.

By March 29, Exxon conceded it had lost the opportunity to contain most of the spill. It admitted that containment booms were not deployed around the leaking tanker until 10 hours after the accident—twice the amount of time called for in the cleanup plan. ''This spill has pretty much blown into Prince William Sound,'' said Don Cornett, Exxon's Alaskan coordinator. ''We will never get back those 240,000 barrels.''

By April 21, Exxon said it had recovered about 31,000 barrels of oil—13 percent of the total spill; the company indicated that only 4,000 additional barrels might be recoverable. Meanwhile, some of the oil had already moved into the Gulf of Alaska, extending the threat to new areas. By mid-April, oil was washing ashore at Kenai Fjords National Park and Katmai National Park, a spectacular wilderness area more than 250 miles (400 kilometers) from the accident.

Under the law, Exxon is responsible for cleaning up the spill. Exxon Chairman L. G. Rawl repeatedly said that the company would take ''full responsibility'' for the spill and would pay cleanup costs. The company also agreed to make "reasonable payments" to fishermen to compensate them for revenues lost as a result of the oil spill.

Entering the Food Chain

Prince William Sound is home to a rich variety of wildlife. Best known are fish such as herring and pink salmon, some 10,000 sea otters, and, in winter, 100,000 birds. In late April an estimated 1 million additional birds arrive at the end of their springtime migration, to use the islands as breeding grounds. This also is the time when whales, seals, and sea lions migrate into the area. The salmon fry migrate from coastal water to the ocean. Adult herring move in toward the shore to spawn their roe on kelp; in June some 50 million adult salmon return to spawn. Along the beaches, bears scavenge, and deer graze on kelp.

Many thousands of animals died in the weeks immediately following the *Valdez* spill. Sea otters froze to death because the oil that covered their fur destroyed the fur's insulating ability. The same happened to birds when their feathers became drenched in the black goo. Other birds, including the Sound's bald eagle population, were at risk because they scavenged on the carcasses of oil-soaked birds. The oil coated the birds' intestines, preventing absorption of water and nutrients and causing the birds to die of a combination of starvation and dehydration.

The spill also meant severe losses for fishermen. Fishing is a $150-million-a-year industry in Prince William Sound. The first casualty was herring fishing, canceled by state officials because of oil in the spawning beds. Officials also canceled the shrimp and sablefish seasons and barred salmon fishing from many parts of the sound. Another worry of scientists was the effect of the oil on the fishes' senses. Would it disorient them, thus affecting either their immediate or long-term behavior?

Volunteers worked around the clock in an effort to catch oil-drenched birds and sea otters so they could be cleaned. Alice Berkner, executive director of the International Bird Rescue Center in Berkeley, California, who was retained by Exxon to direct the effort, uses Dawn dishwashing detergent to clean the animals. "It cuts through this terrible oil quite effectively, but we have to work on the birds pretty hard, even so," she says. "We use the WaterPik dental appliance to dislodge clumps of oil from their

© B. Nation/SYGMA

Thousands of birds died when the oil permeated their feathers. Volunteers used dishwashing detergent to clean the oil-soaked birds (below) before releasing them in areas unthreatened by the spill (above).

© Ron Stapleton/SYGMA

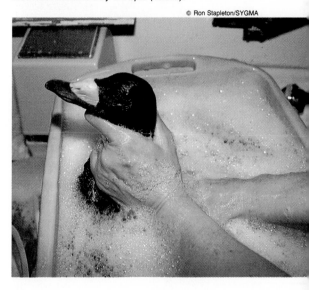

feathers, and we use toothbrushes to get the oil away from eyes and beaks.'' According to Berkner, it takes about 40 minutes to clean a bird, and about twice that time to clean an otter.

Despite heroic efforts, only a small percentage of animals could be rescued and cleaned, and many of the rescued animals died. Various causes of death were cited, including stress and overheating from hair dryers used to dry fur (the practice was discontinued).

As the mousse spread over ever-larger areas and became ever more dispersed, fewer and fewer oil-covered bodies were washed ashore. But the threat to wildlife did not end. Animals will suffer adverse effects from the *Valdez* spill for a long, long time, as the oil makes its way through marine food chains. Microorganisms ingest the oil. They are eaten by small fish, which are eaten by larger fish, which are eaten by still larger creatures. Toxic hydrocarbons from the oil will cause diseases in the animals just as they would in humans.

If there is a positive aspect to the spill, it is the opportunity afforded scientists to learn more

Buoys offered only a temporary safe haven to animals that depend on the oil-soaked waters for food and shelter.

© B. Nation/SYGMA

about the environmental and biological effects of marine oil pollution. Researchers hope to increase their understanding of such issues as how oil affects wildlife, how it enters the food chain, and how it ultimately breaks down.

A Change of Attitude

Traditionally, the conservation ethic has been unpopular among the great majority of Alaskans. Rather, the people saw the land and its treasures as things to be exploited: forests to be cut for lumber, animals to be killed for their fur, ground to be mined for gold and oil. But the *Valdez* spill may change this. Says Governor Steve Cowper: ''Most Alaskans are going to reassess their attitude toward oil and development in this state.''

In early April the state senate's oil and gas committee voted to ask Congress to halt the sale of federal oil leases in Bristol Bay, near the Aleutian Islands. And drilling in the Arctic National Wildlife Refuge suddenly faced stiff opposition.

There was growing reluctance to believe oil industry assurances that their operations seldom had adverse environmental effects, and that spills could be readily handled. Alyeska's contingency plans were expected to be reviewed, and there were calls for the creation of federal contingency plans to deal with offshore spills. People in other parts of the United States also raised questions about contingency plans for spills in their areas. For example, U.S. Senator Joseph I. Lieberman (Conn.) asked the Coast Guard to review contingency plans for a Long Island Sound spill, and determine whether changes were needed. ''We're spending millions cleaning up Long Island Sound, and one major spill could set us back by decades,'' warned Lieberman, pointing out that an estimated 3.3 billion gallons (12 billion liters) of oil entered Connecticut in 1987 from tankers crossing Long Island Sound.

Tighter regulations, bigger contingency funds, stricter enforcement, newer equipment—all will add to the cost of oil recovery. Ultimately, it will be the consumers who will pay this cost, primarily through increased gasoline prices. Which is as it should be, since it is Americans' massive consumption of gasoline that has necessitated drilling in places such as the North Slope. ''Don't blame the oil spill on one drunken sailor,'' says a spokesman for the environmental organization Greenpeace, ''but on oil-drunk America.''

© Chiasson/Gamma-Liaison

HANDLING HOSPITAL WASTE

by Ellen Kunes

© Mike Duffy/News-Times

Alarming amounts of medical waste have washed up on our beaches and accumulated in our landfills. Although the waste poses a distinct threat of infectious disease, government, hospitals, and environmentalists have yet to agree upon an acceptable means of disposal.

AIDS seems to have invaded every aspect of our lives. It has infected the nation's blood supply, curtailed our sex lives. We fear it may somehow taint our food and water. We see AIDS everywhere—even in our garbage. Late last June some Indianapolis, Indiana, schoolchildren kicked off their summer vacation with a hunt for a box in which to keep a baby bird. The children rummaged through an unlocked trash dumpster behind a medical clinic and uncovered one box full of syringes and another packed with vials of blood—two of which were drawn from the clinic's AIDS patients. The kids examined the cache and hid it under a bush, where it was found by another group of neighborhood youngsters. These children took the booty behind an apartment house and divided the spoils; some grabbed the needles and drew in the dirt with them, while others smashed the blood-filled vials against a wall. Of the 13 children who had handled the infectious garbage, seven may have been exposed to the AIDS virus. Two of the children—a brother and sister—who had played with the blood had open sores from poison ivy, making it possible for the deadly virus to enter their bloodstreams. One boy with a cut on his foot walked through the blood. Another tasted it.

In Boardman, Ohio, a second group of kids discovered syringes in an open dumpster and played doctor for an afternoon by jabbing one another in the arms with used needles. And in Ocean County, New Jersey, last August, a 50-mile (80-kilometer) slick of hospital waste fouled the tourist-packed shores with hundreds of hypodermic needles and other infectious detritus. Local officials closed the beaches for 72 hours to clean up the mess. While authorities first suspected it was dumped by unscrupulous

Many hospitals sterilize infectious waste at temperatures high enough to kill harmful bacteria and viruses.

© Jim Heemstra/Picture Group

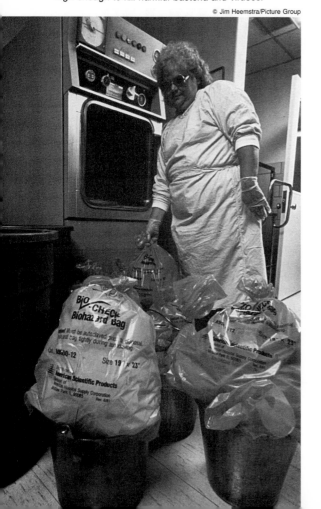

private haulers paid by hospitals to cart their infectious waste off to commercial incinerators, New Jersey officials now believe that the hospital trash was dumped by a New York sanitation barge on its way to a Staten Island landfill.

The Haul from Hospitals

Experts estimate that each day 1.5 million pounds (680,000 kilograms) of infectious, or "red-bag," waste emanates from the well-scrubbed halls of this nation's 7,000 hospitals. In addition, the contaminated garbage from research labs, nursing homes, outpatient clinics, and the offices of private doctors and dentists must be hauled away. In past years many states had no regulations and few guidelines to control the infectious-waste stream. Local and state health departments simply advised that potentially dangerous refuse be handled in a "safe" manner. In most cases this meant that pathological wastes such as tissue specimens, organs, amputated limbs, and body fluids were burned in the hospital incinerator or double-bagged and tossed onto trucks bound for the local landfill. Other types of refuse, including drug waste, "sharps"—hospital materials with sharp points or edges, such as syringes and scalpels—and contaminated bandages and bedding from patients with communicable diseases, were often chucked out with scraps from the hospital cafeteria and the rest of the ordinary garbage.

The AIDS crisis, however, has changed everything. Hospital housekeeping staffs and sanitation workers have never much liked getting stuck by hypodermic needles poking through plastic garbage bags. Now many fear there is a deadly disease lurking on the tips of those needles, and state and local authorities have been forced to act. The race is on to regulate the disposal of infectious waste.

Add in AIDS Hysteria

The offensive nature of hospital garbage—the bloody gauze pads and intravenous tubes and urine bags, the used syringes, and the decaying umbilical cords and diseased organs—have always made us want to keep it out of sight. What we once found revolting—the infectious waste stream—we now fear may be health-threatening as well. After swimming in trash-infested waters, people who contract routine maladies like ear, nose, and throat infections can't help but wonder what else lurks in their bodies. Could they have gotten AIDS from hospital waste-filled waters? Frightening incidents like the ones

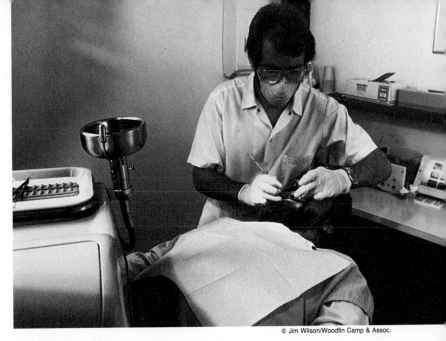

For years, many doctors and dentists in private practice discarded their infectious waste down the drain or threw it out with the regular paper trash. Only recently have laws governing infectious waste disposal in hospitals been expanded to include private practitioners and medical labs.

© Jim Wilson/Woodfin Camp & Assoc.

in New Jersey have mobilized the public's fear of hospital waste. Couple these suspicions with the mysterious deaths of bottle-nosed dolphins along the East Coast: 420 of them washed ashore during the summer of 1987 alone, badly decomposed, apparently having succumbed to some immune-system disorder. A few sea-mammal experts speculated that ocean pollution could have killed the dolphins—and the public wondered whether an AIDS-like virus derived from tainted hospital refuse had infected these animals.

In focusing attention on the garbage problem, AIDS hysteria has performed a valuable public service: the problem of trash is finally receiving widespread attention. In 1978, before anyone had ever heard about AIDS, the Environmental Protection Agency (EPA) tried to set down some rules governing the disposal of infectious waste. Nothing was concluded.

"As far as we could see, health threats from mismanagement of infectious waste didn't exist," says Jacqueline Sales, the EPA's chief of regulation development for land-disposal restrictions. "We know it's a good idea to put needles and scalpels in rigid containers. But what about a Band-Aid with a few drops of blood on it? Is that really going to spread disease? The problem is, we don't have any data." There's nothing out there, according to Sales, that experts can look at and say, "Gee, we know that a tube of blood, once it leaves the hospital and goes to a landfill, will infect somebody with a disease three days later." We also

don't know, Sales explains, whether burying infectious waste in a landfill allows organisms to survive, migrate downward, and contaminate the groundwater.

Researchers must first determine whether infectious waste proves to be really that dangerous—or at least *more* dangerous than the rubbish the average American family creates every day. William Rutala, research associate professor in the Division of Infectious Diseases at the University of North Carolina, and a representative for the Association of Practitioners in Infection Control at congressional hearings, isn't so sure. "From a purely scientific standpoint, there's no microbiological evidence that suggests hospital waste is more infective than residential waste," he says.

AIDS versus Hepatitis

So, does hospital waste spread infectious diseases, or AIDS in particular? No, says Walter W. Bond, research microbiologist in the Hospital Infections Program at the Centers for Disease Control (CDC) in Atlanta, Georgia: "It takes gross and sometimes repeated exposures to blood and/or blood-contaminated body fluids to become infected with the AIDS virus." The reason, according to Bond, is that AIDS has an incredibly low number of viruses per milliliter of blood; and the smaller the number of viruses in the blood, the more difficult it is to transmit the disease.

"For instance, in the HBV [hepatitis B] virus, which is highly infectious, there are a hundred million to a billion viruses per milliliter of blood—equal to about 15 drops,'' Bond explains. ''That's a lot of virus. But the AIDS virus has only one to 100 bugs in a milliliter, depending on the stage of the disease.''

Furthermore, the AIDS virus is a fragile one: even at optimum temperatures, it dies quickly when exposed to the environment. Only three reported cases of health-care workers have tested positive for the AIDS virus. All three were reported to have small cuts or other breaks in the skin through which the virus may have passed, and one was splashed in the mouth with AIDS-contaminated blood.

The hepatitis B virus, however, is not easily killed. According to CDC epidemiologist Craig Shapiro, ''Hepatitis B requires high temperatures to kill it. Dried blood on a surface may still have infectious virus in it several weeks later.'' Hepatitis B, like AIDS, is a blood-borne, sexually transmitted disease: simply touching the virus won't infect you, but a jab with a contaminated syringe, or a splash of infected blood in the eye, can put you at a 10 percent risk of developing the disease. Furthermore, the number of people infected with hepatitis B is escalating: the CDC estimates between 250,000 and 300,000 will become infected with hepatitis B this year.

The bottom line: while the risk of contracting AIDS through infectious waste is very slim, potential exposure to hepatitis B from hospital garbage does exist. ''We should err on the side of caution,'' suggests Rutala. Although he doesn't support federal legislation, he believes that individual states should manage infectious wastes. ''All states should regulate two types of waste,'' he says. ''Stocks and cultures of infectious agents from microbiology labs and other research labs should be carefully controlled.'' The other type of waste, he says, is used sharp objects of any type. ''These should always be placed in rigid containers, out of the public's reach.''

Rutala worries that in the frenzy to regulate, officials are overlooking the dangers posed by small generators of infectious waste: private physicians, dentists, medical labs, small clinics. ''Even the bill before the House of Representatives exempts private physicians and small clinics,'' he says. ''But they throw their waste, untreated, right into a dumpster or a sanitary landfill. Obviously, if you believe that some of this waste is infectious, the origin of that waste makes no difference.''

Patchwork of Regulations

As infectious waste is banned from municipal incinerators and sanitary landfills, hospitals are forced to seek costly alternatives. Some send their waste to expensive commercial incinerators, while others hire private haulers to truck the garbage to the nearest incinerators—often up to 500 miles (800 kilometers) away. What's more, officials find new regulations hard to enforce: the costs of disposing of hospital garbage legally are greater than the penalties for illegal dumping.

Today trying to make sense of the crazy patchwork of infectious-waste guidelines and regulations enacted by local and state governments across the country could be compared to understanding the new federal tax laws. According to the latest survey by the National Solid Waste Management Association, 32 states already regulate infectious-waste disposal. But the laws imposed by each state vary widely: in Rhode Island and Arkansas, rules apply only to hospitals—and not to medical labs or private doctors. Some states *require* that all infectious wastes be incinerated or treated before they are dumped in landfills; others simply *recommend* this. Ohio and Colorado have no regulations and few official recommendations for handling infectious waste. Where state laws are inadequate, some cities enact their own regulations. Last summer, after the Indianapolis children found the infected vials of blood from AIDS patients, the city passed legislation to govern infectious-waste disposal.

Perhaps some of the toughest laws have been passed in New York City, the home of more than 100 hospitals and 11,770 AIDS victims—nearly a quarter of all those diagnosed with the disease in the entire country. Daniel Millstone, chief environmental counsel for the city's department of sanitation, claims that regulations governing the disposal of hypodermic needles and syringes have been on the books ''since time immemorial. But they really haven't been enforced,'' he says. That changed in 1985, when sanitation workers at the Fresh Kills Landfill on Staten Island found bags bursting with hypodermic needles, bloodstained surgical instruments, and dressings—even body parts. ''They were finding livers, umbilical cords, fingers, all kinds of stuff,'' Millstone says. With the AIDS panic at its height, workers didn't want to get near the mess. Reports that some sanitation workers, stuck by contaminated needles, were coming down with hepatitis only increased the workers' fears. A department investigation revealed that several hospitals were sneaking their red-bag waste in with their ordinary "black-bag" rubbish.

Fees and Fines

As the number of AIDS patients in the city rose, so did the amount of red bags hospitals shipped out of state for incineration. In 1985 more than 40,000 pounds (18,000 kilograms) of red-bag waste was produced each day by city institutions. The private-hauling fee could run as high as $2.60 for each bag the size of an average kitchen garbage sack, says Elizabeth Sommers, vice president for regulatory and professional affairs at the Greater New York Hospital Association. "Special haulers, special incinerators—it all makes the price so high," she says. "And garbage is not the item you really want to be paying a lot for in a health-care institution." In New York City, infectious-waste disposal was fast becoming an economic nightmare.

To stem the tide of cheating, the city council enacted Local Law 57 in 1985. It was simple but severe: all refuse emanating from medical, pathological, and research labs; hospital isolation and surgery wards; and infected patients of private physicians and dentists would be barred from municipal incinerators and landfills and instead sent to pathological-waste incinerators. The penalties for violators were enormous: fines of up to $10,000, and suspension of city pickup of noninfectious waste for a minimum of six months. Already strapped, the institutions would be forced to hire private haulers at exorbitant rates to cart the *harmless* stuff away to commercial incinerators. What really distinguished the New York law from any other in the country was how rigorously it would be enforced. Thirteen "environmental police officers," hired to examine ordinary hospital garbage, cracked down hard: in one 18-month period, the new unit handed out fines totaling $449,000 to 110 hospitals and 12 doctor's offices for sneaking infectious waste into black bags.

Most New York hospitals are currently forced to pay a middleman—the private hauler—to cart their truckloads of contagious waste to commercial incinerators out of the state. The private hauler then pays the incinerator operator for burning the infectious waste. But a few opportunistic hauling companies have taken the hospital waste and dumped it in abandoned warehouses, on roadsides, and in other

© Jim Heemstra/Picture Group

Hospital incinerators frequently lack the pollution-control devices required of municipal incinerators to prevent the emission of toxic substances into the air.

places where the public could find it, while keeping the profits. Ironically, New York City's crackdown may actually increase the ordinary citizen's exposure to hospital waste.

• Two years ago, in a New York suburb, a mere 100 feet (30 meters) from the doorstep of a children's dance studio, an abandoned warehouse was found packed with five tons of medical trash, including amputated limbs and hypodermic needles.

• In 1986 truckloads of infectious waste from New York hospitals were dumped on a pig farm in Bucks County, Pennsylvania.

• Late that same year, a Brooklyn warehouse was discovered piled high with 1,400 bags containing blood-soaked gauze pads, hypodermic needles and syringes, containers marked *isolation waste*, and documents with hospitals' and patients' names on them. The bags, dumped there in 1982, had been rummaged through and slept on by vagrants, says Nancy Young, a spokesperson for the Brooklyn district attorney's office.

• The Federal Bureau of Investigation (FBI) is currently investigating a New York City hauler that it suspects is collecting red bags from hospitals, throwing them into innocent-looking black bags, and then carting them off to landfills in New York State, New Jersey, and Pennsylvania.

Tracking laws in most states are weak: no "cradle-to-grave" manifest is needed to prove that the garbage actually reached its final destination. In fact, haulers aren't even required to name the hospitals they've serviced until the end of the year; so it's easy for haulers to dump the waste. New York State officials hope the hauling scams will end when tighter rules for haulers and hospitals take effect in April. Once a year, haulers will be required to show cradle-to-grave manifests—what hospitals they served, how much garbage they carted, which incinerators were used. "Until now, hospitals didn't have to turn their garbage over to a licensed hauler, but now they will," says Gordon Boyd, executive director of the Legislative Commission on Solid Waste. Penalties will be doubled: for each day of violation, haulers and hospitals will be fined between $1,000 and $2,500.

Insidious Incinerators

Perhaps the most dangerous and overlooked aspect of the whole infectious-waste dilemma is the invisible one: on-site hospital incinerators may be spewing a staggering amount of toxic pollutants into the air. A study conducted in 1986 by the EPA demonstrated that most of the country's large municipal incinerators have inadequate pollution controls, emitting some of the most toxic substances into the air—dioxins, furans, hydrochloric acid, and other acid gases and heavy metals such as cadmium and lead.

Not surprisingly, most hospital incinerators have even fewer pollution controls than municipal incinerators. Neither hospital nor city facilities have the stringent controls mandated by the government for hazardous-waste incinerators. "Many of these 'old dog' hospital incinerators emit 1,000 or more times as many poisons into the air as hazardous-waste facilities do," asserts Jack Lauber, an engineer with the New York Department of Environmental Conservation. Hospital incinerators, he contends, weren't built to burn the wide variety of hospital wastes thrown into them. "The biggest problem is the chlorinated plastics—disposable instruments, intravenous tubing, syringes. If not com-pletely combusted," he says, "these can release dioxins and furans—toxic organic substances believed to promote cancer."

Ordinary household waste contains about 3 to 7 percent plastic refuse; hospital waste is made up of between 20 and 30 percent plastics. "Most hospital incinerators weren't built to control the emission of these substances," says Lauber. "They control only the amount of smoke and odor they put in the air." With more hospitals firing up old incinerators, the pollution could get worse. In New York City alone, 24 hospitals use virtually unregulated incinerators to burn their infectious garbage.

Studies conducted by Canada's national environmental board and a state agency in California show that in addition to emitting dioxins and acid gases, many hospital incinerators may release low-level radioactive wastes when substances such as leftover chemotherapy drugs are burned. Some of these drugs are so toxic that they're classified by the Nuclear Regulatory Commission (NRC) as "hazardous" wastes. A recent report published in *Pollution Engineering* concludes that chemotherapy wastes not burned at high enough temperatures may result in the release of cancer-causing contaminants.

"I don't think many hospital administrators realize that these drugs are regulated as hazardous," says the EPA's Sales. "It amazes me; they don't even know that the drugs might cause a problem."

Some materials dumped into hospital burn boxes are harmless by themselves. When combined with other substances, however, they form dangerous compounds. According to Lauber, hydrochloric acid produced by burning plastics may combine with formaldehyde—a chemical used in hospital labs to store tissue samples—to form a very potent human carcinogen called BCME (bichloromethylether). "I think it could happen in these old, inefficient incinerators," says Lauber. "And we don't know if there *is* a safe level of this material that we can be exposed to."

Five thousand "retort," or excess-air, hospital incinerators are operating around the country, according to recent EPA estimates. These antiquated incinerators burn refuse with plenty of air, ensuring incomplete combustion and the release of toxic by-products. Most have absolutely no controls to prevent the emission of acid gases and dioxins.

The remaining hospital incinerators—about 1,600 of them—are more modern. Built

Some experts on sea mammals suspect that the scores of dolphins that washed up along the East Coast in 1987 died from an immune-system disorder contracted from ocean pollution.

according to the "controlled-air" design, they limit the amount of air in the burn chamber, ensuring better incineration, and usually possess a second chamber, where hydrocarbon gases are retained and burned. Yet these models, while slightly less toxic than the old retort incinerators, don't have wet or dry scrubbers, essential equipment that prevents the escape of acid gases and dioxins into the air. Most also lack automatic controls, the latest safety innovation.

Why Not Recycle?

Because of the very nature of infectious waste, recycling is not a viable option. "I'm in favor of recycling," says Lauber. "We just have to find people willing to sort through the infectious material and separate the metals and glass and plastics. That could be dangerous." Infectious trash is still allowed in landfills in many states, but the furor over AIDS may force states to forbid dumping unburned hospital waste in landfills—even if it has been "treated" to make it noninfectious.

The only solution to the infectious-waste dilemma is incineration. Not just any type of incineration will do, obviously. State-of-the-art facilities are needed, with high combustion efficiency, high temperatures in the range of 2,000° F (1,100° C), automatic shutdown controls, and pollution-treatment mechanisms such as scrubbers to prevent the emission of dangerous toxins. New large-scale, regional waste-to-energy hospital incinerators with dry-air scrub-

bers can also be built; one heat-recovery model is being erected at a hospital in Albany, New York. It combines an innovative energy-recovery system with pollution controls, and the recovery system's $80,000 price tag (the pollution controls are extra) has an estimated energy-saving payback time of about two years.

Most of the nation's 6,600 on-site hospital incinerators don't have this kind of sophisticated equipment; many hospitals can't afford the steep cost of upgrading their old incinerators to meet new pollution standards. The best solution for any infectious-waste generator burning less than 1,000 pounds (450 kilograms) per hour, says Lauber, is to send the waste to regional commercial incinerators. "I'd like to see more of these large, highly efficient BACT facilities. The waste could be properly manifested, properly packaged; that way no sanitation worker could get stuck with a needle," he says. Tighter local and state regulations for infectious waste, Lauber says, will encourage private industry to build these safe regional incinerators.

This is the future of infectious waste. The irony is, none of the new disposal measures we envision will control or even hinder the spread of AIDS. It is only the smallest consolation that a deadly epidemic, which could be eradicated before the century's end, may have provided us with the incentive to solve a separate dilemma—one that might have begun to plague us only in the year 2000 and beyond.

FORESTS AFIRE

by Elaine Rascoe

Early on the morning of September 7, 1988, bellhops at the historic Old Faithful Inn in Yellowstone National Park woke guests and told them to prepare for evacuation. The reason: a 200-foot (60-meter) wall of flames, fed by bone-dry trees and brush and fanned by 45-mile (72-kilometer)-per-hour winds, was sweeping toward the tourist complex around the park's famous geyser.

While the 85-year-old log hotel was spared, the flames that day destroyed a dozen park buildings, producing heat so intense that firefighters were forced to flee. By day's end the blaze, known as the North Fork fire, was thought to cover more than 200,000 acres (81,000 hectares). And it was just one of thousands of fires, large and small, that raged out of control in one of the longest and worst U.S. wildfire seasons on record.

By the time rain and snow had snuffed out the last of the flames in November, the fires had swept through an estimated 6 million acres (2.4 million hectares)—an area roughly the size of Massachusetts and Rhode Island combined. Alaska and the western states were hardest hit. The Federal Government had spent more than $580 million fighting the wildfires. Some 30,000 fire fighters had been mobilized, and 10 had been killed.

The most publicized of the fires broke out in Yellowstone National Park and nearby areas, where nearly 1 million acres (400,000 hectares) burned. The extent of damage to the park and the long-term effects on its forests and wildlife are still being assessed. But meanwhile, a sharp debate has broken out over the role that federal policy played in feeding the flames in this and other national parks and forests.

Setting the Stage

When Yellowstone, the country's (and the world's) first national park, was established in 1872, officials modeled their forest management policies on European theories, which held that forest fires were to be promptly put out. That policy held for nearly 100 years despite the fact that it was better suited to the carefully managed plantation forests of Europe than to the vast and tangled wilderness of the western United States.

Occasional severe fire seasons—including that of 1910, when extensive fires in the Rockies burned 5 million acres (2 million hectares) and sent a pall of smoke as far east as Toronto—only served to confirm the view that forest fires should be stopped quickly. Federal officials adopted the so-called "10:00 A.M. policy" (that is, any fire that broke out was to be under control by 10:00 A.M. the next day), and Smokey the Bear became its mascot.

In the early 1960s, however, some forestry experts and environmentalists began to question

Year of the forest fire: flames swept through nearly one million acres of Yellowstone National Park in 1988 (left), and burned millions more in other parks and forests throughout the western states. Thousands of professional and amateur fire fighters arrived to help battle the blazes (right). The record fires sparked sharp debate over the "let-it-burn" policy adopted in 1968 by the federal government.

the fire policy, noting that fire plays an important role in the maintenance of the forest ecosystem. By thinning the dense crown cover of mature forests, fire allows new vegetation to take hold on the forest floor, providing food for deer, elk, and other animals. It also returns nutrients to the soil and promotes the regeneration of certain tree species.

Moreover, environmentalists warned, park and forest officials might be paving the way to disaster by attempting to snuff every ground fire as soon as it broke out. Dry brush and deadwood were building up on the forest floors, setting the stage for much larger and more damaging fires than would otherwise occur. The accumulation of fuel increased the risk that any fire that broke out would rapidly engulf the forest canopy, killing trees and producing intense heat that would make regeneration more difficult.

These concerns were expressed in a 1963 report prepared for the Department of the Interior, and they were reflected in the Wilderness Act of 1964, which called for wild areas to be ''protected and managed so as to preserve natural conditions.'' The result was a new fire policy: beginning in 1968, the National Park Service (which manages forests within national parks) and the Forest Service (which oversees national forests) gradually adopted the view that natural fires should be allowed to burn unless they threatened people, property, or endangered species.

The new natural-burn (or ''let-it-burn'') policy was based in part on the view that most forest fires are self-limiting: mature tree stands burn readily, but fires tend to peter out when they reach stands of young trees, where there is less undergrowth and little deadwood on the ground. In theory, the more forest fires were allowed to go unchecked, the more effective this natural fire control would become—as a result of repeated burning and regeneration, forests would develop in a mosaic pattern of young, middle-aged, and old stands; and the mosaic itself would preclude widespread destruction.

By the time the new policy was in place in the early 1970s many national parks and forests were choked with deadwood and undergrowth, the products of 80 or 90 years of rigorous fire suppression. Still, natural fires that were allowed to burn mostly behaved according to plan and proved to be self-limiting—until 1988.

Unusually dry weather was the biggest factor in the change. The heat and drought that blis-

tered much of the country and damaged crops in the summer of 1988 also dried forests to tinder conditions. In some areas, lack of spring rainfall allowed the wildfire season to get under way as much as six weeks earlier than normal. In other areas the drought came later, but with effects that were just as devastating. In Yellowstone, for example, rainfall was unusually abundant in April and May, but then abruptly stopped, producing the driest season in the 112 years that weather records had been kept for the park.

Drought and policy, then, combined to set the stage for the fires of 1988. Lightning and human carelessness provided the match.

The Fires of 1988

When lightning began to spark fires in Yellowstone in early July, park officials were convinced that, as in past years, rain and the forest mosaic would keep them in check. But by July 21, with no rain in sight, it was clear that the fires were growing out of control. The Interior Department ordered park officials to switch to a policy of total suppression. At this point there were five major fires in the park: the Fan fire, in the northwest corner; the Red and Falls fires, in the southwest; and the Clover and Mist fires, in the east. Together, they covered less than 17,000 acres (6,900 hectares).

But fire fighters were unable to contain the flames, which continued to spread until several of the largest fires merged. And the original fires were soon joined by more—the Shoshone fire, near Yellowstone Lake; the Mint Creek fire, in the southeast; the North Fork fire, which spread into the park from the Targhee National Forest to the west; and others. The North Fork fire, which was thought to have been started by a dropped cigarette, would grow to become the largest in Yellowstone's history, covering almost 500,000 acres (200,000 hectares). And by mid-September, the perimeters of the various fires enclosed nearly half the park's 2.2 million acres (890,000 hectares).

Yellowstone was not alone–elsewhere, federal officials reported major fires burning out of control in more than 20 national parks and forests in six western states. In Alaska 2.2 million acres (890,000 hectares) of tundra and spruce forest were ablaze. In California a 35,000-acre (14,000-hectare) blaze near Sacramento (one of nearly 10,000 wildfires that broke out in the state in 1988) engulfed homes and barns and did roughly $22 million in damage. Nor was the West the only part of the coun-

State forestry officials (above) monitoring the fires kept in constant contact with fire fighters at the scene. Hosing down the flames (below) became a less effective means of containment once the fires grew out of control.

try to be affected—in the Northeast, hot, dry weather was also a problem. Fires burned more than 6,400 acres (2,600 hectares) in New York State in 1988, six times the amount that had burned the year before. Nationwide, the Boise Interagency Fire Center, an Idaho-based agency that coordinates fire-fighting efforts, reported some 60,000 forest fires.

Fire fighters were taxed to the limit. With fires burning in so many areas, states that normally send reinforcements to western wildfire areas were unable to do so. (Even in Alaska, where most of the 1988 fires were allowed to burn unchecked, some 10,000 fire fighters battled those that threatened settlements.) Instead, 6,000 soldiers and marines were called out to help a force of 20,000 professional fire fighters. More reinforcements came from Canada and from some 4,000 largely untrained temporary workers, who included prison inmates, unemployed men and women who wanted the $7.40-an-hour wage that was offered, and adventurers seeking the experience of a lifetime.

Ditches dug ahead of the advancing flames helped prevent the fires from reaching the tinder-dry vegetation.

Working 14-day shifts and sleeping in tents or under the stars (sometimes in mountain areas where nighttime temperatures dropped below freezing), the fire fighters used shovels and bulldozers to dig lines around the fires, hoping to block their spread by stripping away the vegetation that provided them with fuel. Helicopters with 2,300-gallon (8,700-liter) buckets doused the flames with water, while workers on the ground used water hoses on still-smoldering logs or shoveled earth over them to smother the embers. To coordinate these efforts, officials in many areas relied on the Fire Logistics and Mapping System (FLAME), locating the fires and monitoring their spread by means of infrared scanning surveys conducted by aircraft.

Too often, however, the fire fighters battled in vain—the flames simply leaped across the fire lines and spread. Officials in some cases were criticized for doing too little, too late. In Yellowstone, for example, park officials had let the Clover-Mist fire burn for three weeks after full suppression was ordered July 21, mistakenly convinced that cliffs and other natural barriers would contain it. Park officials were also alleged to have hampered fire fighters by discouraging the use of bulldozers, in the belief that the machines would do more lasting damage than the fire, and directing helicopter pilots to fill their water buckets at sites that were distant but not ecologically sensitive.

For the most part, though, fire fighters were simply overwhelmed by natural forces in 1988. "Many fires were so bad that when they started you could have had six battalions of fire fighters just over the hill and they still would have gotten big," a spokesman for the Boise Interagency Fire Center told *The New York Times*. Indeed, some of the largest fires (such as the North Fork fire) had been set by humans, and thus were fought from the moment they broke out. Weather was a major hindrance—whipped by winds of up to 80 miles (130 kilometers) per hour and fueled by dry conditions, the flames hopscotched not only fire breaks but also roads and rivers. In some cases the high winds carried burning brands to start new fires more than a mile from their source.

The fires produced a haze of smoke that hung over much of Montana and Wyoming. They also produced a blitz of media attention, especially at Yellowstone. Reporters converged on the park, describing a moonscape of blackened devastation. Words such as "unprecedented" and "disaster" figured heavily in the

As the inferno grew, helicopters were called in to help douse the flames with 2,300-gallon buckets of water.

accounts. (Officials in Alaska, where the area in flames equaled the total area of Yellowstone, were said to be bemused by the attention the famous park received.)

Although the park attendance was cut in half and some popular areas were closed to visitors, hundreds of tourists nevertheless arrived for a firsthand look at the awesome power of nature. Park officials responded with a special fire information center near the west entrance. Businesses in the surrounding communities, which normally thrive on tourism, made the best of a bad situation with ''fire sales.''

Meanwhile, in Washington, D.C., the ''let-it-burn'' policy came under attack from members of Congress and was questioned by President Reagan, who told reporters, ''I did not even know it existed.'' The policy was reportedly under review by Interior Secretary Donald Hodel and other officials. And a panel of government and outside experts was convened to examine the effects of allowing forest fires to burn, and to make recommendations.

After the Fires

In the end the weather, which had done so much to spread the fires, changed sides and helped put them out. By mid-November, autumn rain and snow had virtually eliminated the fire danger in most areas, although some brush fires continued in southern California.

The job of assessing the damage began, and in many areas, officials reported that the destruction was not as widespread as had initially been feared. In Yellowstone, for example, fire had scorched 995,000 acres (400,000 hectares); but the trees had survived in a third of that area. (In one case of media overstatement, a widely shown scene of charred and fallen trees turned out to depict trees that had been knocked down by a windstorm two years earlier and, as dead timber, had burned on the ground.) Only 2 percent of the burned land had experienced heat intense enough to carry deep into the earth, killing dormant seeds and roots.

Thus the process of regeneration was expected to begin promptly, with a bumper crop of

At Yellowstone, buildings threatened by the encroaching flames (above) were hosed down to reduce their flammability. Nonetheless, a dozen buildings were destroyed, although the park's historic Old Faithful Inn— evacuated as a safety measure (left)—survived.

grasses and wildflowers predicted for the spring of 1989. But that process would take a long time to complete. Officials estimated that it would take 20 years for the charred remnants of trees to decay, with the result that many areas of the park would continue to look burned-out for a long time. Lodgepole pines, which produce cones that open only in the intense heat of a forest fire, would be among the first trees to take root in these areas, along with deciduous shrubs

and trees. Many of the park's aspens survived and were expected to go through a period of regeneration and growth that is typical for this species after a fire.

But it would be 300 years before the burned areas were once again cloaked with the mature pine and fir forests that were there before the fires. Yellowstone officials stressed that the destruction of 1988 was part of a normal cyclical pattern. In fact, they said, most of the forests in the burned areas were 200 to 300 years old—they had gotten their start after a major fire storm that swept through the area of the park in the 1700s.

Still, the damage in this park and elsewhere was extraordinary, and it presented immediate problems for wildlife. While many birds were thought to have been killed by the flames, counts showed that relatively few of Yellowstone's large animals had died. They had, however, lost a significant portion of their food supply. Officials were concerned about the park's grizzly bears, which depend heavily on white-bark pine nuts for food; 10 to 22 percent of the white-bark pines had been destroyed. And matters were especially critical for the park's herds of bison and elk because sections of their winter range had burned.

Environmentalists generally opposed proposals to feed these animals through the winter, arguing that nature should be allowed to take its course. Animals that survived were expected to thrive on the new growth of grass and shrubs in the spring. However, the Park Service proposed feeding some of the herds to prevent them from leaving the park for surrounding areas, where they might compete with ranch cattle for scarce winter feed or fall victim to hunters.

Debate also broke out over proposals to reseed and replant some park areas. While the Park Service generally frowned on reforestation as an unnatural interference, it considered replanting bulldozed areas and some other damaged sections of land, such as streambeds and roadsides, to control erosion. The Forest Service, which normally takes a more active approach in managing its lands, planned an extensive reforestation effort.

Meanwhile, tourists continued to arrive at Yellowstone, encouraged by the Park Service through a major promotional effort. The park was billed as a sort of laboratory where people could see nature at work, and officials were optimistic—they noted that the Mount St. Helens volcano in Washington State had become a major tourist attraction only after a 1980 eruption blasted the forests off its slopes. Other parks soon began similar promotions.

Communities around the parks were not so confident, however; and many added their voices to the chorus calling for revisions in federal fire policy. Critics of the natural-burn policy noted that Canada, which suppresses forest fires in parks because of the risk they pose to its vital timber industry, experienced much less damage in 1988. (Canadian officials, for their part, said luck was responsible for much of the difference.)

Some critics adopted the views of Alston Chase, author of the 1986 book *Playing God in Yellowstone*. Chase argued that the natural-burn policy wasn't natural at all: studies of tree scars showed that, before the 1870s, fires had swept through the park regularly. Many of these blazes were set by Indians, who used them to drive game. The frequency of the fires ensured that they stayed small; but once this practice stopped, fuel began to build up on the forest floor. Thus, Chase argued, the preferred way to prevent fire storms like that of 1988 was with a program of prescribed burning—setting small ground fires in spring and fall, when rain and snow would limit their extent, to produce a mosaic of new growth and firebreaks.

Similar prescribed-burn policies had in fact been used successfully in a few parks, including Everglades in Florida and Sequoia in California. But even if the Park Service stayed with the natural-burn policy elsewhere, it was expected to become more active, clearing away deadwood and acting quickly to put out fires that sprang up near developed areas such as that around Old Faithful.

Yellowstone rebirth: not long after the fires ended, plants and animals began to thrive again.

POLLUTION'S ASSAULT ON ANTIQUITY

by Carl Nylander

Air pollution has dramatically accelerated the deterioration of ancient sculpture and architecture. Throughout Rome, Athens, and elsewhere in the Old World, alarmed archaeologists and environmentalists work feverishly to preserve what remains of the ancient structures (facing page).

When pioneering 19th-century photographers first descended on classical Greek and Roman sites, the Old World ruins were still relatively unmarred. But today these same ruins present a sorry contrast to their appearance of only a century ago. The deterioration of these treasures is, indeed, so shocking that it has turned onetime desk archaeologists into environmental activists.

The Ruin of Ruins

To see this destruction firsthand, one needs only to go to the Temple of the Dioscuri in the Roman Forum, which is being worked on by teams from the Scandinavian academies in Rome. Just by reaching out and, at random, stroking one of the marble blocks, the hand comes away white with the sugarlike powder of disintegrating stone. Not far away, high up on the protective scaffolding around the Column of Marcus Aurelius in Rome's Piazza Colonna, one can see the pitted, leprous limbs and faces that now disfigure the once-smooth sculptures depicting heroic Marcomanni and Romans. All over Rome the ubiquitous green antipollution plastic shrouding temples, arches, and columns snaps and flutters in the breeze, signaling crisis and ruin of ruins.

Why should we be so upset about the ongoing destruction of what are long-studied and apparently well-known monuments? Because whatever exciting new directions archaeology takes in the future, our monuments—the major works of architecture and sculpture—will always remain central to our ongoing dialogue with the past. They constitute the fundamental sources for any future studies.

The ugly fact, however, is that worldwide air pollution is now destroying—rapidly, indiscriminately, and seemingly beyond repair and restoration—many of our most precious monuments of antiquity.

Past and Present Problem

Air pollution is actually not a new phenomenon. Ancient Roman writers complain about smoke blackening Rome's temples and about noxious exhausts from glassmakers' furnaces. In England of 1288, there were already complaints that ''wherein the lime was formerly burnt with logs of wood, it is now burnt by sea-coal, so that air is infected and corrupted. . . .''

This strikingly modern-sounding passage was penned by the diarist John Evelyn in 1661: ''. . . the weary traveler, at many miles distance, sooner smells, than sees the city to which he repairs. This is that pernicious smoke which sullies all her glory, superinducing a sooty crust or fur upon all that it lights [on], spoiling the movables, tarnishing the plate gildings and furniture, and corroding the very iron bars and hardest stones with those piercing and acrimonious spirits which accompany its sulfur; and executing more in one year, than exposed to the pure air of the country it could effect in some hundreds. It is this horrid smoke which obscures our churches, and makes our palaces look old; which fouls our clothes, and corrupts the waters so [that] the very rain, and refreshing dews . . . precipitate this impure vapor, which, with its black and tenacious quality, spots and contaminates whatsoever is exposed to it.'' Here, more than 300 years ago, we are already introduced to destructive sulfur, acid rain, and the resulting corrosion of metal and stone.

Already a serious problem in the past, air pollution has increased tremendously in the modern era, especially since World War II; it is now seriously affecting atmosphere and climate on a global scale. Major contributing factors include extensive industrialization, with its enormous, energy-consuming, and waste-producing production processes; fossil fuel–

Above and facing page: © Fornaciari/Gamma-Liaison

using heat systems; and gasoline consumption by an ever-increasing number of cars. The result is that air pollution has become one of the major problems of modern society, posing serious threats to health and to the environment.

Destruction Mechanics

Pollution is, of course, not a localized phenomenon: tremendous amounts of sulfur, nitrogen, hydrocarbons, ozone, and heavy metals are ejected into the atmosphere and carried far across national boundaries. The amount of airborne pollution—notably sulfur dioxide (SO_2), from industrial and domestic combustion, and nitrogen oxide (NO_x), from combustion in car engines—is today more than 10 times greater than before industrialization. For instance, in 1982 the European countries pumped more than 65 million tons (59 million metric tons) of SO_2

The magnificent Parthenon in Athens (above) has withstood over 2,400 years of weather and wars. In the last 50 years, however, acid rain, automobile exhaust, and industrial pollution have stained the building (left) and decomposed its marble surface at a startling rate. The Greek government has closed the Parthenon to tourist traffic while archaeologists try to save the building from further damage.

into the world atmosphere (more than 200 pounds—90 kilograms—for each of Europe's 600 million inhabitants!). Soil, water, vegetation, and fauna suffer. And—a matter of special concern to archaeologists—the two main pollutants, SO_2 and NO_x, are precisely the chemicals that affect stone most detrimentally. When stone is quarried, the cut surface forms a sort of patina, or skin, that makes the material resistant to normal weathering. This patina can be formed only once. If it is broken by physical stress or by chemical corrosion, the newly exposed surface is relatively weaker than the original one. Weathering then becomes a troublesome problem: the stress of normal expansion and contraction of the stone caused by variations in temperature and humidity is accentuated by the erosive

and other effects of wind, rain, and frost. Biological damage results from the mechanical and chemical activities of plants, algae, and microorganisms. Chemical erosion through air pollution is caused above all by SO_2 and by NO_x. Under special climatic conditions of humidity (such as often occur in Rome), these two pollutants tend to combine synergistically—that is, in ways that drastically increase and accelerate destruction. Acting on limestone and marble, SO_2 transforms the stone into gypsum, which is water-soluble and is washed away on surfaces exposed to rain.

On the other hand, on protected surfaces, where condensation may take place, a crust may be formed with physical properties different from those of the stone beneath. This crust is not waterproof and allows further deterioration to take place underneath it. Meanwhile, the crust formation is accentuated by dust deposits enriched with polluting organic and inorganic particles. Marble is especially sensitive to chemical corrosion and acid rain because of characteristic cracking that increases with age, allowing various kinds of pollutants to penetrate deeper and deeper into the heart of the stone. Eventually these crusts, several millimeters thick, split open because of pressure from the reactions beneath their surface.

Heroic Measures

In many places in the Old World—and elsewhere—the situation for monuments is now critical. One way to preserve ancient treasures is to replace them with plastic models and move the originals indoors. In Athens, for instance, the statues of draped maidens (called caryatids) that support the porch of the Erechtheum temple on the Acropolis are made of plastic; the original marble caryatids have found safety in the Acropolis Museum. In the same museum are the statues of Kekrops and Pandrosos from the Parthenon West Pediment—preserved in a transparent box filled with nitrogen gas. Meanwhile, plastic copies now take the place of these figures in the pediment. Michaelangelo's *David* in Piazza della Signoria in Florence has also been replaced by a copy, and Rome's benevolent guardian spirit, Marcus Aurelius on his powerful horse, has left Piazza Campidoglio, perhaps never to return.

But most monuments have to stay where they are and suffer all the diseases that today can affect marble and limestone. Heroic efforts are being made by archaeological authorities in Rome to study, to clean, to protect and preserve—and, if possible, to slow down the ongoing destructive process. But it is an uphill battle. The destructive onslaught by pollutants has been violent and is rapidly increasing—as is clear, not least, from comparisons with old photographs, which have now become valuable sources, and plaster casts made in the past century or before World War II.

Four important monuments in central Rome have been singled out by the archaeological authorities for special study and for cleaning and treatment: the arches of Septimius Severus and Constantine, and the columns of Trajan and Marcus Aurelius. Scaffolding makes possible a close-up, shocking view of the state of the rich sculptural decoration of these creations.

Everywhere we see the black crust or fur created by dirt, soot, impurities of metal oxides, and advancing corrosion of the surface. We see the raw, nakedly white spots marking surface losses caused by mechanical abrasion, frost, salt, and chemical attack. This, however, is not the end result but work in progress: beneath the surface of such crust or such "white wounds," the pollutants penetrate farther into the stone, together with algae and microorganisms that produce acids and consume the bonding between the stone's crystals.

It is obvious that sculptures, with their intricate plastic forms, and architectural ornamentation provide an excellent foothold for the pollutants carried by wind and rain. Faces, hair, drapery, and bodies in action are the most exposed parts of the statues. So on the sculp-

Pollution has ravaged the statues of the draped maidens that support the porch of the Erechtheum, a temple on the Acropolis in Athens. Archaeologists have replaced each corroded statue (front) with a plastic model (rear), and preserved the originals in a museum.

A corroded statue rescued from the elements requires years of work before it even approaches its former appearance.

tures and ornamentations marred by pollution, we meet faceless armies and deformed people, covered with black accretions and with white wounds, and wearing undefined raiment. The hostile elements are slowly reshaping our monuments in an obtuse style of their own, conveying a message less of triumph than of ultimate, hopeless defeat. Not all parts are equally affected: well-preserved parts stand close to destroyed ones, often those most exposed to wind and rain. But it is important to realize that there is hardly one stone in Rome that has not been affected in one way or another.

Losing Our Heritage?

Experiences like these in Rome could be multiplied with examples from Athens, Ankara (Turkey), Krakow (Poland), Cologne (West Germany), Copenhagen (Denmark), and so on. The international symposium on Air Pollution and Conservation at the Swedish Institute in Rome in October 1986 made this fact clear. There is, indeed, ample evidence that we are now losing our heritage, our sources, at a fright-

ening rate. Already some crucial monuments, like Rome's columns of Trajan and Marcus Aurelius, cannot any longer be fully studied from the originals, but only from the casts made for Napoleon III in 1862 and from the photographic documentation done for the German kaiser in 1898. The same will be true for monuments in many other places.

What can be done about this most serious situation? Any meaningful answer to this question calls for momentous decisions on the political level. But until these decisions are forthcoming, the scientists and conservators are valiantly doing their part, trying to understand the many variables involved in stone degradation. The hope is to develop methods of cleaning and treating the stone so as to protect it and slow down the basically inevitable process of aging and decay. We gratefully acknowledge the fine, committed work done by the archaeological and conservation authorities in Rome, Athens, Ankara, and many other places.

The need for a special contribution from archaeology is twofold. One contribution would be to use our archaeological knowledge and methods to increase the understanding of the creation and long life of these works, to help rescue the crucial monuments of the past, especially those in the heavily polluted centers of our cities, and to collaborate with scientists and conservators.

Documenting Monuments

Another, even more important, contribution—and one much in our self-interest—is to compile as thorough a documentation as possible of other threatened monuments. While air pollution attacks indiscriminately everywhere, only selected monuments can be treated on the intensive scale attempted for the buildings of the Acropolis in Athens and the monuments of central Rome. Others—in the end no less important from a historical point of view—should be well documented for future reference, precisely for the very reason that they may otherwise soon disintegrate and silently disappear as witnesses and partners in any future archaeological dialogue with the past. The challenge to archaeologists is to devise programs, strategies, and techniques to accomplish this undertaking.

A number of such documentation projects are already under way in several countries. A productive recent test case has been the international, interdisciplinary documentation of the 2,600 grave monuments of some 4,000 people in the so-called Protestant Cemetery in Rome (resting place of Keats, Shelley, and other artists and scholars). This undertaking includes creation of a database. Similar activity is carried on in the United States by the American Monument and Outdoor Sculpture Database (AMOS), under the National Park Service and part of the National Acid Precipitation Assessment Program, which is at present handling information on some 5,500 monuments. There is thus growing experience with the problems of broad documentation strategies and projects.

Archaeologists and art historians must now look beyond "business as usual" perspectives. They should step out of libraries, classrooms, and academic dens, and examine firsthand the problem of our endangered monuments. What is needed now is *not* more excavation; what now demands maximum attention is not what is buried deep in the earth, but what is already visible *on its surface.* We now need a wide-ranging international effort, a sort of multinational "Marshall Plan" for the monuments of the Old World. Here is the great, meaningful challenge for the archaeological community: to do the utmost, before it is too late, to Save Our Sources!

Despite their valiant attempts to save classical ruins, archaeologists still despair every time they see the dense layers of smog and haze that shroud ancient cities.

HEALTH
AND
DISEASE

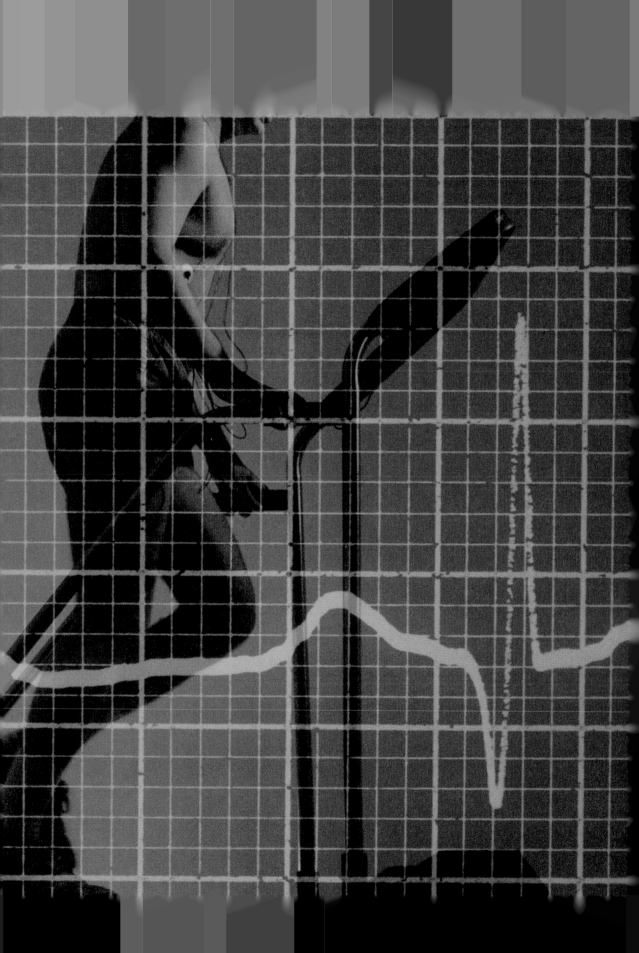

HEALTH AND DISEASE

AIDS, the drug epidemic, cholesterol, and antiacne preparations topped 1988's medical news. Controversy swirled around mammograms and cesarean sections. Bright spots occurred in dentistry and in heart disease research.

by Jenny Tesar

"The Most Alarming Disease of our Times"

By the end of 1988, acquired immune deficiency syndrome (AIDS) had claimed a reported 46,344 lives in the United States. The actual number of deaths is estimated to be higher, however, because in many cases the cause of death is listed as something other than AIDS. For example, AIDS is believed responsible for an increase in pneumonia deaths among young adults.

The soaring number of AIDS cases threatens to overwhelm health-care systems in nations both rich and poor. Treatment costs are staggering. In New York City, it costs about $80,000 to treat an AIDS-infected baby. In Tanzania, where the per capita health budget is $1 a year, it costs up to $631 a year to care for an AIDS patient.

The blood of infected individuals usually contains antibodies—substances produced by the immune system to fight the virus. In late 1988 the U.S. Food and Drug Administration (FDA) approved a new bioengineered test for antibodies to the AIDS virus. Called Recombigen HIV-1 Latex Agglutination, the test is fast, accurate, inexpensive, and can be performed without sophisticated equipment.

The FDA also approved alpha interferon, the first drug specifically developed for treating Kaposi's sarcoma, a cancer that frequently develops in AIDS patients, particularly homosexual men.

The first drug approved for the treatment of AIDS itself, azidothymidine (AZT), cannot be taken by as many as 50 percent of all patients because of side effects, including liver damage and the development of anemia. Many other drugs are being tested in trials involving thousands of AIDS patients.

Desperate patients have flocked to other countries to try drugs not available in the U.S. Following criticism of its lengthy drug-approval procedures, the FDA agreed to allow Americans to import unapproved drugs from abroad in small quantities for personal use. It also changed approval procedures in an effort to make new treatments available more quickly to people suffering from AIDS and other life-threatening diseases. Only two phases of human tests will be required to prove an AIDS drug effective and safe. The third phase, which can take several years, will be dropped.

In the United States, nearly a quarter of all AIDS cases occur in New York City and San Francisco. In Central Park, New Yorkers assembled a memorial quilt from panels that represent local residents who died from the disease.

© Laurie Burnham

"Know Your Cholesterol"

"If you are among the two out of three Americans who do not smoke or drink excessively, your choice of diet can influence your long-term health prospects more than any other action you might take," said Surgeon General Koop as he released the most comprehensive report on nutrition and health ever prepared by the government. The report identified excessive fat consumption as the nation's primary dietary priority, urging Americans to cut their fat intake, which now accounts for at least 37 percent of calorie intake, well above the recommended 30 percent limit.

Closely allied with fats is cholesterol, a fatlike substance found in foods of animal origin that is associated with increased risk of circulatory diseases. For example, for every 1 percent increase in a person's blood cholesterol, his or her risk of a heart attack increases about 2 percent.

"Know Your Cholesterol" advertised the National Heart, Lung and Blood Institute. Public health experts recommend a reading below 200 milligrams for adults, and 140 to 150 milligrams for children age 2 and older. Yet surveys indicate that many children have elevated cholesterol, and that 60 percent exceed the recommended daily maximum intake of 300 milligrams.

Drugs introduced in recent years are proving effective in lowering high cholesterol levels. Other techniques are also being developed. For instance, researchers at Duke University in Durham, North Carolina, are testing a new "Roto-Rooter" device that cuts away the fatty deposits that can narrow the opening of arteries. The device has a cutting blade activated by a hand-held, battery-operated motor. The debris is then removed by suction.

Abused Drugs, Both Legal and Illegal

Each day almost 1,000 Americans quit smoking . . . by dying. Smoking tobacco is the single most preventable cause of death in our society. Many people who try to stop smoking find they cannot overcome their dependence on cigarettes. In May, U.S. Surgeon General C. Everett Koop warned that the nicotine in tobacco is addictive, causing a physical dependence not unlike that caused by heroin and cocaine.

Even people in their seventies can benefit significantly by stopping smoking. A study of people with clogged arteries found that over six years the death rate of older people who continued to smoke was 70 percent greater than the rate of people who had quit shortly before the study began.

For the first time, a tobacco company was found partly responsible for the death of a smoker who developed lung cancer. The suit was filed in the federal district court in Newark, New Jersey, by the widower of the smoker, Rose Cipollone, against the Liggett Group. The jury determined that before 1966, when warnings on cigarette packages were first required by law in the U.S., Liggett had known of the health risks of smoking but had failed to warn consumers.

A new "smokeless" cigarette introduced in 1988 became the target of the American Medical Association (AMA) and other health groups, who asked for a ban on the product's sale and distribution. The AMA contended that these cigarettes should be regarded as a "drug delivery system" designed to introduce nicotine into the users' bodies.

While society found an often losing battle in its fight against the ravages caused by use of crack (the smokable form of cocaine), other illicit drugs surfaced or gained new popularity. Particularly worrisome was the dramatic increase in the production of methamphetamine, a powerful stimulant. A National Institute of Drug Abuse study warned that this drug "looms as a potential national drug crisis for the 1990's."

The misuse of anabolic steroids received widespread publicity following the Summer Olympics, when 10 athletes were expelled for using the banned drugs. The Mayo Clinic estimated that a million Americans take steroids for nonmedical purposes, and a 1987 survey of high school boys indicated that 6.6 percent had used steroids, suggesting that as many as 500,000 adolescents were using or have used the drugs. But any improvements in strength or stamina derived from steroid abuse are more than offset by such potential medical dangers as baldness, severe acne, liver failure, high blood pressure, and cancer of the liver and testicles.

AP/Wide World

Olympic officials stripped Canadian sprinter Ben Johnson of the gold medal in the 100-meter dash when postrace tests revealed he had taken steroids.

Debate on Antiacne Drugs

Sales of Retin-A products, long prescribed to treat acne, soared following publication of a study that found that the chemical could improve skin texture and reduce some of the wrinkles caused by sun damage. The FDA and others warned, however, that many patients develop a rash from using the Retin-A cream, and that long-term effects of the drug are unknown.

New guidelines were recommended for a closely related antiacne compound, Accutane, following reports of severe birth defects in children born to women who used the drug. Apparently, patients ignored package warnings to avoid use of Accutane "if you are or may become pregnant during therapy."

Another related medication, Tegison, used to treat severe cases of psoriasis, was also reported to produce birth defects.

Photos courtesy of Dr. John J. Voorhes, University of Michigan Medical Center

In some patients, a daily application of Retin-A has smoothed out wrinkled, sun-damaged skin in just 17 months.

Caution, Controversy for Women

The most frequently performed surgery in the United States is cesarean section, performed when normal delivery is deemed hazardous for the mother or child. In 1986 the procedure accounted for 24.1 percent of all deliveries, more than five times the 1965 rate. In October 1988, the American College of Obstetricians and Gynecologists recommended that most women who have had a cesarean should attempt to have vaginal deliveries in subsequent births. There is evidence that cesareans increase risks to mothers and infants. And studies indicate that up to 80 percent of women who have had cesareans can have successful vaginal deliveries afterward.

While the incidence of breast cancer continued to increase, the medical establishment remained divided over the value of regular mammograms. Both the American Cancer Society and the American College of Radiology recommend that women undergo the procedure beginning in their late thirties. But one study published in 1988 found that routine mammograms in women under age 50 had little, if any, benefit. Conversely, another study found that mammography can reduce breast-cancer deaths among women in their forties, largely because the procedure detects cancer at an earlier, more curable stage.

Also under dispute is a reported link between alcohol consumption and breast cancer. Some studies indicate that alcohol consumption increases the risk, while others have found no association. And although age, family history, diet, and other factors are known to increase breast-cancer risks, most breast cancer occurs in women without attributable risk, noted Dr. Robert B. Taylor of the Oregon Health Sciences University School of Medicine.

Photos: © Bill Swersey/NYT Pictures

Some breast tumors can be felt and easily detected by mammogram (near right). Mammography finds particular value in detecting tumors that cannot be felt (center). Since mammograms cannot tell a benign cyst (far right) from cancer, a biopsy may be necessary.

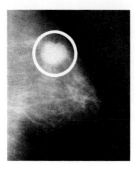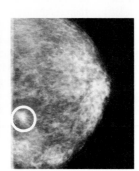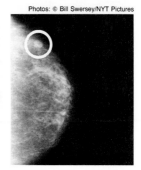

Dentistry Update

Fluoridation of drinking water plus the addition of fluoride to toothpastes have led to a dramatic drop in tooth decay. According to a 1986–87 survey, half the nation's schoolchildren have no cavities or other tooth decay in their permanent teeth. "This is remarkable, especially when you consider that almost all of their parents suffered from tooth decay as children," said Dr. Harold Loe of the National Institutes of Health (NIH).

Those same adults now face another disease: periodontitis, a bacterially induced infection of the bones and gum tissue that support the teeth. Left untreated, teeth become loose and may even fall out. New, still experimental techniques enable dentists to rebuild bone decayed by periodontal disease. One method involves injecting into areas of bone loss synthetic materials that are similar to the mineral crystals found in natural bone. Also under investigation are various procedures to regenerate the connective tissue that anchors teeth to the bone.

The bacteria that cause decay and periodontal disease form a sticky, invisible film called plaque, which enables bacteria and the acids they produce to adhere to the teeth instead of being washed away by saliva. The best weapon against plaque is the toothbrush, used correctly and regularly. In addition, store shelves are being flooded with products proclaiming their ability to combat plaque. But in October the FDA, asserting that it had not received data to support such claims, asked six toothpaste and mouthwash manufacturers to remove the claims from product labels.

Traditional bridges of artificial teeth that sit atop the gums and are anchored to neighboring natural teeth are giving way to implants. These are artificial teeth permanently attached to the jawbone, providing greater convenience and comfort than bridges. In 1978 a type of implant was considered successful if at least 75 percent of the implants lasted 5 years. By 1988 the standard was 85 to 90 percent survival for more than 10 years.

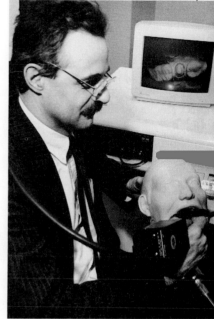

AP/Wide World

French dentists have demonstrated a system of dental restoration that uses computers to prepare and install a finished crown or bridge in one visit.

Increased Incidence of Skin Cancer

More than 500,000 new cases of skin cancer are diagnosed annually in the United States, making it the most common of all cancers. Although 87 percent of adult Americans know that sun exposure can cause skin cancer, four out of 10 say they are not concerned about the exposure they receive from the sun. "We've gotten the message across that excessive sun exposure is bad for our looks and our health, but . . . people don't believe it will happen to them," said Dr. Richard Odom, president of the American Academy of Dermatology.

The growing popularity of tanning salons and equipment that uses artificial sources of ultraviolet radiation is expected to result in an increased incidence of skin cancer. Another danger is the shrinking of the atmosphere's ozone layer. Ozone protects plant and animal life from harmful radiation. Thus the breakdown in ozone protection is expected to contribute to a rise in skin cancer.

Fortunately, improved diagnosis and screening as well as new and more aggressive treatments of cancerous and precancerous lesions have improved the outlook for skin cancer patients.

The alpha ultraviolet radiation that bombards patrons of tanning salons may ultimately promote skin cancer, increase the risk of cataracts, and even cause allergic reactions in people on medication.

© Steve Leonard/*Time* Magazine

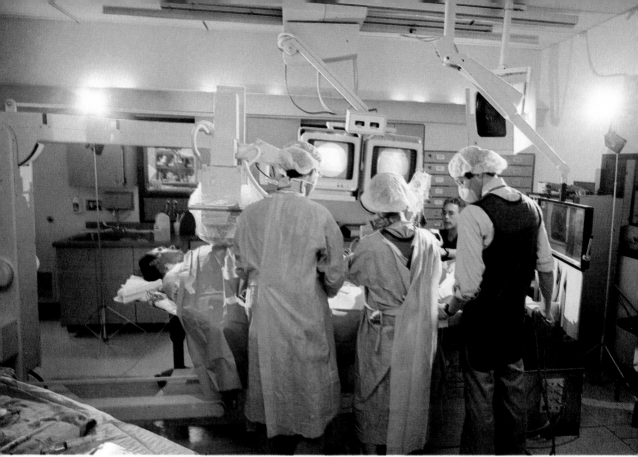

The Revolution in Heart Treatment

by Harold M. Schmeck, Jr.

He awoke shortly after midnight, a 60-year-old man who had always been in good health even though he smoked and was overweight. But now he had a crushing, breath-robbing pain in his chest. He felt nauseated and broke into a cold sweat. Both he and his wife recognized the signs. She called an ambulance, and 30 minutes later he was in the emergency room of Beth Israel Hospital in Boston, Massachusetts. His blood pressure was dropping, and his electrocardiogram warned that a major heart attack was almost certainly developing. Normally, if he was lucky enough to survive it, a special coronary care team would have to watch over his life for days to keep him from slipping over the edge. Even if they succeeded, his heart might well be severely and permanently damaged. That was the expectation, but for this patient there was a crucial dif-

ference. Within five minutes of his arrival at the hospital, doctors had inserted a tube in a vein in his arm and begun infusion of a drug called tissue plasminogen activator, or t-PA. Thirty minutes after the infusion began, the man's pain disappeared completely. And tests later indicated that the attack had been halted—with little heart damage.

Equally dramatic was the case of a Harvard Medical School professor who was driving to his office at the same hospital, when he began having chest pains. He, too, knew what was happening. In spite of his pain, he was able to

A drug called tissue plasminogen activator, or t-PA, can halt a heart attack in its tracks by dissolving artery-blocking blood clots. Using advanced imaging techniques, doctors can then assess the extent of heart damage and determine the course of further treatment.

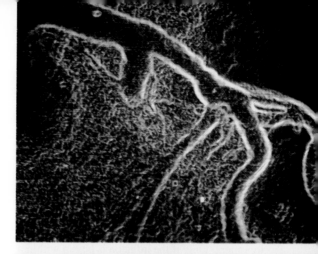

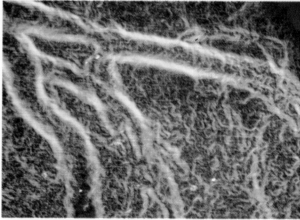

Photos: © Howard Sochurek

A blood clot greatly diminishes the flow of blood to the heart (top). If administered early enough, t-PA restores the blood supply (above) before extensive damage occurs.

continue driving to the hospital himself and went straight to the emergency entrance. He was treated immediately, and about a week later left the hospital, having apparently suffered no permanent heart damage. It appeared that the drug treatment had stopped his heart attack just as it was beginning.

A Clot-dissolving Approach

For the two patients and their families, these events were matters of life and death. But the implications of their stories are immense for the public as well. There is now widespread agreement that the drug infusions they received herald a revolution in coping with heart attacks— the first real revolution in medical treatment that can be credited to the new era of gene-splicing research and biotechnology. This treatment, known as thrombolytic therapy, uses t-PA or other similar drugs to dissolve the blood clots that cause most heart attacks. Every year in the United States, about 1.5 million people suffer heart attacks, and more than 300,000 die before they reach a hospital. Another 230,000 or more die after they arrive, according to government figures, in spite of all that doctors, nurses, and other health professionals can do for them. But many experts believe that the new drugs will dramatically reduce this death toll.

Although this revolution is in its infancy, doctors already see it as changing the whole atmosphere, the timing, and the rhythm of heart attack treatment. "This represents a watershed in the care of what still is the most common cause of hospital death in this country, and for that matter in the industrialized world," says Dr. Eugene Braunwald, chairman of medicine at Beth Israel Hospital and professor of medicine at Harvard Medical School. Dr. Eugene R. Passamani of the National Heart, Lung and Blood Institute, who worked with Dr. Braunwald in evaluating the new clot-dissolving approaches, takes the same view of the revolutionary heart treatments: "I think it is a success story of pretty large proportions."

Sudden Crisis, Prompt Therapy

The muscle that makes up the pumping chambers of the heart demands a continuous supply of oxygen-rich blood. The heart gets this nourishing supply from the coronary arteries, so named because they wreath the heart like a crown of vines. When a clot blocks one of these vital arteries, the portion of the heart that it serves begins to starve for lack of oxygen. The

clot formation is usually a consequence of a crack opening in one of the fatty deposits that narrow the arteries with the advance of atherosclerotic heart disease. But, while atherosclerosis is a gradual disease process, a clot that blocks an artery creates a sudden crisis. Unless the blood supply is restored quickly, some of the heart muscle will die.

Like many other things in modern medicine, the concept of dissolving clots in the heart is not new. But the process of translating that idea into widespread practice is revolutionary. Originally, the benefits of clot-dissolving treatment were demonstrated by infusing the drugs directly into the heart. This might never have been more than a medical curiosity because the mechanics of the procedure are difficult and potentially dangerous. Only specially trained teams at special medical centers would be able to do it well. But more recent studies have shown that a clot can be dissolved by relatively simple infusion through a vein, if the dose is sufficient; more is needed than for direct infusion into the heart.

Indeed, for many patients it does the job beautifully—if use of the drug is begun soon enough. The timing is crucial. "We are now about to enter the thrombolytic era," Dr. Sol Sherry of the Temple University School of Medicine, one of the pioneers in clot dissolving, wrote in a recent survey of the new therapy. But he and his coauthor, Dr. Victor J. Marder of the University of Rochester School of Medicine and Dentistry, stress the urgency of prompt treatment. Only if the infusion is begun within a few hours of the start of a heart attack can dramatic results be expected.

In individual cases, such as that of the 60-year-old man in Boston, it is never possible to be certain what would have happened if clot-attacking drugs had not been used. "I can't swear that he would have had severe damage," says Dr. Braunwald, "but given 10 patients like that, I can tell you that six would have had massive damage."

Early Research

The early focus of research was on three substances: t-PA, a protein that is produced naturally in minute amounts in the blood vessels and some other human tissues; streptokinase, another protein made naturally by one of the great classes of disease-causing bacteria, the streptococci, and urokinase, like t-PA, made in the human body. Long before the era of biotechnology, urokinase was harvested and purified from huge amounts of human urine, and streptokinase was purified painstakingly from the bacteria. T-PA, which was discovered in the late 1940s, was far too scarce for use as a drug—5½ tons of human tissue are needed to produce a single gram. But the skills of genetic engineers have changed that. These scientists have isolated the human gene that constitutes the body's own instructions for making t-PA, and have modified it so that mammalian cells growing in laboratory cultures will follow the instructions faithfully. Then the modified genes are transplanted into cells growing in two-story-high fermentation tanks. There, like workers on an assembly line, the cells produce great quantities of the needed commodity.

Streptokinase and urokinase have been tested for more than 30 years for their usefulness in dissolving dangerous clots within the human body, but outside the heart. Not until the early 1980s was large-scale use of any of the clot-dissolving agents against heart attacks considered seriously.

By 1983 it looked as though thrombolysis might well be more than medical fantasy. Dr. Braunwald, who is also chairman of medicine at Brigham and Women's Hospital in Boston, was named chairman of a study sponsored by the National Institutes of Health (NIH) to evaluate the thrombolytic treatment. One of the first tasks was to decide which of the available drugs worked best. Streptokinase and urokinase seemed to be about equally effective in dissolving clots, but urokinase was far more expensive. So the study group decided to compare streptokinase with what Dr. Braunwald called "the new kid on the block"—t-PA. Dr. Braunwald and many others were skeptical about t-PA.

In a study of 300 patients at several major hospitals, t-PA was shown to cause just as much bleeding as streptokinase, although in neither case was the bleeding sufficient to present a major problem. What was surprising was t-PA's success in reopening clogged arteries. "To my utter amazement," Dr. Braunwald recalls, "t-PA was much, much more effective."

Overall, the study found t-PA twice as effective as streptokinase in reopening totally closed arteries in the heart. The disparity was so great that an independent committee halted the trial prematurely, and preliminary results were published in 1985. Soon afterward the report of a major European study showed essentially the same results.

Course of Action

These studies compared the clot-dissolving abilities of the two substances, not their ultimate effectiveness in reducing deaths from heart attacks. The drugs help dissolve clots in other parts of the body as well. Indeed, streptokinase has been used for that purpose for years, and t-PA has recently been used in research on a few patients to dissolve clots that cause strokes, but the heart attack studies focused on arteries of the heart. To date, there has been little direct comparison of the lifesaving abilities of the various thrombolytic drugs, although large-scale studies are now under way.

Streptokinase and t-PA intercede at a key point in the chain of events by which blood clots form and persist in the body—events that can prevent fatal hemorrhage. One important substance in this process is fibrinogen, which circulates in the bloodstream until it encounters a

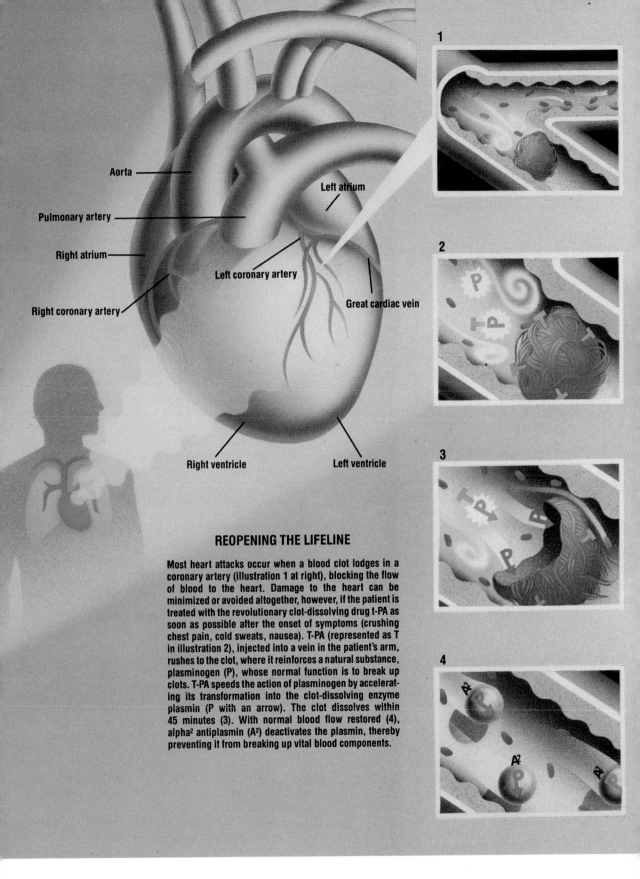

Aorta

Pulmonary artery

Right atrium

Left atrium

Left coronary artery

Right coronary artery

Great cardiac vein

Right ventricle

Left ventricle

1

2

3

4

REOPENING THE LIFELINE

Most heart attacks occur when a blood clot lodges in a coronary artery (illustration 1 at right), blocking the flow of blood to the heart. Damage to the heart can be minimized or avoided altogether, however, if the patient is treated with the revolutionary clot-dissolving drug t-PA as soon as possible after the onset of symptoms (crushing chest pain, cold sweats, nausea). T-PA (represented as T in illustration 2), injected into a vein in the patient's arm, rushes to the clot, where it reinforces a natural substance, plasminogen (P), whose normal function is to break up clots. T-PA speeds the action of plasminogen by accelerating its transformation into the clot-dissolving enzyme plasmin (P with an arrow). The clot dissolves within 45 minutes (3). With normal blood flow restored (4), alpha^2 antiplasmin (A^2) deactivates the plasmin, thereby preventing it from breaking up vital blood components.

Scientists use advanced bioengineering techniques to produce t-PA in large quantities. The drug's high cost—over $2,000 for a single dose—has been widely criticized by the medical community.

© Genentech, Inc.

Aspirin Helps

An international study that started in early 1989 may involve as many as 40,000 patients here and in Europe. It will be the largest study of heart attack treatment ever done, and will compare the lifesaving capabilities of t-PA, APSAC, and streptokinase.

In August 1988 the results of a major study of 17,000 patients here and in Europe showed that streptokinase has a strong beneficial effect in saving heart attack patients, and that, by itself, aspirin given during an attack also exerts powerful protection. The report, published in *The Lancet*, showed that the risk of death during a heart attack and in the month afterward was cut by at least 20 percent by streptokinase. For those patients who received both streptokinase and aspirin, the risk of death was cut about in half if the streptokinase was administered within six hours.

While biotechnology has solved the problem of making t-PA plentiful, it is still extremely expensive. Enough of the drug to treat one patient for one heart attack costs about $2,200—10 times as much as streptokinase. Some doctors privately criticize Genentech for the high price it charges for t-PA. The company recently announced that it will provide the drug free to patients whose annual income is less than $25,000 and who are not covered by private insurance or government reimbursement.

Coronary Care Units

Before the advent of clot-dissolving drugs, the greatest advance in treating heart attacks was the development of the coronary care unit a quarter of a century ago. Until the early 1960s, the death toll among heart attack victims who lived long enough to reach a hospital was about 30 percent. With the coronary care units came the prevention of many deaths from sudden stoppages of the heartbeat or from disastrous disturbances in the heart's rhythm—heart arrhythmias, the most serious of which is ventricular fibrillation. These dangerous disturbances can often be prevented in coronary care units, or else treated by drugs or, at last resort, by electrical shock to the chest—defibrillation.

Five years after coronary care units were first organized, doctors were reporting death rates among heart attack patients treated in some of the units as low as 12 percent. For patients who reached a hospital fast enough, deaths from heart arrhythmias were greatly reduced. But coronary care units did not solve the life-and-

break in a vessel that needs to be plugged. Then and there it is converted to fibrin, a durable, stringy material that forms a framework for a clot, holding it in place. As part of a vital system of checks and balances, another substance, plasminogen, is converted to plasmin in the presence of a clot. Plasmin breaks down fibrin to liquefy and dissolve the clot. Too much clotting stops blood flow and is just as bad as too little. Both streptokinase and t-PA act on the plasminogen-to-plasmin cycle. But t-PA activity is dependent on the presence of fibrin.

T-PA, made by the California biotechnology company Genentech, was approved in 1987 by the Food and Drug Administration (FDA), and now doctors have both it and streptokinase to work with. At least two other drugs are of special interest: APSAC (anisoylated plasminogen-streptokinase complex) and scu-PA (single-chain urokinase-type plasminogen activator). All seem capable of dissolving clots, but experts differ on which is most effective in treating heart attack patients.

death problem of those patients who suffered severe damage to the heart muscle because of a blockage of blood flow to the heart. Probably for that reason, the death rate from heart attacks leveled off and stayed essentially the same for more than two decades.

Presumably, people have died from heart attacks for many thousands of years, but only relatively recently has this become one of the major causes of death in the developed countries of the West. Throughout most of history, the majority of people died of infectious diseases, injuries, and violence or the cumulative effects of malnutrition long before reaching what we now call middle age, when heart attacks become common.

William Harvey, the 17th-century English physician, discovered the role of the coronary arteries in nourishing the heart muscle, but it was not until almost 150 years later that another Englishman, William Heberden, described the arterial hardening, narrowing, and clogging now known as coronary artery disease.

Blood-pressure measurements taken while exercising can be used to evaluate how well a patient's heart functions under stress. If a disorder exists, the patient can take remedial action to avoid suffering a heart attack.

© Arthur Sirdofsky/Medichrome

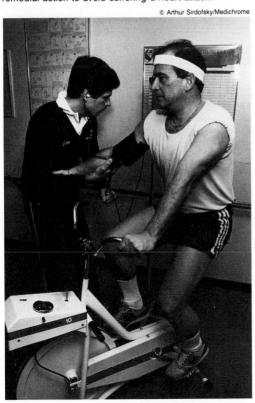

Early in this century, some doctors began to suspect that clots might be the main precipitating cause of heart attacks. This theory was difficult to prove, however, since many clots dissolve spontaneously with the passage of time. It was not until 1980 that the importance of clots was confirmed to most heart specialists' satisfaction. "Having recognized this important fact, attention quickly turned to interventional therapies" to restore blood flow, an editorial in the July 1988 *Archives of Internal Medicine* noted in discussing the future of heart attack treatment. Considering the great amount of time it often takes in medicine to translate an idea into practical and effective treatment, the progress of thrombolytic therapy has been remarkable.

Today clot-dissolving treatment is achieving between a 20 and 50 percent reduction in in-hospital deaths from heart attacks, depending on how early the therapy is begun, which drug is used, and other factors. Scientists note that there are also likely to be long-term advantages—real improvements in the quality of patients' lives because damage to the heart muscle has been kept to a minimum.

Doctors are trying several new methods to help clot-dissolving drugs achieve their best effects. Drugs called beta-blockers are being used experimentally to delay the death of heart muscle cells. An enzyme, superoxide dismutase, has been shown to eliminate the poisonous substances that appear in the heart tissue in the wake of an attack. Measures to make the blood particles called platelets less "sticky," or at least less prone to clump, are also being tried. Platelets are important in the normal clotting process.

Windows of Opportunity

The clot-dissolving drugs seem to make the clearest and most immediate difference to the greatest number of people. According to Rochester's Dr. Marder and Temple's Dr. Sherry, doctors must be rapidly educated about the benefits of thrombolytic therapy. Communities, health workers, and families of patients must be organized and galvanized to cut to a minimum the time between a patient's first symptoms and the start of treatment. Dr. Passamani of the National Heart, Lung and Blood Institute echoes that point. The new drugs, he believes, require a major change in strategy.

"Treatment must begin within minutes," Dr. Braunwald says. "If you treat people within

20 minutes to a half hour (after symptoms begin), you will probably prevent them from losing any heart muscle. Within an hour, you may salvage between 50 and 80 percent.'' He notes, however, that these are very rough numbers, and that lives can be saved even when thrombolytic treatment starts several hours after symptoms begin. One important study has suggested that there may be benefits in giving these drugs as late as 24 hours after an attack starts. But, for many patients, it appears that the ''window of opportunity'' is irrevocably shut after four to six hours.

Possible Misuses

Word of the new treatment has spread at such speed that some doctors worry that incomplete information, excessively enthusiastic claims, and a bandwagon psychology may lead to abuses. Hazards as well as benefits almost always attach to anything new and powerful. Is it not likely, some specialists ask, that doctors will overuse or misuse the new treatment, out of a desperate hope of saving lives or fear of malpractice suits? Dr. Eric R. Powers of the Columbia-Presbyterian Medical Center in New York City says that a risk of misuse certainly exists. Even sophisticated physicians sometimes have difficulty telling quickly whether a patient who has symptoms suggestive of heart attack is really having one.

Misuse of clot-dissolving drugs can occur in two principal ways: if such drugs are given to patients with medical conditions that make the treatment dangerous, and if they are given to patients who are not having heart attacks. Sometimes the two go together. For example, if a patient has a bleeding ulcer, and it is this that is causing the pain in the midsection, not a heart attack, the last thing he or she needs is something that promotes bleeding. The treatment is probably risky for anyone who has had a bleeding ulcer in the past two months. Some experts say that the drugs should not be used in patients who have had major surgery within the previous two weeks, because the treatment might cause bleeding from surgical wounds that are not completely healed. For people who have a history of hemorrhagic strokes, the risk of bleeding inside the brain—the cause of such strokes—must be weighed against the drugs' benefits.

These are never easy decisions. A patient from whom a clot-dissolving drug is withheld might die of a heart attack. Another patient might suffer a fatal stroke or die of uncontrolla-

ble bleeding while damage to the heart is being prevented. New research has surprised doctors by showing that some patients not suspected of being at risk of internal bleeding may have a tendency to hemorrhage that could be aggravated by a clot-dissolving drug. Fortunately, the numbers appear to be small: only one-half of 1 percent of the patients studied.

Research into the clot-dissolving drugs is also producing some surprising discoveries not directly related to heart attack treatment. ''We probably have more fibrin clots in the blood vessels of our brains than we had thought,'' Dr. Braunwald says. ''This means that perhaps four people in 1,000 are walking around with blood vessels safely held together by fibrin, which might be dissolved by a thrombolytic agent.''

Future Potential

Medical researchers and public health workers are studying ways in which clot-dissolving treatment can be started even before a patient gets to a hospital—by properly trained paramedics, for example. Some think that this may be possible within the next two or three years. It is even conceivable that within a decade or so, people who are at very high risk will be trained to start the treatment themselves at home, with the help of a family member. Under such an arrangement, a physician would make the actual decision to start the therapy. At present, it is hard to say how realistic that hope may be.

Many doctors who are concerned with the future of heart treatment often come back in the end to public education, and they're not talking only about how to find a hospital emergency room in a hurry. ''Clearly, the best way to treat a heart attack is not to have it,'' Dr. Passamani says. For many people that means making changes in their diet, quitting smoking, starting an exercise program, or getting treatment for high blood pressure.

It remains to be seen precisely what the impact of thrombolysis will be. But the experts are hopeful. ''Thrombolytic therapy is one of those things that come along rarely,'' Dr. Passamani says, ''a simple, effective therapy for a big public health problem.'' Some normally cautious authorities are not modest in their hopes. They believe that clot-dissolving drugs may eventually bring the death toll from heart attacks among hospitalized patients down as low as 3 percent—one person in 30.

It was only 25 years ago that nearly one in three of these people failed to survive.

Healing with LASERS

by Steven Lally

A barely tangible beam of light zaps artery-clogging cholesterol, then welds the artery shut. A quick flash restores sight to a man who was virtually blind even after conventional cataract-removal surgery. Another beam "energizes" a drug in the body, making cancer cells self-destruct—leaving normal cells unharmed. Scenes from the future? No, just business as usual. These medical procedures are just a few that feature the "Star Wars" technol-

ogy of lasers. Some laser treatments can be performed only at high-tech centers like the Beckman Laser Institute at the University of California, Irvine. Others can be done in your doctor's office. In either case, if lasers are the future, the future is now.

Anatomy of Laser Power

Just for the record, lasers aren't named after a Dr. Igor Laser or a planet Laser. The word *laser* stands for *L*ight *A*mplification by *S*timulated *E*mission of *R*adiation. What this means is that laser beams are created by stimulating atoms in a "core material" (such as argon gas) to emit "packets" of light, then amplifying and focusing the light in a single beam. Lasers differ from light emitted from an ordinary light bulb because of this greater concentration and intensity and because they consist of a single wavelength, or color, of light. Ordinary light is a mixture of all the colors of the light spectrum and therefore looks "white."

Using beams of laser light, doctors can often achieve surgical results without ever touching a scalpel.

Four types of lasers are used regularly in medicine. The *argon* laser emits a blue or green beam of light and is readily absorbed by red objects—perfect for working on arteries and other tissue containing red hemoglobin. The *carbon dioxide* (CO_2) laser emits an infrared beam, which vaporizes water. Since our bodies are mostly water, this laser is an efficient cutting tool. The *neodymium-YAG* (for *Y*ttrium, *A*luminum, and *G*arnet) laser also emits an infrared beam, but at a lower wavelength than the CO_2. The new *"tunable" dye* lasers can be adjusted to the precise wavelength (color) that's best absorbed by whatever is being worked on.

Lasers are impressive in the operating room. They can cut much more precisely than any scalpel. There's less chance of infection because, in most cases, nothing enters the operating field except a beam of light. A laser cauterizes (seals blood vessels) as it cuts, so less blood is lost. There's less damage to surrounding tissue, so most operation wounds heal better and more quickly. And when used carefully, lasers leave little or no scarring.

In many cases, lasers can be cost-effective, too. Many laser procedures can be done on an outpatient basis, which means no hospital stay and fewer days absent from work.

Lasers do have their limits, though. Laser tonsillectomies, for example, can take 20 minutes—but a good surgeon can use a scalpel to cut them out in four or five minutes. "In some cases," says one expert, "lasers are just not a good choice."

Sight-saving Light

Today more ophthalmologists (physicians who specialize in the eye) use lasers than any other specialists. The most common laser procedure is done for diabetic retinopathy, a condition in which tiny extra blood vessels grow in the retina (the back wall of the eye's interior) and into the fluid center of the eye. If not treated in time, these fragile blood vessels rupture and bleed, gradually causing loss of sight. But this slow deterioration can sometimes be stopped by a laser procedure called *pan-retinal photocoagulation*. The argon laser is used to make anywhere from 3,000 to 6,000 microscopic burns in the retina (destroying about 6 to 10 percent of its total area). This halts the growth of new vessels—and the patient usually notices no additional loss of sight due to the treatment.

Linda Rogers is diabetic. When her ophthalmologist told her she needed laser treatment

for retinopathy, she was frightened. But one session changed her mind. "I was surprised at how easy it was." The procedure is usually done over a few sessions—one eye at a time—working from the outer portion in toward the center of the retina. Linda says that her treatments weren't painful, just a bit uncomfortable. "Afterward," she says, "it was like looking through a gray doughnut, but that went away after a few days."

Lasers can also treat another common sight stealer: glaucoma. Fluid inside the eye builds up and causes abnormal pressure. In a procedure called an *iridotomy*, a laser (usually a YAG) makes a tiny hole in the iris (the eye's colored portion) to drain the fluid. This draining used to be done surgically. But now with lasers, it's a painless outpatient procedure that can be done in a matter of minutes—without anesthesia. The same goes for *laser trabeculoplasty*, a similar procedure on the side of the iris.

One popular misconception is that lasers are used to zap cataracts. They aren't—but they are used *after* a cataract is removed, because the capsule that encloses the lens clouds over in about half of all cases. The YAG laser is used to create a shock wave, which makes a tiny hole in the center of the cloudy capsule through which the eye focuses. Literally, the patient is blind one minute and can see the next. It's a very safe procedure that can save hundreds of dollars *per patient* because surgery is avoided.

Getting Under the Skin

In dermatology and plastic surgery, lasers are used to remove birthmarks, warts, and some precancerous lesions. The oldest procedure in this area is the treatment of port-wine-stain birthmarks, which are caused by an excessive growth of tiny blood vessels just under the skin. According to Bruce M. Achauer, M.D., the chief of plastic surgery at Beckman, the argon laser has been the main treatment for port-wine stains since the early 1970s. The beam passes through the skin and selectively "cooks" the stain so the body can absorb it, fading the mark with little scarring.

But like any other medical procedure, this use of an argon laser has its drawbacks. A local anesthetic must be used—with uncomfortable injections. And the procedure isn't usually used on children, because it may produce noticeable scars on their more delicate skin.

Carol Moeller had a port-wine-stain birthmark for 40 years before hearing about the laser.

Ophthalmologists use lasers to treat a number of serious eye disorders, including diabetic retinopathy, glaucoma, and macular degeneration. Typically, the doctor uses a lens to focus the beam on the specific part of the eye under treatment (above). In one highly refined procedure, a laser beam seals pinpoint leaks in the blood vessels of the retina (left), the part of the eye where light focuses.

After two full treatments, her birthmark gradually faded to a pale pink. "It's astonishing," she says. "No pain, and the treatment took only a matter of minutes. I felt a little warmth, but it went away in about an hour. If you can handle a sunburn, you can handle this."

Carol had test patches treated with the argon, but most of her treatment was done with the newer pulsed tunable-dye laser, which requires no anesthesia. This gentler treatment can be used on children for both port-wine stains and strawberry hemangioma, which looks like a raised port-wine stain. Most hemangiomas disappear by themselves after five to 10 years, but this safer laser treatment has made it practical to remove them immediately.

Other skin blemishes involving blood vessels, such as so-called spider veins on the face, can be removed successfully and painlessly with tunable-dye lasers.

"Before lasers, there were no good surgical options for such problems." says Dr. Achauer. "Lasers have really revolutionized the treatment of these types of birthmarks."

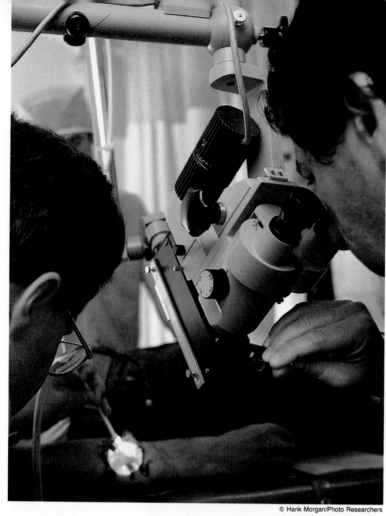

Lasers have found many cosmetic applications, including the virtually painless removal of tattoos.

© Hank Morgan/Photo Researchers

Erasing a Memory

We all do things we later regret, but few things are as regrettably permanent as a tattoo. Until you include lasers in the picture. Formerly, the best that could be done was a procedure called dermabrasion—and it's just as painful as it sounds. Ironically, it often left a negative image of the tattoo. But lasers can remove tattoos with much less scarring and little pain. Just ask Deanna Branch.

Seven years ago Deanna's shoulder was tattooed with a picture of a heart being pierced by a lightning bolt. Seven months ago she had it removed with an argon laser. Was she frightened? "No, I just wanted to get rid of it. And my doctor was so enthusiastic about the laser that I believed in it, too."

Deanna's trust was not misplaced. While she still needs a touch-up to remove some remaining pigment, her tattoo is virtually gone. "The skin is a little faded, but there's no scar," she says.

For Women Only

Lasers have a remarkable number of uses in gynecology. The two main reasons for this: the laparoscope and the CO_2 laser.

The laparoscope is one of several long, thin tubes with high-tech attachments that doctors use to look around inside the body. It's snaked into the abdomen through a small surgical cut, and a fiber-optic thread allows the gynecologist to see and examine the ovaries and other important organs without major surgery. The scope can also transport the light of a laser. The great advantage of this combination is that the laser can be used to treat a problem with a minimal incision the moment it's found, rather than waiting for a more extensive second operation.

Two conditions are regularly treated with laser laparoscopy: endometriosis and infertility. Endometriosis is a painful condition in which uterinelike tissue shows up in other parts of the abdomen—in the stomach, intestines, and ovaries—and begins to bleed. Infertility can be caused by endometriosis or by scar tissue on the fallopian tubes and overies. In each case the laser vaporizes the unwanted tissue with virtually no internal bleeding.

The laser is also used externally on the vulva, vagina, and cervix to remove precancerous lesions and warts caused by the papilloma virus. The real advantages of the laser are precision, speed, and minimal scarring, according to Mark A. Rettenmaier, M.D., a gynecologic oncologist at Beckman. Laser treatments cost a few hundred dollars more than conventional therapies, but they seem to be worth the expense.

One promising laser treatment on the horizon: *laser hysterectomy*. The YAG laser has been used experimentally in a small number of cases to vaporize the lining of the uterus (not to remove the uterus, as in a conventional hysterectomy). It's less traumatic than a regular hysterectomy, but more expensive, and isn't widely available. Its long-term effects aren't yet known.

Ear, Nose, and Throat

If you overuse your voice (as professional singers sometimes do), you can develop tiny polyps on your vocal cords and thus impair your voice, says Roger L. Crumley, M.D., an otolaryngologist (ear, nose, and throat doctor) and chief of head and neck surgery at UC-Irvine. But polyps and small cancers on the vocal cords can be vaporized with the CO_2 laser. "We've got better control over what we're doing than with a scalpel," says Dr. Crumley. "The laser does all the work."

Edward Hughes is a mechanic who went to Dr. Crumley to have polyps removed. Since the operation is performed under general anesthesia, Hughes expected to wake up with a sore throat. "But I had no pain," he says. "In fact, I was supposed to keep quiet for five days, but the minute I woke up, they started asking me questions . . . so I answered them."

Farther down the throat, CO_2 lasers are used to vaporize tumors that obstruct the windpipe. "It's a lifesaving procedure," says Dr. Crumley. "There's no other good way to remove them." And in the nose, lasers are used to destroy polyps caused by allergies. The YAG laser is even used to stop chronic nosebleeds caused by a rare hereditary condition.

The middle ear is another place in which the CO_2 laser is useful. Mastoid disease (any

one of several different infections, inflammations, and growths in the middle ear) used to be treated surgically with tiny surgical instruments. The laser is a big improvement over the earlier procedures.

A brain tumor near the ear (*acoustic neuroma*) is more easily removed with the laser because there's less danger of nerve damage than with scalpels. And stapedectomy—the removal of a tiny bone in the ear—is now a laser procedure in some institutions. When this bone stops functioning properly, it can cause a 70 percent hearing loss, so the laser literally restores hearing.

The laser has revolutionized treatment in these procedures because it can be manipulated in small cavities without disturbing important, delicate structures around it. Lasers don't necessarily lower costs in most of these operations—primarily because they still must be done in an operating room under general anesthesia—but they do improve the outcome. And that's what *really* counts.

Doctors use fiber optic threads to transmit laser energy to hard-to-reach tumors in the throat and elsewhere.

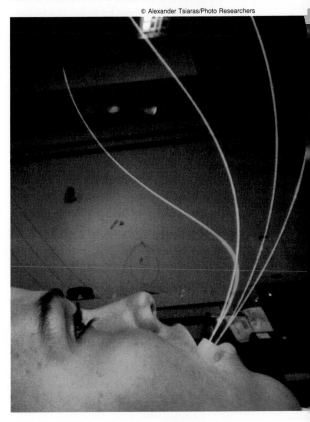

Lasers against Kidney Stones

A nonlaser machine called the *lithotripter*, which breaks up kidney stones with shock waves, has virtually replaced standard kidney-stone surgery. But as pieces of the stones are passed out of the urinary tract, the larger ones can get stuck in the ureter on the way to the bladder. The position of the pelvic bones makes further shock-wave lithotripsy difficult.

Enter the laser. Pulses of laser energy produce shock waves that break up the stone with little risk of damage to any surrounding part of the body.

Conquering Cancer

Although it's only in clinical trials at Beckman and a few other institutions, a cancer therapy using the laser and a drug called HpD (hematoporphyrin derivative) is showing promise for some cancer patients.

Michael W. Berns, Ph.D., director and cofounder of Beckman Laser Institute, says that the procedure works like this: HpD is injected into the body and enters the tumors. Normal tissue expels the drug within 72 hours. Cancer tissue retains it longer. HpD is photodynamic, which means that it initiates a chemical reaction in the cells when stimulated by light. If a laser is beamed at the cancer tissue containing HpD, the drug will kill it.

The Food and Drug Administration (FDA) has approved this therapy for experimental use in lung, bladder, and esophageal cancer.

Scouring Arteries with Light

There's currently only one FDA-approved clinical use for lasers in vascular disease: the "hot-tip" catheter, which has a metal cap that's heated by laser pulses. The metal cap burns through obstructions (cholesterol or a blood clot) so that a balloon catheter can be used to widen blocked arteries. It was approved for use in the legs in February 1987, and is now available in most major cardiovascular centers.

John Eugene, M.D., a cardiovascular surgeon associated with the Beckman Laser Institute since 1982, has pioneered a procedure that may expand the use of lasers in his field. He developed *laser endarterectomy*, an operation in which the laser is used to vaporize plaque (accumulated cholesterol) in an artery, then used to weld the artery back together. In a regular endarterectomy, a scalpel is used to remove plaque, then the artery is sewn up. The laser not only leaves a smoother surface *inside* the artery (discouraging blood-clot formation or further plaque buildup), but it seems to close the artery with less trauma. So far the procedure has been performed on arteries in the legs and the neck. Experiments on the heart are the next step.

Pulses of laser energy can pulverize kidney stones with little risk of injury to surrounding parts of the body.

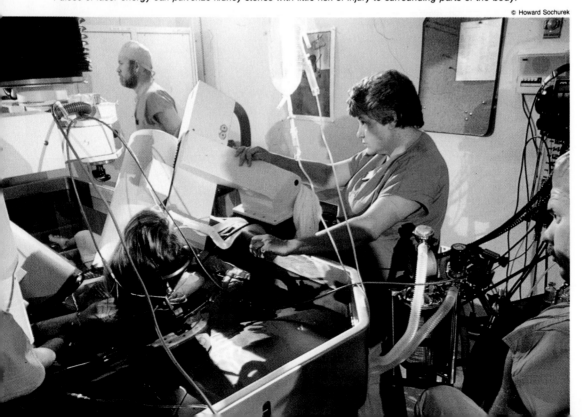

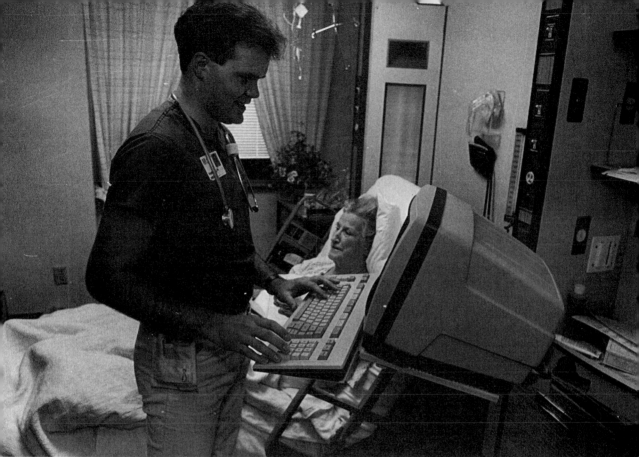

NURSING: *A Changing Profession*

by Jenny Tesar

A hospital bed catches on fire. The patient suffers burns on 40 percent of her body before overworked nurses discover the accident.

• A patient requiring emergency attention almost dies because the only available nurse is dealing with another emergency situation.

• Injured and critically ill patients are denied admission by their local hospitals because there are not enough nurses to work in the intensive-care units.

Horror stories abound as the United States experiences its worst nursing shortage since World War II. According to the American Medical Association (AMA), the nation's hospitals are short an estimated 300,000 nurses—a number that will double by the year 2000 if the current trends continue.

Some 11.3 percent of nursing jobs were unfilled in 1988—nearly triple the 1983 figures. Although shortages are occurring throughout the nation, they are particularly severe in large urban hospitals, where vacancies approach 20 percent, and in nursing homes, where vacancies reach as high as 25 percent.

No one is unaffected. Because of the shortage, hospitals have shut down rooms and decreased the number of beds. In 1987, 18 percent of large urban hospitals and 9.5 percent of rural hospitals had to reduce the number of beds because of insufficient nurses. The American

Computerized medical records and more male practitioners represent just two of the many changes that the nursing profession has undergone in recent years.

Hospital Association found that 15 percent of hospitals surveyed postponed elective surgery because of a nursing shortage, 18 percent turned away patients, and 3.6 percent temporarily closed emergency rooms.

The result: delayed admissions, inadequate care, discharges before patients are well, all supporting one nurse's blunt contention that "patient care is compromised all the time."

Why the Shortage?

Actually, there are more nurses than ever before—some 2 million, an increase of more than 33 percent in the past decade. Approximately 80 percent of these nurses are either working in the profession or looking for work, up significantly from the usual 60 to 70 percent.

But though the number of nurses has increased, the demand for nurses has increased even faster, due to a variety of factors.

One factor is the aging of the American population. The number of elderly patients has almost doubled in the past 20 years. Older

The growing number of AIDS patients has put a strain on hospitals already trying to cope with a lack of nurses.

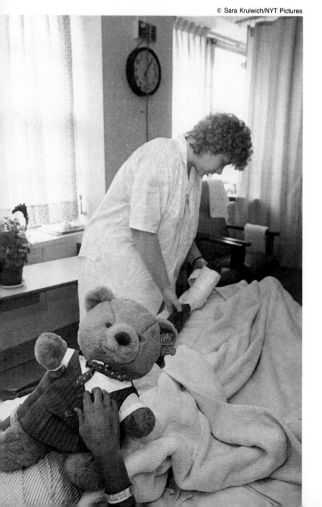

patients tend to be sicker than younger patients. A 1983 report prepared by the Institute of Medicine of the National Academy of Sciences states: "Those at age 75 and older are the most prone to multiple disabilities and chronic diseases. They use hospital, nursing home, and home care services at rates double or triple those of the population as a whole."

Another major reason for the growing demand is the specter of AIDS, a fatal disease unknown prior to 1981, but now claiming thousands of lives each year. The Centers for Disease Control estimates that 1.5 million Americans are infected with the AIDS virus, and experts believe that most infected people eventually contract AIDS itself. The disease causes great suffering and demands extensive care. On an average day, some 1,500 people in the United States are hospitalized with AIDS, a number predicted to at least double by 1992. Already hospitals in some cities are crammed with AIDS patients, thus limiting the number of beds available for other patients. For example, in New York City, which leads the nation in the number of diagnosed cases, AIDS patients take up 9 percent of all available hospital beds.

Effects of Cost-containment Efforts

According to the American Nurses Association, 91 nurses (spread over three shifts) are needed for every 100 patients today, compared to an average of 50 in 1975. This is due not only to the growing number of elderly patients and AIDS patients, but also to efforts to contain health care costs, which have resulted in generally sicker hospital populations. Patients are being released from hospitals faster than in years past. Those remaining are sicker, requiring greater care and more advanced technology.

In 1983 the federal government revised Medicare, the health insurance plan for people age 65 and older and for people under age 65 who are severely disabled. Implemented in 1966 by Title XVIII of the Social Security Act, Medicare reimburses hospitals, physicians, and other health care providers. Prior to 1983 reimbursement was based on the prevailing rates for medical care within a locality, enabling hospitals to usually recover the full cost of care for each patient. Under the new system, Medicare payment to hospitals became a set fee based on the average cost of a specific treatment. Hospitals that treated patients for less than the government payment could keep the difference, while those charging more had to take the difference

Nurses must spend an inordinate amount of time on paperwork and other tasks not directly related to patient care.

out of their profits. It was hoped that this system would act as an incentive for greater efficiency and cost-cutting. In some ways it did. "The problem is that cost containment too often becomes care containment. And it affects the least powerful population sector with the quietest voice," said Dr. Ron Anderson, president of Parkland Hospital in Dallas, Texas.

Even before the new system began, hospitals with large Medicare caseloads looked for ways to reduce the costs of treating these patients. They shortened hospital stays and reduced admissions of less acutely ill patients. The average length of a hospital stay fell 22 percent between 1980 and 1985, from 7.35 days in 1980 to 5.71 days in 1985. Admission declined from 38,892,000 in 1980 to 36,304,000 in 1985.

Government agencies weren't the only forces pressing for lower costs. Employers and private insurers also scrutinized the need for hospitalization, often finding that impressive savings could be attained. For example, over a period of three years, Chrysler Corporation cut $100 million from its health care bill simply by requiring second medical opinions for nonemergency, nonmaternity hospital stays.

Sicker Patients, More Responsibility

At the same time that nurses found themselves caring for sicker patients, they were burdened with responsibilities previously handled by other health care workers. To reduce labor costs, hospitals laid off many medical workers while maintaining or increasing the number of registered nurses (RNs). The RNs found themselves doing the work of licensed practical nurses (LPNs), physical therapists, pharmacists, social workers, and clerks. Their paperwork load increased. Instead of being with patients, they were answering telephones. In some cases they even had to perform such menial tasks as taking out the garbage. According to Dr. Lucille Joel, president of the American Nurses Association, between 10 and 60 percent of a nurse's time is devoted to nonnursing duties.

Understaffing has led many nurses to worry about potential liability and malpractice problems. Nurses can lose their license if they refuse to work in an understaffed unit. But if a patient receives insufficient care because of understaffing and something goes wrong, the nurses may be slapped with a malpractice suit, which can also result in loss of license. Some nurses have taken to filling out forms protesting assignment to understaffed units. If problems arise, they can at least prove that the hospital was aware of the situation.

Despite the heavier workload given to nurses during much of the 1980s, salary increases—at least until very recently—have been minimal. Salaries for a beginning RN start at about $22,000, which is comparable to starting salaries for other professionals. But a nurse's salary doesn't rise very far. According to a survey published in the *American Journal of Nursing*, the average nurse's salary reaches a maximum only 36 percent higher than the starting salary, even after years of experience and increased responsibility. This compares to 106.1 percent for computer programmers, 192 percent for accountants, and 231 percent for chemists.

"Merely a Nurse"

The history of caring for the sick, the weak, and the disabled is as old as the history of human beings. Historically, however, nurses were generally untrained, receiving no medical education, but learning only what was needed for the specific situations in which they worked.

Nursing as a modern profession is traced back to the mid-19th century, to the remarkable Englishwoman Florence Nightingale, whose care of wounded British soldiers during the Crimean War dramatically demonstrated the efficacy of skilled nursing. In 1860 the first nursing school based on Nightingale's methods was founded in affiliation with Saint Thomas' Hospital in London. The first nursing school in the U.S. based on her system was founded at Bellevue Hospital in New York City in 1873.

In the ensuing years, society came to expect much of nurses. But expectations were not matched by admiration. Even today these providers of care are often viewed much as they were by English biographer Lytton Strachey, who expressed surprised admiration for the heroic Florence Nightingale, who was, after all, "merely a nurse."

Overwhelmingly, the nursing profession is dominated by women: only 3 percent of America's nurses are men. In large part the negative view of nursing is related to society's attitudes about women and their "appropriate" roles. Peri Rosenfeld, director of research for the National League for Nursing, writing in *Nursing & Health Care*, said: "Society likens nursing to motherhood and homemaking, which are essential to society but not worthy of economic or political rewards. Furthermore, society considers the female characteristics found in nursing unprofessional because they are emotional rather than objective, passive instead of assertive, and subordinate instead of dominant."

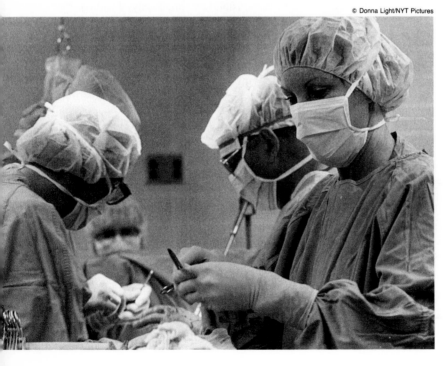

© Donna Light/NYT Pictures

As in many other professions, modern nursing has evolved numerous areas of specialization.

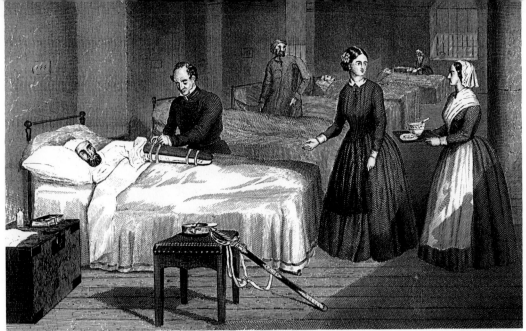

The Bettmann Archive

Modern nursing traces its roots to the methods developed by Florence Nightingale during the Crimean War.

Overworked, underpaid, receiving neither the status nor the respect accorded other professionals—it is not surprising that nurses are angry. Nor is it surprising that many young people who in the past might have chosen nursing are pursuing other careers.

Shrinking Enrollments

There has been a sharp decline in enrollment in nursing schools. According to the American Hospital Association, enrollment in nursing schools dropped 10 percent a year between 1974 and 1987, to fewer than 180,000 students.

Career opportunities for women are far greater today than they were several decades ago. As a result, many bright women are going into law, business, and other fields once closed to them. And those interested in medicine study to be doctors rather than nurses. Indeed, in 1990, for the first time in the nation's history, more women will graduate as physicians than as nurses.

Financing is another problem: in 1983 the Reagan administration cut all aid to nursing education. Hospitals are starting to make up some of the difference. For instance, the community hospital in Danbury, Connecticut, will pay student nurses at a local university $4,000 over two years if they promise to work at the hospital when they graduate. The program is designed to benefit both the hospital, which hopes to ease its nursing shortage, and the uni-

versity, which hopes to attract students to its nursing program.

This type of joint program between hospitals and nursing schools was one of the recommendations of the Connecticut Governor's Task Force on the Nursing Shortage. Doris Armstrong, co-chairwoman of the group, also said that more effort needs to be made to attract minority high school students to nursing, and to lure nontraditional students, such as biology majors, into the field.

Dealing with the Shortage

To ease their nursing shortage, many hospitals have recruited nurses from abroad. About 10,000 foreign nurses work in U.S. hospitals. Many are highly qualified critical-care nurses, working in inner-city hospitals that U.S. nurses consider undesirable. New York City alone has some 4,000 foreign nurses, comprising 12 percent of the nurses in the city's hospitals.

Foreign nurses typically enter the United States on an H-1 visa, which permits them to stay for five years. Efforts in 1988 by the Immigration and Naturalization Service (INS) to strictly enforce the visa limits were widely criticized by health-care facilities and nurses' groups. It was pointed out that these nurses were experienced in working within the U.S. health care system, and that replacing them with new recruits from abroad would cost millions of dollars. Advocates for the nurses also pointed out

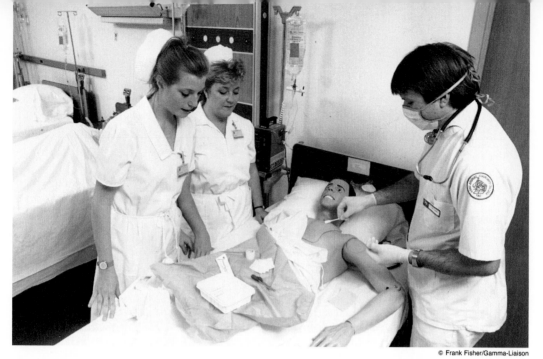

© Frank Fisher/Gamma-Liaison

Hospitals and nursing schools have developed various incentive programs to draw more students into the field.

the irony that while the federal government was trying to force desperately needed nurses to leave, it was conferring amnesty on many illegal aliens.

In May 1988, the INS, bowing to the pressure, agreed to extend the visas for one more year.

The following month the AMA approved a plan to help alleviate the nursing shortage by creating a new category of hospital workers called registered care technologists. According to the plan, these people would receive between two and 18 months of training in apprentice programs at hospitals, and they would be certified and registered by state medical boards. Their responsibilities would include routine bedside chores such as taking temperatures, administering certain medications, and changing bedpans.

The proposal was strongly opposed by nurses' groups, who felt the technologists would duplicate the jobs of licensed practical nurses and nurse's aides. They also feared added confusion on the part of patients, who already must deal with a sometimes bewildering array of workers. "There are so many people doing different things—the respiratory therapist, the physical therapist, the orderly—the patient doesn't know who's who as it is," commented Alice Roye, executive director of the National Federation of Licensed Practical Nurses.

Questions also were raised concerning the financing of the program, who would train and supervise the new workers, and whether the position would be a dead-end, low-paying job and thus unlikely to attract competent, dedicated individuals.

Better Salaries, More Perks

As the demand for nurses is growing, so, too—finally—are salaries. In 1987 Westchester County (New York) Medical Center raised starting salaries 18.5 percent, from $22,350 to $26,500 a year. By mid-1988 the figure approached $30,000. Differentials between salaries of starting and experienced nurses are also increasing. In Los Angeles some hospitals now offer salaries of $32,000 to starting RNs, and up to $58,000 for experienced nurses.

To keep nurses and lure new ones, hospitals and nursing homes are beginning to offer more flexible working hours and on-site day care. Some will reimburse tuition fees for employees who study to become RNs or LPNs. Perhaps most important, they are revamping management systems to give nurses more autonomy and more power, both over patient care and within the hospital as a whole.

Efforts are also being made to reduce the paperwork nurses must handle, either by hiring other, less-skilled workers or by putting the information in computerized databases. While some medical centers are using computer systems to obtain quick access to patient data, most places continue to rely on paper for patient records and clinical information. Often these papers are incomplete, illegible, unorganized, or simply not available to the nurse. Computer systems complete with terminals at nursing stations and bedsides allow rapid, systematic access to the data needed to make decisions on patient treatment.

But more money for nurses' salaries and other benefits means less money somewhere else. "Medicare is increasing payments 0.5 percent, and in our area, the average hospital has increased nursing salaries 5 percent," comments Mary Smithwick, associate administrator for patient care services at El Camino Hospital in Mountain View, California. "You can't continue that very long without something falling apart."

Many hospitals, operating at a loss on Medicare patients, have seen profits plummet. Many, if not all, are increasing prices. Hospital costs are soaring, and are expected to continue to rise into the 1990s. And many hospitals, economically pressed, have closed: 79 during 1987, another 75 in the first 10 months of 1988.

The Coming Years

In January 1988, the U.S. Secretary of Health and Human Services, Otis R. Bowen, appointed a Commission on Nursing to study the nursing shortage and make recommendations. Heading the commission was Carolyne K. Davis, a former administrator of the department's Health Care Financing Administration.

The commission presented its report in December 1988. Among its recommendations was an increase in Medicare hospital rates that would be earmarked for increased nurses' salaries. It also urged Congress to create a payment mechanism that would "assure equity between hospital nursing salaries and salaries for nurses working in nursing homes and home health agencies." Of the RNs currently working, 67 percent work in hospitals, 7 percent in nursing homes, and the rest in doctors' offices and health maintenance organizations (HMOs).

The commission also urged states to evaluate their Medicaid programs to assure that payment levels allowed health care facilities to offer wages adequate to hire and retain nurses. (Medicaid is essentially a health care program for poor people funded jointly by federal and state agencies.)

While the shortage of nurses remains the health care field's most pressing problem, nurses aren't the only health care workers in short supply. Medical institutions also face growing shortages of a variety of other skilled workers. A 1987 survey by the AMA found that enrollment in training programs declined for 12 of 22 health care specialties. The most severe declines were in programs for laboratory technicians, medical technologists, nuclear-medicine technologists, and respiratory therapists. Only the programs for physician's assistants and emergency medical technicians reported significant increases.

Thus the overall outlook for the next few years isn't bright. Hospitals and other health care facilities will continue to scramble for workers; patients will continue to compete for hospital beds and workers' attention. Only nurses may find a silver lining in the cloud, as they finally receive some of the professional and financial recognition they deserve.

Overworked and underpaid, nurses have sometimes resorted to the picket line to make their plight known.

© John Chiasson/Gamma-Liaison

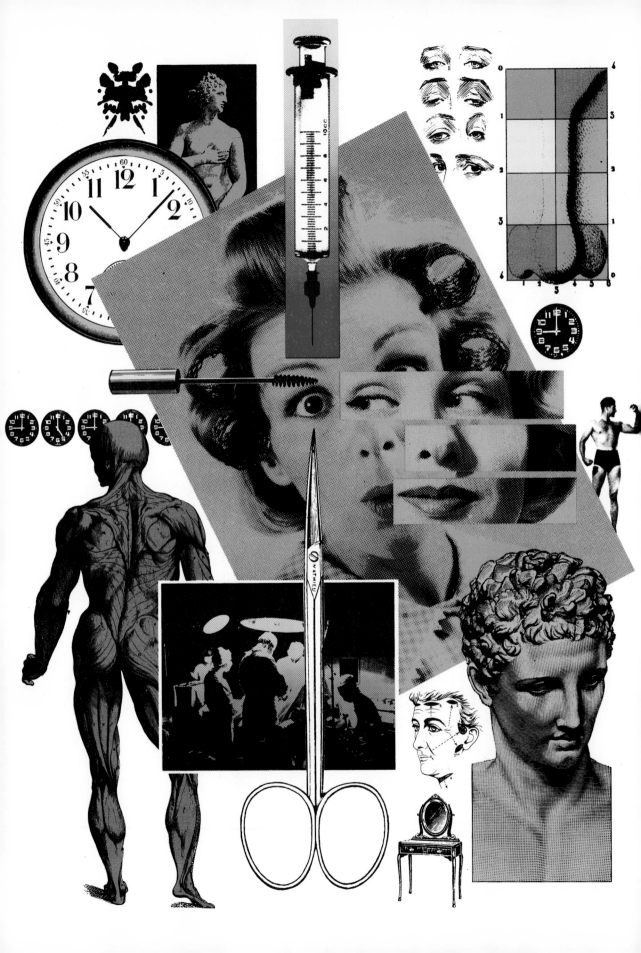

BODIES to ORDER

by Shirley Kraus

Just about everything is possible these days when it comes to cosmetic surgery. With a nip or a tuck, an implant, some suctioning or a lift, surgeons can achieve virtually any desired effect. Even though very little innovation in surgical techniques has occurred in the past decade or so, dramatic changes are taking place in the field. These changes are driven by an increasing number of surgeons—especially in the San Francisco Bay area, which boasts the highest density of plastic and reconstructive surgeons of any metropolitan area in the nation. They're doing everything possible—from sponsoring free seminars to sending mass mailings to community residents—to draw new patients. The result is an overwhelming increase in cosmetic-surgical procedures performed throughout the nation. But in a field where nearly all surgical procedures are elective, many professionals feel that patients are being encouraged to undergo procedures that not only are unnecessary, but perhaps should not even be done.

"When it comes to cosmetic surgery, we are specialists in unnecessary surgery," says plastic and reconstructive surgeon Dr. Mark Gorney, who teaches at Stanford University Medical Center and practices at St. Francis Hospital in San Francisco. An active member of national medical societies as well, Gorney grimaces as he discusses the state of the cosmetic-surgery profession today.

"There are less than 4,000 board-certified plastic surgeons," he says, "but that number has grown totally out of proportion to the growth of society. As a result, there's a glut of plastic surgeons who have to make a living. So they sell, and they sell hard. You now see advertising in the media, seminars, slick brochures, and more. Plastic surgeons are screaming from the rooftops that they are the salvation for people's problems. It's cheapening the profession."

Surgery for the Masses

According to the American Society of Plastic and Reconstructive Surgeons (ASPRS), of which Gorney is a former president, nearly 600,000 Americans had tummy tucks, breast augmentations, eyelid procedures, nose jobs, face-lifts, and other cosmetic-surgery procedures done in 1986, up 24 percent from 1984. These procedures differ from those considered reconstructive surgery, which are medically indicated to correct defects due to trauma or disease. Liposuction, the newest technique to join the cosmetic-surgery arsenal, is the number one surgical procedure performed in the United States. The number of these fat-suctioning procedures performed increased 78 percent between 1984 and 1986. Men are opting for cosmetic surgery more than ever before, and so are younger and younger women.

"Cosmetic surgery now is surgery for the masses," says Dr. Lars Vistnes, who heads up Stanford's plastic and reconstructive surgery division. "People who formerly saved up enough money to get a new dress or a fur coat now save up for a new nose or liposuction."

It's not that there's anything wrong with these procedures, if they're done "under proper circumstances with patients who are properly trained," he stresses. But, unfortunately, in today's climate that's not always the case.

In spite of cosmetic surgery's newfound popularity, many practitioners feel that it's the responsibility of the physicians to select patients they think are appropriate for surgery and to turn away the rest. "As many as one-third of all patients interested in cosmetic surgery should be rejected," Vistnes asserts.

But "nobody is getting turned away," Gorney says. If patients go to one physician who refuses to do a procedure, they will always be able to find another cosmetic surgeon who will agree to do it.

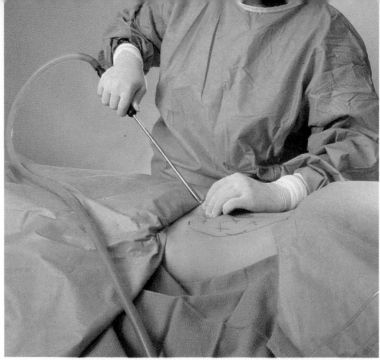

In liposuction, the surgeon inserts a thin tube called a cannula into fatty areas. Much like a vacuum cleaner, the cannula draws out the fat cells using suction. Cosmetic surgeons do not use liposuction as a weight-reduction technique, but as a means to rid individuals of hereditary fat cells that no amount of diet or exercise will eliminate. More Americans now undergo liposuction than any other surgical procedure.

"People considering plastic surgery are treading dangerous waters, and they should navigate very carefully," he cautions. "The decision to undergo cosmetic surgery is irreversible, and it can lead to tragic consequences."

Screening Patients

Trying to figure out if patients *really* want the procedure they express an interest in, and why, is perhaps the greatest challenge surgeons face. "Every experienced plastic surgeon is a good amateur psychiatrist," Vistnes explains. "You have to screen patients very, very carefully."

"Screening is key," agrees Marilee Marshall, a patient counselor for Palo Alto, California, plastic surgeon Dr. George Commons, who also teaches at Stanford. "Not all procedures are for everyone. It's part of my job to tell patients what the limitations are and which procedures may or may not be appropriate. When patients decide to undergo surgery, I discuss with them the actual procedure, recovery, possible complications, and realistic expectations. We have a book of less-than-ideal results that we make sure patients look through. They have to know exactly what can and cannot be accomplished."

Many patients are fairly sophisticated in their knowledge of cosmetic surgery because of today's emphasis on marketing—"a new direction for medicine," Marshall says. But she does have to deal with some outlandish requests that may be rejected by Commons but, unfortunately, may not be rejected by another surgeon. "We have patients come in and give Commons photographs of models from fashion magazines. They'll say, 'I want to look like this, Doctor. What can you do?'

"On the other hand," she continues, "we have people who come in for, say, a face-lift or breast augmentation. When you start questioning their motives, you find out their marriage is on the rocks and they're hoping this will help. We have to explain that cosmetic surgery does not solve marital problems."

Nor will cosmetic surgery resolve a variety of other problems that are much more than skin-deep. "The psychological underpinnings of a potential patient must be determined very carefully," Vistnes says. "Some people I see are clearly emotionally disturbed. I try to very tactfully suggest they seek help for their nonsurgical problems."

There are physicians who practice both plastic surgery and psychiatry to deal with precisely these patients, Vistnes says. Others, such as Commons, refer some patients to a psychiatrist or a clinical psychologist, including one who shares office space with him.

"I make people come back two or three times before I'll even consent to operate on them," Gorney declares. "I want to make sure they really understand what they're getting into, and I want to know what their motivations are and what they expect."

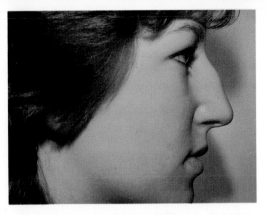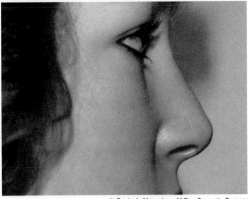

Nose surgery, or rhinoplasty, is perhaps the most familiar cosmetic surgery technique. By making incisions inside the nostrils, surgeons can remove cartilage and bone to smooth out unsightly bumps or otherwise reshape the nose.

"The bottom line is that the motivation for aesthetic surgery should come from within," he adds. "You need to figure out if patients' concerns over a deformity are proportional to the deformity you see. The more the disparity, the faster you should backpaddle."

Magic Changes

Under the right circumstances, cosmetic surgery can be extremely beneficial for patients. "We're three-dimensional surgeons," Gorney explains. "We don't operate only on the flesh, bones, and tissues; we operate on people's souls. If you do something that is needed on the right patient, the changes that occur are explosive. They're magic."

Gorney illustrates that magic with a story of a young Italian girl who had "a cute little button nose until she was about 14 years old." The larger her nose grew, he says, the more "she just withered." So he performed nose surgery, and the change was remarkable. "Her grades improved; her outlook improved; she started dating—it changed her life. And all we did was fix her nose."

Marshall confirms the potential impact of cosmetic surgery. "It's a powerful force. The way you see yourself makes all the difference in your self-confidence. I see people gain a renewed enthusiasm for life. They increase their activity levels socially and professionally. They feel like they've won."

"There's nobody more happy than a happy cosmetic-surgery patient," Vistnes agrees. "But there's nobody more unhappy than an unhappy cosmetic-surgery patient."

Face- and neck-lifts, or facial rhytidectomy, counter the effects of aging by removing loose sagging skin and fat. Although it may take the skin a year or more to regain its natural elasticity, the results can be truly remarkable.

Complications and Drawbacks

The advertisements that promise you a new, younger-looking, more attractive body with cosmetic surgery do not tell you about the possible complications, pitfalls, and long recovery periods. Nor do they tell you the costs of various procedures, which can range from as low as a few hundred dollars for collagen injections to as much as $10,000 for face-lifts.

The advertisements also don't tell you that, with very few exceptions, these fees come out of your pocket because insurance companies, in an attempt to control health-care costs, refuse to pay for cosmetic surgery. And they make light of the fact that when you decide to undergo cosmetic surgery, in many cases you are, in fact, undergoing major surgery.

"Many patients seem to have no comprehension that we are dealing with human flesh and blood," Dr. Mark Gorney marvels.

"Being a good cosmetic surgeon is as much of a challenge, if not more so, than any other type of surgeon," Dr. Lars Vistnes says. "Patients are demanding when it comes to their appearance, especially when they're paying for it. Unfortunately, many patients don't accept the reality of the surgical operation. There's no such thing as guaranteed success."

Dr. Vistnes comments on analogies drawn between cosmetic surgery and art: "Someone once said that if you compare plastic surgery to sculpture, no artist would ever work in this medium. If you take a piece of clay and mold it, it will still look the same after it's fired. But in our work the clay is skin. It can fall by gravity; it can be hiked up to the side by scar contraction; it can look ugly because the scar didn't turn out well. It has nothing to do with the actual surgery—it depends on the individual. And there is no way you can predict what will happen."

3-D Computer Models

Cosmetic-surgery patients may not always have a clear idea of exactly what they want, nor do they always want what they get.

"The fear has always been that you're not going to be able to offer patients what they want," says plastic and reconstructive surgeon Dr. Joseph Rosen. "The real fear should be that you don't understand what it is that patients want."

For example, Rosen explains, if a man wants a nose job, physicians know what they can do technically. "The problem is getting inside the patient's head and figuring out what exactly he wants to see when he looks in the mirror. You can make a nose that's an excellent result technically, but it may not be the nose the patient wants."

"Three out of every 10 patients will say the result of their surgery is not what they expected," Marilee Marshall says. "Two of those three, however, will say the result is an improvement, therefore they're happy. The third patient will want something done."

What may happen, Rosen agrees, is that the same man who comes in for the nose job will come back and say, "That's not me. Make it back to what it was before."

And that, he explains, is difficult. "You try to prevent this scenario by giving patients an idea of what they're going to get."

How? Rosen just happens to be working on the problem.

Always one step ahead of the state of the art, Rosen and engineers at the Massachusetts Institute of Technology (MIT) Media Lab and the National Aeronautics and Space Administration's (NASA's) Ames Research Center are developing a three-dimensional computer-modeling system that would allow physicians to show patients the precise results of cosmetic surgery. What's more, it would allow physicians to determine exactly how much skin, cartilage, muscle, or bone to remove or change in order to get the results patients want—the type of information now available only through personal experience.

And that's not all, Rosen explains. It would eventually be possible to animate such a model, making it possible to see how a new nose, for example, would affect the rest of the face. What would happen when the patient smiles? What would be the effects of aging?

Rosen and his colleagues have already succeeded in developing one version of a low-resolution system. They're now working to improve the resolution to make the image more detailed. "It's about five years away," he predicts. "It depends how quickly hardware can move."

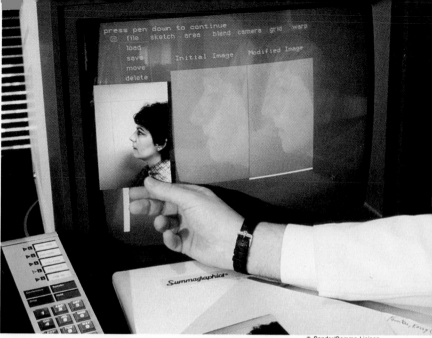

Using computer imaging, doctors can give cosmetic-surgery candidates a realistic idea of how they will look after surgery.

Most procedures can be done on an outpatient basis. Patients are often required to wear bandages or special garments for some time after the surgery, however; and, more often than not, they experience varying amounts of swelling, bruising, and pain. Many patients cannot see the final result of their surgery for a long time because it can take as long as a year for the skin to regain its normal elasticity.

Cosmetic Procedures

In spite of these concerns, more and more Americans are opting to go under the knife. Some of the more popular cosmetic procedures are as follows:

• Liposuction (suction-assisted lipectomy) burst onto the cosmetic-surgery scene about five years ago, and is now the most popular surgical procedure in the U.S. Thin tubes are inserted into the fatty area through small incisions, and the fat cells are suctioned out. Surgeons stress that liposuction is not a weight-reducing technique; rather, it is used to rid individuals of hereditary fat cells that no amount of diet and exercise will eliminate. It can be used on cheeks, chin, and neck, as well as thighs, hips, buttocks, arms, knees, ankles, and abdomen.

• Face- and neck-lifts (facial rhytidectomy) remove loose, sagging skin and fat in an attempt to counter the effects of aging. Surgeons cut the skin near the hairline and the ears, pull it away from the underlying fat and muscle, and then pull it up and back. The extra skin is cut off, and the remaining skin is sewn back into place.

• Breast augmentation involves inserting implants to increase breast size. Breast reduction, on the other hand, involves removing tissue. It is the operation most likely to fail, physicians say, because the incisions, which most often extend from the nipple down to the bottom of the breast, often scar badly. The way individuals scar is unpredictable.

• Nose surgery (rhinoplasty) can change the shape of a nose in any way. Surgeons make incisions inside the nostrils, from which point they can remove cartilage and bone to create the desired result.

• Tummy tucks (abdominoplasty) remove excess fatty tissue and wrinkled skin to rid patients of bulging stomachs. In this procedure, surgeons make a horizontal cut on the lower abdomen and pull the skin away from underlying fat and muscle. They remove the excess tissue, pull the skin down, and trim away the extra before sewing it back together.

In addition to these procedures, which are the most common, plastic surgeons can take the puffiness and sagging out of your eyelids (blepharoplasty); augment your chin with an implant (genioplasty); tuck your ears in closer to your head (otoplasty); "lift" parts of your body such as thighs, arms, buttocks, and breasts; add permanent eyeliner; peel the top layer of skin off your face to remove wrinkles and superficial scarring; and inject collagen to fill out wrinkles and scars. But physicians should point out that none of these procedures provide the final solution to youth and physical perfection.

© Richard Howard

CAFFEINE:
Victim or
Villain ?

by Bruce Paterson

Coffee is still consumers' second choice of beverages (soft drinks are first), but fewer cups are consumed each year: per capita consumption of coffee has fallen to 26.3 gallons (99.5 liters) in 1986 from the high of 37.8 gallons (143 liters) in 1965. Health concerns related to caffeine consumption have been a major influence in this decline (coffee contains more caffeine than any other popular drink).

Despite health concerns about caffeine, people still savor the lift they get from a cup of caffeinated coffee.

What are these concerns? How solid is the medical evidence concerning caffeine?

To determine if caffeine is a villain or actually a victim of alarmists in the health community, you must examine the latest available scientific evidence.

Physiological Effects

Caffeine stimulates the central nervous system and can produce a variety of effects elsewhere in the body. Depending upon how much you consume, it can increase your heartbeat and speed up your metabolism. It also promotes secretion of stomach acid and increases the production of urine. Caffeine acts to dilate certain blood vessels and constrict others, and in some instances to increase the capacity for muscular effort.

Psychologically, the overall effect often has been described as a "lift," a feeling of being wide-awake and able to focus on mental and physical tasks. Unfortunately, caffeine will only "lift" you back to your condition before fatigue or boredom has set in and affected your performance.

There is a great variability among individuals in their physiological response to caffeine. Age and weight are especially important influences on the body's response to caffeine; therefore, moderation in caffeine consumption by children and young adults is warranted because their smaller bodies do not metabolize caffeine as quickly as adults. As a result, the caffeine they get from caffeinated beverages and candy has a much stronger effect on their central nervous system than on an adult's. Parents should ask their family pediatrician about safe levels of consumption for their children.

Questions of Safety

• *Heartburn.* Heartburn occurs when the ring of muscles at the lower end of the esophagus relaxes, allowing the contents of the stomach to "back up" into the esophagus. Anything that makes those muscles relax can cause heartburn. Caffeine alone has almost no effect on these muscles. Coffee, however, has been shown to relax the muscles in some people, and to have the exact opposite effect in others.

• *Ulcers.* Coffee has been shown to stimulate the increased secretion of stomach acid, exacerbating any existing ulcers. However, two studies—one reported in a 1974 *American Journal of Epidemiology*, and the other in a 1974 *New England Journal of Medicine*—failed to correlate coffee consumption with the risk of actually developing peptic ulcers. Also, because regular and decaffeinated coffee both increase the release of stomach acid, it appears that caffeine is not the component of coffee responsible.

• *Heart Disease.* A widely publicized 1972 study, conducted at the Boston University Medical Center with 13,000 patients, did link heart attacks with coffee drinking, with risk increasing in relation to the amount consumed. However, these results ran directly counter to the results of a number of other investigations, notably the Framingham study. This was a 22-year comprehensive health study of 5,000 men and women in Framingham, Massachusetts. In this study, no evidence was found of a relationship between coffee consumption and heart disease.

Studies on the effects of caffeine consumption on blood-cholesterol levels have also produced unclear results. One such study, at the Kaiser-Permanente Medical Center in Oakland, California, examined 43,000 men and women over three years. It showed a significant correlation between coffee intake and higher cholesterol levels, but no relationship was detected in the case of tea drinkers. So, these researchers concluded that caffeine per se was not the causative factor.

A 1983 Norwegian study published in *The New England Journal of Medicine* reported that healthy volunteers who drank coffee had 14 percent higher total blood-cholesterol levels than those who did not drink coffee. It is important to note that these Norwegian coffee drinkers consumed in excess of nine cups of coffee daily.

While common sense suggests that excessive consumption of caffeine is not wise, there is

CAFFEINE CONTENT OF VARIOUS PRODUCTS	
Source of Caffeine	**Amount of caffeine per serving (milligrams)**
Coffee (6 ounces)	
Automatic drip	180
Automatic perk	125
Instant	75
Decaffeinated	5
Tea (6 ounces)	
Iced tea	70
Hot tea (moderate steeping time)	65
Soft Drinks (12 ounces)	
Caffeine-free colas	5
Jolt	72
Sugar-free Mr. PIBB	59
Mountain Dew	54
Mello Yellow	53
Tab	47
Coca-Cola	46
Diet Coke	46
Shasta Cola	44
Shasta Cherry Cola	44
Shasta Diet Cola	44
Shasta Diet Cherry Cola	44
Mr. PIBB	41
Dr Pepper	40
Sugar-Free Dr Pepper	40
Pepsi-Cola	38
Diet Pepsi	36
Pepsi Light	36
Cocoa Products	
Chocolate candy (2 ounces)	45
Baking chocolate (1 ounce)	45
Milk chocolate (2 ounces)	10
Drugs (one tablet or capsule)	
Dexatrim	200
NoDoz	100
Anacin	35
Midol	30
Coricidin	30

Caffeine has a stronger stimulant effect on a child's nervous system than on an adult's. Much of the caffeine children consume comes from candy and soft drinks.

The caffeine level in a cup of coffee depends on the origin of the beans, the grind, and the method of brewing.

no evidence that moderate caffeine intake (about 500 milligrams per day) is a causative factor in heart disease.

• *Cancer.* Coffee drinkers choked when in 1981 the Harvard School of Public Health reported an increased risk of pancreatic cancer among patients who drank as little as one or two cups of coffee a day. (Interestingly, patients who drank tea, which also contains caffeine, were found to have a *decreased* risk of pancreatic cancer.) In 1986 the same group of Harvard researchers published results that essentially reversed their 1981 findings and concluded "no trend in risk" for pancreatic cancer in male and female coffee drinkers.

The largest study to date, completed by cancer scientists at the Institute of Social Medicine, evaluated over 16,000 men and women between 1967 and 1979. It demonstrated no relationship between coffee drinking and cancer incidence anywhere in the body, including the pancreas and the bladder.

Further, no link between coffee consumption and any form of cancer was detected in a 1986 study in Hawaii (at the Kuakini Medical Center in Honolulu) that examined more than 7,000 men.

• *Diabetes.* Of the nearly 6 million diabetics in the United States, about 300,000 people die each year as a result of diabetes and its complications. Any possible adverse effects of caffeine consumption for diabetes must therefore be carefully examined.

While a report published in *Lancet* in 1972 indicated that blood-glucose (sugar) levels rose in rats given caffeine, results from similar human experiments have been inconclusive.

In a Boston University Medical Center study, chronic caffeine users were given decaffeinated coffee, and blood-glucose levels declined. However, when they returned to caffeinated coffee, there was no corresponding elevation in their blood-glucose levels.

Furthermore, literature distributed by the American Diabetes Association (ADA) to help diabetics manage their condition does not say to eliminate caffeine from their diets. The ADA does recommend caffeine should only be consumed in moderation.

• *Birth Defects.* Largely on the evidence of animal tests, the Food and Drug Administration (FDA) in 1980 advised pregnant women to reduce their consumption of caffeine. In these tests, pregnant rats were force-fed daily the human equivalent of caffeine found in 87 cups of strong-brewed coffee at one time. No associations were found, however, between birth defects and the mother's caffeine consumption in eight studies conducted during the past decade. In one particular study, completed at Boston's Brigham and Women's Hospital and published in *The New England Journal of Medicine*, more than 12,000 women were questioned soon after their delivery about their coffee and tea consumption. No relationship was found between coffee and tea intake and premature delivery,

Caffeine Content and Sources

Unless you abstain from eating or drinking almost everything that looks, smells, and tastes good, you will probably consume caffeine in one form or another. Children, adolescents, and adults under 30 take their caffeine largely in the form of soft drinks. A study published in 1986 showed that while 80 percent of Americans in their twenties drank coffee in 1963, this percentage dropped to 40 percent in 1986. Adults over 30 lean primarily toward coffee and tea. After age 60, preference for caffeinated coffee seems to decline, and many senior citizens switch to decaffeinated coffee or tea.

Chemically, caffeine is one of a group of compounds called *methylxanthines*, occurring naturally in more than 60 species of plants. The most familiar and widely used sources of caffeine are coffee and cocoa beans, cola nuts, and the leaves of tea plants. Coffee, tea, and colas are three of the most common beverages in the world, while beverages and confections based on cocoa and chocolate are also very popular.

While coffee, tea, chocolate, cocoa, and colas are all sources of caffeine, the amount of caffeine in any single serving varies considerably. In general, an average mug of coffee contains the most caffeine. A typical cup of tea of the same size usually provides less than one-half as much, and regular colas about one-third that of tea. Cocoa and hot chocolate both contain small amounts of caffeine.

The amount of caffeine in any given cup of coffee or tea depends on a number of factors, including: the variety of coffee bean or tea leaf, where it was grown, the particle size used (the particular coffee "grind" or tea-leaf cut), and the method and length of brewing or steeping. The amount of caffeine in cocoa or chocolate varies less, but still depends on factors such as the origin of the beans.

People also consume caffeine through medicines. Caffeine serves a variety of pharmacologic functions and is found in combination with drugs used as stimulants, pain relievers, diuretics, cold remedies, and weight-control products.

low birth weight, or any birth defects among their babies.

It is important to note that although apparently not responsible for birth defects in humans, caffeine does cross the placenta during pregnancy, and does appear in breast milk while mothers are nursing. Scientific studies show that babies in the last trimester of pregnancy and newborn babies respond to caffeine by exhibiting marked respiratory stimulation and increased urine production. Because of these reasons, along with the limited ability of the developing child to metabolize caffeine, pregnant and nursing mothers are well advised to limit their consumption of caffeine.

What About Decaffeinated Coffee?

Decaffeination has recently come under public scrutiny due to the FDA's proposed ban of methylene chloride in aerosol cosmetic products. This compound has a variety of uses, including extracting caffeine from coffee during the decaffeination process.

In two long-term studies (both conducted at the Harvard School of Public Health), methylene chloride was given to rats and mice in their drinking water in doses roughly equivalent to human consumption of 6 million cups of decaffeinated coffee each day for a lifetime. The chemical did not induce the growth of cancerous tumors in rats and mice.

You may be sacrificing flavor when you drink decaffeinated coffee, but you are certainly not sacrificing your health.

Cutting Back

Caffeine has had a long history of safe use by humans everywhere. While health concerns about the safety of caffeine remain, there is a substantial body of solid scientific evidence supporting the view that moderate caffeine consumption (about 500 milligrams per day) is not a threat to the health of the average adult.

However, if you feel the need to cut back, here are some suggestions: (1) select decaffeinated coffee, tea, or soft drinks; (2) mix caffeinated and decaffeinated coffee grounds together before making coffee; (3) limit your consumption of caffeinated beverages to a preselected number, and then gradually switch to decaffeinated beverages; (4) limit the amount of chocolate that you eat.

If you still have questions regarding the dietary safety of caffeine, you should visit with your physician or a registered dietitian.

PAST, PRESENT, AND FUTURE

PAST, PRESENT, AND FUTURE

Discoveries about early humans and early civilizations provide an ever-clearer picture of the past. But the ever-bleaker condition of many of the world's people darkens the present and troubles the future.

ANTHROPOLOGY AND ARCHAEOLOGY

by Peter S. Wells

Early Humans

Archaeologists in South Africa discovered evidence of the earliest known use of fire by humans. In a cave at Swartkrans, scientists found remains of animal bones that had been charred in a fireplace by early humans of the type *Homo erectus*, sometime between 1 million and 1.5 million years ago. The superimposed layers of burned bones indicate that the early humans used fire repeatedly.

New evidence from the eastern Mediterranean suggests an early date for the appearance of modern humans. Fossil remains of anatomically modern humans from Qafzeh Cave in Israel date to sometime around 90,000 years ago, much earlier than previously dated bones of *Homo sapiens*, or modern humans. This discovery runs contrary to the long-held theory that modern humans first developed around 40,000 or 35,000 years ago, about the time that Neanderthals disappear from the archaeological record, and puts a new slant on the long-debated relationship between Neanderthals and modern humans. If the date is accurate, the Qafzeh Cave discovery would suggest that Neanderthals may represent only a side branch of human evolution (as some anthropologists have long believed), and that modern humans developed quite independently of Neanderthals.

At Tibooburra, Australia, about 530 miles (850 kilometers) northwest of Sydney, scientists found hundreds of thousands of flakes of stoneworking debris where intensive manufacturing apparently occurred some 2,000 years ago.

Secrets of the Shroud

The Shroud of Turin was probably made during the Middle Ages, between A.D. 1260 and 1390. The piece of yellow linen, about 14 feet (4.25 meters) long and 3 feet (1 meter) wide, bears the image of a man thought by some to be Jesus Christ. The Vatican, owner of the shroud, permitted three small samples of the cloth to be analyzed by radiocarbon dating techniques by laboratories at Oxford University in England, the University of Arizona, and the Federal Institute of Technology in Zurich, Switzerland. As a result of the analyses, the Roman Catholic Church announced that the shroud could not be authentic.

Using advanced radiocarbon-dating techniques (right), scientists determined that the Shroud of Turin (top) was made during the Middle Ages.

Photos, this page: AP/Wide World

Early Rome

Excavations on the Palatine Hill in Rome have shed new light on the early development of the city. Rome may have been a sizable community already in the seventh and sixth centuries B.C., earlier than has been believed. Discoveries include a wall that may have formed a defense system for the early town. The new data, after analysis, will likely revise our understanding of the origin and development of this important city.

Recent excavations suggest an earlier settlement date for ancient Rome than has been previously believed.

Peruvian Archaeology

A richly outfitted tomb about 1,500 years old was discovered at Sipan on the north coast of Peru in an excavation supported by the Peruvian Government and the National Geographic Society. The undisturbed burial chamber contains the remains of a high-ranking warrior-priest who died in his thirties, entombed with a great quantity of gold, silver, and copper, including a crown, masks, a knife, necklaces, bells, and a shield. Thousands of ceramic vessels lay nearby. Also entombed were several wives, servants, and a dog. The tomb belongs to the Moche Culture, who dominated the region between A.D. 250 and 750. The discovery—the richest assemblage of gold and silver ever excavated by scientific techniques in the New World—occurs in an area in which robbers have been very active. An intact grave of such wealth is an extremely important discovery that enhances the scientific and historical understanding of the cultural development of the ancient pre-Columbian civilizations of South America.

An undisturbed tomb discovered by archaeologists in Peru contains a rich assortment of luxury items dating from pre-Columbian South America.

Bill Ballenberg/© National Geographic Society

FOOD AND POPULATION

by Martin M. McLaughlin

The world's hungry people suffered more than usually in 1988. Bad weather in many regions (North America, China, Bangladesh), and warfare in others (sub-Saharan Africa, Central America), sharply lowered global food output, thereby reducing consumption for chronically hungry people.

The United Nations Food and Agriculture Organization (FAO) predicts that the world's stocks of cereal grains will fall by a record 119 million tons in 1988–1989, after the second successive drop in annual production, bringing the stocks to 16 percent of consumption, lower than the FAO's minimum for world food security. This drop marks the first time since World War II that grain production has decreased two years running.

Even the modest good news carried a negative aspect. A slight increase in some African production was offset by an unprecedented locust plague. World food aid remained relatively constant, but an increasingly large share went to refugees from civil strife in places like Afghanistan and the horn of Africa.

Although famines (which had perhaps 10 million victims, mainly women and children) continue to receive the major share of public attention, chronic hunger—which affects far more people—is also on the rise: UNICEF estimates a daily death toll of 40,000 children. Brown University's *Hunger Report: 1988* found that 30 percent of the world's people (just under 1.5 billion) received a dietary energy supply less than the basic survival needs in 1985; current estimates could be higher.

In the U.S.—although explicit records of the number of hungry people do not exist—a combination of Census Bureau poverty figures and the report of the Physicians Committee on Social Responsibility suggests that as many as 20 million people (including 12 million children) are hungry in this country.

Besides the restraints on supply and demand that are "internal" to the food system (limitations on land, water, energy, technology, and research; unpredictable weather; population growth; and the increasing gap between rich and poor in both quality and quantity of food consumption), three major "external" factors also bear on the extent and persistence of hunger in many parts of the developing world:

• Armed conflicts.
• The debt burden of the Third World, which now exceeds $1.3 trillion (just over half the U.S. national debt). Making payments on that huge amount (most of it only interest) inhibits the development of debtor countries and consigns their poor people to continuing privation.
• The continuing danger of an agricultural trade war between the U.S. and the European Community (EC), the world's number one and number two food exporters. Both the U.S. and the EC have become increasingly concerned about the sharply rising costs of programs to benefit agricultural producers. The U.S. has proposed that all agricultural subsidies and trade barriers be eliminated by the year 2000. The EC, which has its own ideas about how to reduce these budget outlays, resists the proposal.

For hungry people in the Third World, some liberalization of trade would surely be helpful in providing incentives for their own production; but it is not certain that they could improve their situation in the face of the sort of competition that would follow the elimination of *all* restraints.

Pending further action in these areas, however, most authorities agree that global output must increase by more than 220 million tons in 1989 to replenish depleted stocks, maintain current levels of consumption, and feed the nearly 90 million new people who will be added to the world's population.

The Mystery of Easter Island

by Jeffrey H. Hacker

O n Easter Sunday, 1722, in a remote corner of the southeastern Pacific, surrounded by thousands of miles of ocean, a Dutch explorer named Jacob Roggeveen dropped anchor at a tiny volcanic island and christened the place in honor of the day. Upon exploring the island, Roggeveen and his crew were startled to discover hundreds of stone statues interspersed along the shore, massive humanlike sculptures—immense heads, elongated ears, jutting chins, and disdainful expressions—standing guard over the island's rugged coast. In his log that day, the Dutch explorer wrote of "remarkably tall stone figures . . . [that] caused us to be filled with wonder."

For the more than two and a half centuries since Europeans first set foot on Easter Island, these brooding, monolithic, eerily majestic statues—which range in height from 3 to 32 feet (1 to 10 meters) and weigh up to 70 to 90 tons (63 to 82 metric tons)—have raised questions that generations of scientists have been unable to solve conclusively. What compelled the islanders to sculpt the figures—called *moai* in the native language—on such a colossal scale? How did they move the *moai* from their hillside quarries to the coast? How did they stand them upright? How did this unique and extraordinary culture take root on one of the most remote islands in the Pacific? How did it die?

The Navel of the World

A tiny speck at the easternmost end of Polynesia, Easter Island lies some 1,100 miles (1,700 kilometers) southeast of Pitcairn—the nearest inhabited island—and some 2,300 miles (3,700 kilometers) west of Chile, to which it belongs. The island is roughly triangular in shape, and covers an area of about 62 square miles (160 square kilometers). According to Polynesian legend, it was formed when a supernatural giant named Uoke roamed the Pacific Ocean. Uoke was said to pry up chunks of land with an enormous pole and scatter them across the sea as islands. But when he came to Te Pito O Te Henua—"the navel of the world"—he found that it was made of rock too hard for his pole, and so he left it in its present form, far removed from the rest of the chain.

In reality, Easter Island is volcanic in origin and owes its triangular shape to the three extinct volcanoes—Rano Kau, Maunga Terevaka, and Pua a Katiki—at its corners. The island has no running streams, although there are some prehistoric wells and freshwater crater lakes. There is evidence that thick forests and other vegetation once covered the land, but plant and animal life was always sparse. The landscape is highlighted by sheer ocean cliffs, the towering peaks and broad slopes of the three volcanoes, and the mysterious, hulking statues that dot the coastline.

Settlement

The enigma of Easter Island begins with the origin of its inhabitants. Local legend has it that a sacred chief called Hotu Matu'a was forced to leave his home in the Hiva archipelago after being defeated in battle. With a vision of a new homeland somewhere in the direction of the rising sun, he set out by canoe with a small group of tribesmen and, by virtue of his divine powers, or *mana*, reached the shores of the isolated island—later to be called Rapa Nui.

The most widely accepted scientific theory of the settlement of the Pacific lends credence to the native account. Archaeologists agree that the ancient Polynesians were master navigators who began migrating eastward at least by 2000 B.C. Originating in the western Pacific, they moved gradually across the island chain, adapting to each new environment and giving birth to unique cultural strains. The first settlers of Eas-

Mysterious brooding statues called moai *line the hillsides (facing page) and guard the beaches (below) of Easter Island. How and why the early islanders erected such colossal sculptures still puzzles archaeologists.*

ter Island, or Rapa Nui, are believed to have ventured from the Marquesas or Society Islands and arrived sometime around A.D. 300 or 400, perhaps earlier.

A second theory, promoted by the Norwegian scholar and adventurer Thor Heyerdahl, tells a very different story. While living in the Marquesas Islands during the 1930s, Heyerdahl and his wife heard a legend of how the first Polynesians had sailed from the *east*, led by a king called Tiki. Later, in South America, Heyerdahl was told of a pre-Incan legend about a prince named Kon Tiki who had been expelled from his land and, with a group of his followers, set out across the Pacific in a raft. Based on these accounts, perceived artistic similarities between Polynesian and Incan artifacts, Pacific currents, botanical features, and other evidence, Heyerdahl theorized that the Polynesian race was descended from South American Indians who sailed from the east. To prove the plausibility of his theory, Heyerdahl built a balsawood raft in the Peruvian style and, in his famed *Kon-Tiki* expedition of 1947, sailed it more than 4,000 miles (6,400 kilometers) from the coast of Peru to Polynesia's Tuamotu archipelago.

As even Heyerdahl pointed out, the success of his 101-day voyage merely demonstrated that the original Polynesian settlers *could* have come from South America. Archaeological evidence, however, indicates that eastward-bound voyagers into the Pacific had set out from Southeast Asia. Recent genetic studies also suggest an eastward migration, as present-day Easter Islanders and natives of the Marquesas Islands—which lie far to the west—show a remarkable similarity in gene pools.

The Rise . . .

Beginning with the work of the American W. J. Thomson in the 1880s, archaeologists have conducted extensive research on Easter Island to solve the mystery of the great statues and to trace the growth of Rapa Nui culture. Over the past century, teams of scientists have uncovered, analyzed, and catalogued more than 800 of the giant *moai* and countless other relics. Major scientific expeditions were led by Katherine Routledge of England in the 1910s; Alfred Métraux of France and Henri Lavachery of Belgium in the 1930s; William Mulloy of the United States and Thor Heyerdahl beginning in

---

Ancient Polynesians most likely settled Easter Island, arriving more than 1,600 years ago at the end of a long eastward migration. A westward migration by ancient South American Indians probably never occurred.

© Sélection du Reader's Digest

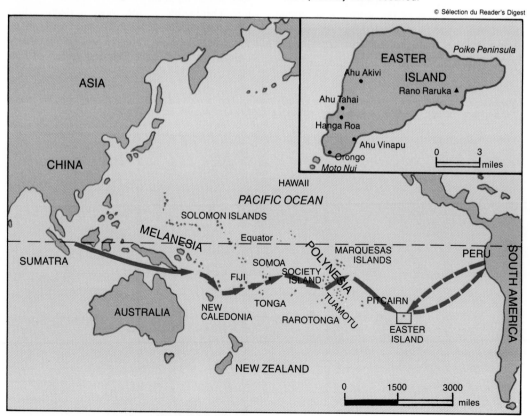

Seven giant moai (above) stand atop an ahu, a masonry platform where the ancient islanders conducted religious rituals. Archaeologists (below) still wonder how the people moved the 16-ton statues from the quarries to the ahus several miles away.

the 1950s; and JoAnne Van Tilburg of the United States in the 1980s. Father Sebastian Englert, the island's priest in the 1930s, also conducted useful scholarly investigations.

Although stone figures have been found elsewhere in Polynesia, the *moai* of Easter Island are by far the largest, most numerous, and most distinctive in style. The vast majority were sculpted out of soft volcanic tuff from Rano Raraku at the eastern end of the island. The Rano Raraku site contains 394 statues, the biggest collection of *moai* on the island. They are found in every stage of workmanship, from the first chinks to completion, thereby providing clues as to the sculpting process. Stone picks and adzes were used to carve the statues, each one taking from 50 to 300 hours.

After quarrying a statue from the stone of Rano Raraku volcano, the islanders hauled it to one of about 240 ceremonial burial shrines, called *ahu*, throughout the island. The *ahu* were long, narrow masonry platforms on which the *moai* were erected and where religious rituals—offerings, sacrifices, prayers, and others—were conducted.

Based on carbon-14 datings, archaeologists have determined that the oldest *ahu* date from about A.D. 690, although none of the classically stylized *moai* were made during this early phase (settlement to A.D. 1100). Most were made and erected during the phase from

1100 to 1680 A.D., when the Rapa Nui culture reached its peak.

Much is known about the early islanders. They lived in thatched huts. Fish constituted the bulk of their diet, supplemented by sugarcane, bananas, taros, and sweet potatoes. But what inspired them to create the statues—especially on such a large scale and in such profusion? The answer is not known with absolute certainty, but legend and science together provide some plausible explanations.

As Chief Hotu Matu'a felt death approaching, he divided the island kingdom among his children. This ultimately gave rise to ten distinct kinship groups, or *mata*, each with its own territory. Most *ahu* were built on lineage or family lands owned by the various *mata*. The *ahu* and the statues that stood upon them were the focus of commemorative rituals. Ceremonies to mark the deaths of sacred chiefs were held there. The bodies were displayed on the *ahu*, which was declared *tapu* (off-limits) until the flesh had fallen from the bones. Some archaeologists suspect that the *ahu*, and later the *moai* themselves, were the products of competition among the various clans.

Two distinct groups of *moai* have been identified. Those erected on *ahu* platforms have clearly delineated eye sockets—originally inlaid with coral—and some also wore a cylindrical *pukao*, or topknot, made of a volcanic rock called red scoria. These statues were set up on pedestals, and all of them faced the central ceremonial space. The second group comprises the 394 statues in the Rano Raraku quarry; they have the further distinction of lacking eyes and topknots.

How did the Rapa Nui islanders move these colossal statues from the quarry to the *ahu*—in some cases up to 6 miles (10 kilometers)? How did they stand them up? And how did they raise the massive topknots? Scientists have puzzled over such questions for more than a century, giving rise to a host of theories. Some have suggested that transportation was accomplished with sleds or bipods (none of which has ever been found), ropes and harnesses, rock or log rollers, or a combination of these methods. Some theorize that the *moai* were transported in an upright position, with the topknot lashed to the head, and raised as a unit; others maintain that they were moved in a prone position and the topknot raised separately.

As for methods of elevating the *moai*, two plausible—and similar—theories have been offered and tested. According to one, the statues on the quarry slopes were tipped over in a hole and hoisted upright by work gangs pulling on ropes. A dirt mound was then piled to the top of the figure, and the topknot was hoisted up the side of the mound. The second theory, successfully tested by archaeologists in the 1950s, involved the construction of a masonry platform under the prone statue's belly and levering up the figure with two long tree trunks.

According to one estimate, the transportation and elevation of so many statues by such a procedure would indicate a population of perhaps 10,000 islanders during the heyday of Rapa Nui society. Whatever method actually was employed and however many men were put to the task, the achievement was truly monumental.

. . . and Fall

The earliest *ahu* known to have served as an altar for the giant statues has been dated to about A.D. 1100–1200. The period of *moai* carving continued for about another 450–500 years, to about the middle of the 17th century. Then, by all archaeological indications, Rapa Nui society seemed to have reached a level of severe social and environmental stress. Population had reached unacceptably high levels. Land had been cleared of vegetation and trees, and heavy erosion resulted. With few large trees left, fishing canoes could not be built, and food was scarce.

The outcome of this environmental destruction was bitter feuding and warfare among the various *mata*. People were forced to seek refuge in caves. During this phase of the island's troubled history, few statues were carved, and countless *ahu* were deliberately destroyed. The warrior class ruthlessly terrorized the populace.

As in a number of other cases, recent scientific evidence coincides with Rapa Nui folklore. The latter tells of a war between two groups: the dominant Hanau Eepe ("long ears" or "heavy-set people") and the lower-class Hanau Momoko ("slender people"), descended from Chief Hotu Matu'a. According to oral tradition, the oppressed Hanau Momoko rose up against the Hanau Eepe and drove them to a hill called Poike, at the eastern end of the island. To protect themselves, the Hanau Eepe built a long fortification trench and filled it with fuel. Ironically, the Hanau Eepe's strategy was their undoing: the Hanau Momoko passed around the sides

Hatlike cylindrical head-
pieces called pukao (above)
cap some of the Easter Island moai. The significance
of the headpieces remains a
mystery. After centuries of
intense monument build-
ing, the islanders abruptly
stopped carving statues and
even abandoned partially
completed sculptures (right).

Top: Photo by David C. Ochsner/© JoAnne Van Tilburg, PhD; above: © David C. Ochsner

of the ditch, attacked the Hanau Eepe from
behind, and threw them into their own flaming
pit. Radiocarbon dating lends support to this
account, placing the events somewhere around
the year 1680.

At about this time also, a new religious cult
called *manutara,* or birdman, took root. Its ceremonial center was Orongo, where hundreds of
carved petroglyphs of birdmen and other figures

still can be seen. The creator god Makemake
came to replace the ancestors as the source of
spiritual power and fertility.

When the Dutch arrived in 1722, they
found a scarcity of vegetation and a society in
violent disarray. Cannibalism was practiced,
and kinship groups were constantly at war. The
population of islanders—described by Roggeveen as being heavily tattooed, with long,

MYSTERIOUS "TALKING BOARDS"

The famous stone statues are not the only Easter Island relics that have puzzled archaeologists over the decades. In 1862 the French missionary Eugene Eyraud discovered an ancient wooden tablet covered with rows of carved symbols. European scholars were fascinated by his find, and mounted an effort to uncover more of these "talking boards." With the islanders using them as firewood, however, a total of only 21 tablets were found. Because so few remained, and because all of the Rapa Nui clan leaders had been killed or kidnapped, researchers had too little evidence with which to reconstruct the language. Some scholars tried to link the designs with ancient Panamanian pictograms; others with Egyptian hieroglyphics, Australian rock paintings, and Indian inscriptions. None could find the answer.

A major breakthrough came in the 1950s with the work of a German linguist named Thomas Barthel. Identifying 120 basic elements in the script, Barthel found that they were combined in various ways to form more than 1,000 compound signs. He concluded that each sign was a stylized pictogram comprised of rebuslike elements that together created a stylized outline of some object or idea. All that he needed now was some key to the symbols, a lexicon.

Barthel's "Rosetta Stone" came in the form of an old journal found in a monastery outside Rome. The journal had belonged to an early Easter Island researcher, French Bishop Tepano Jaussen. On a visit to Tahiti, Bishop Jaussen had met an Easter Islander named Metoro Tauara, who had been trained as a *rongorongo* man, or chanter. Metoro, it turned out, had been able to chant some of the songs on four "talking boards" that Bishop Jaussen had with him. In his notebook, Jaussen noted the Polynesian syllables for each song.

It quickly became clear that Metoro's memory had been sketchy and fragmentary, but Barthel began piecing together the language. According to his translations, the tablets contained prayers, priestly instructions, and mythological accounts. Nevertheless, there were simply too few of the boards to be completely certain, and many experts have rejected Barthel's theory. Scholars now generally believe that the boards were ingenious mnemonic devices (memory aids) used by ritual chanters during important ceremonies.

pierced ears that stretched to their shoulders—had dwindled to about 4,000. *Moai* carving had ceased, and nearly all of the existing statues had been vindictively overturned or destroyed.

The bloodshed, disruption, and upheaval continued for more than another century, followed by more death and violence at the hands of outside exploiters. In 1805 the U.S. schooner *Nancy* abducted 22 islanders and carried them away as slaves. From 1859 to 1862, slave traders from Peru swooped down on the island, rounded up thousands of natives, and shipped them off to dig guano (bird droppings used as fertilizer) off the Peruvian coast. The few who survived eventually were returned to the island, but smallpox came with them. By the late 1870s, the population of Easter Island had dwindled to 111. The last of the kings had died. Christian missionaries had established a strong presence. And the once flourishing Rapa Nui culture lay toppled beneath the giant stone figures, its mysteries left to the ages.

Past and Present

Peace finally came to the island upon its annexation by Chile in 1888. About 2,000 people now live on the island, most of them Rapa Nui and almost all of them in the village of Hanga-Roa on the western coast. Small detachments of the Chilean Navy and Air Force also are based on the island. Spanish is the official language, but the Rapa Nui tongue is commonly spoken. A fledgling tourist trade has developed in recent years.

Still one of the most isolated places on earth and still one of the great enigmas of human civilization, Easter Island was thrust into the space age—as well as the international spotlight—when the U.S. National Aeronautics and Space Administration (NASA) announced in mid-1985 that it was negotiating with the Chilean Government to construct an emergency space shuttle landing site there. Among the terms of the subsequent agreement were strict enforcement of all laws protecting the island's archaeological treasures. In 1986–87, NASA expanded the island's lone runway from 9,000 feet (2,750 meters) to 11,000 feet (3,000 meters) and added the ramps and overruns necessary to accommodate the shuttle. The facility would be used only if a shuttle launched from California's Vandenberg Air Force Base lost power during its ascent and had to be aborted.

Whatever changes have come to Easter Island—from tourist hotels to the space shuttle—the landscape remains shrouded in mystery. Archaeologists continue to study the giant, brooding statues whose hulking figures still stand guard along the island's coast. For with all the theories and explanations that have been promoted over the decades, basic questions remain essentially unanswered. By what route did the islanders arrive? How did a flourishing culture evolve in such a remote place? What compelled the inhabitants to build the giant stone figures? How did they move them? Exactly how did Rapa Nui society meet its demise?

The aura of mystery on Easter Island today remains as palpable as English researcher Katherine Routledge described it in 1915:

"In Easter Island the past is the present, it is impossible to escape from it; the inhabitants of today are less real than the men who have gone; the shadows of the departed builders still possess the land. Voluntarily or involuntarily, the sojourner must hold commune with those old workers; for the whole air vibrates with a vast purpose and energy which has been and is no more. What was it? Why was it?"

Soon after the monument-building phase of Easter Island culture ended, a new religious cult called manutara, *or birdman, took root. At Orongo, the cult's ceremonial center, the island's inhabitants carved hundreds of birdmen and other figures in the rock.*

Bigfoot or BUST

by Jamie James

Cyclops or sea serpent, unicorn or yeti—stories of fabulous beasts have always fascinated us. Yet these creatures, which thrive lustily in the murky realm of myth, seem to vanish in the hard light of the real world. They stay just out of sight, just over the horizon or higher on the mountain, hidden in the forest or the dark depths of the sea.

And that's where most of us are content to leave them. But there are those few who can't let go of the fantasy quite so easily, who must go out themselves to search for the beasts in the shadows. In most cases the dragnets have been laid in vain. Yet occasionally—just often enough to fuel the fires of curiosity—fable becomes fact. When first described by native guides to European explorers, many of the large

African animals that are now so familiar sounded quite as outlandish as the unicorn.

The mountain gorilla, for example, had long been known to the inhabitants of Rwanda as a huge, dark, hairy manlike beast that swung through the treetops emitting a fearful cry. A ridiculous native superstition—until 1901, when Oscar von Beringe brought back the skin of an animal exactly fitting the description. The pygmy hippopotamus, the Komodo dragon, the giant panda—all these animals from the far corners of the world existed only in the mists of superstition, right up to the day they were "found" by white scientist-explorers during the mid-19th to the early 20th century.

Perhaps the most dramatic discovery came in 1938, when a South African deep-sea fisher-

John Butler/© 1988 DISCOVER PUBLICATIONS

man hauled in a very strange fish, the ugly likes of which he had never seen before. The ichthyologists who were brought in to examine it, however, had seen it before—in fossils of the Devonian period. This fish, the coelacanth, had been presumed extinct for 60 million years.

Cryptozoology

The reappearance of the fish is one of the favorite stories of cryptozoologists, the beast seekers. For this small but determined band of scientists and adventurers, the coelacanth is living proof that the elusive *it* is still out there, if only we could find it. Cryptozoologists will tell you that though discussions about the creatures they search for—the yeti in the Himalayas, Sasquatch in the Pacific Northwest, Nessie in Loch

Ness—tend to induce amusement rather than belief, most people had the same reaction to stories about mountain gorillas and Komodo dragons and coelacanths.

Cryptozoology, as a science unto itself, has existed since the term was coined (from Greek, meaning "the study of hidden animals") in 1959 by Belgian zoologist Bernard Heuvelmans. While the International Society of Cryptozoology has only about 800 members, and no more than 100 people are actively engaged in the cryptozoological quest, the field captures the imagination of millions. One recent discovery in particular added some luster to this frequently maligned discipline.

The Elusive Onza

Along the west coast of Mexico, in the province of Sinaloa, the local inhabitants have always known about—and lived in fear of—three kinds of big cat: *el león* (the puma), *el tigre* (the jaguar), and *la onza*, a creature similar to a puma but said to be lankier, faster, and more aggressive. Science, however, has officially recognized only the first two, as *Felis concolor* and *Felis onca*. Although the onza has been part of the indigenous oral history for hundreds of years, gringo zoologists have always considered it just one of the many legendary creatures that abound in the folklore of the Sierra Madre.

But in January 1986, rancher Andres Rodriguez shot a big cat that exactly matched the traditional description of the onza. It was similar to a puma, with the same tawny fur, but with a more slender body, long legs and ears, and distinctive horizontal stripes on the inside of its forelimbs, near the paws.

Richard Greenwell, a cryptozoologist who had been in the Sierra Madre looking for the onza only a few months earlier, was on the scene quickly. He supervised the analysis and dissection of the cat, which had been refrigerated and was therefore in good condition.

A dapper English expatriate given to wearing safari suits, Greenwell is the secretary of the International Society of Cryptozoology, which is run out of an office complex in Tucson, Arizona. Although the president of the society is Heuvelmans, the "father of cryptozoology," it is really Greenwell who keeps the thing going, answering the mail and editing the quarterly newsletter and the annual journal, a meticulously printed, impressive affair.

Greenwell has been very careful not to make any grandiose claims about the onza. "It's so rare to get a specimen of a claimed or mythical animal that I've told my associates that I want us to go very slowly," he says. Assisting him in the dissection of the animal was Troy Best, a University of New Mexico zoologist who has measured 1,600 puma skulls in North American collections.

No one is yet saying exactly what the creature is, whether a previously unknown species of cat, subspecies of puma, or some sort of peculiar hybrid or local variant. Greenwell even allows that it might simply be a weird, skinny puma. To clarify the matter, he is having tissue from the animal examined by a laboratory that specializes in the analysis of mitochondrial DNA, genetic material common to all animals; differences can indicate the closeness of two species' evolutionary branches.

If the onza should indeed "cross over from the somewhat nebulous realm of cryptozoology into the more conventional world of systematic zoology," Greenwell asserts, "both fields will have been enriched—cryptozoology by the demonstration that pursuing anecdotal and native reports can lead to significant zoological discoveries, and zoology by the addition of a large felid to the inventories of our natural world."

Sasquatch

What is significantly present in the onza affair—the animal itself—is what is significantly lacking in most cryptozoological casebooks. The most celebrated no-show of all is bigfoot, or Sasquatch, the huge anthropoid creature said to inhabit the thick forests of the Pacific Northwest. There are abundant eyewitness accounts, plaster casts of footprints, some bad photographs, and a few puzzling hairs, but the star of the show has never appeared.

Its invisibility notwithstanding, the phantom creature commands a wide and loyal following, even among professional scientists. In the February 1981 issue of the journal *Current Anthropology*, Greenwell published the results of a survey he had conducted of physical anthropologists: 13 percent of the respondents accepted bigfoot as a living animal "still unknown to science." Cryptozoologists glumly quote this figure as a discouraging statistic, to show how lonely and misunderstood they are. Yet many people might say that one out of eight isn't bad.

The leading bigfootist at the moment is Grover Krantz, an anthropologist at Washington State University. Krantz has absolutely no doubts about its existence. What tipped the balance for him was a set of plaster casts of huge footprints made in 1970 in northeastern Washington. Altogether Krantz has collected 65 casts of footprints—hikers in this part of the country seem never to be without their bag of plaster of

Mexican folklore telling of the onza gained some legitimacy when a cat fitting the description was shot in 1986.

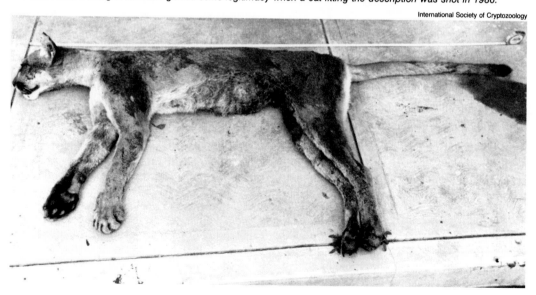

Although dozens of Sasquatch footprints have been reported (right), the creature remains elusive. Indistinct photographs like the one below, supposedly of a bathing Sasquatch, have been rejected by even the most ardent cryptozoologists.

© D. Kirkland/SYGMA

© Amazing Horizons/SYGMA

paris—prints that he claims were made by 20 individual bigfeet.

The casts that have stirred the widest interest were made in 1982 near Walla Walla, Washington, by a Forest Service patrolman. The 15-inch (38-centimeter)-long footprints were impressed in extremely fine soil, and the casts clearly reveal dermal ridges, the little fingerprintlike lines that are found on the soles of anthropoid feet.

Walter Birkby, a respected forensic anthropologist at the University of Arizona who is himself a member of the editorial board of *Cryp-*

tozoology, the annual journal of the society, finds the Walla Walla casts interesting, but he's far from convinced. "I need something that can't be faked before I run out and buy a big block of Sasquatch stock," he says. "Give me a skull and some dentition."

Taxonomic Hastiness?

Krantz, however, is utterly convinced—so much so that he has proposed a genus and species for Sasquatch. In 1986 he published a paper in *Northwest Anthropological Research Notes* in which he applied to Sasquatch the existing fossil name *Gigantopithecus blacki*. This is an enormous (800 pounds [360 kilograms]) ape, known only through fossil teeth and jawbones found in China and northern India, that has been extinct, as far as paleontologists are concerned, since the middle Pleistocene, half a million years ago. Krantz, however, believes that a relict population of *Gigantopithecus* has somehow survived in the Northwest. (Other cryptozoologists have speculated that the Himalayan yeti, too, represents a population of *Gigantopithecus* that managed to elude the evolutionary pink slip, but Krantz offers no opinion about that.)

When asked if he did not jump the gun in assigning the species a name before an actual specimen had been collected, Krantz replies, "People name fossils in the same way, from a few scraps of bone." When it is pointed out that he lacks any scraps at all of Sasquatch, neither flesh nor bone, he is not fazed. "It is an accepted paleontological practice to name life-forms from footprints and spoor." He is, however, unable to cite any specific examples of this; he does remember that there was some 500-million-year-old wormlike organism that was named on the basis of trails in fossilized mud.

Despite the irregularities of his methods, Krantz has attracted the best sort of publicity for his work. In September 1987, in *Newsweek*, there appeared an article titled "Tracking the Sasquatch," which breathlessly described Krantz's work as a major breakthrough: "Discoveries of footprints this spring, plus rigorous analyses of casts of earlier prints, have strengthened the claim that something is out there. . . . Krantz believes the creatures are representatives of a species that eventually led to modern man. If he's right, Sasquatch could be our closest living relative."

Rooting for Discovery

Now, in the first place, neither Krantz nor any other anthropologist believes that *Gigantopithecus* led to modern man. Secondly, this formula could be applied to absolutely any piece of romantic nonsense. ("If Dr. X is right, and the sky is a dome fretted with golden fire, then the world might well be flat.") *Newsweek* goes on to suggest that Krantz is a victim of "mainstream scientists' refusal to consider the evidence." The piece indignantly concludes: "With the potential jackpot so great, perhaps more anthropologists will examine the case for Sasquatch instead of dismissing it out of hand."

This is a complaint often heard from cryptozoologists (though it is surprising to read it, unleavened by any sort of editorial balance, in the pages of *Newsweek*), that "real" scientists ignore the overwhelmingly persuasive case for Sasquatch, or yeti, or Nessie, or whatever it might be, because they are afraid that everything they stand for will be overturned. As Krantz puts it, "All the scientific institutions do not want the waters muddied."

Harvard biologist Stephen Jay Gould, a scientific institution himself, says that this is just not so. "You always hear that charge from people with unconventional views. Yet every natural historian would be delighted if this existed. We all root for these things." Gould believes that no motive exists for the sort of suppression that Krantz fears, and that the only reason Sasquatch hasn't been accepted by mainstream zoologists is the lack of evidence. "If Sasquatch were found, it would overturn no existing theory. It just doesn't seem likely. If it exists, why is it that all we have are fuzzy photographs and footprints?"

If such a large, lumbering creature existed, then we would have one by now, he says. The coelacanth, after all, was swimming about in the immensity of the Indian Ocean, and one of those turned up, followed by many more. Each individual Sasquatch would need a considerable foraging range in order to survive in the inhospitable evergreen forests that are its supposed habitat. And certainly more than one must be living. "People think of Sasquatch as a solitary beast prowling about in the woods, but there can't be just one," says Gould. "There must be a viable population." And, he says, it's unlikely that such a population would not come into contact with humans. "Americans are an active people. There's not a square foot of North America that hasn't been extensively tramped over." He believes that with every Sasquatch-less day, the odds decline a bit further.

Encounter with Yeti

If any evidence were needed that Gould, at least, is not a party to the Great Sasquatch Cover-up, it could be found in his open-minded view about the creature's Asian counterpart, the yeti: "I don't think the yeti is impossible. There are probably 1,000 square miles (2,600 square kilometers) of unexplored territory high in the Himalayas."

As a matter of fact, there has been a flurry of activity on the yeti front. In March 1986, Anthony Wooldridge, an English long-distance runner, undertook a solo marathon in the Garhwal Himalayas, in northern India near Nepal, to raise money for charity. His encounter with a yeti, as described in accounts published in *The New York Times* and *Cryptozoology*, occurred on a snow-covered slope more than 11,000 feet (3,300 meters) above sea level. Wooldridge saw a strange set of footprints that led to a spindly shrub. "Standing behind the shrub was a large, erect shape perhaps up to 2 meters (6.5 feet) tall. . . . It was standing with its legs apart, apparently looking down the slope, with its right shoulder turned toward me. The head was large and squarish, and the whole body appeared to be covered with dark hair, although the upper arm was a slightly lighter color." Wooldridge whipped out his trusty Nikon and shot.

The resulting photographs, in which Wooldridge's "yeti" is a tiny fleck of darkish fuzz (there never seems to be a telephoto lens on hand when such a creature appears), have received mixed reviews. John Napier, former curator of primate collections at the Smithsonian Institution and dean of bigfoot theorists, concluded in 1972 in his book *Bigfoot* (touted on

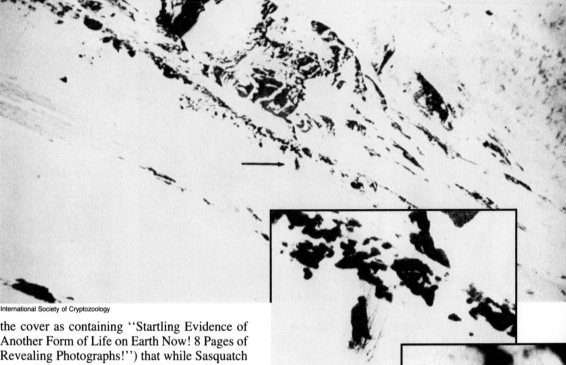

International Society of Cryptozoology

the cover as containing "Startling Evidence of Another Form of Life on Earth Now! 8 Pages of Revealing Photographs!") that while Sasquatch was a definite maybe, yeti was just too shadowy to bother with. Yet, after seeing the Wooldridge photographs, Napier announced that he had been converted to yetiism. His fellow cryptozoologists, however, tactfully suggest that the aged Napier is a bit gaga.

In any case, when Grover Krantz and Stephen Jay Gould agree on something, everyone else ought to take notice: the former avers that Wooldridge's pictures are definitely not of a yeti; the latter says that the photograph is "ridiculous," and the supposed yeti "a stupid-looking blob."

Yeti evidence? In 1986, a runner in the Himalayas snapped the photograph at top. An arrow points to the supposed "creature." The enlargements are claimed to show a hairy, six-foot-tall, manlike shape. Skeptics claim the indistinct form is more likely a dark rock standing out against the snowy, mountainous landscape.

Mysterious Mokele-Mbembe

Perhaps the most exotic cryptozoological quarry of all (and that's saying something) is Mokele-Mbembe, the swamp monster of the equatorial Congo. Its adherents claim that it is nothing less than a relict sauropod, a semiaquatic dinosaur of the Cretaceous period. It is said to inhabit one of the most dangerous and inaccessible places in the world, Lake Telle in the Likouala swamplands of the Congo.

In 1981 two separate Mokele-Mbembe expeditions were launched. One was led by Roy Mackal, vice president of the International Society of Cryptozoology and at the time a biochemist at the University of Chicago (he's now an administrator in the office of the president of the university); the group included Richard Greenwell. The other expedition was led by Herman Regusters, who is an engineering consultant to the Jet Propulsion Laboratory in Pasadena, California—and who seems to be something of an embarrassment to more orthodox cryptozoologists like Mackal and Greenwell.

Originally, the two teams were to have combined forces. But when Regusters issued a press release that made reference to alligators (no such thing in Africa, only crocodiles) and headhunters and cannibals (there are none in the Congo), and sent Mackal T-shirts emblazoned with a brontosaurus orbited by a space satellite and the logo MACKAL-REGUSTERS DINOSAUR TREK, Mackal sundered all connections with him. Thus two expeditions went into the Congo simultaneously, but never met each other.

All the Mackal expedition managed to turn up, according to the society's newsletter, was "a wake in a river caused by a large, unidenti-

In equatorial Congo, local legend holds that Mokele-Mbembe (below), a gigantic lizard-like creature, inhabits the dark waters of Lake Telle. In 1981, an expedition led by cryptozoologists Richard Greenwell and Roy Mackal (with beards, fore and aft, respectively) failed to find any conclusive evidence of the animal's existence.

fied submerging animal (neither elephant nor hippo)'' and ''a trail left by a large, unidentified animal (not an elephant).'' Slim pickings, in other words.

But the flamboyant Regusters' team claimed to have scored a whopping success. Regusters reported that he saw Mokele-Mbembe several times, but his evidence is more than suspect. He brought back photographs of the monster, which no one can decipher, and recordings of its call, which, according to Greenwell—one of the few people who have heard the tape—sounds like nothing more than the trumpeting call of a big animal.

Paucity of Evidence

Two years later an expedition sponsored by the Congolese Government itself also claimed to have met up with the sacred sauropod. This time the observer was Marcellin Agnagna, one of only two zoologists living in the Congo, who received his training at the University of Havana. Here is how his sighting of Mokele-Mbembe at Lake Telle was described in the cryptozoological society's newsletter: ''It had a long neck, small head, and large back, and its length visible above the water was thought to be about 5 meters (16 feet). Agnagna immediately recognized that it was not part of the known fauna of Central Africa, and, in fact, that it greatly resembled a Mesozoic sauropod in morphology.''

Agnagna grabbed his movie camera, which was at the ready for just such an occasion, and waded out into the lake to film the amazing sight. Imagine his dismay when he found that he

Illustrations, above and facing page: International Society of Cryptozoology

had the camera on the wrong setting, which meant that all his footage would turn out to be completely worthless! And by the time he realized his mistake—drat!—the camera had run out of film.

Despite the paucity of evidence, Mackal remains undaunted: ''I don't give a damn what some people in the scientific community say. When I make my case to friends of mine who are atomic physicists, they tell me, 'If we had 10 percent of this amount of evidence for subatomic particles or black holes, we'd be on much more solid ground.' '' Mackal and Greenwell are planning to make another expedition to Lake Telle in the near future.

The Loch Ness Monster

The most celebrated and beloved of the crypto-critters is undoubtedly the monster that inhabits Loch Ness, in Scotland. First sighted in 1933, Nessie has become something of the doyenne of cryptozoology. Yet the creature's appeal extends beyond the ranks of society members. In Greenwell's survey of physical anthropologists, 23 percent of those questioned—nearly twice as many as believe in Sasquatch—said they accepted Nessie as a living animal "still unknown to science."

At the moment there are at least two groups devotedly pursuing Nessie. One is American, led by attorney Robert Rines, president of the Academy of Applied Sciences; the other is British and is called the Loch Ness and Morar Project (Morar being another loch nearby, which is also believed to harbor a monster). The British group, led by a man named Adrian Shine, recently launched a much-publicized "$1.6 million sonar campaign." The figure is misleading, because it reportedly represents the total book value of the boats and sonar equipment (nothing more than ordinary commercial fish-finders), which were used for only two days. Mackal doesn't conceal his disdain for Shine's vaunted sonar search: "It was ridiculous. Why borrow some fish-finders and go up and down the loch in little boats? It did more harm than good."

Rines, on the other hand, is using much more sophisticated equipment, including some highly advanced underwater time-lapse photography technology designed for his group by Harold Edgerton, the inventor of high-speed strobe photography. Both Greenwell and Mackal have high hopes for the Rines group, which is shying away from publicity until it has deployed its arsenal and come up with something to report.

A Limbo of Nonexistence

It is easy to smile at cryptozoologists. However, it would be a mistake, and an unscientific one at that, to dismiss what they do out of hand. "Remember the coelacanth" could serve as a sort of cryptozoological commandment, suitable for needlepoint, a talisman to ward off the intellectual sin of smugness. And now there is the onza. If it turns out to be a new species of New World cat, it would be a major contribution to biology, its discovery the envy of every zoologist.

The onza represents a personal triumph for Greenwell and his relatively low-profile ap-

Indistinct photographs of the Loch Ness monster (top) do not prove its existence to cryptozoologists, who caution not to judge a swimming beast by its neck (above).

proach. Yet it is a rather huge leap from a newly discovered cat to living dinosaurs and *Gigantopithecus* skulking about the wilderness of Washington state.

While there is undoubtedly something wonderful about Sasquatch and Nessie, it has more to do with children's literature than anything else: we would like to believe in them just as we would like to believe in Tinker Bell. Stephen Jay Gould says wistfully, "I'd rather that there were a Sasquatch," and we understand perfectly. It seems terribly boring and humorlessly adult of us to condemn such appealing characters to the limbo of nonexistence. But until they climb out of that state and make a personal appearance, a rational person doesn't have much choice.

SAVING VENICE

by H. Aldersey-Williams

As I make my way through narrow Venice streets, crossing countless bridges over the busy canals, I pass ancient churches and palazzi filled with priceless artworks. Occasionally I see a wall of a building inscribed with the date November 4, 1966.

These inscriptions are high-water marks, a sad reminder that all this splendor is perpetually threatened by the sea. For on that day, the city's official tide gauge, located at the mouth of Venice's Grand Canal, recorded a tide, swollen by strong winds and torrential rain, fully 6 feet (1.8 meters) above mean sea level. As water poured through palaces, hotels, shops, and museums, damage ran in the tens of millions of dollars, not including damage that was done to priceless works of art.

Sinking City

In the 21 years since Venice recorded that catastrophic day of flooding, it may seem that little or nothing has been done to prevent an equally disastrous recurrence. Now, after several false starts, a local construction consortium aptly named Venezia Nuova, or New Venice, has received approval for a plan to build a flood barrier around the Venice lagoon. The action comes none too soon. Venice has been sinking

The floods that periodically inundate Venice, Italy, threaten the city's priceless artwork and historic structures. Engineers have devised a barrier system that holds back the sea but still allows the water exchange needed to remove sewage and pollution from the canals.

some 4 inches (10 centimeters) a century because of geological shifts in the Po Valley region. While experts now believe this sinking has stopped, the tide level in Venice continues to increase by 1/20 inch (1.25 millimeters) each year as the average sea level throughout the world increases. High tides periodically flood Venice's piazzas and do untold damage to the foundations of its historic buildings.

When I enter the Venezia Nuova office, a former ducal palace now updated with computer terminals and modern office furniture, the businesslike hush is broken only by the clacking of keyboards. Beneath an ornate, frescoed ceiling, I meet Dr. Franco de Siervo, the engineer in charge of technical services for the consortium to build the Venice barrier. He lights his pipe, leans back in his chair, and slides toward me the book of matches he has just used. "The barrier is a gate, hinged on the bottom, that runs across the lagoon entrance. In the open position, it will lie in a recess in the concrete foundation," he says as he lays the matchbook on the desk.

In this condition the gates, which are actually rows of 65-foot (20-meter)-long water-filled steel canisters, lie horizontally on the seabed at the three entrances to Venice's lagoon. Tides and ships can pass without hindrance. But under specific conditions, outlined to me later by another engineer, the gates open up. "We inject air so that the water is pushed out of the canisters," de Siervo continues. "Just from buoyancy, the gate rises up." As he speaks, he slowly lifts one edge of the matchbook off the table. "It's simple."

Simple, yes—but not cheap. The $2.6 billion scheme is the latest of many proposals to protect Venice and its surrounding lagoon from floods. But unlike previous comers, including an inflatable rubber dam suggested by Italian tire manufacturer Pirelli, Venezia Nuova's plans have gained government approval and funding.

A Multitude of Requirements

This difficulty in gaining government approval is one reason it's taken over 20 years to formulate a final plan to hold back the Venice floods. Italy's volatile politics may be partly responsible for this delay, but the greater part of it is for good scientific reasons. Venice lies in a large, shallow lagoon that supports not only the people of the city, but also a fragile ecology and a booming chemical and oil-refining industry fed by the continual traffic of large ships.

Any barrier to prevent tidal flooding must not harm plant or animal life in the lagoon, restrict shipping movements, or reduce the water exchange between the lagoon and the sea that helps remove sewage and pollution from inhabited areas. In addition, the barrier must be completely reliable even if it's used only infrequently.

These requirements make the design of the Venice barrier more complex than for existing barriers around the world. "It's the only one of this dimension that has both to stop the water and allow navigation," points out Alberto Scotti, managing director of Technital, a Verona-based consulting firm responsible for computer simulations and mathematical modeling of the Venice design. He explains how this is achieved: "The barrier does not have intermediate concrete support structures. Normally with such a barrier, you can have a maximum of 70 or 80 meters [230 or 260 feet] between supports. In our case we have an open space of 300 meters [984 feet]." The Thames Barrier in Great Britain, by contrast, allows the passage only of minor shipping, while the Dutch Oosterschelde is a different, continuous structure for protection against storm surges rather than high tides, and it does not allow any shipping through.

The special combination of requirements for the Venice barrier ruled out many early designs that were submitted. Some, though, received detailed consideration, including laborious mathematical modeling and physical simulation studies. But in the end, findings always indicated possible damage to the delicate balance of natural forces in the lagoon, and a need for more research.

Tests so far on the Venezia Nuova proposal look considerably more hopeful. So much so that the 27-firm consortium is now in the process of submitting the final proposal for funding the research and construction program. "Our target," says de Siervo, "is to complete everything to start operation at the beginning of 1996." Government funding is provided annually in roughly $250 million batches. The first two such sums have been spent partly on design and modeling studies of possible barriers, but mostly on preliminary work on the fabric of Venice itself, including dredging canals and reinforcing seawalls. A third injection of cash will finance the last of the research, and subsequent grants will be spent on construction of the barrier itself.

Closing Questions

One of the barrier's principal engineers is Augusto Ghetti, president of the Venice region's Institute of Sciences, Arts and Letters, and professor at the Institute of Hydraulics at the ancient University of Padua. While he is enthusiastic about the newest barrier design, Ghetti concedes that there are still some unsolved design problems. For example, a satisfactory design for the hinge that will double as a valve to admit compressed air and expel water during barrier operation has not been agreed upon. Another source of debate concerns the frequency and duration of barrier closings. "If you don't want any flooding in Venice, it is necessary to close the gates at 80 centimeters [about 2.5 feet] on the tide gauge at the Punta della Salute," says Ghetti. "Statistically, that would happen about 40 times a year for flooding to be completely avoided." It is at this 80-centimeter level that a tide officially becomes an *acqua alta*, or high water, and Venetians are warned of its impending arrival by eerie howling sirens.

Such frequent closings, however, would interfere with shipping and would build up excessive pollution in the lagoon. The duration of each closure must be considered, too. Ghetti provides a dramatic illustration: "Here is a tide record from February 1987," he says as he opens up a graph of the most recent severe flood in Venice. He points to a tall peak on the graph. "You see that the level was high—1.75 meters [almost 6 feet] on the tide gauge." The 1966 record flood level was 6.3 feet (1.94 meters). "And the duration was 48 hours. That would be a long closure. But," he adds, with a sigh of relief, "of course, that is only one or two times a year."

Computer Flood Prediction

Rare as such cases are, scientists now favor using a tidal barrier just for these short-lived extreme high waters. Minor flooding would be prevented by other means, such as the construction of low seawalls along the canal sides. Current thinking favors starting the closure at about

Because Venice is built on a group of islands, it is highly vulnerable to the slowly rising levels of the Adriatic.

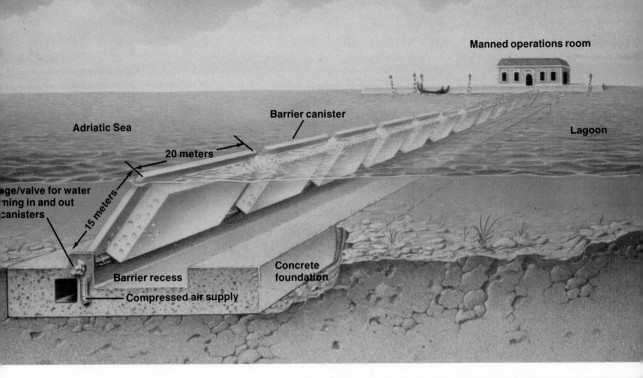

Manned operations room

Barrier canister

Adriatic Sea

20 meters

Lagoon

ge/valve for water
ning in and out
canisters

15 meters

Barrier recess

Concrete
foundation

Compressed air supply

The Venice barrier system will consist of three separate gates lying horizontally at the three entrances to Venice's lagoon. Individual water-filled canisters (above) make up the gates. When the tide begins to rise, generators will pump compressed air into the canisters, replacing the water. As the canisters fill with air, they will float up to about a 45-degree angle, providing a shelf on which the waves can break. Each individual canister will oscillate with the sea, preventing stress from building up in the gate. Such oscillation will also allow wave action to continue past the gates toward the city, thereby preventing stagnation in the lagoon. Construction of the system has begun already (right), with full operation scheduled for early 1996.

Top: © Wendell McClintock; above: © Rudi Frey/*Time* Magazine

3.5 feet (110 centimeters), a water level that would flood about 8 percent of Venice, including St. Mark's Square, a little more than ankle-deep. "In this case," says Ghetti, "only three or four closures a year would be necessary."

Those few occasions arise when a high tide coincides with particular weather phenomena. Says Ghetti: "The water tends to increase gen-

erally when there is sinking pressure at Venice and high pressure in the South Mediterranean." The high atmospheric pressure at the south end of the Adriatic Sea pushes water northward toward Venice, while the low pressure offers no resistance to the water-level rise. This set of weather circumstances is made more threatening because of the likelihood of rain associated with the low-pressure area at Venice's end of the Adriatic Sea.

. Computers will be used to forecast flooding danger, using standard tide data from published tidal-prediction tables in combination with frequently updated atmospheric-pressure readings and wind and rainfall predictions from the Italian state meteorological service. "This should give us a reliable forecast of the actual high tide between six and 12 hours in advance," says de Siervo.

These data will be interpreted in an operations center where a course of action will be decided. If the barriers are to be closed, three operations subcenters—one at each lagoon entrance—will be instructed to begin barrier closing. But first an operator will make a visual check to make sure that the entrance is clear. "It will never be completely automatic," says de Siervo. "There could always be a small boat just fishing on the gate. You have to look and check."

Scale-model studies are being used to see how the gate will behave during closings. At the consulting hydraulic laboratory Estramed, near Rome, Franco Guiducci and his colleagues have constructed a 1/40-scale model of the gate-element designs. "Here we have the tank," Guiducci says as he gestures, standing on the gravel bottom of a large, glass-sided channel constructed in Estramed's laboratory. In a few days, the spot where Guiducci stands will be filled with water for the tests. A hydraulically driven wave generator at the end of the 150-foot (45.75-meter) channel is capable of creating a variety of wave shapes and sizes. The model is halfway along the channel. Three bright yellow barrier canisters lie flush with the foundations at the bottom of the tank. "We are going to test them under varying wave conditions and sea levels that could occur in the lagoon," explains Guiducci.

Two prototype gate-element designs have been tested. One is a rectangular canister, stepped at the edges, looking a bit like a giant block of chocolate. The other has air chambers in the form of cylindrical drums mounted four across the gate. Already the Estramed tests have rejected the cylindrical canisters. The cylinders, Guiducci recalls, rose to nearly vertical position when filled with air. As a result, they hit the waves coming down the tank head-on, setting up wild oscillations that allowed waves inside the lagoon to build up almost to the height of those in the open sea.

Because the barrier must keep storm waves from the Adriatic Sea from entering the lagoon, the gate elements now being tested are designed not to rise to a fully vertical position. Instead, the canisters are designed to float up to about 45 degrees, providing a shelving "beach" on which the waves can break and expend their energy. Each element is independent of its neighbors and is free to swing on its pair of hinges to absorb this energy without stress building up in the structure.

Holding Back the Sea

Estramed's studies are being complemented by tests in a larger hydrological research firm, Delft Hydraulics in the Netherlands. Here tests will be performed using a 1/30-scale complete barrier as well as the surrounding fixed-concrete constructions and models of the islands. "It's a huge model. We are modeling all 15 barrier-gate elements covering an area of 1 by 1 1/2 kilometers [0.6 by 0.9 mile] around the Malamocco entrance," says Wiel Tilmans, the project manager at Delft.

The Delft studies will explore possible instabilities in the barrier design. For example, the order in which the gate elements are swung into position might be important, as well as the order in which they close—should the edge canisters or the center canisters be closed first? Another possibility is that waves of a particular frequency might set huge snakelike oscillations rippling from one element to the next along the entire length of the barrier. Other waves might scour out the seabed near the barrier and threaten its foundations. All these risks must be evaluated.

Work cannot begin on the entrances until all model tests have been completed, says de Siervo. "In the meantime, we are designing all the interventions in the lagoon that do not depend on their completion—dredging of canals, reconstruction of the *barene*, grassy mud flats in the lagoon, which are covered at ordinary high waters, and the maintenance and repair of the boundaries of the small islands which constitute the inhabited part of the lagoon."

Walking over to a giant chart of the Venice lagoon that covers a wall of his office, de Siervo stresses that the barrier is just one step in the general scheme to save Venice: "We are looking at the restoration and preservation of the ecological equilibrium of the lagoon as a whole."

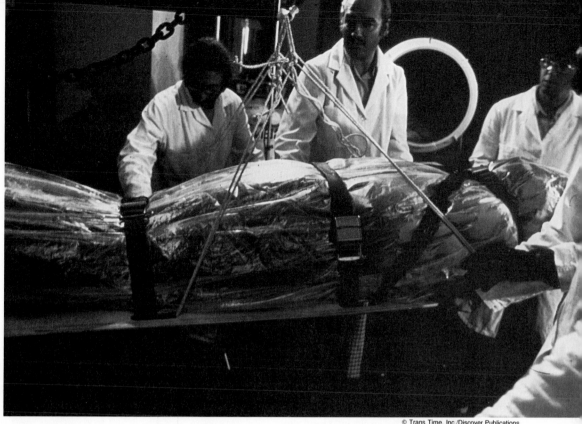

© Trans Time, Inc./Discover Publications

A Cryonic Future

by Miles Cunningham

Dora Kent's head lies in mute repose in a canister of liquid nitrogen, preserved in hope that scientists one day will find a way to thaw it out without damaging the tissues. Perhaps by then they will also have mastered the problem of cloning a new Dora Kent from its cells.

But there is a more immediate problem facing those who placed Dora in her frozen state: a coroner in Riverside, California, has determined that she was still alive when a lethal dose of barbiturates was injected into her 83-year-old body in December 1987. Prosecutors are deciding whether to file criminal charges.

Though the field of cryonics, as the practice of freezing humans is known, has been an obscure one, the last thing those engaged in the work wanted was publicity of the sort generated by Dora Kent. "Cutting off a head is sensational but not very important," says Avi Ben-Abraham, the Israeli-born chairman of the American Cryonics Society, based in San Francisco. Elected chairman of the society last year, Ben-Abraham, 30, has an IQ said to be too high to measure accurately. He is listed in *The Guinness Book of World Records* as the youngest person to become a doctor, having graduated summa cum laude from the University of Perugia, Italy, with a degree in medicine when he was 18. He was nominated for a Nobel Prize when he was 23. "Cryonics is not just raising the dead," he says. "Cryonics is the most exciting field that any scientist can deal with."

Cryonics versus Cryobiology

Not everyone agrees, and especially not those in the related field of cryobiology. "Here you have a group of people trying to freeze people who are already dead in anticipation of their reanimation," says Arthur W. Rowe, editor of

Cryonicists freeze a diseased, dead body in hopes of reviving it once science develops a cure for the disease.

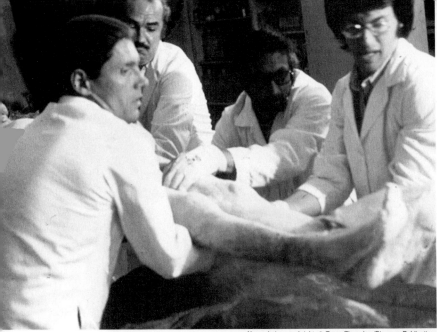

When a cryonics customer dies, technicians cool the dead body to near freezing, replace the blood with a special substitute to prevent ice formation, and then further cool the body in a tub of rubbing alcohol and dry ice (below). When the temperature of the body has cooled to −110°F, cryonicists wrap it in an insulating sleeping bag (left) and place it in a stainless steel capsule filled with liquid nitrogen (right). The head-end down position of the capsule provides the brain with maximum protection from warm air should a malfunction occur.

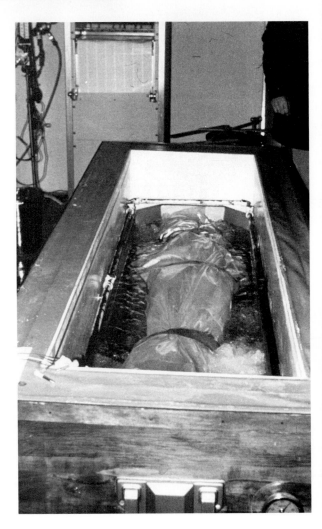

Cryobiology magazine. "They are trying to believe you can make a cow from hamburger."

Cryobiologists work in low-temperature medicine—for instance, freezing white blood cells and the platelets that assist in blood clotting. "Much of our work is done at the single-cell stage," says Rowe. "But a lot is aimed at preserving larger organs—pancreatic tissue, for example—with the eventual goal of tissue banks."

But "there are many, many problems when you get up to larger organs," Rowe says. Freezing and thawing large masses of tissue without damaging the cells, say the cryobiologists, is probably impossible.

"I would agree that any animal frozen and thawed by today's techniques is going to be very dead," says physiologist and cryonicist Paul E. Segall. "But tomorrow is not here yet. A hundred years from now, we may have technologies that are very advanced." One promising area is vitrification, adding such protectives as glycerol to the tissue to prevent the formation of destructive ice crystals.

The cryonicists, who freeze bodies for restoration, see the cryobiologists as cautious minimalists. The cryobiologists, who freeze blood and tissue, see the cryonicists as crackpots. So bad are relations between the two groups that the cryobiologists will not admit cryonicists to their organization, the Society for Cryobiology, though there may be some closet ones among the ranks. It is society policy to deny membership to or expel any member who freezes bodies

request to undergo the procedure despite his family's objections.

Some clients of Trans Time wear bracelets directing immediate application of the cryonics process upon death. At the concrete, one-story Trans Time warehouse, the client's blood is replaced with a blood substitute and glycerol; the body is then wrapped in foil, placed in a polyethylene bag, and suspended upside down in a stainless-steel cylinder filled with liquid nitrogen at $-320°$ F ($-195°$ C). The bodies are placed upside down so that the brain would be last to thaw should there be an accident and some of the nitrogen drain off.

Cryonics' critics do not accuse the cryonicists of dishonesty. James H. Southard, a cryobiologist at the University of Wisconsin Hospital in Madison, says cryonics is "bad science," but "I don't think they go about it in a dishonest manner. . . . It is a religious belief. In America you can do these kinds of things. As far as I know, they don't deceive anybody."

Cryonics is expensive, which would appear to make it an option only for the rich and quirky. The cost of freezing an entire body, says Zinn, is about $125,000. The account is usually

The liquid-nitrogen-filled capsule sits in a concrete block that protects its contents from natural disasters.

with an aim of resurrection. Would a cryonicist be permitted to publish a scientific paper in the 25-year-old *Cryobiology* magazine? "That's hard to say," Rowe says. "I seriously doubt if it would pass muster."

The cryonicists take fierce umbrage at this, in part because they are denied a measure of professional standing and thus have difficulty getting research grants. "It is totally unethical," says Segall. "They are way out to lunch on this."

In the Deep Freeze

There are five cryonics firms in North America: in Florida, Michigan, and California, as well as one in Ontario. Worldwide there are believed to be 16 persons in deep freeze, though there could be others secretly held, according to Jackson Zinn, a lawyer and president of the American Cryonics Society. Five of them are in storage at Trans Time Inc., a cryonics firm in Oakland, California. According to Zinn, since the first body was placed there in 1974, the practice of cryonic suspension has been upheld by the state courts. In one case the court upheld a man's

set up as a trust in the form of life insurance. A portion of the trust pays for the initial processing, and the balance earns interest to pay for maintenance over the years.

The Cutting Edge?

The cryonics society and Ben-Abraham feel they are on the cutting edge of deep advances in the way life is sustained: low-temperature medicine, bloodless surgery, blood substitutes, cloning, and whole-organ freezing among them. "What we are trying to do is buy more time for those patients whose time has run out," says Ben-Abraham. Just as science has largely conquered polio and tuberculosis, he argues, eventually there will be cures for cancer and other deadly diseases.

In 1986 Segall anesthetized a laboratory beagle named Miles (after the protagonist in the Woody Allen movie *Sleeper*) and placed him in a bin of crushed ice, chilling the dog to about 68° F (20° C). Then his blood was removed and replaced with a solution of blood salts, starches, minerals, sugars, buffers, and anticoagulants. As Segall recounts the experiment, Miles was chilled further to about 38° F (3° C), and then the pumps were shut off. For 15 minutes the chilled beagle was without oxygen or pulse. Then the pumps were turned on, Miles was warmed up to 44° F (7° C), and Segall began restoring the blood. When the normal concentration of blood was reached, Miles was sewn up and shipped off to intensive care.

Within hours the dog was active, and after six days he left the clinic. Since then he has lived at the Segall household. "He stands on his hind legs begging for food; he is very well coordinated; there has been little or no brain damage," says Segall. Trans Time intends similar experiments soon with monkeys.

The most significant result of the experiment, says Segall, was that Miles was treated with a relatively cheap blood substitute developed for experiments with hamsters. Answering his critics, Segall readily concedes that similar experiments were performed almost 20 years ago, but with more damage sustained by the specimen.

The cryonicists say that there are a number of potential immediate benefits from their research. Suppose a healthy person dies in Oregon in an auto accident. Usually only one or two organs, if any, can be salvaged. But cryonicists contend that if the body could be chilled quickly, the victim's heart could be shipped out for a recipient in California, the lungs to Florida, the corneas to New England, and so on— all at a great time advantage.

Buying Time

They offer more visionary scenarios as well: an astronaut deep in space, stricken with some malady, might have to wait months for treatment. Cryonic suspension could buy valuable time. "Imagination," says Ben-Abraham, "is more important than knowledge."

Another example: chemotherapy, commonly used in the treatment of cancer patients, requires the injection of toxic chemicals systemically or in various parts of the body. The chem-

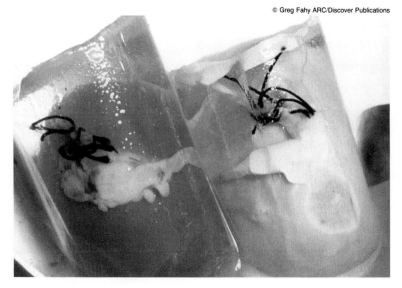

Cryonics research has led to a number of related medical advances, including better ways of preserving organs for future transplantation. Ice crystals have damaged the frozen kidney on the right. But through a process called vitrification—preserving the organ in a liquid that hardens like glass when cooled—the kidney on the left shows no trace of ice.

Physiologist Paul Segall has successfully tested many cryonics techniques on Miles, a laboratory beagle.

icals produce side effects such as loss of hair, dry skin, malaise, infections, tissue damage. So toxic are the chemicals that there is danger of damage to the rest of the body. "But suppose a blood substitute is injected, the body chilled, and the diseased organ warmed," says Segall. "Then the infected organ alone could be targeted for high doses of the anticancer agents and later flushed out without the side effects, but with the added benefit of concentrated chemotherapy."

Segall and Ben-Abraham think these possibilities hold great promise. "We are forming a medical products company to explore and market these spin-offs," says Segall. "We think we are looking at the beginning of a new industry here: low-temperature medicine." Ben-Abraham regards natural death as a gradual shutting down of the body's systems rather than the sudden departure of life. There is an abrupt loss of cardiovascular activity, resulting in clinical death, he says, but organs, tissues, and cells remain "very much alive" for some time.

Through advances in cryonics, he anticipates a major change in the ways that organs are retrieved. But freezing and thawing, with the accompanying damage, is the hurdle. "While cold is really our main ally as to preservation,

it is also our biggest enemy in a way. It is a double-edge sword," he says. "We are trying to halt the death process, hoping that the cold will prevent any further deterioration, so when we get back to the body in 100 years, we will get to it, in effect, 20 minutes after clinical death. By the end of the millennium, we will be able to successfully revive a human body that has been frozen, and that will be the testimony that there is no limitation to the human mind and to the progress of science."

Ben-Abraham, who considers himself "very religious," sees no conflict between cryonics and the promise of an afterlife. "God gave us the intelligence to extend life as much as we can," he says. "Do we accept scientists playing God, playing with the most accepted concept of life, which is death? Is science reaching too far? I'm saying that just because people have always accepted death, we should not continue to accept it. . . . Imagine you are on your deathbed, and every possible medical avenue has been exhausted. If you have anything going in your life, you may be happy that some scientists spent the best years of their lives making progress in science and cryonics. For each of us, there is a point at which we say, 'Nature be damned.' "

PHYSICAL SCIENCES

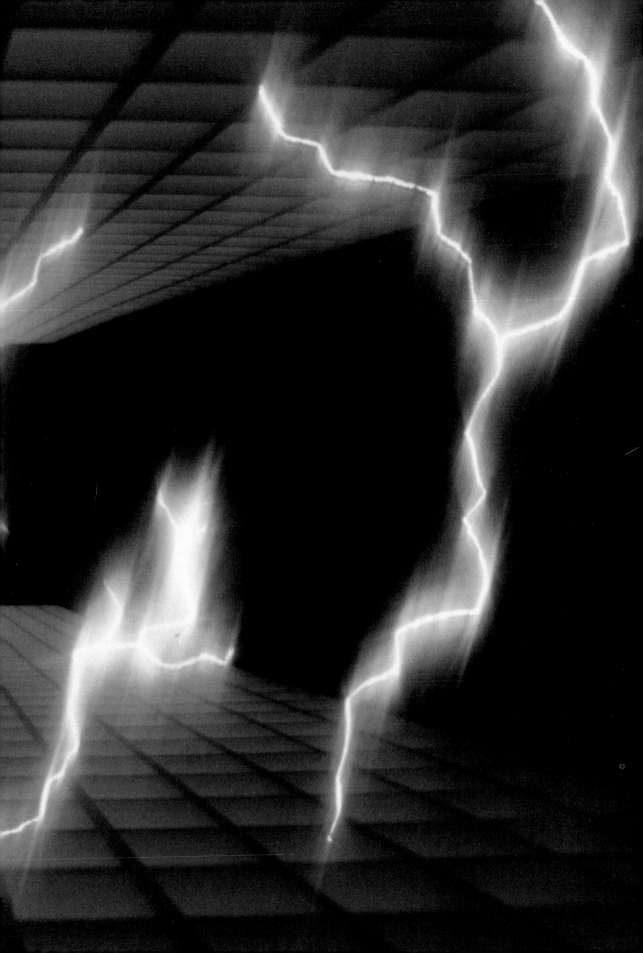

PHYSICAL SCIENCES

Experimenters in the physical sciences synthesized new materials—including superconductors—developed techniques for studying matter, and sought a deeper understanding of the varied, mysterious world of subatomic particles.

by Marc Kusinitz

Lockheed Missiles & Space Company, Inc.

For years, scientists have known that a magnet will levitate over a superconductor. Now scientists have discovered that superconducting material will dangle below a magnet, as though suspended by a thread (above).

Superconductivity

Physicists continued to construct theories to explain why some materials achieve superconductivity (complete loss of electrical resistance) at very low temperatures, and the phenomenon itself was observed in a growing number of substances.

William A. Goddard, III, and his colleagues at the California Institute of Technology (Caltech) in Pasadena developed a theory that they believe explains superconductivity in copper-based materials. In the case of lanthanum copper oxide, substituting strontium atoms for some lanthanum atoms forces some oxygen atoms to lose a single electron and develop a spin. This, in turn, causes each of the spinning copper atoms on either side of the oxygen atoms to line up in the same direction, creating pockets of magnetism. Oxygen atoms deprived of elec-

trons act as "holes" that attract electrons from other, nearby oxygen atoms, which, in turn, lose electrons, forming new holes as they do so. Such holes moving through the pattern would create a trail of magnetic pockets that facilitate the flow of electrons. Goddard's theory is controversial but, if true, would preclude superconductivity at room temperature.

Another theory, developed by Richard L. Martin and his colleagues at the Los Alamos (New Mexico) National Laboratory, suggested that electrons shuttle between oxygen and copper atoms in a way that reinforces the tendency of each atom to release an electron.

But even without a definitive theory of superconductivity, researchers discovered two new families of superconducting materials. Compounds based on bismuth achieve superconductivity at tempera-

tures as high as 110° Kelvin (−261° F); those based on thallium achieve superconductivity at 125° Kelvin (−234° F).

The uncanny "suspension effect" was also discovered. Scientists had known for many years that superconductors could cause magnets to levitate above them. In September, Dr. Brian B. Schwartz of Brooklyn College accidentally discovered that magnets can also suspend a superconductor in space.

New Tools and Techniques

© IBM Corporation/Almaden Research Center

A scanning tunneling microscope produced the first visual proof of benzene's ringed structure. Each cluster is a single benzene molecule.

Cornell University scientists used a device called the undulator to produce a flash of high-energy, tightly focused X rays that was a million times faster than any previous flash, and capable of photographing chemical reactions in a billionth of a second. The technique vastly improves conventional X-ray crystallography, a procedure through which the structure of a crystallized substance is analyzed by shooting X rays for hours or days at the substance.

Researchers at the National Bureau of Standards used lasers to slow the movement of sodium atoms enough to

produce a gas a fraction of a degree above absolute zero (−459°F or −273°C)—an achievement useful in studying low-energy atomic collisions.

Researchers from the IBM Almaden Research Center and the University of California at Berkeley, using a scanning tunneling microscope (STM), produced the first picture of a benzene molecule. German chemist Friedrich August Kekulé von Stradonitz had postulated in 1865 that the benzene molecule is composed of six carbon and six hydrogen atoms arranged in the shape of a ring; the STM image provides visual proof of it.

Materials Science

The ability of researchers to crystallize proteins in order to study their chemical composition by crystallography was enhanced by the discovery that mineral particles such as mica, talc, and topaz facilitate crystallization of proteins that otherwise do so very poorly, or not at all. Researchers at the Jet Propulsion Laboratory (JPL) in Pasadena, California, showed that mineral grains can act as "nucleant" particles, around which protein crystals can grow from solution. The work opens the way for the crystallographic study of many proteins important to the biotechnology industry, and may make it easier to perform crystal-growing experiments in space, where the lack of gravity makes such experiments more productive.

Another advance in understanding the chemistry of biomolecules came when researchers at the Universities of Houston and Illinois reported that there were important differences between the classical physics model of ferrocytochrome C and a quantum mechanical model of the molecule (ferrocytochrome C is an enzyme important to respiration). The differences between the two models could have important ramifications: it may change the perception of how oxygen respiration evolved; and it could influence the design of new proteins and solar-energy devices with better electron-transfer properties.

Chemists at the California Institute of Technology (Caltech) in Pasadena discovered that a type of reaction called ring-opening metathesis polymerization (ROMP), which ordinarily is hobbled by traces of water and oxygen, works very efficiently in the presence of both, if a ruthenium-based catalyst is used to drive the reaction. The modified ROMP process will be important in a number of areas, most notably the paint and coatings industry.

Texas A&M University researchers demonstrated that a lithium–magnesium oxide catalyst can use methane, rather than the more precious petroleum, to produce polyethylene, an important starting material in plastics manufacturing. Florida State University researchers synthesized taxusin, an important step toward the complete synthesis of the anticancer compound taxol. A technique developed at Cornell University would enable the manufacture of gallium arsenide gas (for possible use in making gallium arsenide semiconductors) at much lower temperatures than was previously possible.

Particle Physics

Texas won out over six other states in the competition for the world's most powerful atom smasher, the $4 billion to $6 billion Superconducting Super Collider (SSC). If built, the SSC will be able to smash together beams of subatomic particles at nearly the speed of light, in order to permit physicists to gain insights into the fundamental particles and forces of nature as they study the composition and properties of the postcollision debris. The choice prompted controversy as some critics charged that political favoritism influenced the decision, while others warned that the project will be so expensive that other important research will be crippled for lack of funding.

The Stanford Linear Collider at California's Stanford University represents a new generation of colliders that shoot beams of electrons into opposing beams of positrons, their positively charged antimatter counterparts, in order to produce and study Z-zero particles (heavy, short-lived particles that convey the weak nuclear force) produced by the collision. Determining the weight of Z-zero particles will help physicists in their quest for understanding why subatomic particles have the weight they do, and how various types of subatomic particles combine in different ways to make up all the matter in the universe.

Physicists at the European Center for Nuclear Research's (CERN's) Laboratory for Particle Physics near Geneva, Switzerland, found evidence of a new, theoretical state of matter, a quark gluon plasma. The researchers used an accelerator to slam oxygen nuclei into a gold target, creating a miniature explosion that destroyed protons and neutrons and released traces of quark gluon states. The findings from this study support the idea that the universe was too hot during the first millionth of a second after its creation for neutrons and protons to condense out of the sea of quarks and gluons.

Scientists devised tests for a hypothesis about the existence of a fifth fundamental force in nature (about 1/50th that of gravity). The hypothesis still remains unproven, however, and new research to resolve the matter must still be carried out.

©Stanford Linear Accelerator and the DOE

The linear collider at Stanford University will be used to study the weight of subatomic particles and how they combine to form matter.

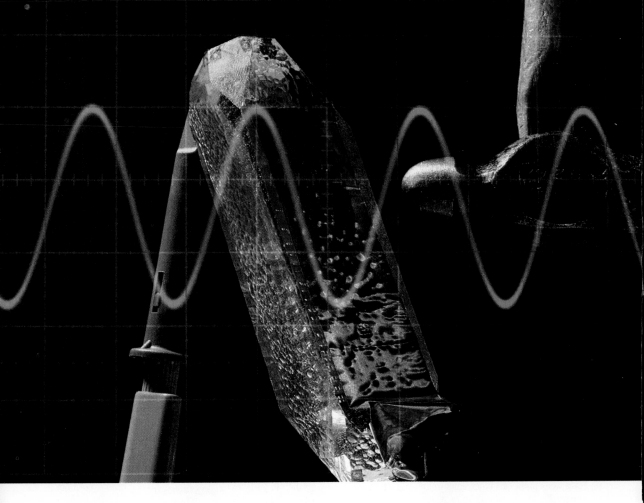

Good Vibes From Quartz

by Bruce Hathaway

W hen you first meet them, you'd never guess that the one thing Joseph Ba- lascio and Uma Silbey have in com- mon is also what's most important to each— crystal vibrations. Balascio is archetypal Radio Shack: pens in his shirt pocket, no-nonsense shoes, and a very efficient-looking haircut. He's an engineer who speaks in clipped phrases and obviously lives in a hard-data world. Silbey, on the other hand, exudes a definite mystical aura: long, flowing blonde hair; intense eyes; and large pieces of crystal jewelry that look as if they'd been made on another planet. Her given name is Marilyn, but she now prefers Uma—a Sanskrit name for a Hindu goddess. She thinks in spiritual terms like ''balancing,'' ''the heart's mind,'' ''cosmic delight,'' and ''inner truth.''

But both of them, in fact, are in the busi- ness of crystal vibrations, and they agree that the best source of these is common quartz. Ba- lascio supervises the hydrothermal operations in- volved in growing quartz crystals for electronic devices at a Motorola facility in Carlisle, Penn- sylvania. ''Mention quartz, and most people think of crystal balls or chandeliers, or something that's of little interest to anyone but a rock- hound,'' he explains. ''However, tiny wafers of quartz are at the heart of umpteen things we use

Quartz crystals find use in electronics based on their ability to transform mechanical force, such as a blow from a ham- mer, into electricity. The crystalline structure of quartz allows it to precisely regulate electrical vibrations (depic- ted by the wave on the oscilloscope screen).

every day—almost everybody's wristwatch, electronic clocks, remote telephones, personal computers, VCRs, CB radios, your color television set, and even washing machines.''

Slivers of quartz embedded in the innards of radio and TV transmitters keep the thousands of broadcast frequencies from jumbling together into a chaos of sound. They allow hundreds of telephone conversations to travel through a single channel without mixing. And quartz crystals are the crux of most precision time systems. They've already made possible wristwatch-size ''data centers'' and smart cards—credit-card-size plates with microprocessors (tiny computers) whose memories can store anything from account records to a person's medical history. Before long, we'll all have fantastic Dick Tracy–type wrist telephones. Thanks to quartz, stopwatches—until recently, expensive pieces of equipment jealously guarded by timers at sports events—are common and cheap.

The gist of modern electronics technology is precision frequency control, which might seem to have nothing to do with a ''common rock'' like quartz. But this crystal's atomic structure allows it to precisely regulate electrical circuits vibrating at millions of cycles per second. ''Fortunately, quartz is one of the most prevalent minerals on earth,'' observes Balascio. ''It's as if Mother Nature foresaw the needs of the Information Age.''

A ''Live Rock''?

Silbey also relates the abundance of quartz to divine benevolence, and even believes that the essence of life itself is represented in its crystalline structure. She and her husband, Ramana Das (also a spiritual name), own Uma Inc., a Marin County, California, company that markets quartz crystal jewelry to New Age spiritualists who feel it can heal the sick and connect souls to the Eternal Light. This interest among the cosmic-culture crowd isn't as far out on the occultist fringe as you might think. Even mainstream publishers list titles on quartz enlightenment, and hundreds of crystal shops, advisers, and lecturers across the country have levitated the metaphysical interest in quartz into a

The Smithsonian's flawless Burmese quartz crystal ball, likely the world's largest, weighs 107 pounds.

Below: © Smithsonian Institution; facing page: © Yoav Levy/Phototake

multimillion-dollar industry. Crystal Adventures and other companies now offer luxury tours of quartz deposits in Brazil and Madagascar so New Age pilgrims can dig their own.

"The recognition that quartz crystals have unique energy-channeling potential is nothing new," observes Silbey. "Throughout history you'll find examples of cultures that believed quartz could magnify psychic energy and healing powers. Many aboriginal medicine men have viewed quartz as a 'live rock' that can treat maladies and fetch the souls of the departed. The Sumerians, Maya, and other civilizations used quartz crystals for curative purposes." New Agers often state authoritatively that the Great Pyramid at Giza originally had a capstone full of quartz crystals. And, they contend, the king's burial chamber inside the pyramid is made entirely of Aswan granite, about 35 percent quartz, because the ancient Egyptians believed that the enormous pressure from the huge blocks above it would cause the quartz to emanate a rejuvenating energy field. In support of this belief, they cite the fact that such a conversion of mechanical force into electrical polarity is one basis for using quartz in electronics.

Abundant Supply and Variety

Though magical and maybe even deservedly sacred, quartz is certainly not rare. In fact, it is a crystalline fusion of our planet's two most common elements: oxygen, which contributes nearly half the weight of the earth's crust; and silicon, which accounts for another quarter of it. Silicon dioxide (SiO_2) abounds; it makes up the bulk of sand on many beaches and is the raw material for most types of glass. However, the word "quartz" describes SiO_2 only in crystalline form—atoms arranged in orderly and infinitely repeated three-dimensional patterns called lattices.

These occur in a wide variety of colors and textures, ranging from vitreous beauties like purple amethyst and yellow citrine to translucent stones such as agate and prase, which often present splendid bands and other patterns. Quartz is harder than steel, and for at least 30,000 years, humans have fashioned it—in the form of flint and jasper—into weapons and tools. The ancient Sumerians made agate signet rings, beads, and ceremonial ax heads, and the Egyptians ground and polished agates into bowls, cups, and bottles.

As time went by, the value of quartz was enhanced by mystique. Agate was thought to allay thirst, so camel drivers would hold a piece of the stone in their mouths as they crossed the desert. And the supposed sobering effects of amethyst made it popular with the spouses of drunkards and of those prone to passion. It was also thought to protect soldiers, to shield any wearer from disease, and even to help hunters

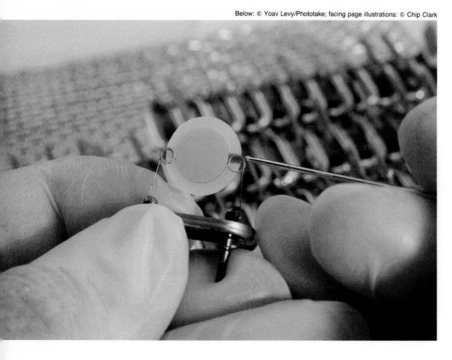

A worker very delicately cements wires to an electrode that will transmit charges between the quartz crystal and the circuit.

Quartz crystals exist in a wide variety of colors and shapes. Sparkling amethyst prisms (above) have the hexagonal shape characteristic of most quartz crystals. A smoky gray quartz (above right) and a lighter variety (below) have collars of rose quartz, the products of later growth and geological change. The brilliant colors of Mexican agates (right and below right) represent the presence of trace minerals in the quartz crystals.

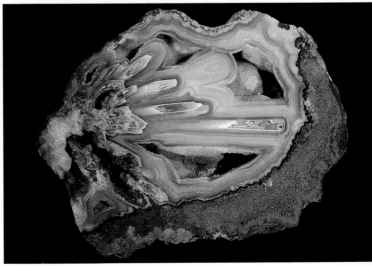

track wild animals. During the Middle Ages, many crusaders swore by quartz amulets.

The most touching quartz legend is expressed in a 16th-century French verse that tells how the god Bacchus, angered at some neglect, determines to avenge himself. He declares that the first human his procession passes will be devoured by tigers. Tragically, the mortal is a beautiful maiden named Amethyst, who is on her way to worship at the shrine of the goddess Diana. As the tigers spring toward her, Amethyst seeks protection from Diana, who turns her into a white stone. On seeing the result of his ire, the repentant Bacchus pours the juice of a grape over the petrified body of the maiden as a libation, thus giving the stone its lustrous violet hue.

The Piezoelectric Phenomenon

Ironically, it is the imperfection, the asymmetry, of the quarz crystal lattice that makes it useful in electronics. Though quartz spiritualists are convinced that the ancient Egyptians were well aware of the mineral's electrical properties, it wasn't until the late 19th century that European scientists demonstrated them. Jacques and Pierre Curie hypothesized that subjecting crystals such as quartz to mechanical stress would generate electrical charges. In 1880 they attached electrodes to opposite sides of a slab of quartz, then placed weights on it. With increasing pressure, their electroscope registered growing polar electrical charges on the crystal's surfaces. Then, a year later, they found that giving a positive charge to one side of the quartz slab and a negative charge to the other caused it to bulge or shrink, depending on the placement of the contacts.

In an asymmetrical crystal such as quartz, pressure displaces positive and negative ions differently: electrical polarity at the surface results. Conversely, an external, alternating electrical field causes rhythmic displacement of ions: in response the crystal quivers. This two-part phenomenon subsequently came to be known as the piezoelectric effect—piezo comes from the Greek word meaning to press or squeeze.

Its first part—pressure on a crystal resulting in electrical polarity—can be seen in many flintless cigarette lighters and pilotless gas stove igniters: a sharp blow on the crystal in them generates a charge and hence a spark. Phonograph cartridges are sometimes piezoelectric—crystals connected to the needle translate vibrations from bumps on the record into electrical signals.

Engineers can modify the properties of industrial quartz through careful cutting and shaping of the crystals.

Quartz crystals can control electronic frequencies in avionic and telecommunication devices.

Crystals have also been used in microphones to translate sound waves into electrical signals. Many transducers—devices that, for example, register the pressure in an oil well—rely on this aspect of piezoelectricity. Quartz strain-sensors already provide early warning of earthquakes, and crystals implanted in future airplanes and buildings might be able to send electrical signals that will warn of an impending structural failure. There are even prospects for piezoelectric power generation, in which crystals will convert the vibrations of a helicopter or ocean waves into usable power.

The flip side of piezoelectricity—alternating electrical charges placed on a crystal causing it to vibrate—is the basis for most applications of quartz in electronics. Virtually all have to do with the control of radio waves or with keeping time. As it turns out, a crystal in an electrical circuit will, in addition to resonating at its own frequency, bring the oscillations of the circuit into exact harmony with the crystal's vibrations. The most common use of this effect likely is in operation on your wrist at this very moment. In a quartz watch, the precise vibrations of a microthin quartz disk regulate the flow of electrons that move the hands or cause the digits to change.

Despite its enormous technological potential, piezoelectricity was little more than a laboratory curiosity for almost three decades after the Curies discovered it. Then, during World War I, French scientists, anxious to find a way of detecting German submarines, found that quartz crystals could transduce sound waves into recognizable electrical signals; they had invented an early form of sonar.

Resonance for Radios

The resonance of quartz also intrigued American radio fans after it was shown, in 1919, that crystals could control radio frequencies. These were the early days of radio, when members of wireless clubs were madly wrapping coils of wire around broken baseball bats or Quaker Oats boxes, attempting to receive various signals on their sets. In attics and barns around the country, the radio pioneers bent intently over their jury-rigged boxes and listened excitedly to ships at sea. At just the wrong instant, the transmitter somehow drifted off frequency, and the operator's voice was lost in a roar of atmospheric sound. So reports of reliable quartz frequency control swept the country, and wildly enthusiastic amateur hams quickly began making their own crystals.

Above: © Manfred Kage/Peter Arnold, Inc.; facing page: © Yoav Levy/Phototake

Crystal oscillators, used in everything from common pocket watches to the space shuttle, have cores of thin wafers carefully cut from quartz bricks.

However, cutting and shaping crystals for radio transmitters was pretty much a hit-or-miss operation until 1934, when a group of students at Dickinson College, in Carlisle, Pennsylvania—now a center of the quartz crystal industry—persuaded Grover Hunt, a college custodian, to help them. His daughter Harriet Fanus, now retired after 22 years at Motorola, recalls: "My father was a chess player, and once, on a visit to the Painted Desert in Arizona, he got the idea that he could make a fortune by carving the petrified wood he saw there into chess pieces. He took out the car seats, loaded boxes on the roof, and creaked along back to Carlisle. The chess piece business fizzled, but the college hams heard about the rock saw he was using. While teaching them how to cut with it, my dad eagerly learned all about quartz electronics from the students. He soon developed a lapping machine that mechanized the process of making quartz radio crystals."

Quartz crystals quickly became the standard means by which radio stations controlled their broadcast frequencies. "The first was WEAF in New York City," notes Virgil Bottom, an Abilene, Texas, piezoelectricity expert.

"They broadcast at 610 on the AM dial, or 610 kilohertz—meaning that they emitted radio waves with a frequency of 610,000 cycles per second. A little piece of quartz the size of a nickel inside their transmitter was cut to vibrate at that same rate, and it kept their broadcasts on the correct frequency." Today radio stations still rely on quartz crystals to do the same thing. The thinner the quartz wafer, the higher the frequency of its vibrations—this holds true for other electronics applications as well.

The 1930s saw a handful of crystal manufacturers emerge, but nowhere near enough to supply the need for quartz radios in World War II. Early on, pilots and tank commanders pleaded for crystal radios capable of keeping frequencies firmly in tune. In response, the U.S. Army Signal Corps fervently recruited companies to manufacture crystals. Indeed, supplying reliable quartz radio crystals was later seen as second in strategic importance only to the Manhattan Project. The demand was desperate. In Carlisle, where quartz residue had been used to make sidewalks, local citizens busily dug them up, scavenging every bit of the precious crystal they could find. By December

1943, industry was working at breakneck speed to keep up.

The value of crystals became especially clear on D-Day. Underpinning the vast Allied armada that moved across the English Channel were thousands of different transmitters, all operating on myriad frequencies—separated by a hairbreadth from one another by means of quartz crystals. Without the slivers of quartz hidden away in the radios, the information that coordinated the movements of the different units in the great battle would have become an incoherent jumble of sound.

Because the United States successfully dominated the quartz trade with Brazil, source of the best crystals, the Germans had to make do with inferior bits and pieces of quartz for their radios—or go without. Clearly, though, they realized the importance of quartz. After the war, American experts, dispatched to interview Nazi scientists, discovered that they were well along with research on how to grow crystals artificially. Building on the work of German and U.S. scientists, Bell Labs and other American groups began to culture crystals, in time so successfully that synthetic crystals came to be preferred by electronics manufacturers. Still, culturing requires natural quartz as a feedstock, and today—in part due to an attempt by Brazil in 1974 to control the quartz market—almost all American firms buy it from domestic mines.

Growing Quartz

The richest quartz deposits in North America are found in the Hot Springs, Arkansas, area—which, predictably, is emerging as a mecca for New Age crystal seekers. ''People have wonderful expectations of what the mines will look like—like bejeweled caverns with the Seven Dwarfs,'' observes Serenity Peterson of Nashville, Tennessee, who teaches workshops on the mystical qualities of quartz and is the author of *Crystal Visioning*. Actually, most of what comes out of the open-pit mines looks more like what you'd use to make a driveway than like something to raise consciousness or guide a missile. But some beautiful pieces are found, and the plain white rocks are still needed to grow quartz for radios and computers.

''We get them in 100-pound (45-kilogram) bags,'' explains Motorola's Joseph Balascio. ''The crystalline structure is already in the rocks; our job is to transform them into bars that can be sawed and polished into wafers.'' The quartz from Arkansas is loaded into the bottom half of an autoclave, a giant, tube-shaped pressure cooker. In the top half, hundreds of thin quartz seed plates are hung in a cluster that looks like a high-tech chandelier. After an alkaline solution is pumped into the autoclave, it is sealed, and electric heaters below raise the temperature in the bottom half to 750° F (398° C). The quartz dissolves, and its elements, bonded to those of the solution, rise to the cooler seeds. As a result, particles are deposited on the seeds, and they grow in accord with the preordained lattice. It is a controlled, much-speeded-up imitation of what happens in nature. After 30 to 45 days, the autoclave is opened to reveal a rack full of glistening bricks of quartz crystals. Even though he's done it hundreds of times, Balascio still loves to watch them come out. Each batch will yield tens of thousands of wafers. Using diamond saws, technicians cut the bricks into bars, which are then shipped to frequency-device manufacturers.

Scientists culture electronics-quality crystal brick from natural quartz using giant autoclaves.

Quartz wafers in clocks are no doubt the most common use of crystals in electronics—everything from wristwatches to the timekeeping circuits in computers and VCRs. A standard watch crystal oscillates at 32.768 cycles per second; a slower rate wouldn't be accurate enough; a faster one would wear down the battery too quickly. These oscillations are divided in half 15 times by step-down circuits in the watch so that they occur precisely once every second.

Quartz and Technology

In addition to people, machines of many kinds also depend on quartz to keep time for them. Microprocessors, which employ crystals, have now replaced mechanical timers in many appliances, such as dishwashers. These little computers have also invaded the engine compartments of automobiles; they adjust the fuel-and-air mixture, and even provide mechanics with an invaluable diagnostic tool by preserving an onboard record of how well the motor is doing.

Personal computers invariably contain quartz crystals. "It's impossible to do those logic and memory functions, and have streams of information flowing around inside the PC and arriving at the right place at the right time, if you don't have precise timing," says Bell Labs' Bob Laudise. "So whenever you have digital information, it's very important to have a quartz clock."

All types of radios depend on quartz to control broadcast frequencies, as does television. The reds, blues, and greens that make up your color picture have to be decoded by a circuit with a little quartz wafer called a colorburst crystal. Before it can be broadcast, the TV signals that carry color information have to be modulated (changed to a different frequency) so they don't interfere with the contrast part of the picture. By oscillating at 3.58 megahertz, the crystal in your set retrieves those color signals, which in turn trigger the pulses that light up your picture tube.

In addition to these applications, quartz and other piezoelectric materials such as piezopolymers enjoy a bright future in a variety of new technologies. Voice-recognition devices, which by the 21st century should permit you and your computer to talk to each other, employ crystals to slice verbal sound waves into pieces and turn them into numbers. The pen you use to endorse checks at the bank of the future may be piezoelectrically controlled. A quartz crystal will translate the vibrations of your handwriting movements into electrical memory. Someone else's hand vibrations in combination with your signature will alert the teller to a forgery.

All of this quartz magic can be easily explained by the theories of mainstream physics. But what about New Age claims that quartz crystals can heal the sick? Richard Gerber, a Livonia, Michigan, internist and author of *Vibrational Medicine,* is an enthusiast who believes there may well be more to crystal healing that just the placebo effect. "We know from Einsteinian theory that all matter is basically energy," he says. "So the body is actually a complex system of energy fields. Quartz crystals apparently produce a subtle energy field that escapes measurement by traditional electromagnetic devices, but is nonetheless capable of influencing biological organisms." Indeed, after 14 years of research, retired IBM scientist Marcel Vogel of San Jose, California, says that with charged quartz crystals he can change the pH value (a measure of acidity versus alkalinity) of water from five to eight and back again, and also reduce the time it takes to age wine from years to seconds, a process now being used experimentally by Sycamore Creek Vineyards in Morgan Hill, California. "I haven't seen reliable data yet, but the work is scientifically important," says William Tiller, a professor of materials science and engineering at Stanford. "Quartz has a very interesting structure, and I think eventually science will discover that it does have some ability to amplify subtle energies."

Many New Age claims for quartz, however, are nothing but pseudoscience. The supposed piezoelectrically generated energy field in the pyramid at Giza is an example. "True, the pressure of all those blocks would cause electric charges in the granite," explains Kurt Nassau, a Bell Labs' crystal expert. "But the grains of quartz are randomly oriented, so there's no way you'd see the charges unifying into any kind of energy field." And there is no established archaeological evidence that the Egyptians knew anything about piezoelectricity.

Engineer Balascio is amused at the thought that he and New Age crystal salvationists like Uma Silbey are colleagues in the quartz vibrations business. But he's enough of a scientist not to dismiss claims like hers until all the data are in. Still, for now, he's certain that she's a lot more likely to listen to one of his radios than he is to be healed by one of her earrings.

© Paul L. Ruben

The Physics of THRILLS

by William J. Broad

The century-old terror machine known as the roller coaster is delivering new thrills as designers, drawing on a series of recent innovations, find ever more devious ways to hurl the human frame toward the limits of its endurance.

Gone are the days when creating amusement rides was an informal affair that often ended in accident or injury. Designers now rely on physics, computers, accelerometers, and a host of high-strength, high-technology parts and materials to create a rush of drops and climbs, twists and turns. They also use new skills to renovate and improve the safety of old coasters.

Engineers apply the laws of physics to maximize the terror but minimize the danger of such roller coasters as "Dragon Fyre" at Canada's Wonderland in Ontario.

"Today we get into the physics of it, the dynamics of it," says William L. Cobb, a long-time coaster designer based in Dallas, Texas. "We know what's going to happen even before we put it on paper."

The Shock Wave

In the language of physics, the coaster designer's goal is to produce as many accelerations on the body as possible. The main breakthrough was the discovery in the 1970s, and the wide application in the 1980s, of several ways to safely turn a trainload of screaming people upside down.

In April 1988, the trend saw its greatest refinement in the opening of the Shock Wave, a new ride at the Six Flags Great America amusement park in Gurnee, Illinois. The Shock Wave

In new and renovated coasters, tracks are banked on turns so that centrifugal forces press riders deep into their seats rather than to the sides of the cars.

© Jerry Wachter/Photo Researchers

is billed as the world's tallest and fastest roller coaster. Riders are lifted almost 17 stories, carried at about 70 miles (110 kilometers) per hour in a hefty drop, sent into a giant loop that turns them upside down, thrown into a "boomerang" that rapidly reverses their direction in a pretzel-like welter of turns, and finally twisted in a series of corkscrew spirals. All told, riders are upended seven times.

"It's pretty wild," says Ronald V. Toomer, a former rocket scientist who designed the ride.

Coaster fans agree. "Technology is creating the ability to send your body through more demented configurations than would have been dreamed possible 10 years ago," says Randy Geisler, president of American Coaster Enthusiasts, a group based in Chicago.

The new generation of coasters is so intriguing scientifically that high school teachers are using it to elucidate basic physics.

"High-tech rides have so many variations that you can illustrate more principles," says John H. McGehee, a physics teacher at Rolling Hills High School in Rolling Hills Estates, California. Each year he leads a field trip of eager students to Six Flags Magic Mountain near Los Angeles.

The source of much of the current excitement is the clothoid loop, a teardrop shape that makes it easy to turn people upside down.

The loop is hardly new. Its mathematical basis was explained by history's most prolific mathematics genius, Leonhard Euler of Switzerland, in the 18th century. But it was only about a decade ago that coaster designers realized that Euler's shape was perfect for achieving the long-sought goal of the vertical somersault. Today there are more than 20 roller coasters around the country with clothoid loops; some have two or three.

"We're building one now for Great Adventure in New Jersey," says Toomer, president of Arrow Dynamics of Clearfield, Utah, a major maker of roller coasters. At the Six Flags Great Adventure Park in Jackson, New Jersey, "they have one right now with a couple of those loops, and we're building another with three," he says.

Designers previously had little success with what would seem to be the logical choice for a loop, a 360-degree circle. When entering such a circle, a speeding coaster car moves rapidly upward, generating a strong centrifugal force that presses riders into seats with too much energy.

The danger at the top is just the opposite. The cars decelerate sharply, and if a car slows too much, gravity can pull riders from their seats while the cars are upside down. As early as 1900, a circular loop was attempted at Coney Island in New York. But it had many limitations and was soon dismantled.

Smoothing Acceleration

By contrast, the clothoid shape smooths out the acceleration so riders speed safely along the interior of the loop. The secret is the loop's changing radius, which controls the speed of the cars, varying it according to a scientific law known as the conservation of angular momentum.

This principle can easily be visualized. The speed of a small weight tied to a string and whirled in a circle will be controlled by the radius of the circle. The weight will move slower if the string is lengthened, and faster if the string is shortened.

Elongating the circle into an ellipse provides radii of varying lengths. Thus a comet in an elliptic orbit about the sun moves faster as it nears the sun, and slower when it is far away.

So, too, a coaster entering a teardrop loop moves relatively slowly as it arcs upward across a large radius at the bottom of the loop, lessening the centrifugal force on riders. At the top the radius is much smaller. The coaster thus moves faster than it would in a circle, creating a greater centrifugal force to counteract gravity and keep riders safely in their seats.

This innovation allows vertical loops to be quite large because coaster cars will not lose as much of their energy at the top as they would in a circle. The biggest of the three clothoid loops on the Shock Wave ride sends riders head over heels while they are 13 stories above the ground.

Designers say the coaster revolution is far from over, despite dozens of patents already filed and a decade of competition that has covered the country with increasingly innovative rides.

"There's a lot of progress yet to be made," says T. Harold Hudson, vice president for engineering at the Six Flags Corporation in Arlington, Texas, one of the world's largest chains of amusement parks. "The limit is probably the economics of it, not the physics."

The origin of the roller coaster is believed to lie with Russian sled riders who, some 400 years ago, hurtled down artificial mountains of ice and snow that were supported by wood frames. In 1804 the French adapted the idea, removing the ice and replacing a sled's runners

Rider safety is the prime concern in coaster designs. Both the suspended "Iron Dragon" (above) at Cedar Point in Sandusky, Ohio, and the "Ultra Twister" (below) at Six Flags Great Adventure in Jackson, New Jersey, have wraparound devices to firmly hold the cars to the tracks.

THE PSYCHOLOGY OF THRILLS

Why do people submit themselves to roller coasters and their mutations, the "scream machines" that seem so ubiquitous on the summer landscape?

Some clearheaded analyses of the allure of wild rides are emerging as scientists study why people seek the thrill of great velocities, upside-down suspensions, and other sensations that the human body reads as pure torment.

The roller coaster question touches on some complex physiological issues. New research suggests, for instance, that the craving of thrills may be hard-wired into those who thrive on the level of primitive brain activity that physical danger stimulates.

Another appeal is that roller coasters, in simulating true danger, provide the illusion of mastering a great peril. It is a deeply satisfying feeling in which mock danger provides the exhilaration of self-affirmation.

Fear is the key component, as has been shown in research into more dangerous activities like skiing and parachute-jumping.

Thrill seekers shriek their way down the stand-up "Shockwave" at King's Dominion in Doswell, Virginia.

with wheels. In 1884 an American inventor, LaMarcus A. Thompson, refined the French idea by setting wheeled cars on an undulating track. Thompson's Switchback Gravity Pleasure Railway at Coney Island reached a top speed of 6 miles (9.6 kilometers) per hour as it moved down a hill. At the bottom, riders got out while attendants pushed the cars up a second incline. Riders then climbed aboard for the return trip.

By 1900 the modern ride was born. In terms of physics, the characteristic feature of the roller coaster is that its potential energy, gained as a chain drive lifts cars through the earth's gravity to the top of that first drop, has been mostly converted to kinetic energy by the time the ride ends. The cars coast to a stop (or close to it, often aided by brakes).

There are no engines, no motors, just gravity pushing riders along. Since speeding cars have no energy of their own, they can never climb higher than that first hill. Secondary hills get progressively smaller as the potential energy is used up.

Centrifugal Forces

Designers who renovate coasters have been hard at work perfecting classic rides, generally for reasons of safety.

"In the old days if people got roughed up, they didn't file a lawsuit," says Curtis D. Summers, a coaster designer in Cincinnati, Ohio.

A key redesign tool is the accelerometer, a device that can show the strength of centrifugal forces acting on coaster riders. Its readings are usually given in "g's," with one g representing the acceleration of gravity. A fighter pilot going through a tight turn can take about 10 or 11 g's before blacking out. Coaster designers generally try to limit centrifugal forces to 3.5 or 4 g's, except for a short spurt where they may achieve even higher levels.

"If you ask accident-prone skiers if they are scared when they are on a high-risk slope, they'll say they wouldn't bother to ski the slope if they weren't scared," says Seymour Epstein, a University of Massachusetts psychologist.

"They want a slope that terrifies them," he says. "Parachuters say the same thing. After you take the plunge, there's an immense relief and sense of well-being in facing a fear that doesn't materialize."

That kind of exhilaration is particularly appealing to a personality type aptly known as "thrill-seekers," people who have been studied by Frank Farley, a psychologist at the University of Wisconsin.

"Not everybody goes on scary rides like roller coasters, or comes back a second time if they try it," Dr. Farley says. "It's those with the thrill-seeking personality who come back again and again. They like adventure, like high diving and hang gliding."

Underlying the propensity for physical thrills, Dr. Farley believes, may be a neurological need for the biochemical state that comes from intense physical excitement.

One theory holds that the brains of thrill-seekers are usually at a lower level of arousal compared with most other people. This theory holds that the sense of danger and the extremes of a roller coaster ride prime a neural network at the base of the brain called the reticular activating system, which in turn heightens the level of activation throughout the rest of the brain.

"They feel fully alive when something raises their level of brain arousal," Dr. Farley says of thrill-seekers.

Another theory, put forth by Marvin Zuckerman, a psychologist at the University of Delaware, proposes that those who need to seek out intense stimulation, the roller coaster being a prime example, have an imbalance in a brain chemical, monoamine oxidase, which has also been implicated in some forms of depression. Excitement seems to change the levels of the chemical in some people, lifting them from torpor to elation.

Heightened concentration is at play, too. "Being totally absorbed is in itself pleasurable," Dr. Epstein says. "Complete concentration that blanks out everything else temporarily relieves you from all conflicts."

Dr. Epstein adds: "It makes you feel very alive to be so scared. When you react to something that demands your full attention so forcefully, all your senses engage. It's a very different feeling from being in your usual semiawake state."

Daniel Goleman

On old coasters, accelerometers often reveal that cars rapidly going over the crest of a small hill develop negative g's, meaning a coaster car is accelerating downward faster than the rider—a potentially dangerous situation.

"Some of the old rides had a tendency to lift you out of your seat," Summers says. His usual goal in redesigning the rides, he adds, is to smooth out the hills so riders going over them always experience a slightly positive force of about 0.3 g.

"Negative g's are thrilling," he says, "but you don't want people to get the sensation that they're being thrown out of the car."

Banking the Turns

Another goal in redesign efforts has been to bank turns more steeply. On old coasters the centrifugal forces of sharp turns often threw riders to the side of the cars, in some cases causing injuries. In renovated coasters, tracks are banked on turns so that centrifugal forces press riders deep into their seats rather than to the side of the cars.

"All the time we're looking for ways to keep from having accidents," says William Cobb, the Dallas coaster designer.

Of course, all the improvements based on physics do not guarantee safety if basic riding rules are ignored or forgotten. Riders still must wear safety harnesses, for example, or risk falling out of a car at any stage in the ride. In June 1987, a 19-year-old woman who was not secured by a harness was thrown to her death from a roller coaster at the Six Flags Great Adventure Park in New Jersey. She was thrown from her seat when her car began its downward run as it was leaving the loading platform.

One of the biggest innovations in the business has been based not on physics or mathematics but on a simple change of building materials. Old coasters were made of wood, while new ones often have support structures made of steel, which lasts longer and needs less maintenance. More important, giant steel coasters usually have tracks made out of steel tubes rather than flat rails. The wheels of coaster cars firmly grip the tubular track from top and bottom, increasing safety and giving designers greater freedom to try wild ideas.

On a recent Saturday at Coney Island, patrons clearly seemed attracted to the new high-technology rides. The 61-year-old Cyclone, a wooden roller coaster, was half empty. But the steel Double Loop, a traveling attraction, was packed with riders.

CIRCLE VERSUS TEARDROP

Circular loops were tried and rejected decades ago because roller coaster cars moved too fast at the bottom and too slowly at the top. The rapid upward climb created excessive centrifugal force that pressed riders into seats uncomfortably. But the slowdown at the top could let upside-down riders fall out of their seats as centrifugal force weakened and gravity became the dominant force. Today's designers realize that they control the speed of a roller coaster by modifying the radii of the loop. Thus, in a teardrop-shaped loop, the cars move more slowly across the large lower radius than they would in a perfect circle, and more quickly at the top, where the radius is small.

"This is better," says Walter Gonzales, who describes himself as a Coney Island expert. "You'll see. You go upside down."

Ronald Toomer is a pioneer of the steel-tube rides. His company, Arrow Dynamics, helped Disneyland get off the ground. After a quarter century of innovation, its rides, including a host of roller coaster designs, have been widely copied around the world.

In 1975 Toomer and a colleague discovered the industry's first way of reliably and safely turning riders upside down. Their idea was to build a series of corkscrew spirals relatively close to the ground using tracks made of the new steel tubes.

"We went through a great deal of agonizing," Toomer recalls. "Even when we built a full-scale prototype, we were worried about putting people on board. Our accelerometer found heavy g loads."

However, a research trip to an old roller coaster in Santa Cruz, California, showed that it developed forces as great as 5 g's, easing apprehension about the forces of the new ride. The first rider was a company salesman, not Toomer, who says he hates the quick motions of roller coasters. "I get sick," he admits.

Breakthrough of the 1980s

The success of the corkscrew was followed in 1977 by the giant clothoid loop, which Toomer says was independently developed by several designers.

"It's logical," he says. "If it was perfectly round, you'd have way too high g's at bottom, and way too low at the top."

The breakthrough of the 1980s has been the suspended coaster, in which speeding cars dangle from movable pivots hooked to steel tubes, generating unusual new accelerations as cars swing around turns. "It's a totally different sensation," says Geisler of American Coaster Enthusiasts. "You can swing out 120 degrees. The thrill is entirely different."

Toomer would not talk about new designs he and his colleagues are working on, saying the industry is becoming increasingly secretive as competition heats up for another round of innovation.

"Back 15 years, before there were any upside-down coasters, I wouldn't have dreamed what's happened," he says. "I think there's still some pretty exciting stuff to do. We've got a lot of far-out ideas down on paper that we haven't cracked yet."

GLIMPSES of CREATION

by Ric Dolphin

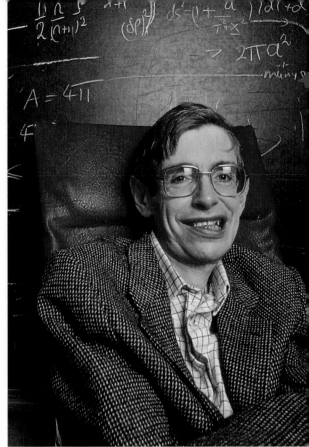

© Abe Frajndlich/SYGMA

Physicist Steven Hawking seeks the "Grand Unification," a theory that would explain the origin of the universe by linking relativity and quantum mechanics.

I n an ordinary academic office overlooking an ordinary parking lot sits an extraordinary man with his head in the stars. Physically, Stephen W. Hawking, 46, professor of mathematics at Cambridge University, England, could scarcely be more terrestrial. Afflicted for 25 years with a progressive and incurable neurological disorder, amyotrophic lateral sclerosis (Lou Gehrig's disease), Hawking has withered. He can no longer talk and has lost practically all muscle control. He is constantly attended by nurses, one of whom sits with him in his office. But behind the slack-jawed countenance lives a brain that has been compared to Einstein's and Galileo's—a brain capable of somersaulting through space and time. And with the first three fingers of his twisted right hand, Hawking has just enough movement to work his wheelchair-mounted computer, through which his thoughts are converted into a tinny, American-accented voice synthesizer. "Why was the universe formed?" he is asked. "If I knew that," he says, "there would be nothing else to find out."

Publishing Phenomenon

What Hawking does claim to know something about is how the universe came into being. His reputation in the arcane scientific field known as cosmology has lately blossomed outside its usual academic realm. Hawking's latest book, *A Brief History of Time,* which in 198 pages marries Einstein's general theory of relativity with quantum mechanics in an attempt to explain the formation of the universe, has become a publishing phenomenon. It has topped the nonfiction best-seller lists this summer in Canada, the United States, and the United Kingdom. According to Albert Zuckerman, Hawking's New York City literary agent, Bantam Books Inc. of New York City has already shipped 500,000 copies of the book across North America. "We can't keep it in stock," says Paul McFedries,

buyer for the Toronto retail outlet that calls itself the World's Biggest Bookstore.

Rarely, if ever, has a book so hard to understand sold so well. Even those involved in its publication admit difficulty with the book's content, which touches such things as universal gravitation, the expanding universe, quarks (a type of subatomic particle), and "naked singularities" (areas of infinite destiny in the universe). Peter Guzzardi, a Bantam editor who spent two years editing Hawking's words into something that he hoped would be accessible to a wide reading public, openly admits that he still has difficulty understanding all of Hawking's book. "But in my mind," he says in an interview, "I at least came up with the shapes of things—a great improvement over my previous ideas about little nuclei with little things spinning around them." Says Mark Barty-King of Bantam Press, the company's London subsidiary: "I feel that I would need to read the book 500 times to fully comprehend it."

The Grand Unification Theory

Explanations for the success of Hawking's book range from curiosity to the mystical. Bantam London's press manager, Jeannette Wilford, describes Hawking as the ideal combination of human-interest story and genius. "People have been so taken by him," she says. "He is so physically disabled but has this fantastic brain." Bantam New York's publicity director, Sally Williams, says: "My own personal theory is that people are keenly interested in things that offer an alternative vision of reality." Indeed, many people believe that Hawking is offering them the closest glimpse of creation they may ever have.

In his book, Hawking presents in a relatively simplified form a concept known as the Grand Unification Theory (GUT). After outlining the history of cosmological thought from ancient times to the present, Hawking takes readers into a mirrored world of advanced physics that seeks to unite the four physical forces binding the universe. He also seeks to explain what happened in the moment of the so-called Big Bang, the fiery instant in history when the universe was set into motion. Isaac Newton described one of the forces, gravity, 300 years ago. It was further developed in this century by the great German-born American scientist Albert Einstein to create a model for a universe that is curved in space and time.

The later concept of quantum mechanics involves itself with the other end of the scale, where three forces—the electromagnetic, strong nuclear, and weak nuclear forces—hold together atoms. Grand Unification Theory—which exists only in the minds of leading theoretical physicists—attempts to explain how all of those forces acted in that first millisecond. In doing so, such theories go one vast step further than Einstein's. Although Einstein produced a model of how the universe grew out of the Big Bang, he was unable to explain how subatomic forces came into being.

Einstein continued to believe that, at a fundamental level, nothing random can exist. But Hawking and some other contemporary cosmologists have drawn on the possibility of random events postulated by quantum mechanics in the 1920s. Einstein had rejected such randomness; he and other scientists of his period were able to describe the development of the universe only from the Big Bang onward. Hawking, by adding a random component, can speculate on what caused the universe to develop. As a result, he says that the four dimensions accepted in modern physics—three of space and one of time—may have grown out of any number of dimensions that originally existed. In the first milliseconds of creation, those extra dimensions—inconceivable except in the equations of mathematicians—curled up or flipped over into

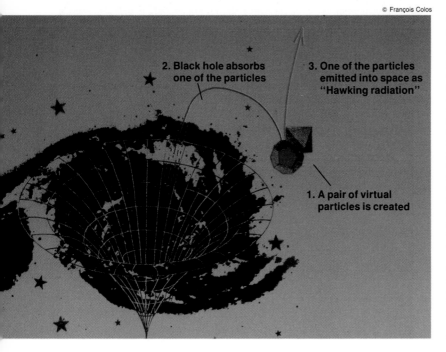

© François Colos

2. Black hole absorbs one of the particles

3. One of the particles emitted into space as "Hawking radiation"

1. A pair of virtual particles is created

Hawking's best-known research concerns black holes—regions of extreme density in which the extraordinary gravity prevents anything, even light, from escaping. Hawking, however, believes that black holes can emit radiation in the form of subatomic particles that do not obey the traditional laws of physics. Such "virtual" particles, Hawking theorizes, can be created in pairs out of empty space, only to instantly collide and annihilate one another. But if such a pair came into being in the neighborhood of a black hole, one particle would be sucked into the black hole while the other would escape into space as "Hawking radiation." Hawking's theory, in that it suggests the creation of something from nothing, represents a step toward understanding the origin of the universe.

Unable to speak and virtually paralyzed by Lou Gehrig's disease, Hawking communicates with his family and colleagues by means of a computer. By squeezing a switch held in his lap, Hawking can construct sentences from a library of 2,600 preprogrammed words at a rate of about 10 words per minute.

Next Page of Words

naked	need	new	nor
name	negative	Newcastle	normal
napkin	neglect	newspaper	normally
nation	negligible	newton	north
national	neighbour	Newton's	nose
natural	neither	next	nostril
nature	nerve	nhs	not
near	nervous	nice	notably
nearer	network	night	notation
nearest	neurone	no	note
nearly	neutrino	nobel	nothing
necessaril	neutron	noise	notice
necessary	never	non	now
neck	neverthele	none	nu

TALKING 70/69/360

It doesn't matter what the exact numbers are. The point is there are

the dimensions we know. The dimension of time, nonexistent before that moment, came into being. And the four forces of the universe—taking the form of invisible, subatomic, so-called superstrings—comprise the atoms, stars, planets, and galaxies that form the expanding universe, a universe both finite and without boundaries as we know them.

Before the Big Bang

In dismissing the commonsense concept of time having always existed, Hawking enters what was once considered difficult territory. The Russian-American physicist George Gamow, when asked in the 1950s what had happened before the Big Bang, replied, "Hell is reserved for people who ask such questions." But Hawking has alleviated his fate somewhat by subscribing in part to the dictum of the fourth-century Christian philosopher Saint Augustine, who speculated that time is a property of the universe that God created, but which did not exist before the beginning of the universe.

When considering what he calls the "boundary conditions" at the beginning of time, Hawking writes: "One possible answer is to say that God chose the initial configuration of the universe for reasons that we cannot hope to understand. This would certainly have been within the power of an omnipotent being, but if he had started it off in such an incomprehensible way, why did he choose to let it evolve according to laws that we could understand? The whole history of science has been the gradual realization that events do not happen in an arbitrary manner, but that they reflect a certain underlying order, which may or may not be divinely inspired." In his conclusion, however, Hawking leaves the door open. "Why does the universe go to all the bother of existing?" he asks. "Is the unified theory so compelling that it brings about its own existence? Or does it need a creator and if so, does He have any other effect on the universe?"

Most of Hawking's fellow scientists clearly find his reasoning compelling. One of them, Werner Israel, 56, a University of Alberta physicist who has coedited two academic books with Hawking, says that "the subtlety and power of his arguments are without parallel in mathematical physics," adding, "His vision of creation is too beautiful not to be true." Edward Kolb, a physicist at Fermi National Accelerator Laboratory (Fermilab) near Batavia, Illinois, says: "It's like Michael Jordan playing basketball. No one can tell Jordan what moves to make. It's intuition. Hawking has a remarkable amount of intuition."

Defying Medical Predictions

Through the years, Hawking has also displayed remarkable perseverance. The son of a London doctor, Hawking became an undistinguished, though popular, physics student at Oxford. He later moved to Cambridge for postgraduate work in cosmology because, as he once said, "it really did seem to involve the big question: Where did the universe come from?" Hawking's universe almost fell apart in 1963, when his illness, also known as Lou Gehrig's disease, after the New York Yankee baseball player who was stricken with it, was diagnosed. At first, Hawking was given only two years to live.

But even though the disease has reduced Hawking almost to a state of mute quadriplegia, he has defied medical predictions. In 1965 he married a language student named Jane Wilde; the couple now have three children. Meanwhile, Hawking launched himself into a challenging postgraduate project, involving the phenomenon of black holes, with British theoretician Roger Penrose, and later began teaching and writing. Hawking seems unconcerned about his own fate. Asked what he thinks will become of him after he dies, Hawking, displaying matter-of-fact wit, says, "I will probably be cremated and my ashes will be recycled."

His *A Brief History of Time* is the culmination of a long-standing desire to make his work more accessible to a mass audience. "My original aim was to write a book that would sell on airport bookstalls," he recalls. He was contacted in 1983 by Zuckerman, whose brother-in-law, an American scientist, had told him about Hawking. Zuckerman suggested that Hawking collaborate with another writer in writing a book. But Hawking, who is known for his stubbornness, would allow only an editor. Three New York publishers bid amounts in the region of $500,000 as an advance on the work, but Hawking says that he decided to choose Bantam because of its reputation as a publisher of popular nonfiction works.

Beating Out Astrology

The easy sale to a publisher in New York City contrasted sharply with the book's reception in London. Four major publishers turned it down because the subject was too esoteric. Bantam's Barty-King finally advanced Hawking $60,000 after beating down Hawking's demand for $150,000. Now, with his book expected to have sold an unprecedented 150,000 copies in Britain by Christmas 1988, the other British publishers are wistful. "I'm kicking myself like hell," says Century Hutchinson managing director Anthony Cheetham. "My mistake was thinking that the reader would lose the arguments two-thirds of the way through and that this mattered." When the book was finally launched in London in June 1988, Hawking delightedly informed a group of booksellers that in the United States, his work had already pushed a book about clairvoyance in the White House, by former President Ronald Reagan's chief of staff, Donald Regan, off the top of *The New York Times* best-seller list. "Cosmology," Hawking declared, "has finally beaten out astrology."

Now Hawking is gamely bearing up to the rigors of being a celebrity, touring the globe to give lectures and attending cocktail parties where he occasionally drinks a glass of wine. Recent travels have taken him to Switzerland, the United States, and the Soviet Union. His book has sold better than even he had anticipated. Currently continuing his work on the unification theory, Hawking is also considering another foray into the world of popular nonfiction. "It would be hard to write an equal to *A Brief History of Time,*" he says. "If I do write another book, it will probably be my autobiography." It seems likely that Hawking's new-found public would find such a story as dazzling as his insights into the cosmos.

The Science of **FOUL PLAY**

by Dan Gutman

O n the morning of August 7, 1987, a battery of emergency X rays was run in the
diagnostic unit of Executive Health Ex-
aminers in Manhattan. Five men nervously
waited outside the radiology room while technicians inside went through their paces. When the
film was processed, the pictures were snapped
onto a light box. The X rays were negative.
Everyone breathed a collective sigh of relief.
New York Mets third baseman Howard Johnson's bat was a solid piece of wood.

In the year of Iranscam, a pot-smoking
Supreme Court nominee, and a philandering
presidential candidate, even all-American major
league baseball lost its squeaky-clean image.
Pitchers were reportedly giving up the fastball
and the curveball in favor of the spitball and the
scuffball. Hitters were concerned less with
swinging bats than with doctoring them: drilling
them, stuffing them with cork or some other foreign substance to gain an illegal edge.

Baseball has always had its cheaters, even
back in 1908, when a bogus committee of historians concocted the myth that Abner Double-
day invented the sport. But a virtual crime wave
has gripped the game, and the commissioner's
office has stopped winking at the delinquency
on the diamond and started cracking down.

*Caught in the act: a baseball player who swings a stuffed
bat or pitches a scuffed ball may unnecessarily risk drawing the ire of fans and umpires now that physicists have
begun to doubt whether such cheating gives the player
even a slight competitive edge.*

Paragons of Innocence?

The season's most celebrated bust took place on August 3, 1987. After Minnesota Twins pitcher Joe Niekro fired a particularly wicked knuckleball to Brian Downing of the California Angels, the umpires converged on the mound and demanded that Niekro empty his pockets. The 42-year-old veteran turned his back pockets inside out and held his palms in the air. As Niekro raised his hands, out of his pockets flipped an emery board and a piece of sandpaper contoured to the shape of a finger. Nabbed in front of 33,983 witnesses! The umps put six scuffed baseballs they had collected during the game into a plastic bag and sent them off to league officials. And they sent Niekro packing.

A week later Philadelphia Phillies pitcher Kevin Gross was caught with sandpaper glued in the pocket of his glove. Mike Scott of the Houston Astros, Don Sutton of the California Angels, Tommy John and Rick Rhoden of the New York Yankees—at some point during the season, all were accused of doctoring the ball.

The hitters were hardly paragons of innocence. After a while suspicions ran so high that on-field arrests were being made two at a time.

On August 19, Howard Johnson and San Francisco Giant Candy Maldonado both had their bats confiscated in the same game. (Johnson had never before hit more than 12 four-baggers in a season; in this game he had already whacked his 30th of the season.) Two weeks later, as Houston's leading hitter, Billy Hatcher, took a swing, the barrel of his bat split open, spraying a rain of cork over the infield.

Some fans feel that doctoring the bat or ball is simply an enhancement of the game, like the oversize racket was to tennis. Others believe cheating masks the true talent of the players. But still others argue something even more fundamental: cheating doesn't matter—because cheating doesn't work. Doctored balls, the argument goes, fly just as true as untouched ones. Loaded bats have no more power than solid ones. Players can gouge and scuff and stuff all they want, but they're simply mutilating a lot of perfectly good sports equipment.

When the 1988 season opened, the issue had not been decided. But increasingly the debate is being taken out of the hands of players and fans and turned over to the folks who might finally settle it: the physicists.

Those players who illegally stuff bats with cork, foam, sawdust, latex (below), and other materials less dense than wood do so to lighten the bat and therefore gain a supposed advantage when hitting. X rays invariably expose the material.

Life Extension Institute/© 1988 DISCOVER PUBLICATIONS

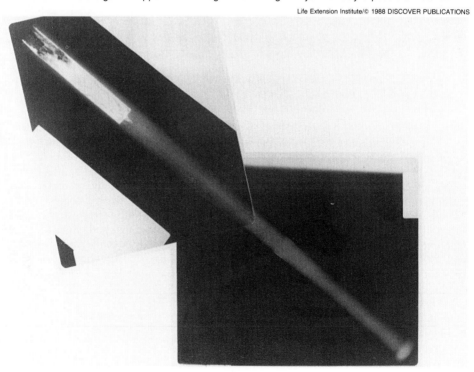

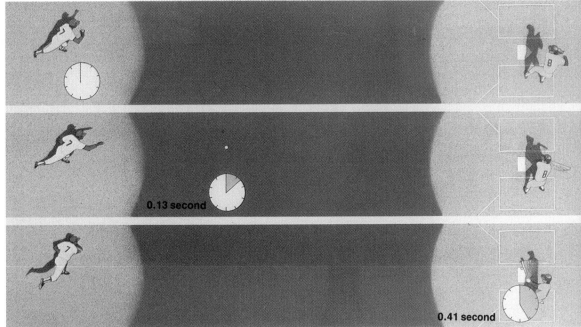

0.13 second

0.41 second

Greg Harlin, S.R.W./© 1988 DISCOVER PUBLICATIONS

A split-second drama unfolds as the pitcher winds up and the batter stands poised (top). The batter must begin his swing 0.13 seconds after the pitcher has released the ball (center). In 0.41 second, ball and bat meet (bottom).

Baseball Physicist

Peter Brancazio is the guy sports announcers love to hate. The Brooklyn College physics professor and author of *SportScience* has spent the past seven years telling the baseball establishment that it's all wet. Brancazio has argued that much of what athletes, umps, and coaches have long taken as physical givens actually violates gravity and common sense. Players and sportscasters can rail all they want, but Brancazio insists that it is simply impossible for a fastball to rise or a peg from third to first to travel in a horizontal line.

"I'm sitting at home watching a ball game and minding my own business, when I hear Tim McCarver call me an idiot," he says. "I mean, what do announcers know about physics?"

Brancazio *does* know something about both science and sport. In fact, he is one of a handful of physicists who have published research papers or magazine stories on baseball.

Brancazio remembers what was probably the most outrageous illegal-bat tale in baseball history. Back in 1974 Graig Nettles of the Yankees took a vicious swing in the fifth inning of a game against Detroit, splitting his bat as it made contact. Out bounced six Super Balls.

Nettles was simply heir to a rich tradition of cheating that preceded him by decades. In the 1950s Ted Kluszewski of the Cincinnati Reds used to sink tenpenny nails into his bat barrel. St. Louis Browns first baseman "Gorgeous" George Sisler banged in Victrola needles. Nellie Fox, among others, used to hit one side of his bat with a sledgehammer to flatten it out and give him more hitting surface. Tony Kubek would carve out the dark, softer grain of the wood and fill it with pine tar. Kansas City Royals star Amos Otis admitted after he retired that he had used a corked bat for 14 years. Otis claimed that it added 193 home runs to his statistics. (He had a career home run total of 193.) Nowadays, it's been estimated, up to 20 percent of all hitters in baseball may be using some kind of illegal bat.

But according to Brancazio, all this criminality is a simple waste of time. "Stuffing Super Balls in your bat and doing all those other things is absolute nonsense," he says. What the athletes believe, Brancazio explains, is that a hollowed-out bat with rubber, cork, or something else inside somehow becomes "springier" and is thus likelier to loft a ball out of the park. But this, he insists, is a myth. "Loading bats just doesn't do anything like that."

Brancazio cites tests that were run last season by Hillerich & Bradsby—the makers of the Louisville Slugger—at the request of baseball commissioner Peter Ueberroth. Company technicians hollowed out bats and filled them with polyurethane foam. They then hit baseballs with the doctored clubs and recorded the distances. "It really didn't have much effect," says Brancazio. "The tests showed that stuffing some foreign substance into a bat simply cannot make an average hitter a great hitter."

A Little More Oomph

Brancazio does not maintain that tampering with bats does nothing to improve hitting; both on the field and in the lab, it has been shown that adulterated bats do propel baseballs with just a little more oomph. But Brancazio explains that this phenomenon has nothing at all to do with some magical property of cork or sawdust or polyurethane foam. What actually happens when doctoring takes place is that the bat simply becomes lighter. This allows the player to swing just a little bit faster and propel the ball just a little bit farther. A quicker swing also gives a batter an additional split second to hold the bat on his shoulder and decide if he wants to swipe at the ball at all, thus reducing the chance that he will chase a bad or tricky pitch.

"Speed is a more important consideration than weight," claims Brancazio, who has worked all this out on his TRS-80 Model III computer. "It takes up to 2,000 pounds (900 kilograms) of force to hit a ball out of the park. Given that fact, it's more effective to swing the lightest bat you can. If a player wants to get more hits, he should forget about cheating and simply select a lighter bat from the bat rack."

History bears Brancazio out. Great hitters like Ted Williams, Rod Carew, and Stan Musial all used light bats, in the range of 31 to 33 ounces (879 to 936 grams). When Roger Maris whacked his 61 home runs in 1961, his favorite bat was a lean 33-ouncer. Hank Aaron, too, was known for using one of the lightest bats in the game, and no one has ever hit more home runs than he did.

The problem with swinging a lighter bat, however, is that the more ounces the lumber loses, the smaller it gets. Brancazio has estimated that the optimum bat weight for maximum speed and power would be a toothpick-light 20 ounces. But to come anywhere near that featherweight figure, the manufacturer would have to shave away so much wood that the "perfect" bat would be absolutely useless.

This leaves cheating. If you bore a half-inch (1.25-centimeter)-diameter hole 8 inches (20 centimeters) into the barrel of the bat and fill it with sawdust or cork (which is one-third the density of wood), the bat becomes an ounce lighter. A wider bore or a deeper hole removes more weight still. With just a little clever handiwork, a player can have it both ways: a light, high-speed whip of a bat with the fat hitting surface of a heavyweight model. The bat can be made even lighter by leaving out the cork, but it will be more likely to crack, and it will make a hollow sound when it hits the ball.

Brutally Tough

The reason players are willing to go to all this work to gain even a tiny advantage is simple: hitting is a brutally tough job. The sport's very best batters fail to get a hit almost seven out of every 10 times they step up to the plate. Ted Williams, former left fielder for the Boston Red Sox and now a hitting instructor for the team, has said that hitting a baseball is the single most difficult thing to do in any sport. In the 47 years since Williams became the last player to have a full-season batting average of .400, there has never been much argument with his views.

An average 90-mile (145-kilometer)-per-hour fastball reaches the batter just .41 second after it leaves the pitcher's hand. To hit the ball a batter must decide to swing after seeing just .13 second of its flight. A difference of a thousandth of a second in the speed of a swing will determine whether the ball goes up the middle or down the foul line. A change of three thousandths of a second—either too early or too late—means no contact with the ball at all. Making matters even tougher is the rather small size of both bat and ball.

All this would seem to give the pitcher a pronounced advantage over the hitter, but this is by no means the case. Stymieing good batters seven out of 10 times means that three out of 10 times the ball *does* get whacked. The pitcher who consistently lets the other guys hit .300 will not last long in the major leagues. So there is as much to be gained by cheating on the pitcher's mound as there is in the batter's box.

To Spin or Not to Spin

To understand why it's worth a pitcher's while to learn the spitball, the scuffball, or other unwholesome tricks, it's necessary to understand what makes a baseball dance or curve in the first place. Popular legend credits development of the curveball to Hall of Famer Candy Cummings, who was inspired in the summer of

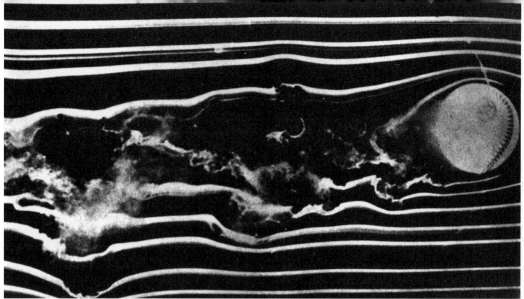

A well-pitched ball can make as many as 16 complete turns as it spins its way to the plate. In a wind tunnel, smoke jets reveal how air and a spinning ball interact. The top of the ball rotates into the wind, increasing resistance; the bottom moves with the wind, lowering resistance. The ball therefore drops, taking the path of least resistance.

1863 when he noticed that he could throw a clamshell and make it veer off-course. In the decades that followed, Cummings' invention was adopted and adapted by countless other pitchers, who called their creations benders, jughandles, and pretzels. Despite the popularity of the curve, however, for decades, people outside the sports community were not convinced that it was really possible for a baseball to change its course. In 1941 a *Life* photographer armed with high-speed strobes attempted to settle the controversy by photographing the curveball in flight. The magazine concluded that "this stand-by of baseball [may be], after all, only an optical illusion." Twelve years later *Life* repeated the test. The curve, the editors decided after improving their photographic techniques, indeed existed.

Basically, there are two legal ways to make a baseball curve: spin it or don't spin it. Most pitches spin. A good fastball, slider, or curve can rotate as many as 30 times per second, or 16 complete turns on its way to the plate. Anyone who has stuck a hand out a car window on the freeway can appreciate the forces acting on a pitched baseball. The flow of air rushing by can't go through the ball, just as it can't go through your hand, so it is forced to go above or below. If the baseball didn't spin, and if it were perfectly smooth like a billiard ball, the wake of air around the ball would be perfectly symmetrical, and the pitch wouldn't curve.

But when a baseball spins, the flow of air around it becomes asymmetrical. The ball is both moving forward and spinning; one side of the ball is spinning against the air as the ball moves toward the plate, creating greater pressure on that side. The ball veers in the opposite direction, where the pressure is lower.

When a left-handed pitcher throws a curve, he spins the ball clockwise, and it curves away from a left-handed batter. Spinning it counterclockwise results in a screwball, which curves toward the batter. If he gives the ball topspin, it will sink, while backspin will make it rise (or, strictly speaking, it will not drop as much as it would under the force of gravity alone). Indeed, since there is *some* spin on any pitch, it is almost impossible for a pitcher not to make a ball curve at least a few inches; a good, deliberate curve, however, can deviate by more than a foot. The rule for the degree of movement is simple: the greater the rotation, the greater the break.

The Knuckleball

Oddly, on some occasions the *less* rotation a pitcher puts on the ball, the more it may break also. A knuckleball is thrown with little or no spin by keeping the wrist stiff and pushing the ball off the fingertips (not the knuckles). The ball flutters to the plate at about 65 miles (100 kilometers) per hour and is notoriously hard to hit, catch, or umpire. When asked how he handled the knuckleball, former catcher and celebrity beer-drinker Bob Uecker has said he would simply pick it up after it stopped rolling.

It was once believed that knuckleballs behaved erratically because they were buffeted about by puffs of wind (which if true would make the pitch useless in any domed stadium). In 1975, however, Tulane University engineers Robert Watts and Eric Sawyer published "Aerodynamics of a Knuckleball" in the *American Journal of Physics*.

Placing a baseball in a wind tunnel, Watts and Sawyer found that it is not the wind but the raised stitches on the baseball that cause the knuckleball's unpredictable path. The stitches disrupt the flow of air around the ball, creating an asymmetrical wake that pushes the ball this way and that on its way to the plate.

Engineer Joel Hollenberg of Cooper Union in New York City recently updated Watts and Sawyer's knuckleball research with a computer

Yvonne Gensurowsky, S.R.W./© 1988 DISCOVER PUBLICATIONS

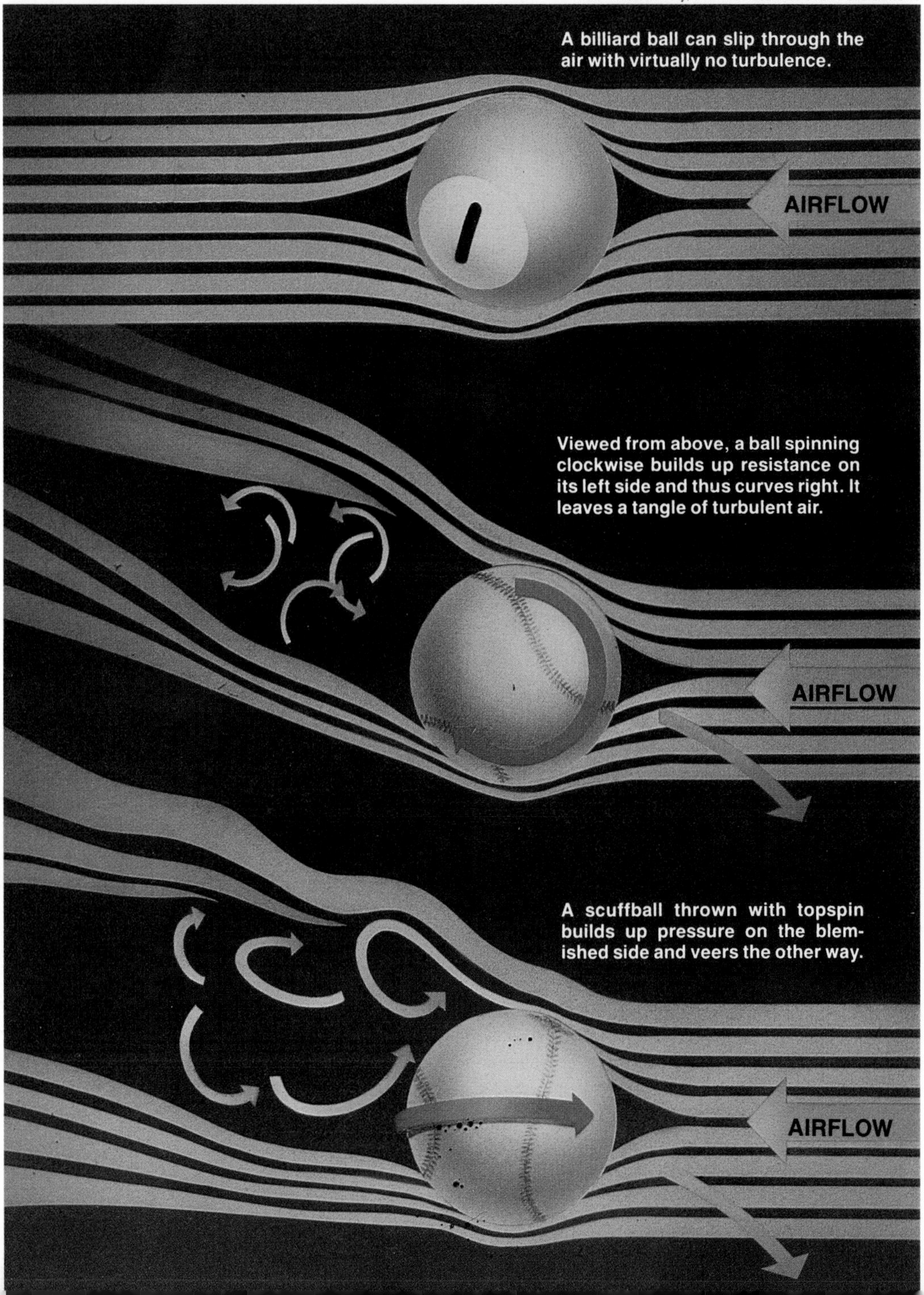

A billiard ball can slip through the air with virtually no turbulence.

AIRFLOW

Viewed from above, a ball spinning clockwise builds up resistance on its left side and thus curves right. It leaves a tangle of turbulent air.

AIRFLOW

A scuffball thrown with topspin builds up pressure on the blemished side and veers the other way.

AIRFLOW

simulation that does just that. Since the knuckleball's path depends on the position of the stitches, the key inputs to Hollenberg's computer are angles describing the orientation of the ball at the moment the pitcher lets go of it. According to the computer, if the pitcher holds the ball at a "tilt angle" of 15 degrees relative to a line from first base to third, and a "release angle" of 3 degrees relative to a line from home plate to the mound, and throws a 70-mile (112-kilometer)-per-hour knuckleball that spins 10 degrees per second, the ball will cross the plate 2.81 feet above the ground and .42 foot to the first-base side. Piece of cake—that is, as long as the temperature outside is 75° F (23° C), and the barometric pressure is ideal.

The knuckleball is so tough to hit because it does most of its movement after the batter has started his swing. Although every Little Leaguer is told to keep his eye on the ball, recent research shows that to be an impossible feat. University of Arizona engineer Terry Bahill measured the eye and head movements of baseball players and found that even the quickest batters lose sight of the ball once it closes to within 5.5 feet (1.6 meters) of the plate. At that point the ball is moving three times faster than the human eye can track. The batter has to plan his swing after seeing only a portion of the incoming trajectory. If the pitcher can make the ball change course within that critical 5.5-foot space, the ball is virtually unhittable. That's exactly what a good knuckleball does.

"If you can throw a pitch that exhibits its most erratic motion in the last portion of its flight, the batter will have a very difficult time," says Hollenberg, who became intrigued with pitching when, from a 75-cent bleacher seat, he watched Don Larsen's perfect game in the 1956 World Series.

A good knuckleball may be a powerful weapon, but that there are only four or five knuckleballers in the major leagues suggests how exquisitely difficult it is to throw the pitch. To compensate, pitchers have come up with other means to make a baseball hop even more than a knuckleball does.

Doctoring the Ball

Regulation number 3.02 of the baseball rule book states that "No player shall intentionally discolor or damage the ball by rubbing it with soil, rosin, paraffin, licorice, sandpaper, emery paper, or other foreign substance." So far, nobody has been caught tossing licorice balls, but pitchers have used everything from belt buckles and wedding rings to bent eyelets on their gloves to scar the skin of the baseball.

The most blatant scuffer in baseball history had to be Rick Honeycutt of the 1980 Seattle Mariners. While Niekro and others could argue that emery boards and sandpaper are necessary tools for precise nail filing, there wasn't much Honeycutt could say when caught on the mound with a thumbtack sticking through a Band-Aid on his finger. He became the first pitcher to be

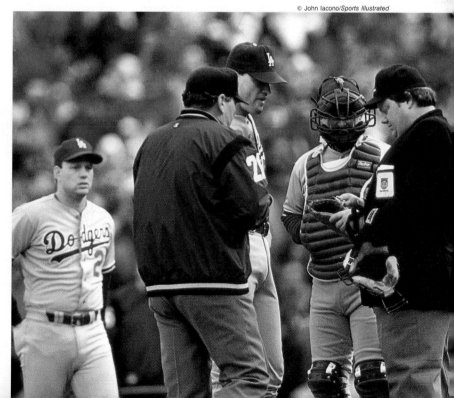

The unpredictable path taken by a doctored ball (facing page) makes it easier for a pitcher to strike out a batter. In the 1988 National League playoffs, Jay Howell (the tallest player at right), a Dodgers relief pitcher, dabbed his glove with pine tar, purportedly to gain a better grip on the ball in the chilly weather. Any use of a foreign substance by a pitcher violates baseball rules, however, and Howell ultimately found himself ejected from the game and suspended for two days.

suspended for throwing a scuffball since the pitch was banned 60 years earlier.

Scuffing or scraping the ball or putting a glob of spit on it does the same thing for an ordinary pitch that the raised stitches do for a knuckleball. If the surface of the ball becomes irregular, the airflow around it is disrupted. Air resistance is increased on the side of the ball that has been altered, and the throw veers the other way.

"To me, the whole idea of roughing the ball up is absurd," says Hollenberg. "A pitcher who understands how to use the roughness of the stitches doesn't have to do anything to the ball."

Ballplayers, however, believe that cutting or scuffing the surface of the ball has more of an effect than the stitches alone do. According to New York Mets catcher Gary Carter, "An illegal pitch moves in so many different directions; many more than a good knuckleball."

The way to throw the best possible scuffer is to cut the ball in one of the four large areas that are free of stitching and throw with the same backspin motion used for a fastball. The ball is gripped so that the scuff faces first or third base. The idea is for the scuff mark to stay in one place and disrupt the airflow on that side. If you put the scuff facing to your right (toward third), the ball will break left. If the scuff faces left, the ball will break right.

It's also possible to legally make one side of the ball rougher than the other. In the 1982 World Series, Cardinals pitcher Bruce Sutter was observed throwing a "shiner." By rubbing the ball briskly against his uniform, Sutter made part of the ball smoother, which in effect made the rest of the ball rougher. Ted Williams says in his autobiography that "pitchers as a breed are dumb and hardheaded," but it cannot be denied that they are also quite resourceful.

The success of the scuffball has taken the classic spitball off the front pages, at least for the time being. Aerodynamically, the spitter works the same way as the scuffer does, but it's an ever so much more colorful way to cheat. We'll miss characters like John Wyatt, a pitcher with the 1960s Kansas City A's who used to hide a syringe filled with Vaseline in the thumb of his glove. After that trick was exposed, Wyatt came to the mound with a tube of Vaseline in his mouth; he squeezed out however much he needed by using his teeth.

Gaylord Perry, dubbed "The Great Expectorator" by admiring fellow pitchers and angry enemy batters, made Wyatt look positively scrupulous. Like Edison searching for the perfect filament for his incandescent bulb, Perry used baby oil, suntan lotion, fishing-line wax, and even K-Y jelly to dress up and mess up his baseballs. He must have known something: he spent 22 years in the majors, won 314 games, and received a Cy Young Award at the age of 40; he'll probably make it to Cooperstown. Perry was caught only once, in 1982, and he paid with a ten-day suspension.

Early in the history of the sport, the spitball was perfectly legal, while the innocent curveball was verboten. This meant that the original spitters could juice up the ball in all manner of stomach-turning ways. Ed Walsh, who pitched for the White Sox, would stick out his tongue and actually lick the ball to wet it down. His opponents, unable to complain to league officials, foiled Walsh by smearing the baseballs with horse manure. (Of course, that simply added a new pitch to Walsh's repertoire, and he eventually made it to the Hall of Fame.)

What's Next?

It appears that pitchers in general have more weapons at their disposal than batters do, and the rules of baseball are continually being tweaked to give the hitters an even chance. (Good illegal pitching beats good illegal hitting.) If it is any consolation to batters, a baseball that has been scuffed up or wetted down travels farther when hit than one that has been left alone. The irregular surface causes air to stick to the ball, reducing its wake and providing less drag, the same way dimples give a golf ball a lift. That is, of course, if the batter can manage to get a piece of the illegal pitch in the first place.

What's next in cheating technology? Brancazio has conducted an unpublished study demonstrating that aluminum bats have a larger "sweet spot" than wooden ones because the center of gravity is closer to the handle. "I've got this idea I'm going to start playing around with," he whispers, as if A. Bartlett Giamatti, the new baseball commissioner, were hiding in the next office. "You take a wooden bat, and you stick a lead disk near the knob, under your hands. The mathematics work out so that the added weight gives you a better hitting response. You get the effects of an aluminum bat, even though you're using a wooden one."

Sounds promising. Are you listening out there, umpires?

PHYSICS AND CHEMISTRY

by Elaine Pascoe

A landmark experiment in particle physics and a breakthrough in the understanding of photosynthesis brought Nobel prizes to six scientists in 1988.

The prize in physics was awarded to three Americans—Leon M. Lederman of the Fermi National Accelerator Laboratory (Fermilab) in Illinois, Melvin Schwartz of Digital Pathways Inc. in California, and Jack Steinberger of the European Center for Nuclear Research (CERN) in Geneva—for work done at Columbia University in the early 1960s. In their experiment the three scientists created the first laboratory-produced beam of the subatomic particles known as neutrinos, and they identified a previously unknown form of neutrino. The discovery led to a new theory of fundamental particles that became part of the foundation of modern physics.

The chemistry prize went to three West Germans—Johann Deisenhofer of the Howard Hughes Medical Institute in Dallas, Robert Huber of the Technical University in Munich, and Hartmut Michel of the Max Planck Institute for Biophysics in Frankfurt. In the early 1980s, they collaborated on research that revealed the structure of proteins that are essential to photosynthesis, the process by which plants convert the energy in sunlight into nourishment. The work increased understanding of photosynthesis and opened the way to the development of artificial photosynthetic materials.

The Prize in Physics

At the time that Lederman, Schwartz, and Steinberger conceived their experiment, neutrinos were considered virtually impossible to detect, let alone study. With no electrical charge and no detectable mass, a neutrino does not respond to the so-called strong force, which binds atomic nuclei together, or to electromagnetic force. Thus neutrinos can pass through matter without interacting with other particles or atoms; in fact, billions of them pass through the earth undetected every second.

The researchers' interest in neutrinos stemmed from the particle's relation to the so-called weak force, which is involved in some forms of radioactive decay. The weak force was known, for example, to cause beta decay, in which a neutron becomes a proton by shedding an electron and a neutrino. The problem was that the theories that explained the force's action didn't hold together in certain situations, particularly when particles collided at high energies. Yet studying weak-force interactions in high-energy collisions seemed impossible because they would be obscured by the more powerful electromagnetic and strong-force interactions that would also result.

Schwartz hit on the idea of studying weak-force interactions through neutrinos, which interact only through this force, and proposed it to the others. The first step was to create a high-energy neutrino beam. The group used the nearby Brookhaven accelerator on Long Island to fire a stream of protons at 15

The Physics Nobel laureates created the first laboratory-produced beam of neutrinos—uncharged fundamental particles of matter with no detectable mass. First, they energized protons in a particle accelerator and fired them into a beryllium block. The collision produced a shower of protons, neutrons, and pions. The pions decayed into muons and neutrinos. A thick steel wall blocked the forward movement of all the particles except the neutrinos, which emerged as a pure beam.

THE ELUSIVE NEUTRINO

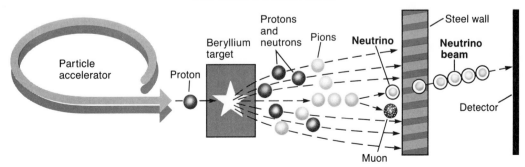

Dr. Jack Steinberger (right), one of the 1988 Physics Nobel Prize winners, taught at the University of California and Columbia University before joining the European Center for Nuclear Research (CERN) in Geneva.

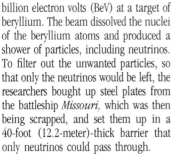

Two others shared the physics Nobel. Dr. Leon Lederman (above) teaches at the University of Chicago. Dr. Melvin Schwartz (right) founded Digital Pathways, a computer-security company.

billion electron volts (BeV) at a target of beryllium. The beam dissolved the nuclei of the beryllium atoms and produced a shower of particles, including neutrinos. To filter out the unwanted particles, so that only the neutrinos would be left, the researchers bought up steel plates from the battleship *Missouri,* which was then being scrapped, and set them up in a 40-foot (12.2-meter)-thick barrier that only neutrinos could pass through.

To detect the neutrinos, the researchers built a 10-ton (9-metric-ton) aluminum detection chamber in which neutrino collisions would be revealed by sparks from any electrically charged particles that resulted. In eight months, the team recorded 56 collisions.

Significantly, while previously observed neutrino interactions had produced electrons, every one of these interactions produced a different particle—the mu-meson, or muon. Thus, the researchers concluded, the neutrinos were of a different type. Their "two-neutrino" experiment led ultimately to the development of the standard model theory, which holds that several types of matter exist side by side.

Leon Max Lederman was born in New York City on July 15, 1922. He earned a bachelor's degree in chemistry at the City College of New York, received his doctorate in physics from Columbia in 1951, and remained at Columbia as a professor. In 1979 he became director of Fermilab near Chicago. At the time he received the Nobel award, he had announced plans to return to teaching, at the University of Chicago.

Jack Steinberger was born in Bad Kissingen, Germany, on May 25, 1921, and moved to the United States with his family in 1934. He studied at the Illinois Institute of Technology, Massachusetts Institute of Technology (MIT) (where he was assigned to the radiation lab and worked on radar bombsights during World War II), and the University of Chicago, where he received his doctorate in 1948. He taught at the University of California as well as Columbia before joining CERN.

Melvin Schwartz was born in New York City on November 2, 1932, and studied at Columbia, earning a doctorate in physics in 1958. He was on the faculty at Columbia until 1966, when he became a professor of physics at Stanford University. In 1979 he left the school to devote his energies to Digital Pathways, a company he had founded to produce security systems for computers.

The Prize in Chemistry

Since plants stand at the base of the food chain, all living things ultimately depend on photosynthesis for survival. By mapping the precise three-dimensional structure of proteins that are essential to photosynthesis, the winners of the Nobel for chemistry were able to shed new light on the complex process by which plants convert the Sun's energy into food.

The researchers used bacteria, *Rhodopseudomonas viridas,* in which photosynthesis is simpler than it is in plants; but enough similarities exist to give the work broad applications. They focused on the photosynthetic reaction centers at the bacterial cell surfaces. Here a complex of four proteins is bound together in such a way that it spans the cell's outer membrane—some projecting outside the cell, some within the membrane, and some inside the cell. When sunlight strikes this protein complex, it triggers a wave of electron transfers that travels into the cell, where the energy is used to form adenosine triphosphate (ATP), one of life's basic energy sources.

Before they could reveal the protein structure and map the path of the energy transfer, however, the researchers faced a technical problem: membrane-bound proteins such as those in the photosynthetic reaction centers had proved virtually impossible to reduce to crystalline form for study through X-ray crystallography. (In this technique, which is used to reveal the structure of proteins and other large molecules, the molecules are bombarded with X rays, and the structure is deduced from the way the X rays bounce back.) Michel solved this problem in 1982, when he succeeded in growing crystals of the proteins.

The research was then taken over by Huber, an expert in X-ray crystallography, and Deisenhofer. By 1985 the researchers had succeeded in mapping all the roughly 10,000 atoms that make up the protein complex. Their success had implications for other biological processes as well, since membrane-bound proteins are involved in the actions of viruses and of many body hormones. And knowledge of the specific protein structure involved in photosynthesis increased the possibility that researchers might one day be able to reproduce this complex process artificially, creating systems for energy storage.

Johann Deisenhofer was born in Zusamaltheim, Bavaria, on September 30, 1943, and earned his doctorate at the Max Planck Institute for Biochemistry in Martinsried, West Germany. In 1987 he moved to Texas to join the Howard Hughes Medical Institute and the University of Texas at Dallas, to help establish a center for X-ray crystallography.

Robert Huber was born in Munich, Germany, on February 10, 1937. He earned his doctorate at the Technical University at Munich and has remained on the faculty there, directing a major X-ray crystallography lab and developing an international reputation in that field.

Hartmut Michel, who initiated the award-winning work, was born in Ludwigsburg, West Germany, on July 18, 1948. After earning a doctorate at the University of Würzburg in 1977, he spent eight years at the Max Planck Institute in Martinsried. He then moved to Frankfurt to become divisional head of the Max Planck Institute there.

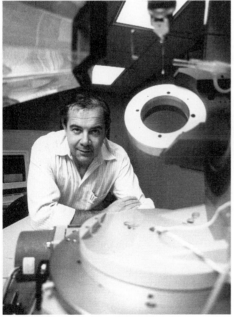

Three West Germans shared the 1988 Chemistry Nobel Prize. Drs. Johann Deisenhofer (left), Robert Huber (center), and Hartmut Michel (right) determined the structures of proteins that are essential to photosynthesis, the process by which plants convert the Sun's energy into food. Their discovery opens the way to developing artificial photosynthetic materials.

TECHNOLOGY

TECHNOLOGY

Technological progress went beyond isolated inventions with narrow application. New trends were in evidence, new directions were explored, and advances were made in the development of unified, integrated technological systems.

by Jeffrey H. Hacker

© 1988 Peter Menzel

Research on the U.S. Strategic Defense Initiative, a space-based antimissile defense system, has led to new developments in laser technology.

Defense

In military technology, always the focus of intensive research and development, the highlight of the year for the Pentagon was the unveiling of the Stealth bomber—officially designated the B-2. The long-range strategic bomber takes its nickname from its ability to fly without being detected by radar. (See also the article on stealth technology beginning on page 330.)

Work continued on the U.S. Strategic Defense Initiative (SDI), the elaborate space-based antimissile defense system proposed by President Reagan in 1983. In February 1988, the Defense Department conducted its most complex test to date of such "Star Wars" technology, launching a highly computerized satellite into space. The satellite ejected a variety of objects, and then used special sensors to identify and track them. Despite the successful test, SDI remained politically controversial and technologically suspect. The Office of Technology Assessment (OTA), a congressional research agency, concluded after a two-year study that SDI would probably "suffer a catastrophic failure" in its first use. In the spring of 1989, the Bush Administration scaled back funding for SDI research.

At the same time, the Pentagon proceeded with another long-term project begun in 1983, the 10-year Strategic Computing Initiative (SCI). The largest computer research project in the United States, SCI is an effort to develop intelligent computers for warfare. In addition to advances in artificial intelligence and large-scale computing, technicians have been working on automated battlefields and robotic weaponry. Examples of the latter, still in their early simulation stages, include a pilotless combat plane and an unmanned land vehicle.

Health Care

© NYT Pictures

Electronic sensors built into the fingertips of artificial hands can provide a partial sense of touch.

They still don't wash dishes or vacuum floors, but robots are performing many new and vital tasks—and not just in factories. Following a trend toward more service-industry uses, a company in Danbury, Connecticut, has developed a robot that delivers meal trays to hospital patients. It memorizes floor corridors and uses electronic sensors to avoid people. The robot got on-the-job training at a local hospital.

The hearing-impaired are benefiting from a new generation of smaller, smarter hearing aids. Unlike models that attach to the ear and are wired to bulky control boxes, the new devices fit into the ear canal and adjust automatically (or by remote control) to volume and frequency. Among the users is former President Reagan, who was fitted just before leaving office. His two tiny aids not only amplify wanted sounds, but filter out distracting background noises. With a remote control the size of a credit card, he can also control the volume or switch the aids off completely.

A New Jersey doctor developed electronic sensors for the fingertips of an artificial hand. In response to pressure, the sensors generate signals in the form of high-frequency vibrations. The vibrations are transmitted to the base of the plastic hand, which is attached to the end of the arm. The person feels vibrations in the arm and learns to distinguish the signals from different fingers.

Communications

In a joint venture of 29 telephone companies from Europe and North America, the first fiber-optic telephone cable across the Atlantic Ocean went into service in December 1988. Strung along the ocean floor, the new light-wave cable doubles the number of calls that can be placed between the United States and Europe at one time—from 20,000 by existing copper wires and satellites, to 40,000. A single fiber-optic cable, which uses pulses of laser light in digital form to transmit voice and computer data, can carry more than 8,000 conversations; a standard copper wire can carry 48. A fiber-optic cable across the Pacific Ocean also neared completion.

The United States government moved forward on replacing its aging, outmoded telephone system with a high-tech, all-digital network featuring high-capacity, high-speed switching equipment. Called FTS-2000, the new network will be the world's largest and most sophisticated private communications system, serving 1.3 million people in 3,500 locations. The basic network was expected to be working in three years, with special features—such as video conferencing, voice mail, and high-speed data transfer—coming into use during the next 10 years. Total cost of the project: $25 billion.

The goal of a super communications system—called the Integrated Services Digital Network (ISDN)–neared realization with a series of successful trials. ISDN will provide high-speed digital transmission and switching of combined voice, data, and video signals. The first demonstration was made early in 1988 between locations in Colorado, New Jersey, and Florida. Trials were being planned in 20 U.S. exchanges and more than a dozen other countries.

Civil Engineering

Work continued, though slightly behind schedule, on the largest civil-engineering project in the history of Western Europe—a tunnel under the English Channel connecting France and Great Britain. The so-called Chunnel project, begun in December 1986, employs some of the world's most advanced tunnel-boring technology in digging three parallel shafts 31 miles (50 kilometers) between Cheriton in southern England and Frethun in northern France. Two of the tunnels will handle electric shuttle trains that carry cars, trucks, and buses. The middle shaft will be a service-ventilation tunnel linked to the other two. The project is scheduled for completion in May 1993 at an expected cost of $10.3 billion. In 1988 French workers crossed the shoreline and began digging under the Channel itself. Hitting easier ground, British workers made swifter progress.

A centuries-old dream was realized in Japan, as that nation's four main islands were fully linked by bridge and tunnel. The northern island of Hokkaido and the largest island of Honshu were joined by the new Seikan Tunnel, at 33.5 miles (54 kilometers) the longest in the world. The first passenger and freight trains rolled through Seikan in March. Then, in April, Japan's southern island of Shikoku was linked to Honshu by a new 23-mile (37.3-kilometer) series of road-and-rail crossings collectively known as the Seto Great Bridge. The fourth main island, Kyushu, already was connected to Honshu by a bridge and tunnel.

In Chicago, substantial progress was made on what soon would be the world's tallest concrete building. Standing 967 feet (296 meters) tall, the new high rise featured a top-down method of construction. Thus underground excavation of the foundation could proceed simultaneously with tower-frame construction.

Inside and out, engineers use the latest technology to dig the Chunnel, a set of tunnels under the English Channel connecting France and Britain.

Photography and Video

Billed as a "photographic time machine," a system developed at the National Institute of Standards and Technology allows scientists to photograph events after they happen. Called an image-preserving optical delay, the device is an arrangement of optical components, including a series of mirrors. The mirrors bounce the image back and forth for a tiny fraction of a second before delivering it to the camera's lens. The device is used for events that last from 100 nanoseconds (billionths of a second) to 10 microseconds (millionths of a second)—such as a spark or a lightning bolt. The system stores the image long enough for the shutter of a high-speed camera to be opened and the photograph taken. One application is the study of materials used by the electric power industry.

For the more casual photographer, a new product bridges the gap between conventional still snapshots and home video. It is the electronic still video camera, a device that captures an image on electronic sensors instead of film. The image is stored on built-in magnetic disks that can be played back on a unit connected to a television. The result is an instant photo displayed on the TV screen. Consumer versions of the system were expected in 1989, at a cost (camera and playback unit) of about $1,000.

TV itself was on the verge of a revolution, as a technology called high-definition television (HDTV) emerged clearly on the horizon. As its name suggests, HDTV offers a vastly sharper picture than a conventional television. Introduced in the early 1980s by Japanese manufacturers, the system more than doubles the number of lines on a standard TV screen and increases the width-to-height ratio. The result is a picture five times clearer than on a standard TV. HDTV receivers are not yet available in the United States, but in September 1988 the Federal Communications Commission (FCC) announced technical guidelines that will bring HDTV to the American public in the 1990s. Already, though, HDTV videotape is beginning to replace 35-millimeter film because it is cheaper and easier to edit. In the fall of 1989, CBS will air its first movie—*Innocent Victims*—made with the HDTV videotape technology.

And the video revolution took another step forward with the introduction of the Sony Video Walkman, a 2.5-pound (1.1-kilogram) videocassette recorder with a 3-inch (7.6-centimeter) color screen. The device, which sells for about $1,300, plays 8-millimeter videocassettes and also includes a timer for automatic recording.

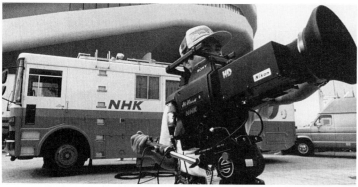

© A. Tannenbaum/SYGMA

Japanese networks sent HDTV transmissions back home from the Seoul Olympics.

Transportation

Increasing concern over airline safety has led to several technological innovations in recent years. Under 1987 legislation, U.S. commercial airlines are required to install an electronic device called the Traffic Alert and Collision Avoidance System (TCAS) on all planes by 1992. The equipment tracks nearby planes by radar, displays their positions on a cockpit screen, and sounds a warning when evasive action is needed. In 1988 several airlines completed testing on the TCAS and began installation.

Increasing air traffic has led some airline officials to predict a new age of supersonic air transportation over long-haul routes. The first-generation supersonic passenger plane, the British-French Concorde, would fly at a snail's pace compared with the next generation. The Concorde, launched in 1976, flies at about 1,350 miles (2,175 kilometers) per hour. Some analysts expect 250 to 350 such planes to be in demand by the year 2010. Meanwhile, even faster *hyper*sonic planes were in the planning or experimental stages. The Orient Express passenger plane, for example, would soar at 10,000 miles (16,000 kilometers) per hour—or 14 times the speed of sound. At that speed, it could cross the Pacific Ocean in a cool two hours.

Back on the ground, the computerization of the automobile gained momentum. American automakers made progress in developing smaller, more durable, less costly "smart sensors" that will make computer-controlled features more practical and affordable in the 1990s. Among the expected applications are antiskid brakes (already available on a few high-priced cars), which sense when the wheels are about to lock, and alter pressure to prevent it; traction control to prevent wheel spins; and motorized suspension adjustment for a smoother ride. (See also the article beginning on p. 334.)

Automation and Industry

In the late 1970s, the spread of assembly-line robots and computerized manufacturing equipment created visions of fully automated industrial plants. While workers feared for their jobs, executives and engineers saw the coming of "lights out" factories that could operate on their own, literally in the dark. Now, however, that thinking appears to be changing. Many major companies have recognized the importance of smart workers to manage smart machines. In the manufacture of automobiles, electric equipment, household appliances, and a variety of other goods, plant workers have been given more information and a greater decision-making role. At such companies as Mazda, General Electric, and Weyerhaeuser, for example, plant workers may have as much production data as the plant manager, a television screen to monitor operations, the expertise to correct technical problems, and the authority to make improvements. Manufacturing experts have

dubbed this new system the "informated" factory.

Meanwhile, progress continued to be made in the effort to speed up and integrate automation itself. At a June 1988 convention in Baltimore, Maryland, called Enterprise 88, representatives of the world's leading industrial companies and engineering groups joined in promoting international standards for the linking of high-tech factory and office systems. Known as the Manufacturing Automation Protocol (MAP) and the Technical and Office Protocol (TOP), the guidelines would enable computers and other equipment across the globe to communicate as easily as telephones. According to supporters, the interconnection of equipment and cooperation of effort would enhance automation and lower the cost of final products.

To build support for MAP/TOP, participants in the conference displayed a "minifactory" that brought together more than 50 companies. This model

© Duane Hall/NYT Pictures

In "informated" factories, the person who operates a programmable manufacturing machine can also service it.

global enterprise, employing some one hundred high-tech operations and support systems, manufactured the first real product—a souvenir desk top organizer—under the guidelines. Promoters of MAP/TOP see it as a major boost to the continued growth of automation. "This is a coming of age," said one chief executive.

Law Enforcement

Robots are turning up in *a lot* of new places, including roadside speed traps and jails. In the town of Paradise Valley, Arizona, a hidden robot aims radar signals at oncoming traffic. When it detects a vehicle moving faster than a designated speed, it automatically trips a camera shutter. The vehicle's owner is identified by tracing the license plate number, and a speeding ticket is mailed to the offender.

At a prison in Alameda County, California, robotic carts have been introduced to feed the facility's 3,000 inmates. Guided by computers and embedded magnetic wires, the carts ferry food trays from the kitchen to separate prison units. Guards distribute the food.

At a time when many prison systems are severely overcrowded, special devices are being employed for nonviolent offenders placed under house arrest rather than in jail. In Anne Arundel County, Maryland, for example, officials can

Photos: © Michael Spector/NYT Pictures

A photo-radar device (above) snaps pictures of speeding cars. The driver, identified by license plate (right), receives a ticket by mail.

check on such convicts via two-way video telephones. For drunk-driving offenders, hand-held breath analyzers display blood alcohol levels on the monitor. In a New York State house-arrest program, convicts wear an electronic bracelet that trips an alarm when they leave the house.

SKY SCRAPING

by Doug Stewart

Erecting a supertall building poses no insurmountable problems to today's engineers. Skyscrapers a half mile high may someday dwarf Manhattan's World Trade towers.

Like many of his colleagues, structural engineer William LeMessurier has a plan for the world's tallest building. He keeps an architectural model of it outside his cluttered third-floor office at LeMessurier Consultants in Cambridge, Massachusetts. Affixed to the sturdy plywood obelisk are markers showing how existing skyscrapers would measure up: the Eiffel Tower would be at eye level, the Empire State Building a couple of feet above that. LeMessurier's model pokes up through the stairwell next to his corner office and tops out just beyond the level of the receptionist's desk on the floor above. Nearly 15 feet (4.5 meters) tall, but only 18 inches (45 centimeters) wide at the base, the model is something of a structural tour de force all by itself.

"There's no likelihood of it ever being built," LeMessurier says of his half-mile (800-meter)-high, 207-story Erewhon Center, "because there's no site I could imagine where it would make sense." (Indeed, the name he chose for the building is an anagram for *nowhere*.) LeMessurier (pronounced "le measure"), a relaxed, chain-smoking architect-turned-engineer, is utterly confident that he could construct his tower should the need arise. All he needs is a client with about a billion dollars and the proper building permits.

Skyscraper Science

Similar architectural models perch in plastic display cases or on windowsills in the offices of at least half a dozen other high-thinking builders in New York City; Chicago, Illinois; and Houston, Texas. At 1,454 feet (436 meters), the Sears Tower in Chicago has looked down on all rivals for 15 years, but no one's betting it will do so much longer. Within the next five years, it's all but certain that a rash of new supertall buildings will be poking through the clouds in U.S. cities and in boomtowns like Sydney, Australia; Hong Kong; and Singapore.

The science of skyscraping has come of age. Most of today's high-rise builders say that erecting supertall structures poses no insurmountable challenges. "Right now," says Hal Iyengar, a partner at Chicago-based Skidmore, Owings & Merrill, which designed the 110-floor Sears Tower, "we can comfortably build up to 150 stories, perhaps even up to 200 stories. The technology is there."

A number of technological advances are responsible for such confidence. Wind-tunnel testing has become a routine tool, letting builders know how a tall building will react to the stresses of even the worst gale. Computer-aided design (CAD) programs have shortened the time needed to produce drawings, consider alternatives, and make changes. High-strength steel and concrete let builders go tall without the penalty in extra material, and thus extra cost, that was exacted in the 1920s and 1930s, the era of the Chrysler and the Empire State buildings.

To the average pedestrian on Fifth Avenue, a future building rising 200 stories above the sidewalk may summon up disquieting images of giant towers collapsing under their own weight or simply crushing the ground beneath them. However, engineers respond that the weight of a supertall building—its "gravity load," in engineering lingo—is a perfectly manageable burden. Both steel and concrete are wonderfully resistant to the compression forces that such a building would exert on its lower-floor columns. Similarly, the ground itself, provided it isn't a swamp, withstands such pressure well. Office buildings are, after all, mostly air. In fact, the rock removed in digging a foundation hole 100 feet (30 meters) deep would weigh more than a 1,000-foot (300-meter) building. While designers are forever trying to come up with better methods for making supertall buildings stand, they have not had to concern themselves with discovering new ways to support unprecedented gravity loads.

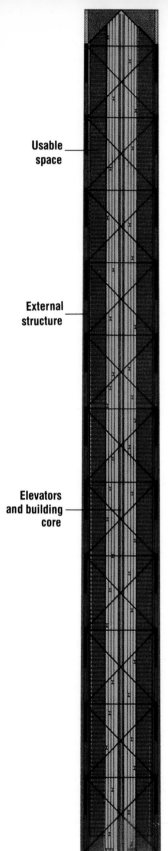

Usable space

External structure

Elevators and building core

William LeMessurier claims that construction on his dream building, the 207-story Erewhon Center, could begin tomorrow if he could obtain the right site, adequate financing, and the proper building permits.

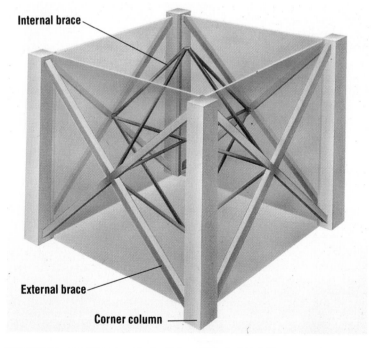

Internal brace

External brace

Corner column

New designs using high-strength steel let engineers build tall. The exposed braces of the Erewhon Center (left) would crisscross every 18 stories. Inside each multifloor segment (above), smaller steel beams would support the weight of the floors and radiate it out to the side beams, which, in turn, would transfer the weight to the corner columns.

The slant-topped Citicorp Center in midtown Manhattan, engineered by LeMessurier, is a case in point. Instead of containing thousands of short vertical columns supporting horizontal beams for floor after floor, the 915-foot (280-meter) building is supported by just a relative handful of long diagonal steel braces. The frame of the building is divided into six sections stacked one atop the next, and the diagonals are arranged in a series of downward-pointing triangles. The triangles span the four exterior faces of each nine-story section, their points seeming to perch on large load-bearing columns at the midpoints of the building's sides. The diagonals of these triangles shoulder the loads of the floors above and channel them directly to the exterior columns. As a result, Citicorp Center, although only a few hundred feet shorter than the Empire State Building, exerts less than half as much pressure on each square foot of ground below.

Lightness has its drawbacks, however. Without the forests of steel columns and the heavy masonry walls of the traditional high rise, New Wave skyscrapers are vulnerable to the buffeting of wind. This problem tends to grow geometrically with a building's height. On average, winds battering the top of a 100-story building are four times as powerful as those swirling around the top floor of a 50-story building. A hurricane can exert over 4,000 tons (3,600 metric tons) of force on the side of a very tall skyscraper—4,000 tons that are working to topple the building.

No wind has actually "overturned" a skyscraper (to use the engineer's tidy-sounding term), and building codes with built-in safety margins make that extremely unlikely in the future. Although high winds have occasionally popped out windows, high rises now routinely use flexible panes with high-strength gaskets that can easily take the punishment. The real wind problem isn't structural failure—it's seasickness on the upper floors. LeMessurier compares a very tall, very narrow building to a flycaster's fishing rod. "I can whip it all around, and it doesn't break," he says, "but you wouldn't want to be sitting on the end of it."

Hancock Building Havoc

When the narrow, lightweight John Hancock insurance building in Boston, Massachusetts, was completed in the early 1970s, the top of the 790-foot (240-meter) tower began shimmying more than a foot whenever strong winds whistled through Copley Square. On the upper

© Ron Benvensti/Magnum

Wind-generated oscillations shattered the windows of the 60-story John Hancock Tower in Boston. Engineers solved the problem by using different windowpane assemblies and installing devices called tuned mass dampers that reduce the natural sway of skyscrapers.

floors, doors opened and closed by themselves, and water sloshed in the toilet bowls. Architect Henry Cobb of the I. M. Pei firm called in LeMessurier to remedy the situation. Rather than simply recommending that the building be stiffened with a few thousand extra tons of steel, LeMessurier chose an arrangement that he was already planning for Citicorp: a tuned mass damper. Boston's Hancock Tower now has two of these devices at opposite ends of its 58th floor. The business part of each is a tray 17 feet (5.1 meters) square and 4 feet (1.2 meters) deep, resting on a thin sheet of oil and guided by a track. Inside the trays are lead ingots, stacked to the brim. BB shot fills the cracks. Each tray weighs 600,000 pounds (272,000 kilograms), slightly more than a fully loaded DC-10.

The purpose of the dampers is simple. Like a tuning fork, a tall building in a strong wind tends to sway back and forth in a set period of time, regardless of the wind's force. The Hancock's back-and-forth wobble takes seven sec-

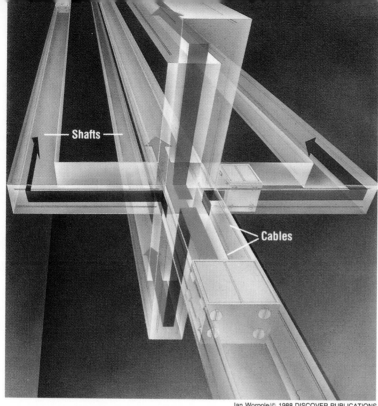

Shafts

Cables

Efficient and sufficient vertical transportation poses one of the greatest challenges to skyscraper builders. Engineers have designed forking shafts and cables that let elevators move in two axes.

onds. When the building starts to move, sensors detect the motion and pump oil under the trays. Aided by enormous electric motors, the dampers slide in a direction opposite to the one in which the building is moving. This motion disrupts the building's natural rhythm, like a child on a swing who pumps at the wrong times and soon stops swinging. In a storm straight from Hell—say, with sustained winds of more than 100 miles (160 kilometers) per hour—the dampers are capable of sliding back and forth nearly 7 feet (2 meters), though a mere 4 feet (1.2 meters) is the record so far. With the dampers the building barely budges at all.

Stop the Sway

It is not height alone that causes a building to sway; it is the ratio of height to width. Indeed, Chicago architect Harry Weese explains that the narrow base of many modern high rises can present more of a challenge than sheer height does. "Sliver" buildings—residential towers squeezed onto tiny lots—can sway as much as supertall buildings do.

Weese, who once submitted a plan for a low-rise, earthquake-resistant library that would float on a pond, has every reason to learn as much as he can about how to keep buildings stationary: displayed in his office atrium is a model of another would-be world's tallest building, one that would soar several hundred feet past the Erewhon Center. To make the structure stand, Weese and structural engineer Charles Thornton refined the idea of a guyed tower. Like a radio tower held steady by taut steel cables leading to the ground, Weese and Thornton's tapered building would have heavy diagonal columns under its skin, stretching from the corners of the roof to anchorages deep underground. In a high wind, the diagonals on the windward side would go into tension: instead of holding the building up, they would be holding it down.

Weese designed the building as a stack of seven 30-story modules. One variation called for two-story openings between the sections that would let the wind swirl through and help prevent oscillations. To cut down on the monolith's monthly electric bills, Weese even toyed with the idea of placing windmills in the openings.

During a wind-tunnel test, the tip of a 5-foot (1.5-meter) model of the tower (without the holes) began to oscillate ferociously. In the full-size version, the motion would have been 50-foot (15-meter) round-trips three times a minute; the building would stay intact, but only a test pilot would be able to hold down his lunch. Thornton decided to try something different. He

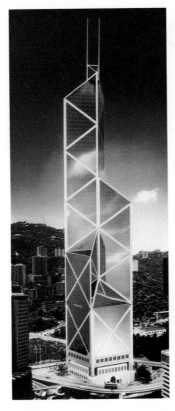

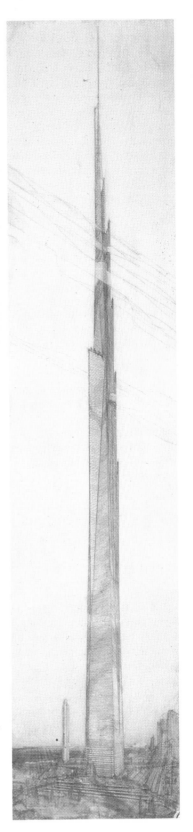

Frank Lloyd Wright's mile-high skyscraper (right) and Harry Weese's 210-story spire (center) remain unbuilt. I.M. Pei's 70-story Bank of China (model at left), under construction in Hong Kong, will be Asia's tallest building.

added a makeshift damper to the model: a 6-inch (15-centimeter) rubber tube in the middle of one of the upper stories, protruding through floors and ceilings above for three levels. Stuck on the rubber tube was an adjustable metal nut, for tuning. The rubber damper would wiggle back and forth, out of phase with the building's natural period. Back in the wind tunnel, the model hardly moved.

Thornton has worked out a variation on the idea: a lead pendulum inside the building that would swing in response to the building's motion. The pendulum needed to stabilize a 210-story office building would be considerably bigger than the 6-inch (15-centimeter) model Thornton first built. "A 200-foot (61-meter) pendulum weighing about 2,000 tons (1,800 metric tons) ought to do it," he says. This is still far lighter than the extra steel beams and columns traditionally used to stiffen a structure.

Other techniques for making lightweight skyscrapers stand still are less dramatic but equally clever. The tallest skyscrapers now being designed are structurally much closer to lightweight metal bridges than to old-fashioned brick buildings. Skidmore, Owings & Merrill's John Hancock Center in Chicago, the sixth-tallest building in the world at the moment, is a good example. Like a suspension bridge or a railroad trestle, the 1,127-foot (344-meter) tower doesn't try to conceal its load-bearing system. A set of steel X braces crisscross the building's outer walls like sheet-metal bands holding together a shipping carton—"expressed structure," the architects call it.

Another example of expressed structure is I. M. Pei's Bank of China building, now under construction in Hong Kong. Asia's tallest building will be an enormous network of steel diagonals and pyramids resembling an oversize section of an airplane-hangar roof. No one can honestly label either of these buildings beautiful, but in the age of supertall, it is the dictates of the engineer, not the aesthetic urges of the artist-architect, that take precedence.

Vertical Transportation

Perhaps more problematic than designing the shells of supertall buildings is designing their innards. A building is useless if its occupants can't work, live, or move about comfortably. One of the thorniest challenges is coming up with what engineers call vertical transportation. Engineer William Lewis has designed elevator systems for some of the world's tallest buildings. His office at Jaros, Baum & Bolles, on Park Avenue in New York, is located, strangely enough, in a windowless subbasement.

"In conventional elevatoring, all rides originate at street level," Lewis says, "so the bottom of the building is filled with elevator shafts." In effect, the building is a pyramid of rentable space surrounding a pyramid of unrentable space. Above a certain height, the building would actually lose office space with each additional floor because of the need for additional shafts. Developers who skimp on shaft space end up with fuming tenants who spend their time waiting for elevators. "But," says Lewis, "you can get rid of all those shafts running through the lower part of the building by putting in sky lobbies."

A sky lobby is to vertical transportation what an express subway stop is to horizontal transportation. People might catch an express elevator to a sky lobby at the 40th floor, the 80th, or the 120th, for example, then take a local to their destination. As a result, a single local shaft can accommodate several cars at different heights, and that leaves more room for offices. The Sears Tower, for example, has 87 elevators but only 40 shafts.

As for speed, physical comfort limits how fast elevators can move. Today's fastest average only 20 miles (32 kilometers) per hour. Even then, the starts and stops make some passengers dizzy. An eventual reduction in the time needed to get to a lofty destination may come not from faster-moving cars but instead from computer-controlled switching. If an elevator were an independent vehicle instead of a cage hung on a cable (as all elevators today are), and if it contained the appropriate sensing and logic system, it could switch horizontally to unused shafts as needed, like a train on a siding. But engineers agree that the technology this requires is still a long way off.

Other elevator problems, however, can be solved today. One of the quirkiest characteristics of very tall buildings is something called the stack effect. This is the tendency of a large building to act like a smokestack on a cold day: as warm air leaks out the top, cold air rushes into the lobby at the bottom. An unbroken top-to-bottom elevator shaft can turn into a screaming wind tunnel. On a recent afternoon at the Sears Tower, the wind racing through the elevator doors on the observation deck sounded like the wailing of banshees.

Accommodating Enormity

But elevators and wind management are not the only elements that make supertall buildings radically different from their more modest predecessors. Other mechanical systems—plumbing, heating, ventilation, power—all must be changed to accommodate enormity. Simply installing stretched-out versions of the same old systems would never do. A toilet flushed on the 150th floor would put the wastewater into free-fall for a third of a mile (0.5 kilometer), a situation that would tax the gaskets and fittings of a submarine. Similarly, the chilled-water pipes for a single, roof-to-ground air-conditioning system in a 150-story building would be gargantuan. The pipes that bring Hudson River water into the cooling system of New York's World Trade Center are already 5 feet (1.5 meters) wide, close to the limit of practicality—especially if there's not a major river out back.

To make things manageable, new skyscrapers are likely to be broken up into mechanically independent chunks. As with the sky-lobby system for elevators, a 150-story building might be a stack of three 50-story sections, each with its own heating and ventilation system, its own air-conditioning plant, and its own holding tanks for tap water. In the future, cities might demand that a supertall building with a population of 25,000 come equipped with its own internal waste-treatment plant, thus sparing the local infrastructure from sewer-line Armageddon. Separate power plants for each section are a distant fantasy, but some engineers suggest that high-voltage power transmission inside the building could hold down the size of copper cables, as is done with high-tension power lines. Some even envision chilled wiring for superconductive electric transmission.

There is less high-flying fantasizing when it comes to safety—specifically, what to do when a supertall building catches fire. The current wisdom, albeit inelegant, is probably the best: contain it. Evacuating the building is no longer a practical solution when a skyscraper encloses as much acreage as 83 football fields, as does the Sears Tower. Instead, occupants of burning areas first evacuate just the affected floors. Then fans blow air into the stories above and below the fire, slightly pressurizing them and the staircases to keep the smoke from spreading. Sears Tower manager Philip Chinn recalls that the movie *The Towering Inferno* was released not long after the building opened: ''I spent a lot of time that year explaining how sprinklers work.''

Although not all the problems associated with designing supertall buildings have the same life-and-death implications, all require the same inventiveness. In his New York office, architect Robert Sobel of Emery Roth and Sons has a model of a 500-story building with a triangular base that would stretch for four blocks on a side. Houston engineer Joseph Colaco has designed a 1-mile (1.6-kilometer)-high tower made entirely of concrete. Other designers snort at this escalating game of show-and-tell as mere publicity seeking, even as they ready blueprints for their own two-mile-high designs.

Big Shadows

For many of those on the ground, the game is a disturbing one. Citizens' groups around the country are leading efforts to block approval of new skyscrapers, citing worries about gigantic shadows, doomed residential neighborhoods, and ungodly traffic congestion. Making the up-

AP/Wide World

Firefighter's nightmare: one person perished when a Los Angeles skyscraper caught fire in 1988; many more might have died if the blaze occurred during business hours. In new skyscrapers, fans pressurize stories above and below the fire to keep flames and smoke from spreading.

ward surge all the more frightful to critics is the skyscrapers' essential permanence. Says architect Richard Roth of Emery Roth and Sons: ''Skyscrapers don't have life spans. When they're torn down, it's either because they haven't been maintained or because they no longer bring in enough rent for the site.''

Despite all these problems, LeMessurier is sure of one thing: people simply like to be way up high. He hasn't made a model of his tallest dream building yet, but he has a vivid picture of it in his mind's eye: ''It would be a hollow tube with people living like cliff dwellers around the outside. Don't bother putting floors across the inside—just leave it hollow. It's the space around the edge that's most valuable. That's where the light is, and the views. It could be 800 feet [224 meters] in diameter,'' he says in a conspiratorial whisper, ''and 8,000 feet [2,440 meters] high.'' He muses for a moment. ''Of course, it would cast a bloody big shadow.''

STEALTH TECHNOLOGY

by Tom Heppenheimer

The Air Force's stealth bombers and fighters may not show up on radar screens, but they are becoming visible on the nation's TV screens. Early in November 1988, the Pentagon released the first photo of the stealth fighter, a project so secret its very name had never been disclosed. Later that month, for the first time, the Air Force put its new stealth bomber on public display, allowing journalists to view it from a distance. Meanwhile, the stealthiest weapon of all—the submarine—has recently become quieter than ever, and more difficult to detect.

Stealth aircraft got their start during the 1970s, with the realization that advances in airplane design were bringing in features that had the unintended side effect of making aircraft harder to detect. For instance, engineers were increasingly interested in building future aircraft from composites—high-tech materials resembling fiberglass. These offered strength and light weight. In addition, they tended to absorb radar waves or let them pass on through, rather than reflecting them back to a receiver. A plane built of composites thus could be not only lighter but stealthier.

The Air Force set out to push the trend as far as possible, seeking to build planes that were nearly invisible to radar except at close range, and hard to detect with other techniques—such as heat-sensing infrared detectors—as well. In particular, the stealth designers tried to avoid right-angled corners—such as those formed where wings meet a fuselage or where tail surfaces join together in a conventional design—because such corners reflect radar signals particularly well. As it happens, trends in aircraft design have favored "blending," smoothing the transition from wings to fuselage. Blended shapes have less drag; they also have less of a radar reflection.

The ultimate in blending is the flying wing, which dispenses almost entirely with both fuselage and tail surfaces. This is the shape of the stealth bomber, the B-2.

A Flying Wing Reborn

Flying wings have long tantalized designers, but have had their problems. They can carry enormous loads, because they dispense with the weight of the tail and fuselage. But they have had a tendency to go out of control and crash.

The stealth bomber's composite construction and sleek, rounded edges help it elude detection by radar.

Flying-wing aircraft have also demanded thick wings, to provide room for engines and other equipment; and such wings produce high drag and slow speeds. Both of these problems have been solved, however. Improved autopilots—flying by computer—react quickly to a plane's motion and thus stabilize its flight. And "supercritical airfoils," an invention of the National Aeronautics and Space Administration (NASA), offer thick wings with low drag, capable of high speed. Taken together, these advances make the flying wing a practical airplane.

Engines, too, have been made stealthy. The compressor blades at the front of a jet engine are superb radar reflectors; some fighters carry radar that can actually count the number of blades and hence identify the type of engine and the aircraft. Moreover, engine exhausts have traditionally been quite hot, emitting intense infrared signals that can be readily detected by advanced sensors.

To overcome these problems, stealth aircraft bury their engines deep within the aircraft and bring air to the engines via a twisting duct. This design hides the compressor—a potential source of radar echoes—from incoming radar signals. Modern jet engines are turbofans, which mix a cooling stream of air into the exhaust to increase fuel efficiency, but which also reduce the infrared emissions. Stealth aircraft carry this development further, mixing extra air into the exhaust for still more cooling, and spreading the exhaust into a thin sheet that is not concentrated enough for infrared detectors to see.

Radar-absorbing coatings and materials on the body of the planes appear to intensify the stealth effect. In radar test chambers, for example, walls designed to get rid of all stray radar beams are fitted with closely spaced cones of radar-absorbing material; the radar waves are trapped in the spaces between the cones and not reflected. Similar cones or wedges, with radar-transparent material such as fiberglass within the gaps, can form the leading edge of a wing, making it hard to detect by radar stations ahead of the plane's path.

Rubberized Coatings Absorb Radar

Radar-absorptive coatings are full of iron particles that pick up the beam's electromagnetic energy and convert it to heat. The coatings themselves are believed to be dense, rubberized materials somewhat like linoleum floor coverings. Even a thin coating can absorb high-frequency radar waves of the type generated by the small radar carried by fighter planes and missiles.

All these features appear to be part of the B-2. The newly disclosed stealth fighter, the F-117A, adds two more. Its tail surfaces meet at a sharp angle, avoiding right-angled corners that would reflect a radar beam back in the direction it came from. Also, its skin is formed from panels that meet in ridges, rather than being smoothly curved. This design makes the F-117A the counterpart for radar of a glitter ball at a disco. Its panels break up a radar beam into numerous reflected beamlets aimed in a variety of directions, so that a radar receiver cannot pick up a strong signal.

The composite materials that form this skin are highly secret. In July 1986, when one of

HOW THE STEALTH BOMBER EVADES RADAR

A. CONTROL SURFACES

Spoilers

Flaps

Elevons

B. ENGINE AIRFLOW

Radar-absorbent liner

Turbine compressor

Air intake

Boundary-layer gutter

S-duct

Exhaust mixer

Exhaust diffuser

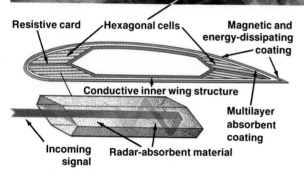

C. RADAR ABSORPTION

Resistive card

Hexagonal cells

Magnetic and energy-dissipating coating

Conductive inner wing structure

Multilayer absorbent coating

Incoming signal

Radar-absorbent material

In the official Air Force painting of the stealth bomber, the boomerang-shaped plane has a sawtooth trailing edge and three raised pods on the wing (two for engines, one for crew and weapons). Elevons (A) provide directional control. Air flows through intakes (B) and into a radar-proof duct where the compressor—a potential source of radar echoes—lies hidden. A diffuser flattens exhaust into a plume invisible to infrared sensors. The wing (C), covered with a multilayered material and edged with hexagonal honeycomb tubes, effectively absorbs radar. Unlike a contoured surface, the faceted surface of the wing pods (D) deflects radar signals away from their source. The stealth bomber might be detected by bistatic radar (E), in which signals from a ground or satellite transmitter bounce off the target and are received by a separate ground station.

these fighters crashed near Bakersfield, California, the Air Force immediately sealed off the area and imposed the strictest security, lest souvenir hunters carry off any pieces. And if this special composite skin suffers even slight damage, it cannot simply be patched like aluminum. Instead, an entire damaged panel must be cut loose and a new one glued into place using epoxy adhesives.

Through such means, the B-2 and F-117A appear to attain high levels of radar invisibility, without compromising their qualities as flying machines. Air Force officials have said that no existing air-defense system can be sure of detecting these planes at great enough distances to intercept or shoot them down. The cost of inte-

grating many stealth technologies into an operational warplane, however, is apparently high: estimated costs for the B-2 range from $400 million to $600 million per plane.

Even Stealthier—Submarines

Stealth is a relatively new idea for airplanes, but it has long been the essence of submarine strategy. Even in World War II, when subs could not stay submerged for long and were nearly as noisy as a clanking merchant ship, they were called "the silent service." In part that is because the ocean is far more opaque—and is noisier—than the atmosphere.

Searching for subs is done mostly by listening, using devices known as hydrophones to

D. FACETS

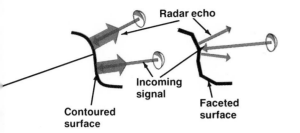

Radar echo

Incoming signal

Contoured surface

Faceted surface

E. BISTATIC RADAR

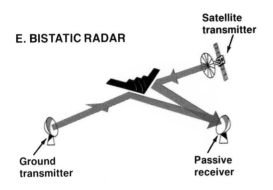

Satellite transmitter

Ground transmitter

Passive receiver

pick out the noise they make, amid the constant sounds of a very noisy ocean. Stealth under the ocean thus calls for noiseless operation.

Most of a submarine's noise comes from propulsion machinery, which in old-style subs amounts to a powerful sound generator coupled directly to a steel drumhead, the sub's hull. Beginning in the mid-1960s, the U.S. Navy mounted the gears, turbines, condensers, and turbogenerators on a ''bedplate,'' a steel foundation that is separated from the hull by sound-absorbing material.

Such noise-isolating mountings add weight to a sub and take up more room. Their effectiveness, however, was dramatically demonstrated in a 1984 incident involving a quiet Soviet attack sub, which appears to use a bedplate. Long-range sonar arrays detected the sub in a large area of ocean off the coast of South Carolina. This triggered an intensive and initially unsuccessful hunt. A ship towing a string of hydrophones very near the Soviet sub failed to detect it; but the towing cable for the hydrophones became tangled in the sub's propeller, forcing it to surface.

Propellers are another major source of noise. Their rapidly rotating blades produce zones of low pressure in which seawater vaporizes, forming bubbles that collapse in loud ''pops.'' Large propellers that rotate slowly avoid the phenomenon, but are harder to fabricate without computerized milling machines.

The importance of large propellers—and the machines that make them—became clear in a scandal involving the Japanese firm of Toshiba, which had falsified records to obtain export licenses so as to send advanced milling machines to the Soviets. The incident came to light when a U.S. Navy sub followed a characteristically noisy Soviet sub to its home port. ''A few months later,'' reported the *Washington Post,* ''the Soviet sub returned to the open sea quietly, thanks to the installation'' of this quiet propeller.

Still quieter propulsion systems are found in the missile-carrying Trident nuclear subs. These vessels use a nuclear reactor designed to eliminate another source of noise: the pumps that circulate water to carry away the reactor's heat. Pumps are rather noisy and cannot be acoustically insulated from the hull. So the Trident reactors don't use pumps. Instead, they use the buoyancy of heated water, which rises naturally and displaces the cooler water that has given up its heat. Circulating the cooling water through natural convection is very silent, but requires a reactor design that is heavy and very bulky. As a result of these and other quieting techniques, Trident subs cannot accelerate quickly, and they weigh more than World War II aircraft carriers. But they are so quiet that they reputedly could pass within 1,000 yards (900 meters) of another sub and not be detected, even with sensitive listening instruments.

Attack subs need to move quickly and cannot use pumpless reactors. But the newest attack subs apparently reduce propeller noise even further by placing the propeller within a tunnellike duct. There the propeller directs the water it pushes against a set of vanes that straighten out the flow and prevent it from swirling to form a turbulent and noise-producing wake.

Fewer, More Expensive Weapons

How effective is all this stealthiness, both beneath the sea and in the air? Evidently the Navy has confidence in its quiet subs: it has been buying fewer but larger and costlier submarines, putting its eggs into fewer baskets. The Air Force, for its part, hopes to buy 132 B-2 stealth bombers, which—in combination with its 98 B-1B planes—will replace a bomber force that 25 years ago numbered 1,526. Stealth apparently figures strongly in future military strategies.

Untangling Traffic's Troubled Future

by Glenn Emery

Technology to untie tie-ups: a traffic-flow display map in Los Angeles pinpoints congestion. Transportation officials can help unclog the jam electronically by adjusting the timing of stoplights on freeway on-ramps.

The facts are grim: the bridges and highways are being beaten to death. Billions of dollars in time, productivity, and fuel are squandered each year in traffic jams. Pollution is threatening to alter the atmosphere irreversibly. In the United States, nearly 50,000 people a year die in crashes; countless others are crippled and maimed. One would think the average motorist would be panicked.

On the contrary, more people are driving more cars more places more often. The explana-

tion is simple. With apologies to Winston Churchill, the automobile is the worst form of transport in the world—except for all the others. All its attendant problems are simply the price humans are willing to pay for flexible mobility.

In 1901, when the automobile was in its infancy, and the dominant mode of personal travel was the horse-drawn carriage, the Mercedes-Benz Company predicted that the worldwide market for automobiles would be 1 million—tops. That was reached within 15 years;

today there are more than 400 million automobiles throughout the world.

Common sense dictates that the auto will dominate transportation for at least a while longer. "The four-wheeled vehicle has been around for over 5,000 years," says Howard Ross, a consultant to the Program on Advanced Technology for the Highway in California. "The automobile is simply the most recent manifestation."

Gridlock in the Offing?

Already there are more than 180 million registered automobiles (about 75 percent of the total), trucks, and buses in the United States, and the number is increasing. In fact, since 1986 there have been more registered vehicles in the United States than licensed drivers—about 1.1 vehicles for every driver. (Or, put another way, less than one driver per vehicle. "I always say maybe that's why we have so many traffic problems," quips Francis B. Francois, executive director of the American Association of State Highway and Transportation Officials.)

With only a finite amount of road space, the prospect of doubling the number of cars and trucks over the next 30 years is giving transportation planners nightmares. "If we continue to add vehicles at the rate we have been, by the year 2020 we'll have at least twice [as many vehicle-miles traveled, a projected 2 trillion this year], and at least twice as many vehicles on the road as we do now. Obviously, something will have to be done, because this means gridlock in many urban areas," says Francois, whose organization in early 1987 began Transportation 2020, a program to assess the nation's transport needs into the next century. "One of the big problems with the American highway system is the average occupancy of our vehicles is about 1.2 to 1.3 people, and dropping slightly. If we could get it up to 2.0, most of our problems would vanish."

For years the prevailing logic to solve congestion has been two-pronged: build new highways, but discourage people from using them. The flaw in the logic is obvious. Nature abhors a vacuum; by the same token, automobiles abhor an empty highway.

Thinking is starting to flow the other way: build fewer highways and maximize the potential of existing ones. "No society can afford to build enough highways so there's no congestion at the peak hour," says Ed Weiner, a Transportation Department senior policy analyst. "For a 10-week period each summer, everyone wants to go to the beach on Friday night and come home on Sunday night. That's a lot of money to spend to make sure that people for two days a week for 10 weeks don't have to worry about congestion."

Besides, the economic history of the world shows that where the roads go, development follows. Development begets traffic, and traffic begets congestion. New roads can be built and old ones expanded, but they, too, eventually become congested. It is a natural phenomenon in a growing economy.

Accidents create many traffic jams. Huge mobile cranes can clear even the most sizable objects from the roadway.

Electronic innovations destined for the family car include a computerized navigation system whose dashboard video screen (top) warns of upcoming road conditions and terrain, and a collision-avoidance device (above), which uses radar to analyze oncoming vehicles.

Highway Automation

Managing the traffic flow has always been a major part of the overall strategy, but with the era of interstate highway construction winding down and the future of the nation's highway program up in the air, the issue in recent years has assumed a new urgency. Proposals from the mundane to the fantastic are on the table in the United States, Europe, and Japan.

In Los Angeles, sensors are being installed in the roadways to spot bottlenecks and adjust traffic lights accordingly. New York City has found that keeping delivery trucks off the streets during peak hours and towing illegally parked

cars has helped significantly. In Norway the world's first fully automatic tollgates, called Premid, use electronic scanners and special identity plates on vehicles to allow drivers to pay tolls without slowing down.

But the most ambitious and revolutionary concept is to automate the highways, removing from the driver control over the vehicle. The rationale is not merely technology for its own sake. "We all know that when the freeway system is working, it works pretty darn good. But it's subject to perturbation," says Lyle G. Saxton, chief of the Federal Highway Administration's Traffic Systems Division.

"You drive into the west with the sun in your eyes, and everybody drops 10 to 15 miles [16 to 24 kilometers] per hour. There's a very minor incident off to the side of the road, and everybody is slowing down to watch. You've got the disparity in driver performance: the little-old-lady syndrome versus the guy who thinks he's Juan Fangio," a 1950s champion race driver. "You've got the fact that when the weather deteriorates slightly, you get this wide disparity of speeds. Even when you don't have an accident or something in the lane itself, you still have all these problems, and your whole freeway flow goes down the tubes."

And when there is an accident, like a recent series of fiery truck crashes on the Washington Beltway, the overburdened system collapses. "All of our problems on the highway are caused by driver failures," says Ross. "The mistakes that are made are due to the fact that one in 10 drivers is drunk or on drugs, and that a fairly large percentage shouldn't drive at all because their judgment and reflexes are bad."

In theory, vehicles under the control of a computerized guidance system would not need as much headway between other vehicles on the roadway, thereby dramatically increasing the highway's capacity. Says Saxton: "Instead of talking about 2,000 vehicles per hour per lane, which is the accepted maximum you can get under reasonably stable flow [50 to 55 miles (80 to 88 kilometers) per hour] and good weather, people conjecture that you could get 2,400 to 3,000—perhaps under some conditions up to 3,600—vehicles per lane per hour, reliably and safely under automated flow conditions. The reason is, you're putting in constant headways and constant speeds and not getting all the variations that upset traffic flow."

Developers of the automated highway say it is a logical evolution of the lanes for high-occupancy vehicles in place around the country. And a new generation of ''smart'' vehicles, now under development, is the necessary counterpart. ''Where the auto industry seems to be going is at electric power steering, computer-controlled transmissions and speed control, and so forth,'' says Saxton. ''So with a few sensors in the road to interface with those systems that already exist in the car, you essentially can automate it.''

Drivers Out of Control?

The practical problem in such an approach is the disparity in performance from one automobile to the next, even among identical makes and models. Instead of speeding up and slowing down in unison (while maintaining headways of perhaps less than 2 feet [0.5 meter]), vehicles would quickly get out of sync, creating the so-called ''Slinky'' effect—a line of cars alternately spreading out and bunching up whenever the speed changes.

Besides the practical problem, there is also a powerful sociological barrier that could be impossible to overcome: drivers may obdurately resist anything that takes control of their vehicles away from them.

''If you think about how society presses in on people and the stress and intensity and competition at work or at school or even when you go to recreate—there are lines to get into all the national parks, parking at the beach is a pain in the butt, and that sort of thing—the only time you're totally alone anymore, the only space individuals control by themselves anymore, is the space within their car,'' says Richard Katz, chairman of the California Assembly's Transportation Committee.

''You can sing without anyone telling you you're a lousy singer; you can scream at the umpire; you can listen to whatever weird sounds you want, and nobody can tell you to turn it off; you can control who comes into your space. If you want passengers in your car, you agree to it

Using computer models, highway engineers can design streamlined expressways that handle four times as much traffic volume as the older highways. Although still incomplete, Atlanta's ''Spaghetti Junction'' (right) has all but eliminated traffic congestion in the city's northern suburbs.

Decaying infrastructure? Several fatal bridge collapses have graphically dramatized the need for better maintenance of the U.S. interstate highway system.

California's $56 million advanced highway technology program has other projects under way besides automation of the roadways. The Santa Barbara Electric Bus project is designed to show how a battery-powered vehicle, which in the past was burdened with many heavy power cells, can absorb energy inductively from electric cables buried in the road, enabling it to run all day without recharging. Such a system, if it proved economically viable for use on interstate highways, could enable an electric vehicle to go coast-to-coast nonstop.

Advanced Navigation

Obviously, widespread application of such vehicles and highways is years away. Much more immediate is the possibility of advanced navigation systems—really an old idea brought up-to-date. Just as the citizens band (CB) radio craze of the 1970s brought instantaneous traffic information to millions of drivers, and frequent rush-hour traffic reports are common fare in urban radio markets, the envisioned system would link the automobile directly to a vast network of computerized sensors throughout a metropolitan area and guide the driver along the optimum route.

"The Europeans have got Project Prometheus, in which most of the major European automobile manufacturers and government transportation departments have contributed money to try to develop hardware for this kind of process," says Weiner. "You need monitoring devices for traffic flow; you need communication devices to get this information from the monitoring devices to some central computer and from the central computer to the drivers. So they've been spending a lot of money developing this hardware."

The California project is testing a navigation system along a 12-mile (19-kilometer) stretch of the Santa Monica Freeway in Los Angeles, using 25 specially equipped cars with access to traffic information from sensors along the corridor. Over the testing period, 500 drivers will try the system for one week each.

It is easy to imagine such a system being extremely useful, but there is also the possibility that it would become self-defeating, just like CB radios when they became too widespread to give anyone a leg up. A system that provides instantaneous traffic information to everyone is going to be of the most benefit only to the drivers that get to the alternate route first. But at least traffic will be more spread out.

or they don't come in. You are in total control and total mastery of that space, and that's the only place that happens today."

The most likely first candidate for passenger travel on an automated highway is a small bus, according to Ross. "An automated vehicle like that could go anywhere, pick up at their doors, get out on the highway, and deliver them to multiple destinations. This is a door-to-door public transit system. I think that could be very big."

The reasons for the current and projected traffic congestion have been well documented. Both Transportation 2020's preliminary report, ''Beyond Gridlock,'' and the Eno Foundation for Transportation's ''Commuting in America'' detail the problem: the population bulge of baby boomers, who are now in their prime working years, and the dramatic rise of women in the work force account for the unprecedented crush of commuters filling the highways each day. In addition, there is a burgeoning of suburban development.

While this has definitely put a strain on existing facilities and heightened the call for more roads and transit systems, the problem, though serious, may not justify all the alarmist rhetoric. ''We're going up the hill now, but somewhere in 2010 or around there, things should flatten out,'' says Weiner. ''We're in sort of this catch-up period now, trying to patch the potholes at the same time we're trying to expand facilities. We're just getting hit with it all at once, but it's not a never-ending problem. I think we're just in a bad part of the curve.''

Decaying Interstates

A much more vexing problem is the infrastructure itself. Much of it is decaying, and basic rehabilitation—never mind automated highways—promises to be very expensive. ''The

level of investment in the nation's 3.85 million miles (6.2 million kilometers) of streets, roads, and highways in 1987 was about $66 billion,'' says Francois. ''At a minimum, it should be in the $80 billion level, just to hold our own. And if you try to solve some of these congestion problems, the $100 billion level is about where we think we have to be.''

The interstate highway system, perhaps the most advanced mass-transit system in the world and the backbone of ground transportation in the United States, is scheduled for completion in the early 1990s, at an estimated total cost (since 1956) of $122 billion—an average of roughly $2.8 million per mile—90 percent of it federally financed using a pay-as-you-go system. The present highway bill, which contains the final $1.4 billion in federal aid to construct the last connecting links of the nearly 43,000-mile (69,000-kilometer) network, expires in 1991. (The interstates represent slightly more than 1 percent of the nation's streets and roads, but carry about 20 percent of the traffic.)

Americans got their first glimpse of the interstate at the 1939 World's Fair in New York, where a model of a modern highway—complete with cloverleafs, median, shoulders, and overpasses—seemed too fantastic to believe. But the country quickly bought into the idea of driving coast-to-coast without traffic lights.

With highway construction winding down, drivers will find fewer new roads to accommodate a greater traffic volume.

"There's one key player in the whole thing, and that's Dwight David Eisenhower," says Francois. "In the mid-1920s, Eisenhower was in charge of a military convoy that set as its goal getting from the East Coast to the West Coast. It was quite an undertaking. He didn't enjoy it too much."

As a general in Europe during World War II, Eisenhower observed Hitler's ability to move men and equipment from one part of Germany to another over a modern highway system. So in the mid-1950s, when the concept of such a highway was being discussed in the United States, Eisenhower immediately saw the military value of it. In fact, the proper name of the system is the National System of Interstate and Defense Highways: the standard 15-foot (4.5-meter) clearance of bridges and overpasses was designed to accommodate the military equipment of the day. (The beltways, Francois says, were also products of the war experience: built several miles out from urban centers, the military believed such roads would survive the bombing of cities during a war, allowing troops and matériel to bypass the destruction. Modern weapons have rendered that concept obsolete.)

For more than 30 years, the interstate highway program has given federal and state transportation planners an object upon which to focus their collective energies. But what comes next? That was the principal reason the American Association of State Highway and Transportation Officials began the Transportation 2020 project, to help form over the next several years a national consensus on the future of American transportation. "There no longer is a central, unifying theme that brings urgency to a new highway bill," says Sunny Mays Schust, the organization's director of communications and publications. "It is the end of an era."

But even as the final miles of concrete are poured, it is obvious that many existing segments are aging and inadequate. Built to last 20 years, whole corridors are being ground to dust in half that time by heavy trucks and unprecedented numbers of cars.

Rep. Glenn M. Anderson, a Democrat from California and chairman of the Public Works and Transportation Committee, asserted in a recent position paper that "since 1975, the portion of our interstate system rated in a very good condition or better decreased from nearly one-half to less than one-third, and the total in fair or poor condition rose from 19 percent to 28 percent."

That does not begin to address the secondary roads, state highways, and interstate connectors. According to Transportation 2020's "Beyond Gridlock," "The Federal Highway Administration's 1986 report on the pavement condition by functional classification nationwide rates 218,087 miles (350,901 kilometers) of urban roadways. About 60 percent of that mileage—all urban principal arterials, freeways, major arterials, and connectors—are reported in fair or poor condition. Some 42 percent of the nation's total estimated 575,607 bridges are classified as structurally deficient or functionally obsolete."

Solutions and Skepticism

Already there is serious discussion of a new national program to build additional interstate-type highways, including bypasses to the bypasses, to replace those highways, especially beltways, that have been all but overwhelmed by commuter traffic. Whereas commuting to work was once almost exclusively a suburb-to-downtown trip, today the predominant commuting pattern is suburb-to-suburb. "In point of fact, those beltways . . . have become the new Main Streets of metropolitan areas," says Francois.

A number of innovations have been mentioned to deal with traffic, including spreading out the workday and staggering shifts, limiting truck travel to off-peak hours, and restricting the use of private automobiles within urban areas. But many look to the communications industry to relieve the congestion through "telecommuting." Rather than drive to a downtown office, the average worker in the 21st century may work primarily from home or neighborhood centers and "commute" by telephone.

Others are skeptical for the simple reason that upward mobility usually depends on face-to-face interaction. That translates into a continuing need for lateral mobility.

"What you can expect in 2020 is going to depend on some decisions that are going to be made in the next three years," says California Assemblyman Katz. "If, in the next three years, Californians get serious about solving transportation problems, then you'll see a lot of cars, but you'll see a system that functions. . . . If, on the other hand, people plod along like they are right now, 2020 in L.A. is going to be a massive gridlock, and you'll be able to walk where you're going on the rooftops of the cars that are all sitting in traffic."

Have Office, Will Travel

by Ellen Hoffman

Sandra Gill, an independent health-care consultant in Illinois, travels by plane four out of five days a week. While on the road, she keeps in constant touch with her clients and her office by phone and fax machine. She uses spare time on airplanes and in hotels to write speeches and papers on her portable typewriter. Her productivity "has zoomed," she says, since she began this system.

Andre Delbecq, dean of the School of Business Administration at Santa Clara University in California, uses his time on airplanes for reflection, not for writing. But when he drives 56 miles (90 kilometers) two or three times a week to San Francisco, he spends the time answering his correspondence. "When you're going eight miles an hour on a congested freeway, you can make very good use of a Dictaphone," he explains.

No More Imposed Downtime

In the old days, traveling business executives knew that they would be incommunicado for much of their trip. They might have to check in periodically, but their bosses didn't expect them to be available at all times. Nor could they be expected to return from a week of negotiations in Brussels or Tokyo with a contract or report fully written. One of the perks—or pitfalls, depending on your point of view—of business traveling was imposed downtime. Those days are gone forever.

During the past few years, technology and miniaturization have brought us portable

Airborne workplace: laptop computers, cellular telephones, and a host of other portable office equipment can transform virtually any location into a conference room.

Hotel "business centers" give traveling executives access to computers, fax machines, and secretarial services.

computers, long-distance beepers, tiny Dicta-
phones, compact photocopiers, and the ubiquitous telephone—now found in cars, planes,
trains, and your back pocket. The old line "I
couldn't find a phone" is no longer an excuse
for being out of touch. Whether you are taking a
shower in your hotel bathroom or en route to
your next destination, the phone need be only an
arm's length away.

More than 2,600 calls have been made
each week from Amtrak's Northeast Corridor
Metroliner trains since phones were installed on
that line in 1986. The Comtec Division of the
Gartner Group, an information consulting firm,
estimates that there are 1.1 million cellular
phones as well as 3.3 million portable computers in use in this country.

Those who find carrying their own compact computer too cumbersome can simply bor-
row one at one of the many "business centers"
that have sprung up in hotels and airports around
the country. The Wall Street Journal Business
Center at the New York Hilton offers personal
computers, as well as word processing, photocopying, fax machines, Dow Jones News/
Retrieval, a reference library, and 24-hour dic-
tation. Driven executives can dictate into a hotel
telephone at 3:00 A.M. and receive the typed
copy on their tray with coffee and the paper first
thing in the morning.

Executives traveling to New York City can
turn to the tony Rockefeller Center Club for the
antidote to office withdrawal. The club, which
manager Jane Fincke Ellis refers to as "the prototype for the business club of the future,"
offers everything from secretarial services to a
nine-screen "video wall" carrying CNN, Reu-
ters, C-Span, and the Financial News Network.
The club can also give you a conference room
complete with private elevator and phones
linked to a computer network.

The cellular phone has already transformed
hundreds of cars into mobile offices. An ultra-
deluxe limousine, offered by Dillinger/Gaines
Coachbuilders for $80,000, takes this concept a
few steps further. This office on wheels contains not one but two cellular phones, a fax
machine, rosewood writing desks to hold a portable computer, and a paper shredder.

Help or Hindrance?

In a new and perhaps more urgent form, these
developments raise the age-old questions about
the impact of technology: Does it help or hurt?
Does it make us more productive or more har-
ried? Do we control it, or does it run us? Are
high-tech tools turning managers into more isolated, independent, and self-sufficient workers?

In recent years, most research on this issue
has focused on lower-level workers threatened

by having their activities monitored by computers or even losing their jobs to technological replacements. But the explosion and availability of new products and services for business travelers—often overworked executives already sabotaged by jet lag—expose a new class of worker to high-tech stress.

For the executive who can pick and choose his portable, computerized tools and decide when to use them, the ever-present laptop or phone can be liberating. "There's probably no problem when the person using it is in charge," observes Michael J. Smith, professor of industrial engineering at the University of Wisconsin. His specialty is occupational stress.

As a world traveler who sometimes makes phone calls from an altitude of 30,000 feet or higher confirms, "I like knowing the telephone is there. I get uptight being 12 or 13 hours away and not in touch." Unfortunately for this traveler, airplane phones are subject to the vicissitudes of weather and other flight conditions. And down on the ground, Amtrak phones often lose the connection when the train goes through a tunnel.

High tech's negatives are more likely to affect mid-level managers who are forced to use these gadgets, says Daniel A. Araoz, a psychologist at Long Island University in Brookville, New York. "The fact that they can be reached at any time, by anybody, means that they have no privacy," he says. Araoz, who conducts a seminar in "executive effectiveness" for the American Management Association, says he sees executives "who feel obliged to use these things because competition is too fierce. The company expects them to be available."

Whether the impact of the new technology for travelers is positive or negative depends to some degree on the personality of the user. "People who are more insecure, have a poorer self-image, and who can't believe they've reached the heights they've reached in business" are most vulnerable to the negative impact of the travel-related technology, Araoz explains.

Gadget Freaks

On the other hand, those who are confident in their positions may even thrive on the opportunities new high-tech tools offer. Health consultant Gill, for example, is a self-diagnosed "gadget freak" who appreciates knowing that she can choose from a continually changing parade of time-saving products and services.

When New York investment banker Jeffrey E. Garten was living and working in Tokyo, Japan, he learned to "play the time zones" to the benefit of his work and his psyche. "I had a Dictaphone installed with a secretary in New

A fax machine converts printed matter into electronic signals that then travel through the telephone system to a fax machine at the other end of the line. The receiving machine reconverts the signals to the original images and prints them out on paper. The entire process occurs in seconds.

PHONING FROM A CELL

Only recently a novelty, cellular phones are fast becoming a "must" for salespeople and other business people on the go. Over a million cellular phones are now in use in the United States, a number that is expected to more than double by 1990.

Many are mobile phones, designed to operate from a car. The handset is attached by wire to a power pack installed in the trunk of the car and to a special phone antenna mounted on the car.

Gaining in popularity are portable cellular phones, which can be used at home, on the road, or even in a boat in the middle of a lake. They operate off a battery pack and require no installation. There is, however, a trade-off between size and weight on the one hand, and power and "talk time" on the other. The smaller the battery pack, the shorter the period of time a user can talk before having to change or recharge the battery.

A call from a cellular phone travels via radio waves to a nearby transmission site equipped with antenna, receiver, transmitter, and controller computer. The site is linked to a Mobile Telephone Switching Office (MTSO), which connects to the local phone company.

Each transmission site covers an area called a *cell*. A cell isn't very large; depending on geographical location, it generally averages some 4 to 20 miles (6 to 32 kilometers) in diameter. If a person moves from one cell to another while using the cellular phone, the MTSO switches transmission from one site to the next. Called a *handoff*, this takes but a fraction of a second and may occur several times, depending on how far the person travels during a conversation.

Like other telephones, many models and many features are available. Most cellular phones offer one-button dialing for frequently called numbers. Many have speakers that can be attached to the car visor, so that the user need only lift the handset briefly when placing or receiving a call. Some models are voice-activated; just tell the phone whom you want to call, and it will dial the number itself.

JENNY TESAR

© Jon Feingersh/The Stock Market

Business travelers maintain close contact with the home office using mobile communication devices.

York so that anytime I wanted to, I could pick up the phone and dictate. Since I was 13 hours ahead, I could just dictate all day (night back in New York). When I woke up in the morning, it was all back to me, sent by fax or telex."

"I suspect that the key personality variable is self-discipline," says James Campbell Quick, professor of organizational behavior at the University of Texas at Arlington. Quick theorizes that the executive who can say "no" as well as "yes" is likely to get more positive results from the new gadgetry. "We need to turn off often enough to rejuvenate ourselves," he says. "The risk in being able to work around the clock anywhere in the world is that you'll do just that," Quick says. "You may get a lot done, but you also may be dead sooner."

Even the once-sacred vacation can fall prey to the demands and interruptions of beepers, cellular phones, and overnight mail. Kerry Bunker, a psychologist who conducted research on occupational stress for AT&T before joining the Center for Creative Leadership in Greensboro,

North Carolina, has met people who tell him, ''I never get away from work. It always follows me. Even when I'm on vacation, I'm not on vacation.''

Technology Management

Businesses that want to protect the psychological well-being of their executives can learn to manage the latest communication technology to their benefit, according to Quick. ''At some time during travel time, it is necessary to program in relaxation,'' he says. In other words, give them the gadgets, but state clearly that management does not expect them to be used 24 hours a day.

Another strategy is to ''schedule things so that all the responsibility is not on one person's shoulders,'' adds Araoz. ''If the top figure in the company has three middle-management people to rely on, have a schedule so that one covers for another. Doctors do it. They can go away on vacation and their patients don't die.''

Smith counsels employers to respect individual differences when formulating policies and demands on communications or productivity. ''People have their own styles,'' he says. Companies should provide the users with ''some input and choice about what they feel they need. A very flexible policy benefits the corporation.''

As the availability of devices increases, so does the incidence of fitness centers in hotels and business centers, offering an opportunity to relieve or escape from the concerns of the office. ''I'd recommend that no person be allowed to bring a beeper'' into the exercise or locker room, Araoz says.

As surely as the power wrench can be a lifesaver or a killer for the assembly-line worker, the laptop or the long-distance beeper can be the salvation or the downfall of the globe-trotting manager. Unfortunately, many companies and individuals have not gotten that message. In the interest of getting it across, Quick proposes, with tongue slightly in cheek, that producers of ''these new devices should have a warning or caution that excess use can be dangerous to your health.''

Araoz adds his own warning: ''Technology is advancing so rapidly that if people are not careful, it may dehumanize the work force. . . . Then it will really be true that we are selling our lives and our souls to the company for which we work.''

GETTING THE FAX

Telephone calls are no longer limited to voice communications. Thanks to facsimile machines, many calls now are voiceless, used instead to send letters, diagrams, pictures, orders, and other images on paper. The phenomenon has even given birth to a new group of words. Facsimile machines generally are known as fax machines, the materials they send and receive are called faxes, and the process of sending something is called faxing.

A fax machine plugs into a standard electrical outlet and a telephone line. It can be placed on the same line as a telephone used for voice calls, but putting it on a separate line is more convenient.

The user places the letter or other printed matter to be copied in the machine, and dials the telephone number of the fax machine to which it is to be sent. Once the connection is made, a scanner in the fax machine converts the images on the paper to electrons. The electronic message travels through the telephone system to the fax machine at the other end of the line, which reconverts the image and prints it on paper. The entire process takes only a few seconds and is relatively inexpensive—big advantages over regular and even overnight mail.

Most fax machines have a G-3 protocol, which enables communication with other fax machines worldwide. Image quality will improve when people switch to the G-4 protocol, which requires digital phone lines, still rare in many places.

In addition to the basics, many fax machines offer such features as a built-in telephone answering machine, an auto-dialer for frequently called numbers, a photocopying option, an automatic document feeder, and a paper cutter. Some machines can be programmed to transmit at other times, perhaps late at night to take advantage of low nighttime phone rates.

Some fax machines are light enough to be portable. Powered by batteries, they can be used wherever there's a telephone. It's even possible to hook your fax machine to a cellular phone to transmit or receive documents from your car.

JENNY TESAR

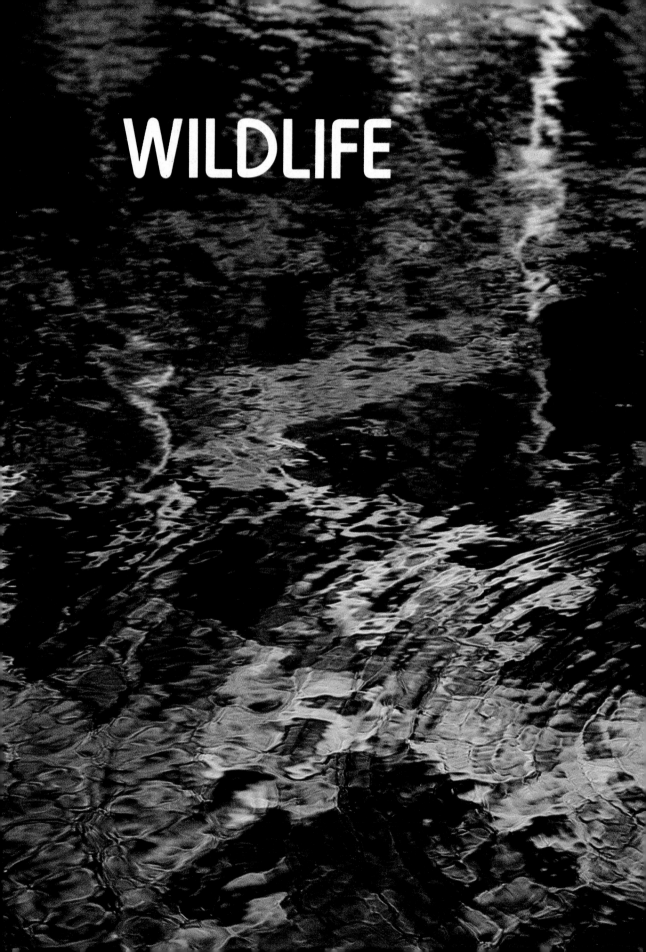

WILDLIFE

WILDLIFE

A dramatic whale rescue, a condor chick born in captivity, and the ramifications of a severe drought topped wildlife news in 1988. Concern continued to mount over endangered species and the condition of wildlife refuges.

by Bob Strohm

AP/Wide World

The California condor born in captivity in 1988 has grown into a healthy adolescent (top). Another condor was born in 1989. Florida held its first alligator hunt in years (above) to help control the creature's booming population.

Drought Disaster

The drought of 1988 wreaked havoc on wildlife. A dramatic population decline occurred among the ducks and geese that nest in the northern U.S. and Canada and migrate south for the winter. The arid spring and summer weather dried up about one-third of the usual 3 million rain-fed "prairie potholes" that several major duck species use for mating and nesting. Those potholes that remained were rapidly overcrowded, inhibiting the waterfowl from reproducing. Insufficient food in the secondary wetlands further compounded the problem. In the fall, ornithologists estimated that only 66 million ducks and geese made the southward migration—a drop of 8 million since 1987. Alarmed U.S. Fish and Wildlife Service officials restricted autumn hunting, and warned that another drought year might eliminate fall hunting altogether. Other migratory birds—including swans, whooping cranes, and plover—also depend on open ponds in the Midwest for survival. The extent to which the drought affected their population remains unclear.

Other wildlife suffered later from the consequences of the drought. A poor nut crop in the fall affected squirrels, chipmunks, deer, and turkeys. With fewer squirrels and chipmunks, fox populations declined for lack of prey. Hawks and owls found mice in short supply. Such ground-nesting birds as quail and pheasant lost the ground cover that hides them from predators. The lack of water even killed insects that songbirds depend on for food.

Endangered Species

The Fish and Wildlife Service announced that it had added 59 species to the list of endangered and threatened species—the second-highest number of additions ever in one year. Still, many conservationists claimed that the agency moved at a snail's pace in listing wildlife species in danger—in the case of the spotted owl, for instance. These critics concede that some species—including the American alligator, the red wolf, and the bald eagle—may have been rescued in the U.S. Nonetheless, several important species have died out since the Endangered Species Act was passed, notably the dusky seaside sparrow and the Palos Verde blue butterfly. Other celebrated species still hover on the brink of extinction, including the California condor. Critics complain that dozens of species have become extinct while awaiting formal listing, and hundreds more may have passed the point of no return.

At present there are 993 species on the list, 553 of which live only in foreign countries; about 1,000 species still await formal listing. When a species is added to the list, the government is then required to take action to foster its survival, and to make no moves to threaten it.

Habitat Restoration

Individuals and groups continue work on many fronts to restore lost or damaged habitats to their original state, and thereby encourage the revival of wildlife. One company, Environmental Concern, has created 200 marshes from Maine to Virginia by planting former wetlands with native plant species. In Costa Rica, Daniel Janzen is trying to re-create 150 square miles (389 square kilometers) of dry tropical forests. David Simpson and his neighbors in northern California have spent a decade rehabilitating a salmon stream. And in northern Illinois, Robert Betz is restoring 100 acres (41 hectares) a year of prairie by planting tall native grasses. After several seasons, Betz burns the prairie, thereby killing pesky invaders while allowing the deep-rooted native grasses to thrive.

Whale Rescue

In October 1988, three gray whales became trapped by ice near Barrow, Alaska. Two of the whales eventually escaped after a massive international rescue operation coordinated by the U.S. National Oceanic and Atmospheric Administration (NOAA). The third whale apparently died before a path through the ice was cleared. (See also p. 350.)

Neglected Refuges

Last year the ability of the National Wildlife Refuge System to support wildlife came under scrutiny. A Wilderness Society study showed that the entire refuge system has been neglected in the 1980s. Specific problems include: dams in poor condition; water projects that pollute refuges; damage from off-road vehicles; poisonous runoff from agriculture, mining, and oil drilling; and the effect of military aircraft on training flights. In some refuges even the water is too toxic for animals to drink. Concerned individuals use noisemakers to keep the wildlife from the polluted water. The report included a list of the ten "most endangered" of the 445 wildlife refuges that make up the national system.

Reintroductions to the Wild

Human intercession into wildlife survival saw some success in 1988. California condors continued to hold on—albeit in captivity—with 30 individuals, including two chicks born in captivity, the latest in April 1989. Zoologists need a more viable population before reintroducing the species to the wild.

A zoological success story did occur in the North Carolina lowlands, where two pairs of red wolves, previously extinct in the wild, were reintroduced into their natural habitat. During their first year in the wild, the wolves produced several pups, a very encouraging sign for wildlife specialists.

Other programs only recently got under way. In New York's Adirondack Mountains, five lynx were released, a century after they disappeared from the area. Thirty-six immature bald eagles were set free 80 miles (130 kilometers) west of Boston, Massachusetts, in a pine wilderness with no known breeding population of eagles since at least 1903.

Some proposed introductions have caused a minor uproar in New Mexico, currently the home of Persian ibex, Siberian ibex, oryx, and Barbary sheep, all imported as game animals for hunters. The exotic imports already compete with the native desert bighorn sheep for the little available grass. Ecologists oppose the introduction of two more exotics— the African kudu and the Persian gazelle—on the grounds that the introduction of more exotic species will further threaten native species.

© Steve Miller/NYT Pictures

An American eagle that turned up in Ireland was brought back to join 36 other eagles being used to repopulate a forest near Boston.

Wild Horses

The population of free-ranging wild horses west of the Rockies has skyrocketed since 1971, when Congress passed a law protecting the animals. Later laws allowed individuals to pay the government $125 per horse. Beginning in 1985, the Bureau of Land Management (BLM) gave free title to as many as 100 "unadoptable" horses to almost anyone. Then, in 1988, animal-rights groups convinced the government that some people were "adopting" horses simply to slaughter them and use their meat for dog food. The bureau is now prohibited from giving wild horses to anyone known to use them for pet food, rodeos, or other "exploitive" purposes.

Tough adoption procedures may help protect wild horses from mistreatment.

© Lane Stewart/*Sports Illustrated*

© Flip Nicklin

A Whale of a Tale

by Robert Sullivan

O n October 7, 1988, Roy Ahmaogak was scanning the waters of the Arctic Ocean near Barrow, Alaska, when he spotted three gray whales breaching. That's odd, he thought. Grays rarely come this far north. Bowheads, sure, but not grays. And any that did would have migrated south by mid-September. Ahmaogak then had another thought: the sea ice is growing, and if these three don't get out of here soon, they will be trapped.

As just about everyone from Barrow to Bangkok now knows, the whales—all thought to be one or two years old—did indeed become trapped. Three weeks later, through the extraordinary efforts of the residents of Barrow, the U.S. Government, and two Soviet icebreakers, two of the whales swam free. (The third had apparently drowned seven days before.) While no one was certain the grays would safely reach their wintering waters off Baja California, the high drama in Barrow was over.

However, something lingered: a renewed curiosity about the fate of whales—not just these whales, but the order as a whole. "We thought the phone would stop ringing when they got free, but it hasn't," says Howard Braham, an ecologist who is director of the National Marine Mammal Laboratory in Seattle, Washington. "People now are asking better questions, looking for perspective. They want to know how whales are doing. Not just those two, but all the great whales."

Conservation Success Story

T-shirt slogans to the contrary, whales—and gray whales in particular—have quietly become one of the conservation movement's most grati-

Whale resurgence: thanks to years of protection, nearly every species of whale has posted a dramatic gain in population. Frequent sightings of giant barnacled tails ripping through the water bear testimony to the successful comeback of the once critically endangered mammals.

fying success stories. Not since the early 1600s have things looked so rosy for these leviathans: most species are either holding their own or prospering. "It's generally going quite, quite well," says Ray Gambell, a British biologist and secretary of the International Whaling Commission. The IWC is a 38-nation organization, based in Cambridge, England, that was chartered to conserve and regulate whaling worldwide. "There are threats, of course," says Gambell. "The moratorium on commercial whaling, which we passed in 1982, will be reviewed in 1990. We expect a war on that. But right now the news for whales is positive."

The Verge of Extinction

This news reverses centuries of decline for the animals. But while whales have been extensively hunted for 400 years, chiefly for their oil, a critical point came in 1712. That was the year a ship out of Nantucket, Massachusetts, blundered upon a pod of sperm whales in the open North Atlantic. Shoreline whaling—a dangerous method of hunting some species of whales—quickly was superseded by the more efficient deep-sea whaling. By the mid-1800s, American whalers were prospecting for whales in every ocean of the world, and many species had been hunted to near extinction in temperate waters.

Then, in the early 1900s, Antarctic explorers discovered that the frigid southern oceans were teeming with the mammals. Steam engines and the explosive harpoon made it possible to reach and kill these whales easily, and at a profit. While the introduction of petroleum as an industrial lubricant had lessened the market, there was still a demand for whale flesh and bone for uses as diverse as food, fertilizer, perfume, candles, and stays for men's shirts and women's corsets. In 1934 Norway launched the first open-ocean factory ship. This type of vessel allowed the animals to be safely processed on board. Previously the dead whales were towed to land or—a far more dangerous procedure—flayed at shipside in rolling waters. By 1930 and 1931, blue whales, the largest of the whales—a mature adult weighs about 160 tons (145 metric tons)—were being slaughtered at a rate of nearly 30,000 a year. The figures for bowhead and right whales (so named because they were easy to catch, floated when killed, were filled with oil, and were therefore the "right whale" to hunt) were far lower because, ominously, there were few of them left.

In 1946 the IWC was founded. "The 14 signatories constituted little more than a sailing club," Gambell says. "It was a gentlemen's club, and its mission was to make sure that there would always be enough whales to hunt."

Initially, the IWC did little to diminish the kill. This century's peak of 66,090 whales slaughtered was attained in the 1961–62 season. But by the end of the decade, the environmental and conservation movement had grown substantially. The first call for a commercial-whaling moratorium came at the 1972 IWC convention. The U.S., which had banned all commercial whaling as of December 1971 and had recently passed a Marine Mammal Protection Act, gave strong support to the proposal. Nevertheless, the measure failed, with only four of the IWC's 14 member nations voting for a moratorium.

So conservationists adopted a new strategy: if you can't beat 'em, join 'em. Nations whose only interest in whaling was to see it stopped—Switzerland and India, for example—enrolled in the IWC. "There was a total switch in attitude on the part of the IWC," says Gambell. "In a decade, it became a conservation organization." When the moratorium was proposed again, in 1982, the save-the-whales side won, 25 to seven, with five abstentions.

Scientific Research?

But whaling—and controversy—didn't end with that vote. The IWC has no power to enforce the country-by-country commercial quotas it sets, and some IWC member nations continue to kill whales for "scientific research."

When Patty Warhol, executive director of the American Cetacean Society, is asked if the harvests are truly for scientific purposes, she answers, "Give me a break!" A source close to the IWC, who wishes to remain anonymous, says of the quotas: "Norway's perhaps is legitimate. Perhaps. But Japan took 273 minkes from Antarctic waters both last year and this. That's too small a sample for scientific study, but too large to be called negligible. It's definitely a perpetuation of Japan's commercial whaling."

Conservation groups are lobbying for economic reprisals to be leveled against Japan, which, in addition to importing whale meat from countries like Iceland, hunts the mammals with its own fleet. These groups are suggesting severe cuts in the $500 million in seafood the U.S. imports annually from Japan.

In October 1988, three gray whales found themselves trapped in the sea ice near Barrow, Alaska. The whales' predicament sparked an extraordinary international rescue effort. Racing against time, a Soviet icebreaker (below) cleared an escape route for two of the whales; the third whale had already drowned. The episode served an additional purpose: it sparked renewed curiosity about whales and the success of whale-conservation programs.

Meanwhile, Greenpeace, the environmental organization, has made Iceland its target and is urging a worldwide boycott of fish products from that country. "They have lost $12 million in contracts in the last few weeks," says Dean Wilkinson, legislative director for ocean ecology issues for Greenpeace. "The owners of Long John Silver's restaurants in the U.S. and a West German grocery store chain have just agreed to the boycott. We have more than 20 American school districts boycotting."

Besides real or purported scientific harvests, the only whaling now being done is by or for aboriginal peoples who depend upon whales for subsistence. The Inuit of Alaska, for example, are allowed to kill 41 bowheads per year; Ahmaogak was scouting for bowheads when he discovered the distressed grays off Barrow. The Soviet Union's aging whaling fleet catches approximately 200 grays a year. Those whales are supposedly intended for the Chukchi Eskimo of Siberia, but Greenpeace claims some of them end up as feed on Soviet mink farms.

"No, we can't call it a true moratorium because whaling is indeed continuing," says Wilkinson, "but, yes, the moratorium is working. This year, for the first time in more than two centuries, fewer than 1,000 whales will be killed worldwide.'' Warhol concurs in this assessment and adds, ''The North Atlantic right whale is the only whale that might not be with us in 100, 200, 500 years.''

Population Resurgence

This quiet optimism is based on the latest analysis of whale populations. It should be noted that whale counting has become a much more sophisticated science in recent years, and the higher numbers may, in part, reflect that fact. Nevertheless, a quick species-by-species review shows that not only are many great whales doing better, but they also are doing, as Gambell says, ''quite, quite well.''

By chance, the incident in the Arctic Ocean off Alaska drew attention to this success story. Or was it by chance?

''Those three probably got caught precisely *because* the gray whale is doing great,'' says Geoff Carroll, a marine biologist with the borough of North Slope, a huge chunk of Alaska in which Barrow is located. ''When a species burgeons as the grays have, some of the immature animals start venturing beyond their normal range. With more and more grays out there, grays are going to get into more and more places and situations that they should not be in.''

The idea of gray whales overrunning their habitat was something that, until recently, seemed inconceivable. Centuries ago, grays were hunted to extinction in the North Atlantic, and late in the past century, they were nearly extinct in the Pacific. Whalers would wait for the grays to gather in the calving lagoons off Baja, and then would descend on their prey. Some hunters used explosives, which quickly killed the big animals. Others harpooned the calves so that the mothers would swim closer and become easy targets.

Several international agreements have been signed in this century (in 1911, 1931, and 1946) granting protection to whales, but they seemed meaningless gestures. Since the early 1900s, grays were rarely seen off Baja in the calving season, and scientists thought they had disappeared. In fact, the species had experienced an unexplained behavioral change, and was no longer migrating close to the West Coast or using the Baja lagoons as its calving ground.

Then, ever so slowly, as this century progressed, grays were sighted with increasing frequency along their 6,000-mile (9,650-kilometer)-long migration route, most of which lies within 10 miles (16 kilometers) of the North American coast. In the past decade, it has become evident that the recovery of the West Coast population is complete. ''We think there are more than 21,000 of them [gray whales]

For over 400 years, hunters have slaughtered whales to satisfy the demand for whale oil, flesh, and bone.

North Wind Picture Archives

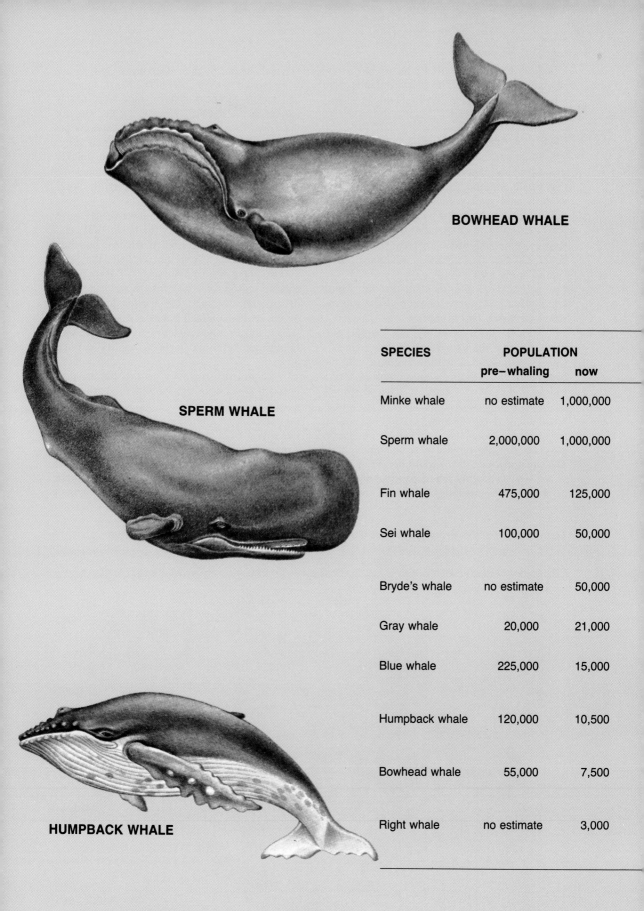

BOWHEAD WHALE

SPERM WHALE

HUMPBACK WHALE

SPECIES	POPULATION	
	pre–whaling	now
Minke whale	no estimate	1,000,000
Sperm whale	2,000,000	1,000,000
Fin whale	475,000	125,000
Sei whale	100,000	50,000
Bryde's whale	no estimate	50,000
Gray whale	20,000	21,000
Blue whale	225,000	15,000
Humpback whale	120,000	10,500
Bowhead whale	55,000	7,500
Right whale	no estimate	3,000

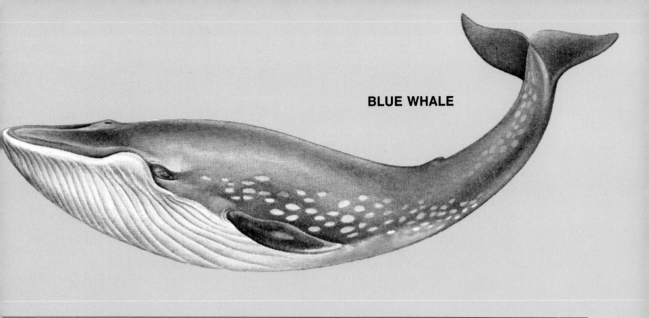

BLUE WHALE

GREAT NEWS FOR THE GREAT WHALES

Population believed stable. The smallest of the great whales, it was once thought to be a minor whale. The Japanese consider it the primary target animal for any return to commercial whaling.

Population estimate is probably conservative. The largest of the toothed whales and the inspiration for Moby Dick. A Japanese whaler claims to have spotted a white sperm whale in the 1950s, but it got away.

Data on fins are difficult to gather because the breed migrates in the open ocean. Strongest gains have been made in North Pacific and Antarctic waters.

Population rising. It may be 80 percent recovered in its North Pacific habitat and is making a comeback in the Southern Hemisphere as well. Initial population estimate is unreliable because it was often confused with Bryde's whale.

Population stable. Because it was long confused with the sei, it never made the endangered-species list—no one knew a different species was out there.

Population may be at all-time peak and is rising. The gray hasn't shown any sign of a comeback in the North Atlantic, but in the eastern North Pacific, it's thriving.

Population estimate very conservative. The blue is the largest animal ever—twice the size of the heaviest dinosaur. It has a gestation period of 12 months, but although its comeback from near extinction has been slow, it is confirmed.

Current population estimate probably conservative. A hopeful sign: the humpback stock in the western North Atlantic might be larger than ever. Can stocks in the Indian and Pacific oceans and the Southern Hemisphere follow suit?

Population rising. The bowhead looked like a goner, but improved census techniques have revealed that there are more than had been estimated. Species is increasing in the Arctic, but recovery of the once-dominant stock off Greenland is in question.

Population struggling. So named because its stores of blubber and oil made it the "right" whale to hunt. Although its population in the North Atlantic has dwindled to almost nothing, two stocks—one off South Africa, the other off Argentina—show signs of increasing.

© Plowden/Greenpeace

Greenpeace and other environmental groups have staged daring protests against countries that continue to hunt whales.

now,'' says Carrol. ''That's the historic high for the species.''

The abandonment of the Baja calving grounds was doubtless a major factor in the gray's comeback, but the fact that the gray is smaller than most great whales was probably a factor as well. An adult gray is 36 to 50 feet (11 to 15 meters) long and weighs between 16 and 45 tons (14.5 and 40 metric tons), which is about half the size of a fin whale and only one-third the size of a mature blue whale. Therefore, the gray doesn't require the same quantities of food as its bigger relatives.

Not to be discounted are man's efforts. The gray is the first to support the notion that a whale not hunted is a whale on the rebound. ''We simply do not know why the gray whale has recovered so well,'' says the National Marine Mammal Laboratory's Braham, who coedited the latest National Marine Fisheries report on the status of endangered whales. ''We always hoped that the minute we stopped killing a spe-

cies, it would start to come back, but we've never been sure. Because whales have long gestation periods, they don't come back fast. It takes generations to see a rebound, and we're seeing it now with the grays.''

Happy Quandary

This rebound has put environmental groups in a happy quandary. ''We don't know whether to pop champagne over the whale's success, or stay quiet and try to keep the gray on the endangered species list and, therefore, superprotected,'' says Wilkinson.

In 1972, after the whales began to return annually to their Baja calving grounds, Mexico designated a major calving lagoon as a sanctuary. The other lagoons used by those whales came under similar protection by 1979. In the U.S. and Canada, environmental officials are monitoring the effects of whale-watching excursions on the whales. The gray's biannual trips— a 10-week period in the fall when the whales head south from Alaska, and the 10 weeks in the spring when they swim north from Baja—are major drawing cards for this thriving industry.

"Researchers are making recommendations on how to proceed with whale-watching so as not to disrupt the animals," says Whitney Tilt, project manager for the National Fish & Wildlife Foundation headquartered in Washington, D.C. "I'm happy to say that the industry has been receptive."

The gray whale has responded to all this tender loving care in a most extraordinary way. Scientists call it "the friendly whale syndrome." In 1976 a calf approached a dinghy full of whale-watchers in San Ignacio Lagoon off Baja. The curious little whale, nicknamed Bumper, even submitted to being patted on the head. Since the first close encounter, trusting whales have become increasingly playful with human visitors. It's easy to anthropomorphize such occurrences, and, indeed, the gray's apparent friendliness strikes some observers as an act of forgiveness, for it occurs in the very waters where gray whales were once slaughtered by the thousands.

Heightened Awareness

Certainly the publicity that the grays have generated—Bumper and now the Barrow trio—has helped all whales. "Awareness is always good," says Braham. And it also makes life more difficult for proponents of commercial whaling. "I think even before the incident in Alaska, Japan would have had a tough time getting the moratorium lifted for any species, even the minke," says Warhol. "The new group of whale lovers makes it that much tougher. We'll win next year."

Conservationists hope for even more fallout from the Barrow whale incident. The 1972 Marine Mammal Protection Act was reauthorized by Congress last month. Oceanic pollution, already a hot topic, could get hotter because it affects whales. The practice of drift netting, which often entangles and drowns small whales, dolphins, and porpoises, will come under closer scrutiny. There already is heightened concern about the depletion of the ozone layer that protects the planet from damaging levels of ultraviolet light. Several recent studies maintain that even a slight increase in the amount of ultraviolet light reaching the earth's surface would kill off krill, the shrimplike organisms that are the main food of many whales.

"Some people asked if all the effort in Alaska was worth it for just a couple of whales," says Braham. "But I don't think that's the point. First, it had value as a story about humans. It was a finite problem with a beginning and an end that people could feel good about. It was valuable on that level.

"And unquestionably it was valuable for whales. That story fanned interest in whales. We still know pathetically little about them— who they are, how they're growing, where they are in their life history and in their interaction with the environment. What happened in Alaska was good for the whales."

© Larry Kokzak/Earthwatch

The increased population of whales and their regular migratory routes have made whale-watching excursions a thriving industry. Although seemingly harmless, such excursions may ultimately disrupt the whales' migration patterns.

© Margot Conte/Animals Animals

An Abundance of Swans

by Wendy Williams

A weather-beaten hand, still wet from paddling across the windblown bay out to the isolated island, reaches gently down, disappearing below the rim of a giant nest. When it reappears, it grips a 4-inch (10-centimeter) mute-swan egg, still warm with life from the roosting hen. Back and forth, up and down, the hand shakes the egg, scrambling the yolk and destroying the swan embryo.

The pen and the cob swim nearby, watching. Later they return to the nest and continue to watch over their now-lifeless eggs. Fooled, the thwarted parents will try to hatch the clutch for several more weeks, until it is too late to lay a second clutch successfully.

This past spring, Charlie Allin, Rhode Island's senior wildlife biologist, and his staff visited nearly 100 such nests, shaking more than 500 eggs. The program, a decade old, is designed to control the spread of the destructive, nonnative birds.

Populations of mute swans—an exotic species introduced to North America from Europe in the early 1900s—are increasing by an alarm-

As menacing as they are majestic, mute swans have begun to wear out their welcome in North America. Since their introduction from Europe less than a century ago, mute swans have multiplied at a rate high enough to threaten the habitats of less-aggressive native waterfowl.

ing 30 to 40 percent annually in some states. Most wildlife biologists believe the majestic white creatures, with their tendency to destroy a pond's plant life and drive away native waterfowl, might create havoc on the scale of the gypsy moth, starling, or English sparrow. Limit the exploding mute population now, they strongly advise, before the numbers become unmanageable.

Yet biologists' principles are sometimes difficult to reconcile with human emotions. As the egg-shaking continues, human heartstrings often tug. Few species inspire such images of romance and classic beauty as the mute swan. Destroying tree-killing gypsy moths on biological grounds is one thing. Destroying these handsome birds, which many people are strongly attracted to, is quite another.

For the past decade, the genial, good-humored Allin and the staff at the Rhode Island Division of Fish and Wildlife have spent one month each year seeking out and shaking mute-swan eggs. "The only way to control these birds is to shake eggs throughout the Atlantic Flyway," says Allin. Yet the swan population continues to grow. From a total of about 200 to 300 in the 1950s, the number of feral mute swans in the Atlantic Flyway has swollen to more then 6,000. Without controls, he says, that figure could double before the year 2000. Allin's staff finds more nests every year. "We're losing the battle despite our work," he says, "because our neighboring states haven't done anything."

Astounding Growth Rate

If some 6,000 mute swans sounds harmless enough, keep in mind that in some states during the 1960s and 1970s, the growth rate hovered at about 40 percent, and that one of these birds can live as long as 50 years. Also consider that a nesting pair of mute swans might usurp a whole pond, sometimes killing other waterfowl. "When you put that many 30-pound [13.5-kilogram] birds into the Atlantic coastal zone, it's too much stress," explains James Myers, Rhode Island's principal wildlife biologist. "These birds should be controlled now, before they do considerable damage."

Of the six species in the swan genus, only two are native to North America. The trumpeter swan, the largest of the group, breeds in the northern United States and Alaska, and was nearly wiped out during the 19th-century craze for elaborately feathered hats. The whistling swan, which winters in large flocks on the Ches-

apeake Bay, has recently been renamed the tundra swan because it breeds and summers on the northernmost tundra regions of the continent.

Both native species are wild and require large areas of uninhabited summer ground for nesting and feeding. Mutes, however, are semi-domesticated and accustomed to people. As many as three or four pairs can nest on one small coastal pond, which can burden delicate and environmentally essential brackish ponds.

Symbols of wealth and European royalty, mute swans became fashionable on Long Island and upstate New York estates earlier this century. Their population has since blossomed into feral groups in seven Atlantic Flyway states: Rhode Island, New York, Connecticut, Massachusetts, New Jersey, Pennsylvania, and Maryland. Isolated pockets also thrive in Michigan, Wisconsin, on the coasts of the Great Lakes, Yellowstone National Park, Ontario, and British Columbia.

Most biologists would like to see feral mute populations limited, but they have encountered

As the number of mute swans continues to skyrocket, some states have adopted controversial methods of population control. In one such method, biologists briskly shake unhatched swan eggs to destroy the embryos.

© Dann Blackwood

Mute swans conduct elaborate courtship displays before mating. A pair of swans (left) generally bonds for life. The female usually assumes responsibility for incubating the eggs, although either parent may guard the nest.

Above: © Fred Whitehead/Animals Animals; below: © Dann Blackwood

fierce opposition from people. One third-grade class from a school in Rhode Island sent Allin a packet of hate mail. "Charlie Allin is a very bad man," one child wrote. "He kills baby animals."

A man who saw Rhode Island wildlife biologist Lori Suprock shaking eggs prophesied disaster for Suprock's children because she was willing to "kill another mother's babies." On another pond, fans of the local cob and pen built them a house on the edge of the marsh. A sobbing woman once begged Allin not to touch the eggs by a pond behind her house. "You would have thought they were her own children," Allin says. "It's difficult to get people to see that the birds are becoming a real problem."

Wildlife agencies in the affected states must decide within the next several years whether to impose Allin's proposed controls or face runaway swan populations. While agency heads may agree with the egg-shaking plan—which is supported by the Atlantic Flyway Council, a waterfowl advisory group representing the flyway states—most hesitate to say so publicly. Making the biologists' job even tougher, some states with large swan populations—New York, New Jersey, and Massachusetts, for example—indirectly protect mutes by excluding them from lists of harvestable birds.

In Great Britain the Crown controlled ownership of mute swan population, even employing a Royal Swanherd to organize an annual swan roundup. Around the turn of the century, however, the budding American aristocracy began importing swan pairs from Britain as symbols of prestige.

Finding a Niche

The pinioned birds produced plentiful and fertile offspring, which soon left the estates to nest in other ponds. These escaped, semidomesticated mutes found what scientists call a biological niche, "the total set of circumstances an organism needs to survive,'' explains Alfred Hawkes, executive director of the Audubon Society of Rhode Island. ''When an invading species survives by locating an unoccupied niche,'' he says, ''it is likely to explode in its population and become a nuisance. The mute swan is shaping up as such a problem.''

Human encroachment had driven off native wild waterfowl. But the mutes, bred to nest near humans, flourished in the coastal waters—brackish ponds filled with eelgrass. The only predators were snapping turtles and an occasional human seeking black-market cygnets.

Cape Cod cranberry grower Arthur Handy is painfully aware of the trouble the birds can bring. Mute swans wintering in nearby coastal waters discovered that Handy's bogs made good winter grazing grounds. Shortly after eight pairs found a tasty 56-acre (22-hectare) bog on his property last winter, the bog's bottom looked like an exploded minefield. The swans cleared whole sections, digging foot-wide craters and

uprooting every plant. Damage assessment for one small corner: $5,000. Whole cranberry bogs have disappeared down those beautifully curved white throats.

Although Canada geese share this relish for bog foraging, the mute's unique body type gives it an edge. A powerful jaw enables it to tear plants into small pieces, and its long, agile neck helps the mute search for and uproot plants 18 inches (45 centimeters) or more below the water's surface.

The law allows Handy recourse to a rifle, but he feels constrained by the neighbors. One summer a conservation officer ousted a pair and their cygnets three times, but the family kept coming back. ''They cleaned out one whole section of the bog and started on another,'' says Handy. He finally ordered the birds shot. ''Well, shooting them straightened out the problem,'' he says, ''but it sure upset the neighborhood.'' Shortly afterward a message appeared on a bog outbuilding: ''Kill Arthur Handy.''

The plumage of mute swans changes from a light gray as juveniles, or cygnets, to entirely white as adults.

Natural ponds and bogs also sustain similar damage from mute swans. Yet far greater than any financial losses are the effects on the environment. "There's no question that a breeding pair of mute swans can have significant impact in reducing aquatic vegetation," says Connecticut wildlife biologist Greg Chasko. In one experiment, Chasko sealed off an area of a pond, then sampled random spots available to the swans outside the exclosure. After a summer of feeding, he checked the results. "In some cases there would be no vegetation outside the exclosure at all," says the biologist.

Fastidious but Indiscriminate

Although they are fastidious eaters, consuming only the choicest roots, mute swans uproot natural vegetation indiscriminately in their search for the tastiest morsels. Other birds graze, of course, but few rival the mutes' capacity for destruction. And overgrazing can destroy the delicate balance in the coast's brackish ponds. The birds upend their bodies and dig with their bills in the mud on the pond bottom, clearing holes and pulling out plants, roots and all.

The brackish ponds are highly productive environments containing a great diversity of species, says Alfred Hawkes, who cautions, "These areas need to be protected very carefully." That means discouraging swan housekeeping on smaller ponds. As Cape Cod conservation officer William Richardson explains, "These water bodies are filtration systems, designed to clean the poisons out of the marsh areas." A 25-pound (11-kilogram) adult mute swan eats upwards of 8 pounds (3.6 kilograms) of vegetation daily and leaves behind pounds of droppings. "If you look at what the swans eat, and consider what they leave behind that will not be absorbed by the declining vegetation," Richardson says, "you are looking at a pond that will have severe problems."

Every summer for several decades, more than 400 unmated mute swans have visited the mammoth marsh at Briggs Marsh, Rhode Island, gathering into large, temporary flocks during the molt. "If you go out and look at the bottom of Briggs Marsh, it looks like the surface of the moon," says J. Stanley Cobb, a University of Rhode Island zoologist. Underwater defoliation, in turn, harms aquatic animal populations: tiny pond fish depend on vegetation for food and cover, and the pond bottom needs several years to recover from the Swiss-cheese devastation the birds usually leave behind.

Displacing Natives

Mutes also drive native waterfowl from their natural nesting sites, say researchers. Nesting males defend large territories, often attacking other birds and animals. They even stand on other birds' nests and prevent females from sitting, says Ontario biologist Harry Lumsden, who has found dead goslings on swan nests and has seen swans kill goslings and ducklings. In the spring of 1983, Lumsden counted 13 Canada-goose nests destroyed by mutes.

What is an acceptable number of mute swans? For Lumsden, not many. "We want to get rid of them," he says. "We don't want any at all. We realize that if we wait, it won't be possible to do anything about them." Definitive statistics are unavailable, but Lumsden and other biologists believe as mute-swan populations rise, numbers of other waterfowl will fall. "They scare away native waterfowl and nest early, before the others," explains Rhode Island's Lori Suprock. "The birds defend their territories against native waterfowl, which should have first dibs."

Willis Gelston, an amateur ornithologist who has studied Michigan's mute swans for more than a decade, says he once saw one of the birds attack and drown a gosling. Even so, Gelston—executive director of Grand Traverse Swan, Inc., a nonprofit group that feeds Michigan's mutes in winter—dismisses as "tommyrot" the charge that mutes will eradicate other waterfowl: "Of course the male is going to protect his territory. That's why the female selected him. He's just doing his job."

It is a job the birds do energetically. Once, on a pond at Rhode Island's Gilbert Stuart Birthplace, swans accustomed to being fed attacked a father and son who came empty-handed. As Charlie Allin tells it, the male followed their boat to shore and chased them across the beach all the way to their car. The same swan once demanded food from a fisherman. When none was forthcoming, the bird attacked the boat, rising with arched wings out of the water and half-entering the craft. The fisherman, though unhurt, lost two expensive rods. "He was a preacher," recalls caretaker William Geary. "I'll tell you, for a preacher, this guy was . . . pretty upset."

The mute swan's most potent weapon is an exceptionally large wing joint—the manus joint, similar to the human elbow. "Imagine the power behind that joint if it enables a 6½ foot [2-meter] wing to lift a 30-pound [13-kilogram]

© Margot Conte/Animals Animals

The aggressive nature of mute swans may ultimately endanger the survival of other waterfowl. Mute swans threaten native ducks and geese by damaging their nests, killing their young, and driving them from their breeding grounds.

bird into the air,'' says James Myers. ''Imagine what it can do to little kids and dogs.'' Though trumpeter and tundra swans have a similar wing structure, they don't generally nest near people.

In a full-fledged attack, the bird rushes across the water with wings flapping, then spins wildly, turns sideways, and strikes out with that joint. ''It's like throwing a roundhouse punch,'' says Charlie Willey, a former Rhode Island biologist who conducted one of the first studies of mutes in 1972. ''They can crush a galvanized bucket with that joint.''

Justified Egg-shaking

In Delaware, wildlife managers do not allow the birds in wildlife reserves. ''The mute swan has the status of, for example, a chicken,'' says Delaware biologist Tom Whittendale. ''A wildlife area should be for native wildlife, not for exotics.'' State wildlife managers generally destroy the birds, letting a few live in specific areas for the public.

Ontario's Harry Lumsden, spurred by a decision by Canadian wildlife biologists in 1982 to reestablish decimated trumpeter-swan populations, has begun substituting trumpeter eggs in the nest with mute eggs. However, the experiment has yet to yield substantial numbers of the native species.

By far the most likely program to achieve flyway-wide adoption is egg-shaking. Every spring, Charlie Allin and Lori Suprock take an aerial survey of mute-swan nests. Then Allin and the staff spend the next month seeking out those nests and shaking the incubating eggs.

Allin figures the time-consuming program, which costs the state between $5,000 and $6,000 annually, is the least likely to raise a public row. But unless other states join in, he warns, the effort will have been in vain: in 1988 more mute swans than ever chose Rhode Island as the place in which to raise their cygnets. Last spring, Allin's team found more than 90 nests and shook more than 500 eggs. ''Our previous all-time high was 350 eggs,'' he says. ''Imagine how many birds would be out there if we hadn't done anything to control them.''

Alfred Hawkes justifies egg-shaking as proper self-defense against a formidable intruder. ''The mute swan is such a handsome bird, but it's also an invading species—an exotic. Why compound the problems our native wildlife already have? Biologically,'' he insists, ''we're doing the right thing.''

Tracking the
Rain Forest Giraffe

by Terese B. Hart and John A. Hart

I t takes six hours to walk from the village of Epulu to Afarama, our research camp. Porters carrying our supplies always announce their imminent arrival while still 10 minutes away by pounding a stout stick against the thin buttress of an ironwood tree. The hollow sound carries more than half a mile (800 meters) through the forest. It is the standard form of long-distance announcement. There is only one path in from town, and the porters never arrive before midafternoon. So when rhythmic thuds broke through the drone of cicadas well before

noon, we all knew what it meant: an okapi had fallen into a pit.

We had dug and camouflaged more than a hundred pits in groups of 10 to 15 throughout our study area. Every morning, three teams, each made up of two Mbuti (Pygmy) assistants, set out to make the rounds of the pits. Our forest team of 20 is comprised of Mbuti hunters and Bantu farmers. Because of their greater expertise in the rain forest, the Mbuti were the obvious choice for the swift and silent inspection of the various pits.

sensitive ears, just visible over the rim of the pit, turn in their direction, and the animal stamps and snorts. Abeli peers in. It is a "glistening" (as he later describes it), adult male okapi. Quickly, Abeli and Lui cut some 3-foot (1-meter)-long poles and set them across the pit, then lay leafy branches on top of the poles. Now in darkness, the okapi grows quiet.

Lui starts back to camp to get the capture kit, which contains a radio collar and the tools to fasten it. He pauses only to beat out a summons to the field crew. It will take him an hour to reach camp and then make the return trip to the capture site.

Abeli speeds off to find us. He knows the approximate direction we have taken to track an already-collared okapi. He follows the leaf sign we have left at each path crossing—Marantaceae leaves with the stems pointing the route. Nimbly and fast as a startled duiker, Abeli leaps logs and tree roots, shoots through our network of paths, and delivers the news to us in less than 45 minutes.

Author John Hart (left) crosses a stream in Zaire's Ituri Forest as he follows the elusive okapi (below). The okapi's zebra-like stripes and dark color help the animal blend with the sun-dappled background.

It is Abeli and Lui who discover Asoma, our fourth okapi. As always, they approach each pit cautiously, with spear ready just in case; leopards fall into the pits more often than okapis do. So far, the cats have always gotten out on their own before anyone arrives. Nevertheless, the Mbuti approach the pits as they do the forest: with a respectful caution born from experience. One time a team met three restless red buffalo at the rim of the pit into which a fourth had fallen. On another round, a giant forest hog was encountered at a pit in which a second hog was trapped. Releasing these large mammals can be a difficult and dangerous operation. Even more dangerous is approaching a pit unprepared.

Abeli and Lui move silently and quickly from one pit to another. From a distance they see that the vegetation covering one pit has been disturbed. They creep closer. A pair of large,

Recent Discovery

The existence of the okapi was first brought to the attention of the scientific world in 1900, in a brief report by British explorer Sir Harry Johnston to a meeting of the Zoological Society of London. Though preceded by earlier erroneous reports of a forest donkey, the finding of a short-necked giraffe living in the middle of a rain forest astonished the zoologists of the day, who had presumed that all the world's large mammals had already been discovered by earlier explorers.

The okapi, *Okapia johnstoni,* whose name is probably derived from a local tribal name, *o'api,* appears to be related to an extinct group of giraffids, the paleotragines, which disappeared from Eurasia and Africa 2 million years ago, before the Pleistocene. Since its discovery, the okapi has generated intense interest and excitement; yet the life of this secretive creature in its forest home has remained essentially unknown. Even the local villagers and the Mbuti hunters, who accord the animal a special respect and status, infrequently encounter it in the forest. The species has long been considered rare and has been protected under national law since 1933, but because the okapi lives only in a limited area of the forests of northeastern Zaïre, it is vulnerable to habitat destruction. Before we could recommend additional measures to ensure the survival of the species, we needed to have information about its natural density, habitat requirements, and social interactions.

Collaring an okapi. Local members of the research team camouflage a shallow pit with arrowroot leaves (above). When an okapi falls into the pit, researchers fit the captured animal with a radio collar (below) to track its movements, and then release it.

With funding from Wildlife Conservation International, we returned to Epulu in 1986—accompanied by our two daughters and John's sister, Natalie—to conduct the first study of okapis in the wild. Some of the basic biological information could be acquired by working closely with the Mbuti, who are skilled at interpreting okapi signs. With our own preliminary knowledge of the flora, we could outline broad patterns of habitat use and diet. But because these animals are so difficult to observe, detailed information could be acquired only by trapping and collaring a number of them.

Collaring a Male

When Abeli runs up to us, breathless and shining with perspiration, he delivers the news we have been hoping for. We have already equipped three female okapis with radio collars, but have not equipped any males. Full of anticipation, we hurry to the pit, where we pull back the branches and find a magnificent mature male. His velvety dark chestnut back, 5 feet (1.5 meters) high at the shoulder, slopes down to his rump, where striking stripes, white against black, begin. There is a maroon sheen on his neck, which tapers up toward the delicate gray head. Dark eyes watch from his fine, long face, and his large ears are attentive.

We replace the branches with a large navy cotton cloth to keep the okapi in the dark and calm. The field crew moves away to make a barrier, the sound of their machetes dulled by the surrounding trees. We check the new collar; the radio signal is clear. In less than half an hour, the crew has fashioned a tall, gatelike barrier, which we slip under the cloth at an angle to the bottom of the pit, placing one end near the okapi's front hooves. As we push the barrier upright, the okapi takes one, two steps backward and snorts slightly, but is otherwise quiet. When his rump touches the back wall of the pit, we fix the barrier in place with two poles.

While two men hold John's legs to prevent his falling into the pit, he slips his head and shoulders under the cloth. The okapi shies a little, but in the dark confined space, John is able to maneuver the sturdy canvas collar around his neck and fasten it in place. The rest of us start throwing dirt back into the pit to form a ramp in front of the barrier. Next to every pit we leave a pile of excavated gravel and clay camouflaged with transplanted shrubs and dead leaves. The pile looks like a termite mound, but the dirt is loose. Very soon the okapi's path is ready.

We remove the barrier and the cloth. Most of the workers have dispersed to nearby pits, which they have uncovered and are guarding, to make sure the animal does not fall into one of them. The okapi remains standing in the pit, apparently calm, ears turning in every direction. We retreat out of sight, and 10 minutes later, without warning, he bounds out and gallops off. Perhaps he has decided the coast is clear.

Though we have captured a number of animals, we are awed each time in that brief moment when the okapi is before us, free and startlingly tall and powerful. It is difficult to believe that this animal, as large as a horse, can live so secretively in the forest.

Observing Okapi

Trail cutting is one of our major tasks, and it seems a never-ending one. Okapis basically are solitary. Each of our (now) eight collared animals (three males and five females) uses roughly 1 square mile (2.6 square kilometers) of forest. In order to locate them and map their movements, we have divided their home ranges by a grid of narrow paths.

Cutting our trail system reveals hitherto unknown worlds: a hill where we can stand on capping boulders and see far over the unbroken canopy; a natural spring dripping into a deep, rock-sheltered pool; an elephant wallow crossed with fresh spoor and the sad litter of old bones, testimony to past ivory hunting. The element of surprise, no doubt, comes from the constant constraints on vision in the forest. Unless something is close at hand, you may not see it at all.

Even when radio-collared, okapis are difficult to observe. We know them primarily from occasional glimpses or a snort and the staccato of receding hoofbeats on forest duff. Our trail system permits us to get relatively close, but actual observation is another matter. We have often sat within 50 feet (15 meters) of one of our collared subjects without seeing so much as the stripes of its hindquarters. To be unobtrusive, we try to mimic its exemplary stillness, always wishing we could see or at least hear it.

More frequently, some other creature catches our attention. An elephant shrew scampers near our feet, or an exquisite high-stepping blue duiker picks its way among roots and trunks, nuzzling the leaf litter at each step. We once sit in attempted immobility as a troop of colobus monkeys ravages the young foliage of a tree over our heads. For more than 15 minutes, we are showered by large leaves, each

Even a collared okapi can prove difficult to track. An okapi frequently remains perfectly still for an hour or more, frustrating even the most patient observer. Then, without a sound, the okapi seemingly vanishes into the forest, maintaining a silence amazing for an animal the size of a horse.

Above and facing page: © John and Terese Hart

having had the base of its stem neatly nipped off. Every once and again, a white-whiskered black face peers in our direction, as though the monkeys are taking aim.

Not infrequently, an okapi will remain inactive for half an hour to an hour or more. After a while we turn on the receiver for a periodic check, only to discover that the individual has moved off, maintaining a silence amazing for so large an animal.

As we hurry to catch up with it, we must be careful to approach slowly and silently. If the animal is browsing, we can locate it relatively simply by the sound of ripping leaves as it strips branches with its long, prehensile tongue. But if it has paused, we may inadvertently walk right up to it without seeing it. Even in open forest, the pattern of stripes, the dark flanks, and the pale face materialize slowly out of the mottled sun and shadow of the understory. Just as we realize the animal has been watching us, it has vanished.

Leaf Eater

The okapi's mystery is not only its invisibility but also its unique eating habits. No other large mammal of the Ituri Forest survives on a diet comprised entirely of understory foliage. The elephant eats foliage but also a great deal of fruit; seedlings sprout from its droppings. The six species of forest duikers and the water chevrotain, which share the forest with the okapi, have, like the elephant, eclectic diets. They eat some leaves and flowers, most scavenged from the forest floor, but the bulk of their food is fallen fruits and seeds. The okapi alone specializes in leaves.

Within its home range an okapi has no special feeding sites to which it returns daily, no trails it follows to regular sources of food. Openings created by tree falls often show the most signs of browsing, but okapis forage widely under the closed canopy and even in swamp forest. Wherever an okapi stops to browse, it selects only young leaves and tender shoot tips, and these from only a small number of the plants within easy reach.

Okapis weave back and forth over their home ranges, often covering well more than half a mile (800 meters) in a day, eating as they walk. In just a few days, they may forage on more than a hundred plant species; no single species accounts for more than a fraction of their diet.

Conserving the Okapi

Our preliminary observations suggest that the okapi is thinly distributed throughout its range. Conservation of large tracts of continuous forest is necessary to maintain viable populations. Although there is no imminent menace to okapis in the Ituri Forest, neither is there security for their future. Despite the absence of large-scale deforestation, the Ituri is not safe from change. Areas of continuous forest will eventually attract logging companies. In the meantime, there is a gradual gnawing at the forest edge.

Over the past 10 years, we have witnessed slow changes that attest to the inexorable growth of the human population impinging on the eastern and northern borders. These people see the forest as a settlement frontier. Small homesteads pop up along the roadside and expand on a scale never achieved by the traditional shifting cultivators.

Temporary gold camps, with their raucous treasure-seekers, appear and disappear along the rivers. Ivory hunters, also invariably outsiders, come to plunder and then quickly move on. More long-lasting damage is wrought by the expanding charcoal industry and the coffee plantations of new immigrants. The influx of settlers will continue to increase; the pressure from growing human populations around the forest shows no signs of abating.

The Zaïre Institute for the Conservation of Nature (IZCN) has recently taken the first steps toward an ambitious project to ensure the survival of the okapi in the Ituri Forest. Using recommendations and findings from our research, IZCN has established ecological requirements for the species. With technical assistance from the World Wildlife Fund and financial support from TABAZAÏRE, a private Zaïrian company, it has drawn up plans to designate a core region of the Ituri Forest as a national park and forest reserve.

Local farmers and Mbuti are becoming aware that the vast wilderness beyond their homes will soon be protected. These people have lived in and with the forest for generations, and they are well aware that the okapi is found only in the Ituri. We hope to nurture local pride into a force for wildlife conservation. Already, the people's voices have been joined by a national call for the conservation of the okapi, the living symbol of Zaïre's valuable natural forests. But we know that effective conservation of the okapi can be realized only when the effort to save the rain forest giraffe and its habitat becomes an international one.

Unlike other large mammals, the okapi feeds exclusively on leaves and shoot tips growing near the forest floor.

Frogs That Sweat POISON

by J. S. Bainbridge, Jr.

In the South America of lore and legend, an Indian raises a long blowgun, takes aim at his quarry, and lets fly. The prey drops, paralyzed almost instantly—not by the dart itself, but by the poison on its tip. Among the hunters of our sister continent, the knowledge and use of deadly natural compounds became a refined art.

Most of these poisonous compounds were extracted from plants and were often used on arrows as well as on darts. The compounds came to be known generally as curare, a substance administered in thrillers and murder mysteries. The word derives from three similar Indian words for poison, and, technically, chemists now reserve it for a specific group of plant-derived alkaloids. On the Pacific slopes of Colombia, however, the Choco Indians tipped their darts with a poison excreted from the skin of small, brilliantly colored frogs.

As long ago as 1820, Captain Charles Stuart Cochrane, on leave from the British Navy, explored Colombia and described how Choco hunters got poison for their darts by tormenting the unfortunate frogs until they "perspire very much." The frog sweat takes the form of white froth, in which "they dip or roll the points of their arrows, which will preserve their destruc-

More than 100 species of the tiny but colorful dart-poison frog thrive in Central and South American forests.

tive power for a year. Afterwards, below this white substance, appears a yellow oil, which is carefully scraped off, and retains its deadly influence for four or six months, according to the goodness [as they say] of the frog. By this means, from one frog sufficient poison is obtained for about 50 arrows.''

Today most of the surviving Indians have turned to firearms. Only a few still use darts to hunt. But the knowledge and use of their dart-poison frogs has not been lost. What was once a hunter's art has been taken up by modern scientists, who study the toxins for possible application as anesthetics and cardiac stimulants.

Stronger than Strychnine

There are more than 100 species of dart-poison frogs that belong to the family Dendrobatildae. Only about half are toxic, and only three species are actually used for poisoning the darts. The poison secreted by *Phyllobates terribilis,* the most toxic species, is stunningly powerful.

John Daly, a chemist at the National Institutes of Health [NIH] and an expert on dart-poison frog toxins, learned just how powerful while studying *P. terribilis* on the Pacific coast of Colombia during the 1970s. Daly and his colleague Charles Myers, a curator at the American Museum of Natural History's Department of Herpetology, were staying with a family of Indians while collecting specimens. The scientists had put on rubber gloves when handling the frogs and burned the gear afterward.

One morning, after rains had doused their trash fire, they awoke to find the bodies of a chicken and a dog near the contaminated garbage. The Indians concluded that the poisons from the frogs had killed their animals. Myers and Daly had to pay for the chicken but not the dog, which the family agreed was worthless. The secretions from the frogs ''made strychnine look like table salt,'' Daly observes.

To determine toxicity of other frog species, researchers use an inelegant test—simply touching the tip of their tongue to the back of a frog under stress (usually pinching its leg creates stress enough). They have found that such a test on a *Phyllobates* species less toxic than *P. ter-*

A vivid stripe (below) warns potential predators to stay clear. The heavy granular skin (right) oozes a milky, toxic secretion when the frog is stressed.

Photos, below and facing page: © Robert Noonan

ribilis, produces a bitter taste and ''a lingering, almost numb sensation on the tongue, followed by a disagreeable tightening sensation in the throat.'' With *P. terribilis,* the taste test could be deadly. For this virulent, bright yellow amphibian carries 20 times more poison under its skin than other species, enough to kill several people. The Indians always use leaves to protect their hands when touching them. There is no known antidote.

Even so, the deadliness of dart-poison frogs is not always as great as their reputation suggests. Four years ago a Brazilian naturalist named Augusto Ruschi blamed his liver disease on a dart-poison frog he had handled more than a decade earlier. With much fanfare, the president of Brazil brought to Ruschi's rescue a chief and a shaman from the country's Txukahamae and Kamayura Indian tribes. Both agreed that the frog was the culprit. The cure: massages, herbal baths, and smoke puffed from hallucinogenic cigars and blown over Ruschi's body. Scientists familiar with the dart poisons and their toxins, however, said that the cause of the disease had to be something else: frog poisons act quickly and primarily affect nerve and muscle, not the liver. In any case, Ruschi died.

Warning Coloration

In nature the frogs' known deadliness serves to protect not only *P. terribilis,* but many less-toxic species as well. Most share a dazzling array of color schemes that stand out from the dark green hues of the rain forest. Some are bright red; others blue with black spots, yellow with black bands, orange-swirled, or three-toned. Their bold colors warn a legion of predators who normally eat frogs to stay away, and most species hop about safely during the day. The bright colors aren't so obvious at night, but these frogs for the most part lie low after dark.

Dart-poison frogs are found only in lower Central America and the northern half of South America. They are tiny, ranging from ½ to 2 inches (1¼ to 5 centimeters) in length. They can live along stream banks, in lowlands, or high in the mountains. Some can survive dry, open countryside, keeping moist in the shade. Many are territorial. Males (and even some females) stake out private turf, and warn off invaders and attract females with an assortment of chirps, peeps, or trills. When the frogs clash, their battles can be fierce, but rarely life-threatening, for they are immune to their own toxins.

Unlike the familiar American pond frogs, many of these frogs breed away from water. And because the dart-poison frogs lay fairly few eggs—never more than 40 at a time, often far fewer—protecting them is critical. Dart-poison frogs tend to remain at the egg site, keeping the eggs moist until they hatch.

Once that happens, one of the parents will taxi the young to a watery site for the next stage of development. Such ''nurse frogs'' secrete

© Michael Fogden/Animals Animals

Many dart-poison frogs tend their eggs away from water. Once the eggs hatch, the tadpoles wriggle their way onto the back of a parent, who then taxis them to a nearby pool of water.

Dart-poison frogs, immune to each other's poison, will fight for their turf (above). Indians extract poison from only three species, including the yellow frog below. Some less-toxic frogs mimic the coloration of their more-dangerous cousins to confuse predators (right).

Top: © Michael Fogden/Animals Animals; both photos above: © Robert Noonan

mucus from their skin, and the tadpoles wriggle onto their backs, literally glued there for the duration of the journey. In some species the tadpoles stay attached for more than a week until the nurse frog finds a proper pool, where the water loosens the mucus bond, setting the tadpoles free. Once loose, they begin to swim.

Sorting out the puzzling relationships among these frog species has been a longtime passion of taxonomist Charles Myers. Dozens of dots on a wall map of Central and South America in his New York City office show where he has found specimens to help him analyze and classify dart-poison species. One of many mysteries he is exploring concerns dramatic changes in the color of one species. A *Dendrobates pumilio* with a red torso and black-and-blue limbs lives in an area that stretches roughly from Nicaragua down to Panama. But surprisingly, in the Panama area ''an explosion of different colors" occurs in the *D. pumilio* populations.

Their behavioral aspects suddenly vary, too. Some frogs in Panama are easily caught; others are more elusive, swiftly disappearing into natural cover. These differences are so great that Myers wonders if what passes for *D. pumilio* is in fact several species.

Frog Fanciers

With increasing knowledge of the dart-poison frogs has come greater interest in them—even, believe it or not, as pets. Because of their beauty and their ability to live in a tiny terrarium, they have been popular in public exhibits and even serve as models for jewelry. "Europeans like to keep frogs the way we keep tropical fish," says Myers. For the serious frog fancier, there is even an international society for the study of dart-poison frogs, complete with its own newsletter. Though Myers' museum laboratory has been visited by the occasional jewelry designer looking for inspiration in his frogs' brilliant hues, he has yet to see any of them immortalized as a bauble.

Getting the tiny frogs to breed in captivity is a problem. At the National Aquarium in Baltimore, Maryland, which houses one of the world's more extensive collections of dart-poison frogs, herpetologists Jack Cover and Anthony Wisnieski have been working with several species. A year ago, for the first time in the United States, they succeeded in breeding a blue dart-poison frog from Suriname, *Dendrobates azureus*. In a small room near the aquarium's rooftop "tropical rain forest," dozens of frogs of several species can be heard chirping at one another from terrariums complete with special ground cover, mock tropical mist, and nourishing bromeliads. After experimenting with various naturelike breeding containers, Cover and Wisnieski discovered that *D. azureus* preferred the overturned plastic casing that's fastened to the bottom of 2-liter soda pop bottles. Its dimensions seem to provide just enough room for courtship, while being small enough to give the frogs a sense of security.

Medical Applications

Meanwhile, NIH scientist John Daly and others are exploring the medical applications of frog toxins. Daly has isolated the alkaloids secreted by the three most virulent species and has labeled them batrachotoxins. Used in research as neuromuscular probes, batrachotoxins are enabling scientists to "find out basic things about how nerves and muscles work," says Daly. Another class of alkaloids acts as a heart stimulant and might aid cardiac patients by replacing more-dangerous drugs now used. A third class of frog alkaloids may prove clinically useful as muscle relaxants or anesthetics.

There is a major problem attached to studying the poisons of these frogs in laboratories. Frogs caught in the wild keep their dangerous qualities until they die, although toxicity levels do fall off. Unlike individuals born in the wild, those born in captivity do not secrete toxins, though they retain their genetic immunity to the poisons of other members of their species. Thus far no one knows why this is so.

Much remains to be discovered in the wild, too. About half the species known to us have been described since 1970. Is it likely that new types of dart-poison frogs are waiting to be discovered?

"Absolutely," says Myers. "New species are being found almost every year." Even now, on top of a remote South American mountain or in a dense, untrammeled rain forest, unique kinds of frogs—brilliant as enameled rainbows, but perhaps capable of getting into a deadly sweat—are now calling to one another.

Although only 1.5 inches long, a blue frog from Suriname is one of the largest of the dart-poison family.

© Zig Leszczynski/Animals Animals

The Peculiar Platypus

by Eric Hoffman

In 1798 scientists at the British Museum opened a box sent by colleagues in Australia. It contained the furry pelt of a creature with webbed feet, a flat tail like a beaver's, a long bill like a duck's, and various appendages and anatomical curiosities that made it unlike anything they had ever seen before.

The reaction was immediate disbelief: the scientists dismissed the specimen as a fake, the clever ruse of irreverent Australian colonials.

Today that pelt is still in the museum's research collection, complete with scalpel marks where skeptical scientists tried to locate the stitchery that attached the bill to the body. The animal, it turns out, was no fake, but a real creature now commonly known as the duck-billed platypus, *Ornithorhynchus anatinus*.

The curious creature still confuses and bemuses scientists. Only now are they finally be-

The platypus (top) has the distinction of being one of the oddest mammals in existence. The furry aquatic creature lays eggs, has a rudder-like paddle for a tail, propels itself through the water with webbed feet, and sports a bill (above) remarkably like that of a duck.

ginning to solve the mystery of what it is and does, and the picture they are assembling is of an animal far more bizarre than anything the scientists at the British Museum could have imagined.

A Taciturn Oddity

For the field biologist, part of the difficulty in piecing together the platypus' story is the creature's incredible wariness. Even though the ani-

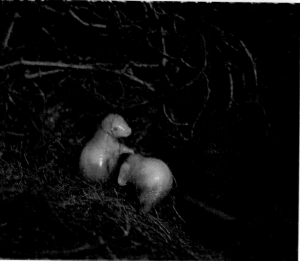

Photos: © The Walt Disney Company

Platypus eggs (top) take 10 to 14 days to hatch. The newborn young (above)—hairless, blind, and only as big as a quarter—receive months of devoted care from their mother before venturing out on their own.

mals are paddling about in substantial numbers in the slow-moving, shallow watercourses throughout eastern Australia's Great Dividing Range, the east coast tablelands, upper Murray River drainage, and in Tasmania, only the most dedicated and keen-eyed observers have seen one. Jack Throp, the former director of Sydney's Taronga Zoo, estimates that "fewer than 5 percent of Australians have ever seen a platypus in the wild."

The platypus is nocturnal. The best time to catch a glimpse of one is at the crack of dawn,

overlooking a glass-smooth pool in a secluded stream. Usually the first sign of a platypus is its small wake, which at first glance could be mistaken for that of a large fish or turtle swimming close to the surface. Just the eyes, the nostrils in the bill, and the upper back of the animal poke above the surface.

A platypus is surprisingly small. Adults seldom weigh more than 4 pounds (1.8 kilograms), and rarely measure longer than 24 inches (60 centimeters), bill to tail. Except for its broad bill and webbed feet, the animal's entire body is covered with dark, otterlike fur that is often the same color as the murky rivers it inhabits. Unlike other aquatic mammals, such as the beaver, which pushes through water with its hind legs and tail, the platypus pulls itself along with its extensively webbed, oversized front feet. It is a strong swimmer, churning along at twice the speed of ducks or geese.

A platypus in a quiet pool is a delight to see. It dives, captures small invertebrates, and returns to the surface to eat. Ripples and faint splashing radiate out from its busy bill as it transfers its catch from cheek pouches to mouth, and grinds its food between horny pads in the upper and lower jaws. It may interrupt its eating to groom, or paddle after other platypuses in courtship, to settle territorial squabbles, or to play. But at the slightest movement on the bank, the show is over. The animal disappears. It is the platypus' steadfast shyness and adherence to a nocturnal schedule that, for the better part of the past two centuries, has kept under wraps such basics as how the animal catches food, reproduces, and behaves.

Platypus-induced Paralysis

During the 1800s Australians used dogs to hunt platypuses. Probably because the animals are so difficult to locate and have such small, tough-skinned pelts, platypus fur never caught on as a commercial export, or even as a domestic money-maker. It took around forty pelts to make a single rug or bedspread.

To supply humans with small apparel such as furry slippers and hats in the late 1800s, platypuses were victims of target practice, fishing nets, and hunting. While an animal relaxed on the surface, the hunter shot just below it. This stunned the platypus while a dog retrieved it. Shooting a hole in the platypus would defeat the purpose of collecting its pelt.

Hunters and dogs alike found that even a stunned or dying platypus could trade tit for tat.

tive tract was found to be more like a bird's, suggesting it laid eggs instead of bearing live young. The classification quandary was temporarily resolved when someone hit on the concept of the "primitive mammal," a possible bridging link to reptiles.

Platypuses were assigned to the lonely mammalian order of Monotremata, which means "one hole" for both excreting waste and reproduction. Only the echidna, the two species of spiny anteater found in Australia and New Guinea, share the order with them. In the eyes of most scientists, this classification placed platypuses below both placental mammals (humans, dogs, cats, etc.) and marsupials (kangaroos, koalas, wombats) in evolutionary development. Those trying to classify its genus and species were befuddled. Initially the "duck mole," as many Australian colonials had come to know it, was named *Platypus anatinus* (meaning flat-footed and ducklike). However, scientists scrubbed *Platypus* for *Ornithorhynchus* when it was discovered that a group of beetles was already known as *Platypus*. Probably because *Ornithorhynchus* is such a mouthful, the species name is used only by scientists. "Platypus" has survived for popular usage, despite the beetles.

Egg-layers

The fact that the platypus lays eggs wasn't conclusively established until 100 years after the animal's discovery. The mammary glands of female platypuses are very large in proportion to the size of the animal, and the nipples have evolved to accommodate young platypuses' bills. The skeletal structure, with splayed front legs and distinctive pectoral girdle, is similar to that of a reptile.

From 1800 until the 1930s, the platypus was ignored by science. In the 1940s and 1950s, Australian naturalists Harry Burrell and David Fleay, working on a shoestring budget, made great strides in understanding platypus behavior and diet. In 1944 Fleay's efforts culminated in the only hatching of a platypus in captivity—a feat that has never been duplicated.

During the century and a half of inattention to the platypus, a wealth of misinformation and

Top: © Eric Hoffman; above: © Jean-Paul Ferrero/AUSCAPE International

Male platypuses have sharp spurs on their hind legs that dispense a strong toxin. The struggling platypus would clamp its legs around the dog's muzzle, drive in the spurs, and release the poison, often killing the dog. Occasionally people were spurred. That could result in severe pain, swelling, and weeks of partial paralysis.

Platypus-induced paralysis of another sort struck 19th-century taxonomists when they grappled with classifying the platypus. The battle raged over its paradoxical makeup. Though it suckles its young like a mammal, its reproduc-

half-truths accumulated. It was popularly believed that platypuses breathe through their backs, because air bubbles rise from their bodies when they swim underwater. This turned out to be nothing more than trapped air escaping from their thick, insulating fur. Among scientists, it had become "common knowledge" that platypuses, like reptiles and unlike mammals, couldn't regulate their body temperatures in water. But in 1972 New South Wales University doctoral student Tom Grant, using telemetry equipment, found that platypuses thermoregulate in near-freezing water as well as any aquatic mammal.

The scientific community was beginning to focus on the platypus. Interesting discoveries followed.

Underwater Guidance

The platypus' bill, which had so often been compared to a duck's bill, proved to be astonishingly sophisticated. Both ducks and platypuses use their bills to collect food, but the platypus' bill is broader, pliable, and leathery, and possesses a sensory system that functions like a scanner in locating live food. Underwater, a flap of skin covers the eyes and ears, and the animal's nostrils close tight. A hungry platypus wags its bill back and forth as it paddles along in an attempt to get a fix on prey. "What guided them underwater was the question we'd been asking for years," says Grant.

The mystery was solved in 1986, when Henning Scheich, of the Technical University of Darmstadt in West Germany, received a platypus bill in the mail from Australian mammalogist Chris Tidemann. Scheich is an expert on electric eels. He, Tidemann, and other Australian scientists conducted experiments with captive platypuses and determined that the animals are extremely efficient at detecting very low-voltage electrical fields. The fields the researchers created using 1.5-volt batteries were similar to those created by the platypus' favorite food: small crustaceans, worms, larvae, and freshwater shrimp that hide in the nooks and crannies of murky river bottoms. Tidemann elaborates, "Their electroreception is passive—nothing is put out—but they're very good at pinpointing a source of low-voltage emissions, even if it's a hollow brick."

Subsequent research has shown that the platypus' bill is highly sensitive. It possesses approximately 850,000 tactile and electrical receptors, which feed information to the brain.

The platypus is the only creature in the world with aquatic and terrestrial sensory systems that work independently from one another. The eyes, ears, and nose let the platypus know what's happening on land. The highly sensitized bill directs the foraging platypus to food and warns him of submerged boulders and logs.

"It makes sense that the bill is highly developed," says Grant, "considering that the platypus is a nocturnal animal that feeds during dark nights at the bottom of even darker rivers." Because the sensory system is so unique in structure, Scheich and Tidemann are confident the finely tuned bill is an independent adaptation. It's not related to any other known biological electroreceptor system, such as those common to some sharks.

Though it is not a high-tech appendage like the bill, the platypus' tail has also been misunderstood. It is often compared to a beaver's tail, perhaps because it is broad and flat and both animals share an affinity for water. But a beaver's tail is hairless, scaly-looking, muscular, and used to propel the animal through the water. In contrast, the platypus' fur-covered tail is a fat-filled appendage used not for propulsion, but as a rudder. For scientists conducting field research, the tail has become a useful barometer to judge an animal's health. "Generally, the fatter the tail, the healthier the animal," says Grant. The tail also acts as a portable heater. When they curl up to sleep or incubate their eggs in their riverbank burrows, platypuses wrap their tails around the front half of their bodies.

Out of water, platypuses steadfastly pursue an underground life-style. They block their burrow entrances by backfilling them. Nesting burrows, which are the most elaborate, may extend 100 feet (30 meters) or more. Resting burrows may be just a few yards long.

Platypus Babies

Scientists have never observed mating between wild platypuses, and much of how they care for their young is not known. During nesting in the spring and summer, females will seal themselves into their burrows for days. Gestation is thought to take about a month, and the eggs hatch in 10 to 14 days. Young are born naked and blind, the size of a quarter, and three months of vigilant care are required before the mother brings them out for their first swim. The babies spend their first months literally confined to a plugged hole in the ground. This behavior intrigued Grant. "It's a great strategy against predators, but I wondered how they acquire enough oxygen to survive in their burrows. Especially since the oxygen they use is replaced by exhaled carbon dioxide."

Grant took blood samples and found platypuses have an inordinate number of red blood cells. "Their high red blood cell count is similar to that of a prairie dog," explains Grant. "The two species aren't related, but they've come up with a similar evolutionary response to combat hypoxia (low amounts of oxygen)."

Dr. Frank Carrick of the University of Queensland has studied platypus reproduction and ecology for 20 years, and has come up with surprising findings. "To begin with, the platypus egg is extremely porous. It is so porous that nutrients and waste can pass through it." According to Carrick, this is unique. He has also found that the hormonal changes in a pregnant platypus are remarkably similar to changes in other mammals.

As for the male part in reproduction, Carrick says, "The sperm is unique among mammals. It resembles the sperm of a bird in its structural simplicity."

While Carrick's findings may not explain conclusively where the platypus fits into the evolutionary development of mammals, he believes new information uncovered by him and others dispels many popular erroneous notions. "Simplistic dogma that attempts to explain evolution as a lineal process doesn't hold up with the platypus," he explains. "For example, all reptiles with venomous systems have modified salivary glands. How do you explain the platypus' venomous system placed on the hind legs?"

Some scientists feel that the platypus' splayed legs and reptilianlike pectoral girdle link it with reptiles. Carrick believes this can be explained just as easily as ". . . molelike. After all, both mammals dig tunnels. Their skeletal structure is as apt to be a response to function as it is anything else."

Successful Species

Overspecialized or not, the platypus seems to fare well enough, if it's left alone. Besides its wide distribution and broad-spectrum diet, the combination of extreme wariness and adherence to tunnel living has made it nearly predator-proof (though a crocodile may gulp one down in the tropics, or an eagle or dingo might snatch one traveling across land).

Carrick adds, "Success of a species is the only final measure of its evolutionary development, and the platypus has 100 million years under its highly sophisticated mammalian bill. That's success."

A young platypus pair basks in the sun. Although seemingly asleep, the ever-vigilant creatures will disappear into the water at the first sign of danger.

IN MEMORIAM

ALLEGRO, JOHN (65), British classicist best known for his work during the 1950s in deciphering the Dead Sea Scrolls, the oldest known manuscripts from the Old Testament. His book, *The Dead Sea Scrolls* (1956) was a best-seller. Allegro later was ridiculed by the scientific community for his theory that Judaism and Christianity were products of an ancient cult that worshipped sex and mushrooms, proposed in *The Sacred Mushroom and the Cross* (1970); d. London, Feb. 17.

ALVAREZ, LUIS W. (77), U.S. physicist who won the 1968 Nobel Prize in Physics for his use of a hydrogen bubble chamber to detect new subatomic particles. Alvarez also developed a type of radar to help airplanes land in fog; worked on the development of the atomic bomb at Los Alamos, N. Mex., during World War II; and proved that there were no hidden chambers in the Chephren pyramid at Giza, Egypt, by using radiation from space to scan its interior. In the 1970s Alvarez and his son developed and promoted a controversial theory that the extinction of dinosaurs was caused by one or more extraterrestrial impacts 65 million years ago; d. Berkeley, Calif., Sept. 1.

ANABLE, GLORIA HOLLISTER (87), U.S. scientist, explorer, and conservationist who in 1931 set a women's world record for ocean descent in a bathysphere. She was the chief assistant to oceanographer William Beebe during his exploration of the 1920s and 1930s, made other expeditions with the New York Zoological Society, and in 1936 led an exploration through the jungles of British Guiana; d. Fairfield, Conn., Feb. 19.

ANDERSON, HERBERT L. (74), U.S. physicist regarded as a pioneer in the development of the atomic bomb and nuclear energy. He received the Department of Energy's highest scientific honor, the Enrico Fermi Award, from President Reagan in 1983; d. Santa Fe, N. Mex., July 16.

ANDREWES, SIR CHRISTOPHER (92), British virologist who helped discover and isolate the influenza virus; d. London, Dec. 31.

ASLAN, ANA (92?), Romanian gerontologist whose Parhon Institute of Geriatrics in Bucharest attracted wealthy and prominent people from throughout the world in search of renewed youth; d. Bucharest, May 20.

AUSTIN, OLIVER L. (85), U.S. ornithologist who wrote the definitive *Birds of the World* (1961) and was curator of ornithology at the Florida Museum of Natural History; d. Gainesville, Fla., Dec. 31.

BEJEROT, NILS (67), Swedish physician and psychiatrist recognized for developing an epidemiology of drug abuse and for investigating ways to prevent addiction to amphetamines, cocaine, and other narcotics; d. Stockholm, Nov. 29.

BOURNE, GEOFFREY H. (78), Australian-born U.S. anatomist and primatologist who wrote extensively on his studies of, and experiences with, apes and other primates. He appeared on television's "Tonight Show" to demonstrate how he taught chimpanzees to communicate by typing on a computer; d. New York, N.Y., July 19.

BRAINERD, JOHN G. (83), U.S. electrical engineer and computer scientist who served as director of a project that built ENIAC, one of the earliest electronic computers, in 1946; d. Kennett Square, Pa., Feb. 1.

BURK, DEAN (84), U.S. chemist who served as chief chemist at the National Institute of Cancer from 1949 to 1974. In 1952 he won the Hildebrand Prize for his work on photosynthesis. He also developed a process for distinguishing the difference between normal cells and those damaged by cancer; codeveloped a prototype of the nuclear magnetic resonance scanner, an imaging device often used instead of X rays; and was a codiscoverer of biotin, one of the B-complex vitamins; d. Washington, D.C. (of cancer), Oct. 6.

CLARK, JOHN D. (80), U.S. rocket-fuel developer who directed a team of Navy civilian scientists that produced a revolutionary new family of high-energy, storable liquid propellants in 1959; d. Denville, N.J., July 6.

CLOWES, GEORGE H. A., JR. (73), U.S. medical researcher and surgeon who studied the activities of human cells that cause the muscle tissue of sick people to weaken during the healing process. He was professor of surgery at Harvard Medical School from 1965 to 1985; d. Woods Hole, Mass., Sept. 10.

COOL, RODNEY L. (68), U.S. experimental physicist whose work in the 1970s helped establish the existence of the quark, a subatomic particle. His experiments at the European Center for Nuclear Research in Geneva helped demonstrate that the quark is a building block of neutrons and protons, previously regarded as the basic particles of nature; d. New York, N.Y., April 16.

CORBIN, HAZEL (93), Canadian-born U.S. health-care expert who crusaded for improved maternal and infant care through demonstration projects, research, and the education of professionals and childbearing families. She served as general director of the Maternity Center Association in New York City from 1923 to 1965; d. New Smyrna Beach, Fla., May 18.

COURNAND, ANDRÉ F. (92), French-born U.S. medical researcher and surgeon who shared the 1956 Nobel Prize in Medicine (with Dickinson Richards and Werner Forssmann) for perfecting a method of exploring the heart through catheterization. His long collaboration with Richards at Bellevue Hospital and Columbia University in New York City also included the development of research and teaching programs on the history of medicine and science and human affairs; d. Great Barrington, Mass., Feb. 19.

DART, RAYMOND A. (95), Australian-born South African anatomist and paleoanthropologist whose discovery of an early human fossil in South Africa in 1924 revolutionized the study of human origins. The skull—known as the "Taung child" and of a species that Dart called *Australopithecus africanus*—was the first early human fossil found in Africa, and inspired extensive searches on that continent for the "missing link" between apes and humans; d. Johannesburg, Nov. 22.

DECKER, ALBERT (93), U.S. expert on infertility best known as the founder and director of the nonprofit Fertility Research Foundation in New York City, one of the first centers devoted entirely to the diagnosis and treatment of infertility. He was also the author of numerous articles and books on the subject; d. New York, N.Y., Nov. 27.

DISCHE, ZACHARIAS (92), Austrian-born U.S. biochemist known for his work on the nature of DNA and human metabolism. He was a professor of biochemistry at Columbia University from 1943 to 1963; d. Englewood, N.J., Jan. 17.

DUBOS, JEAN PORTER (70), U.S. biological and environmental researcher who collaborated with her husband, the late René Dubos, on the study of tuberculosis and on several books proposing a philosophy of the human environment. She was a founder of the René Dubos Center for Human Environments in New York City; d. New York, N.Y., Aug. 6.

FERRETTI, JULIUS J. (92), Italian-born U.S. inventor whose patents included a 1923 matchbook-making machine and several air-pollution-control devices; d. Bridgeport, Conn., Oct. 17.

FEYNMAN, RICHARD P. (69), U.S. theoretical physicist regarded as one of the most brilliant and influential of his generation. Feynman shared the 1965 Nobel Prize in Physics (with Julian S. Schwinger and Shinichiro Tomonaga) for his work in the 1940s remaking the theory of quantum electrodynamics. Many believed he could have won it again for his later work with Murray Gell-Mann in developing a theory of weak interactions. He was also a group leader on the atomic bomb project at Los Alamos, N. Mex., during World War II, and invented the commonly used "Feynman diagram" system for representing complicated events in particle physics. Feynman became known to the general public in 1986, when he served on the presidential commission investigating the explosion of the U.S. space shuttle *Challenger*. He taught at Cornell University during the late 1940s, and went to the California Institute of Technology in 1950, where he spent the rest of his life; d. Los Angeles, Calif., Feb. 15.

GOLLAN, FRANK (78), Czech-born U.S. medical researcher and inventor who isolated the polio virus in the 1940s and was instrumental in the invention of the first heart-lung machine in the 1950s. Himself a victim of polio since childhood, Gollan and his wife, Alice, died in what appeared to be a double suicide (he left a note expressing concern over their deteriorating health); d. Miami, Fla., Oct. 6.

GORDON, HARRY H. (81), U.S. pediatrician considered a pioneer in the fields of neonatology (the treatment of newborn babies) and child development. He was the author of more than 100 scientific papers in these fields, and in 1965 became the founding director of the Rose F. Kennedy Center for Research in Mental Retardation at the Albert Einstein College of Medicine in New York City. He headed that facility until his retirement in 1972; d. New York, N.Y., July 20.

HATEM, GEORGE (78), U.S. public health worker who spent some 50 years in China, playing a major role in the fight against venereal disease and leprosy. Known as Ma Haide, he was one of the most beloved Americans in China; d. Beijing, Oct. 2.

KILLIAN, JAMES R., JR. (83), U.S. science administrator who was named the first U.S. presidential assistant for science and technology in 1957. In that capacity, he played a central role in the organization of NASA. Prior to serving in the Eisenhower administration, he had been president of the Massachusetts Institute of Technology for ten years. Later, as chairman of the Carnegie Commission on Educational Television (1965–67) and chairman of the Corporation for Public Broadcasting (1973–74), he became known as the father of public broadcasting; d. Cambridge, Mass., Jan. 29.

LAMB, THOMAS B. (91), U.S. inventor and industrial designer whose products ranged from a pulsating armchair to rifles for the Army. At various times he was also a cartoonist, writer, and textile designer. One of his passions was designing handles— for cutlery, kitchen utensils, and anything else that needed them—which were the subject of a one-man show at New York's Museum of Modern Art in 1948; d. Fairfield, Conn., Feb. 2.

LEGASOV, VALERY A. (51), Soviet physical chemist who headed the commission that investigated the April 1986 accident at the Chernobyl nuclear power plant; d. Soviet Union, April 27.

LEVCHENKO, ANATOLY (47), Soviet cosmonaut and test pilot being trained to fly the Soviet space shuttle *Buran*, expected to make its first manned voyage in 1989. Levchenko, one of two pilots preparing to fly the shuttle, died of a brain tumor; d. Soviet Union, Aug. 9.

LEWYT, ALEXANDER M. (79), U.S. inventor and manufacturer best known for the Lewyt vacuum cleaner, a compact machine with no dust bag, designed to operate without disrupting television or radio signals; d. Sands Point, N.Y., March 18.

MAURER, JOHN A. (83), U.S. inventor who developed 16- and 18-millimeter sound-recording and reproduction systems. His more than 60 patents also included a photoelectric eye that could identify a fingerprint in five seconds; d. New Brunswick, N.J., March 20.

MORSE, RICHARD S. (76), U.S. inventor and commercial technologist who helped develop frozen orange juice concentrate and a variety of industrial vacuum processes. In 1940 he founded the National Research Corporation to develop products and techniques and then persuade manufacturers to produce or use them. The company also helped develop instant coffee, antibiotics, and machines for television production. Morse advised the government on chemical, biological, and radiological warfare and later became involved in efforts to reduce automobile pollution; d. Falmouth, Mass., July 1.

MURRAY, HENRY A. (95), U.S. psychologist who pioneered the development of personality theory. He was a coinventor of the Thematic Apperception Test (TAT), commonly used in psychiatric diagnosis and research, and was one of the first American-born practitioners of psychoanalysis. He taught at Harvard University for almost 40 years, until his retirement in 1962. Murray was also an authority on the life and works of Herman Melville; d. Cambridge, Mass., June 23.

MYLONAS, GEORGE E. (89), Turkish-born U.S. archaeologist who directed a number of excavations in Greece and the Middle East. In 1970 he won the Gold Medal of the Archaeological Institute of America, of which he was president from 1956 to 1960. His several books included the seminal *Mycenae and the Mycenaean Age* (1966); d. Athens, April 15.

NAUMOV, BORIS N. (61), Soviet computer scientist who sought joint ventures with U.S. companies and led efforts to develop computer science as part of President Mikhail Gorbachev's program to revitalize the economy. Since 1983 he served as head of the Institute of Informatics Problems, which conducts research in computer technology; d. Soviet Union, June 11.

NUTTLI, OTTO (61), U.S. seismologist known as an expert on earthquakes and the New Madrid fault in southeastern Missouri; d. St. Louis, Mo., Feb. 9.

PAGE, RICHARD W. (76), U.S. dental surgeon and inventor who developed the first high-speed dental drill in the 1950s. Known as the Page-Chayes handpiece, it operated up to 40 times faster than conventional drills and was adopted by dentists across the country. Other inventions included an air-and-water sprayer for the drill that cools, flushes, and dries the tooth so the dentist can examine the surface, and a hydraulic chair with revolving platform; d. Hudson, N.Y., Feb. 2.

PAGELS, HEINZ R. (49), U.S. physicist and author who wrote several books explaining the complexities of physics and cosmology to the lay public, including *The Cosmic Code* (1982), *Perfect Symmetry* (1985), and *The Dreams of Reason* (1987). He was killed in a mountain climbing accident on Colorado's Pyramid Peak; d. July 24.

PAIGE, RICHARD E. (83), U.S. inventor, author, and musician who held 170 patents, including folding boxes, corrugated display stands, and others in the packaging field. During World War II, he developed an instructional sighting device used by the military. His books included *The Complete Guide to Making Money With Your Ideas and Inventions* and *The Science of Creating Ideas for Industry*. In the early days of radio, he wrote theme songs and singing commercials; d. New York, N.Y., Aug. 15.

PANOFSKY, HANS A. (70), German-born U.S. atmospheric scientist credited with several advances in meteorological research. He was one of the first to study the lower 300 feet (90 meters) of the atmosphere for pollution control and other purposes. He also developed theories of wind flow over complex terrain and contributed to the understanding of air turbulence as a cause of airplane crashes. He taught at Pennsylvania State University for 30 years; d. San Diego, Calif., Feb. 28.

PHELPS, WILLIAM H., JR. (85), Venezuelan ornithologist, conservationist, and explorer who, with his father and wife, built the foremost collection of birds in Latin America. He described more than 150 previously undocumented forms of bird life and wrote more than 75 scientific articles. He led several expeditions through unexplored regions of Venezuela; Pico Phelps, one of the highest points in the country, is named in his honor.

As a conservationist, he was Venezuela's delegate to the 1972 Stockholm Conference on the Human Environment and a trustee of the American Museum of Natural History. He was also the founder of Radio Caracas and its television counterpart; d. Caracas, Aug. 13.

POLK, B. FRANK (46), U.S. epidemiologist and medical researcher who was a leading figure in the study and treatment of AIDS. He was a professor of epidemiology at the Johns Hopkins School of Public Health, as well as a professor of medicine and obstetrics and gynecology at the Johns Hopkins School of Medicine. Under his direction, Johns Hopkins became a center for research on the control of the AIDS epidemic. He also directed the AIDS outpatient clinic and was active in public education on the dangers of the disease; d. Boston, Mass., Oct. 11.

POMERANCE, LEON (81), U.S. businessman and patron of archaeology whose financial contributions made possible the excavation of an important Bronze Age palace on the island of Crete in the 1960s. The president of the Forest Paper Company, he began an annual grant in 1962 that enabled the Greek Archaeological Society to begin a dig on Crete's eastern shore. The excavation revealed a 250-room palace built in 1600 B.C.; d. New York, N.Y., Nov. 11.

RABI, ISIDOR I. (89), Austria-Hungary-born U.S. physicist considered a pioneer in the exploration of the atom and a major figure in 20th-century physics. He won the 1944 Nobel Prize in Physics for developing a method of measuring the magnetic properties of atoms, molecules, and atomic nuclei—essential to the development of lasers, masers, atomic clocks, and nuclear magnetic resonance for diagnostic scanning of the human body. He conceived the CERN nuclear research center in Geneva, instrumental in the rebirth of science in postwar Europe, and helped found the Brookhaven National Laboratory on Long Island, N.Y. At New York's Columbia University for nearly 60 years, he became known as an advocate for the reform of science education in the United States and as a moral influence in the debate over controlling atomic energy; d. New York, N.Y., Jan. 11.

RUBEN, SAMUEL (88), U.S. electrochemical engineer and inventor whose work led to more than 300 patents, including the alkaline battery. Other inventions included a dry electrolytic condenser that was used in every television and radio for decades and in the starters of most electric motors. He had no formal education beyond high school; d. Milwaukie, Oreg., July 16.

RUSKA, ERNST A. F. (81), German electrical engineer who shared the 1986 Nobel Prize in Physics for his invention of the electron microscope in 1931. The instrument, one of the most significant biological research tools developed in the 20th century, enormously magnifies an image by accelerating a beam of electrons (rather than light) through a specimen. Ruska devoted the rest of his career to perfecting the invention; d. West Berlin, May 30.

SCOTT, SHEILA (61), British aviatrix who in 1971 became the first woman to circle the world by way of the North Pole in a light aircraft. A former actress, she made three solo flights around the world and claimed more than 100 flying records, trophies, and awards; d. London, Oct. 20.

SHEPARD, LEONARD F. (61), U.S. engineer who helped develop space suits and other technology for the U.S. space program. He founded and headed Time System Technology, a company that developed precision instruments. Shepard had also been a concert pianist, appearing with the New York City Symphony in the late 1940s; d. Stony Brook, N.Y., April 9.

SHERIF, MUZAFER (82), Egyptian-born U.S. social psychologist known for his pioneering studies of intergroup conflict, hostility, and prejudice. He is best known for his "Robber's Cave" experiment, in which boys at a summer camp were divided into two groups, pitted against each other in competition, and then brought together for common work projects. The study was a seminal one for social psychologists interested in intergroup relations, especially during the civil rights movement of the 1960s. Sherif was the coauthor of 17 books on social psychology; d. Fairbanks, Alaska, Oct. 16.

STEPTOE, PATRICK C. (74), British obstetrician who ushered in the era of "test-tube" babies in 1978, when one of his patients gave birth to a baby girl, Louise Brown, conceived in a laboratory container. In this now-commonplace procedure, known as in vitro fertilization, eggs are fertilized by sperm in a glass dish and allowed to develop briefly. The resulting embryos are then inserted in the uterus, where they develop normally. Steptoe and his colleague, Dr. Robert G. Edwards, became world-famous after the birth of Louise Brown and were made Commanders of the British Empire. Steptoe received one of the highest honors in the scientific world in 1987, when he was named a Fellow of the Royal Society; d. Canterbury, England, March 21.

THOMPSON, LUCILLE S. HURLEY (66), Latvian-born U.S. nutritionist whose research linked dietary deficiencies in expectant mothers with birth defects in their children. Beginning in the 1950s, she studied the effects of the trace metals manganese, zinc, iron, and copper on fetal development. She was a professor at the University of California at Davis, editor of The Journal of Nutrition, and head of several national scientific organizations; d. Sacramento, Calif., July 28.

TINBERGEN, NIKOLAAS (81), Dutch-born British zoologist who shared the 1973 Nobel Prize in Medicine for "discoveries in the field of the organization and occurrence of individual and social behavior patterns" in animals. He became well known in the late 1930s as one of the founders of ethology, the study of animal behavior in their natural environments. His many writings included what was considered the first handbook in that field, The Study of Instinct (1951). Tinbergen was a professor in animal behavior at Oxford University from 1966 to 1974; d. Oxford, England, Dec. 21.

TUSHINSKY, JOSEPH S. (78), U.S. inventor, business executive, and musician who was the first U.S. importer of Sony audiotape recorders. With his brother Irving, he invented a process called Superscope, which optically squeezed film images for wide-screen projection. Introduced in 1953, Superscope helped usher in the era of wide-screen motion pictures. While marketing Superscope in Japan, he discovered the small Sony company and began importing their products in 1957. In addition to being chairman of the Superscope Corporation and the Marantz stereo company, he was a trumpeter for several orchestras, including the NBC Symphony under Toscanini, and a Hollywood screenwriter; d. Encino, Calif., March 21.

WILLIAMS, ROGER L. (94), Indian-born U.S. biochemist and nutritionist who discovered the growth-promoting vitamin pantothenic acid and was credited with significant advances in the study of how nutrients affect health, aging, psychological disorders, alcoholism, and mental retardation. A professor at the University of Texas from 1934 until 1971, he wrote 26 books and more than 275 scholarly articles. His first book, Introduction to Organic Chemistry (1928), was a standard text in hundreds of colleges. In 1957 he became the first biochemist to serve as president of the American Chemical Society, then the largest scientific body in the world; d. Austin, Tex., Feb. 20.

WILSON, LOIS BURNHAM (97), U.S. family-health organizer who helped found the Al-Anon Family Groups for relatives and friends of alcoholics. The wife of reformed alcoholic William G. Wilson, a cofounder of Alcoholics Anonymous in 1935, she began holding informal self-help groups for family members of alcoholics. In 1951 she set up an information center in New York City for similar groups that had developed throughout the United States, and the movement took its name shortly thereafter. Today there are some 30,000 Al-Anon groups worldwide, with a membership of 500,000. As Lois W., she was known as "the first lady of Al-Anon"; d. Mount Kisco, N.Y., Oct. 5.

WRIGHT, SEWALL (98), U.S. geneticist regarded as the leading American evolutionary theorist of the 20th century. His major contribution is considered the establishment of a mathematical basis for evolution, based on decades of study of the genetics of populations. His statistical technique, called "path analysis," has been widely adopted in such fields as sociology, econometrics, and behavioral genetics. Wright is also known for the theory of "genetic drift," which holds that random fluctuations in gene frequency play a key role in the evolutionary process of small groups; d. Madison, Wis., March 3.

INDEX